C000100315

SAXON BRITAIN:

being a Map of

ENGLAND & WALES;

to illustrate

Bede's Ecclesiastical History;
and

The Saxon Chronicle.

Bishops See ...8

10 20 30 40 50 60 70

English Miles

55°

Streoneshalch
Whitby

Scarborough

ngham

Beverley

Barton

Sidnacrester
Stow
Bardney
Lincoln   Parteney

Howaford
Seaford

Cranhoe
Boston

Grantham
Elmham

E A S T   Burgh Castle

Greyland
Northwich
Norwich

hamstede
borough

A N G L I A

indle

Theodford
Thetford

Elig
Ely

untendune
Huntingdon

Holm

Soham

S Neots

Badricesworth
Bury St Edmunds

Domuc
Dmouch

Grantabridge
Cambridge

Gipeswic
Ipswich

oceaster

Sudbury
Sithbert

Deaninge
Felixstow

unstable

Glaester
Harwich

EAST SAXONS

Hegerford
Hertford

St Osyth Chich

rd
chester

St Albans

Barking

London

R. Thames

Tilbury

Kingston
Hrofescester
Rochester

Othna Rituper
Richborough

ortead
ertsey

K E N T

Guildford

Ockley

Cantwarabr
Canterbry

Dofre
Dover

easter
chester

Peterfield

S O U T H

Cicester
Chichester

S A X O N S

Hastings

bury

50°

Drawn & Engraved by J.&C.Walker

LONDON

Drawn & Engraved. by J.&C.Walker

THE

VENERABLE BEDE'S

ECCLESIASTICAL HISTORY

OF ENGLAND.

ALSO THE

ANGLO-SAXON CHRONICLE.

WITH

ILLUSTRATIVE NOTES, A MAP OF ANGLO-SAXON ENGLAND,
AND A GENERAL INDEX.

EDITED

BY J. A. GILES, D.C.L.,

LATE FELLOW OF CORPUS CHRISTI COLLEGE, OXFORD.

———

LONDON:

HENRY G. BOHN, YORK STREET, COVENT GARDEN.

M.DCCC.XLVII.

BODLEIAN
D
1 7 J... 1931
LIBRARY

PREFACE.

CHAP. I.—INTRODUCTION.

THE period of six hundred years (from about A.D. 466 to 1066), during which the Anglo-Saxons were dominant in England, has always been viewed with much interest and attention by the modern English, particularly of our own day. Nor are we at a loss to discover the true explanation of this fact. A nation will always be most attached to that portion of its former history which developes a state of things, polity, and institutions, similar to their own, and adapted to become a model for their imitation. Now the tendency of the present times is to enlarge the rights and privileges of the people, that they may—all, and not merely a section of them—enjoy as much happiness in their social life and during their existence on the earth, as the constitution of their nature requires; and, moreover, that they shall, as a body, have the privilege of judging for themselves in what way the largest share of enjoyment may be obtained. Hence has arisen that renewal of attention which the people of England at present devote to that part of English history which preceded the Norman conquest. Then are supposed to have been planted those seeds of national liberty which, under every form of cutting and pruning to which the plant may occasionally have been subjected, have nevertheless continually germinated, until the tree, like that which sprang from the grain of mustard-seed, bids fair to overshadow all of us.

To such a spirit of inquiry must be attributed the fact that the Anglo-Saxon Ecclesiastical History by the Venerable Bede, has already, before the appearance of this volume, been published in three separate editions in about seven years; and to the same cause must be ascribed the publication of this volume, in which, at an unprecedented low price, are now for the first time presented to the public the two great

Chronicles of Anglo-Saxon History. Although of limited dimensions, they present us with a most extraordinary number of facts arranged chronologically, and form a mass of history such as no other nation of Europe possesses.

CHAP. II.—LIFE OF BEDE.

Sect. 1.—*Of his birth.*

THE year of our Lord 673, remarkable for one of the most important of our early English councils, held at Hertford, for the purpose of enforcing certain general regulations of the church, has an equal claim on our attention, as the year in which that great teacher of religion, literature, and science, the Venerable Bede, first saw the light.

The time of his birth has, however, been placed by some writers as late as A.D. 677, but this error arose from not perceiving that the last two or three pages of his Chronological Epitome, attached to the Ecclesiastical History, were added by another hand.*

Bede's own words appear decisive in fixing the date of his birth:—" This is the present state of Britain, about 285 years since the coming of the Saxons, and in the seven hundred and thirty-first year of our Lord's incarnation." To this he subjoins a short chronology which comes down to 731, and was continued to 734, either by another hand or by Bede himself, at a later period just before his death: he then gives a short account of the principal events of his own life, and says, that he has attained *(attigisse)* the fifty-ninth year of his life. Gehle, in his recent publication on the life of Bede, has not scrupled to fix the year 672, interpreting Bede's expression that he had attained his fifty-ninth year as implying that he was entering on his sixtieth. On the other hand, another learned critic,† whose opinion has been adopted by Stevenson in his Introduction [p. 7], has endeavoured to show that 674 is the true date. But in so unimportant a particular it is hardly worth while to weigh the conflicting opinions, and the intermediate date, so long ago settled by

* Mabill. in v. Bed. sect. ii.   Sim. Dun. de Ecc. D. 8, and Ep. de Archie. Ebor.   Stubbs's Act. Pont. Eborac.   Sparke's Hist. Ang. Scrip. 1723. Surtees' Hist. of Durham, ii. p. 69.

† Pagi Critic. in Baron. Ann. A.D. 693, sect. 8.

Mabillon, and apparently so well borne out by Bede's own words, is perhaps the best that can be adopted.

It is always to be regretted, when little is known of the early life of eminent men, as in all cases where many facts have been handed down concerning the years of their youth, something or other has invariably broken forth significant of their future life and fortunes. So very little, however, is known of this great ornament of England and father of the universal church, that, except his own writings, the letter of Cuthbert his disciple, and one or two other almost contemporary records, we have no means whatever of tracing his private history.

The place of his birth is said by Bede himself to have been in the territory afterwards belonging to the twin-monasteries of St. Peter and St. Paul, at Wearmouth and Jarrow. The whole of this territory, lying along the coast near the mouths of the rivers Tyne and Wear, was granted to abbat Benedict by king Egfrid two years after the birth of Bede. William of Malmesbury points out more minutely the spot where our author first saw the light. His words are these: "Britain, which some writers have called another world, because, from its lying at a distance, it has been overlooked by most geographers, contains in its remotest parts a place on the borders of Scotland, where Bede was born and educated. The whole country was formerly studded with monasteries, and beautiful cities founded therein by the Romans; but now, owing to the devastations of the Danes and Normans, it has nothing to allure the senses. Through it runs the Wear, a river of no mean width, and of tolerable rapidity. It flows into the sea, and receives ships, which are driven thither by the wind, into its tranquil bosom. A certain Benedict built two churches on its banks, and founded there two monasteries, named after St. Peter and St. Paul, and united together by the same rule and bond of brotherly love."* The birth of Bede happened in the third year of Egfrid, son of Oswy, the first of the kings of Northumberland, after the union of the provinces Deira and Bernicia into one monarchy. The dominions of this king extended from the Humber to the Frith of Forth, and comprehended all the six northern counties of England, and the

* Hist. of the Kings of England, book i. chap. iii., p. 54.

whole of the southern part of Scotland. The piety of Egfrid induced him to grant the large tract of land above mentioned to one Biscop, surnamed Benedict, who had formerly
been one of his thanes, but now became a monk, and built
thereon a monastery, which he dedicated to St. Peter, on the
north bank of the river Wear, and which from this circumstance derived the name of Wearmouth. The same pious
abbat, eight years after [A.D. 682], built another monastic
establishment, which he dedicated to St. Paul, at Jarrow, on
the banks of the Tyne, at the distance of about five miles
from the former. In memory of this, the following inscription, which has been preserved, was carved on a tablet in the
church at Jarrow :—

> Dedicatio Basilicæ
> S. Pauli VIII Kal. Maii
> Anno XV Egfridi regis
> Ceolfridi Abb. ejusdemque
> Ecclesiæ Deo auctore
> Conditoris anno IV.

> The Dedication of the Church
> of Saint Paul, on the 24th of April
> in the fifteenth year of king Egfrid
> and in the fourth year of abbat Ceolfrid,
> who, under God, founded the same church.

These two establishments were for many years ruled by
Benedict himself, and his associates Ceolfrid, Easterwin, and
Sigfrid, and from the unity and concord which prevailed
between the two, deserved rather, as Bede expresses it, to
be called "one single monastery built in two different
places."*

We cannot be certain as to the exact spot, but it is sufficiently near the mark to ascertain that Bede was born in the
neighbourhood of these two monasteries, and probably in the
village of Jarrow.

Of his parents nothing has been recorded. He tells us, in
his own short narrative of himself, that he was placed, at
the age of seven years, under the care of abbat Benedict, in
the abbey of Wearmouth, that of Jarrow being not yet
built. When, however, this second establishment was
founded, Bede appears to have gone thither under Ceolfrid

* Leland. Antiq. de Reb. Brit. Coll. ed. Hearne, iii. 42.

its first abbat, and to have resided there all the remainder of his life.

Sect. 2.—*Of his youth.*

For a youth of such studious habits and indefatigable industry, no situation could have been more appropriate than that in which he was now placed. Benedict Biscop, the founder of the monasteries, was a man of extraordinary learning and singular piety. Though a nobleman by birth, he was unwearied in the pursuit of knowledge, and in ameliorating the condition of his country. In order to accomplish his benevolent intentions, he travelled into other countries, and introduced not only foreign literature, but arts hitherto unknown, into our island. He was the first who brought masons and glaziers home with him, having need of their services in the noble buildings which he erected. He travelled four or five times to Rome, and became intimate with Pope Agatho. Here he was much captivated with the liturgy of the Roman church, and their manner of chanting, for until then the Gallican or Mozarabic liturgy was used both in Britain and Ireland, as is alluded to in Augustine's Questions to pope Gregory. Each time, on his return to England, Benedict carried back with him the most valuable books and costly relics and works of art which could be procured for money. This collection, which was, by his orders, preserved with peculiar care, received considerable augmentations from the zeal and munificence of his successors. Bede's thirst for study was here, no doubt, satisfied : so large and valuable a library could scarcely have been within his reach elsewhere, even among the other Benedictines of the day, however well qualified that order was to encourage a taste for learning, and to provide means for gratifying that taste among its fosterlings. In so large a community, too, as that of Wearmouth, there were doubtlessly many scholars of mature age, who would all assist in promoting the studies of so talented a youth as he who was now introduced within their walls.

Bede was not, however, left to chance, or the untutored dictates of his own youthful fancy, to find his way as he could through the years spent in the rudiments of learning. In the study of theology and the Holy Scriptures, he received, as he himself tells us,* the instructions of Trumhere, a monk,· who had been educated under the holy Chad, bishop of Lichfield. The art of chanting, as it was practised at Rome, was taught him by John, the arch-chanter of St. Peter's at Rome, who had been, by the consent of pope Agatho, brought into Britain by Biscop Benedict. This celebrated singer attracted multitudes of people from the counties adjoining to the monastery of Wearmouth to witness his performances. It has also been said by Stubbs,† that Bede received instructions from John of Beverley, the disciple of archbishop Theodore ; and possibly this may have been the case, as he might also from others learned in the Greek and Latin tongue who were in the company of that famous archbishop ; but Mabillon thinks that the author above referred to has made a confusion between the two Johns, for there is no other mention whatever made of his being a pupil of John of Beverley. It is certain, however, that Bede possessed considerable knowledge, not only in the Latin and Greek languages, but also in the Hebrew, although nothing remains which has been ascribed to him in that language, save a vocabulary, entitled "Interpretatio Nominum Hebraicorum," which is now admitted to be the production of another. In the Greek tongue he must have made considerable proficiency, as appears from his "Ars Metrica," and from his having translated the life of Anastasius and the Gospel of St. John out of that language into Latin. The last two of these productions are no longer extant.

Whatever advantages, however, Bede may have enjoyed, the greatest was his own ardour in the pursuit of learning ; and let us remember, that the rules of the monastic institutions did not leave the student the uncontrolled disposal of his own time. Many offices, not wholly menial, were performed by the brethren ; he himself instances Biscop the founder, and says, that, like the rest of the brothers, he delighted to exercise himself in winnowing the corn, and threshing it, in giving milk to the lambs and calves, in the bakehouse, in the garden, in the kitchen, and in the other employments of the monastery ; a considerable portion of the day was spent in discharging the duties required by the monastic rules, and in the daily service and psalmody of the

* Ecclesiastical Hist. iv. 3, page 177.　† Act. Pontif. Eborac.

church. All his leisure time was not even then occupied in reading; part was devoted to writing and to the instruction of others. His own words are here in point: "All my life I spent in that same monastery, giving my whole attention to the study of the Holy Scriptures, and in the intervals between the hours of regular discipline and the duties of singing in the church, I always took pleasure in learning, or teaching, or writing something."

Sect. 3.—*Of his admission to Holy Orders.*

THE twenty-fifth year of one's age, was then, as the twenty-fourth at present, the limit of admission to Deacon's Orders. Of his own entry into this holy ordination, let us hear what he says himself, "In the nineteenth year of my life I was made deacon, and in the thirtieth was ordained priest; both ordinances were conferred on me by bishop John, at the bidding of abbat Ceolfrid."

This John was bishop of Hagulstad, now Hexham, in the county of Northumberland, and the monasteries of Wearmouth and Jarrow were in his diocese, for the see of Durham did not exist until a later period, when the brotherhood of Lindisfarne settled there, carrying with them the bones of St. Cuthbert. This John is also better known by the name of John of Beverley, and is mentioned in high terms by Bede in his History.

So remarkable a deviation from the general rule as the ordination of a candidate for Holy Orders in the nineteenth year of his age, is in itself a sufficient proof of the estimation in which the young student was held. His piety, moreover, must have been well known to the abbat who sent him for ordination, and to the bishop, who hesitated not to admit him so prematurely to that holy rite. It is moreover said of him that, in his ardour for study, he declined to be raised to the dignity of an abbat, lest the distraction to which the care of such an establishment, or *family*, as the historian expresses it, would subject him, might allow him less time and leisure for his favourite pursuits. "The office," as he expressed it, "demands thoughtfulness, and thoughtfulness brings with it distraction of the mind, which impedes the pursuit of learning."*

* Trithem. de Viris illust. ord. Bened. ii. 21, 34.

This, however, no doubt happened after he took priest's orders in his thirtieth year, though the eleven years which intervened must have been sedulously spent in laying up that store of erudition which afterwards enabled him to shine forth to the world in every department of literature. For it does not appear that he published any thing in writing until after he had undergone the second of the church's ordinances. This we have from his own words, "From the time of my taking priest's orders, to the fifty-ninth year of my age, I have occupied myself in making these short extracts from the works of the venerable fathers for the use of me and mine, or in adding thereto somewhat of my own, after the model of their meaning and interpretation."

If, however, he was admitted unusually early to the orders of deacon, he was in no mind, on the other hand, to rush hastily, or without long and patient study, into the full duty of the priest's office; and thus he devoted eleven patient years to qualify himself for the various services which he was preparing to render to the literature of his country, and the interests of the church.

Sect. 4.—*Of his clerical and literary labours.*

THE office of priest, or *mass-priest*, as he is called in king Alfred's Anglo-Saxon translation, brought with it a considerable portion of duties which would not allow him to devote the whole of his time to his favourite occupations. His employment was to say mass in the church, by which we are to understand that he officiated at the various masses which were performed at different hours in the day, besides perhaps assisting in the morning and evening prayers of the monastery. The following extracts from Anglo-Saxon writers, quoted by Sharon Turner, will well describe the responsible functions which were supposed to belong to the priest's office.

"Priests! you ought to be well provided with books and apparel as suits your condition. The mass-priest should at least have his missal, his singing-book, his reading-book, his psalter, his hand-book, his penitential, and his numeral one. He ought to have his officiating garments, and to sing from sun-rise, with the nine intervals and nine readings. His sacramental cup should be of gold or silver, glass or tin, and not of earth, at least not of wood. The altar should be always clean, well clothed, and not defiled with dirt. There should be no mass without wine.

"Take care that you be better and wiser in your spiritual craft than worldly men are in theirs, that you may be fit teachers of true wisdom. The priest should preach rightly the true belief; read fit discourses; visit the sick; and baptize infants, and give the unction when desired. No one should be a covetous trader, nor a plunderer, nor drunk often in wine-houses, nor be proud or boastful, nor wear ostentatious girdles, nor be adorned with gold, but to do honour to himself by his good morals.

"They should not be litigious nor quarrelsome, nor seditious, but should pacify the contending; nor carry arms, nor go to any fight, though some say that priests should carry weapons when necessity requires; yet the servant of God ought not to go to any war or military exercise. Neither a wife nor a battle becomes them, if they will rightly obey God and keep his laws as becomes their state." *

Their duties are also described in the Canons of Edgar in the following terms : —

"They are forbidden to carry any controversy among themselves to a lay-tribunal. Their own companions were to settle it, or the bishop was to determine it.

"No priest was to forsake the church to which he was consecrated, nor to intermeddle with the rights of others, nor to take the scholar of another. He was to learn sedulously his own handicraft, and not put another to shame for his ignorance, but to teach him better. The high-born were not to despise the less-born, nor any to be unrighteous or covetous dealers. He was to baptize whenever required, and to abolish all heathenism and witchcraft. They were to take care of their churches, and apply exclusively to their sacred duties; and not to indulge in idle speech, or idle deeds, or excessive drinking; nor to let dogs come within their church-inclosure, nor more swine than a man might govern.

"They were to celebrate mass only in churches, and on the altar, unless in cases of extreme sickness. They were

* Elfric, in Wilkins's Leges Anglo-Saxon. 169—171.

to have at mass their corporalis garment, and the subucula under their alba; and all their officiating garments were to be woven. Each was to have a good and right book. No one was to celebrate mass, unless fasting, and unless he had one to make responses; nor more than three times a day; nor unless he had, for the eucharist, pure bread, wine and water. The cup was to be of something molten, not of wood. No woman was to come near the altar during mass. The bell was to be rung at the proper time.

"They were to preach every Sunday to the people; and always to give good examples. They were ordered to teach youth with care, and to draw them to some craft. They were to distribute alms, and urge the people to give them, and to sing the psalms during the distribution, and to exhort the poor to intercede for the donors. They were forbidden to swear, and were to avoid ordeals. They were to recommend confession, penitence, and compensation; to administer the sacrament to the sick, and to anoint him if he desired it; and the priest was always to keep oil ready for this purpose and for baptism. He was neither to hunt, or hawk, or dice; but to play with his book as became his condition." *

But the duties pointed out in these extracts do not seem to have satisfied the Venerable Bede; he applied himself to every branch of literature and science then known, and besides study, and writing comments on the Scriptures, he treated on several subjects, on history, astrology, orthography, rhetoric, and poetry; in the latter of which he was not inferior to other poets of that age, as appears by what he has left us on the life of St. Cuthbert, and some verses in his Ecclesiastical History; he wrote likewise two books of the Art of Poetry, which are not now extant; a book of Hymns, and another of Epigrams. Bede's own writings inform us of the names of some of his literary friends; among whom were Eusebius or Huetbert, to whom he inscribed his book, De Ratione Temporum, and his Interpretation on the Apocalypse, and who was afterwards abbat of Wearmouth: Cuthbert, called likewise Antonius, to whom he inscribed his book, De Arte Metrica, and who succeeded Huetbert, and was afterwards abbat of Jarrow; he wrote of his master's death, but of this hereafter: also Constantine, to whom he

* Wilkins's Leges Anglo-Saxonicæ, 85—87.

inscribed his book, De Divisione Numerorum; and Nothelm, then priest at London, and afterwards archbishop of Canterbury, to whom he wrote his Questions on the Books of Kings; to which we may add several in other monasteries; whilst others have improperly classed amongst them Alcuinus, afterwards preceptor to Charles the Great.

Thus was the time of that excellent man employed in doing good to mankind, seldom or never moving beyond the limits of his own monastery, and yet in the dark cloister of it surveying the whole world, and dispensing to it the gifts entrusted to him; it seems not a little surprising, that one who had scarcely moved away from the place of his nativity, should so accurately describe those at a distance; and this quality in his writings, when considered with reference to the age in which he lived, is the more remarkable, as there is but one other recorded in history who possessed it in equal perfection,—the immortal Homer.

Sect. 5.—*Of his supposed journey to Rome.*

THE peaceful- tenor of Bede's monastic life was apparently uninterrupted by absence or travel, and his own words might be thought to afford sufficient authority for the supposition. A controversy, however, on this subject has arisen from a letter first published by William of Malmesbury, which to this hour has not been satisfactorily decided. This historian says that Bede's learning and attainments were so highly esteemed, that pope Sergius wished to see him at Rome, and consult him on questions of importance and difficulty relating to the church. He accordingly quotes a letter, addressed by Sergius to abbat Ceolfrid, in which he is requested to send Bede without delay to Rome. Now it is argued, and apparently with truth, that Bede would not have dared to decline an invitation coming from so high a quarter; and yet it is all but certain that Bede never was out of England. He tells us distinctly that his whole life was spent in the neighbourhood of Jarrow; and that the letters, which he has inserted in his Ecclesiastical History, had been procured for him at Rome by Nothelm, which would certainly lead us to infer that Bede *was not* there himself. Moreover, he tells us in his treatise, De Natura Rerum [46], that he was not with the monks of Yarrow,

who went to Rome in the year 701. It is therefore certain
that Bede, if invited, never went to Rome; and it is most
probable, as has been stated by Gehle in his Latin Life of
Bede, that the unexpected death of Pope Sergius, which
happened shortly after, was the cause of his not undertaking
the journey.

Sect. 6.—Of his pretended residence at Cambridge.

IT has been also asserted, that Bede resided at the University of Cambridge, and taught there in the office of Professor.
This has been maintained by certain members of that University, who have been eager to claim such an illustrious
man as their own; whilst other writers of the University of
Oxford have been induced, by a corresponding jealousy, to
deny the fact.

The principal authority for this ill-supported statement is
found in a volume called *Liber Niger*, preserved in the University of Cambridge. Out of that book, Hearne, in the
year 1719, published "Nicolai Cantalupi Historiola de Anti-
quitate et Origine Universitatis Cantabrigiensis, simul cum
Chronicis Sprotti Ox."*

In this history Bede is said, "at the request of doctor
Wilfred, and at the bidding of abbat Ceolfrid, to have left
the territory belonging to the monastery of St. Peter and
St. Paul, and being even then a monk in mind and regular
discipline, though not in dress, to have gone, in the year
682, to Cambridge, where by sowing the seeds of knowledge
for himself and others, by writing books and teaching the
ignorant, he was of use before God and man in eradicating
prevailing errors.

It is hardly necessary to observe, that this is said to have
happened at a time when Bede was little more than nine
years old! Seven years after he is stated to have had public
honours conferred on him by the University, and at a later
period to be still pursuing the duties of a teacher.

In support of these statements a letter is produced,
purporting to be addressed to the Students of the University

---

* This work has been twice published in English, under the following
titles, "History and Antiquities of the University of Cambridge, in two
parts, by Richard Parker, B.D., and Fellow of Caius College, in 1622.
London, 1721; and again printed for J. Marcus, in the Poultry, London."

of Cambridge, by Alcuin, in which allusion is made to Bede as still alive, but Alcuin was fifty years later than Bede, and the supposed letter is consequently a forgery.

Sect. 7.—*Of his occasional visits to his friends.*

WE may therefore infer without hesitation that Bede did not travel far from the monastery. This is both plainly asserted in his own account of his secluded life, and appears also from the want of any evidence to the contrary. Yet it is certain he made visits and excursions to other places; nor can we suppose that he confined himself entirely within the monastery, and never indulged the pleasure of seeing and conversing with his friends. In his own letter to Egbert, archbishop of York, and nephew to king Ceolwulf, he alludes to a visit which he paid to that nobleman and prelate, and acknowledges an invitation to go there for the sake of conferring with him on their common pursuits in the year following. He was unable to comply with this request, in consequence of illness, and therefore communicated with his friend by letter. In another letter, still extant, addressed to Wictred* on the celebration of Easter, he speaks of the kindness and affability with which he had been received by him on a former occasion. It is not improbable that he might sometimes likewise pay visits to the court; for Ceolwulf, king of the Northumbrians, in one of whose provinces, *i. e.* Bernicia, Bede lived, was himself a man of singular learning, and a very great encourager of it in others; and had, doubtlessly, an extraordinary respect for Bede, as appears by his request to him to write the Ecclesiastical History, and by Bede's submitting the papers to him for his perusal. That prince was not only a lover of learned men in general, but especially of that part of them who led a monastic life, insomuch that, about three years after Bede's death, he resigned his crown, and became a monk at Lindisfarne.

Sect. 8.—*Of his death.*

THE tranquillity of Bede's life, passed, as we have seen, entirely in the monastery of Jarrow, has left it a difficult task for his biographers to extend their accounts of him to

* King of Kent.

c

that length which might seem suitable to his reputation and the value of his works. It has been truly remarked that scholars and persons of sedentary habits, though liable to frequent petty illnesses from want of bodily exercise and too great mental exertion, are nevertheless on the whole rather a long-lived race. This rule was not exemplified in the case of Bede. He seems to have contracted at a somewhat early period a complaint in his stomach, accompanied with short-ness of breath : "So that," says Malmesbury, "he suffered in his stomach, and drew his breath with pains and sighs."[*] An attack of this disorder had lately prevented him from visiting his friend archbishop Egbert, and led to his writing him the valuable letter on the duties of a bishop, which we have still extant. We are not informed whether the dis-order left him at that time, and came on afresh, when it at last killed him ; but it is most probable that he enjoyed general ill health during the last few years of his existence. He was ill some weeks before he died, and was attended by Cuthbert, who had been one of his pupils, and after Huetbert became abbat of the monastery. The Christian piety with which he suffered the dispensation which awaited him, has been the universal theme of panegyric. The whole scene of his increasing malady, his devout resignation, and fervent prayers for all his friends, together with his paternal admo-nitions for the regulation of their lives, and his uncontrollable anxiety to dictate to the boy who was his amanuensis, even to his last moments, are so beautifully recorded in the letter of his pupil Cuthbert, that we shall not attempt here to describe it in other terms.[†]

CUTHBERT'S LETTER ON THE DEATH OF VENERABLE BEDE.

" To his fellow reader Cuthwin, beloved in Christ, Cuth-bert, his school-fellow ; health for ever in the Lord. I have received with much pleasure the small present which you sent me, and with much satisfaction read the letters of your devout erudition ; wherein I found that masses and holy

---

[*] Hist. of the Kings of England, lib. i. c. 2.

[†] See Simeon. Dunelm. de Ecc. Dun. ap. Twysdeni Scrip. X. I. 15, p. 8. Leland, Collect. Hearne, IV. iii. 77. Mabilloni Act. Bened. Sec. iii.

prayers are diligently celebrated by you for our father and master, Bede, whom God loved : this was what I principally desired, and therefore it is more pleasing, for the love of him (according to my capacity), in a few words to relate in what manner he departed this world, understanding that you also desire and ask the same. He was much troubled with shortness of breath, yet without pain, before the day of our Lord's resurrection, that is, about a fortnight ; and thus he afterwards passed his life, cheerful and rejoicing, giving thanks to Almighty God every day and night, nay, every hour, till the day of our Lord's ascension, that is, the seventh before the kalends of June [twenty-sixth of May], and daily read lessons to us his disciples, and whatever remained of the day, he spent in singing psalms ; he also passed all the night awake, in joy and thanksgiving, unless a short sleep prevented it ; in which case he no sooner awoke than he presently repeated his wonted exercises, and ceased not to give thanks to God with uplifted hands. I declare with truth, that I have never seen with my eyes, nor heard with my ears, any man so earnest in giving thanks to the living God.

"O truly happy man ! He chanted the sentence of St. Paul the apostle, 'It is dreadful to fall into the hands of the living God,' and much more out of Holy Writ ; wherein also he admonished us to think of our last hour, and to shake off the sleep of the soul ; and being learned in our poetry, he said some things also in our tongue, for he said, putting the same into English,

"'For tham neod-fere
Nenig wyrtheth
Thances snottra
Thonne him thearf sy
To gehiggene
Ær his heonen-gange
Hwet his gaste
Godes oththe yveles
Æfter deathe heonen
Demed wurthe.'

which means this :—

"'No man is wiser than is requisite, before the necessary departure ; that is, to consider, before the soul departs hence, what good or evil it hath done, and how it is to be judged after its departure.'

"He also sang antiphons according to our custom and his own, one of which is, 'O glorious King, Lord of all power, who, triumphing this day, didst ascend above all the heavens ; do not forsake us orphans ; but send down upon us the Spirit of truth which was promised to us by the Father. Hallelujah!' And when he came to that word, 'do not forsake us,' he burst into tears, and wept much, and an hour after he began to repeat what he had commenced, and we, hearing it, mourned with him. By turns we read, and by turns we wept, nay, we wept always whilst we read. In such joy we passed the days of Lent, till the aforesaid day ; and he rejoiced much, and gave God thanks, because he had been thought worthy to be so weakened. He often repeated, 'That God scourgeth every son whom he receiveth;' and much more out of Holy Scripture ; as also this sentence from St. Ambrose, 'I have not lived so as to be ashamed to live among you ; nor do I fear to die, because we have a gracious God.' During these days he laboured to compose two works well worthy to be remembered, besides the lessons we had from him, and singing of Psalms ; viz. he translated the Gospel of St. John as far as the words : 'But what are these among so many,' etc. [St. John, vi. 9.] into our own tongue, for the benefit of the church ; and some collections out of the Book of Notes of bishop Isidorus, saying : 'I will not have my pupils read a falsehood, nor labour therein without profit after my death.' When the Tuesday before the ascension of our Lord came, he began to suffer still more in his breath, and a small swelling appeared in his feet ; but he passed all that day and dictated cheerfully, and now and then among other things, said, 'Go on quickly, I know not how long I shall hold out, and whether my Maker will not soon take me away.' But to us he seemed very well to know the time of his departure ; and so he spent the night, awake, in thanksgiving ; and when the morning appeared, that is, Wednesday, he ordered us to write with all speed what he had begun ; and this done, we walked till the third hour with the relics of saints, according to the custom of that day. There was one of us with him, who said to him, 'Most dear master, there is still one chapter wanting : do you think it troublesome to be asked any more questions ?' He answered, 'It is no trouble. Take your pen, and make ready, and write fast.' Which he did, but at the ninth hour he said to me, 'I have some little articles of value in my chest, such as pepper, napkins, and incense : run quickly, and bring the priests of our monastery to me, that I may distribute among them the gifts which God has bestowed on me. The rich in this world are bent on giving gold and silver and other precious things. But I, in charity, will joyfully give my brothers what God has given unto me.' He spoke to every one of them, admonishing and entreating them that they would carefully say masses and prayers for him, which they readily promised; but they all mourned and wept, especially because he said, 'They should no more see his face in this world.' They rejoiced for that he said, 'It is time that I return to Him who formed me out of nothing: I have lived long; my merciful Judge well foresaw my life for me; the time of my dissolution draws nigh; for I desire to die and to be with Christ.' Having said much more, he passed the day joyfully till the evening; and the boy, above mentioned, said: 'Dear master, there is yet one sentence not written.' He answered, 'Write quickly.' Soon after, the boy said, 'The sentence is now written.' He replied, 'It is well, you have said the truth. It is ended. Receive my head into your hands, for it is a great satisfaction to me to sit facing my holy place, where I was wont to pray, that I may also sitting call upon my Father.' And thus on the pavement of his little cell, singing: 'Glory be to the Father, and to the Son, and to the Holy Ghost,' when he had named the Holy Ghost, he breathed his last, and so departed to the heavenly kingdom. All who were present at the death of the blessed father, said they had never seen any other person expire with so much devotion, and in so tranquil a frame of mind. For as you have heard, so long as the soul animated his body, he never ceased to give thanks to the true and living God, with expanded hands exclaiming: 'Glory be to the Father, and to the Son, and to the Holy Ghost!' with other spiritual ejaculations. But know this, dearest brother, that I could say much concerning him, if my want of learning did not cut short my discourse. Nevertheless, by the grace of God, I purpose shortly to write more concerning him, particularly of those things which I saw with my own eyes, and heard with my own ears."

As we learn from this letter of Cuthbert that Bede died on St. Ascension-day which he states to have been that year the seventh before the kalends of June, this fact enables us to fix it on the 26th May, in the year of our Lord 735.

The remains of the venerable Bede were placed first under

the south porch of the church. After being removed to a
more honourable situation within the church, they were
stolen from the monastery by Elfred a priest of Durham,
who used for some years previously to offer up his prayers
at Bede's tomb, on the anniversary of his death.

"On one of these occasions," says Simeon of Durham,
"he went to Jarrow as usual, and having spent some days
in the church in solitude, praying and watching, he returned
in the early morning alone to Durham, without the knowledge of his companions—a thing which he had never done
before—as though he wished to have no witness to his secret.
Now, although he lived many years afterwards, yet he never
again visited Jarrow, and it appeared as if he had achieved
the object of his desires. When, also, he was asked by his
most intimate friends, 'Where were the bones of venerable
Bede?' he would reply, 'No one can answer that question
so well as I. You may be assured, my brethren, beyond all
doubt, that the same chest which holds the hallowed body of
our father Cuthbert, also contains the bones of Bede, our
reverend teacher and brother. It is useless to search beyond that little corner for any portion of his relics.' "

By this artifice the cathedral of Durham obtained possession of a valuable source of revenue in the offerings which
were sure to be made at the tomb of so venerable a man.
The theft was kept secret by the brethren until all who
could have reclaimed the body were dead, and so Bede's
bones remained until A.D. 1104, when St. Cuthbert's relics
were removed, and those of Bede were placed alone in a
linen bag in the same chest. Fifty years afterwards Hugh
Pudsey, bishop of Durham, erected a shrine of gold and
silver, adorned with jewels, in which he enclosed the relics
of venerable Bede, with an inscription placed on it, which
may be translated thus:

Within this chest Bede's mortal body lies.

In the reign of Henry VIII this beautiful shrine was
demolished, and the saintly relics were treated with every
indignity by the insane and ignorant mob. The only memorial now remaining in Durham cathedral of its having
once been the resting-place of Bede's remains, is a long

inscription to his memory concluding with the well known monkish rhyme :—

"Hac sunt in fossa Bedæ venerabilis ossa."

Here lie beneath these stones—venerable Bede's bones.

CHAP. III.—ANALYSIS OF BEDE'S ECCLESIASTICAL HISTORY.

THE Ecclesiastical History of venerable Bede was first published on the Continent: numerous editions of it have been printed, which it is here necessary to enumerate.

It was first published in England by Wheloc, fol. Cantab. 1643-4, with an Appendix containing the Anglo-Saxon translation by king Alfred the Great.

To this succeeded the edition of Smith, printed at Cambridge in 1722, which superseded all the preceding. The basis of this edition was a MS. formerly belonging to More, bishop of Ely, and now deposited in the public library at Cambridge. [Kk, 5, 16.] At the end of the MS., which is written in Anglo-Saxon letters, are several notes in a somewhat later handwriting, by which it would appear that the volume was copied in the year 737, i.e. two years after Bede's death, and probably from the author's original manuscript.

The last edition of this celebrated and valuable work is that of Stevenson, published by the English Historical Society, Lond. 8vo. 1838. The editor professes to have used the same MS. of bishop More, and to have occasionally collated four others [Cotton. Tib. C, II, Tib. A, XIV, Harl. 4978, and King's MS. 13 C, V.]. Prefixed to the volume is a copious and valuable notice of the author and his work, from which we take the liberty of making the following long extract, as containing the most judicious account of this our author's greatest work.

"The scope of this valuable and justly esteemed work is sufficiently indicated by its title. After some observations upon the position, inhabitants, and natural productions of Britain, the author gives a rapid sketch of its history from the earliest period until the arrival of Augustine in A.D. 597, at which era, in his opinion, the ecclesiastical history of our nation had its commencement. After that event, he treats, as was to be expected, for a time exclusively of the circumstances which occurred in Kent; but, as Christianity extended itself over the other kingdoms into which England was then divided, he gradually includes their history in his narrative, until he reaches the year 731. Here he concludes his work, which embraces a space of one hundred and thirty-four years, with a general outline of the ecclesiastical state of the island.

"The Introduction, which extends from the commencement of the work to the conversion of the Saxons to Christianity, is gleaned, as Bede himself informs us, from various writers. The chief sources for the description of Britain are Pliny, Solinus, Orosius, and Gildas; St. Basil is also cited; and the traditions which were current in Bede's own day are occasionally introduced. The history of the Romans in Britain is founded chiefly upon Orosius, Eutropius, and Gildas, corrected, however, in some places by the author, apparently from tradition or local information, and augmented by an account of the introduction of Christianity under Lucius, of the martyrdom of St. Alban, copied apparently from some legend, and of the origin of the Pelagian heresy,—all of them circumstances intimately connected with the ecclesiastical history of the island. The mention of Hengist and Horsa, and the allusion to the tomb of the latter at Horstead, render it probable that the account which Bede gives of the arrival of the Teutonic tribes, and their settlement in England, was communicated by Albinus and Nothelm. It is purely fabulous, being, in fact, not the history, but the tradition, of the Jutish kingdom of Kent, as appears from circumstances mentioned elsewhere in this work, as well as from the authorities there quoted. The two visits of Germanus to England, so important in the history of its religion, are introduced in the very words of Constantius Lugdunensis, and must therefore have been copied from that author. The ante-Augustine portion of the history is terminated by extracts from Gildas, relative to the conflicts between the Saxons and Britons. As the mission of Augustine in A.D. 596 is the period at which Bede ceases to speak of himself as a compiler, and assumes the character of an historian, it becomes incumbent upon us to examine into the sources upon which he has founded this, by far the most interesting portion of his history. The materials which he employed seem to have consisted of (I.) written documents, and (II.) verbal information. (I.) The written materials may be divided into (1.) Historical information drawn up and communicated by his correspondents for the express purpose of being employed in his work; (2.) documents pre-existing in a narrative form, and (3.) transcripts of official documents.

" (1.) That Bede's correspondents drew up and communicated to him information which he used when writing this history, is certain from what he states in its prologue; and it is highly probable that to them we are indebted for many particulars connected with the history of kingdoms situated to the south of the river Humber, with which a monk of Jarrow, from his local position, was probably unacquainted. Traces of the assistance which he derived from Canterbury are perceptible in the minute acquaintance which he exhibits not only with the topography of Kent, but with its condition at the time when he wrote; and the same remark is applicable, although in a more limited degree, to most of the southern kingdoms.

"(2.) Documents pre-existing in an historical form are seldom quoted: amongst those of which use has been made may be numbered the Life of Gregory the Great, written by Paulus Diaconus; the miracles of Ethelberga, abbess of Barking; the Life of Sebbi, king of the East Saxons; the Legend of Fursey; and that of Cuthbert of Lindisfarne, formerly written by Bede, but now augmented by himself, with additional facts. These, together with some extracts from the Treatise of Arculf de Locis Sanctis, are all the written documents to which the author refers.

" That other narratives, however, were in Bede's possession, of which he has made liberal use, is certain from his express words, and may also be inferred from internal evidence. Albinus and Nothelm appear to have furnished him with chronicles, in which he found accurate and full information upon the pedigrees, accessions, marriages, exploits, descendants, deaths, and burials of the kings of Kent. From the same source he derived his valuable account of the archbishops of Canterbury, both before and after ordination, the place and date of consecration, even though it took place abroad the

days on which they severally took possession of that see, the
duration of their episcopate, their deaths, burial-places, and
the intervals which elapsed before the election of a successor.
It is evident that the minuteness and accuracy of this information could have been preserved only by means of contemporary written memoranda. That such records existed
in the time of the Saxons cannot be doubted, for Bede intro-
duces a story by which it appears that the abbey of Selsey
possessed a volume in which were entered the obits of
eminent individuals; and the same custom probably prevailed throughout the other monastic establishments of England.

"The history of the diocese of Rochester was communicated by Albinus and Nothelm. It is exceedingly barren of
particulars, and probably would have been even more so, had
it not been connected with the life of Paulinus of York, concerning whom Bede appears to have obtained information
from other quarters.

"The early annals of East Anglia are equally scanty, as
we have little more than a short pedigree of its kings, an
account of its conversion to Christianity, the history of
Sigebert and Anna, and a few particulars regarding its
bishops, Felix, Thomas, Bertgils, and Bisi, which details
were communicated in part by Albinus and Nothelm.

"The history of the West Saxons was derived partly
from the same authorities, and partly from the information of
Daniel, bishop of Winchester. It relates to their conversion
by Birinus, the reigns of Cædwalla and of Ina, and the pontificate of Wini, Aldhelm, and Daniel. To this last named
bishop we are indebted for a portion of the little of what is
known as to the early history of the South Saxons and the
Isle of Wight, the last of the Saxon kingdoms which embraced the Christian faith. It relates to the conversion of
those districts by the agency of Wilfrid. A few unimportant additions are afterwards made in a hurried and incidental
manner, evidently showing that Bede's information upon this
head was neither copious nor definite.

"The monks of Lastingham furnished materials relative
to the ministry of Cedd and Chad, by whose preaching the
Mercians were induced to renounce paganism. The history
of this kingdom is obscure, and consists of an account of its

conversion, the succession of its sovereigns and its bishops. The neighbouring state of Middle Anglia, which, if ever independent of Mercia, soon merged in it, is similarly circumstanced, and we are perhaps indebted to its connexion with the princes and bishops of Northumbria for what is known of its early history.

"Lindsey, part of Lincolnshire, although situated so near to the kingdom of Northumbria, was both politically and ecclesiastically independent of it, and Bede was as ignorant of the transactions of that province as of those which were much more remote from Jarrow. He received some materials from bishop Cynebert, but they appear to have been scanty, for the circumstances which relate to Lincolnshire are generally derived from the information of other witnesses.

"The history of East Saxony is more copious, and is derived partly from the communications of Albinus and Nothelm, and partly from the monks of Lastingham. To the first of these two sources we must probably refer the account of the pontificate of Mellitus, and the apostasy of the sons of Sabert,—circumstances too intimately connected with the see of Canterbury to be omitted in its annals. To the latter we are indebted for the history of the reconversion of Saxony,—an event in which the monks of Lastingham were interested, as it was accomplished by their founder Cedd. From them Bede also received an account of the ministry of Chad. Some further details respecting its civil and ecclesiastical affairs, the life of Earconwald, bishop of London, and the journey of Offa to Rome, conclude the information which we have respecting this kingdom.

"In the history of Northumbria Bede, as a native, was particularly interested, and would probably exert himself to procure the most copious and authentic information regarding it. Although he gives no intimation of having had access to previous historical documents, when speaking of his sources of information, yet there seems reason to believe that he has made use of such materials. We may infer from what he says of the mode in which Oswald's reign was generally calculated, that in this king's time there existed Annals or Chronological Tables, in which events were inserted as they occurred, the regnal year of the monarch who then filled the throne being at the time specified. These annals appear to have extended beyond the period of the conversion of Northumbria to Christianity, although it is difficult to imagine how any chronological calculation or record of events could be preserved before the use of letters had become known. But the history of Edwin, with its interesting details, shows that Bede must have had access to highly valuable materials which reached back to the very earliest era of authentic history; and we need not be surprised at finding information of a similar character throughout the remainder of his history of Northumbria. Accordingly we have minute accounts of the pedigrees of its kings, their accession, exploits, anecdotes of them, and sketches of their character, their deaths, and the duration of their reigns,—details too minute in themselves, and too accurately defined by Bede, to have been derived by him from tradition. Similar proofs might, if necessary, be drawn from the history of its bishops.

"(3.) The Historia Ecclesiastica contains various transcripts of important official documents. These are of two classes, either such as were sent from the Papal Court to the princes and ecclesiastics of England, or were the production of native writers. The first were transcribed from the Papal Regesta by Nothelm of London, during a residence at Rome, and were sent to Bede by the advice of his friend Albinus of Canterbury. They relate to the history of the kingdoms of Kent and Northumbria. The letters of archbishops Laurentius and Honorius, concerning the proper time for celebrating Easter, were probably furnished by the same individual. The proceedings of the councils of Hertford and Hatfield may have been derived from the archives of Bede's own monastery, since it was customary in the early ages of the church for each ecclesiastical establishment to have a 'tabularium' in which were deposited the synodal decrees by which its members were governed.

"(II.) A considerable portion of the Historia Ecclesiastica, especially that part of it which relates to the kingdom of Northumberland, is founded upon local information which its author derived from various individuals. On almost every occasion Bede gives the name and designation of his informant, being anxious, apparently, to show that nothing is inserted for which he had not the testimony of some respectable witness.   Some of these persons are credible from having been present at the event which they related; others, from the high rank which they held in the church, such as Acca, bishop of Hexham, Guthfrid, abbat of Lindisfarne, Berthun, abbat of Beverley, and Pechthelm, bishop of Whitherne.   The author received secondary evidence with caution, for he distinguishes between the statements which he received from eye-witnesses, and those which reached him through a succession of informants.   In the last of these instances, the channel of information is always pointed out with scrupulous exactness, whatever opinion we may entertain, as in the case of some visions and miracles, of the credibility of the facts themselves."

Of the value of this work we can have no better evidence than the fact of its having been so often translated into the vernacular tongue.   King Alfred thought it not beneath his dignity to render it familiar to his Anglo-Saxon subjects, by translating it into their tongue.

The first version in modern English was that of Stapleton, bearing the following title, " The History of the Church of Englande, compiled by Venerable Bede, Englishman, translated out of Latin into English by Thomas Stapleton, Student in Divinity.   Antw. by John Laet, 1565."   The object of the translator was to recall the affections of the people to the theological forms and doctrines which in his time were being exploded.   In the dedication to queen Elizabeth occurs the following passage :—" In this History Your Hignes shall see in how many and weighty pointes the pretended reformers of the Church in Your Graces dominions have departed from the patern of that sounde and catholike faith planted first among Englishmen by holy S. AUGUSTIN our Apostle, and his virtuous company, described truly and sincerely by *Venerable* BEDE, so called in all Christendom for his passing vertues and rare learning, the Author of this History.   And to thentent Your Highnes intention bent to weightier considerations and affaires may spende no longe time in espying oute the particulars, I have gathered out of the whole History a number of diversities betwene the pretended religion of Protestants, and the primitive faith of the English Church."

The work was again translated into English by John Stevens, Lond. 8vo. 1723; and a third time (with some omissions) by W. Hurst, Lond. 8vo. 1814, and apparently with the same object which influenced Stapleton.

In 1840, the editor of the present volume published a new edition of Stevens's translation, altering it in many respects, and correcting the orthography of proper names, according to the modern and generally received standard. A second edition of the same volume was published in 1842. In the same year also it was introduced, to accompany the Latin text, in the second volume of an edition of the complete works of Venerable Bede, and is now a fourth time printed with the other works contained in this volume. As the translation has on each occasion received certain corrections, it is hoped that the English reader will now find it to convey a tolerably accurate notion of the style and sense of the original.

CHAP. IV.—OF THE SAXON CHRONICLE.

THE work, which passes under the name of the Saxon Chronicle, is a continued narrative written at different dates, and in the Anglo-Saxon language, of the most important events of English History from the earliest period to the year of our Lord 1154. As it is evident, both from the antiquity of the very manuscripts of it now extant, as well as from certain allusions and forms of speech which occur in it, that the latter part of it at least was written by a person contemporary with the events which he relates, it cannot but be an object of interest and of great historical importance to examine so ancient a writing according to all the modes which literary criticism can suggest; and this inquiry becomes the more imperative from the extreme probability that the earlier part of the Chronicle is also of a contemporary character, and therefore ascends to a very earlier period of Saxon history, even to the time of the Heptarchy itself. This opinion rests upon the remarkable fact, that whilst the dialect of the latter portion of the Chronicle approaches very nearly to our modern English, the early part of it bears the impress of times much more rude and ancient, and the language in which it is written is absolutely unintelligible to the modern Englishman, who has not made the Anglo-Saxon tongue a serious object of his study.

The first point which suggests itself to the inquirer, concerns the form in which so valuable a national monument has come down to us. I shall not deem it necessary to delay the reader's attention by an account of the mode in which our large public and private collections of manuscripts have been formed. It is sufficient to observe that in all our collections of MSS. there are now only six ancient copies of the Saxon Chronicle known to be in existence. We will proceed to enumerate and describe them in order.

I. The first copy of this Chronicle is generally known by the name of the Benet or Plegmund MS., so called because it is preserved in Benet [now Corpus Christi] College, Cambridge, and because Plegmund, archbishop of Canterbury, in the reign of king Alfred, is thought to have had some hand in compiling the first part of it.

"From internal evidence of an indirect nature," says Dr. Ingram, "there is great reason to presume that archbishop Plegmund transcribed or superintended this very copy of the Saxon Annals to the year 891, the year in which he came to the see. Wanley observes it is written in one and the same hand to this year, and in hands equally ancient to the year 924, after which it is continued in different hands to the end.

"At the end of the year 890 is added, in a neat but imitative hand, the following interpolation, which is betrayed by the faintness of the ink, as well as by the Norman cast of the dialect and orthography:

"Her wæs Plegemund gecoron of gode and of eallen his halechen.

"There are many other interpolations in this MS.;* a particular account of which, however curious, would necessarily become tedious. A few only are here selected, with a view to illustrate the critical apparatus of this work, and the progressive accumulation of historical facts. They are generally very short, except where an erasure has been made to find room for them. The notice of the birth of St. Dunstan, as of every thing else relating to him, appears to be a monastic interpolation. His death is mentioned in the margin, in a very minute hand, in Latin. There seems to be nothing of any great value in this MS. beyond the time of Alfric, whose

* The death of Plegmund for instance.

death is recorded, after a considerable chasm, in the year 1006. After this period the notices of events and transactions are very scanty and defective. The royal donation of the haven of Sandwich to Christ Church, Canterbury, is placed to the year 1031, but evidently written after the conquest, and left unfinished. The Saxon part ends in the year 1070, with the words, - - bletsungan underfeng ; after describing at full length the dispute between the archbishops of Canterbury and York."*

II. The second copy of the Saxon Chronicle is in the British Museum. [MS. COTTON, TIBERIUS A. vi.] It is "written in the same hand with much neatness and accuracy, from the beginning to the end," and "is of very high authority and antiquity. It was probably written c. 977, where it terminates. The hand-writing resembles that ascribed to St. Dunstan. It narrowly escaped destruction in the fire at Westminster, previous to its removal to its present place of custody, being one of Sir R. Cotton's MSS., formerly belonging to the monastery of St. Augustine's, Canterbury."†

III. A third MS. is also in the British Museum. [Cott. Tib. B. i.]

"This MS., though frequently quoted by Somner in his Dictionary under the title of 'Chronica Abbendoniæ,' or the Abingdon Chronicle, and said to have been transcribed by him, seems not to have been known to Gibson, though noticed by Nicolson within a few years after the appearance of his edition.‡ It contains many important additions to the former Chronicles, some of which are confirmed by C. T. B. iv. ; but many are not to be found in any other MS., particularly those in the latter part of it. These are now incorporated with the old materials. Wanley considers the handwriting to be the same to the end of the year 1048. The orthography, however, varies about the year 890 (889 of the printed Chronicle). The writer seems to have been startled at Offæ for Oththan, i. e. Othoni, A.D. 925 ; for there is a chasm from that place to the year 934, when a slight notice is introduced of the expedition of Athelstan into Scotland.§

---

* Dr. Ingram's preface, p. xx.   † Ibid.
‡ English Historical Library, Part I. p. 116.
§ Most of the MSS. are defective here; and the thread of history, during this turbulent period, appears to have been often disturbed. But

In the year 982 are some curious particulars respecting the wars of Otho II. in Greece, and his victories there over the Saracens, now first printed. From the same source, and from *C. T.* B. iv., we have been enabled to present to the reader of English history a more copious and accurate account than has hitherto appeared, of the Danish invasions, the civil wars in the reign of Edward the Confessor, and the battles of Harold previous to the Norman Conquest. The MS. terminates imperfectly in 1066, after describing most minutely the battle of Stanford-bridge ; the few lines which appear in the last page being supplied by a much later hand."

IV. A fourth copy of the Saxon Chronicle occurs also in the British Museum. [Cott. Tiberius B. iv.]

"This MS. like the preceding, though of invaluable authority, was unknown to Gibson. It is written in a plain and beautiful hand, with few abbreviations, and apparently copied in the early part, with the exception of the introductory description of Britain, from a very ancient MS. The defective parts, from A.D. 261 to 693, were long since supplied from four excellent MSS. by Josselyn ; who also collated it throughout with the same ; inserting from them, both in the text and in the margin, such passages as came within his notice ; which are so numerous, that very few seem to have eluded his vigilant search. A smaller but elegant hand commences fol. 68, A.D. 1016 ; and it is continued to the end, A.D. 1079, in a similar hand, though by different writers. Wanley notices a difference in the year 1052. The value and importance of this MS., as well as of the preceding, will be best exemplified by a reference to the notes and various readings in the present edition. The last notice of it will be found in page 456."

V. The fifth MS. is in the Bodleian Library at Oxford. [Laud E, 80.]

It is so "well known, from being made the basis of Gibson's edition where Wheloc's was deficient, that it will not be so necessary to enlarge on it here. It is a fair copy of older Chronicles, with a few inaccuracies, omissions, and interpolations, to the year 1122 ; therefore no part of it was written

poetry took advantage of the circumstance, and occasionally filled a chasm with some of the earliest specimens of the northern muse ; the preservation of which we owe exclusively to the Saxon Chronicle.

d

before that period. The next ten years rather exhibit different ink than a different writer. From 1132 to the end,
A.D. 1154, the language and orthography became gradually
more Normanized, particularly in the reign of king Stephen;
the account of which was not written till the close of it.
The dates not being regularly affixed to the last ten years,
Wanley has inadvertently described this MS. as ending
A.D. 1143; whereas it is continued eleven years afterwards."

VI. The sixth and last copy is in the British Museum.
[Cotton, Domitian A. viii.]

"This is a singularly curious MS., attributed generally to
a monk of Christ Church, Canterbury, on account of the
monastic interpolations. It is often quoted and commended
by H. Wharton, in his Anglia Sacra, because it contains
much ecclesiastical and local information. We consider it,
however, of the least authority among the Cotton MSS.,
because the writer has taken greater liberties in abridging
former Chronicles, and inserting translations of Latin documents in his own Normanized dialect. Frithstan, bishop of
Winchester, who died A.D. 931 according to this Chronicle,
is called biscop Wentanus; and Byrnstanus [Brinstan] is said
to have been consecrated on his loh—*in ejus* locum. *lieu*, Fr.
Its very peculiarities, nevertheless, stamp a great value on
it; and its frauds are harmless, if possible, because they are
easily detected. Towards the end the writer intended to
say something about prince Edward, the father of Edgar and
Margaret; but it is nearly obliterated, and the MS. soon
after concludes, A.D. 1058. It is remarkable for being
written both in Latin and Saxon; but for what purpose it is
now needless to conjecture. It is said to have been given to
Sir Robert Cotton by Camden. The passages printed from
it by Gibson, and the variations in the margin, marked *Cot.*,
are from the collations of Junius inserted in his copy of
Wheloc. There does not appear to have been any entire
transcript of the MS., as we find it sometimes stated.* Gibson takes no notice of the introductory description of Britain
as being in this MS., and he dates its termination in the
wrong place. We have therefore had recourse to it again in
the British Museum, where it is deposited."

* Vid. Wanl. Cat. p. 220.

Besides these six, no other ancient copy is known to exist; but there is a single leaf of an ancient copy in the British Museum. [Cotton, Tiberius A iii.] There are also three modern transcripts, two of which are in the Bodleian library, [Junian MSS. and Laud G. 36,] and one in the Dublin library. [E 5, 15.] The Bodleian transcripts are taken from two of the Cotton MSS., and therefore are of little critical value; but the Dublin transcript appears to be taken from an original, now lost, [Cott. Otho B. xi.] and therefore it possesses an independent authority.

" At the end of the Dublin transcript is this note, in the hand-writing of archbishop Usher : ' These Annales are extant in Sr R. Cotton's Librarye at the ende of Bede's Historye in the Saxon Tongue.' This accords with the description of the MS. in Wanley's Catalogue, p. 219 ; to which the reader is referred for more minute particulars. As this MS. was therefore in existence so late as 1705, when Wanley published his Catalogue, there can be little doubt that it perished in the lamentable fire of 1731, which either destroyed or damaged so many of the Cotton MSS. while deposited in a house in Little Dean's Yard, Westminster."

" This transcript is become more valuable from the loss of the original. It appears from dates by Lambard himself, at the beginning and end, that it was begun by him in 1563, and finished in 1564, when he was about the age of twenty-five. In the front is this inscription in Saxon characters :

Willm lambarde, 1563 ; and, wulfhelm lambheord ; with this addition, wæccath thine leoht-fæt ; which may be thus translated :

' Lambard, arise ; awake thy lamp.'

At the end is the following memorandum : ' Finis : 9 Aprilis, 1564. W. L. propria manu.' I am informed by several gentlemen of Trinity College, Dublin, to whom I am indebted for most of the particulars relating to this transcript, that it was once in the possession of archbishop Usher, and is the same mentioned in his Ecclesiastical History, p. 182, which Nicolson says ' is worth the inquiring after.'[*] It came into the Dublin Library with the other MSS. of the archbishop, according to his original intention, after the restoration of Charles II."

[*] English Historical Library, Part I. p. 117.

· To these six, or if we include the Dublin MS., seven, copies of the Saxon Chronicle, must our inquiry therefore be confined ; and the first point worthy of notice, is the fact, that no two of them agree in the date at which they terminate. Thus :

No. 2. comes down no later than A.D. 977.

„ 7. ends at A.D. 1001.

„ 6. ends imperfectly at 1058.

„ 3. ends at 1066.

„ 1. ends at 1070.

„ 4. ends abruptly at 1080.

„ 5. ends imperfectly at 1154.

· This diversity can hardly be accounted for on any other view of the case, than that which applies to a large number of other ancient writings, and is peculiarly forcible as applied to a series of annals like the work before us.

Almost every monastery had its own historiographer or historian, whose business or at least whose general practice it was to copy the history of preceding times from those who were already known to have written of them with success, and to continue the narrative, during his own times, in his own words, to the best of his ability. Now in the case of the Saxon Chronicle we may reasonably suppose that its original groundwork consisted of little more than a meagre string of events, arranged chronologically with a few genealogies and notices of the deaths and births of the kings and other distinguished personages. In the limited dimensions within which learning was confined during the Anglo-Saxon Heptarchy, and in consequence also of the paucity of scholars, it is more likely that such a record would become generally used than that new ones would be written, and most of the monasteries would probably possess a copy of the early part of these annals, which afterwards they would bring down to their own times. Consistent with this theory is the evident fact that the existing MSS. coming from different religious houses, all differ in the year at which they terminate, as if the last transcriber of the shortest had not been aware that the copy which he followed was less complete than those which existed elsewhere.*

* A case exactly in point to illustrate this suggestion occurs in the letters of Arnulf bishop of Lisieux under Henry II. Seven MSS. only exist :

But there is another peculiarity in the MSS. of the Saxon Chronicle which almost proves for certain the account above given. Some of these MSS. are more diffuse than the others about the affairs of the particular monastery in which they are believed to have been written. Thus one of them, especially, is most minute concerning the affairs of Peterborough,—a fact, which, almost without other evidence, would prove it to have been transcribed within the walls of that monastery.

However this theory, which lies upon the surface of the inquiry concerning the mode in which the Saxon Chronicle was compiled, may be thought worthy or not of the reader's attention, I am not disposed to waive it in favour of any other ; for numerous writers have already tried to go more deeply into the subject, and have failed in eliciting more than vague and remote probabilities. The following remarks are taken from the Preface of Dr. Ingram, and I do not scruple to insert them, although the quotation is rather long, because they show the train of thought which arose in the mind of one who as yet stands foremost among the translators and illustrators of the Anglo-Saxon Chronicle.

"It is now time to examine, who were probably the writers of these annals. I say probably, because we have very little more than rational conjecture to guide us.

"The period antecedent to the times of Bede, except where passages were afterwards asserted, was perhaps little else, originally, than a kind of chronological table of events, with a few genealogies, and notices of the death and succession of kings and other distinguished personages. But it is evident from the preface of Bede and from many passages in his work, that he received considerable assistance from Saxon bishops, abbats and others ; who not only communicated certain traditional facts *viva voce*, but also transmitted to him many written documents. These, therefore, must have been the early chronicles of Wessex, of Kent, and of the other provinces of the Heptarchy ; which formed together the groundwork of his history. With greater honesty than most of his followers, he has given us the names of those

six of which contain about seventy letters only. On coming to examine the seventh in St. John's College Library, I was at once enabled to augment the number to 130.

learned persons who assisted him with this local information. The first is Alcuinus or Albinus, an abbat of Canterbury, at whose instigation he undertook the work; who sent by Nothelm, afterwards archbishop of that province, a full account of all ecclesiastical transactions in Kent, and in the contiguous districts, from the first conversion of the Saxons. From the same source he partly derived his information respecting the provinces of Essex, Wessex, East Anglia, and Northumbria. Bishop Daniel communicated to him by letter many particulars concerning Wessex, Sussex, and the Isle of Wight. He acknowledges assistance more than once '*ex scriptis priorum;*' and there is every reason to believe that some of these preceding records were the Anglo-Saxon annals; for we have already seen that such records were in existence before the age of Nennius. In proof of this we may observe, that even the phraseology sometimes partakes more of the Saxon idiom than the Latin. If, therefore, it be admitted, as there is every reason to conclude from the foregoing remarks, that certain succinct and chronological arrangements of historical facts had taken place in several provinces of the Heptarchy before the time of Bede, let us inquire by whom they were likely to have been made.

"In the province of Kent, the first person on record, who is celebrated for his learning, is Tobias, the ninth bishop of Rochester, who succeeded to that see in 693. He is noticed by Bede as not only furnished with an ample store of Greek and Latin literature, but skilled also in the Saxon language and erudition. It is probable, therefore, that he left some proofs of this attention to his native language; and, as he died within a few years of Bede, the latter would naturally avail himself of his labours. It is worthy also of remark, that Berthwald, who succeeded to the illustrious Theodore of Tarsus in 690, was the first English or Saxon archbishop of Canterbury. From this period, consequently, we may date that cultivation of the vernacular tongue which would lead to the composition of brief chronicles,* and other vehicles of instruction, necessary for the improvement of a rude and illiterate people. The first chronicles were, perhaps, those of Kent or Wessex; which seem to have been regularly

* "The materials, however, though not regularly arranged, must be traced to a much higher source.

continued, at intervals, by the archbishops of Canterbury, or by their direction,* at least as far as the year 1001, or even 1070; for the Benet MS. which some call the Plegmund MS. ends in the latter year; the rest being in Latin. From internal evidence indeed, of an indirect nature, there is great reason to presume, that archbishop Plegmund transcribed or superintended this very copy of the Saxon annals to the year 891; † the year in which he came to the see; inserting, both before and after this date, to the time of his death in 923, such additional materials as he was well qualified to furnish from his high station and learning, and the confidential intercourse which he enjoyed in the court of king Alfred. The total omission of his own name, except by another hand, affords indirect evidence of some importance in support of this conjecture. Whether king Alfred himself was the author of a distinct and separate Chronicle of Wessex, cannot now be determined. That he furnished additional supplies of historical matter to the older chronicles is, I conceive, sufficiently obvious to every reader who will take the trouble of examining the subject. The argument of Dr. Beeke, the present dean of Bristol, in an obliging letter to the editor on this subject, is not without its force;—that it is extremely improbable, when we consider the number and variety of king Alfred's works, that he should have neglected the history of his own country. Besides a genealogy of the kings of Wessex from Cerdic to his own time, which seems never to have been incorporated with any MS. of the Saxon Chronicle, though prefixed or annexed to several, he undoubtedly preserved many traditionary facts; with a full and circumstantial detail of his own operations, as well as those of his father, brother, and other members of his family; which scarcely any other person than himself could have supplied. To doubt this, would be as incredulous a thing as to deny that Xenophon wrote his Anabasis, or Cæsar his Commentaries. From the time of Alfred and Plegmund to

---

* "Josselyn collated two Kentish MSS. of the first authority; one of which he calls the History or Chronicle of St. Augustine's, the other that of Christ Church, Canterbury. The former was perhaps the one marked in our series C. T. A vi.; the latter the Benet or Plegmund MS.

† "Wanley observes, that the Benet MS. is written in one and the same hand to this year, and in hands equally ancient to the year 924; after which it is continued in different hands to the end. Vid. Cat. p. 130.

a few years after the Norman Conquest, these chronicles seem to have been continued by different hands, under the auspices of such men as archbishops Dunstan, Alfric, and others, whose characters have been much misrepresented by ignorance and scepticism on the one hand, as well as by mistaken zeal and devotion on the other. The indirect evidence respecting Dunstan and Alfric is as curious as that concerning Plegmund ; but the discussion of it would lead us into a wide and barren field of investigation ; nor is this the place to refute the errors of Hickes, Cave, and Wharton, already noticed by Wanley in his preface. The Chronicles of Abingdon, of Worcester, of Peterborough, and others, are continued in the same manner by different hands ; partly, though not exclusively, by monks of those monasteries, who very naturally inserted many particulars relating to their own local interests and concerns ; which, so far from invalidating the general history, render it more interesting and valuable. It would be a vain and frivolous attempt to ascribe these latter compilations to particular persons,* where there were evidently so many contributors ; but that they were successively furnished by contemporary writers, many of whom were eye-witnesses of the events and transactions which they relate, there is abundance of internal evidence to convince us. Many instances of this the editor had taken some pains to collect, in order to lay them before the reader in the preface ; but they are so numerous that the subject would necessarily become tedious ; and therefore every reader must be left to find them for himself. They will amply repay him for his trouble, if he takes any interest in the early history of England, or in the general construction of authentic history of any kind. He will see plagiarisms without end in the Latin histories, and will be in no danger of falling into the errors of Gale and others ; not to mention those of our historians, who were not professed antiquaries, who mistook that for original and authentic testimony which was only translated. It is remarkable that the Saxon Chronicle gradually expires with the Saxon language, almost melted into modern English, in the year 1154.

* "Hickes supposed the *Laud* or Peterborough Chronicle to have been compiled by Hugo Candidus (Albus, or White), or some other monk of that house.

From this period almost to the Reformation, whatever knowledge we have of the affairs of England has been originally derived either from the semi-barbarous Latin of our own countrymen, or from the French chronicles of Froissart and others.

"The revival of good taste and of good sense, and of the good old custom adopted by most nations of the civilized world—that of writing their own history in their own language—was happily exemplified at length in the laborious works of our English chroniclers and historians.

"Many have since followed in the same track; and the importance of the whole body of English history has attracted and employed the imagination of Milton, the philosophy of Hume, the simplicity of Goldsmith, the industry of Henry, the research of Turner, and the patience of Lingard. The pages of these writers, however, accurate and luminous as they generally are, as well as those of Brady, Tyrrel, Carte, Rapin, and others, not to mention those in black letter, still require correction from the Saxon Chronicle; without which no person, however learned, can possess any thing beyond a superficial acquaintance with the elements of English history, and of the British Constitution.

"Some remarks may here be requisite on the CHRONOLOGY of the Saxon Chronicle. In the early part of it * the reader will observe a reference to the grand epoch of the creation of the world. So also in Ethelwerd, who closely follows the Saxon annals. It is allowed by all, that considerable difficulty has occurred in fixing the true .epoch of Christ's nativity,† because the Christian era was not used at all till about the year 532,‡ when it was introduced by Dionysius Exiguus; whose code of canon law, joined afterwards with the decretals of the popes, became as much the standard of authority in ecclesiastical matters as the pandects of Justinian among civilians. But it does not appear that in

---

* " See A.D. XXXIII. the era of Christ's crucifixion.

† " See Playfair's System of Chronology, p. 49.

‡ " Playfair says 527: but I follow Bede, Florence of Worcester, and others; who affirm that the great paschal cycle of Dionysius commenced from the year of our Lord's incarnation 532—the year in which the code of Justinian was promulgated. Vid. Flor. an. 532, 1064, and 1073. See also M. West. an. 532.

the Saxon mode of computation this system of chronology
was implicitly followed. We mention this circumstance,
however, not with a view of settling the point of difference,
which would not be easy, but merely to account for those
variations observable in different MSS.; which arose, not
only from the common mistakes or inadvertencies of tran-
scribers, but from the liberty, which the original writers
themselves sometimes assumed in this country, of computing
the current year according to their own ephemeral or local
custom. Some began with the incarnation or Nativity of
Christ; some with the Circumcision, which accords with the
solar year of the Romans as now restored; whilst others
commenced with the Annunciation; a custom which became
very prevalent in honour of the Virgin Mary, and was not
formally abolished · here till the year 1752; when the
Gregorian calendar, commonly called the New Style, was
substituted by Act of Parliament for the Dionysian. This
diversity of computation would alone occasion some confusion; but in addition to this, the INDICTION, or cycle of
fifteen years, which is mentioned in the latter part of the
Saxon Chronicle, was carried back three years before the
vulgar era, and commenced in different places at four
different periods of the year! But it is very remarkable
that, whatever was the commencement of the year in the
early part of the Saxon Chronicle, in the latter part the
year invariably opens with Midwinter-day or the Nativity.
Gervase of Canterbury, whose Latin Chronicle ends in
1199, the era of *legal* memory, had formed a design, as he
tells us, of regulating his chronology, by the Annunciation;
but from an honest fear of falsifying dates he abandoned his
first intention, and acquiesced in the practice of his predecessors; who for the most part, he says, began the new year
with the Nativity."*

Let us now see what has been done by previous editors
and translators of this valuable national document.

Gerard Langbaine was the first who entertained thoughts
of publishing this Chronicle; but he relinquished his design,
as appears from his papers in the Bodleian library, because
Wheloc had anticipated him.

The first edition therefore of the original text of this

* " Vid. Prol. in Chron. Gervas. *ap.* X. Script. p. 1338."

work is due to Wheloc, professor of Arabic at Cambridge. His work entitled *Chronologia Anglo-Saxonica*, [A.D. 1644], occupying about sixty folio pages, forms a supplement to his edition of Bede's Ecclesiastical History. But as Wheloc had the use of only the Bennet or Plegmund MS. [No. 1 in our summary of the MSS.], and of an original, now lost, of which our No. 7, the Dublin transcript, is supposed to be a copy, it is manifest that the editor had no opportunity of inserting those parts of the Chronicle—forming about one half of the whole—which do not occur in those two manuscripts.

Forty-eight years after Wheloc, Gibson, a young man of Queen's College, Oxford, and afterwards bishop of London, published a more complete edition of the Chronicle, for which he used three additional MSS. which had come into notice since the time of Wheloc.

More than 120 years passed before this historical record again attracted the notice of the public, or the labours of an editor. It was then translated into English throughout from the text of Gibson by a learned lady still living, Miss Gurney; to whom, both my enterprising publisher and myself are largely indebted for her kindness in facilitating the present edition, and to whom we gladly take this opportunity of acknowledging the debt.

Miss Gurney's translation was printed for private circulation, and did not receive the final polish of the fair translator, who was deterred from bestowing further labour upon a work which was shortly to be undertaken by one of our ablest antiquaries.

In 1823 appeared an edition of the Saxon Chronicle by Dr. Ingram, now President of Trinity College, accompanied with an English translation, a map of Saxon-England, coins of the Saxon kings, &c., &c.

At the same time that this learned work made its appearance, it was understood that the late Mr. Petrie, keeper of the records in the Tower, was devoting his laborious attention to prepare the Chronicle for publication at the expense of the Record Commission. Accuracy and laborious research were shining features in the literary character of Petrie: but he was less remarkable for discriminating how far an author's text may be illustrated without being overlaid by various readings, and he carried his mode of arrangement to such extremities, mutilated and subdivided his authors to such a degree, and so encumbered his pages with references, stars, accents, and brackets, that it is doubtful whether the learned and laborious folio, which he superintended to its completion, will ever see the light of publication. It remains in the possession of the Master of the Rolls, a mighty storehouse of collations for all future editions of Gildas, Nennius, Bede, the Saxon Chronicle, Florence of Worcester, Henry of Huntingdon, &c., &c.

In 1830 appeared a small anonymous volume, entitled, *Ancient History, English and French, exemplified in a regular dissection of the Saxon Chronicle, &c., &c.*, London, Hatchard, 1830; containing some lively dissertations in which much genius is displayed, unhappily not leading to clear or satisfactory results.

Such being the editions and translations already in existence, it became a serious question with the publisher and editor of the present volume, what would be the best plan to be pursued, in order that the work might be placed before the public in a form the best adapted to secure general approbation. As the result of this deliberation, it was judged expedient to take the edition of Petrie as a basis, because it was found to contain the most perfect collations of all the six existing manuscripts, and therefore to present a more complete text than any other printed volume. The style of the translation is as literal as the idiom of our language will allow.

But, as the edition of Mr. Petrie extends only to the year 1066, it has been necessary to form a text for the latter portion of the Chronicle from other sources. To effect this the translation of Miss Gurney, has, with the consent of that amiable lady, been taken as a ground-work, and numerous additions, variations, and notes, have been introduced by a collation of her text with that of Dr. Ingram.

As the result of these various modes, the public have now the advantage of reading the whole of this very interesting chronicle, not only in a perfect form, but even to an extent that might, perhaps, by some be deemed superfluous, with all the variations which can be gathered from all the manuscript copies now known to be in existence.

J. A. G.

Bampton, Oxfordshire, July, 1847.

THE ECCLESIASTICAL HISTORY

OF THE

ENGLISH NATION.

BY VENERABLE BEDE.

BOOK I.

PREFACE.

To the most glorious king Ceolwulph,* Bede, the servant of Christ and Priest.

I FORMERLY, at your request, most readily transmitted to you the Ecclesiastical History of the English Nation, which I had newly published, for you to read, and give it your approbation ; and I now send it again to be transcribed, and more fully considered at your leisure. And I cannot but commend the sincerity and zeal, with which you not only diligently give ear to hear the words of the Holy Scripture, but also industriously take care to become acquainted with the actions and sayings of former men of renown, especially of our own nation. For if history relates good things of good men, the attentive hearer is excited to imitate that which is good ; or if it mentions evil things of wicked persons, nevertheless the religious and pious hearer or reader, shunning that which is hurtful and perverse, is the more earnestly excited to perform those things which he knows to be good, and worthy of God. Of which you also being deeply sensible, are desirous that the said history should be more fully made familiar to yourself, and to those over whom

---

* Ceolwulph king of Northumberland, not the king of Wessex, who reigned about A.D. 527 ; nor the king of Mercia, who reigned about A.D. 819.

B

the Divine Authority has appointed you governor, from your
great regard to their general welfare.   But to the end that
I may remove all occasion of doubting what I have written,
both from yourself and other readers or hearers of this history, I will take care briefly to intimate from what authors I
chiefly learned the same.

My principal authority and aid in this work was the learned
and reverend Abbot Albinus ; who, educated in the Church
of Canterbury by those venerable and learned men, Archbishop Theodore of blessed memory, and the Abbot Adrian,
transmitted to me by Nothelm, the pious priest of the Church
of London,* either in writing, or by word of mouth of the
same Nothelm, all that he thought worthy of memory, that
had been done in the province of Kent, or the adjacent parts,
by the disciples of the blessed Pope Gregory, as he had
learned the same either from written records, or the traditions
of his ancestors.   The same Nothelm, afterwards going to
Rome, having, with leave of the present Pope Gregory,†
searched into the archives of the holy Roman Church, found
there some epistles of the blessed Pope Gregory, and other
popes ; and returning home, by the advice of the aforesaid
most reverend father Albinus, brought them to me, to be inserted in my history.   Thus, from the beginning of this
volume to the time when the English nation received the
faith of Christ, have we collected the writings of our predecessors, and from them gathered matter for our history ; but
from that time till the present, what was transacted in the
Church of Canterbury, by the disciples of St. Gregory or
their successors, and under what kings the same happened,
has been conveyed to us by Nothelm through the industry of
the aforesaid Abbot Albinus.   They also partly informed
me by what bishops and under what kings the provinces of
the East and West Saxons, as also of the East Angles, and
of the Northumbrians, received the faith of Christ.   In short
I was chiefly encouraged to undertake this work by the per-
suasions of the same Albinus.   In like manner, Daniel, the
most reverend Bishop of the West Saxons, who is still living,
communicated to me in writing some things relating to the
Ecclesiastical History of that province, and the next adjoin-

* Afterwards Archbishop of Canterbury, A.D. 736.
† Gregory the Third, who began to reign, A.D. 731.

ing to it of the South Saxons, as also of the Isle of Wight. But how, by the pious ministry of Cedd and Ceadda, the province of the Mercians was brought to the faith of Christ, which they knew not before, and how that of the East Saxons recovered the same, after having expelled it, and how those fathers lived and died, we learned from the brethren of the monastery, which was built by them, and is called Lastingham. What ecclesistical transactions took place in the province of the East Angles, was partly made known to us from the writings and tradition of our ancestors, and partly by relation of the most reverend Abbot Esius. What was done towards promoting the faith, and what was the sacerdotal succession in the province of Lindsey, we had either from the letters of the most reverend prelate Cunebert, * or by word of mouth from other persons of good credit. But what was done in the Church throughout the province of the Northumbrians, from the time when they received the faith of Christ till this present, I received not from any particular author, but by the faithful testimony of innumerable witnesses, who might know or remember the same ; besides what I had of my own knowledge. Wherein it is to be observed, that what I have written concerning our most holy father, Bishop Cuthbert, either in this volume, or in my treatise on his life and actions, I partly took, and faithfully copied from what I found written of him by the brethren of the Church of Lindisfarne ;† but at the same time took care to add such things as I could myself have knowledge of, by the faithful testimony of such as knew him. And I humbly entreat the reader, that if he shall in this that we have written find anything not delivered according to the truth, he will not impute the same to me, who, as the true rule of history requires, have laboured sincerely to commit to writing such things as I could gather from common report, for the instruction of posterity.

Moreover, I beseech all men who shall hear or read this history of our nation, that for my manifold infirmities both of mind and body, they will offer up frequent supplications

---

* Bishop of Sidnacester, the present see of Lincoln.
† Lindisfarne, now called Holy Island, is situated on the north of Northumberland, in its southern extremity. Here stood a monastery in Bede's time, and it was for four centuries the seat of the present see of Durham.

to the throne of Grace.   And I further pray, that in recompense for the labour wherewith I have recorded in the several countries and cities those events which were most worthy of note, and most grateful to the ears of their inhabitants, I may for my reward have the benefit of their pious prayers.

CHAP. I.

Of the Situation of Britain and Ireland, and of their ancient inhabitants.

BRITAIN, an island in the ocean,* formerly called Albion, is situated between the north and west, facing, though at a considerable distance, the coasts of Germany, France, and Spain, which form the greatest part of Europe.   It extends 800 miles in length towards the north, and is 200 miles in breadth, except where several promontories extend further in breadth, by which its compass is made to be 3675 miles.†
To the south, as you pass along the nearest shore of the Belgic Gaul, the first place in Britain which opens to the eye, is the city of Rutubi Portus, by the English corrupted into Reptacestir.‡   The distance from hence across the sea to Gessoriacum,§ the nearest shore of the Morini, is fifty miles, or as some writers say, 450 furlongs.   On the back of the island, where it opens upon the boundless ocean, it has the islands called Orcades.   Britain excels for grain and trees, and is well adapted for feeding cattle and beasts of burden.   It also produces vines in some places, and has plenty of land and water-fowls of several sorts ; it is remarkable also for rivers abounding in fish, and plentiful springs.   It has the greatest plenty of salmon and eels ; seals are also frequently taken, and dolphins, as also whales ; besides many sorts of shell-fish, such as muscles, in which are often found excellent

---

* The expression, " an island in the ocean," seems to be used to distinguish Britain from the other islands known to the ancients, almost all of which were in the Mediterranean sea.
† This total varies in different authors : some make it 4875. The first few pages of Bede are of not much value, being copied out of Pliny, Solinus, and other Roman authors. See the Appendix to my History of the Ancient Britons.
‡ Richborough, Kent.   § Boulogne.

pearls of all colours, red, purple, violet, and green, but
mostly white.   There is also a great abundance of cockles, of
which the scarlet dye is made ; a most beautiful colour, which
never fades with the heat of the sun or the washing of the
rain ; but the older it is, the more beautiful it becomes.   It
has both salt and hot springs, and from them flow rivers
which furnish hot baths, proper for all ages and sexes,
and arranged according.   For water, as St. Basil says,
receives the heating quality, when it runs along certain
metals, and becomes not only hot but scalding.   Britain
has also many veins of metals, as copper, iron, lead, and
silver ; it has much and excellent jet, which is black and
sparkling, glittering at the fire, and when heated, drives
away serpents ; being warmed with rubbing, it holds fast
whatever is applied to it, like amber.   The island was formerly embellished with twenty-eight noble cities, besides innumerable castles, which were all strongly secured with walls,
towers, gates, and locks.   And, from its lying almost under
the North Pole, the nights are light in summer, so that at
midnight the beholders are often in doubt whether the evening twilight still continues, or that of the morning is coming
on ; for the sun, in the night, returns under the earth,
through the northern regions at no great distance from them.
For this reason the days are of a great length in summer, as,
on the contrary, the nights are in winter, for the sun then
withdraws into the southern parts, so that the nights are
eighteen hours long.   Thus the nights are extraordinarily
short in summer, and the days in winter, that is, of only six
equinoctial hours.   Whereas, in Armenia, Macedonia, Italy,
and other countries of the same latitude, the longest day or
night extends but to fifteen hours, and the shortest to nine.

   This island at present, following the number of the books
in which the Divine law was written, contains five nations,
the English, Britons, Scots,* Picts,† and Latins, each in its

   * The *Scots* were the relatives of the Cymri, being another branch of the
great Celtic nation, who, at a period far beyond all authentic history,
had established themselves in Hibernia, Erin, or Ireland.   Hence that
island, from its predominant population, was generally called Scotia, or
Insula Scotorum, by the writers of the sixth and seventh centuries.   The
name of *Scotia*, or Scotland, as applied to the northern portion of Britain,
is comparatively of modern origin.
   † The original of the *Picts*, has caused various opinions.   Hector Boe-

own peculiar dialect cultivating the sublime study of Divine truth. The Latin tongue is, by the study of the Scriptures, become common to all the rest. At first this island had no other inhabitants but the Britons, from whom it derived its name, and who, coming over into Britain, as is reported, from Armorica, possessed themselves of the southern parts thereof. When they, beginning at the south, had made themselves masters of the greatest part of the island, it happened, that the nation of the Picts, from Scythia, as is reported, putting to sea, in a few long ships, were driven by the winds beyond the shores of Britain, and arrived on the northern coasts of Ireland, where, finding the nation of the Scots, they begged to be allowed to settle among them, but could not succeed in obtaining their request. Ireland is the greatest island next to Britain, and lies to the west of it ; but as it is shorter than Britain to the north, so, on the other hand, it runs out far beyond it to the south, opposite to the northern parts of Spain, though a spacious sea lies between them. The Picts, as has been said, arriving in this island by sea, desired to have a place granted them in which they might settle. The Scots answered that the island could not contain them both ; but "We can give you good advice," said they, "what to do ; we know there is another island, not far from ours, to the eastward, which we often see at a distance, when the days are clear. If you will go thither, you will obtain settlements ; or, if they should oppose you, you shall have our assistance." The Picts, accordingly, sailing over into Britain, began to inhabit the northern parts thereof, for the Britons were possessed of the southern. Now the Picts had no wives, and asked them of the Scots ; who would not consent to grant them upon any other terms, than that when any difficulty should arise, they should choose a king from the female royal race rather than from the male : which custom, as is well known, has been observed among the Picts to this day. In process of time, Britain, besides the Britons and the Picts, received a third nation, the Scots,

thius derives them from the Agathyrsi, others from the Germans, Bede from Scythia, and the author of the Saxon Annals from the southern parts of Scythia. Mr. Camden is of opinion that they were originally Britons, who fled into the northern parts of the island from the Roman invasions, as the Welsh into the western. But this is opposed by Bishop Stillingfleet, who was of opinion that they came from Scandinavia, Orig. Brit c. 5.

who, migrating from Ireland under their leader, Reuda, either by fair means, or by force of arms, secured to themselves those settlements among the Picts which they still possess. From the name of their commander, they are to this day called Dalreudins; for, in their language, Dal signifies a part.*

Ireland, in breadth, and for wholesomeness and serenity of climate, far surpasses Britain; for the snow scarcely ever lies there above three days: no man makes hay in the summer for winter's provision, or builds stables for his beasts of burden. No reptiles are found there, and no snake can live there; for, though often carried thither out of Britain, as soon as the ship comes near the shore, and the scent of the air reaches them, they die. On the contrary, almost all things in the island are good against poison. In short, we have known that when some persons have been bitten by serpents, the scrapings of leaves of books that were brought out of Ireland, being put into water, and given them to drink, have immediately expelled the spreading poison, and assuaged the swelling. The island abounds in milk and honey, nor is there any want of vines, fish, or fowl; and it is remarkable for deer and goats. It is properly the country of the Scots, who, migrating from thence, as has been said, added a third nation in Britain to the Britons and the Picts. There is a very large gulf of the sea, which formerly divided the nation of the Picts from the Britons; which gulf runs from the west very far into the land, where, to this day, stands the strong city of the Britons, called Alcluith. The Scots, arriving on the north side of this bay, settled themselves there.

CHAP. II.

Caius Julius Cæsar, the first Roman that came into Britain.

BRITAIN had never been visited by the Romans, and was, indeed, entirely unknown to them before the time of Caius Julius Cæsar, who, in the year 693 after the building of Rome, but the sixtieth† year before the incarnation of our

---

* Hence Dalrieta, or Dalreuda may be explained *Dal-Ri-Eta*, the portion of *Reuda* or *Rieta,* i.e. king Eta.
† This date, like many others in Bede, is not correct. Cæsar's invasion happened, B. C. 54.

Lord, was consul with Lucius Bibulus, and afterwards while
he made war upon the Germans and the Gauls, which were
divided only by the river Rhine, came into the province of
the Morini, from whence is the nearest and shortest passage
into Britain. Here, having provided about eighty ships of
burden and vessels with oars, he sailed over into Britain ;
where, being first roughly handled in a battle, and then
meeting with a violent storm, he lost a considerable part of
his fleet, no small number of soldiers, and almost all his
horses. Returning into Gaul, he put his legions into winter-
quarters, and gave orders for building six hundred sail of
both sorts. With these he again passed over early in spring
into Britain, but, whilst he was marching with a large army
towards the enemy, the ships, riding at anchor, were, by a
tempest either dashed one against another, or driven upon
the sands and wrecked. Forty of them perished, the rest
were, with much difficulty, repaired. Cæsar's cavalry was,
at the first charge, defeated by the Britons, and Labienus,
the tribune, slain. In the second engagement, he, with
great hazard to his men, put the Britons to flight. Thence
he proceeded to the river Thames, where an immense multitude of the enemy had posted themselves on the farthest side
of the river, under the command of Cassibellaun,* and fenced
the bank of the river and almost all the ford under water
with sharp stakes : the remains of these are to be seen to this
day, apparently about the thickness of a man's thigh, and being
cased with lead, remain fixed immovably in the bottom of the
river. This, being perceived and avoided by the Romans, the
barbarians, not able to stand the shock of the legions, hid
themselves in the woods, whence they grievously galled the
Romans with repeated sallies. In the meantime, the strong
city of Trinovantum,† with its commander Androgeus, sur-

* Cassibellaun, or as he is sometimes called, Cassibelinus, seems to have
maintained an extent of power and territory superior to most of the British
kings. His own possessions originally comprised that portion of the island
which is now divided into the counties of Hertford, Bedford, and Buckingham, together, as Horsley supposes, with part of Huntingdonshire and
Northamptonshire. To these he added, by conquest, part of the territory
of the Trinobantes, who occupied that tract which now comprises the
counties of Essex, Middlesex, and part of Surrey.

† Supposed to be London, and erroneously interpreted " New-Troy,"
by Geoffery of Monmouth and his followers.

rendered to Cæsar, giving him forty hostages. Many other cities, following their example, made a treaty with the Romans. By their assistance, Cæsar at length, with much difficulty, took Cassibellaun's town,* situated between two marshes, fortified by the adjacent woods, and plentifully furnished with all necessaries. After this, Cæsar returned into Gaul, but he had no sooner put his legions into winter-quarters, than he was suddenly beset and distracted with wars and tumults raised against him on every side.

CHAP. III.

Claudius, the second of the Romans who came into Britain, brought the islands Orcades into subjection to the Roman empire; and Vespasian, sent by him, reduced the Isle of Wight under their dominion.

IN the year of Rome 798,† Claudius, fourth emperor from Augustus, being desirous to approve himself a beneficial prince to the republic, and eagerly bent upon war and conquest, undertook an expedition into Britain, which seemed to be stirred up to rebellion by the refusal of the Romans to give up certain deserters. He was the only one, either before or after Julius Cæsar, who had dared to land upon the island; yet, within a very few days, without any fight or bloodshed, the greatest part of the island was surrendered into his hands. He also added to the Roman empire the Orcades,‡ which lie in the ocean beyond Britain, and then, returning to Rome the sixth month after his departure, he gave his son the title of Britannicus. This war he concluded in the fourth year of his empire, which is the forty-sixth from the incarnation of our Lord. In which year there happened a most grievous famine in Syria, which, in the Acts of the Apostles is recorded to have been foretold by the prophet Agabus. Vespasian, who was emperor after Nero, being sent into Britain by the same Claudius, brought also under the Roman dominion the Isle of Wight, which is next to Britain on the south, and is about thirty miles in length from east to west, and twelve from north to south; being six miles distant from the southern coast of Britain at the east

---

* Supposed to be St. Alban's.   † Claudius came to Britain, A.D. 44.
    ‡ This also is a mistake; it was probably Agricola who first subdued the Orkneys.

end, and three only at the west. Nero, succeeding Claudius in the empire, attempted nothing in martial affairs ; and, therefore, among other innumerable detriments brought upon the Roman state, he almost lost Britain ; for under him two most noble towns were there taken and destroyed.

CHAP. IV.

Lucius, king of Britain, writing to Pope Eleutherus, desires to be made a Christian.

IN the year of our Lord's incarnation 156, Marcus Antoninus Verus, the fourteenth from Augustus, was made emperor, together with his brother, Aurelius Commodus.* In their time, whilst Eleutherus, a holy man, presided over the Roman church, Lucius, king of the Britons, sent a letter to him, entreating that by his command he might be made a Christian. He soon obtained his pious request, and the Britons preserved the faith, which they had received, uncorrupted and entire, in peace and tranquillity until the time of the Emperor Diocletian.

CHAP. V.

How the Emperor Severus divided that part of Britain, which he subdued from the rest by a Rampart.

IN the year of our Lord 189, Severus, an African, born at Leptis, in the province of Tripolis, received the imperial purple. He was the seventeenth from Augustus, and reigned seventeen years. Being naturally stern, and engaged in many wars, he governed the state vigorously, but with much trouble. Having been victorious in all the grievous civil wars which happened in his time, he was drawn into Britain by the revolt of almost all the confederate tribes ; and, after many great and dangerous battles, he thought fit to divide that part of the island, which he had recovered from the other unconquered nations, not with a wall, as some imagine, but with a rampart. For a wall is made of

* It is not to be wondered that Bede shows himself very confused on subjects connected with Roman history. In this passage are several glaring errors. No such emperors as the two mentioned ever reigned together, nor is the date or the name of the Roman bishop more correct than the names of the emperors. Eleutherus flourished between A.D. 176 and 190; and Marcus Antoninus was made emperor A.D. 161.

stones, but a rampart, with which camps are fortified to repel the assaults of enemies, is made of sods, cut out of the earth, and raised above the ground all round like a wall, having in front of it the ditch whence the sods were taken, and strong stakes of wood fixed upon its top.　Thus Severus drew a great ditch and strong rampart, fortified with several towers, from sea to sea ; and was afterwards taken sick and died at York, leaving two sons, Bassianus and Geta ; of whom Geta died, adjudged a public enemy ; but Bassianus, having taken the surname of Antoninus, obtained the empire.

CHAP. VI.

The reign of Diocletian, and how he persecuted the Christians

IN the year of our Lord's incarnation 286, Diocletian, the thirty-third from Augustus, and chosen emperor by the army, reigned twenty years, and created Maximian, surnamed Herculius, his colleague in the empire.　In their time, one Carausius, of very mean birth, but an expert and able soldier, being appointed to guard the sea-coasts, then infested by the Franks and Saxons, acted more to the prejudice than to the advantage of the commonwealth ; and from his not restoring to its owners the booty taken from the robbers, but keeping all to himself, it was suspected that by intentional neglect he suffered the enemy to infest the frontiers. Hearing, therefore, that an order was sent by Maximian that he should be put to death, he took upon him the imperial robes, and possessed himself of Britain, and having most valiantly retained it for the space of seven years, he was at length put to death by the treachery of his associate, Allectus. The usurper, having thus got the island from Carausius, held it three years, and was then vanquished by Asclepiodotus, the captain of the Prætorian bands, who thus at the end of ten years restored Britain to the Roman empire.　Meanwhile, Diocletian in the east, and Maximian Herculius in the west, commanded the churches to be destroyed, and the Christians to be slain.　This persecution was the tenth since the reign of Nero, and was more lasting and bloody than all the others before it ; for it was carried on incessantly for the space of ten years, with burning of churches, outlawing of innocent persons, and the slaughter of martyrs. At length, it reached Britain also, and many persons, with the constancy of martyrs, died in the confession of their faith.

CHAP. VII.

The Passion of St. Alban and his Companions, who at that time shed their blood for our Lord. [A.D. 305.]

At that time suffered St. Alban,* of whom the priest Fortunatus, in the Praise of Virgins, where he makes mention of the blessed martyrs that came to the Lord from all parts of the world, says—

In Britain's isle was holy Alban born.

This Alban, being yet a pagan, at the time when the cruelties of wicked princes were raging against Christians, gave entertainment in his house to a certain clergyman, flying from the persecutors. This man he observed to be engaged in continual prayer and watching day and night ; when on a sudden the Divine grace shining on him, he began to imitate the example of faith and piety which was set before him, and being gradually instructed by his wholesome admonitions, he cast off the darkness of idolatry, and became a Christian in all sincerity of heart. The aforesaid clergyman having been some days entertained by him, it came to the ears of the wicked prince, that this holy confessor of Christ, whose time of martyrdom had not yet come, was concealed at Alban's house. Whereupon he sent some soldiers to make a strict search after him. When they came to the martyr's house, St. Alban immediately presented himself to the soldiers, instead of his guest and master, in the habit or long coat which he wore, and was led bound before the judge.

It happened that the judge, at the time when Alban was carried before him, was standing at the altar, and offering sacrifice to devils. When he saw Alban, being much enraged that he should thus, of his own accord, put himself into the hands of the soldiers, and incur such danger in behalf of his guest, he commanded him to be dragged up to the

---

* There are great chronological difficulties in the story of the martyrdom of St. Alban. Whilst the persecution lasted, Britain was first alienated from the Roman empire by Carausius and Allectus, and was then under Constantius and his son Constantine the Great. It is difficult to believe that either of these would sanction a bloody persecution in their dominions.

images of the devils, before which he stood, saying, "Because you have chosen to conceal a rebellious and sacrilegious person, rather than to deliver him up to the soldiers, that his contempt of the gods might meet with the penalty due to such blasphemy, you shall undergo all the punishment that was due to him, if you abandon the worship of our religion." But St. Alban, who had voluntarily declared himself a Christian to the persecutors of the faith, was not at all daunted at the prince's threats, but putting on the armour of spiritual warfare, publicly declared that he would not obey the command. Then said the judge, "Of what family or race are you?"— "What does it concern you," answered Alban, "of what stock I am? If you desire to hear the truth of my religion, be it known to you, that I am now a Christian, and bound by Christian duties."—"I ask your name," said the judge; "tell me it immediately."—"I am called Alban by my parents," replied he; "and I worship and adore the true and living God, who created all things." Then the judge, inflamed with anger, said, "If you will enjoy the happiness of eternal life, do not delay to offer sacrifice to the great gods." Alban rejoined, "These sacrifices, which by you are offered to devils, neither can avail the subjects, nor answer the wishes or desires of those that offer up their supplications to them. On the contrary, whosoever shall offer sacrifice to these images, shall receive the everlasting pains of hell for his reward."

The judge, hearing these words, and being much incensed, ordered this holy confessor of God to be scourged by the executioners, believing he might by stripes shake that constancy of heart, on which he could not prevail by words. He, being most cruelly tortured, bore the same patiently, or rather joyfully, for our Lord's sake. When the judge perceived that he was not to be overcome by tortures, or withdrawn from the exercise of the Christian religion, he ordered him to be put to death. Being led to execution, he came to a river, which, with a most rapid course, ran between the wall of the town and the arena where he was to be executed.*

* There is either a corruption or great obscurity in the text of this passage. All the MSS. however agree, and yet it is impossible to translate the passage grammatically. I believe the text above gives the intended meaning.

He there saw a multitude of persons of both sexes, and of several ages and conditions, who were doubtlessly assembled by Divine instinct, to attend the blessed confessor and martyr, and had so taken up the bridge on the river, that he could scarce pass over that evening. In short, almost all had gone out, so that the judge remained in the city without attendance. St. Alban, therefore, urged by an ardent and devout wish to arrive quickly at martyrdom, drew near to the stream, and on lifting up his eyes to heaven, the channel was immediately dried up, and he perceived that the water had departed and made way for him to pass. Among the rest, the executioner, who was to have put him to death, observed this, and moved by Divine inspiration hastened to meet him at the place of execution, and casting down the sword which he had carried ready drawn, fell at his feet, praying that he might rather suffer with the martyr, whom he was ordered to execute, or, if possible, instead of him.

Whilst he thus from a persecutor was become a companion in the faith, and the other executioners hesitated to take up the sword which was lying on the ground, the reverend confessor, accompanied by the multitude, ascended a hill, about 500 paces from the place, adorned, or rather clothed with all kinds of flowers, having its sides neither perpendicular, nor even craggy, but sloping down into a most beautiful plain, worthy from its lovely appearance to be the scene of a martyr's sufferings. On the top of this hill, St. Alban prayed that God would give him water, and immediately a living spring broke out before his feet, the course being confined, so that all men perceived that the river also had been dried up in consequence of the martyr's presence. Nor was it likely that the martyr, who had left no water remaining in the river, should want some on the top of the hill, unless he thought it suitable to the occasion. The river having performed the holy service, returned to its natural course, leaving a testimony of its obedience. Here, therefore, the head of our most courageous martyr was struck off, and here he received the crown of life, which God has promised to those who love him. But he who gave the wicked stroke, was not permitted to rejoice over the deceased; for his eyes dropped upon the ground together with the blessed martyr's head.

At the same time was also beheaded the soldier, who

before, through the Divine admonition, refused to give the stroke to the holy confessor. Of whom it is apparent, that though he was not regenerated by baptism, yet he was cleansed by the washing of his own blood, and rendered worthy to enter the kingdom of heaven. Then the judge, astonished at the novelty of so many heavenly miracles, ordered the persecution to cease immediately, beginning to honour the death of the saints, by which he before thought they might have been diverted from the Christian faith. The blessed Alban suffered death on the twenty-second day of June, near the city of Verulam,* which is now by the English nation called Verlamacestir, or Varlingacestir, where afterwards, when peaceable Christian times were restored, a church of wonderful workmanship, and suitable to his martyrdom, was erected.† In which place, there ceases not to this day the cure of sick persons, and the frequent working of wonders.

At the same time suffered Aaron and Julius, citizens of Chester,‡ and many more of both sexes in several places; who, when they had endured sundry torments, and their limbs had been torn after an unheard-of manner, yielded their souls up, to enjoy in the heavenly city a reward for the sufferings which they had passed through.

---

* Now St. Albans in Hertfordshire.

† The place where St. Alban suffered was called Holmhurst, in the Saxon, signifying a woody place, near the city of Verulamium, or Verulam, where Bede says there was a beautiful church in his time; since when, Offa, king of the Mercians, anno 793, founded in this place the stately monastery of St. Alban, and procured and granted it extraordinary privileges, upon which arose the town of St. Albans, in Hertfordshire. As the saint of this church was the first martyr in England, Pope Honorius granted the abbat a superiority over all others. In the time of Henry VIII. it fell with the rest, but the townsmen preserved the church from ruin, by a purchase of £400. The ruins of the ancient Verulam are even now to be seen; and the church is built out of them, being, as Bishop Gibson observes, of British bricks.

‡ Gildas says, that Aaron and Julius were citizens of Carlisle; but others make them to have been inhabitants of the Roman city of Caerleon upon Usk, where according to Walter, Geoffrey of Monmouth, as well as Giraldus Cambrensis, two or three illustrious churches were dedicated to their memory.

CHAP. VIII.

The persecution ceasing, the Church in Britain enjoys peace till the time of the Arian heresy. [A.D 307—337.]

WHEN the storm of persecution ceased, the faithful Christians, who, during the time of danger, had hidden themselves in woods and deserts, and secret caves, appearing in public, rebuilt the churches which had been levelled with the ground; founded, erected, and finished the temples of the holy martyrs, and, as it were, displayed their conquering ensigns in all places; they celebrated festivals, and performed their sacred rites with clean hearts and mouths. This peace continued in the churches of Britain until the time of the Arian madness, which, having corrupted the whole world, infected this island also, so far removed from the rest of the globe, with the poison of its arrows; and when the plague was thus conveyed across the sea, all the venom of every heresy immediately rushed into the island, ever fond of something new, and never holding firm to any thing.

At this time, Constantius, who, whilst Diocletian was alive, governed Gaul and Spain, a man of extraordinary meekness and courtesy, died in Britain. This man left his son Constantine, born of Helen his concubine, emperor of the Gauls. Eutropius writes, that Constantine, being created emperor in Britain, succeeded his father in the sovereignty. In his time the Arian heresy broke out, and although it was detected and condemned in the Council of Nice, yet it nevertheless infected not only all the churches of the continent, but even those of the islands, with its pestilent and fatal doctrines.

CHAP. IX.

How during the reign of Gratian, Maximus, being created Emperor in Britain, returned into Gaul with a mighty army. [A.D. 383.]

IN the year of our Lord's incarnation 377, Gratian, the fortieth from Augustus, held the empire six years after the death of Valens; though he had long before reigned with his uncle Valens, and his brother Valentinian. Finding the state of the commonwealth much impaired, and almost gone to ruin, he looked around for some one whose abilities might

remedy the existing evils ; and his choice fell on Theodosius,
a Spaniard.   Him he invested at Sirmium with the royal
robes, and made him emperor of Thrace and the Eastern
provinces.   At which time, Maximus, a man of valour and
probity, and worthy to be an emperor, if he had not broken
the oath of allegiance which he had taken, was made emperor by the army, passed over into Gaul, and there by
treachery slew the Emperor Gratian, who was in a consternation at his sudden invasion, and attempting to escape
into Italy.   His brother, Valentinian, expelled from Italy,
fled into the East, where he was entertained by Theodosius
with fatherly affection, and soon restored to the empire.
Maximus the tyrant, being shut up in Aquileia, was there
taken and put to death.

CHAP. X.

*How, in the reign of Arcadius, Pelagius, a Briton, insolently impugned
the Grace of God.*

In the year of our Lord 394, Arcadius, the son of Theodosius, the forty-third from Augustus, taking the empire upon
him, with his brother Honorius, held it thirteen years.   In
his time, Pelagius, a Briton,* spread far and near the infection of his perfidious doctrine against the assistance of the
Divine grace, being seconded therein by his associate Juli-
anus of Campania, whose anger was kindled by the loss of
his bishopric, of which he had been just deprived.   St,
Augustine, and the other orthodox fathers, quoted many
thousand catholic authorities against them, yet they would
not correct their madness ; but, on the contrary, their folly
was rather increased by contradiction, and they refused to
embrace the truth ; which Prosper, the rhetorician, has
beautifully expressed thus in heroic verse :—

> " A scribbler vile, inflamed with hellish spite,
> Against the great Augustine dared to write ;
> Presumptuous serpent ! from what midnight den
> Durst thou to crawl on earth and look at men !
> Sure thou wast fed on Britain's sea-girt plains,
> Or in thy breast Vesuvian sulphur reigns."

* Pelagius was a native of Wales ; his real name is supposed to have
been Morgan. He was a man of learning, and is said to have written the
following works :—" A Commentary on the Epistles of St. Paul, attributed

C

CHAP. XI.

How during the reign of Honorius, Gratian and Constantine were created tyrants in Britain; and soon after the former was slain in Britain, and the latter in Gaul.

IN the year 407, Honorius, the younger son of Theodosius, and the forty-fourth from Augustus, being emperor, two years before the invasion of Rome by Alaric, king of the Goths, when the nations of the Alani, Suevi, Vandals, and many others with them, having defeated the Franks and passed the Rhine, ravaged all Gaul, Gratianus Municeps was set up as tyrant and killed. In his place, Constantine, one of the meanest soldiers, only for his name's sake, and without any worth to recommend him, was chosen emperor. As soon as he had taken upon him the command, he passed over into France, where being often imposed upon by the barbarians with faithless treaties, he caused much injury to the Commonwealth. Whereupon Count Constantius by the command of Honorious, marching into Gaul with an army, besieged him in the city of Arles, and put him to death. His son Constans, whom of a monk he had created Cæsar, was also put to death by his own Count Gerontius, at Vienne.

Rome was taken by the Goths, in the year from its foundation, 1164. Then the Romans ceased to rule in Britain, almost 470 years after Caius Julius Cæsar entered the island. They resided within the rampart, which, as we have mentioned, Severus made across the island, on the south side of it, as the cities, temples, bridges, and paved roads there made, testify to this day; but they had a right of dominion over the farther parts of Britain, as also over the islands that are beyond Britain.

to St. Jerome; a Letter to Demetria, and some others in the last volume of St. Jerome; A Confession of Faith to Pope Innocent; Fragment of a Treatise of the Power of Nature and Free Will, in St. Augustine; these are extant. He wrote likewise a Treatise of the Power of Nature, and several books concerning Free Will, which are lost."—*Collier's Eccles. Hist.* vol. i. p. 42, folio. For further particulars respecting Pelagius, see Du Pin's Hist. of the Church, vol. ii. pp. 184—194, 12mo. 1724.

CHAP. XII.

The Britons, being ravaged by the Scots and Picts, sought succour from the Romans, who, coming a second time, built a wall across the island; but the Britons being again invaded by the aforesaid enemies, were reduced to greater distress than before.

FROM that time, the south part of Britain, destitute of armed soldiers, of martial stores, and of all its active youth, which had been led away by the rashness of the tyrants, never to return, was wholly exposed to rapine, as being totally ignorant of the use of weapons. Whereupon they suffered many years under two very savage foreign nations, the Scots from the west, and the Picts from the north. We call these foreign nations, not on account of their being seated out of Britain, but because they were remote from that part of it which was possessed by the Britons ; two inlets of the sea lying between them, one of which runs in far and broad into the land of Britain, from the Eastern Ocean, and the other from the Western, though they do not reach so as touch one another. The eastern has in the midst of it the city Giudi. The western has on it, that is, on the right hand thereof, the city Alcluith,* which in their language signifies the Rock Cluith, for it is close by the river of that name.

On account of the irruption of these nations, the Britons sent messengers to Rome with letters in mournful manner, praying for succours, and promising perpetual subjection, provided that the impending enemy should be driven away. An armed legion was immediately sent them, which, arriving in the island, and engaging the enemy, slew a great multitude of them, drove the rest out of the territories of their allies, and having delivered them from their cruel oppressors, advised them to build a wall between the two seas across the the island, that it might secure them, and keep off the enemy ; and thus they returned home with great triumph. The islanders raising the wall, as they had been directed, not of stone, as having no artist capable of such a work, but of sods, made it of no use. However, they drew it for many miles between the two bays or inlets of the seas, which we have spoken of ; to the end that where the defence of the

* Alcluith is the modern Dunbarton : the situation of Giudi is not known.

water was wanting, they might use the rampart to defend their borders from the irruptions of the enemies. Of which work there erected, that is, of a rampart of extraordinary breadth and height, there are evident remains to be seen at this day. It begins at about two miles' distance from the monastery of Abercurnig,* on the west, at a place called in the Pictish language, Peanfahel,† but in the English tongue, Penneltun, and running to the westward, ends near the city Alcluith.

But the former enemies, when they perceived that the Roman soldiers were gone, immediately coming by sea, broke into the borders, trampled and overran all places, and like men mowing ripe corn, bore down all before them. Hereupon messengers are again sent to Rome, imploring aid, lest their wretched country should be utterly extirpated, and the name of a Roman province, so long renowned among them, overthrown by the cruelties of barbarous foreigners, might become utterly contemptible. A legion is accordingly sent again, and, arriving unexpectedly in autumn, made great slaughter of the enemy, obliging all those that could escape, to flee beyond the sea; whereas before, they were wont yearly to carry off their booty without any opposition. Then the Romans declared to the Britons, that they could not for the future undertake such troublesome expeditions for their sake, advising them rather to handle their weapons, like men, and undertake themselves the charge of engaging their enemies, who would not prove too powerful for them, unless they were deterred by cowardice; and, thinking that it might be some help to the allies, whom they were forced to abandon, they built a strong stone wall from sea to sea, in a straight line between the towns that had been there built for fear of the enemy, and not far from the trench of Severus. This famous wall, which is still to be seen, was built at the public and private expense, the Britons also lending their assistance. It is eight feet in breadth, and

* Now called Abercorn, a village on the south bank of the Frith of Forth.

† Pean-fahel, or vahel, or wahel, [for f, v, w, are kindred consonants,] evidently is to be interpreted in English, " wall-head," i. e. the " head," or beginning of the wall. *Pen* means head in the Celtic dialect; thus, Pendennis in Cornwall.

twelve in height, in a straight line from east to west, as is still visible to beholders.* This being finished, they gave that dispirited people good advice, with patterns to furnish them with arms. Besides, they built towers on the sea-coast to the southward, at proper distances, where their ships were, because there also the irruptions of the barbarians were apprehended, and so took leave of their friends, never to return again.

After their departure, the Scots and Picts, understanding that they had declared they would come no more, speedily returned, and growing more confident than they had been before, occupied all the northern and farthest part of the island, as far as the wall. Hereupon a timorous guard was placed upon the wall, where they pined away day and night in the utmost fear. On the other side, the enemy attacked them with hooked weapons, by which the cowardly defendants were dragged from the wall, and dashed against the ground. At last, the Britons, forsaking their cities and wall, took to flight and were dispersed. The enemy pursued, and the slaughter was greater than on any former occasion; for the wretched natives were torn in pieces by their enemies, as lambs are torn by wild beasts. Thus, being expelled their dwellings and possessions, they saved themselves from starvation, by robbing and plundering one another, adding to the calamities occasioned by foreigners, by their own domestic broils, till the whole country was left destitute of food, except such as could be procured in the chase.

CHAP. XIII.

In the reign of Theodosius the younger, Palladius was sent to the Scots that believed in Christ; the Britons begging assistance of Ætius, the consul, could not obtain it. [A.D. 446.]

IN the year of our Lord 423, Theodosius, the younger, next to Honorius, being the forty-fifth from Augustus, governed the Roman empire twenty-six years. In the eighth year of

* This wall extended from Cousin's House, near the mouth of the river Tyne, on the east, to Boulness on the Solway Frith on the west, and was sixty-eight English miles in length. For an account of this wall consult Horsley's Brit. Romana, b. i. c 8 pp. 121, 122, and Whitaker's Manchester, b. i. c. 12.

his reign, Palladius was sent by Celestinus, the Roman pontiff, to the Scots that believed in Christ, to be their first bishop. In the twenty-third year of his reign, Ætius, a renowned person, being also a patrician, discharged his third consulship with Symmachus for his colleague. To him the wretched remains of the Britons sent a letter, which began thus :—"To Ætius, thrice Consul, the groans of the Britons." And in the sequel of the letter they thus expressed their calamities :—"The barbarians drive us to the sea ; the sea drives us back to the barbarians : between them we are exposed to two sorts of death ; we are either slain or drowned." Yet neither could all this procure any assistance from him, as he was then engaged in most dangerous wars with Bledla and Attila, kings of the Huns. And, though the year before this, Bledla had been murdered by the treachery of his brother Attila, yet Attila himself remained so intolerable an enemy to the Republic, that he ravaged almost all Europe, invading and destroying cities and castles. At the same time there was a famine at Constantinople, and shortly after, a plague followed, and a great part of the walls of that city, with fifty-seven towers, fell to the ground. Many cities also went to ruin, and the famine and pestilential state of the air destroyed thousands of men and cattle.

CHAP. XIV.

The Britons, compelled by famine, drove the barbarians out of their territories ; soon after there ensued plenty of corn, luxury, plague, and the subversion of the nation. [A.D. 426—447.]

IN the meantime, the aforesaid famine distressing the Britons more and more, and leaving to posterity lasting memorials of its mischievous effects, obliged many of them to submit themselves to the depredators ; though others still held out, confiding in the Divine assistance, when none was to be had from men. These continually made excursions from the mountains, caves, and woods, and, at length, began to inflict severe losses on their enemies, who had been for so many years plundering the country. The Irish robbers thereupon returned home, in order to come again soon after. The Picts, both then and afterwards, remained quiet in the farthest part of the island, save that sometimes they would do some mischief, and carry off booty from the Britons.

When, however, the ravages of the enemy at length ceased, the island began to abound with such plenty of grain as had never been known in any age before ; with plenty, luxury increased, and this was immediately attended with all sorts of crimes ; in particular, cruelty, hatred of truth, and love of falsehood ; insomuch, that if any one among them happened to be milder than the rest, and inclined to truth, all the rest abhorred and persecuted him, as if he had been the enemy of his country. Nor were the laity only guilty of these things, but even our Lord's own flock, and his pastors also, addicting themselves to drunkenness, animosity, litigiousness, contention, envy, and other such like crimes, and casting off the light yoke of Christ. In the meantime, on a sudden, a severe plague fell upon that corrupt generation, which soon destroyed such numbers of them, that the living were scarcely sufficient to bury the dead : yet, those that survived, could not be withdrawn from the spiritual death, which their sins had incurred, either by the death of their friends, or the fear of their own. Whereupon, not long after, a more severe vengeance, for their horrid wickedness, fell upon the sinful nation. They consulted what was to be done, and where they should seek assistance to prevent or repel the cruel and frequent incursions of the northern nations ; and they all agreed with their King Vortigern to call over to their aid, from the parts beyond the sea, the Saxon nation ; which, as the event still more evidently showed, appears to have been done by the appointment of our Lord himself, that evil might fall upon them for their wicked deeds.

CHAP. XV.

The Angles, being invited into Britain, at first obliged the enemy to retire to a distance ; but not long after, joining in league with them, turned their weapons upon their confederates. [A.D. 450—456.]

In the year of our Lord 449, Martian being made emperor with Valentinian, and the forty-sixth from Augustus, ruled the empire seven years. Then the nation of the Angles, or Saxons,* being invited by the aforesaid king, arrived in

* It is now beginning to be generally understood that the Saxons

Britain with three long ships, and had a place assigned them
to reside in by the same king, in the eastern part of the
island, that they might thus appear to be fighting for their
country, whilst their real intentions were to enslave it. Accordingly they engaged with the enemy, who were come
from the north to give battle, and obtained the victory;
which, being known at home in their own country, as also
the fertility of the country, and the cowardice of the Britons,
a more considerable fleet was quickly sent over, bringing a
still greater number of men, which, being added to the former, made up an invincible army. The new comers received
of the Britons a place to inhabit, upon condition that
they should wage war against their enemies for the peace
and security of the country, whilst the Britons agreed to
furnish them with pay. Those who came over were of the
three most powerful nations of Germany—Saxons, Angles,
and Jutes. From the Jutes are descended the people of
Kent, and of the Isle of Wight, and those also in the province of the West-Saxons who are to this day called Jutes,
seated opposite to the Isle of Wight. From the Saxons,
that is, the country which is now called Old Saxony, came
the East-Saxons, the South-Saxons, and the West-Saxons.
From the Angles, that is, the country which is called Anglia,
and which is said, from that time, to remain desert to this
day, between the provinces of the Jutes and the Saxons, are
descended the East-Angles, the Midland-Angles, Mercians,
all the race of the Northumbrians, that is, of those nations
that dwell on the north side of the river Humber, and the
other nations of the English. The two first commanders are
said to have been Hengist and Horsa. Of whom Horsa, being afterwards slain in battle by the Britons,* was buried in
the eastern parts of Kent, where a monument, bearing his
name, is still in existence. They were the sons of Victgil-
sus, whose father was Vecta, son of Woden; from whose
stock the royal race of many provinces deduce their original.
In a short time, swarms of the aforesaid nations came over

acquired their settlement in Britain rather by a long course of predatory
inroads than in the rapid, and somewhat dramatic manner related by our
native historians.

 * This battle was fought between Vortimer, the eldest son of Vortigern,
and Hengist, at Aylesford in Kent.

into the island, and they began to increase so much, that they became terrible to the natives themselves who had invited them.   Then, having on a sudden entered into league with the Picts, whom they had by this time repelled by the force of their arms, they began to turn their weapons against their confederates.   At first, they obliged them to furnish a greater quantity of provisions ; and, seeking an occasion to quarrel, protested, that unless more plentiful supplies were brought them, they would break the confederacy, and ravage all the island ; nor were they backward in putting their threats in execution.   In short, the fire kindled by the hands of these pagans, proved God's just revenge for the crimes of the people ; not unlike that which, being once lighted by the Chaldeans, consumed the walls and city of Jerusalem.   For the barbarous conquerors acting here in the same manner, or rather the just Judge ordaining that they should so act, they plundered all the neighbouring cities and country, spread the conflagration from the eastern to the western sea, without any opposition, and covered almost every part of the devoted island.   Public as well as private structures were overturned ; the priests were everywhere slain before the altars ; the prelates and the people, without any respect of persons, were destroyed with fire and sword ; nor was there any to bury those who had been thus cruelly slaughtered. Some of the miserable remainder, being taken in the mountains, were butchered in heaps.   Others, spent with hunger, came forth and submitted themselves to the enemy for food, being destined to undergo perpetual servitude, if they were not killed even upon the spot. Some, with sorrowful hearts, fled beyond the seas.   Others, continuing in their own country, led a miserable life among the woods, rocks, and mountains, with scarcely enough food to support life, and expecting every moment to be their last.

CHAP. XVI.

The Britons obtained their first victory over the Angles, under the command of Ambrosius, a Roman.

WHEN the victorious army, having destroyed and dispersed the natives, had returned home to their own settlements, the Britons began by degrees to take heart, and gather strength,

sallying out of the lurking places where they had concealed
themselves, and unanimously imploring the Divine assistance,
that they might not utterly be destroyed. They had at that
time for their leader, Ambrosius Aurelius,* a modest man, who
alone, by chance, of the Roman nation had survived the
storm, in which his parents, who were of the royal race, had
perished. Under him the Britons revived, and offering battle
to the victors, by the help of God, came off victorious. From
that day, sometimes the natives, and sometimes their enemies,
prevailed, till the year of the siege of Baddesdown-hill, when
they made no small slaughter of those invaders, about
forty-four years after their arrival in England. But of this
hereafter.

CHAP. XVII.

*How Germanus the Bishop, sailing into Britain with Lupus, first quelled
the tempest of the sea, and afterwards that of the Pelagians, by Divine
power.* [A.D. 429.]

SOME few years before their arrival, the Pelagian heresy,
brought over by Agricola, the son of Severianus, a Pelagian
bishop, had sadly corrupted the faith of the Britons. But
whereas they absolutely refused to embrace that perverse
doctrine, so blasphemous against the grace of Christ, and
were not able of themselves to confute its subtilty by force
of argument, they thought of an excellent plan, which was
to crave aid of the Gallican prelates in that spiritual war.
Hereupon having gathered a great synod, they consulted together what persons should be sent thither, and by unanimous
consent, choice was made of the apostolical priests, Germanus,
bishop of Auxerre,† and Lupus of Troyes,‡ to go into Britain
to confirm it in the faith. They readily complied with the
request and commands of the holy Church, and putting to
sea, sailed half way over from Gaul to Britain with a fair
wind. There on a sudden they were obstructed by the

* Ambrosius, according to Whitaker, was the hereditary sovereign of the
Damnonii, the inhabitants of Devon, Cornwall, and the west of Somerset.
Their capital was Isca Damnoniorum, supposed to be the present Exeter.

† The Life of St Germanus was written by Constantius, a priest of the
Gallican Church, whom Bede follows.

‡ Lupus was brother to Vincent of Lerins, author of an able treatise,
entitled, Commonitorium, for the Antiquity and Universality of the
Catholic Faith against the Profane Novelties of all Heretics.

malevolence of demons, who were jealous that such men
should be sent to bring back the Britons to the faith.   They
raised storms, and darkened the sky with clouds.   The sails
could not bear the fury of the winds, the sailors' skill was
forced to give way, the ship was sustained by prayer, not by
strength, and as it happened, their spiritual commander and
bishop, being spent with weariness, had fallen asleep.   Then
the tempest, as if the person that opposed it had given way,
gathered strength, and the ship, overpowered by the waves,
was ready to sink.   Then the blessed Lupus and all the rest
awakened their elder, that he might oppose the raging elements.   He, showing himself the more resolute in proportion
to the greatness of the danger, called upon Christ, and having,
in the name of the Holy Trinity, sprinkled a little water,
quelled the raging waves, admonished his companion, encouraged all, and all unanimously fell to prayer.   The Deity
heard their cry, the enemies were put to flight, a calm
ensued, the winds veering about applied themselves to forward their voyage, and having soon traversed the ocean, they
enjoyed the quiet of the wished-for shore.   A multitude
flocking thither from all parts, received the priests, whose
coming had been foretold by the predictions even of their adversaries.   For the wicked spirits declared what they feared,
and when the priests afterwards expelled them from the
bodies they had taken possession of, they made known the
nature of the tempest, and the dangers they had occasioned,
and that they had been overcome by the merits and authority
of the saints.

In the meantime, the apostolical priests filled the island
of Britain with the fame of their preaching and virtues ; and
the word of God was by them daily administered, not only
in the churches, but even in the streets and fields, so that
the Catholics were everywhere confirmed, and those who had
gone astray, corrected.   Like the Apostles, they had honour
and authority through a good conscience, obedience to their
doctrine through their sound learning, whilst the reward of
virtue attended upon their numerous merits.   Thus the
generality of the people readily embraced their opinions ;
the authors of the erroneous doctrines kept themselves in the
back-ground, and, like evil spirits, grieved for the loss of the
people that were rescued from them.   At length, after

mature deliberation, they had the boldness to enter the lists, and appeared for public disputation,* conspicuous for riches, glittering in apparel, and supported by the flatteries of many ; choosing rather to hazard the combat, than to undergo the dishonour among the people of having been silenced, lest they should seem by saying nothing to condemn themselves. An immense multitude was there assembled with their wives and children. The people stood round as spectators and judges ; but the parties present differed much in appearance ; on the one side was Divine faith, on the other human presumption ; on the one side piety, on the other pride ; on the one side Pelagius, on the other Christ. The holy priests, Germanus and Lupus, permitted their adversaries to speak first, who long took up the time, and filled the ears with empty words. Then the venerable prelates poured forth the torrent of their apostolical and evangelical eloquence. Their discourse was interspersed with scriptural sentences, and they supported their most weighty assertions by reading the written testimonies of famous writers. Vanity was convinced, and perfidiousness confuted ; so, that at every objection made against them, not being able to reply, they confessed their errors. The people, who were judges, could scarcely refrain from violence, but signified their judgment by their acclamations.

CHAP. XVIII.

The same holy man gave sight to the blind daughter of a Tribune, and then coming to St. Alban's, there received some of his relics, and left others of the blessed Apostles, and other martyrs.

AFTER this, a certain man, who had the quality of a tribune, came forward with his wife, and presented his blind daughter, ten years of age, for the priests to cure. They ordered her to be set before their adversaries, who, being convinced by guilt of conscience, joined their entreaties to those of the child's parents, and besought the priests that she might be cured. The priests, therefore, perceiving their adversaries

* Matthew Florilegus informs us, that this conference was held at St. Alban's, where, says Camden, near the ruins of the old city, stands a chapel dedicated to St. Germanus, built upon the spot where he held this dispute.

to yield, made a short prayer, and then Germanus, full of
the Holy Ghost, invoked the Trinity, and taking into his
hands a casket with relics of saints, which hung about his
neck, applied it to the girl's eyes, which were immediately
delivered from darkness and filled with the light of truth.
The parents rejoiced, and the people were astonished at the
miracle; after which, the wicked opinions were so fully
obliterated from the minds of all, that they ardently embraced
the doctrine of the priests.

This damnable heresy being thus suppressed, and the authors
thereof confuted, and all the people's hearts settled in the
purity of the faith, the priests repaired to the tomb of the
martyr, St. Alban, to give thanks to God through him.
There Germanus, having with him relics of all the Apostles,
and of several martyrs, after offering up his prayers, commanded the tomb to be opened,* that he might lay up therein
some precious gifts; judging it convenient, that the limbs of
saints brought together from several countries, as their equal
merits had procured them admission into heaven, should be
preserved in one tomb.   These being honourably deposited,
and laid together, he took up a parcel of dust from the place
where the martyr's blood had been shed, to carry away with
him, which dust having retained the blood, it appeared that
the slaughter of the martyrs had communicated a redness to
it, whilst the persecutor was struck pale.   In consequence of
these things, an innumerable multitude of people was that
day converted to the Lord.

CHAP. XIX.

*How the same holy man, being detained there by an indisposition, by his
prayers quenched a fire that had broken out among the houses, and was
himself cured of a distemper by a vision. [A.D. 429.]*

As they were returning from thence, Germanus fell and
broke his leg, by the contrivance of the Devil, who did not
know that, like Job, his merits would be enhanced by the

---

* Bede here follows Constantius, lib. i. cap. 25, who asserts the same.
In the year 1257, was dug up this old inscription in St. Alban's Church.—
"In this mausoleum was found the venerable corpse of St. Alban, the
protomartyr of Britain." It was in lead, and supposed to have been laid
in king Offa's time.

affliction of his body. Whilst he was thus detained some
time in the same place by illness, a fire broke out in a cottage
neighbouring to that in which he was; and having burned
down the other houses which were thatched with reed, was
carried on by the wind to the dwelling in which he lay. The
people all flocked to the prelate, entreating that they might
lift him in their arms, and save him from the impending danger.
He, however, rebuked them, and relying on faith, would not
suffer himself to be removed. The multitude, in despair, ran
to oppose the conflagration; however, for the greater mani-
festation of the Divine power, whatsoever the crowd endeavoured to save, was destroyed; but what he who was
disabled and motionless occupied, the flame avoided, sparing
the house that gave entertainment to the holy man, and
raging about on every side of it; whilst the house in which
he lay appeared untouched, amid the general conflagration.
The multitude rejoiced at the miracle, and praised the superior power of God. An infinite number of the poorer sort
watched day and night before the cottage; some to heal their
souls, and some their bodies. It is impossible to relate what
Christ wrought by his servant, what wonders the sick man
performed: for whilst he would suffer no medicines to be
applied to his distemper, he one night saw a person in garments as white as snow, standing by him, who reaching out
his hand, seemed to raise him up, and ordered him to stand
boldly upon his feet; from which time his pain ceased, and
he was so perfectly restored, that when the day came on, he,
without any hesitation, set forth upon his journey.

CHAP. XX.

*How the same Bishops procured the Britons assistance from Heaven in a
battle, and then returned home.* [A.D. 429.]

IN the meantime, the Saxons and Picts, with their united
forces, made war upon the Britons, who, being thus by fear
and necessity compelled to take up arms, and thinking themselves unequal to their enemies, implored the assistance of
the holy bishops; who, hastening to them as they had promised, inspired so much courage into these fearful people,
that one would have thought they had been joined by a
mighty army. Thus, by these holy apostolic men, Christ

himself commanded in their camp. The holy days of Lent were also at hand, and were rendered more religious by the presence of the priests, insomuch that the people being instructed by daily sermons, resorted in crowds to be baptized; for most of the army desired admission to the saving water; a church was prepared with boughs for the feast of the resurrection of our Lord, and so fitted up in that martial camp, as if it were in a city. The army advanced, still wet with the baptismal water; the faith of the people was strengthened; and whereas human power had before been despaired of, the Divine assistance was now relied upon. The enemy received advice of the state of the army, and not questioning their success against an unarmed multitude, hastened forwards, but their approach was, by the scouts, made known to the Britons; the greater part of whose forces being just come from the font, after the celebration of Easter, and preparing to arm and carry on the war, Germanus declared he would be their leader. He picked out the most active, viewed the country round about, and observed, in the way by which the enemy was expected, a valley encompassed with hills.* In that place he drew up his inexperienced troops, himself acting as their general. A multitude of fierce enemies appeared, whom as soon as those that lay in ambush saw approaching, Germanus, bearing in his hands the standard, instructed his men all in a loud voice to repeat his words, and the enemy advancing securely, as thinking to take them by surprise, the priests three times cried, Hallelujah. A universal shout of the same word followed, and the hills resounding the echo on all sides, the enemy was struck with dread, fearing, that not only the neighbouring rocks, but even the very skies, were falling upon them; and such was their terror, that their feet were not swift enough to deliver them from it. They fled in disorder, casting away their arms, and well satisfied if, with their naked bodies, they could escape the danger; many of them, in their precipitate and hasty flight, were swallowed up by the river which they were passing. The Britons, without the loss of a man, beheld

* According to Usher, in Flintshire, near the village called *Mold*, or *Guid Cruc* in Welsh; the name of the field where the armies met still retains the name of *Maes Garmon*, or the Field of Germanus. Llanarmon Church now occupies the site of the wattled edifice.

their vengeance complete, and became inactive spectators of their victory.* The scattered spoils were gathered up, and the pious soldiers rejoiced in the success which Heaven had granted them. The prelates thus triumphed over the enemy without bloodshed, and gained a victory by faith, without the aid of human force ; and, having settled the affairs of the island, and restored tranquillity by the defeat, as well as of the invisible, as of the carnal enemies, prepared to return home. Their own merits, and the intercession of the holy martyr Alban, obtained them a safe passage, and the happy vessel restored them in peace to their rejoicing people.

CHAP. XXI.

The Pelagian heresy again reviving, Germanus, returning into Britain with Severus, first healed a lame youth, then having condemned or converted the Heretics, they restored spiritual health to the people of God. [A.D. 447.]

NOT long after, advice was brought from the same island, that certain persons were again attempting to set forth and spread abroad the Pelagian heresy. The holy Germanus was entreated by all the priests, that he would again defend the cause of God, which he had before asserted. He speedily complied with their request ; and taking with him Severus, a man of singular sanctity, who was disciple to the most holy father, Lupus, bishop of Troyes, and afterwards, as bishop of Treves, preached the word of God in the adjacent parts of Germany, put to sea, and was calmly wafted over into Britain. †

In the meantime, the wicked spirits flying about the whole island, foretold by constraint that Germanus was coming, inosmuch, that one Elafius, a chief of that region, hastened to meet the holy men, without having received any certain news, carrying with him his son, who laboured under a weakness of his limbs in the very flower of his youth ; for the nerves being withered, his leg was so contracted that the

---

* The account of this miraculous victory is given by Constantius, and is copied by Bede in nearly the same words. It does not appear that the Welsh MSS. take any notice of it ; and the truth of it is doubted by Whitaker in his Ancient Cathedral of Cornwall, (Appendix, No. III.)

† This second voyage of St. Germanus is supposed to have taken place eighteen years after the first.

limb was useless, and he could not walk. All the country followed this Elafius. The priests arrived, and were met by the ignorant multitude, whom they blessed, and preached the word of God to them. They found the people constant in the faith as they had left them ; and learning that but few had gone astray, they found out the authors, and condemned them. Then Elafius cast himself at the feet of the priests, presenting his son, whose distress was visible, and needed no words to express it. All were grieved, but especially the priests, who put up their prayers for him before the throne of mercy ; and Germanus, causing the youth to sit down, gently passed his healing hand over the leg which was contracted ; the limb recovered its strength and soundness by the power of his touch, the withered nerves were restored, and the youth was, in the presence of all the people, delivered whole to his father. The multitude was amazed at the miracle, and the Catholic faith was firmly planted in the minds of all ; after which, they were, in a sermon, warned and exhorted to make amends for their errors. By the judgment of all, the spreaders of the heresy, who had been expelled the island, were brought before the priests, to be conveyed up into the continent, that the country might be rid of them, and they corrected of their errors. Thus the faith in those parts continued long after pure and untainted. All things being settled, the blessed prelates returned home as prosperously as they came.

But Germanus, after this, went to Ravenna to intercede for the tranquillity of the Armoricans, where, being very honourably received by Valentinian and his mother, Placidia, he departed to Christ ; his body was conveyed to his own city with a splendid retinue, and numberless deeds of charity accompanied him to the grave. Not long after, Valentinian was murdered by the followers of Ætius, the Patrician, whom he had put to death, in the sixth year of the reign of Marcianus, and with him ended the empire of the West.

CHAP. XXII.

The Britons, being for a time delivered from foreign invasions, wasted themselves by civil wars, and then gave themselves up to more heinous crimes.

IN the meantime, in Britain, there was some respite from foreign, but not from civil war. There still remained the ruins of cities destroyed by the enemy, and abandoned ; and the natives, who had escaped the enemy, now fought against each other. However, the kings, priests, private men, and the nobility, still remembering the late calamities and slaughters, in some measure kept within bounds ; but when these died, and another generation succeeded, which knew nothing of those times, and was only acquainted with the present peaceable state of things, all the bonds of sincerity and justice were so entirely broken, that there was not only no trace of them remaining, but few persons seemed to be aware that such virtues had ever existed. Among other most wicked actions, not to be expressed, which their own historian, Gildas,* mournfully takes notice of, they added this—that they never preached the faith to the Saxons, or English, who dwelt amongst them ; however, the goodness of God did not forsake his people, whom he foreknew, but sent to the aforesaid nation much more worthy preachers, to bring it to the faith.

CHAP. XXIII.

How Pope Gregory sent Augustine, with other monks, to preach to the English nation, and encouraged them by a letter of exhortation, not to cease from their labour. [A.D. 596.]

In the year of our Lord 582, Maurice, the fifty-fourth from Augustus, ascended the throne, and reigned twenty-one years. In the tenth year of his reign, Gregory, a man renowned for learning and behaviour, was promoted to the apostolical see of Rome, and presided over it thirteen years, six months and ten days. He, being moved by Divine inspiration, in the fourteenth year of the same emperor, and about the one hundred and fiftieth after the coming of the English into Britain, sent the servant of God, Augustine,† and with him several other monks, who feared the Lord, to preach the word of God to the English nation. They having, in obedience to the pope's commands, undertaken that work, were,

---

* Called Badonicus. He is supposed to have been born in the year 520, of a Bardic family and connexion, and to have studied at the College of Lantwit Major, Glamorganshire. His querulous "History of the Britons," is all we have of his works.

† Augustine was prior of St. Gregory's Monastery dedicated to St. Andrew in Rome.

on their journey, seized with a sudden fear, and began to think of returning home, rather than proceed to a barbarous, fierce, and unbelieving nation, to whose very language they were strangers ; and this they unanimously agreed was the safest course.   In short, they sent back Augustine, who had been appointed to be consecrated bishop in case they were received by the English, that he might, by humble entreaty, obtain of the holy Gregory, that they should not be compelled to undertake so dangerous, toilsome, and uncertain a journey.   The pope, in reply, sent them a hortatory epistle, persuading them to proceed in the work of the Divine word, and rely on the assistance of the Almighty.   The purport of which letter was as follows :—

"*Gregory, the servant of the servants of God, to the servants of our Lord.*   Forasmuch as it had been better not to begin a good work, than to think of desisting from that which has been begun, it behoves you, my beloved sons, to fulfil the good work, which, by the help of our Lord, you have undertaken.   Let not, therefore, the toil of the journey, nor the tongues of evil speaking men, deter you ; but with all possible earnestness and zeal perform that which, by God's direction, you have undertaken ; being assured, that much labour is followed by an eternal reward.   When Augustine, your chief, returns, whom we also constitute your abbat, humbly obey him in all things ; knowing, that whatsoever you shall do by his direction, will, in all respects, be available to your souls.   Almighty God protect you with his grace, and grant that I may, in the heavenly country, see the fruits of your labour.   Inasmuch as, though I cannot labour with you, I shall partake in the joy of the reward, because I am willing to labour.   God keep you in safety, my most beloved sons.   Dated the 23rd of July, in the fourteenth year of the reign of our pious and most august lord, Mauritius Tiberius, the thirteenth year after the consulship of our said lord.   The fourteenth indiction."

CHAP. XXIV.

How he wrote to the bishop of Arles to entertain them. [A.D. 596.]

THE same venerable pope also sent a letter to Ætherius,

D 2

bishop of Arles,* exhorting him to give favourable entertainment to Augustine on his way to Britain; which letter was in these words :—

"*To his most reverend and holy brother and fellow bishop Ætherius, Gregory, the servant of the servants of God.* Although religious men stand in need of no recommendation with priests who have the charity which is pleasing to God ; yet as a proper opportunity is offered to write, we have thought fit to send you this our letter, to inform you, that we have directed thither, for the good of souls, the bearer of these presents, Augustine, the servant of God, of whose industry we are assured, with other servants of God, whom it is requisite that your holiness assist with priestly affection, and afford him all the comfort in your power. And to the end that you may be the more ready in your assistance, we have enjoined him particularly to inform you of the occasion of his coming ; knowing, that when you are acquainted with it, you will, as the matter requires, for the sake of God, zealously afford him your relief. We also in all things recommend to your charity, Candidus, the priest, our common son, whom we have transferred to the government of a small patrimony in our church. God keep you in safety, most reverend brother. Dated the 23rd day of July, in the fourteenth year of the reign of our most pious and august lord, Mauritius Tiberius, the thirteenth year after the consulship of our lord aforesaid. The fourteenth indiction."

CHAP. XXV.

Augustine, coming into Britain, first preached in the Isle of Thanet to King Ethelbert, and having obtained licence, entered the kingdom of Kent, in order to preach therein. [A.D. 597.]

AUGUSTINE, thus strengthened by the confirmation of the blessed Father Gregory, returned to the work of the word of God, with the servants of Christ, and arrived in Britain. The powerful Ethelbert was at that time king of Kent ;†

---

* This is a palpable error in Bede, as it appears from the catalogues of the Archbishops of Arles and Lyons, that Vergilius filled that see at this time, and that Ætherius was his contemporary Archbishop at Lyons. Dr. Lingard attributes the origin of the error to Nothelm, who was deputed by Bede to search the papal archives, and to copy from them documents for his work. The same error occurs in chaps. xxvii. xxviii. pp. 40, 53.

† Ethelbert was the third Bretwalda, or dominant king.

he had extended his dominions as far as the great river Humber, by which the Southern Saxons are divided from the Northern.   On the east of Kent is the large Isle of Thanet containing according to the English way of reckoning, 600 families, divided from the other land by the river Wantsum,* which is about three furlongs over, and fordable only in two places, for both ends of it run into the sea.   In this island landed the servant of our Lord, Augustine, and his companions, being, as is reported, nearly forty men.   They had, by order of the blessed Pope Gregory, taken interpreters of the nation of the Franks,† and sending to Ethelbert, signified that they were come from Rome, and brought a joyful message, which most undoubtedly assured to all that took advantage of it everlasting joys in heaven, and a kingdom that would never end, with the living and true God.   The king having heard this, ordered them to stay in that island where they had landed, and that they should be furnished with all necessaries, till he should consider what to do with them.   For he had before heard of the Christian religion, having a Christian wife of the royal family of the Franks, called Bertha ;‡ whom he had received from her parents, upon condition that she should be permitted to practise her religion with the Bishop Luidhard,§ who was sent with her to preserve her faith.   Some days after, the king came into the island, and sitting in the open air, ordered Augustine and his companions to be brought into his presence.   For he had taken precaution that they should not come to him in any house, lest, according to an ancient superstition, if they practised any magical arts, they might impose upon him, and so get the better of him.   But they

---

* Thanet is now divided from the rest of Kent by a narrow rill, crossed by an arch of the smallest span.   In Bede's time the two arms of the Stour were a channel nearly a mile in width, which received several streams besides the Greater and Lesser Stour.   This channel was called the Wantsum.

† The Franks and English Saxons were equally German nations ; the former came 130 years earlier from beyond the Rhine ; the latter from the countries about the mouths of the Rhine and the Elbe, and about Holstein, on the continent of Denmark, still called Jutland.   Hence the French and English both had the same language, as Bishop Godwin observes from the circumstance.   This is confirmed by other clear proofs by the learned William Howel, in his Institution of General History.

‡ Daughter of Charibert, king of Paris.

§ Bishop of Senlis.

came furnished with Divine, not with magic virtue, bearing
a silver cross for their banner, and the image of our Lord
and Saviour painted on a board ; and singing the litany, they
offered up their prayers to the Lord for the eternal salvation
both of themselves and of those to whom they were come.
When he had sat down, pursuant to the king's commands, and
preached to him and his attendants there present, the word
of life, the king answered thus :—" Your words and promises
are very fair, but as they are new to us, and of uncertain
import, I cannot approve of them so far as to forsake that
which I have so long followed with the whole English nation.
But because you are come from far into my kingdom, and,
as I conceive, are desirous to impart to us those things which
you believe to be true, and most beneficial, we will not molest
you, but give you favourable entertainment, and take care to
supply you with your necessary sustenance ; nor do we forbid you to preach and gain as many as you can to your
religion."* Accordingly he permitted them to reside in the
city of Canterbury, which was the metropolis of all his
dominions, and, pursuant to his promise, besides allowing
them sustenance, did not refuse them liberty to preach. It
is reported that, as they drew near to the city, after their
manner, with the holy cross, and the image of our sovereign
Lord and King, Jesus Christ, they, in concert, sung this
litany : " We beseech thee, O Lord, in all thy mercy, that
thy anger and wrath be turned away from this city, and from
thy holy house, because we have sinned.   Hallelujah."†

* It would appear, from the humanity and kindness with which St.
Augustine was received immediately on his arrival, that Bishop Luidhard
was his precursor, and opened a way for his success ; and that the piety and
prayers of Queen Bertha herself are not likely to have been without their
effect in causing Ethelbert to lend an attentive ear to the preaching of St.
Augustine.

† With St. Augustine, it is recorded, that St. Gregory sent the following
books :—a Bible in two vols. ; a Psalter, and a book of the Gospels ; a
book of Martyrology ; Apocryphal Lives of the Apostles ; and expositions
of certain Epistles and Gospels.   The Canterbury Book, in the library of
Trinity Hall, Cambridge, closes the brief catalogue in these expressive
words : " These are the foundation, or beginning, of the library of the whole
English church, A.D. 601." See Wanley's Catalogue of Saxon manuscripts in vol. ii. of Dr. Hickes's Thesaurus, p. 172.

CHAP. XXVI.

St. Augustine in Kent followed the doctrine and manner of living of the primitive church, and settled his episcopal see in the royal city. [A.D. 597]

As soon as they entered the dwelling-place assigned them, they began to imitate the course of life practised in the primitive church; applying themselves to frequent prayer, watching and fasting; preaching the word of life to as many as they could; despising all worldly things, as not belonging to them; receiving only their necessary food from those they taught; living themselves in all respects conformably to what they prescribed to others, and being always disposed to suffer any adversity, and even to die for that truth which they preached. In short, several believed and were baptized, admiring the simplicity of their innocent life, and the sweetness of their heavenly doctrine. There was on the east side of the city, a church dedicated to the honour of St. Martin,* built whilst the Romans were still in the island, wherein the queen, who, as has been said before, was a Christian, used to pray. In this they first began to meet, to sing, to pray, to say mass, to preach, and to baptize, till the king, being converted to the faith, allowed them to preach openly, and build or repair churches in all places.

When he, among the rest, induced by the unspotted life of these holy men, and their delightful promises, which, by many miracles, they proved to be most certain, believed and was baptized, greater numbers began daily to flock together to hear the word, and, forsaking their heathen rites, to associate themselves, by believing, to the unity of the church of Christ. Their conversion the king so far encouraged, as that he compelled none to embrace Christianity, but only showed more affection to the believers, as to his fellow citizens in the heavenly kingdom. For he had learned from his instructors and leaders to salvation, that the service of Christ ought to be voluntary, not by compulsion. Nor was

* The present church of St. Martin near Canterbury is not the old one spoken of by Bede, as it is generally thought to be, but is a structure of the thirteenth century, though it is probable that the materials of the original church were worked up in the masonry on its re-construction, the walls being still composed in part of Roman bricks.

it long before he gave his teachers a settled residence in his
metropolis of Canterbury, with such possessions of different
kinds as were necessary for their subsistence.

CHAP. XXVII.

*St. Augustine, being made bishop, sends to acquaint Pope Gregory with
what had been done, and receives his answer to the doubts he had proposed to him.*   [A.D. 597.]

IN the meantime, Augustine, the man of God, repaired to
Arles, and, pursuant to the orders received from the holy
Father Gregory, was ordained archbishop of the English
nation,* by Ætherius,† archbishop of that city. Then returning into Britain, he sent Laurentius the priest, and Peter
the monk, to Rome, to acquaint Pope Gregory, that the
nation of the English had received the faith of Christ, and
that he was himself made their bishop.   At the same time, he
desired his solution of some doubts that occurred to him.
He soon received proper answers to his questions, which we
have also thought fit to insert in this our history :—

*The First Question of Augustine, Bishop of the Church
of Canterbury.*—Concerning bishops, how they are to behave
themselves towards their clergy ? or into how many portions
the things given by the faithful to the altar are to be divided ?
and how the bishop is to act in the church ?

Gregory, Pope of the City of Rome, answers.—Holy Writ,
which no doubt you are well versed in, testifies, and particularly St. Paul's Epistle to Timothy, wherein he endeavours to
instruct him how he should behave himself in the house of
God ; but it is the custom of the apostolic see to prescribe

---

* Augustine was not consecrated as archbishop either of London or Canterbury ; but by the general title of the " Bishop of the English," (Anglorum Episcopus,) that he might be at liberty to fix his seat in whatever part
of the country he pleased.—*Parker, Antiq. Britan.* p. 18. The primacy of
Canterbury is owing to the fact of Kent being the first and chief of the
Saxon kingdoms, extending to the Humber.

† For Ætherius read Vergilius, see note at p. 36. Arles is situated in the
extreme south of France, not far from the Mediterranean. Early in the
fifth century, the emperor Honorius erected this city into a metropolis over
seven of the sixteen provinces into which Gaul was at that time divided ;
the bishop of Rome, apprehensive that the archbishop of Arles might
elevate himself into a patriarch of the whole kingdom, appointed him his
apostolic vicar in Gaul.

rules to bishops newly ordained, that all emoluments which accrue, are to be divided into four portions ;—one for the bishop and his family, because of hospitality and entertainments ; another for the clergy ; a third for the poor ; and the fourth for the repair of churches. But in regard that you, my brother, being brought up under monastic rules, are not to live apart from your clergy in the English church, which, by God's assistance, has been lately brought to the faith ; you are to follow that course of life which our forefathers did in the time of the primitive church, when none of them said anything that he possessed was his own, but all things were in common among them.

But if there are any clerks not received into holy orders, who cannot live continent, they are to take wives, and receive their stipends abroad ; because we know it is written, that out of the same portions above-mentioned a distribution was made to each of them according to every one's wants. Care is also to be taken of their stipends, and provision to be made, and they are to be kept under ecclesiastical rules, that they may live orderly, and attend to singing of psalms, and, by the help of God, preserve their hearts, and tongues, and bodies from all that is unlawful. But as for those that live in common, why need we say anything of making portions, or keeping hospitality and exhibiting mercy ? inasmuch as all that can be spared is to be spent in pious and religious works, according to the commands of Him who is the Lord and Master of all, "Give alms of such things as you have, and behold all things are clean unto you."

Augustine's Second Question.—Whereas the faith is one and the same, why are there different customs in different churches ? and why is one custom of masses observed in the holy Roman church, and another in the Gallican church ?

Pope Gregory answers.—You know, my brother, the custom of the Roman church in which you remember you were bred up. But it pleases me, that if you have found anything, either in the Roman, or the Gallican,* or any other

* It is presumed that Luidhard, bishop of Senlis, who accompanied Bertha from Paris on her marriage with Ethelbert, would use the Gallican rites in the church of St. Martin, at Canterbury, and that this must have attracted the attention of St. Augustine on his landing in our island. It is not improbable too that St. Germanus effected a great change in the eccle-

church, which may be more acceptable to Almighty God, you carefully make choice of the same, and sedulously teach the church of the English, which as yet is new in the faith, whatsoever you can gather from the several churches. For things are not to be loved for the sake of places, but places for the sake of good things. Choose, therefore, from every church those things that are pious, religious, and upright, and when you have, as it were, made them up into one body, let the minds of the English be accustomed thereto.

Augustine's Third Question.—I beseech you to inform me, what punishment must be inflicted, if any one shall take anything by stealth from the church?

Gregory answers.—You may judge, my brother, by the person of the thief, in what manner he is to be corrected. For there are some, who, having substance, commit theft; and there are others, who transgress in this point through want. Wherefore it is requisite, that some be punished in their purses, others with stripes; some with more severity, and some more mildly. And when the severity is more, it is to proceed from charity, not from passion; because this is done to him who is corrected, that he may not be delivered up to hell-fire. For it behoves us to maintain discipline among the faithful, as good parents do with their carnal children, whom they punish with stripes for their faults, and yet design to make those their heirs whom they chastise; and they preserve what they possess for those whom they seem in anger to persecute. This charity is, therefore, to be kept in mind, and it dictates the measure of the punishment, so that the mind may do nothing beyond the rule of reason. You may add, that they are to restore those things which they have stolen from the church. But, God forbid, that the church should make profit from those earthly things which it seems to lose, or seek gain out of such vanities.

Augustine's Fourth Question.—Whether two brothers may marry two sisters, which are of a family far removed from them?

Gregory answers.—This may lawfully be done; for nothing is found in holy writ that seems to contradict it.

siastical customs of the ancient British church, which he would naturally wish to regulate after the model of the Gallican. For an account of the Gallican Liturgy, and its variations from that of the Roman, consult Palmer's Origines Liturgicæ, vol. i. page 144.

Augustine's Fifth Question.—To what degree may the faithful marry with their kindred ? and whether it is lawful for men to marry their stepmothers and relations ?

Gregory answers.—A certain worldly law in the Roman commonwealth allows, that the son and daughter of a brother and sister, or of two brothers, or two sisters, may be joined in matrimony ; but we have found, by experience, that no offspring can come of such wedlock ; and the Divine Law forbids a man to "uncover the nakedness of his kindred." Hence of necessity it must be the third or fourth generation of the faithful, that can be lawfully joined in matrimony ; for the second, which we have mentioned, must altogether abstain from one another.   To marry with one's stepmother is a heinous crime, because it is written in the Law, "Thou shalt not uncover the nakedness of thy father :" now the son, indeed, cannot uncover his father's nakedness ; but in regard that it is written, "They shall be two in one flesh," he that presumes to uncover the nakedness of his stepmother, who was one flesh with his father, certainly uncovers the nakedness of his father.   It is also prohibited to marry with a sister-in-law, because by the former union she is become the brother's flesh.   For which thing also John the Baptist was beheaded, and ended his life in holy martyrdom.   For, though he was not ordered to deny Christ, and indeed was killed for confessing Christ, yet in regard that the same Jesus Christ, our Lord, said, "I am the Truth," because John was killed for the truth, he also shed his blood for Christ.

But forasmuch as there are many of the English, who, whilst they were still in infidelity, are said to have been joined in this execrable matrimony, when they come to the faith they are to be admonished to abstain, and be made to know that this is a grievous sin.   Let them fear the dreadful judgment of God, lest, for the gratification of their carnal appetites, they incur the torments of eternal punishment. Yet they are not on this account to be deprived of the communion of the body and blood of Christ, lest they seem to be punished for those things which they did through ignorance before they had received baptism.   For at this time the Holy Church chastises some things through zeal, and tolerates some through meekness, and connives at some things through discretion, that so she may often, by this forbearance and connivance, suppress the evil which she disapproves. But all that come to the faith are to be admonished not to do such things. And if any shall be guilty of them, they are to be excluded from the communion of the body and blood of Christ. For as the offence is, in some measure, to be tolerated in those who did it through ignorance, so it is to be strenuously prosecuted in those who do not fear to sin knowingly.

Augustine's Sixth Question.—Whether a bishop may be ordained without other bishops being present, in case there be so great a distance between them, that they cannot easily come together ?

Gregory answers.—As for the church of England, in which you are as yet the only bishop, you can no otherwise ordain a bishop than in the absence of other bishops ; unless some bishops should come over from Gaul, that they may be present as witnesses to you in ordaining a bishop. But we would have you, my brother, to ordain bishops in such a manner, that the said bishops may not be far asunder, that when a new bishop is to be ordained, there be no difficulty, but that other bishops, and pastors also, whose presence is necessary, may easily come together. Thus, when, by the help of God, bishops shall be so constituted in places everywhere near to one another, no ordination of a bishop is to be performed without assembling three or four bishops. For, even in spiritual affairs, we may take example by the temporal, that they may be wisely and discreetly conducted. It is certain, that when marriages are celebrated in the world, some married persons are assembled, that those who went before in the way of matrimony, may also partake in the joy of the succeeding couple. Why, then, at this spiritual ordination, wherein, by means of the sacred ministry, man is joined to God, should not such persons be assembled, as may either rejoice in the advancement of the new bishop, or jointly pour forth their prayers to Almighty God for his preservation ?

Augustine's Seventh Question.—How are we to deal with the bishops of France and Britain ?

Gregory answers.—We give you no authority over the bishops of France, because the bishop of Arles received the pall* in ancient times from my predecessor, and we are not to

* The pallium, or pall, consisted of a long strip of fine woollen cloth,

deprive him of the authority he has received. If it shall therefore happen, my brother, that you go over into the province of France, you are to concert with the said bishop of Arles, how, if there be any faults among the bishops, they may be amended. And if he shall be lukewarm in keeping up discipline, he is to be corrected by your zeal ; to whom we have also written, that when your holiness shall be in France, he may also use all his endeavours to assist you, and put away from the behaviour of the bishops all that shall be opposite to the command of our Creator. But you, of your own authority, shall not have power to judge the bishops of France, but by persuading, soothing, and showing good works for them to imitate ; you shall reform the minds of wicked men to the pursuit of holiness ; for it is written in the Law, "When thou comest into the standing corn of thy neighbours, then thou mayest pluck the ears with thine hand ; but thou shalt not move a sickle unto thy neighbours' standing corn." For thou mayest not apply the sickle of judgment in that harvest which seems to have been committed to another ; but by the effect of good works thou shalt clear the Lord's wheat of the chaff of their vices, and convert them into the body of the Church, as it were, by eating. But whatsoever is to be done by authority, must be transacted with the aforesaid bishop of Arles, lest that should be omitted, which the ancient institution of the fathers has appointed.* But as for all the bishops of Britain, we commit them to your care, that the unlearned may be taught, the weak strengthened by persuasion, and the perverse corrected by authority.

Augustine's Eighth Question.—Whether a woman with child ought to be baptized ? Or how long after she has brought forth, may she come into the church ? As also, after how many days the infant born may be baptized, lest he be prevented by death ? Or how long after her husband may

ornamented with crosses, the middle of which was formed into a loose collar resting on the shoulders, while the extremities before and behind hung down nearly to the feet. In the east it is called *omophorion*, the bishops wearing it above the phenolion, or vestment, during the eucharist. It originally formed part of the imperial habit, of which Collier has given some interesting particulars, in his Eccles. Hist. vol. i. 69, folio.

* St. Gregory probably alludes to the third œcumenical council, held at Ephesus, A.D. 431.

have carnal knowledge of her ?   Or whether it is lawful for
her to come into the church when she has her courses ?   Or
to receive the holy sacrament of communion ?   Or whether
a man, under certain circumstances, may come into the
church before he has washed with water ?   Or approach to
receive the mystery of the holy communion ?   All which
things are requisite to be known by the rude nation of the
English.

Gregory answers.—I do not doubt but that these questions
have been put to you, my brother, and I think I have already
answered you therein.   But I believe you would wish the
opinion which you yourself might give to be confirmed by
mine also.   Why should not a woman with child be baptized,
since the fruitfulness of the flesh is no offence in the eyes of
Almighty God ?   For when our first parents sinned in
Paradise, they forfeited the immortality which they had received, by the just judgment of God.   Because, therefore,
Almighty God would not for their fault wholly destroy the
human race, he both deprived man of immortality for his sin,
and, at the same time, of his great goodness, reserved to him
the power of propagating his race after him.   On what
account then can that which is preserved to the human race,
by the free gift of Almighty God, be excluded from the privilege of baptism ?   For it is very foolish to imagine that
the gift of grace opposes that mystery in which all sin is
blotted out.   When a woman is delivered, after how many
days she may come into the church, you have been informed
by reading the Old Testament, viz. that she is to abstain for
a male child thirty-three days, and sixty-six for a female.
Now you must know that this is to be taken in a mystery ;
for if she enters the church the very hour that she is delivered, to return thanks, she is not guilty of any sin ; because
the pleasure of the flesh is in fault, and not the pain ; but
the pleasure is in the copulation of the flesh, whereas there
is pain in bringing forth the child.   Wherefore it is said to
the first mother of all, "In sorrow shalt thou bring forth
children."   If, therefore, we forbid a woman that has brought
forth, to enter the church, we make a crime of her very punishment.   To baptize either a woman who has brought forth, if
there be danger of death, even the very hour that she brings
forth, or that which she has brought forth the very hour it

is born, is no way prohibited, because, as the grace of the holy mystery is to be with much discretion provided for the living and understanding, so is it to be without any delay offered to the dying ; lest, while a further time is sought to confer the mystery of redemption, a small delay intervening, the person that is to be redeemed is dead and gone.

Her husband is not to approach her, till the infant born be weaned. A bad custom is sprung up in the behaviour of married people, that is, that women disdain to suckle the children which they bring forth, and give them to other women to suckle ; which seems to have been invented on no other account but incontinency ; because, as they will not be continent, they will not suckle the children which they bear. Those women, therefore, who, from bad custom, give their children to others to bring up, must not approach their husbands till the time of purification is past. For even when there has been no child-birth, women are forbidden to do so, whilst they have their monthly courses, insomuch that the Law condemns to death any man that shall approach unto a woman during her uncleanness. Yet the woman, nevertheless, must not be forbidden to come into the church whilst she has her monthly courses ; because the superfluity of nature cannot be imputed to her as a crime ; and it is not just that she should be refused admittance into the church, for that which she suffers against her will. For we know, that the woman who had the issue of blood, humbly approaching behind our Lord's back, touched the hem of his garment, and her distemper immediately departed from her. If, therefore, she that had an issue of blood might commendably touch the garment of our Lord, why may not she, who has the monthly courses, lawfully enter into the church of God ? But you may say, Her distemper compelled her, whereas these we speak of are bound by custom. Consider, then, most dear brother, that all we suffer in this mortal flesh, through the infirmity of our nature, is ordained by the just judgment of God after the fall ; for to hunger, to thirst, to be hot, to be cold, to be weary, is from the infirmity of our nature ; and what else is it to seek food against hunger, drink against thirst, air against heat, clothes against cold, rest against weariness, than to procure a remedy against distempers ? Thus to a woman her monthly courses are a distemper. If, therefore,

it was a commendable boldness in her, who in her disease
touched our Lord's garment, why may not that which is
allowed to one infirm person, be granted to all women, who,
through the fault of their nature, are distempered ?

She must not, therefore, be forbidden to receive the mystery
of the holy communion during those days. But if any
one out of profound respect does not presume to do it, she is
to be commended; yet if she receives it, she is not to be
judged. For it is the part of noble minds in some manner
to acknowledge their faults, even where there is no offence ;
because very often that is done without a fault, which, nevertheless, proceeded from a fault. Therefore, when we are
hungry, it is no crime to eat ; yet our being hungry proceeds
from the sin of the first man. The monthly courses are no
crime in women, because they naturally happen ; however,
because our nature itself is so depraved, that it appears to be
so without the concurrence of the will, the fault proceeds
from sin, and thereby human nature may herself know what
she is become by judgment. And let man, who wilfully
committed the offence, bear the guilt of that offence. And,
therefore, let women consider with themselves, and if they
do not presume, during their monthly courses, to approach
the sacrament of the body and blood of our Lord, they are to
be commended for their praiseworthy consideration ; but
when they are carried away with love of the same mystery
to receive it out of the usual custom of religious life, they are
not to be restrained, as we said before. For as in the Old
Testament the outward works are observed, so in the New
Testament, that which is outwardly done, is not so diligently
regarded as that which is inwardly thought, in order to
punish it by a discerning judgment. For whereas the Law
forbids the eating of many things as unclean, yet our Lord
says in the Gospel, "Not that which goeth into the mouth
defileth a man ; but that which cometh out of the mouth,
this defileth a man." And presently after he added, ex-
pounding the same, "Out of the heart proceed evil thoughts."
Where it is sufficiently shown, that that is declared by
Almighty God to be polluted in fact, which proceeds from
the root of a polluted thought. Whence also Paul the Apostle
says, " Unto the pure all things are pure, but unto them that
are defiled and unbelieving, nothing is pure." And pre-

sently after, declaring the cause of that defilement, he adds,
"For even their mind and conscience is defiled." If, therefore, meat is not unclean to him who has a clean mind, why
shall that which a clean woman suffers according to nature,
be imputed to her as uncleanness?

A man who has approached his own wife is not to enter
the church unless washed with water, nor is he to enter immediately although washed. The Law prescribed to the
ancient people, that a man in such cases should be washed
with water, and not enter into the church before the setting
of the sun. Which, nevertheless, may be understood spiritu-
ally, because a man acts so when the mind is led by the
imagination to unlawful concupiscence; for unless the fire of
concupiscence be first driven from his mind, he is not to
think himself worthy of the congregation of the brethren,
whilst he thus indulges an unlawful passion. For though
several nations have different opinions concerning this affair,
and seem to observe different rules, it was always the custom
of the Romans, from ancient times, for such an one to be
cleansed by washing, and for some time respectfully to forbear entering the church. Nor do we, in so saying, assign
matrimony to be a fault; but forasmuch as lawful intercourse cannot be had without the pleasure of the flesh, it is
proper to forbear entering the holy place, because the pleasure itself cannot be without a fault. For he was not born
of adultery or fornication, but of lawful marriage, who said,
"Behold I was conceived in iniquity, and in sin my mother
brought me forth." For he who knew himself to have been
conceived in iniquity, lamented that he was born from sin,
because the tree in its bough bears the moisture it drew from
the root. In which words, however, he does not call the
union of the married couple iniquity, but the pleasure of the
copulation. For there are many things which are proved to
be lawful, and yet we are somewhat defiled in doing them.
As very often by being angry we correct faults, and at the
same time disturb our own peace of mind; and though that
which we do is right, yet it is not to be approved that our
mind should be discomposed. For he who said, "My eye
was disturbed with anger," had been angry at the vices of
those who had offended. Now, in regard that only a sedate
mind can apply itself to contemplation, he grieved that his

E

eye was disturbed with anger ; because, whilst he was correcting evil actions below, he was obliged to be withdrawn and disturbed from the contemplation of things above.   Anger against vice is, therefore, commendable, and yet painful to a man, because he thinks that by his mind being agitated, he has incurred some guilt.   Lawful commerce, therefore, must be for the sake of children, not of pleasure ; and must be to procure offspring, not to satisfy vices.   But if any man is led not by the desire of pleasure, but only for the sake of getting children, such a man is certainly to be left to his own judgment, either as to entering the church, or as to receiving the mystery of the body and blood of our Lord, which he, who being placed in the fire cannot burn, is not to be forbidden by us to receive.   But when, not the love of getting children, but of pleasure prevails, the pair have cause to lament their deed.   For this the holy preaching allows them, and yet fills the mind with dread of the very allowance.   For when Paul the Apostle said, " Let him that cannot contain, have his wife ;" he presently took care to subjoin, " But this I say by way of indulgence, not by way of command."   For that is not granted by way of indulgence which is lawful, because it is just ; and, therefore, that which he said he indulged, he showed to be an offence.

It is seriously to be considered, that when God was to speak to the people on Mount Sinai, he first commanded them to abstain from women.   And if so much cleanness of body was there required, where God spoke to the people by the means of a subject creature, that those who were to hear the words of God should not do so ; how much more ought women, who receive the body of Almighty God, to preserve themselves in cleanness of flesh, lest they be burdened with the very *greatness* of that unutterable mystery ?   For this reason, it was said to David, concerning his men, by the priest, that if they were clean in this particular, they should receive the shewbread, which they would not have received at all, had not David first declared them to be clean.   Then the man, who, afterwards, has been washed with water, is also capable of receiving the mystery of the holy communion, when it is lawful for him, according to what has been before declared, to enter the church.

Augustine's Ninth Question.—Whether after an illusion,

such as happens in a dream, any man may receive the body of our Lord, or if he be a priest, celebrate the Divine mysteries ?

Gregory answers.—The Testament of the Old Law, as has been said already in the article above, calls such a man polluted, and allows him not to enter into the church till the evening after being washed with water. Which, nevertheless, spiritual people, taking in another sense, will understand in the same manner as above ; because he is imposed upon as it were in a dream, who, being tempted with filthiness, is defiled by real representations in thought, and he is to be washed with water, that he may cleanse away the sins of thought with tears ; and unless the fire of temptation depart before, may know himself to be guilty as it were until the evening. But discretion is very necessary in that illusion, that one may seriously consider what causes it to happen in the mind of the person sleeping ; for sometimes it proceeds from excess of eating or drinking ; sometimes from the superfluity or infirmity of nature, and sometimes from the thoughts. And when it happens, either through superfluity or infirmity of nature, such an illusion is not to be feared, because it is rather to be lamented, that the mind of the person, who knew nothing of it, suffers the same, than that he occasioned it. But when the appetite of gluttony commits excess in food, and thereupon the receptacles of the humours are oppressed, the mind from thence contracts some guilt ; yet not so much as to obstruct the receiving of the holy mystery, or celebrating mass, when a holy day requires it, or necessity obliges the sacrament to be administered, because there is no other priest in the place ; for if there be others who can perform the ministry, the illusion proceeding from over-eating is not to exclude a man from receiving the sacred mystery ; but I am of opinion he ought humbly to abstain from offering the sacrifice of the mystery ; but not from receiving it, unless the mind of the person sleeping has been filled with some foul imagination. For there are some, who for the most part so suffer the illusion, that their mind, even during the sleep of the body, is not defiled with filthy thoughts. In which case, one thing is evident, that the mind is guilty even in its own judgment ; for though it does not remember to have seen any thing whilst the body was sleeping, yet it calls to mind that when waking it fell into bodily gluttony. But if the sleeping illusion proceeds from evil thoughts when waking, then the guilt is manifest to the mind ; for the man perceives from whence that filth sprung, because what he had knowingly thought of, that he afterwards unwittingly revealed. But it is to be considered, whether that thought was no more than a suggestion, or proceeded to enjoyment, or, which is still more criminal, consented to sin. For all sin is fulfilled in three ways, viz., by suggestion, by delight, and by consent. Suggestion is occasioned by the Devil, delight is from the flesh, and consent from the mind. For the serpent suggested the first offence, and Eve, as flesh, was delighted with it, but Adam consented, as the spirit, or mind. And much discretion is requisite for the mind to sit as judge between suggestion and delight, and between delight and consent. For if the evil spirit suggest a sin to the mind, if there ensue no delight in the sin, the sin is in no way committed ; but when the flesh begins to be delighted, then sin begins to grow. But if it deliberately consents, then the sin is known to be perfected. The beginning, therefore, of sin is in the suggestion, the nourishing of it in delight, but in the consent is its perfection. And it often happens that what the evil spirit sows in the thought, the flesh draws to delight, and yet the soul does not consent to that delight. And whereas the flesh cannot be delighted without the mind, yet the mind struggling against the pleasures of the flesh, is somewhat unwillingly tied down by the carnal delight, so that through reason it contradicts, and does not consent, yet being influenced by delight, it grievously laments its being so bound. Wherefore that principal soldier of our Lord's host, sighing, said, "I see another law in my members warring against the law of my mind, and bringing me into captivity to the law of sin, which is in my members." Now if he was a captive, he did not fight ; but if he did fight, how was he a captive ? he therefore fought against the law of the mind, which the law that is in the members opposed; if he fought so, he was no captive. Thus, then, man is, as I may say, a captive and yet free. Free on account of justice, which he loves, a captive by the delight which he unwillingly bears within him.

CHAP. XXVIII.

Pope Gregory writes to the bishop of Arles to assist Augustine in the work of God. [A.D. 601.]

THUS far the answers of the holy Pope Gregory, to the questions of the most reverend prelate, Augustine. But the epistle, which he says he had written to the bishop of Arles, was directed to Vergilius, successor to Ætherius, the copy whereof follows :—

" *To his most reverend and holy brother and fellow bishop, Vergilius; Gregory, servant of the servants of God.* With how much affection brethren, coming of their own accord, are to be entertained, is well known, by their being for the most part invited on account of charity. Therefore, if our common brother, Bishop Augustine, shall happen to come to you, I desire your love will, as is becoming, receive him so kindly and affectionately, that he may be supported by the honour of your consolation, and others be informed how brotherly charity is to be cultivated. And, since it often happens that those who are at a distance, sooner than others, understand the things that need correction, if any crimes of priests or others shall happen to be laid before you, you will, in conjunction with him, sharply inquire into the same. And do you both act so strictly and carefully against those things which offend God, and provoke his wrath, that for the amendment of others, the punishment may fall upon the guilty, and the innocent may not suffer an ill name. God keep you in safety, most reverend brother. Given the 22nd day of June, in the nineteenth year of the reign of our pious and august emperor, Mauritius Tiberius, and the eighteenth year after the consulship of our said lord. The fourth indiction."

CHAP. XXIX.

The same Pope sends Augustine the Pall, an Epistle, and several Ministers of the word. [A.D. 601.]

MOREOVER, the same Pope Gregory, hearing from Bishop Augustine, that he had a great harvest, and but few labourers, sent to him, together with his aforesaid messengers, several fellow labourers and ministers of the word of whom the first

and principal were* Mellitus, Justus, Paulinus, and Rufinianus,
and by them all things in general that were necessary for the
worship and service of the church, viz., sacred vessels and
vestments for the altars, also ornaments for the churches, and
vestments for the priests and clerks, as likewise relics of the
holy apostles and martyrs; besides many books. He also
sent letters, wherein he signified that he had transmitted the
pall to him, and at the same time directed how he should
constitute bishops in Britain. The letters were in these
words :—

" *To his most reverend and holy brother and fellow bishop,
Augustine; Gregory, the servant of the servants of God.*
Though it be certain, that the unspeakable rewards of the
eternal kingdom are reserved for those who labour for Almighty God, yet it is requisite that we bestow on them the
advantage of honours, to the end that they may by this re-
compence be enabled the more vigorously to apply themselves
to the care of their spiritual work. And, in regard that the
new church of the English is, through the goodness of the
Lord, and your labours, brought to the grace of God, we
grant you the use of the pall in the same, only for the performing of the solemn service of the mass; so that you in
several places ordain twelve bishops, who shall be subject to
your jurisdiction, so that the bishop of London shall, for the
future, be always consecrated by his own synod, and that he
receive the honour of the pall from this holy and apostolical
see, which I, by the grace of God, now serve. But we will
have you send to the city of York such a bishop as you shall
think fit to ordain; yet so, that if that city, with the places
adjoining, shall receive the word of God, that bishop shall
also ordain twelve bishops, and enjoy the honour of a metropolitan; for we design, if we live, by the help of God, to
bestow on him also the pall; and yet we will have him to be
subservient to your authority; but after your decease, he
shall so preside over the bishops he shall ordain, as to be in
no way subject to the jurisdiction of the bishop of London.
But for the future let this distinction be between the bishops

---

* Mellitus was consecrated bishop of London, A.D. 604; and succeeded
Laurentius in the see of Canterbury, A.D. 619; in 624 Justus was translated
from Rochester to the primacy. In the following year Paulinus was made
archbishop of York. Rufinianus was the third abbot of St. Augustine's abbey.

of the cities of London and York, that he may have the precedence who shall be first ordained.* But let them unanimously dispose, by common advice and uniform conduct, whatsoever is to be done for the zeal of Christ; let them judge rightly, and perform what they judge convenient in a uniform manner.

"But to you, my brother, shall, by the authority of our God, and Lord Jesus Christ, be subject not only those bishops you shall ordain, and those that shall be ordained by the bishop of York, but also all the priests in Britain; to the end that from the mouth and life of your holiness they may learn the rule of believing rightly, and living well, and fulfilling their office in faith and good manners, they may, when it shall please the Lord, attain the heavenly kingdom. God preserve you in safety, most reverend brother.

"Dated the 22nd of June, in the nineteenth year of the reign of our most pious lord and emperor, Mauritius Tiberius, the eighteenth year after the consulship of our said lord. The fourth indiction."

CHAP. XXX.

A copy of the letter which Pope Gregory sent to the Abbot Mellitus, then going into Britain. [A.D. 601.]

THE aforesaid messengers being departed, the holy father, Gregory, sent after them letters worthy to be preserved in memory, wherein he plainly shows what care he took of the salvation of our nation. The letter was as follows:—

"*To his most beloved son, the Abbot Mellitus; Gregory, the servant of the servants of God.* We have been much concerned, since the departure of our congregation that is with you, because we have received no account of the success of your journey. When, therefore, Almighty God shall bring you to the most reverend Bishop Augustine, our brother, tell him what I have, upon mature deliberation on the affair of the English, determined upon, viz., that the temples of the idols in that nation ought not to be destroyed;

* York and London constituted the first metropolitan sees among the ancient Britons. On this account, probably, Gregory invested them with metropolitical dignity on the re-establishment of Christianity in those places. It was some time after the death of both Gregory and Augustine, however, that this project, as respects York, was carried into effect.

but let the idols that are in them be destroyed; let holy water be made and sprinkled in the said temples, let altars be erected, and relics placed. For if those temples are well built, it is requisite that they be converted from the worship of devils to the service of the true God; that the nation, seeing that their temples are not destroyed, may remove error from their hearts, and knowing and adoring the true God, may the more familiarly resort to the places to which they have been accustomed. And because they have been used to slaughter many oxen in the sacrifices to devils, some solemnity must be exchanged for them on this account, as that on the day of the dedication, or the nativities of the holy martyrs, whose relics are there deposited, they may build themselves huts of the boughs of trees, about those churches which have been turned to that use from temples, and celebrate the solemnity with religious feasting, and no more offer beasts to the Devil, but kill cattle to the praise of God in their eating, and return thanks to the Giver of all things for their sustenance; to the end that, whilst some gratifications are outwardly permitted them, they may the more easily consent to the inward consolations of the grace of God. For there is no doubt that it is impossible to efface every thing at once from their obdurate minds; because he who endeavours to ascend to the highest place, rises by degrees or steps, and not by leaps. Thus the Lord made himself known to the people of Israel in Egypt; and yet he allowed them the use of the sacrifices which they were wont to offer to the Devil, in his own worship; so as to command them in his sacrifice to kill beasts, to the end that, changing their hearts, they might lay aside one part of the sacrifice, whilst they retained another; that whilst they offered the same beasts which they were wont to offer, they should offer them to God, and not to idols; and thus they would no longer be the same sacrifices. This it behoves your affection to communicate to our aforesaid brother, that he, being there present, may consider how he is to order all things. God preserve you in safety, most beloved son.

"Given the 17th of June, in the nineteenth year of the reign of our lord, the most pious emperor, Mauritius Tiberius, the eighteenth year after the consulship of our said lord. The fourth indiction."

CHAP. XXXI.

Pope Gregory, by letter, exhorts Augustine not to glory in his miracles.
[A.D. 601.]

AT which time he also sent Augustine a letter concerning the miracles that he had heard had been wrought by him ; wherein he admonishes him not to incur the danger of being puffed up by the number of them.   The letter was in these words :—

"I know, most loving brother, that Almighty God, by means of your affection, shows great miracles in the nation which he has chosen.   Wherefore it is necessary that you rejoice with fear, and tremble whilst you rejoice, on account of the same heavenly gift ; viz., that you may rejoice because the souls of the English are by outward miracles drawn to inward grace ; but that you fear, lest, amidst the wonders that are wrought, the weak mind may be puffed up in its own presumption, and as it is externally raised to honour, it may thence inwardly fall by vain-glory.   For we must call to mind, that when the disciples returned with joy after preaching, and said to their heavenly Master, 'Lord, in thy name, even the devils are subject to us ;' they were presently told, 'Do not rejoice on this account, but rather rejoice for that your names are written in heaven.'   For they placed their thoughts on private and temporal joys, when they rejoiced in miracles ; but they are recalled from the private to the public, and from the temporal to the eternal joy, when it is said to them, 'Rejoice for this, because your names are written in heaven.'   For all the elect do not work miracles, and yet the names of all are written in heaven.   For those who are disciples of the truth ought not to rejoice, save for that good thing which all men enjoy as well as they, and of which their enjoyment shall be without end.

"It remains, therefore, most dear brother, that amidst those things, which, through the working of our Lord, you outwardly perform, you always inwardly strictly judge yourself, and clearly understand both what you are yourself, and how much grace is in that same nation, for the conversion of which you have also received the gift of working miracles. And if you remember that you have at any time offended our Creator, either by word or deed, that you always call it to mind, to the end that the remembrance of your guilt may crush the vanity which rises in your heart. And whatsoever you shall receive, or have received, in relation to working miracles, that you consider the same, not as conferred on you, but on those for whose salvation it has been given you."

CHAP. XXXII.

Pope Gregory sends letters and presents to King Ethelbert.

THE same holy Pope Gregory, at the same time, sent a letter to King Ethelbert, with many presents of several sorts ; being desirous to glorify the king with temporal honours, at the same time that he rejoiced that through his labour and zeal he had attained the knowledge of the heavenly glory. The copy of the said letter is as follows :—

" *To the most glorious Lord, and his most excellent son, Ethelbert, king of the English, Bishop Gregory.* Almighty God advances all good men to the government of nations, that he may by their means bestow the gifts of his mercy on those over whom they are placed. This we know to have been done in the English nation, over whom your glory was therefore placed, that by means of the goods which are granted to you, heavenly benefits might also be conferred on the nation that is subject to you. Therefore, my illustrious son, do you carefully preserve the grace which you have received from the Divine goodness, and hasten to promote the Christian faith, which you have embraced, among the people under your subjection ; multiply the zeal of your uprightness in their conversion ; suppress the worship of idols ; overthrow the structures of the temples ; edify the manners of your subjects by much cleanness of life, exhorting, terrifying, soothing, correcting, and giving examples of good works, that you may find him your rewarder in heaven, whose name and knowledge you shall spread abroad upon earth. For he also will render the fame of your honour more glorious to posterity, whose honour you seek and maintain among the nations.

"For even so Constantine, our most pious emperor, recovering the Roman commonwealth from the perverse

worship of idols, subjected the same with himself to our
Almighty God and Lord Jesus Christ, and was himself, with
the people under his subjection, entirely converted to him.
Whence it followed, that his praises transcended the fame of
former princes ; and he as much excelled his predecessors in
renown as he did in good works.   Now, therefore, let your
glory hasten to infuse into the kings and people that are subject to you, the knowledge of one God, Father, Son, and
Holy Ghost ; that you may both surpass the ancient kings
of your nation in praise and merit, and become by so much
the more secure against your own sins before the dreadful
judgment of Almighty God, as you shall wipe away the sins
of others in your subjects.

"Willingly hear, devoutly perform, and studiously retain
in your memory, whatsoever you shall be advised by our
most reverend brother, Bishop Augustine, who is instructed
in the monastical rule, full of the knowledge of the holy
Scripture, and, by the help of God, endued with good works ;
for if you give ear to him in what he speaks for Almighty
God, the same Almighty God will the sooner hear him praying for you.   But if (which God avert!) you slight his
words, how shall Almighty God hear him in your behalf,
when you neglect to hear him for God ?   Unite yourself,
therefore, to him with all your mind, in the fervour of faith,
and further his endeavours, through the assistance of that
virtue which the Divinity affords you, that He may make
you partaker of his kingdom, whose faith you cause to be
received and maintained in your own.

"Besides, we would have your glory know, we find in the
holy Scripture, from the words of the Almighty Lord, that
the end of this present world, and the kingdom of the saints,
is about to come, which will never terminate.   But as the
same end of the world approaches, many things are at
hand which were not before, viz. changes of air, and terrors
from heaven, and tempests out of the order of the seasons,
wars, famines, plagues, earthquakes in several places ; which
things will not, nevertheless, happen in our days, but will
all follow after our days.   If you, therefore, find any of
these things to happen in your country, let not your mind be
in any way disturbed ; for these signs of the end of the
world are sent before, for this reason, that we may be solicit-

ous for our souls, suspicious of the hour of death, and may be found prepared with good works to meet our Judge. Thus much, my illustrious son, I have said in few words, to the end that when the Christian faith shall increase in your kingdom, our discourse to you may also be more copious, and we may be pleased to say the more, in proportion as joy for the conversion of your nation is multiplied in our mind.

"I have sent you some small presents, which will not appear small, when received by you with the blessing of the holy apostle, Peter. May Almighty God, therefore, perfect in you his grace which He has begun, and prolong your life here through a course of many years, and after a time receive you into the congregation of the heavenly country. May heavenly grace preserve your excellency in safety.

" Given the 22nd day of June, in the nineteenth year of the reign of the most pious emperor, Mauritius Tiberius, in the eighteenth year after his consulship. Fourth indiction."

CHAP. XXXIII.

Augustine repairs the church of our Saviour, and builds the monastery of St. Peter the apostle ; Peter the first abbat of the same. [A.D. 602.]

AUGUSTINE having his episcopal see granted him in the royal city, as has been said, and being supported by the king, recovered therein a church, which he was informed had been built by the ancient Roman Christians, and consecrated it in the name of our holy Saviour, God and Lord, Jesus Christ, and there established a residence for himself and his successors.* He also built a monastery not far from the city to the eastward, in which, by his advice, Ethelbert erected from the foundation the church of the blessed apostles, Peter and Paul,† and enriched it with several donations ; wherein the bodies of the same Augustine, and of all the bishops of Canterbury, and of the kings of Kent, might be buried. However, Augustine himself did not consecrate that church, but Laurentius, his successor.

The first abbat of that monastery was the priest Peter, who, being sent ambassador into France, was drowned in a

* This church is now the cathedral of Canterbury ; but the present structure, although ancient, is of date long subsequent to the age of St. Augustine.
† Afterwards called St. Augustine's Abbey.

bay of the sea, which is called Amfleat,* and privately
buried by the inhabitants of the place ; but Almighty God,
to show how deserving a man he was, caused a light to be
seen over his grave every night ; till the neighbours who
saw it, perceiving that he had been a holy man that was buried
there, inquiring who, and from whence he was, carried away
the body, and interred it in the church, in the city of Boulogne, with the honour due to so great a person.

CHAP. XXXIV.

*Ethelfrid, king of the Northumbrians, having vanquished the nations of
the Scots, expels them from the territories of the English.* [A.D. 603.]

AT this time, Ethelfrid, a most worthy king, and ambitious
of glory, governed the kingdom of the Northumbrians, and
ravaged the Britons more than all the great men of the
English, insomuch that he might be compared to Saul, once
king of the Israelites, excepting only this, that he was ignorant of the true religion. For he conquered more territories
from the Britons, either making them tributary, or driving the
inhabitants clean out, and planting English in their places,
than any other king or tribune. To him might justly be
applied the saying of the patriarch blessing his son in the
person of Saul, "Benjamin shall ravin as a wolf ; in the
morning he shall devour the prey, and at night he shall divide the spoil." Hereupon, Ædan, king of the Scots that
inhabit Britain, being concerned at his success, came against
him with an immense and mighty army, but was beaten by
an inferior force, and put to flight ; for almost all his army
was slain at a famous place, called Degsastan, that is, Degsa-
stone.† In which battle also Theodbald, brother to Ethelfrid, was killed, with almost all the forces he commanded.
This war Ethelfrid put an end to in the year 603 after the
incarnation of our Lord, the eleventh of his own reign,
which lasted twenty-four years, and the first year of the
reign of Phocas, who then governed the Roman empire.
From that time, no king of the Scots durst come into Britain
to make war on the English to this day.

* Now probably Ambleteuse, a small sea-port village about two miles
to the north of Boulogne.
† Perhaps Dalston, near Carlisle : or Dauston, near Jedburgh.

BOOK II.

CHAPTER I.

On the death of the blessed Pope Gregory. [A.D. 605.]

AT this time, that is, in the year of our Lord 605, the blessed Pope Gregory, after having most gloriously governed the Roman apostolic see thirteen years, six months, and ten days, died, and was translated to the eternal see of the heavenly kingdom. Of whom, in regard that he by his zeal converted our nation, the English, from the power of Satan to the faith of Christ, it behoves us to discourse more at large in our Ecclesiastical History, for we may and ought rightly to call him our apostle; because, whereas he bore the pontifical power over all the world, and was placed over the churches already reduced to the faith of truth, he made our nation, till then given up to idols, the church of Christ, so that we may be allowed thus to attribute to him the character of an apostle; for though he is not an apostle to others, yet he is so to us; for we are the seal of his apostleship in our Lord.

He was by nation a Roman, son of Gordian, deducing his race from ancestors that were not only noble, but religious. And Felix, once bishop of the same apostolical see, a man of great honour in Christ and his church, was his great-grandfather.* Nor did he exercise the nobility of religion with less virtue of devotion than his parents and kindred. But that worldly nobility which he seemed to have, by the help of the Divine Grace, he entirely used to gain the honour of eternal dignity; for soon quitting his secular habit, he repaired to a monastery, wherein he began to behave himself with so much grace of perfection that (as he was afterwards wont with tears to testify) his mind was above all transitory things; that he despised all that is subject to change; that he used to think of nothing but what was heavenly; that whilst detained by the body, he by contemplation broke through the bonds of flesh; and that he

---

* Felix IV. was bishop of Rome, A.D. 526.

loved death, which is a terror to almost all men, as the entrance into life, and the reward of his labours. This he said of himself, not to boast of his progress in virtue, but rather to bewail the decay, which, as he was wont to declare, he imagined he sustained through the pastoral care. In short, when he was, one day, in private, discoursing with Peter, his deacon, after having enumerated the former virtues of his mind, he with grief added, "But now, on account of the pastoral care, it is entangled with the affairs of laymen, and, after so beautiful an appearance of repose, is defiled with the dust of earthly action. And after having wasted itself by condescending to many things that are without, when it desires the inward things, it returns to them less qualified to enjoy them. I therefore consider what I endure, I consider what I have lost, and when I behold that loss, what I bear appears the more grievous."

This the holy man said out of the excess of his humility. But it becomes us to believe that he lost nothing of his monastic perfection by his pastoral care, but rather that he improved the more through the labour of converting many, than by the former repose of his conversation, and chiefly because, whilst exercising the pontifical function, he provided to have his house made a monastery. And when first drawn from the monastery, ordained to the ministry of the altar, and sent as respondent to Constantinople from the apostolic see, though he now mixed with the people of the palace, yet he intermitted not his former heavenly life; for some of the brethren of his monastery, having out of brotherly charity followed him to the royal city, he kept them for the better following of regular observances, viz. that at all times, by their example, as he writes himself, he might be held fast to the calm shore of prayer, as it were with the cable of an anchor, whilst he should be tossed up and down by the continual waves of worldly affairs; and daily among them, by the intercourse of studious reading, strengthen his mind whilst it was shaken with temporal concerns. By their company he was not only guarded against earthly assaults, but more and more inflamed in the exercises of a heavenly life.

For they persuaded him to give a mystical exposition of the book of holy Job, which is involved in great obscurity;

nor could he refuse to undertake that work, which brotherly affection imposed on him for the future benefit of many; but in a wonderful manner, in five and thirty books of exposition, taught how that same book is to be understood literally; how to be referred to the mysteries of Christ and the church; and in what sense it is to be adapted to every one of the faithful. This work he began when legate in the royal city, but finished it at Rome after being made pope. Whilst he was still in the royal city, he, by the assistance of the Divine grace of Catholic truth, crushed in its first rise a heresy newly started, concerning the state of our resurrection. For Eutychius, bishop of that city, taught, that our body, in that glory of resurrection, would be impalpable, and more subtile than the wind and air; which he hearing, proved by force of truth, and by the instance of the resurrection of our Lord, that this doctrine was every way opposite to the Christian faith. For the Catholic faith is that our body, sublimed by the glory of immortality, is rendered subtile by the effect of the spiritual power, but palpable by the reality of nature; according to the example of our Lord's body, of which, when risen from the dead, he himself says to his disciples, "Touch me and see, for a spirit hath not flesh and bones, as ye see me have." In asserting which faith, the venerable Father Gregory so earnestly laboured against the rising heresy, and by the assistance of the most pious emperor, Tiberius Constantine, so fully suppressed it, that none has been since found to revive it.

He likewise composed another notable book, called "Liber Pastoralis," wherein he manifestly showed what sort of persons ought to be preferred to govern the church; how such rulers ought to live; with how much discretion to instruct every one of their hearers, and how seriously to reflect every day on their own frailty. He also wrote forty homilies on the Gospel, which he equally divided into two volumes; and composed four books of dialogues, into which, at the request of Peter, his deacon, he collected the miracles of the saints whom he either knew, or had heard to be most renowned in Italy, for an example to posterity to lead their lives; to the end that, as he taught in his books of Expositions, what virtues ought to be laboured for, so by describing the miracles of saints, he might make known the glory of those virtues. He further, in twenty-two homilies, discovered how much light there is concealed in the first and last parts of the prophet Ezekiel, which seemed the most obscure. Besides which, he wrote the "Book of Answers," to the questions of Augustine, the first bishop of the English nation, as we have shown above, inserting the same book entire in this history ; besides the useful little "Synodical Book," which he composed with the bishops of Italy on the necessary affairs of the church ; and also familiar letters to certain persons. And it is the more wonderful that he could write so many and such large volumes,* in regard that almost all the time of his youth, to use his own words, he was often tormented with pains in his bowels, and a weakness of his stomach, whilst he was continually suffering from slow fever. But whereas at the same time he carefully reflected that, as the Scripture testifies, "Every son that is received is scourged," the more he laboured and was depressed under those present evils, the more he assured himself of his eternal salvation.

Thus much may be said of his immortal genius, which could not be restrained by such severe bodily pains ; for other popes applied themselves to building, or adorning of churches with gold and silver, but Gregory was entirely intent upon gaining souls. Whatsoever money he had, he diligently took care to distribute and give to the poor, that his righteousness might endure for ever, and his horn be exalted with honour ; so that what blessed Job said might be truly said of him, "When the ear heard me, then it blessed me ; and when the eye saw me, it gave witness to me : because I delivered the poor that cried, and the fatherless, and him that had none to help him. The blessing of him that was ready to perish came upon me, and I caused the widow's heart to sing for joy. I put on righteousness, and it clothed me ; my judgment was as a robe and diadem. I was the eye to the blind, and feet was I to the lame. I was father to the poor ; and the cause which I knew not, I searched out. And I brake the jaws of the wicked, and plucked the spoil out of his teeth." And a little after : "If I have withheld," says he,

---

* St. Gregory's numerous works have been collected and published by the Benedictines of St. Maur, in 4 vols. fol. Paris, 1707, and still more complete in the reprints of Venice and Verona.

"the poor from their desire ; or have caused the eye of the
widow to fail ; or have eaten my morsel myself alone, and
the fatherless hath not eaten thereof. For of my youth com-
passion grew up with me, and from my mother's womb it
came forth with me."

To these works of piety and righteousness this also may
be added, that he saved our nation, by the preachers he sent
hither, from the teeth of the old enemy, and made it partaker
of eternal liberty ; in whose faith and salvation rejoicing,
and worthily commending the same, he in his exposition on
holy Job, says, " Behold, a tongue of Britain, which only
knew how to utter barbarous language, has long since begun
to resound the Hebrew Hallelujah ! Behold, the once swelling ocean now serves prostrate at the feet of the saints ; and
its barbarous motions, which earthly princes could not subdue with the sword, are now, through the fear of God, bound
by the mouths of priests with words only ; and he that when
an infidel stood not in awe of fighting troops, now a believer,
fears the tongues of the humble ! For by reason that the
virtue of the Divine knowledge is infused into it by precepts,
heavenly words, and conspicuous miracles, it is curbed by
the dread of the same Divinity, so as to fear to act wickedly,
and bends all its desires to arrive at eternal glory." In
which words holy Gregory declares this also, that St. Augustine and his companions brought the English to receive the
truth, not only by the preaching of words, but also by showing of heavenly signs. The holy Pope Gregory, among
other things, caused masses to be celebrated in the churches
of the apostles, Peter and Paul, over their bodies. And in
the celebration of masses, he added three phrases full of great
goodness and perfection : " And dispose our days in thy
peace, and preserve us from eternal damnation, and rank us
in the number of thy elect, through Christ our Lord."

He governed the church in the days of the Emperors
Mauritius and Phocas, but passing out of this life in the
second year of the same Phocas, he departed to the true life
which is in heaven. His body was buried in the church of
St. Peter the Apostle, before the sacristy, on the 4th day of
March, to rise one day in the same body in glory with the
rest of the holy pastors of the church. On his tomb was
written this epitaph :—

Earth ! take that body which at first you gave,.
Till God again shall raise it from the grave.
His soul amidst the stars finds heavenly day ;
In vain the gates of darkness make essay
On him whose death but leads to life the way.
To the dark tomb, this prelate, though decreed,
Lives in all places by his pious deed.
Before his bounteous board pale Hunger fled ;
To warm the poor he fleecy garments spread ;
And to secure their souls from Satan's power,
He taught by sacred precepts every hour.
Nor only taught ; but first th' example led,
Lived o'er his rules, and acted what he said.
To English Saxons Christian truth he taught,
And a believing flock to heaven he brought.
This was thy work and study, this thy care,
Offerings to thy Redeemer to prepare.
For these to heavenly honours raised on high,
Where thy reward of labours ne'er shall die.

Nor is the account of St. Gregory, which has been handed
down to us by the tradition of our ancestors, to be passed by
in silence, in relation to his motives for taking such interest
in the salvation of our nation. It is reported, that some
·merchants, having just arrived at Rome on a certain day,
exposed many things for sale in the market-place, and abundance of people resorted thither to buy : Gregory himself
went with the rest, and, among other things, some boys were
set to sale, their bodies white, their countenances beautiful,
and their hair very fine.. Having viewed them, he asked, as
is said, from what country or nation they were brought ? and
was told, from the island of Britain, whose inhabitants were
of such personal appearance. He again inquired whether
those islanders were Christians, or still involved in the errors
of paganism ? and was informed that they were pagans.
Then fetching a deep sigh from the bottom of his heart,
' Alas ! what pity," said he, " that the author of darkness is
possessed of men of such fair countenances ; and that being
remarkable for such graceful aspects, their minds should be
void of inward grace." He therefore again asked, what was
the name of that nation ? and was answered, that they were
called Angles. "Right," said he "for they have an Angelic
face, and it becomes such to be co-heirs with the Angels in
heaven. What is the name," proceeded he, " of the province
from which they are brought ?" It was replied, that the

natives of that province were called Deiri. "Truly are they
De ira," said he, "withdrawn from wrath, and called to the
mercy of Christ. How is the king of that province called?"
They told him his name was Ælla; and he, alluding to the
name, said, "Hallelujah, the praise of God the Creator must
be sung in those parts."

Then repairing to the bishop of the Roman apostolical see,*
(for he was not himself then made pope,) he entreated him to
send some ministers of the word into Britain to the nation of
the English, by whom it might be converted to Christ; declaring himself ready to undertake that work, by the assistance of God, if the apostolic pope should think fit to have it
so done. Which not being then able to perform, because,
though the pope was willing to grant his request, yet the
citizens of Rome could not be brought to consent that so
noble, so renowned, and so learned a man should depart the
city; as soon as he was himself made pope, he perfected the
long-desired work, sending other preachers, but himself by
his prayers and exhortations assisting the preaching, that it
might be successful. This account, as we have received it
from the ancients, we have thought fit to insert in our Ecclesiastical History.

CHAP. II.

*Augustine admonished the bishops of the Britons to Catholic peace and
unity, and to that effect wrought a heavenly miracle in their presence;
and of the vengeance that pursued them for their contempt. [A.D. 603.]*

In the meantime, Augustine, with the assistance of King Ethelbert, drew together to a conference the bishops, or doctors, of
the next province of the Britons, at a place which is to this
day called Augustine's Ac, that is, Augustine's Oak,† on the
borders of the Wiccii and West Saxons; and began by brotherly
admonitions to persuade them, that preserving Catholic unity
with him, they should undertake the common labour of preach-

* Benedict I. Gregory was made bishop of Rome, A.D. 590.
† The date of this synod is not accurately known: Florence of Worcester gives A.D. 603: Sigebert, A.D. 602; Spelman, A.D. 601; and Randolph of Chester, A.D. 599. It was held probably near Aust, formerly
called *Austre Clive*, Gloucestershire, near the site of the ancient *Vectis* of
the Romans.

ing the Gospel to the Gentiles. For they did not keep Easter Sunday at the proper time, but from the fourteenth to the twentieth moon; which computation is contained in a revolution of eighty-four years. Besides, they did several other things which were against the unity of the church. When, after a long disputation, they did not comply with the entreaties, exhortations, or rebukes of Augustine and his companions, but preferred their own traditions before all the churches in the world, which in Christ agree among themselves, the holy father, Augustine, put an end to this troublesome and tedious contention, saying, "Let us beg of God, who causes those who are of one mind to live in his Father's house, that he will vouchsafe, by his heavenly tokens, to declare to us, which tradition is to be followed; and by what means we are to find our way to his heavenly kingdom. Let some infirm person be brought, and let the faith and practice of those, by whose prayers he shall be healed, be looked upon as acceptable to God, and be adopted by all." The adverse party unwillingly consenting, a blind man of the English race was brought, who having been presented to the priests of the Britons, found no benefit or cure from their ministry; at length, Augustine, compelled by real necessity, bowed his knees to the Father of our Lord Jesus Christ, praying that the lost sight might be restored to the blind man, and by the corporeal enlightening of one man, the light of spiritual grace might be kindled in the hearts of many of the faithful. Immediately the blind man received sight, and Augustine was by all declared the preacher of the Divine truth. The Britons then confessed, that it was the true way of righteousness which Augustine taught; but that they could not depart from their ancient customs without the consent and leave of their people. They therefore desired that a second synod might be appointed, at which more of their number would be present.

This being decreed, there came (as is asserted) seven* bishops of the Britons, and many most learned men, particularly from their most noble monastery, which, in the English

---

* Modern writers enumerate the seven sees, to which these bishops belonged: they are Worcester, Hereford, Chester, Bangor, St. Asaph's, Landaff, and Menevia or St. David's, but there is not the slightest authority for this list.

tongue, is called Bancornburg,* over which the Abbat Dinooth
is said to hath presided at that time.   They that were to go
to the aforesaid council, repaired first to a certain holy and
discreet man, who was wont to lead an eremitical life among
them, advising with him, whether they ought, at the preaching of Augustine, to forsake their traditions.   He answered,
"If he is a man of God, follow him."—"How shall we know
that ?" said they.   He replied, "Our Lord saith, Take my
yoke upon you, and learn of me, for I am meek and lowly in
heart ; if therefore, Augustine is meek and lowly of heart, it
is to be believed that he has taken upon him the yoke of
Christ, and offers the same to you to take upon you.   But,
if he is stern and haughty, it appears that he is not of God,
nor are we to regard his words."   They insisted again,
"And how shall we discern even this ?"—"Do you contrive,"
said the anchorite, "that he may first arrive with his company at the place where the synod is to be held ; and if at
your approach he shall rise up to you, hear him submissively,
being assured that he is the servant of Christ ; but if he
shall despise you, and not rise up to you, whereas you are
more in number, let him also be despised by you."

They did as he directed ; and it happened, that when they
came, Augustine was sitting on a chair, which they observing,
were in a passion, and charging him with pride, endeavoured
to contradict all he said.   He said to them, "You act in
many particulars contrary to our custom, or rather the
custom of the universal church, and yet, if you will comply
with me in these three points, viz. to keep Easter at the
due time ; to administer baptism, by which we are again
born to God, according to the custom of the holy Roman
Apostolic Church ; and jointly with us to preach the word of
God to the English nation, we will readily tolerate all the
other things you do, though contrary to our customs."   They
answered they would do none of those things, nor receive

* This was the station *Banchorium* of Richard of Cirencester, and ·is
now called Bangor-Iscoed, Flintshire, to distinguish it from the city of
Bangor, in Carnarvonshire.   This monastery was one of the most eminent
in Britain.   William of Malmesbury, who lived shortly after the conquest,
says, there remained only in his time the footsteps of so great a place, so
many ruinous churches, and such heaps of rubbish, as were hardly elsewhere to be met with.   See Gibson's Annotations to Camden's Britannia,
Flintshire.

him as their archbishop ; for they alleged among themselves, that "if he would not now rise up to us, how much more will he contemn us, as of no worth, if we shall begin to be under his subjection ?" To whom the man of God, Augustine, is said, in a threatening manner, to have foretold, that in case they would not join in unity with their brethren, they should be warred upon by their enemies ; and, if they would not preach the way of life to the English nation, they should at their hands undergo the vengeance of death. All which, through the dispensation of the Divine judgment, fell out exactly as he had predicted.

For afterwards the warlike king of the English, Ethelfrid, of whom we have already spoken, having raised a mighty army, made a very great slaughter of that perfidious nation, at the City of Legions, which by the English is called Legacestir, but by the Britons more rightly Carlegion.* Being about to give battle, he observed their priests, who were come together to offer up their prayers to God for the soldiers, standing apart in a place of more safety ; he inquired who they were ? or what they came together to do in that place ? Most of them were of the monastery of Bangor, in which, it is reported, there was so great a number of monks, that the monastery being divided into seven parts, with a ruler over each, none of those parts contained less than three hundred men, who all lived by the labour of their hands. Many of these, having observed a fast of three days, resorted among others to pray at the aforesaid battle, having one Brocmail appointed for their protector, to defend them whilst they were intent upon their prayers, against the swords of the barbarians. King Ethelfrid† being informed of the occasion of their coming, said, "If then they cry to their God against us, in truth, though they do not bear arms, yet they fight against us, because they oppose us by their prayers." He, therefore, commanded them to be attacked first, and then destroyed the rest of the impious army, not without considerable loss of his own forces. About twelve hundred‡ of those

* Chester, the Roman colony Deva, the work of the twentieth legion, called Victrix.

† King of Northumbria.

‡ The Saxon Chronicle (A.D. 607) mentions but two hundred. The destruction of the monastery of Bangor-Iscoed followed the massacre of its

that came to pray are said to have been killed, and only fifty
to have escaped by flight. Brocmail turning his back with
his men, at the first approach of the enemy, left those whom
he ought to have defended, unarmed and exposed to the
swords of the enemies. Thus was fulfilled the prediction of
the holy Bishop Augustine, though he himself had been long
before taken up into the heavenly kingdom ;* that those perfidious men should feel the vengeance of temporal death also,
because they had despised the offer of eternal salvation.

CHAP. III.

How St. Augustine made Mellitus and Justus bishops; and of his death.
[A.D. 604.]

In the year of our Lord 604, Augustine, archbishop of Britain, ordained two bishops, viz. Mellitus and Justus ; Mellitus to preach to the province of the East-Saxons, who are
divided from Kent by the river Thames, and border on the
Eastern sea. Their metropolis is the city of London, which
is situated on the bank of the aforesaid river, and is the
mart of many nations resorting to it by sea and land. At
that time, Sabert, nephew to Ethelbert by his sister Ricula,
reigned over the nation, though he was under subjection to
Ethelbert, who, as has been said above, had command over
all the nations of the English as far as the river Humber.
But when this province also received the word of truth, by

members, and the calamity must have caused a great diminution in the
number of the British clergy.
   * Those who would throw the odium of this murder upon Augustine's
curse, make this passage to have been added to Bede some years after his
death, and it is certain the royal paraphraser has made no mention of his
death. Mr. Whelock and Dr. Smith assert it to be in all the ancient Latin
manuscripts they had seen. The time of this battle is placed by the Saxon
Annals in 607. Bishop Godwin asserts his seeing an instrument signed by
Augustine in 605, which Sir Henry Spelman proves spurious, no instruments being used till 700. But the learned Mr. Wharton proves, beyond
dispute, St. Augustine's death to be in 604, which was long before this, if
we follow the Saxon Annals, which place it in 607 ; and very long before, if
we follow Archbishop Usher's and the Ulster Annals, which place it in
613; to this we may add Bede's authority, that Pope Gregory had obiits
said over him in the church at Canterbury; which plainly shows his death
to have been before that pope's. And though we find him in the next
chapter consecrating two bishops, this is frequent with Bede to go backwards for the series of every distinct part of his history, or to work through
a branch of it at once.

the preaching of Mellitus, King Ethelbert built the church
of St. Paul, in the city of London, where he and his successors should have their episcopal see. As for Justus, Augustine ordained him bishop in Kent, at the city which the English nation named Rhofescestir,* from one that was formerly
the chief man of it, called Rhof. It was almost twenty-four
miles distant from the city of Canterbury to the westward,
and contains a church dedicated to St. Andrew, the apostle.
King Ethelbert, who built it, bestowed many gifts on the
bishops of both those churches, as well as on that of Canterbury, adding lands and possessions for the use of those who
were with the bishops.

After this, the beloved of God, Father Augustine, died,
and his body was deposited without, close by the church of
the apostles, Peter and Paul, above spoken of, by reason that
the same was not yet finished, nor consecrated, but as soon
as it was dedicated,† the body was brought in, and decently
buried in the north porch thereof ; wherein also were interred the bodies of all the succeeding archbishops, except
two only, Theodorus and Berthwald, whose bodies are within that church, because the aforesaid porch could contain no
more. Almost in the midst of this church is an altar dedicated in honour of the blessed Pope Gregory, at which every
Saturday their service is solemnly performed by the priest of
that place. On the tomb of the said Augustine is written
this epitaph :—

"Here rests the Lord Augustine, first archbishop of Canterbury, who, being formerly sent hither by the blessed Gregory, bishop of the city of Rome, and by God's assistance
supported with miracles, reduced King Ethelbert and his na-

---

* Now Rochester. A chapter of secular priests was first established
here, which was endowed by Ethelbert with a portion of land called Priest-
field, to the south of the city; he afterwards gave other parcels of land
within and without the walls of the city for its support.—*Dugdale's Mon-
asticon,* i. 153.

† Which was in A.D. 613. The body of St. Augustine was afterwards
removed by Thomas Fyndon, the abbat, A.D. 1300, and placed near the
high altar in a sumptuous monument with this inscription :

    Inclytus Anglorum Præsul, pius, et decus altum,
    Hic Augustinus requiescit corpore sanctus ;
    Ad tumulum laudis Patris almi ductus amore
    Abbas hunc tumulum Thomas dictavit honore.

                    Dugdale's Monast. i. 81.

tion from the worship of idols to the faith of Christ, and
having ended the days of his office in peace, died the 26th
day of May, in the reign of the same king."

CHAP. IV.

Laurentius and his bishops admonish the Scots to observe the unity of the
Holy Church, particularly in keeping of Easter ; Mellitus goes to
Rome. [A.D. 605.]

LAURENTIUS succeeded Augustine in the bishopric, having
been ordained thereto by the latter, in his lifetime, lest, upon
his death, the state of the church, as yet unsettled, might
begin to falter, if it should be destitute of a pastor, though
but for one hour.   Wherein he also followed the example
of the first pastor of the church, that is, of the most blessed
prince of the apostles, Peter, who, having founded the
church of Christ at Rome, is said to have consecrated Clement his assistant in preaching the Gospel, and at the same
time his successor.   Laurentius, being advanced to the degree of an archbishop, laboured indefatigably, both by frequent exhortations and examples of piety, to raise to perfection the foundations of the church, which had been so nobly
laid.   In short, he not only took care of the new church
formed among the English, but endeavoured also to employ
his pastoral solicitude among the ancient inhabitants of Britain, as also the Scots, who inhabit the island of Ireland,
which is next to Britain.   For when he understood that the
course of life and profession of the Scots in their aforesaid
country, as well as of the Britons in Britain, was not truly
ecclesiastical, especially that they did not celebrate the
solemnity of Easter at the due time, but thought that the
day of the resurrection of our Lord was, as has been said
above, to be celebrated between the 14th and 20th of the
moon ; he wrote, jointly with his fellow bishops, an exhort-
atory epistle, entreating and conjuring them to observe unity
of peace, and conformity with the church of Christ spread
throughout the world.   The beginning of which epistle is
as follows :—

" *To our most dear brothers, the lords bishops and abbats*
throughout all Scotland,* Laurentius, Mellitus, and Justus,

* Ireland. See ante, page 5.

servants of the servants of God. When the apostolic see, according to the universal custom which it has followed elsewhere, sent us to these western parts to preach to pagan nations, we came into this island, which is called Britain, without possessing any previous knowledge of its inhabitants. We held both the Britons and Scots in great esteem for sanctity, believing that they had proceeded according to the custom of the universal church ; but coming acquainted with the errors of the Britons, we thought the Scots had been better ; but we have been informed by Bishop Dagan,* coming into this aforesaid island, and the Abbat Columbanus† in France, that the Scots in no way differ from the Britons in their behaviour ; for Bishop Dagan coming to us, not only refused to eat with us, but even to take his repast in the same house where we were entertained."

The same Laurentius and his fellow bishops wrote a letter to the priests of the Britons, suitable to his rank, by which he endeavoured to confirm them in Catholic unity ; but what he gained by so doing the present times still declare.

About this time, Mellitus, bishop of London, went to Rome, to confer with Pope Boniface about the necessary affairs of the English church. And the same most reverend pope, assembling a synod of the bishops of Italy, to prescribe orders for the life and peace of the monks, Mellitus also sat among them, in the eighth year of the reign of the Emperor Phocas, the thirteenth indiction, on the 27th of February, to the end that he also by his authority might confirm such things as should be regularly decreed, and at his return into Britain might carry the same to the churches of the English, to be prescribed and observed ; together with letters which the same pope sent to the beloved of God, Archbishop Laurentius, and to all the clergy ; as likewise to King Ethelbert and the English nation. This pope was Boniface, who came fourth after Pope Gregory, and who obtained of the Emperor Phocas that the temple called by the ancients Pantheon, as representing all the gods, should be given to the Church of Christ ; wherein he, having purified it from contamina-

---

* Dagan is said to have come from the monastery of Banchor, Ireland, and was bishop to the Scots. Bale says, he wrote a book on the British churches.

† Columbanus was the founder of monasteries in France and Italy. ·

tion, dedicated a church to the holy mother of God, and to all Christ's martyrs, to the end that, the devils being excluded, the blessed company of the saints might have therein a perpetual memorial.

CHAP. V.

How, after the death of the kings Ethelbert and Sabert, their successors restored idolatry; for which reason, both Mellitus and Justus departed out of Britain. [A.D. 616.]

IN the year of our Lord's incarnation 616, which is the twenty-first year after Augustine and his companions were sent to preach to the English nation, Ethelbert, king of Kent, having most gloriously governed his temporal kingdom fifty-six years, entered into the eternal joys of the kingdom which is heavenly. He was the third of the English kings that had the sovereignty* of all the southern provinces that are divided from the northern by the river Humber, and the borders contiguous to the same; but the first of the kings that ascended to the heavenly kingdom. The first who had the like sovereignty was Elli, king of the South-Saxons; the second, Celin, king of the West-Saxons, who, in their own language, is called Ceaulin; the third, as has been said, was Ethelbert, king of Kent; the fourth was Redwald, king of the East-Angles, who, whilst Ethelbert lived, had been subservient to him. The fifth was Edwin, king of the nation of the Northumbrians, that is, of those who live on the north side of the river Humber, who, with great power, commanded all the nations, as well of the English as of the Britons who inhabit Britain, except only the people of Kent, and he reduced also under the dominion of the English, the Mevanian Islands† of the Britons, lying between Ireland and Britain; the sixth was Oswald, the most Christian king of the Northumbrians, who also had the same extent under his command; the seventh, Oswy, brother to the former, held the same dominions for some time, and for the most part subdued and made tributary the nations of the Picts and Scots, which possess the northern parts of Britain: but of these hereafter.

King Ethelbert died on the 24th day of the month of

---

* As Bretwalda, or paramount sovereign.   † Anglesea and Man.

February, twenty-one years after he had received the faith,
and was buried in St. Martin's porch within the church of the
blessed apostles Peter and Paul, where also lies his queen,
Bertha. Among other benefits which he conferred upon the
nation, he also, by the advice of wise persons,* introduced
judicial decrees, after the Roman model ; which, being written in English, are still kept and observed by them. Among
which, he in the first place set down what satisfaction should
be given by those who should steal anything belonging to
the church, the bishop, or the other clergy, resolving to give
protection to those whose doctrine he had embraced.

This Ethelbert was the son of Irminric, whose father was
Octa, whose father was Orric, surnamed Oisc, from whom
the kings of Kent are wont to be called Oiscings. His
father was Hengist, who, being invited by Vortigern, first
came into Britain, with his son Oisc, as has been said above.

But after the death of Ethelbert, the accession of his son
Eadbald proved very prejudicial to the new church ; for he
not only refused to embrace the faith of Christ, but was also
defiled with such a sort of fornication, as the apostle testifies,
was not heard of, even among the Gentiles ; for he kept his
father's wife. By both which crimes he gave occasion to
those to return to their former uncleanness, who, under his
father, had, either for favour, or through fear of the king,
submitted to the laws of faith and chastity. Nor did the
perfidious king escape without Divine punishment and correction ; for he was troubled with frequent fits of madness,
and possessed by an evil spirit. This confusion was increased by the death of Sabert, king of the East Saxons, who
departing to the heavenly kingdom, left three sons, still
pagans, to inherit his temporal crown. They immediately
began to profess idolatry, which, during their father's reign,
they had seemed a little to abandon, and they granted free
liberty to the people under their government to serve idols.
And when they saw the bishop, whilst celebrating mass in
the church, give the eucharist to the people, they, puffed up
with barbarous folly, were wont, as it is reported, to say to
him, " Why do you not give us also that white bread, which
you used to give to our father Saba, (for so they used to call

* The Witena-Gemot, the legislative and supreme judicial assembly.

him,) and which you still continue to give to the people in
the church?" To whom he answered, "If you will be
washed in that laver of salvation, in which your father was
washed, you may also partake of the holy bread of which he
partook; but if you despise the laver of life, you may not
receive the bread of life." They replied, "We will not enter
into that laver, because we do not know that we stand in
need of it, and yet we will eat of that bread." And being
often earnestly admonished by him, that the same could not
be done, nor any one admitted to partake of the sacred oblation without the holy cleansing, at last, they said in anger,
"If you will not comply with us in so small a matter as that
is which we require, you shall not stay in our province."
And accordingly they obliged him and his followers to depart from their kingdom. Being forced from thence, he came
into Kent, to advise with his fellow bishops, Laurentius and
Justus, what was to be done in that case; and it was unanimously agreed, that it was better for them all to return to their
own country, where they might serve God in freedom, than
to continue without any advantage among those barbarians,
who had revolted from the faith. Mellitus and Justus
accordingly went away first, and withdrew into France, designing there to await the event of things. But the kings,
who had driven from them the preacher of the truth, did not
continue long unpunished in their heathenish worship. For
marching out to battle against the nation of the Gewissæ,*
they were all slain with their army. However, the people,
having been once turned to wickedness, though the authors
of it were destroyed, would not be corrected, nor return to
the unity of faith and charity which is in Christ.

CHAP. VI.

*Laurentius, being reproved by the apostle, converts King Eadbald to Christ;
Mellitus and Justus are recalled.* [A.D. 616.]

LAURENTIUS, being about to follow Mellitus and Justus, and
to quit Britain, ordered his bed to be laid the night before in
the church of the blessed apostles, Peter and Paul, which has
been often mentioned before; wherein having laid himself to

* West Saxons.

take some rest, after he had poured out many prayers and tears to God for the state of the church, he fell asleep; in the dead of night, the blessed prince of the apostles appeared to him, and scourging him a long time with apostolical severity, asked of him, "Why he would forsake the flock which he had committed to him? or to what shepherds he would commit Christ's sheep that were in the midst of wolves? Have you," said he, "forgotten my example, who, for the sake of those little ones, whom Christ recommended to me in token of his affection, underwent at the hands of infidels and enemies of Christ, bonds, stripes, imprisonment, afflictions, and lastly, the death of the cross, that I might at last be crowned with him?" Laurentius, the servant of Christ, being excited by these words and stripes, the very next morning repaired to the king, and taking off his garment, showed the scars of the stripes which he had received. The king, astonished, asked, "Who had presumed to give such stripes to so great a man?" And was much frightened when he heard that the bishop had suffered so much at the hands of the apostle of Christ for his salvation. Then abjuring the worship of idols, and renouncing his unlawful marriage, he embraced the faith of Christ, and being baptized, promoted the affairs of the church to the utmost of his power.

He also sent over into France, and recalled Mellitus and Justus, and commanded them freely to return to govern their churches, which they accordingly did, one year after their departure. Justus, indeed, returned to the city of Rochester, where he had before presided; but the Londoners would not receive Bishop Mellitus, choosing rather to be under their idolatrous high priests; for King Eadbald had not so much authority in the kingdom as his father, nor was he able to restore the bishop to his church against the will and consent of the pagans. But he and his nation, after his conversion to our Lord, diligently followed the Divine precepts. Lastly, he built the church of the holy Mother of God,* in the monastery of the most blessed prince of the apostles, which was afterwards consecrated by Archbishop Mellitus.

* Eadbald, besides building St. Mary's chapel, endowed it with the manor of Northbourne. This chapel was taken down by the abbat Scotland in the time of Lanfranc, and a new and more splendid church erected in its place. *Thorn*, col. 1768.

CHAP. VII.

Bishop Mellitus by prayer quenches a fire in his city.   [A.D. 619.]

In this king's reign, the holy Archbishop Laurentius was taken up to the heavenly kingdom : he was buried in the church and monastery of the holy Apostle Peter, close by his predecessor Augustine, on the 2nd day of the month of February.   Mellitus, who was bishop of London, was the third archbishop of Canterbury from Augustine ; Justus, who was still living, governed the church of Rochester.   These ruled the church of the English with much industry and labour, and received letters of exhortation from Boniface, bishop of the Roman apostolic see, who presided over the church after Deusdedit, in the year of our Lord 619.   Mellitus laboured under an infirmity of body, that is, the gout ; but his mind was sound, cheerfully passing over all earthly things, and always aspiring to love, seek, and attain to those which are celestial.   He was noble by birth, but much nobler in mind.

In short, that I may give one testimony of his virtue, by which the rest may be guessed at, it happened once that the city of Canterbury, being by carelessness set on fire, was in danger of being consumed by the spreading conflagration ; water was thrown over the fire in vain ; a considerable part of the city was already destroyed, and the fierce flame advancing towards the bishop, when he, confiding in the Divine assistance, where human failed, ordered himself to be carried towards the raging fire, that was spreading on every side.   The church of the four crowned Martyrs was in the place where the fire raged most.   The bishop being carried thither by his servants, the sick man averted the danger by prayer, which a number of strong men had not been able to perform by much labour.   Immediately, the wind, which blowing from the south had spread the conflagration throughout the city, turning to the north, prevented the destruction of those places that had lain in its way, and then ceasing entirely, the flames were immediately extinguished.   And thus the man of God, whose mind was inflamed with the fire of Divine charity, and who was wont to drive away the powers of the air by his frequent prayers, from doing harm to himself, or his people, was deservedly allowed to prevail over the worldly winds and flames, and to obtain that they should not injure him or his.

This archbishop also, having ruled the church five years, departed to heaven in the reign of King Eadbald, and was buried with his predecessors in the monastery and church, which we have so often mentioned, of the most blessed prince of the apostles, in the year of our Lord's incarnation 624, on the 24th day of April.

CHAP. VIII.

Pope Boniface sends the Pall and an Epistle to Justus, successor to Mellitus. [A.D. 624.]

JUSTUS, bishop of Rochester, immediately succeeded Mellitus in the archbishopric. He consecrated Romanus bishop of that see in his own stead, having obtained leave of ordaining bishops from Pope Boniface, whom we mentioned above to have been successor to Deusdedit : of which licence this is the form :

" *Boniface, to his most beloved brother Justus.* Not only the contents of your letter, but the perfection which your work has obtained, has informed us how devoutly and diligently you have laboured, my brother, for the Gospel of Christ ; for Almighty God has not forsaken either the mystery of his name, or the fruit of your labours, having himself faithfully promised to the preachers of the Gospel, 'Lo ! I am with you alway, even unto the end of the world;' which promise his mercy has particularly manifested in this ministry of yours, opening the hearts of nations to receive the mystery of your preaching. For he has enlightened the acceptable course of your endeavours, by the approbation of his grace ; granting a plentiful increase to your faithful management of the talents committed to you, and which you may secure for many generations. This is by that reward conferred on you, who, constantly adhering to the ministry enjoined you, with laudable patience await the redemption of that nation, whose salvation is set on foot that they may profit by your merits, our Lord himself saying, ' He that perseveres to the end shall be saved.' You are, therefore, saved by the hope of patience, and the virtue of endurance,

to the end that the hearts of infidels, being cleansed from
their natural and superstitious disease, might obtain the
mercy of their Redeemer : for having received the letters of
our son Ethelwald, we perceive with how much knowledge
of the sacred word your mind, my brother, has brought over
his mind to the belief in real conversion and the true faith.
Therefore, firmly confiding in the long-suffering of the
Divine clemency, we believe there will, through the ministry
of your preaching, ensue most full salvation not only of the
nations subject to him, but also of those that neighbour round
about ; to the end, that as it is written, the reward of a perfect
work may be conferred on you by our Lord, the giver of all
good things ; and that the universal confession of all nations,
having received the mystery of the Christian faith, may
declare, that their ' Sound went into all the earth, and their
words unto the ends of the world.'

" We have also, my brother, encouraged by zeal for what
is good, sent you by the bearer of these, the pall, which we
have only given leave to use in the celebration of the sacred
mysteries ; granting you likewise to ordain bishops when
there shall be occasion, through the mercy of our Lord ; that
so the Gospel of Christ, by the preaching of many, may be
spread abroad in all the nations that are not yet converted.
You must, therefore, endeavour, my brother, to preserve with
unblemished sincerity of mind that which you have received
through the favour of the Apostolic See, as an emblem
whereof you have obtained so principal an ornament to be
borne on your shoulders.   And make it your business, imploring the Divine goodness, so to behave yourself, that you
may present before the tribunal of the Supreme Judge that
is to come, the rewards of the favour granted you, not with
guiltiness, but with the benefit of souls.

" God preserve you in safety, most dear brother !"

CHAP. IX.

*The reign of King Edwin, and how Paulinus, coming to preach the gospel,
first converted his daughter and others to the faith of Christ.* [A.D. 625.]

AT this time the nation of the Northumbrians, that is, the
nation of the Angles that live on the north side of the river
Humber, with their king, Edwin, received the faith through

the preaching of Paulinus, abovementioned.   This Edwin,
as a reward of his receiving the faith, and as an earnest of
his share in the heavenly kingdom, received an increase of
that which he enjoyed on earth, for he reduced under his
dominion all the borders of Britain that were provinces
either of the aforesaid nation, or of the Britons, a thing
which no British king had ever done before ; and he in like
manner subjected to the English the Mevanian islands, as
has been said above.   The first whereof, which is to the
southward, is the largest in extent, and most fruitful, containing nine hundred and sixty families, according to the
English computation ; the other above three hundred.

The occasion of this nation's embracing the faith was,
their aforesaid king, being allied to the kings of Kent, having taken to wife Ethelberga, otherwise called Tate, daughter
to King Ethelbert.   He having by his ambassadors asked
her in marriage of her brother Eadbald, who then reigned
in Kent, was answered, " That it was not lawful to marry a
Christian virgin to a pagan husband, lest the faith and the
mysteries of the heavenly King should be profaned by her
cohabiting with a king that was altogether a stranger to the
worship of the true God."   This answer being brought to
Edwin by his messengers, he promised in no manner to act
in opposition to the Christian faith, which the virgin professed ; but would give leave to her, and all that went with
her, men or women, priests or ministers, to follow their faith
and worship after the custom of the Christians.   Nor did he
deny, but that he would embrace the same religion, if, being
examined by wise persons, it should be found more holy
and more worthy of God.

Hereupon the virgin was promised, and sent to Edwin,
and pursuant to what had been agreed on, Paulinus, a man
beloved of God, was ordained bishop, to go with her, and by
daily exhortations, and celebrating the heavenly mysteries, to
confirm her and her company, lest they should be corrupted
by the company of the pagans.   Paulinus was ordained bishop
by the Archbishop Justus, on the 21st day of July, in the
year of our Lord 625, and so he came to King Edwin with
the aforesaid virgin as a companion of their union in the flesh.
But his mind was wholly bent upon reducing the nation to
which he was sent to the knowledge of truth ; according

to the words of the apostle, "To espouse her to one husband, that he might present her as a chaste virgin to Christ." Being come into that province, he laboured much, not only to retain those that went with him, by the help of God, that they should not revolt from the faith, but, if he could, to convert some of the pagans to a state of grace by his preaching. But, as the apostle says, though he laboured long in the word, "The god of this world blinded the minds of them that believed not, lest the light of the glorious Gospel of Christ should shine unto them."

The next year there came into the province a certain assassin, called Eumer, sent by the king of the West-Saxons, whose name was Cuichelm, in hopes at once to deprive King Edwin of his kingdom and his life. He had a two-edged dagger, dipped in poison, to the end, that if the wound were not sufficient to kill the king, it might be performed by the venom. He came to the king on the first day of Easter, at the river Derwent, where then stood the regal city,* and being admitted as if to deliver a message from his master, whilst he was in an artful manner delivering his pretended embassy, he started on a sudden, and drawing the dagger from under his garment, assaulted the king ; which Lilla, the king's beloved minister, observing, having no buckler at hand to secure the king from death, interposed his own body to receive the stroke ; but the wretch struck so home, that he wounded the king through the knight's body. Being then attacked on all sides with swords, he in that confusion also slew another soldier, whose name was Forthhere.

On that same holy night of Easter Sunday, the queen had brought forth to the king a daughter, called Eanfled. The king, in the presence of Bishop Paulinus, gave thanks to his gods for the birth of his daughter ; and the bishop, on the other hand, returned thanks to Christ, and endeavoured to persuade the king, that by his prayers to him he had obtained that the queen should bring forth the child in safety, and without much pain. The king, delighted with his words, promised, that in case God would grant him life and victory

* Supposed to be near the Roman city Derventione, on the Derwent, near Stamford Bridge, between seven and eight miles from York. It is now a village called Alby, i. e. the old habitation, and near it are the ruins of an ancient castle.

over the king by whom the assassin had been sent, he would
cast off his idols, and serve Christ; and as a pledge that he
would perform his promise, he delivered up that same daughter to Paulinus, to be consecrated to Christ. She was the
first baptized of the nation of the Northumbrians, on Whitsunday, with twelve others of her family.* At that time, the
king, being recovered of the wound which he had received,
marched with his army against the nation of the West-
Saxons; and having begun the war, either slew or subdued
all those that he had been informed had conspired to murder
him. Returning thus victorious into his own country, he would
not immediately and unadvisedly embrace the mysteries of
the Christian faith, though he no longer worshipped idols,
ever since he made the promise that he would serve Christ;
but thought fit first at leisure to be instructed, by the venerable Paulinus, in the knowledge of faith, and to confer with
such as he knew to be the wisest of his prime men, to advise what they thought was fittest to be done in that case.
And being a man of extraordinary sagacity, he often sat
alone by himself a long time, silent as to his tongue, but de-
liberating in his heart how he should proceed, and which
religion he should adhere to.

CHAP. X.†

Pope Boniface, by letter, exhorts the same king to embrace the faith.
[A.D. 625.]

At this time he received letters from Pope Boniface [IV] exhorting him to embrace the faith, which were as follows:—

COPY OF THE LETTER OF THE HOLY AND APOSTOLIC POPE OF
THE CHURCH OF ROME, BONIFACE, TO THE GLORIOUS EDWIN,
KING OF THE ENGLISH.

To the illustrious Edwin, king of the English, Bishop
Boniface, the servant of the servants of God. Although the
power of the Supreme Deity cannot be expressed by human
speech, as consisting in its own greatness, and in invisible

* The Saxon Chronicle mentions no number. Matthew Paris says
thirty; but several manuscripts of Bede have twelve.

† This and the following chapter should have been placed before the former, which takes in the year 626; for Pope Boniface died on October 22, 625.

and unsearchable eternity, so that no sharpness of wit can comprehend or express it; yet in regard that the goodness of God, to give some notion of itself, having opened the doors of the heart, has mercifully, by secret inspiration, infused into the minds of men such things as he is willing shall be declared concerning himself, we have thought fit to extend our priestly care to make known to you the fulness of the Christian faith; to the end that, informing you of the Gospel of Christ, which our Saviour commanded should be preached to all nations, they might offer to you the cup of life and salvation.

"Thus the goodness of the Supreme Majesty, which, by the word of his command, made and created all things, the heaven, the earth, the sea, and all that is in them, disposing the order by which they should subsist, hath, with the counsel of his co-eternal Word, and the unity of the Holy Spirit, formed man after his own likeness, out of the slime of the earth; and granted him such supereminent prerogative, as to place him above all others; so that, observing the command which was given him, his continuance should be to eternity. This God,—Father, Son, and Holy Ghost, which is an undivided Trinity,—mankind, from the east unto the west, by confession of faith to the saving of their souls, do worship and adore, as the Creator of all things, and their own Maker; to whom also the heights of empire, and the powers of the world, are subject, because the bestowal of all kingdoms is granted by his disposition. It hath pleased him, therefore, of his great mercy, and for the greater benefit of all his creatures, by his Holy Spirit wonderfully to kindle the cold hearts also of the nations seated at the extremities of the earth in the knowledge of himself.

"For we suppose your excellency has, from the country lying so near, fully understood what the clemency of our Redeemer has effected in the enlightening of our glorious son, King Eadbald, and the nations under his subjection; we therefore trust, with assured confidence of celestial hope, that his wonderful gift will be also conferred on you; since we understand that your illustrious consort, which is known to be a part of your body, is illuminated with the reward of eternity, through the regeneration of holy baptism. We have, therefore, taken care by these presents, with all possible affection, to exhort your illustrious selves, that, abhorring idols and their worship, and contemning the follies of temples, and the deceitful flatteries of auguries, you believe in God the Father Almighty, and his Son Jesus Christ, and the Holy Ghost, to the end that, being discharged from the bonds of captivity to the Devil, by believing you may, through the co-operating power of the holy and undivided Trinity, be partaker of the eternal life.

"How great guilt they lie under, who adhere to the pernicious superstitions and worship of idolatry, appears by the examples of the perdition of those whom they worship. Wherefore it is said of them by the Psalmist, 'All the gods of the Gentiles are devils, but the Lord made the heavens.' And again, they have eyes and do not see, they have ears and do not hear, they have noses and do not smell, they have hands and do not feel, they have feet and do not walk. Therefore they are like those that confide in them.' For how can they have any power to yield assistance, that are made for you out of corruptible matter, by the hands of your inferiors and subjects, to wit, on whom you have by human art bestowed an inanimate similitude of members? Who, unless they be moved by you, will not be able to walk; but, like a stone fixed in one place, being so formed, and having no understanding, but absorbed in insensibility, have no power of doing harm or good. We cannot, therefore, upon mature deliberation, find out how you come to be so deceived as to follow and worship those gods, to whom you yourselves have given the likeness of a body.

"It behoves you, therefore, by taking upon you the sign of the holy cross, by which the human race is redeemed, to root out of your hearts all those arts and cunning of the Devil, who is ever jealous of the works of the divine goodness, and to lay hold and break in pieces those which you have hitherto made your material gods. For the very destruction and abolition of these, which could never receive life or sense from their makers, may plainly demonstrate to you how worthless they were which you till then had worshipped, when you yourselves, who have received life from the Lord, are certainly better than they, as Almighty God has appointed you to be descended, after many ages and through many generations, from the first man whom he formed. Draw near, then, to the knowledge of Him who created you, who breathed the breath of life into you, who sent his only-begotten Son for your redemption, to cleanse you from original sin, that being delivered from the power of the Devil's wickedness, He might bestow on you a heavenly reward.

"Hear the words of the preachers, and the Gospel of God, which they declare to you, to the end that, believing, as has been said, in God the Father Almighty, and in Jesus Christ his Son, and the Holy Ghost, and the indivisible Trinity, having put to flight the sensualities of devils, and driven from you the suggestions of the venomous and deceitful enemy, and being born again by water and the Holy Ghost, you may, through his assistance and bounty, dwell in the brightness of eternal glory with Him in whom you shall believe. We have, moreover, sent you the blessing of your protector, the blessed Peter, prince of the apostles, that is, a shirt, with one gold ornament, and one garment of Ancyra, which we pray your highness to accept with the same good-will as it is friendly intended by us."

CHAP. XI.

Pope Boniface advises Queen Ethelberga to use her best endeavours for the salvation of her consort, King Edwin. [A.D. 625.]

THE same pope also wrote to King Edwin's consort, Ethelberga, to this effect :—

THE COPY OF THE LETTER OF THE MOST BLESSED AND APOS-
TOLIC BONIFACE, POPE OF THE CITY OF ROME, TO ETHEL-
BERGA, KING EDWIN'S QUEEN.

" *To the illustrious lady his daughter, Queen Ethelberga, Boniface, bishop, servant of the servants of God:* The goodness of our Redeemer has with much providence offered the means of salvation to the human race, which he rescued, by the shedding of his precious blood, from the bonds of captivity to the Devil ; so that making his name known in divers ways to the Gentiles, they might acknowledge their Creator by embracing the mystery of the Christian faith, which thing, the mystical purification of your regeneration plainly shows to have been bestowed upon the

mind of your highness by God's bounty. Our mind, therefore, has been much rejoiced in the benefit of our Lord's
goodness, for that he has vouchsafed, in your conversion, to
kindle a spark of the orthodox religion, by which he might
the more easily inflame in his love the understanding, not
only of your glorious consort, but also of all the nation that
is subject to you.

"For we have been informed by those, who came to
acquaint us with the laudable conversion of our illustrious
son, King Eadbald, that your highness, also, having received
the wonderful sacrament of the Christian faith, continually
excels in the performance of works pious and acceptable to
God. That you likewise carefully refrain from the worship
of idols, and the deceits of temples and auguries, and having
changed your devotion, are so wholly taken up with the love
of your Redeemer, as never to cease lending your assistance
for the propagation of the Christian faith. And our fatherly
charity having earnestly inquired concerning your illustrious
husband, we were given to understand, that he still served
abominable idols, and would not yield obedience or give ear
to the voice of the preachers. This occasioned us no small
grief, for that part of your body still remained a stranger to
the knowledge of the supreme and undivided Trinity.
Whereupon we, in our fatherly care, did not delay to admonish your Christian highness, exhorting you, that, with
the help of the Divine inspiration, you will not defer to do
that which, both in season and out of season, is required of
us ; that with the co-operating power of our Lord and
Saviour Jesus Christ, your husband also may be added to
the number of Christians ; to the end that you may
thereby enjoy the rights of marriage in the bond of a holy
and unblemished union. For it is written, 'They two shall
be in one flesh.' How can it be said, that there is unity
between you, if he continues a stranger to the brightness
of your faith, by the interposition of dark and detestable
error ?

"Wherefore, applying yourself continually to prayer, do not
cease to beg of the Divine Mercy the benefit of his illumina-
tion ; to the end, that those whom the union of carnal affection has made in a manner but one body, may, after death,
continue in perpetual union, by the bond of faith. Persist,

therefore, illustrious daughter, and to the utmost of your
power endeavour to soften the hardness of his heart by in-
sinuating the Divine precepts ; making him sensible how
noble the mystery is which you have received by believing,
and how wonderful is the reward which, by the new birth,
you have merited to obtain. Inflame the coldness of his
heart by the knowledge of the Holy Ghost, that by the
abolition of the cold and pernicious worship of paganism, the
heat of Divine faith may enlighten his understanding through
your frequent exhortations ; that the testimony of the holy
Scripture may appear the more conspicuous, fulfilled by you,
' The unbelieving husband shall be saved by the believing
wife.' For to this effect you have obtained the mercy of our
Lord's goodness, that you may return with increase the fruit
of faith, and the benefits entrusted in your hands ; for
through the assistance of His mercy we do not cease with
frequent prayers to beg that you may be able to perform the
same.

"Having premised thus much, in pursuance of the duty
of our fatherly affection, we exhort you, that when the
opportunity of a bearer shall offer, you will as soon as possible
acquaint us with the success which the Divine Power shall
grant by your means in the conversion of your consort, and
of the nation subject to you ; to the end, that our solicitude,
which earnestly expects what appertains to the salvation of
you and yours, may, by hearing from you, be set at rest ; and
that we, discerning more fully the brightness of the Divine
propitiation diffused in you, may with a joyful confession
abundantly return due thanks to God, the Giver of all good
things, and to St. Peter, the prince of apostles. We have,
moreover, sent you the blessing of your protector, St. Peter,
the prince of the apostles, that is, a silver looking-glass, and
a gilt ivory comb, which we entreat your glory will receive
with the same kind affection as it is known to be sent by us."

CHAP. XII.

*King Edwin is persuaded to believe by a vision which he had seen when
he was in exile.* [BEFORE A.D. 625.]

THUS the aforesaid Pope Boniface wrote for the salvation of
King Edwin and his nation. But a heavenly vision, which

the Divine Mercy was pleased once to reveal to this king, when he was in banishment at the court of Redwald, king of the Angles,* was of no little use in urging him to embrace and understand the doctrines of salvation. Paulinus, therefore, perceiving that it was a very difficult task to incline the king's lofty mind to the humility of the way of salvation, and to embrace the mystery of the cross of life, and at the same time using both exhortation with men, and prayer to God, for his and his subjects' salvation ; at length, as we may suppose, it was shown him in spirit what was the vision that had been formerly revealed to the king. Nor did he lose any time, but immediately admonished the king to perform the vow which he made, when he received the oracle, promising to put the same in execution, if he was delivered from the trouble he was at that time under, and should be advanced to the throne.

The vision was this. When Ethelfrid, his predecessor, was persecuting him, he for many years wandered in a private manner through several places and kingdoms, and at last came to Redwald, beseeching him to give him protection against the snares of his powerful persecutor. Redwald willingly admitted him, and promised to perform what he requested. But when Ethelfrid understood that he had appeared in that province, and that he and his companions were hospitably entertained by Redwald, he sent messengers to offer that king a great sum of money to murder him, but without effect. He sent a second and a third time, bidding more and more each time, and threatening to make war on him if he refused. Redwald, either terrified by his threats, or gained by his gifts, complied with his request, and promised either to kill Edwin, or to deliver him up to the ambassadors. This being observed by a trusty friend of his, he went into his chamber, where he was going to bed, for it was the first hour of the night ; and calling him out, discovered what the king had promised to do with him, adding, "If, therefore, you think fit, I will this very hour conduct you out of this province, and lead you to a place where neither Redwald

---

* Redwald, was king of East Anglia, which included Norfolk, Suffolk, Cambridge, and part of Bedfordshire. He was the fourth Bretwaida, and reigned A.D. 617—633.

nor Ethelfrid shall ever find you." He answered, " I thank
you for your good will, yet I cannot do what you propose,
or be guilty of breaking the compact I have made with so
great a king, when he has done me no harm, nor offered me
any injury ; but, on the contrary, if I must die, let it rather
be by his hand than by that of any meaner person. For
whither shall I now fly, when I have for so many years
been a vagabond through all the provinces of Britain, to
escape the hands of my enemies ?" His friend being gone,
Edwin remained alone without, and sitting with a heavy
heart before the palace, began to be overwhelmed with many
thoughts, not knowing what to do, or which way to turn
himself.

When he had remained a long time in silence, brooding
over his misfortunes in anguish of mind, he, on a sudden, in
the dead of night, saw approaching a person, whose face and
habit were equally strange, at which unexpected sight he
was not a little frightened. The stranger coming close up,
saluted him, and asked him, " Why he sat there alone and
melancholy on a stone at that time, when all others were
taking their rest, and were fast asleep ?" Edwin, in his turn,
asked, "What it was to him, whether he spent the night
within doors or abroad ?" The stranger, in reply, said,
" Do not think that I am ignorant of the cause of your grief,
your watching, aud sitting alone without. For I know who
you are, and why you grieve, and the evils which you fear
will fall upon you. But tell me, what reward you will give
the man that shall deliver you out of this anguish, and persuade Redwald neither to do you any harm himself, nor to
deliver you up to be murdered by your enemies." Edwin
replied, " That he would give that person all that he was
able for so singular a favour." The other further added,
" What if I also assure you, that you shall overcome your
enemies, and surpass in power, not only all your own progenitors, but even all that have reigned before you over the
English nation ?" Edwin, encouraged by these questions, did
not hesitate to promise that he would make a suitable return
to him who should so highly oblige him. Then said the
other, "But if he who foretells so much good as is to befall you,
can also give you better advice for your life and salvation
than any of your progenitors or kindred ever heard of, do

you consent to submit to him, and to follow his wholesome counsel?" Edwin did not hesitate to promise that he would in all things follow the directions of that man who should deliver him from so many calamities, and raise him to a throne.

Having received this answer, the person that talked to him laid his hand on his head saying, "When this sign shall be given you, remember this present discourse that has passed between us, and do not delay the performance of what you now promise." Having uttered these words, he is said to have immediately vanished, that the king might understand it was not a man, but a spirit, that had appeared to him.

Whilst the royal youth still sat there alone, glad of the comfort he had received, but seriously considering who he was, or whence he came, that had so talked to him, his above-mentioned friend came to him, and saluting him with a pleasant countenance, "Rise," said he, "go in and compose yourself to sleep without fear; for the king's resolution is altered, and he designs to do you no harm, but rather to perform the promise which he made you; for when he had privately acquainted the queen with his intention of doing what I told you before, she dissuaded him from it, declaring it was unworthy of so great a king to sell his good friend in such distress for gold, and to sacrifice his honour, which is more valuable than all other ornaments, for the lucre of money." In short, the king did as he was advised, and not only refused to deliver up the banished man to his enemy's messengers, but assisted him to recover his kingdom. For as soon as the ambassadors were returned home, he raised a mighty army to make war on Ethelfrid; who, meeting him with much inferior forces, (for Redwald had not given him time to gather all his power,) was slain on the borders of the kingdom of Mercia, on the east side of the river that is called Idle.* In this battle, Redwald's son, called Regnhere, was killed; and thus Edwin, pursuant to the oracle he had received, not only escaped the danger from the king his enemy, but, by his death, succeeded him in the throne.

King Edwin, therefore, delaying to receive the word of God at the preaching of Paulinus, and using for some time,

* Near Retford in the southern part of Nottinghamshire.

as has been said, to sit several hours alone, and seriously to ponder with himself what he was to do, and what religion he was to follow, the man of God came to him, laid his right hand on his head, and asked, " Whether he knew that sign ?" The king in a trembling condition, was ready to fall down at his feet, but he raised him up, and in a familiar manner said to him, " Behold, by the help of God you have escaped the hands of the enemies whom you feared. Behold you have of his gift obtained the kingdom which you desired. Take heed not to delay that which you promised to perform ; embrace the faith, and keep the precepts of Him who, delivering you from temporal adversity, has raised you to the honour of a temporal kingdom ; and if, from this time forward, you shall be obedient to his will, which through me he signifies to you, he will not only deliver you from the everlasting torments of the wicked, but also make you partaker with him of his eternal kingdom in heaven."

CHAP. XIII.

Of the Council he held with his chief men about embracing the faith of Christ, and how the high priest profaned his own altars. [A.D. 627.]

THE king, hearing these words, answered, that he was both willing and bound to receive the faith which he taught ; but that he would confer about it with his principal friends and counsellors, to the end that if they also were of his opinion, they might all together be cleansed in Christ the Fountain of Life. Paulinus consenting, the king did as he said ; for, holding a council with the wise men, he asked of every one in particular what he thought of the new doctrine, and the new worship that was preached ? To which the chief of his own priests, Coifi, immediately answered, " O king, consider what this is which is now preached to us ; for I verily declare to you, that the religion which we have hitherto professed has, as far as I can learn, no virtue in it. For none of your people has applied himself more diligently to the worship of our gods than I ; and yet there are many who receive greater favours from you, and are more preferred than I, and are more prosperous in all their undertakings. Now if the gods were good for any thing, they would rather forward me, who have been more careful to serve them. It

remains, therefore, that if upon examination you find those
new doctrines, which are now preached to us, better and
more efficacious, we immediately receive them without any
delay."

Another of the king's chief men, approving of his words
and exhortations, presently added : " The present life of man,
O king, seems to me, in comparison of that time which is
unknown to us, like to the swift flight of a sparrow through
the room wherein you sit at supper in winter, with your
commanders and ministers, and a good fire in the midst,
whilst the storms of rain and snow prevail abroad ; the sparrow, I say, flying in at one door, and immediately out at
another, whilst he is within, is safe from the wintry storm ;
but after a short space of fair weather, he immediately
vanishes out of your sight, into the dark winter from which
he had emerged. So this life of man appears for a short
space, but of what went before, or what is to follow, we are
utterly ignorant. If, therefore, this new doctrine contains
something more certain, it seems justly to deserve to be followed." The other elders and king's counsellors, by Divine
inspiration, spoke to the same effect.

But Coifi added, that he wished more attentively to hear
Paulinus discourse concerning the God whom he preached ;
which he having by the king's command performed, Coifi,
hearing his words, cried out, "I have long since been sensible
that there was nothing in that which we worshipped ; because
the more diligently I sought after truth in that worship, the
less I found it. But now I freely confess, that such truth
evidently appears in this preaching as can confer on us the
gifts of life, of salvation, and of eternal happiness. For
which reason I advise, O king, that we instantly abjure and
set fire to those temples and altars which we have consecrated without reaping any benefit from them." In short,
the king publicly gave his licence to Paulinus to preach the
Gospel, and renouncing idolatry, declared that he received
the faith of Christ : and when he inquired of the high priest
who should first profane the altars and temples of their idols,
with the enclosures that were about them, he answered, " I ;
for who can more properly than myself destroy those things
which I worshipped through ignorance, for an example to all
others, through the wisdom which has been given me by the

true God?" Then immediately, in contempt of his former
superstitions, he desired the king to furnish him with arms
and a stallion; and mounting the same, he set out to destroy
the idols; for it was not lawful before for the high priest
either to carry arms, or to ride on any but a mare: Having,
therefore, girt a sword about him, with a spear in his hand,
he mounted the king's stallion and proceeded to the idols.
The multitude, beholding it, concluded he was distracted; but
he lost no time, for as soon as he drew near the temple he
profaned the same, casting into it the spear which he held;
and rejoicing in the knowledge of the worship of the true
God, he commanded his companions to destroy the temple,
with all its enclosures, by fire. This place where the idols
were is still shown, not far from York, to the eastward, beyond the river Derwent, and is now called Godmundingham,*
where the high priest, by the inspiration of the true God,
profaned and destroyed the altars which he had himself consecrated.

CHAP. XIV.

King Edwin and his nation become Christians; Paulinus baptises them.
[A.D. 627.]

KING EDWIN, therefore, with all the nobility of the nation,
and a large number of the common sort, received the faith,
and the washing of regeneration, in the eleventh year of his
reign, which is the year of the incarnation of our Lord 627,
and about one hundred and eighty after the coming of the
English into Britain. He was baptized at York, on the holy
day of Easter, being the 12th of April, in the church of St.
Peter the Apostle, which he himself had built of timber,
whilst he was catechising and instructing in order to receive
baptism. In that city also he appointed the see of the
bishopric of his instructor and bishop, Paulinus. But as
soon as he was baptized, he took care, by the direction of the
same Paulinus, to build in the same place a larger and nobler
church of stone, in the midst whereof that same oratory which

---

* Or, "The home of the protection of the gods." Its modern name is
Goodmanham, in Harthill wapentake, East Riding of York. Stukeley
says, "The Apostle Paulinus built the parish church of Godmundham,
where is the font in which he baptized the heathen priest Coifi."

he had first erected should be enclosed.* Having, therefore, laid the foundation, he began to build the church square, encompassing the former oratory. But before the whole was raised to the proper height, the wicked assassination of the king left that work to be finished by Oswald his successor. Paulinus, for the space of six years from that time, that is, till the end of the reign of that king, by his consent and favour, preached the word of God in that country, and all that were preordained to eternal life believed and were baptized. Among whom were Osfrid and Eadfrid, King Edwin's sons, who were both born to him, whilst he was in banishment, of Quenberga, the daughter of Cearl, king of the Mercians.

Afterwards other children of his by Queen Ethelberga were baptized, viz. Ethelhun and his daughter Etheldrith, and another, Wuscfrea, a son; the first two of which were snatched out of this life whilst they were still in their white garments, and buried in the church at York. Iffi, the son of Osfrid, was also baptized, and many more noble and illustrious persons. So great was then the fervour of the faith, as is reported, and the desire of the washing of salvation among the nation of the Northumbrians, that Paulinus at a certain time coming with the king and queen to the royal country-seat, which is called Adgefrin,† stayed there with them thirty-six days, fully occupied in catechising and baptizing; during which days, from morning till night, he did nothing else but instruct the people resorting from all villages and places, in Christ's saving word; and when instructed, he washed them with the water of absolution in the river Glen,‡ which is close by. This town, under the following kings, was abandoned, and another was built instead of it, at the place called Melmin.§

* Parts of this fabric were discovered beneath the choir of the present Cathedral during the repairs rendered necessary by the mad act of the incendiary Jonathan Martin. In the first number of Brown's History of the Edifice of the Metropolitan Church of St. Peter, York, in plate III. is given a plan of Paulinus' second edifice; where the probable position of the wooden baptistery, enclosing a spring still remaining, is pointed out, and, though obscured by several successive subsequent erections, this discovery is very valuable to the ecclesiastical antiquary.—*Rev. A. Poole's Lectures on Churches.*

† Yeverin in Glendale, near Wooler in Northumberland.
‡ The River Bowent.   § Milfield.

H

These things happened in the province of the Bernicians ;
but in that of the Deiri also, where he was wont often to be
with the king, he baptized in the river Swale, which runs by
the village of Cataract ;* for as yet oratories, or fonts, could
not be made in the early infancy of the church in those parts.
But he built a church in Campodonum,† which afterwards
the pagans, by whom King Edwin was slain, burnt, together
with all the town. In the place of which the later kings
built themselves a country-seat in the country called Loidis.‡
But the altar, being of stone, escaped the fire and is still preserved in the monastery of the most reverend abbat and
priest, Thridwulf, which is in Elmete wood.§

CHAP. XV.

The province of the East Angles receives the faith of Christ. [A. D. 627.]

EDWIN was so zealous for the worship of truth, that he
likewise persuaded Eorpwald, king of the East Saxons, and
son of Redwald, to abandon his idolatrous superstitions, and
with his whole province to receive the faith and sacraments
of Christ. And indeed his father Redwald had long before
been admitted to the sacrament of the Christian faith in
Kent, but in vain ; for on his return home, he was seduced
by his wife and certain perverse teachers, and turned back
from the sincerity of the faith ; and thus his latter state was
worse than the former ; so that, like the ancient Samaritans,
he seemed at the same time to serve Christ and the gods
whom he had served before ; and in the same temple he had
an altar to sacrifice to Christ, and another small one to offer
victims to devils ; which temple, Aldwulf, king of that same
province, who lived in our time, testifies had stood until his
time, and that he had seen it when he was a boy. The

* Or Catterick, in Gilling-East wapentake, North Riding of York. This
is a place of great antiquity, having been the site of a Roman station called
Cataractonium, where the Ermin Street branches off in two directions.

† Either Doncaster, or Castle-hill near Almondbury. (Archæol. i. p.
224—6.) In the Saxon paraphrase it is called Donafeida, which Dr. Gale
thinks to be Tanfield, near Ripon.   ‡ Leeds.

§ Probably Barwick-in-Elmett, in Skyrack wapentake, West Riding of
York. Here was anciently a castle of considerable extent and importance,
supposed to have been the residence of some of the Northumbrian monarchs.

aforesaid King Redwald was noble by birth, though ignoble
in his actions, being the son of Tytilus, whose father was
Uuffa, from whom the kings of the East Angles are called
Uuffings. *

Eorpwald was, not long after he had embraced the
Christian faith, slain by one Richbert, a pagan; and from
that time the province was under error for three years, till
the crown came into the possession of Sigebert, brother to
the same Eorpwald, a most Christian and learned man, who
was banished, and went to live in France during his
brother's life, and was there admitted to the sacraments of
the faith, whereof he made it his business to cause all his
province to partake as soon as he came to the throne.   His
exertions were much promoted by the Bishop Felix, who,
coming to Honorius, the archbishop, from Burgundy, where
he had been born and ordained, and having told him what
he desired, he sent him to preach the word of life to the
aforesaid nation of the Angles.   Nor were his good wishes
in vain; for the pious husbandman reaped therein a large
harvest of believers, delivering all that province (according
to the signification of his name, Felix) from long iniquity
and infelicity, and bringing it to the faith and works of
righteousness, and the gifts of everlasting happiness.   He
had the see of his bishopric appointed him in the city
Dommoc,† and having presided over the same province with
pontifical authority seventeen years, he ended his days there
in peace.

CHAP. XVI.

*How Paulinus preached in the province of Lindsey; and of the reign of
Edwin.* [A.D. 628.]

PAULINUS also preached the word to the province of
Lindsey,‡ which is the first on the south side of the river

---

* As the kings of Kent were known as Æscingas, so were the sovereigns
of East Anglia distinguished by the patronymic of Uffingas, or sons of
Uffa.   But their annals have been almost wholly lost; and the history of
East Anglia is nearly a blank in the Chronicles of England.—*Palgrave.*

† Afterwards Dunwich, but now no longer in existence, having been
overwhelmed by the sea.   The name of this bishop appears to be still
preserved by the village of Felixstow, "the dwelling of Felix," on the
Suffolk coast.

‡ Lindsey is by Camden computed to be the third part of Lincolnshire,
and appears to have been a subordinate state dependent upon Mercia.

Humber, stretching out as far as the sea; and he first converted the governor of the city of Lincoln, whose name was Blecca, with his whole family. He likewise built, in that city, a stone church of beautiful workmanship; the roof of which having either fallen through age, or been thrown down by enemies, the walls are still to be seen standing and every year some miraculous cures are wrought in that place, for the benefit of those who have faith to seek the same. In that church, Justus having departed to Christ, Paulinus consecrated Honorius bishop in his stead, as will be hereafter mentioned in its proper place. A certain abbat and priest of the monastery of Peartaneu,* a man of singular veracity, whose name was Deda, in relation to the faith of this province told me that one of the oldest persons had informed him, that he himself had been baptized at noon-day, by the Bishop Paulinus, in the presence of King Edwin, with a great number of the people, in the river Trent, near the city, which in the English tongue is called Tiovulfingacestir; † and he was also wont to describe the person of the same Paulinus, that he was tall of stature, a little stooping, his hair black, his visage meagre, his nose slender and aquiline, his aspect both venerable and majestic. He had also with him in the ministry, James, the deacon, a man of zeal and great fame in Christ's church, who lived even to our days.

It is reported that there was then such perfect peace in Britain, wheresoever the dominion of King Edwin extended, that, as is still proverbially said, a woman with her new-born babe might walk throughout the island, from sea to sea, without receiving any harm. That king took such care for the good of his nation, that in several places where he had seen clear springs near the highways, he caused stakes to be fixed, with brass dishes hanging at them, for the conveniency of travellers; nor durst any man touch them for any other purpose than that for which they were designed, either through the dread they had of the king, or for the affection which they bore him. His dignity was so great throughout his dominions, that his banners were not only borne before

---

* Or Parteney, a cell to Bardney Abbey. Deda was the first abbat.
† Southwell, Nottinghamshire.

him in battle, but even in time of peace, when he rode about his cities, towns, or provinces, with his officers, the standard-bearer was wont to go before him. Also, when he walked along the streets, that sort of banner which the Romans call Tufa, * and the English, Tuuf, was in like manner borne before him.

CHAP. XVII.

Edwin receives letters of exhortation from Pope Honorius, who also sends Paulinus the Pall. [A.D. 634.]

AT that time Honorius, successor to Boniface, was prelate of the apostolic see, who, when he understood that the nation of the Northumbrians, with their king, had been, by the preaching of Paulinus, converted to the faith and confession of Christ, sent the pall to the said Paulinus, and with it letters of exhortation to King Edwin, exciting him, with fatherly charity, that his people should persist in the faith of truth, which they had received. The contents of which letter were as follow :—

" *To his most noble son, and excellent lord, Edwin king of the Angles, Bishop Honorius, servant of the servants of God, greeting :* The integrity of your Christian character, in the worship of your Creator, is so much inflamed with the fire of faith, that it shines out far and near, and, being reported throughout the world, brings forth plentiful fruits of your labours. For your conduct as a king is based upon the knowledge which by orthodox preaching you have obtained of your God and Creator, whereby you believe and worship him, and as far as man is able, pay him the sincere devotion of your mind. For what else are we able to offer to our God, but in endeavouring to worship, and to pay him our vows, persisting in good actions, and confessing him the Creator of mankind ? And, therefore, most excellent son, we exhort you with such fatherly charity as is requisite, that you with careful mind, and constant prayers, every way labour to preserve this gift, that the Divine Mercy has vouchsafed to call you to his grace ; to the end, that He, who has been pleased to deliver you from all errors, and bring you to the knowledge of his name, may likewise

---

* A globe, or a tuft of feathers fixed on a spear.

prepare you mansions in the heavenly country. Employing
yourselves, therefore, in reading the works of my Lord
Gregory, your preacher, of apostolical memory, represent
before yourself the tenderness of his doctrine, which he
zealously employed for the sake of your souls; that his
prayers may increase your kingdom and people, and present
you blameless before Almighty God. We are preparing with
a willing mind immediately to grant those things which you
hoped would be by us ordained for your priests, which we
do on account of the sincerity of your faith, which has been
often made known to us in terms of praise by the bearers of
these presents. We have sent two palls to the two
metropolitans, Honorius and Paulinus; to the intent, that
when either of them shall be called out of this world to his
Creator, the other may, by this authority of ours, substitute
another bishop in his place; which privilege we are induced
to grant, as well in regard to your charitable affection, as of
the large and extensive provinces which lie between us and
you; that we may in all things afford our concurrence to
your devotion, according to your desires. May God's grace
preserve your excellency in safety!"

CHAP. XVIII.

*Honorius, who succeeded Justus in the bishopric of Canterbury, receives
the pall and letters from Pope Honorius.* [A.D. 634.]

In the meantime, Archbishop Justus was taken up to the
heavenly kingdom, on the 10th of November,[*] and Honorius,
who was elected to the see in his stead, came to Paulinus to
be ordained, and meeting him at Lincoln was there consecrated the fifth prelate of the church of Canterbury from
Augustine. To him also the aforesaid Pope Honorius sent
the pall, and a letter, wherein he ordains the same that he
had before established in his epistle to King Edwin, viz. that
when either of the bishops of Canterbury or of York shall
depart this life, the survivor of the same degree shall have
power to ordain a priest in the room of him that is departed;
that it might not be necessary always to travel to Rome, at
so great a distance by sea and land, to ordain an archbishop.

[*] Bede does not mention the year of his death. The Saxon Chronicle
places it in 627, and Dr. Smith in 630.

Which letter we have also thought fit to insert in this our history :—

"*Honorius to his most beloved brother Honorius :* Among the many good gifts which the mercy of our Redeemer is pleased to bestow on his servants, the munificent bounty of love is never more conspicuous than when he permits us by brotherly intercourse, as it were face to face, to exhibit our mutual love.   For which gift we continually return thanks to his majesty ; and we humbly beseech him, that he will ever confirm your piety in preaching the Gospel, and bringing forth fruit, and following the rule of your master and head, his holy servant, St. Gregory ; and that, for the advancement of his church, he may by your means add further increase ; to the end, that the souls already won by you and your predecessors, beginning with our Lord Gregory, may grow strong and be further extended by faith and works in the fear of God and charity; that so the promises of the word of God may hereafter be brought to pass in you ; and that this voice may call you away to the everlasting happiness.   'Come unto me all ye that labour and are heavy laden, and I will give you rest.'   And again, 'Well done, thou good and faithful servant ; thou hast been faithful over a few things, I will make thee ruler over many things ; enter thou into the joy of thy Lord.'   And we, most beloved brothers, offering you these words of exhortation, out of our abundant charity, do not hesitate further to grant those things which we perceive may be suitable for the privileges of your churches.

" Wherefore, pursuant to your request, and to that of the kings our sons, we do by these presents, in the name of St. Peter, prince of the apostles, grant you authority, that when the Divine Grace shall call either of you to himself, the survivor shall ordain a bishop in the room of him that is deceased.   To which effect also we have sent a pall to each of you, for celebrating the said ordination ; that by the authority of our precept, you may make an ordination acceptable to God ; because the long distance of sea and land that lies between us and you, has obliged us to grant you this, that no loss may happen to your church in any way, on account of any pretence whatever, but that the devotion of the people committed to you may be more fully extended.

God preserve you in safety, most dear brother ! Given the
11th day of June, in the twenty-fourth year of the reign of
our most pious emperor, Heraclius, and the twenty-third
after his consulship; and in the twenty-third of his son
Constantine, and the third after his consulship; and in
the third year of the most illustrious Cæsar, his son Heraclius, the seventh indiction ; that is, in the year of the incarnation of our Lord, 634."

CHAP. XIX.

*How the aforesaid Honorius first, and afterwards John, wrote letters to
the nation of the Scots, concerning the observance of Easter, and the
Pelagian heresy.* [A.D. 634.]

THE same Pope Honorius also wrote to the Scots [Irish],
whom he had found to err in the observance of Easter, as
has been shown above, earnestly exhorting them not to think
their small number, placed in the utmost borders of the earth,
wiser than all the ancient and modern churches of Christ,
throughout the world; and not to celebrate a different
Easter, contrary to the Paschal calculation, and the synodical
decrees of all the bishops upon earth.   Likewise John,* who
succeeded Severinus,† successor to the same Honorius, being
yet but pope elect, sent to them letters of great authority and
erudition for correcting the same error ; evidently showing,
that Easter Sunday is to be found between the fifteenth
moon and the twenty-first, as was proved in the Council of
Nice.‡   He also in the same epistle admonished them to be

* John IV.   † Who was Pope for a few months only.

‡ It has been erroneously supposed that the dispute between the British
and Saxon clergy respecting the Easter festival was the same as that which
disturbed the peace of the church in the time of Polycarp; and consequently
it has been assumed that the former were Quartodecimans, who observed
it at the Jewish passover, the fourteenth day of Nisan. But this was
never the case, except when that day happened to fall on a Sunday. It
was owing to the disturbed state of Britain in the fifth century that the
Irish and British clergy were unacquainted with the improved cycle of
nineteen years observed at Rome in the time of Pope Hilarius, (A.D.
463); but continued to use the ancient but incorrect cycle of eighty-
four years. Dr. Smith, in his Appendix to Bede (No. IX.), observes,
" that it ought to be particularly borne in mind, that those who think
that the Britons were taught the paschal rite by the Orientals, or
Eastern church, and not by the Roman or Western church, give way to a
very great error."

careful to crush the Pelagian heresy, which he had been informed was reviving among them. The beginning of the epistle was as follows :—

"*To our most beloved and most holy Tomianus, Columbanus,* Cromanus, Dimanus, and Baithanus, bishops; to Cromanus, Hernianus, Laistranus, Scellanus, and Segenus, priests; to Saranus and the rest of the Scottish doctors, or abbats, health from Hilarius, the arch-priest, and keeper of the place of the holy Apostolic See; John, the deacon, and elect in the name of God; from John, the chief secretary and keeper of the place of the holy Apostolic See, and from John, the servant of God, and counsellor of the same Apostolic See.* The writings which were brought by the bearers to Pope Severinus, of holy memory, were left, at his death, without an answer to the things contained in them. Lest such intricate questions should remain unresolved, we opened the same, and found that some in your province, endeavouring to revive a new heresy out of an old one, contrary to the orthodox faith, do through ignorance reject our Easter, when Christ was sacrificed ; and contend that the same should be kept on the fourteenth moon with the Hebrews."

By this beginning of the epistle it evidently appears that this heresy sprang up among them of very late times, and that not all their nation, but only some of them, had fallen into the same.

After having laid down the manner of keeping Easter, they add this concerning the Pelagians in the same epistle.

" And we have also understood that the poison of the Pelagian heresy again springs up among you ; we, therefore, exhort you, that you put away from your thoughts all such venomous and superstitious wickedness. For you cannot be ignorant how that execrable heresy has been condemned ; for it has not only been abolished these two hundred years, but it is also daily anathematized for ever by us ; and we exhort you, now that the weapons of their controversy have been burnt, not to rake up the ashes. For who will not detest that insolent and impious proposition, ' That man can live without sin of his own free will, and not through God's grace ?' And in the first place, it is the folly of blasphemy

* This Columbanus, most likely, was bishop of Clunirard, who died A.D. 652.

to say that man is without sin, which none can be, but only
the Mediator of God and man, the man Christ Jesus, who
was conceived and born without sin ; for all other men, being born in original sin, are known to bear the mark of
Adam's prevarication, even whilst they are without actual
sin, according to the saying of the prophet, ' For behold,
I was shapen in iniquity ; and in sin did my mother conceive me.' "

CHAP. XX.

Edwin being slain, Paulinus returns into Kent, and has the bishopric of
of Rochester conferred upon him. [A.D. 633.]

EDWIN reigned most gloriously seventeen years over the nations of the English and the Britons, six whereof, as has been
said, he also was a servant in the kingdom of Christ.   Cadwalla, king of the Britons, rebelled against him, being supported by Penda, a most warlike man of the royal race of
the Mercians, and who from that time governed that nation
twenty-two years with various success. A great battle being
fought in the plain that is called Heathfield,* Edwin was
killed on the 12th of October,† in the year of our Lord 633,
being then forty-seven years of age, and all his army was
either slain or dispersed.   In the same war also, before him,
fell Osfrid, one of his sons, a warlike youth ; Eanfrid, another of them, compelled by necessity, went over to King
Penda, and was by him afterwards, in the reign of Oswald,
slain, contrary to his oath.   At this time a great slaughter
was made in the church or nation of the Northumbrians ;
and the more so because one of the commanders, by whom
it was made, was a pagan, and the other a barbarian, more
cruel than a pagan ; for Penda, with all the nation of the
Mercians, was an idolater, and a stranger to the name of
Christ ; but Cadwalla,‡ though he bore the name and professed himself a Christian, was so barbarous in his disposi-

* Hatfield, in the West Riding of Yorkshire, about seven miles to the
north-east of Doncaster.
† In the Saxon Chronicle, the date is the second before the Ides of
October, [Oct. 14.]
‡ King of the Western Britons.   For an account of Cadwalla's victories,
see Llewarch Hen, as quoted in Turner's History of the Anglo-Saxons,
i. 367.

tion and behaviour, that he neither spared the female sex, nor the innocent age of children, but with savage cruelty put them to tormenting deaths, ravaging all their country for a long time, and resolving to cut off all the race of the English within the borders of Britain. Nor did he pay any respect to the Christian religion which had newly taken root among them ; it being to this day the custom of the Britons not to pay any respect to the faith and religion of the English, nor to correspond with them any more than with pagans.   King Edwin's head was brought to York, and afterwards into the church of St. Peter the Apostle, which he had begun, but which his successor Oswald finished, as has been said before.   It was deposited in the porch of St. Gregory, Pope, from whose disciples he had received the word of life.

The affairs of the Northumbrians being in confusion, by reason of this disaster, without any prospect of safety except in flight, Paulinus, taking with him Queen Ethelberga, whom he had before brought thither, returned into Kent by sea, and was honourably received by the Archbishop Honorius and King Eadbald.   He came thither under the conduct of Bassus, a most valiant soldier of King Edwin, having with him Eanfleda, the daughter, and Wuscfrea, the son of Edwin, as also Iffi, the son of Osfrid, his son, whom afterwards the mother, for fear of Eadbald and Oswald, sent over into France to be bred up by King Dagobert, who was her friend ; and there they both died in infancy, and were buried in the church with the honour due to royal children and to innocents of Christ.   He also brought with him many rich goods of King Edwin, among which were a large gold cross, and a golden chalice, dedicated to the use of the altar, which are still preserved, and shown in the church of Canterbury.

At that time the church of Rochester had no bishop, for Romanus, the prelate thereof, being sent to Pope Honorius, by Archbishop Justus, as his legate, was drowned in the Italian Sea ; and thereupon, Paulinus, at the request of Archbishop Honorius, and King Eadbald, took upon him the charge of the same, and held it until he departed to heaven, with the glorious fruits of his labours ; and, dying in that church, he left there the pall which he had received from the pope of Rome. He had left behind him in his church at York, James, the deacon, a holy ecclesiastic, who continuing long after in that church, by teaching and baptizing, rescued much prey from the power of the old enemy of mankind; from whom the village,* where he mostly resided, near Cataract, has its name to this day. He was extraordinarily skilful in singing, and when the province was afterwards restored to peace, and the number of the faithful increased, he began to teach many of the church to sing, according to the custom of the Romans, or of the Cantuarians. And being old and full of days, as the Scripture says, he went the way of his forefathers.

BOOK III.

CHAPTER I.

How King Edwin's next successors lost both the faith of their nation and the kingdom; but the most Christian King Oswald retrieved both. [A.D. 633.]

EDWIN being slain in battle, the kingdom of the Deira, to which province his family belonged, and where he first began to reign, devolved on Osric, the son of his uncle Elfric, who, through the preaching of Paulinus, had also received the faith. But the kingdom of the Bernicians—for into these two provinces the nation of the Northumbrians was formerly divided†—was possessed by Eanfrid, the son of Ethelfrid, who derived his origin from the royal family of that province. For all the time that Edwin reigned, the sons of the aforesaid Ethelfrid, who had reigned before him, with many of the nobility, lived in banishment among the Scots or Picts, and were there instructed according to the doctrine of the

---

* Now called Akeburgh, near Richmond.

† The kingdom of the Northumbrians was divided into two provinces, Deira and Bernicia. Deira reached from the Humber to the Tyne; Bernicia from the Tyne to the Tweed. Though not united into one community, the two states were generally governed by one monarch, and became, at such times, the most powerful of the Anglo-Saxon kingdoms.

Scots, and received the grace of baptism. Upon the death of the king, their enemy, they returned home, and Eanfrid, as the eldest of them, mentioned above, became king of the Bernicians. Both those kings, as soon as they obtained the government of their earthly kingdoms, renounced and lost the faith of the heavenly kingdom, and again delivered themselves up to be defiled by the abominations of their former idols.

But soon after, the king of the Britons, Cadwalla, slew them both, through the rightful vengeance of Heaven, though the act was base in him. He first slew Osric, the next summer; for, being besieged by him in a strong town, he sallied out on a sudden with all his forces, by surprise, and destroyed him and all his army. After this, for the space of a year, he reigned over the provinces of the Northumbrians, not like a victorious king, but like a rapacious and bloody tyrant, and at length brought to the same end Eanfrid, who unadvisedly came to him with only twelve chosen soldiers, to sue for peace. To this day, that year is looked upon as unhappy, and hateful to all good men; as well on account of the apostacy of the English kings, who had renounced the faith, as of the outrageous tyranny of the British king. Hence it has been agreed by all who have written about the reigns of the kings, to abolish the memory of those perfidious monarchs, and to assign that year to the reign of the following king, Oswald, a man beloved by God. This last king, after the death of his brother Eanfrid, advanced with an army, small, indeed, in number, but strengthened with the faith of Christ; and the impious commander of the Britons was slain, though he had most numerous forces, which he boasted nothing could withstand, at a place in the English tongue called Denisesburn, that is, Denis's-brook.*

CHAP. II.

How, among innumerable other miraculous cures wrought by the cross, which King Oswald, being ready to engage against the barbarians, erected, a certain youth had his lame arm healed. [A.D. 635.]

THE place is shown to this day, and held in much veneration, where Oswald, being about to engage, erected the sign of the

* Dilston is identified with the ancient Denisesburn, but on no authority. Nennius says the battle took place at Catscaul.

holy cross, and on his knees prayed to God that he would assist his worshippers in their great distress. It is further reported, that the cross being made in haste, and the hole dug in which it was to be fixed, the king himself, full of faith, laid hold of it and held it with both his hands, till it was set fast by throwing in the earth; and this done, raising his voice, he cried to his army, "Let us all kneel, and jointly beseech the true and living God Almighty, in his mercy, to defend us from the haughty and fierce enemy; for He knows that we have undertaken a just war for the safety of our nation." All did as he had commanded, and accordingly advancing towards the enemy with the first dawn of day, they obtained the victory, as their faith deserved. In that place of prayer very many miraculous cures are known to have been performed, as a token and memorial of the king's faith; for even to this day, many are wont to cut off small chips from the wood of the holy cross, which being put into water, men or cattle drinking thereof, or sprinkled with that water, are immediately restored to health.

The place in the English tongue is called Heavenfield, or the Heavenly Field,[*] which name it formerly received as a presage of what was afterwards to happen, denoting, that there the heavenly trophy would be erected, the heavenly victory begun, and heavenly miracles be wrought to this day. The same place is near the wall with which the Romans formerly enclosed the island from sea to sea, to restrain the fury of the barbarous nations, as has been said before. Hither also the brothers of the church of Hagulstad,[†] which is not far from thence, repair yearly on the day before that on which King Oswald was afterwards slain, to watch there for the health of his soul, and having sung many psalms, to offer for him in the morning the sacrifice of the holy oblation. And since that good custom has spread, they have lately

* Dr. Smith (App. to Bede, p. 730) says, that about a mile beyond Bingfield to the north is Hallington, anciently Havenfelth, or Heavenfield; though probably the whole country for two miles from Hallington through Bingfield to the wall was called Havenfelth. On the place where Oswald erected a cross a church was afterwards built.

† Hexham. About 673, Wilfrid, archbishop of York, founded a monastery and erected a church at this place, which, according to Richard of Hexham, was the most beautiful and magnificent ecclesiastical edifice in the kingdom. The ancient name is also written Hagustald,

built and consecrated a church there, which has attached
additional sanctity and honour to that place : and this with
good reason ; for it appears that there was no sign of the
Christian faith, no church, no altar erected throughout all the
nation of the Bernicians, before that new commander of the
army, prompted by the devotion of his faith, set up the cross
as he was going to give battle to his barbarous enemy.

Nor is it foreign to our purpose to relate one of the many
miracles that have been wrought at this cross.   One of the
brothers of the same church of Hagulstad, whose name is
Bothelm, and who is still living, a few years since, walking
carelessly on the ice at night, suddenly fell and broke his
arm ; a most raging pain commenced in the broken part, so
that he could not lift his arm to his mouth for the violence
of the anguish.   Hearing one morning that one of the
brothers designed to go to the place of the holy cross, he
desired him, at his return, to bring him a bit of that venerable wood, saying, he believed that with the help of God
he might thereby be healed.   The brother did as he was
desired ; and returning in the evening, when the brothers
were sitting at table, gave him some of the old moss which
grew on the surface of the wood.   As he sat at table,
having no place to lay up that which was brought him,
he put the same into his bosom ; and forgetting when he
went to bed to put it by, left it in his bosom.   Awaking in
the middle of the night, he felt something cold lying by his
side, and putting his hand to feel what it was, he found his
arm and hand as sound as if he had never felt any such
pain.

CHAP. III.

*The same king Oswald, asking a bishop of the Scottish nation, had Aidan
sent him, and granted him an episcopal see in the Isle of Lindisfarne.*
[A. D. 635.]

THE same Oswald, as soon as he ascended the throne, being
desirous that all his nation should receive the Christian
faith, whereof he had found happy experience in vanquish-
ing the barbarians, sent to the elders of the Scots, among
whom himself and his followers, when in banishment, had
received the sacrament of baptism, desiring they would send

him a bishop, by whose instruction and ministry the English
nation, which he governed, might be taught the advantages,
and receive the sacraments of the Christian faith.   Nor
were they slow in granting his request; but sent him Bishop
Aidan, a man of singular meekness, piety, and moderation;
zealous in the cause of God, though not altogether according
to knowledge; for he was wont to keep Easter Sunday ac-
-cording to the custom of his country, which we have before
so often mentioned, from the fourteenth to the twentieth
moon; the northern province of the Scots, and all the
nation of the Picts, celebrating Easter then after that manner, and believing that they therein followed the writings of
the holy and praiseworthy Father Anatolius; the truth of
which every skilful person can discern.   But the Scots
which dwelt in the South of Ireland had long since, by
the admonition of the bishop of the Apostolic See, learned
to observe Easter according to the canonical custom.

On the arrival of the bishop, the king appointed him
his episcopal see in the isle of Lindisfarne,* as he desired.
Which place, as the tide flows and ebbs twice a day, is enclosed by the waves of the sea like an island; and again,
twice in the day, when the shore is left dry, becomes contiguous to the land.   The king also humbly and willingly in
all cases giving ear to his admonitions, industriously applied
himself to build and extend the church of Christ in his
kingdom; wherein, when the bishop, who was not skilful
in the English tongue, preached the gospel, it was most
delightful to see the king himself interpreting the word of
God to his commanders and ministers, for he had perfectly
learned the language of the Scots during his long banishment.   From that time many of the Scots came daily into

* From the monastery of Lindisfarne, or Holy Island, all the churches
of Bernicia, from the Tyne to the Tweed, had their beginning; as had also
some of those of the Deira, from the Tyne to the Humber.   The prospect
from the island is beautiful; to the northward you command the town of
Berwick, over an arm of the sea, about seven miles in breadth.   At near the
same distance, to the south you view Bambrough Castle, on a bold promontory.   On the one hand you have a view of the open sea, which at the
time of our observation, was calm and resplendent, scattered over with vessels;
and on the other hand a narrow channel, by which this land is insulated,
about two miles in width.   The distant shore exhibits a beautiful hanging
landscape of cultivated country, graced with a multitude of hamlets, villages, and woodlands.

Britain, and with great devotion preached the word to those provinces of the English, over which King Oswald reigned, and those among them that had received priest's orders, administered to them the grace of baptism. Churches were built in several places; the people joyfully flocked together to hear the word; money and lands were given of the king's bounty to build monasteries; the English, great and small, were, by their Scottish masters, instructed in the rules and observance of regular discipline; for most of them that came to preach were monks. Bishop Aidan was himself a monk of the island called Hii,* whose monastery was for a long time the chief of almost all those of the northern Scots, and all those of the Picts, and had the direction of their people. That island belongs to Britain, being divided from it by a small arm of the sea, but had been long since given by the Picts, who inhabit those parts of Britain, to the Scottish monks, because they had received the faith of Christ through their preaching.

CHAP. IV.

When the nation of the Picts received the faith. [A. D. 565.]

In the year of our Lord 565, when Justin, the younger, the successor of Justinian, had the government of the Roman empire, there came into Britain a famous priest and abbat, a monk by habit and life, whose name was Columba, to preach the word of God to the provinces of the northern Picts, who are separated from the southern parts by steep and rugged mountains; for the southern Picts, who dwell on this side of those mountains, had long before, as is reported, forsaken the errors of idolatry, and embraced the truth, by the preaching of Ninias,† a most reverend bishop and holy

---

* The ancient name of Iona was I, or Hi, or Aoi, which was Latinized into Hyona, or Iona. The common name of it now is, I-colum-kill, the Island of Colum of the Cells. It is one of the most fertile and most romantic of the Scottish islands, separated from the west point of Ross by a narrow channel, called the Sound of I; and is about three miles long, and nearly a mile in breadth. A chart of the island may be seen in Pinkerton's Collection of the Lives of the Ancient Saints in Scotland.

† St. Ninias was a native of North Wales, where the British church was then flourishing. His faith was rewarded by the conversion of the

I

man of the British nation, who had been regularly instructed at Rome, in the faith and mysteries of the truth;
whose episcopal see, named after St. Martin the bishop, and
famous for a stately church, (wherein he and many other
saints rest in the body,) is still in existence among the
English nation. The place belongs to the province of the
Bernicians, and is generally called the White House,* because he there built a church of stone, which was not usual
among the Britons.

Columba came into Britain in the ninth year of the reign
of Bridius, who was the son of Meilochon,† and the powerful
king of the Pictish nation, and he converted that nation to
the faith of Christ, by his preaching and example, whereupon
he also received of them the aforesaid island for a monastery,
for it is not very large, but contains about five families,
according to the English computation. His successors hold
the island to this day; he was also buried therein, having
died at the age of seventy-seven, about thirty-two years after
he came into Britain to preach. Before he passed over into
Britain, he had built a noble monastery in Ireland, which,
from the great number of oaks, is in the Scottish tongue
called Dearm-ach—The Field of Oaks.‡ From both which
monasteries, many others had their beginning through his
disciples, both in Britain and Ireland; but the monastery
in the island where his body lies, is the principal of
them all.

That island has for its ruler an abbat, who is a priest, to
whose direction all the province, and even the bishops,
contrary to the usual method, are subject, according to the
example of their first teacher, who was not a bishop, but a

southern Picts. He maintained the catholic faith when the teaching of
Pelagius, his contemporary and countryman, was making great advances.
St. Ninias wrote a comment on the Psalms, and he visited and corresponded with St. Martin, bishop of Tours.

* Whitherne, or Candida Casa, Galloway. Usher supposes that St.
Ninias's diocese extended from the modern Glasgow to Stanmore Cross,
on the borders of Westmoreland; Bishop Nicolson, however, is of opinion,
that the bishops of Scotland had anciently no fixed sees; but that every
prelate exercised his episcopal office indiscriminately, in whatever part of
the kingdom he resided. (Scottish Hist. Lib. p. 74.)

† Elsewhere called Mailcuin.

‡ Now Derry.

priest and monk; * of whose life and discourses some
writings are said to be preserved by his disciples. But
whatsoever he was himself, this we know for certain, that
he left successors renowned for their continency, their love
of God, and observance of monastic rules. It is true they
followed uncertain rules in their observance of the great
festival, as having none to bring them the synodal decrees
for the observance of Easter, by reason of their being so far
away from the rest of the world; wherefore they only
practised such works of piety and chastity as they could
learn from the prophetical, evangelical, and apostolical
writings. This manner of keeping Easter continued among
them for the space of 150 years, till the year of our Lord's
incarnation 715.

But then the most reverend and holy father and priest,
Egbert, of the English nation, who had long lived in
banishment in Ireland for the sake of Christ, and was most
learned in the Scriptures, and renowned for long perfection
of life, came among them, corrected their error, and reduced
them to the true and canonical day of Easter; the which
they nevertheless did not always keep on the fourteenth
moon with the Jews, as some imagined, but on Sunday,
although not in the proper week. † For, as Christians, they
knew that the resurrection of our Lord, which happened on
the first day after the Sabbath, was always to be celebrated
on the first day after the Sabbath; but being rude and
barbarous, they had not learned when that same first day
after the Sabbath, which is now called the Lord's day, should
come. But because they had not laid aside the fervent grace
of charity, they were worthy to be informed in the true
knowledge of this particular, according to the promise of
the apostle, saying, "And if in any thing ye be otherwise
minded, God shall reveal even this unto you." Of which
we shall speak more fully in its proper place.

* This statement of Bede gave rise to a keen controversy on Church
government at the close of the seventeenth century. The reader may consult Mr. Goodall's Preface to Keith's Catalogue of Scottish Bishops, and
Bishop Lloyd's Historical Account of Church Government.
    † See note, at page 104.

CHAP. V.

Of the life of Bishop Aidan. [A.D. 635.]

FROM the aforesaid island, and college of monks, was Aidan sent to instruct the English nation in Christ, having received the dignity of a bishop at the time when Segenius,* abbat and priest, presided over that monastery; whence, among other instructions for life, he left the clergy a most salutary example of abstinence or continence; it was the highest commendation of his doctrine, with all men, that he taught no otherwise than he and his followers had lived; for he neither sought nor loved any thing of this world, but delighted in distributing immediately among the poor whatsoever was given him by the kings or rich men of the world. He was wont to traverse both town and country on foot, never on horseback, unless compelled by some urgent necessity; and wherever in his way he saw any, either rich or poor, he invited them, if infidels, to embrace the mystery of the faith; or if they were believers, to strengthen them in the faith, and to stir them up by words and actions to alms and good works.

His course of life was so different from the slothfulness of our times, that all those who bore him company, whether they were shorn monks or laymen, were employed in meditation, that is, either in reading the Scriptures, or learning psalms. This was the daily employment of himself and all that were with him, wheresoever they went; and if it happened, which was but seldom, that he was invited to eat with the king, he went with one or two clerks, and having taken a small repast, made haste to be gone with them, either to read or write. At that time, many religious men and women, stirred up by his example, adopted the custom of fasting on Wednesdays and Fridays, till the ninth hour, throughout the year, except during the fifty days after Easter. He never gave money to the powerful men of the world, but only meat, if he happened to entertain them; and, on the contrary, whatsoever gifts of money he received from the rich, he either distributed them, as has been said, to the use of the poor, or bestowed them in ransoming such as had

* The fourth abbat from St. Columba.

been wrongfully sold for slaves. Moreover, he afterwards made many of those he had ransomed his disciples, and after having taught and instructed them, advanced them to the order of priesthood.

It is reported, that when King Oswald had asked a bishop of the Scots to administer the word of faith to him and his nation, there was first sent to him another man of more austere disposition, who, meeting with no success, and being unregarded by the English people, returned home, and in an assembly of the elders reported, that he had not been able to do any good to the nation he had been sent to preach to, because they were uncivilized men, and of a stubborn and barbarous disposition. They, as is testified, in a great council seriously debated what was to be done, being desirous that the nation should receive the salvation it demanded, and grieving that they had not received the preacher sent to them. Then said Aidan, who was also present in the council, to the priest then spoken of, "I am of opinion, brother, that you were more severe to your unlearned hearers than you ought to have been, and did not at first, conformably to the apostolic rule, give them the milk of more easy doctrine, till being by degrees nourished with the word of God, they should be capable of greater perfection, and be able to practise God's sublimer precepts." Having heard these words, all present began diligently to weigh what he had said, and presently concluded, that he deserved to be made a bishop, and ought to be sent to instruct the incredulous and unlearned ; since he was found to be endued with singular discretion, which is the mother of other virtues, and accordingly being ordained, they sent him to their friend, King Oswald, to preach ; and he, as time proved, afterwards appeared to possess all other virtues, as well as the discretion for which he was before remarkable.

CHAP. VI.

Of King Oswald's wonderful piety. [A.D. 635.]

KING OSWALD, with the nation of the English which he governed being instructed by the teaching of this most reverend prelate, not only learned to hope for a heavenly kingdom unknown to his progenitors, but also obtained of

the same one Almighty God, who made heaven and earth,
larger earthly kingdoms than any of his ancestors. In short,
he brought under his dominion all the nations and provinces
of Britain, which are divided into four. languages, viz. the
Britons, the Picts, the Scots, and the English. When raised
to that height of dominion, wonderful to relate, he always continued humble, affable, and generous to the poor and strangers.

In short, it is reported, that when he was once sitting at
dinner, on the holy day of Easter, with the aforesaid bishop,
and a silver dish full of dainties before him, and they were
just ready to bless the bread, the servant, whom he had
appointed to relieve the poor, came in on a sudden, and told
the king, that a great multitude of needy persons from all
parts were sitting in the streets begging some alms of the
king; he immediately ordered the meat set before him to be
carried to the poor, and the dish to be cut in pieces and
divided among them. At which sight, the bishop who sat
by him, much taken with such an act of piety, laid hold of
his right hand, and said, "May this hand never perish."
Which fell out according to his prayer, for his arm and hand,
being cut off from his body, when he was slain in battle,
remain entire and uncorrupted to this day, and are kept in a
silver case, as revered relics, in St. Peter's church in the
royal city,* which has taken its name from Bebba, one of its
former queens. Through this king's management the
provinces of the Deiri and the Bernicians, which till then
had been at variance, were peacefully united and moulded
into one people. He was nephew to King Edwin by his
sister Acha; and it was fit that so great a predecessor should
have in his own family so great a person to succeed him in
his religion and sovereignty.

CHAP. VII.

*How the West Saxons received the word of God by the preaching of
Birinus; and of his successors, Agilbert and Eleutherius.* [A.D. 635.]

AT that time, the West Saxons, formerly called Gewissæ,†

---

* Bambrough, where the remains of a noble castle now stand on a bold
promontory called Bambrough Head.

† Smith observes, in his edition of Bede's Ecclesiastical History, that
Gewissæ is the Saxon word for "West" or "Occidentales:" he instances
Visigoths as a word of similar signification.

in the reign of Cynegils, embraced the faith of Christ, at the
preaching of Bishop Birinus, who came into Britain by the
advice of Pope Honorius; having promised in his presence
that he would sow the seed of the holy faith in the inner
parts beyond the dominions of the English, where no other
teacher had been before him.   Hereupon he received episcopal consecration from Asterius, bishop of Genoa; but on
his arrival in Britain, he first entered the nation of the
Gewissæ, and finding all there most confirmed pagans, he
thought it better to preach the word of God there, than to
proceed further to seek for others to preach to.

Now, as he preached in the aforesaid province, it happened
that the king himself, having been catechised, was baptized
together with his people, and Oswald, the most holy and
victorious king of the Northumbrians, being present, received
him as he came forth from baptism,* and by an alliance most
pleasing and acceptable to God, first adopted him, thus regenerated, for his son, and then took his daughter in marriage.
The two kings gave to the bishop the city called Dorcic,†
there to settle his episcopal see; where having built and consecrated churches, and by his labour called many to the Lord,
he departed this life, and was buried in the same city; but
many years after, when Hedda was bishop,‡ he was translated
thence to the city of Winchester, and laid in the church of
the blessed apostles, Peter and Paul.

The king also dying, his son Coinwalch succeeded him in
the throne, but refused to embrace the mysteries of the faith,
and of the heavenly kingdom; and not long after also he
lost the dominion of his earthly kingdom; for he put away
the sister of Penda, king of the Mercians, whom he had
married, and took another wife; whereupon a war ensuing,
he was by him expelled his kingdom, and withdrew to Anna,
king of the East Saxons, where living three years in banishment, he found and received the true faith, and was baptized;
for the king, with whom he lived in his banishment, was a
good man, and happy in a good and pious offspring, as we
shall show hereafter.

---

* The baptism of Cynegils, or Kingil, by Bishop Birinus, is still represented on an old font in Winchester Cathedral.

† Dorchester, 8½ miles from Oxford.   From this see arose the bishopric
of Lincoln, A.D. 1088.   ‡ See book iv. c. 12.

But when Coinwalch was restored to his kingdom, there came into that province out of Ireland, a certain bishop called Agilbert, by nation a Frenchman, but who had then lived a long time in Ireland, for the purpose of reading the Scriptures. This bishop came of his own accord to serve this king, and preach to him the word of life. The king, observing his erudition and industry, desired him to accept an episcopal see, and stay there as his bishop. Agilbert complied with the prince's request, and presided over those people many years. At length the king, who understood none but the language of the Saxons, grown weary of that bishop's barbarous tongue, brought into the province another bishop of his own nation, whose name was Wini, who had been ordained in France; and dividing his province into two dioceses, appointed this last his episcopal see in the city of Winchester, by the Saxons called Wintancestir. Agilbert, being highly offended, that the king should do this without his advice, returned into France, and being made bishop of the city of Paris, died there, aged and full of days. Not many years after his departure out of Britain, Wini was also expelled from his bishopric, and took refuge with Wulfhere, king of the Mercians, of whom he purchased for money the see of the city of London, and remained bishop thereof till his death. Thus the province of the West Saxons continued no small time without a bishop.

During which time, the king of that nation, sustaining very great losses in his kingdom from his enemies, at length bethought himself, that as he had been before expelled from the throne for his infidelity, and had been restored when he received the faith of Christ, his kingdom, being destitute of a bishop, was justly deprived of the Divine protection. He, therefore, sent messengers into France to Agilbert, humbly entreating him to return to the bishopric of his nation. But he excused himself, and affirmed that he could not go, because he was bound to the bishopric of his own city; however, that he might not seem to refuse him assistance, he sent in his stead thither the priest Eleutherius, his nephew, who, if he thought fit, might be ordained his bishop, saying, "He thought him worthy of a bishopric." The king and the people received him honourably, and entreated Theodore, then archbishop of Canterbury, to consecrate him their bishop.

He was accordingly consecrated in the same city, and many years zealously governed the whole bishopric of the West Saxons by synodical authority.

CHAP. VIII.

How Earconbert, King of Kent, ordered the idols to be destroyed; and of his daughter Earcongota, and his kinswoman Ethelberga, virgins consecrated to God. [A.D. 640.]

IN the year of our Lord 640, Eadbald, king of Kent, departed this life, and left his kingdom to his son Earconbert, which he most nobly governed twenty-four years and some months.   He was the first of the English kings that of his supreme authority commanded the idols, throughout his whole kingdom, to be forsaken and destroyed, and the fast of forty days before Easter to be observed; and that the same might not be neglected, he appointed proper and condign punishments for the offenders.   His daughter Earcongota, as became the offspring of such a parent, was a most virtuous virgin, always serving God in a monastery in France, built by a most noble abbess, called Fara,* at a place called Brie; for at that time but few monasteries being built in the country of the Angles, many were wont, for the sake of monastic conversation, to repair to the monasteries of the Franks or Gauls; and they also sent their daughters there to be instructed, and delivered to their heavenly bridegroom, especially in the monasteries of Brie, of Chelles,† and Andelys.   Among whom was also Sethrid, daughter of the wife of Anna, king of the East Angles, above mentioned; and Ethelberga,‡ natural daughter of the same king; both of whom, though strangers, were for their virtue made abbesses of the monastery of Brie.   Sexberga, that king's eldest daughter, wife to

---

* Or Faremoutier monastery, founded about A.D. 616, by St. Fara, sometimes called Burgundofara.   When first established it followed the rule of St. Columban.

† Chelles, four leagues from Paris.   This monastery was founded by St. Clotilda.   St. Bathildes so much enlarged it, as to be considered the principal foundress.

‡ Called by the French St. Aubierge.   Bede styles her the *natural* daughter of Anna, which in his time did not mean illegitimate; but was used in opposition to an adopted child.

Earconbert, king of Kent, had a daughter called Earcongota, of whom we are about to speak.

Many wonderful works and miracles of this virgin, dedicated to God, are to this day related by the inhabitants of that place; but it shall suffice us to say something briefly of her passage out of this world to the heavenly kingdom. The day of her departure drawing near, she visited the cells of the infirm servants of Christ, and particularly those that were of a great age, or most noted for probity of life, and humbly recommending herself to their prayers, let them know that her death was at hand, as she knew by revelation, which she said she had received in this manner. She had seen a number of men, all in white, come into the monastery, and being asked by her, "What they wanted, and what they did there?" they answered, "They had been sent thither to carry away with them the gold medal that had been brought thither from Kent." That same night, at the dawn of morning, leaving the darkness of this world, she departed to the light of heaven. Many of the brethren of that monastery that were in other houses, declared they had then plainly heard concerts of angels singing, and the noise as it were of a multitude entering the monastery. Whereupon going out immediately to see what it might be, they saw an extraordinary great light coming down from heaven, which conducted that holy soul, set loose from the bonds of the flesh, to the eternal joys of the celestial country. They add other miracles that were wrought the same night in the same monastery; but as we must proceed to other matters, we leave them to be related by those to whom such things belong. The body of this venerable virgin and bride of Christ was buried in the church of the blessed protomartyr, Stephen. It was thought fit, three days after, to take up the stone that covered the grave, and to raise it higher in the same place, which whilst they were doing, so great a fragrancy of perfume rose from below, that it seemed to all the brothers and sisters there present, as if a store of the richest balsams had been opened.

Her aunt also, Ethelberga above mentioned, preserved the glory so pleasing to God, of perpetual virginity, in great continency of body. but the extent of her virtue became more conspicuous after her death. Whilst she was abbess,

she began to build in her monastery a church, in honour of
all the apostles, wherein she desired her body might be
buried; but when that work was advanced half way, she
was prevented by death from finishing it, and buried in the
very place of the church where she had desired. After her
death, the brothers occupied themselves with other things,
and this structure was intermitted for seven years, at the
expiration whereof they resolved, by reason of the greatness
of the work, wholly to lay aside the building of the church,
but to remove the abbess's bones from thence to some other
church that was finished and consecrated; but, on opening
her tomb, they found the body as free from decay as it had
been from the corruption of carnal concupiscence, and having washed it again and put on it other clothes, they removed the same to the church of St. Stephen, Martyr, whose
nativity (or commemoration-day) is celebrated with much
magnificence on the 7th of July.

CHAP. IX.

*How miraculous cures have been frequently done in the place where King
Oswald was killed; and how, first, a traveller's horse was restored and
afterwards a young girl cured of the palsy.* [A.D. 642.]

OSWALD, the most Christian king of the Northumbrians,
reigned nine years, including that year which is to be held
accursed for the brutal impiety of the king of the Britons,
and the apostacy of the English kings; for, as was said
above, it is agreed by the unanimous consent of all, that the
names of the apostates should be erased from the catalogue
of the Christian kings, and no date ascribed to their reign.
After which period, Oswald was killed in a great battle, by
the same pagan nation and pagan king of the Mercians, who
had slain his predecessor Edwin, at a place called in the
English tongue Maserfield,* in the thirty-eighth year of his
age, on the fifth day of the month of August.

How great his faith was towards God, and how remark-

* Some difference of opinion exists respecting Maserfield. Camden,
Capgrave, and others, place it at Oswestry, in Shropshire, and the name
certainly favours their opinion. Alban Butler, Powell, and Dr. Cowper
place it at Winwick in Lancashire, and to support this their view there is
an inscription on the outside of the south wall of the parish church.

able his devotion, has been made evident by miracles since
his death; for, in the place where he was killed by the
pagans, fighting for his country, infirm men and cattle are
healed to this day. Whereupon many took up the very dust
of the place where his body fell, and putting it into water,
did much good with it to their friends who were sick. This
custom came so much into use, that the earth being carried
away by degrees, there remained a hole as deep as the height
of a man. Nor is it to be wondered that the sick should be
healed in the place where he died; for, whilst he lived, he
never ceased to provide for the poor and infirm, and to bestow alms on them, and assist them. Many miracles are
said to have been wrought in that place, or with the earth
carried from thence; but we have thought it sufficient to
mention two, which we heard from our ancestors.

It happened, not long after his death, that a man was travelling near that place, when his horse on a sudden began to
tire, to stand stock still, hang down his head, and foam at
the mouth, and, at length, as his pain increased, he fell to
the ground; the rider dismounted, and throwing some straw
under him, waited to see whether the beast would recover or
die. At length, after much rolling about in extreme anguish, the horse happened to come to the very place where
the aforesaid king died. Immediately the pain ceased, the
beast gave over his struggles, and, as is usual with tired
cattle, turned gently from side to side, and then starting up,
perfectly recovered, began to graze on the green herbage:
which the man observing, being an ingenious person, he
concluded there must be some wonderful sanctity in the
place where the horse had been healed, and left a mark
there, that he might know the spot again. After which he
again mounted his horse, and repaired to the inn where he
intended to stop. On his arrival he found a girl, niece to
the landlord, who had long languished under the palsy; and
when the friends of the family, in his presence, lamented the
girl's calamity, he gave them an account of the place where
his horse had been cured. In short, she was put into a cart
and carried and laid down at the place. At first she slept
awhile, and when she awaked found herself healed of her
infirmity. Upon which she called for water, washed her
face, put up her hair, and dressed her head. and returned

home on foot, in good health, with those who had brought
her.

CHAP. X.

The power of the earth of that place against fire.   [A.D. 642.]

ABOUT the same time, another person of the British nation,
as is reported, happened to travel by the same place, where
the aforesaid battle was fought, and observing one particular
spot of ground greener and more beautiful than any other
part of the field, he judiciously concluded with himself that
there could be no other cause for that unusual greenness,
but that some person of more holiness than any other in the
army had been killed there.   He therefore took along with
him some of that earth, tying it up in a linen cloth, supposing it would some time or other be of use for curing sick
people, and proceeding on his journey, came at night to a
certain village, and entered a house where the neighbours
were feasting at supper ; being received by the owners of
the house, he sat down with them at the entertainment,
hanging the cloth, in which he had brought the earth, on a
post against the wall.   They sat long at supper and drank
hard, with a great fire in the middle of the room ; it happened that the sparks flew up and caught the top of the
house, which being made of wattles and thatch, was presently in a flame ; the guests ran out in a fright, without
being able to put a stop to the fire.   The house was consequently burnt down, only that post on which the earth hung
remained entire and untouched.   On observing this, they
were all amazed, and inquiring into it diligently, understood
that the earth had been taken from the place where the
blood of King Oswald had been shed.   These miracles being
made known and reported abroad, many began daily to frequent that place, and received health to themselves and
theirs.

CHAP. XI.

*Of the heavenly light that appeared all the night over the bones of King
Oswald, and how persons possessed with devils were delivered by his
bones.*   [A.D. 697.]

AMONG the rest, I think we ought not to pass over, in

silence, the heavenly favours and miracles that were shown
when King Oswald's bones were found, and translated into
the church where they are now preserved. This was done
by the zealous care of Osthrida, queen of the Mercians, the
daughter of his brother Oswy, who reigned after him, as
shall be said hereafter.

There is a noble monastery in the province of Lindsey,
called Beardeneu,* which that queen and her husband Ethelred much loved, and conferred upon it many honours and
ornaments. It was here that she was desirous to lay the
venerable bones of her uncle. When the wagon in which
those bones were carried arrived towards evening at the
aforesaid monastery, they that were in it refused to admit
them, because, though they knew him to be a holy man, yet,
as he was originally of another province, and had reigned
over them as a foreign king, they retained their ancient aver-
sion to him even after death. Thus it came to pass that the
relics were left in the open air all that night, with only a
large tent spread over them ; but the appearance of a heavenly miracle showed with how much reverence they ought
to be received by all the faithful ; for during that whole
night, a pillar of light, reaching from the wagon up to
heaven, was seen by almost all the inhabitants of the province of Lindsey. Hereupon, in the morning, the brethren
who had refused it the day before, began themselves earnestly to pray that those holy relics, so beloved by God, might
be deposited among them. Accordingly, the bones, being
washed, were put into a shrine which they had made for that
purpose, and placed in the church, with due honour ; and
that there might be a perpetual memorial of the royal person of this holy man, they hung up over the monument his
banner made of gold and purple ; and poured out the water
in which they had washed the bones, in a corner of the
sacred place. From that time, the very earth which received that holy water, had the virtue of expelling devils
from the bodies of persons possessed.

Lastly, when the aforesaid queen afterwards made some

---

* Bardney in Lincolnshire. The foundation of Bardney Abbey is fixed
by Bishop Tanner before the year 697, because Ofthrida, or Osthryda, queen
of Mercia, who caused Oswald's bones to be brought to it, was murdered
in that year.

stay in that monastery, there came to visit her a certain venerable abbess, who is still living, called Ethelhilda, the sister of the holy men, Ethelwin and Aldwin, the first of whom was bishop in the province of Lindsey,* the other abbat of the monastery of Peartaneu;† not far from which was the monastery of Ethelhilda.   When this lady was come, in a conversation between her and the queen, the discourse, among other things, turning upon Oswald, she said, that she also had that night seen a light reaching from the relics up to heaven.   The queen thereupon added, that the very dust of the pavement on which the water that washed the bones had been spilt, had already   healed   many   sick   persons.   The   abbess thereupon desired that some of the said dust might be given her, which she tied up in a cloth, and, putting it into a casket, returned home.   Some time after, when she was in her monastery, there came to it a guest, who was wont often in the night to be on a sudden grievously tormented with an evil spirit; he being hospitably entertained, and gone to bed after supper, was on a sudden seized by the Devil, and began to cry out, to gnash his teeth, to foam at the mouth, and to distort his limbs in a most strange manner.   None being able to hold or bind him, the servant ran, and knocking at the door, acquainted the abbess.   She, opening the monastery door, went out herself with one of the nuns to the men's apartment, and calling a priest, desired he would go with her to the sufferer.   Being come thither, and seeing many more present, who had not been able, though they endeavoured it, to hold the tormented person and prevent his convulsive motions, the priest used exorcisms, and did all he could to assuage the madness of the unfortunate man, but, though he took much pains, could not prevail.   When no hopes appeared of easing him, the abbess bethought herself of the dust, and immediately ordered her servant to go and fetch her the casket in which it was.   As soon as she came with what she had been sent for into the porch of the house, in the inner part whereof the possessed person was tormented, he was presently silent, and laid down his head, as if he had been falling asleep, stretching out all his limbs to rest.   All

---

* Bishop of Sidnacester, afterwards removed to Lincoln.
† Pearteneu, or Parteney, was a cell to Bardney.   Deda (see p. 100), was the first abbat, and Aldwin the second.—*Willis's Mitred Abbeys*, i. 29.

present were silent, and stood attentive to see the end of the affair. After some time, the man that had been tormented sat up, and fetching a deep sigh, said, "Now I am like a sound man, for I am restored to my senses." They earnestly inquired how that came to pass, and he answered, "As soon as that virgin drew near the porch of this house, with the casket she brought, all the evil spirits that vexed me departed, and were no more to be seen." Then the abbess gave him a little of that dust, and the priest having prayed, he had a very quiet night ; nor did he, from that time forward, receive the least disturbance from his old enemy.

CHAP. XII.

Of a boy cured of an ague at St. Oswald's tomb. [A.D. 642.]

SOME time after, there was a certain little boy in the said monastery, who had been long troubled with an ague ; he was one day anxiously expecting the hour that his fit was to come on, when one of the brothers, coming in to him, said, "Shall I tell you, child, how you may be cured of this distemper ? Rise, go into the church, and get close to St. Oswald's tomb ; stay there quiet, and do not leave it ; do not come away, or stir from the place, till the time that your fit is to go off: then I will go in and fetch you away." The boy did as he was advised, and the disease durst not affect him as he sat by the saint's tomb ; but fled so absolutely, that he felt it no more, either the second or third day, or ever after. The brother that came from thence, and told me this, added, that at the time when he was talking with me, the young man was then still living in the monastery, on whom, when a boy, that miraculous cure had been wrought. Nor is it to be wondered that the prayers of that king who was then reigning with our Lord, should be very efficacious with him, since he, whilst yet governing his temporal kingdom, was also wont to pray and take more pains for that which is eternal. In short, it is reported, that he often continued in prayer from the hour of morning thanksgiving till it was day ; and that by reason of his constant custom of praying or giving thanks to God, he was wont always, wherever he sat, to hold his hands turned up on his knees.

It is also given out, and become a proverb, " That he ended
his life in prayer ;" for when he was beset with weapons
and enemies, he perceived he must immediately be killed,
and prayed to God for the souls of his army.   Whence it is
proverbially said, " Lord have mercy on their souls, said
Oswald, as he fell to the ground."   His bones, therefore,
were translated to the monastery which we have mentioned,
and buried therein : but the king that slew him commanded
his head, hands, and arms to be cut off from the body, and
set upon stakes.   But his successor in the throne, Oswy,
coming thither the next year with his army, took them down,
and buried his head in the church of Lindisfarne, and the
hands and arms in his royal city.*

CHAP. XIII.

*Of a certain person in Ireland that was recovered, when at the point of
death, by the bones of King Oswald.*   [A.D. 642.]

NOR was the fame of the renowned Oswald confined to Britain, but, spreading the rays of his healing brightness even
beyond the sea, reached also to Germany and Ireland.   In
short, the most reverend prelate, Acca,† is wont to relate,
that when, in his journey to Rome, he and his bishop Wilfrid
stayed some time with Wilbrord, now the holy bishop of the
Fresons, he had often heard him talk of the wonders which
had been wrought in that province at the relics of that most
reverend king.   And that in Ireland, when, being yet only
a priest, he led a pilgrim's life therein for love of the eternal
country, the fame of that king's sanctity was already spread
far and near.   One of the miracles, among the rest, which
he related, we have thought fit to insert in our history.

"At the time," said he, "of the mortality which made
such great havoc in Britain and Ireland, among others,
the infection reached a certain scholar of the Scottish race,
a man indeed learned in worldly literature, but in no way
solicitous or studious of his eternal salvation ; who, seeing

* Of the translation of these relics from Bardney to St. Oswald's, Gloucestershire, A.D. 910, by Ethelred, earl of Mercia, and Elfleda, the daughter
of King Alfred, see Sim. Dunelm, col. 152, Script. x. Twysden.   See
also Leland, Collectanea, London, 1770, vol. ii. p. 367; and iii. p. 299.
   † Bishop of Hexham.

K

his death near at hand, began to fear, lest, as soon as he was dead he should be hurried away to hell for his sins. He sent for me, who was in that neighbourhood, and whilst he was trembling and sighing, with a mournful voice made his complaint to me, in this manner : 'You see that my distemper increases, and that I am now reduced to the point of death. Nor do I question but that after the death of my body, I shall be immediately snatched away to the perpetual death of my soul, and cast into the torments of hell, since for a long time, amidst all my reading of divine books, I have rather addicted myself to vice, than to keep the commandments of God. But it is my resolution, if the Divine Mercy shall grant me a new term of life, to correct my vicious habits, and totally to reform my mind and course of life in obedience to the Divine will. But I am sensible, that I have no merits of my own to obtain a prolongation of life, nor can I confide in it, unless it shall please God to forgive me, through the assistance of those who have faithfully served him. We have heard, and the report is universal, that there was in your nation a king, of wonderful sanctity, called Oswald, the excellency of whose faith and virtue is become renowned even after his death by the working of miracles. I beseech you, if you have any relics of his in your custody, that you will bring the same to me ; in case the Lord shall be pleased, through his merits, to have mercy on me.' I answered, 'I have indeed some of the stake on which his head was set up by the pagans, when he was killed, and if you believe, with a sincere heart, the Divine Goodness may, through the merit of so great a man, both grant you a longer term of life here, and render you worthy of admittance into eternal life.' He answered immediately, 'That he had entire faith therein.' Then I blessed some water, and put into it a chip of the aforesaid oak, and gave it the sick man to drink. He presently found ease, and, recovering of his sickness, lived a long time after ; and, being entirely converted to God in heart and actions, wherever he came, he spoke of the goodness of his merciful Creator, and the honour of his faithful servant."

CHAP. XIV.

On the death of Paulinus, Ithamar was made bishop of Rochester in his stead. Of the wonderful humility of King Oswin, who was cruelly slain by Oswy. [A. D. 642.]

OSWALD being translated to the heavenly kingdom, his brother Oswy, a young man of about thirty years of age, succeeded him on the throne of his earthly kingdom, and held it twenty-eight years with much trouble, being harassed by the pagan king, Penda, and by the pagan nation of the Mercians, that had slain his brother, as also by his son Alfred, and by his cousin-german Ethelwald, the son of his brother who reigned before him. In his second year, that is, in the year of our Lord 644, the most reverend Father Paulinus, formerly bishop of York, but then of the city of Rochester, departed to our Lord, on the 10th day of October, having held the bishopric nineteen years, two months, and twenty-one days; and was buried in the sacristy of the blessed Apostle Andrew, which King Ethelbert had built from the foundation, in the same city of Rochester. In his place, Archbishop Honorius ordained Ithamar, of the Kentish nation, but not inferior to his predecessors for learning and conduct of life.

Oswy, during the first part of his reign, had a partner in the royal dignity called Oswin, of the race of King Edwin, and son to Osric, of whom we have spoken above, a man of wonderful piety and devotion, who governed the province of the Deiri seven years in very great prosperity, and was himself beloved by all men. But Oswy, who governed all the other northern part of the nation beyond the Humber, that is, the province of the Bernicians, could not live at peace with him; but on the contrary, the causes of their disagreement being heightened, he murdered him most cruelly. For when they had raised armies against one another, Oswin perceived that he could not maintain a war against one who had more auxiliaries than himself, and he thought it better at that time to lay aside all thoughts of engaging, and to preserve himself for better times. He therefore dismissed the army which he had assembled, and ordered all his men to return to their own homes, from the place that is called

Wilfares-dun,* that is, Wilfar's Hill, which is almost ten
miles distant from the village called Cataract, towards the
north-west.   He himself, with only one trusty soldier, whose
name was Tondhere, withdrew and lay concealed in the
house of Earl Hunwald, whom he imagined to be his most
assured friend.   But, alas! it was otherwise; for the earl
betrayed him, and Oswy, in a detestable manner, by the
hands of his commander, Ethilwin, slew him and the soldier
aforesaid.   This happened on the 20th of August, in the
ninth year of his reign, at a place called Ingethlingum,†
where afterwards, to atone for his crime, a monastery was
built, wherein prayers were to be daily offered up to God
for the souls of both kings, that is, of him that was murdered, and of him that commanded him to be killed.

King Oswin was of a graceful aspect, and tall of stature,
affable in discourse, and courteous in behaviour; and most
bountiful, as well to the ignoble as the noble; so that he was
beloved by all men for his qualities of body and mind, and
persons of the first rank came from almost all provinces to
serve him.   Among other virtues and rare endowments, if I
may so express it, humility is said to have been the greatest,
which it will suffice to prove by one example.

He had given an extraordinarily fine horse to Bishop
Aidan, which he might either use in crossing rivers, or in
performing a journey upon any urgent necessity, though he
was wont to travel ordinarily on foot.   Some short time after,
a poor man meeting him, and asking alms, he immediately
dismounted, and ordered the horse, with all his royal
furniture, to be given to the beggar; for he was very
compassionate, a great friend to the poor, and, as it were, the
father of the wretched.   This being told to the king, when
they were going in to dinner, he said to the bishop, "Why
would you, my lord bishop, give the poor man that royal
horse, which was necessary for your use?   Had not we
many other horses of less value, and of other sorts, which
would have been good enough to give to the poor, and not to
give that horse, which I had particularly chosen for

---

* Though the distance of this place from Catterick is so accurately laid
down by Bede, Smith was unable to find any modern name of a place at
all answering to it, at the required distance from Catterick.
† Gilling, in the North Riding of Yorkshire.

yourself?" To whom the bishop instantly answered, "What
is it you say, O king? Is that foal of a mare more dear to
you than the Son of God?" Upon this they went in to
dinner, and the bishop sat in his place; but the king, who
was come from hunting, stood warming himself, with his
attendants, at the fire. Then, on a sudden, whilst he was
warming himself, calling to mind what the bishop had said
to him, he ungirt his sword, and gave it to a servant, and in
a hasty manner fell down at the bishop's feet, beseeching him
to forgive him; "For from this time forward," said he, "I
will never speak any more of this, nor will I judge of what,
or how much of our money you shall give to the sons of
God." The bishop was much moved at this sight, and
starting up, raised him, saying, "He was entirely reconciled
to him, if he would sit down to his meat, and lay aside all
sorrow." The king, at the bishop's command and request,
beginning to be merry, the bishop, on the other hand, grew
so melancholy as to shed tears. His priest then asking him,
in the language of his country, which the king and his
servants did not understand, why he wept, "I know," said
he, "that the king will not live long; for I never before saw
so humble a king; whence I conclude that he will soon be
snatched out of this life, because this nation is not worthy of
such a ruler." Not long after, the bishop's prediction was
fulfilled by the king's death, as has been said above. But
Bishop Aidan himself was also taken out of this world,
twelve days after the king he loved, on the 31st of August,
to receive the eternal reward of his labours from our Lord.

CHAP. XV.

*How Bishop Aidan foretold to certain seamen a storm that would happen,
and gave them some holy oil to lay it.* [A.D. 651.]

HOW great the merits of Aidan were, was made manifest by
the all-seeing Judge, with the testimony of miracles, whereof
it will suffice to mention three as a memorial. A certain
priest, whose name was Utta, a man of great gravity and
sincerity, and on that account honoured by all men, even the
princes of the world, being ordered to Kent, to bring from
thence, as wife for King Oswy, Eanfleda, the daughter of
King Edwin, who had been carried thither when her father

was killed; and intending to go thither by land, but to
return with the virgin by sea, repaired to Bishop Aidan,
entreating him to offer up his prayers to our Lord for him
and his company, who were then to set out on their journey.
He, blessing and recommending them to our Lord, at the
same time gave them some holy oil, saying, "I know that
when you go abroad, you will meet with a storm and
contrary wind; but do you remember to cast this oil I give
you into the sea, and the wind shall cease immediately;
you will have pleasant calm weather, and return home
safe."

All which fell out as the bishop had predicted. For in
the first place, the winds raging, the sailors endeavoured to
ride it out at anchor, but all to no purpose; for the sea
breaking in on all sides, and the ship beginning to be filled
with water, they all concluded that certain death was at
hand; the priest at last, remembering the bishop's words,
laid hold of the phial and cast some of the oil into the sea,
which, as had been foretold, became presently calm. Thus
it came to pass that the man of God, by the spirit of
prophecy, foretold the storm that was to happen, and by
virtue of the same spirit, though absent, appeased the
same. Which miracle was not told me by a person of little
credit, but by Cynemund, a most faithful priest of our
church, who declared that it was related to him by Utta, the
priest, on and by whom the same was wrought.

CHAP. XVI.

*How the same Aidan, by his prayers, saved the royal city when fired by
the enemy.* [A.D. 651.]

ANOTHER notable miracle of the same father is related by
many such as were likely to have knowledge thereof; for
during the time that he was bishop, the hostile army of the
Mercians, under the command of Penda, cruelly ravaged the
country of the Northumbrians far and near, even to the
royal city;* which has its name from Bebba, formerly its
queen. Not being able to enter it by force, or by a long
siege, he endeavoured to burn it; and having destroyed all
the villages in the neighbourhood of the city, he brought to it

* Bambrough.

an immense quantity of planks, beams, wattles and thatch,
wherewith he encompassed the place to a great height on
the land side, and when the wind set upon it, he fired the mass,
designing to burn the town.

At that time, the most reverend Bishop Aidan resided in
the isle of Farne,* which is nearly two miles from the city ;
for thither he was wont often to retire to pray in private,
that he might be undisturbed. Indeed, this solitary residence
of his is to this day shown in that island. When he saw the
flames of fire and the smoke carried by the boisterous wind
above the city walls, he is reported, with eyes and hands
lifted up to heaven, to have said, "Behold, Lord, how great
mischief Penda does !" Which words were hardly uttered,
when the wind immediately turning from the city, drove
back the flames upon those who had kindled them, so that
some being hurt, and all frightened, they forbore any further
attempts against the city, which they perceived was protected
by the hand of God.

CHAP. XVII.

*How the post of the church on which Bishop Aidan was leaning when he
died, could not be burnt when the rest of the Church was consumed by
fire ; and of his inward life.* [A.D. 651.]

AIDAN was in the king's country-house, not far from the city
of which we have spoken above, at the time when death
separated him from his body, after he had been bishop sixteen years ; for having a church and a chamber there, he was
wont often to go and stay there, and to make excursions to
preach in the country round about, which he likewise did at
other of the king's country-seats, having nothing of his own
besides his church and a few fields about it. When he was
sick they set up a tent for him close to the wall at the west
end of the church, by which means it happened that he gave
up the ghost, leaning against a post that was on the outside
to strengthen the wall. He died in the seventeenth year of
his episcopacy, the last day of the month of August. His
body was thence translated to the isle of Lindisfarne, and

---

* A small island in the parish of Holy Island, Durham, about two miles
eastward of Bambrough castle ; it is remarkable as the spot where St.
Cuthbert passed a few of the latter years of his life.

buried in the churchyard belonging to the brethren. Some time after, when a larger church was built there and dedicated in honour of the blessed prince of the apostles, his bones were translated thither, and deposited on the right hand of the altar, with the respect due to so great a prelate.

Finan, who had likewise come from the same monastery of Hii in the Scottish island, succeeded him, and continued a considerable time in the bishopric. It happened some years after, that Penda, king of the Mercians, coming into these parts with a hostile army, destroyed all he could with fire and sword, and burned down the village and church above mentioned, where the bishop died; but it fell out in a wonderful manner that the post, which he had leaned upon when he died, could not be consumed by the fire which consumed all about it. This miracle being taken notice of, the church was soon rebuilt in the same place, and that very post was set up on the outside, as it had been before, to strengthen the wall. It happened again, some time after, that the same village and church were burned down the second time, and even then the fire could not touch that post; and when in a most miraculous manner the fire broke through the very holes in it wherewith it was fixed to the building, and destroyed the church, yet it could do no hurt to the said post. The church being therefore built there the third time, they did not, as before, place that post on the outside as a support, but within, as a memorial of the miracle; and the people coming in were wont to kneel there, and implore the Divine mercy. And it is manifest that since then many have been healed in that same place, as also that chips being cut off from that post, and put into water, have healed many from their distempers.

I have written thus much concerning the person and works of the aforesaid Aidan, in no way commending or approving what he imperfectly understood in relation to the observance of Easter; nay, very much detesting the same, as I have most manifestly proved in the book I have written, "De Temporibus;" but, like an impartial historian, relating what was done by or with him, and commending such things as are praiseworthy in his actions, and preserving the memory thereof for the benefit of the readers; viz. his love of peace and charity; his continence and humility; his mind superior to anger and

avarice, and despising pride and vainglory; his industry in
keeping and teaching the heavenly commandments; his dili-
gence in reading and watching; his authority becoming a
priest in reproving the haughty and powerful, and at the
same time his tenderness in comforting the afflicted, and
relieving or defending the poor.   To say all in a few words,
as near as I could be informed by those that knew him, he
took care to omit none of those things which he found in the
apostolical or prophetical writings, but to the utmost of his
power endeavoured to perform them all.

These things I much love and admire in the aforesaid
bishop; because I do not doubt that they were pleasing to
God; but I do not praise or approve his not observing Easter
at the proper time, either through ignorance of the canonical
time appointed, or, if he knew it, being prevailed on by the
authority of his nation, not to follow the same.   Yet this I
approve in him, that in the celebration of his Easter, the
object which he had in view in all he said, did, or preached,
was the same as ours, that is, the redemption of mankind,
through the passion, resurrection and ascension into heaven
of the man Jesus Christ, who is the mediator betwixt God
and man.   And therefore he always celebrated the same, not
as some falsely imagine, on the fourteenth moon, like the
Jews, whatsoever the day was, but on the Lord's day, from
the fourteenth to the twentieth moon; and this he did from
his belief of the resurrection of our Lord happening on the
day after the Sabbath, and for the hope of our resurrection,
which also he, with the holy Church, believed would happen
on the same day after the Sabbath, now called the Lord's
day.

CHAP. XVIII.

Of the life and death of the religious King Sigebert.   [A.D. 635.]

AT this time, the kingdom of the East Angles, after the
death of Earpwald, the successor of Redwald, was subject to
his brother Sigebert, a good and religious man, who long
before had been baptized in France, whilst he lived in banishment, flying from the enmity of Redwald; and returning
home, as soon as he ascended the throne, being desirous to

imitate the good institutions which he had seen in France, he
set up a school for youth* to be instructed in literature, and
was assisted therein by Bishop Felix, who came to him from
Kent, and who furnished him with masters and teachers after
the manner of that country.

This king became so great a lover of the heavenly kingdom,
that quitting the affairs of his crown, and committing the
same to his kinsman Ecgric, who before held a part of that
kingdom, he went himself into a monastery, which he had
built, and having received the tonsure, applied himself rather
to gain a heavenly throne. Some time after this, it happened
that the nation of the Mercians, under King Penda, made
war on the East Angles; who, finding themselves inferior in
martial affairs to their enemy, entreated Sigebert to go with
them to battle, to encourage the soldiers. He refused, upon
which they drew him against his will out of the monastery,
and carried him to the army, hoping that the soldiers would
be less disposed to flee in the presence of him, who had once
been a notable and a brave commander. But he, still keeping in mind his profession, whilst in the midst of a royal
army, would carry nothing in his hand but a wand, and was
killed with King Ecgric; and the pagans pressing on, all
their army was either slaughtered or dispersed.

Anna, the son of Eni, of the blood royal, a good man, and
father of an excellent family of children, succeeded them in
the kingdom. Of whom we shall speak hereafter; he being
also slain by the same pagan commander as his predecessor
had been.

CHAP. XIX.

*How Fursey built a monastery among the East Angles, and of his visions
and sanctity, of which, his flesh remaining uncorrupted after death, bore
testimony.* [A.D. 633.]

WHILST Sigebert still governed the kingdom, there came out
of Ireland a holy man called Fursey renowned both for his
words and actions, and remarkable for singular virtues, being
desirous to live a stranger for our Lord, wherever an opportunity should offer. On coming into the province of the
East Saxons, he was honourably received by the aforesaid

* Either at Seaham or Dunwich, according to later writers.

king, and performing his usual employment of preaching the Gospel, by the example of his virtue and the efficacy of his discourse, converted many unbelievers to Christ, and confirmed in his faith and love those that already believed.

Here he fell into some infirmity of body, and was thought worthy to see a vision from God; in which he was admonished diligently to proceed in the ministry of the word which he had undertaken, and indefatigably to continue his usual watching and prayers; inasmuch as his end was certain, but the hour of it would be uncertain, according to the saying of our Lord, "Watch ye therefore, because ye know not the day nor the hour." Being confirmed by this vision, he applied himself with all speed to build a monastery on the ground which had been given him by King Sigebert, and to establish regular discipline therein. This monastery was pleasantly situated in the woods, and with the sea not far off; it was built within the area of a castle, which in the English language is called Cnobheresburg, that is, Cnobher's Town;* afterwards, Anna, king of that province, and the nobility, embellished it with more stately buildings and donations. This man was of noble Scottish blood, but much more noble in mind than in birth. From his boyish years, he had particularly applied himself to reading sacred books, and following monastic discipline, and, as is most becoming to holy men, he carefully practised all that he learned was to be done.

In short, he built himself the monastery, wherein he might with more freedom indulge his heavenly studies. There, falling sick, as the book about his life informs us, he fell into a trance, and quitting his body from the evening till the cock crew, he was found worthy to behold the choirs of angels, and to hear the praises which are sung in heaven. He was wont to declare, that among other things he distinctly heard this : "The saints shall advance from one virtue to another." And again, "The God of gods shall be seen in Sion." Being restored to his body at that time, and again taken from it three days after, he not only saw the greater joys of the blessed, but also extraordinary combats of evil spirits, who by frequent accusations wickedly endeavoured to obstruct his journey to heaven; but the angels protecting him, all their

* Burghcastle in Suffolk.

endeavours were in vain. Concerning which particulars, if
any one desires to be more fully informed, that is, with what
subtle fraud the devils represented both his actions and superfluous words, and even his thoughts, as if they had been
written down in a book; and what pleasing or disagreeable
things he was informed of by the angels and saints, or just
men who appeared to him among the angels; let him read
the little book of his life which I have mentioned, and I believe he will thereby reap much spiritual profit.

But there is one thing among the rest, which we have
thought may be beneficial to many if inserted in this history. When he had been lifted up on high, he was ordered
by the angels that conducted him to look back upon the
world. Upon which, casting his eyes downward, he saw,
as it were, a dark and obscure valley underneath him. He
also saw four fires in the air, not far distant from each
other. Then asking the angels, what fires those were? he
was told, they were the fires which would kindle and consume the world. One of them was of falsehood, when we
do not fulfil that which we promised in baptism, to renounce
the Devil and all his works. The next of covetousness,
when we prefer the riches of the world to the love of heavenly things. The third of discord, when we make no
difficulty to offend the minds of our neighbours even in
needless things. The fourth of iniquity, when we look
upon it as no crime to rob and to defraud the weak. These
fires, increasing by degrees, extended so as to meet one
another, and being joined, became an immense flame. When
it drew near, fearing for himself, he said to the angel, "Lord,
behold the fire draws near me." The angel answered, "That
which you did not kindle shall not burn you; for though
this appears to be a terrible and great fire, yet it tries every
man according to the merits of his works; for every man's
concupiscence shall burn in the fire; for as every one burns
in the body through unlawful pleasure, so when discharged
of the body, he shall burn in the punishment which he has
deserved."

Then he saw one of the three angels, who had been his
conductors throughout both visions, go before and divide
the flame of fire, whilst the other two, flying about on both
sides, defended him from the danger of that fire. He also

saw devils flying through the fire, raising conflagrations of
wars against the just.   Then followed accusations of the
wicked spirits against him, the defence of the good angels
in his favour, and a more extended view of the heavenly
troops ; as also of holy men of his own nation, who, as he
had long since been informed, had been deservedly advanced to the degree of priesthood, from whom he heard
many things that might be very salutary to himself, or to
all others that would listen to them.   When they had ended
their discourse, and returned to heaven with the angelic
spirits, the three angels remained with the blessed Fursey,
of whom we have spoken before, and who were to bring
him back to his body.   And when they approached the
aforesaid immense fire, the angel divided the flame, as he
had done before ; but when the man of God came to the
passage so opened amidst the flames, the unclean spirits,
laying hold of one of those whom they tormented in the
fire, threw him at him, and, touching his shoulder and jaw,
burned them.   He knew the man, and called to mind that
he had received his garment when he died ; and the angel,
immediately laying hold, threw him back into the fire, and
the malignant enemy said, "Do not reject him whom you
before received ; for as you accepted the goods of him who
was a sinner, so you must partake of his punishment."   The
angel replying, said, "He did not receive the same through
avarice, but in order to save his soul."   The fire ceased, and
the angel, turning to him, added, "That which you kindled
burned in you ; for had you not received the money of this
person that died in his sins, his punishment would not burn
in you."   And proceeding in his discourse, he gave him
wholesome advice for what ought to be done towards the
salvation of such as repented.

Being afterwards restored to his body, throughout the
whole course of his life he bore the mark of the fire which
he had felt in his soul, visible to all men on his shoulder and
jaw ; and the flesh publicly showed, in a wonderful manner,
what the soul had suffered in private.   He always took care,
as he had done before, to persuade all men to the practice of
virtue, as well by his example, as by preaching.   But as for
the matter of his visions, he would only relate them to those
who, from holy zeal and desire of reformation, wished to

learn the same. An ancient brother of our monastery is still living, who is wont to declare that a very sincere and religious man told him, that he had seen Fursey himself in the province of the East Angles, and heard those visions from his mouth ; adding, that though it was in most sharp winter weather, and a hard frost, and the man was sitting in a thin garment when he related it, yet he sweated as if it had been in the greatest heat of summer, either through excessive fear, or spiritual consolation.

To return to what we were saying before, when, after preaching the word of God many years in Scotland, [Ireland] he could no longer bear the crowds that resorted to him, leaving all that he seemed to possess, he departed from his native island, and came with a few brothers through the Britons into the province of the English, and preaching the word of God there, as has been said, built a noble monastery. These things being rightly performed, he became desirous to rid himself of all business of this world, and even of the monastery itself, and forthwith left the same, and the care of souls, to his brother Fullan, and the priests Gobban and Dicull, and being himself free from all that was worldly, resolved to end his life as a hermit. He had another brother called Ultan, who, after a long monastical probation, had also adopted the life of an anchorite. Repairing all alone to him, he lived a whole year with him in continence and prayer, and laboured daily with his hands.

Afterwards seeing the province in confusion by the irruptions of the pagans, and presaging that the monasteries would be also in danger, he left all things in order, and sailed over into France, and being there honourably entertained by Clovis, king of the Franks, or by the patrician Erconwald, he built a monastery in the place called Latiniacum,* and falling sick not long after, departed this life. The same Erconwald took his body, and deposited it in the porch of a church he was building in his town of Perrone, till the church itself should be dedicated. This happened twenty-seven days after, and the body being taken from the porch, to be re-buried near the altar, was found as entire as if he had just then died. And again, four years after, a more decent tabernacle or chapel being built for the same

* Lagny, about six miles to the north of Paris on the Marne.

body to the eastward of the altar, it was still found free from corruption, and translated thither with due honour ; where it is well known that his merits, through the divine operation, have been declared by many miracles. These things and the incorruption of his body we have taken notice of, that the sublimeness of this man may be the better known to the readers. All which, whosoever will read it, will find more fully described, as also about his fellow-labourers, in the book of his life before mentioned.

CHAP. XX.

Honorius dying, Deusdedit is chosen archbishop of Canterbury, of those who were at that time bishops of the East Angles, and of the church of Rochester. [A.D. 653.]

In the meantime, Felix, bishop of the East Angles, dying, when he had held that see seventeen years, Honorius ordained Thomas his deacon, of the province of the Girvii,* in his place ; and he departing this life when he had been bishop five years, Bertgils, surnamed Boniface, of the province of Kent, was appointed in his stead. Honorius himself also, having run his course, departed this life in the year of our Lord 653, on the 30th of September ; and when the see had been vacant a year and six months, Deusdedit, of the nation of the South Saxons, was chosen the sixth archbishop of Canterbury. To ordain whom, Ithamar, bishop of Rochester, came thither. His ordination was on the 26th of March, and he ruled nine years, four months, and two days ; when he also died. Ithamar consecrated in his place Damian,† who was of the race of the South Saxons.

CHAP. XXI.

How the province of the Midland Angles became Christian under King Peada. [A.D. 653.]

At this time, the Middle Angles,‡ under their Prince Peada, the son of King Penda, received the faith and sacraments of

---

* The Girvii inhabited the counties of Rutland, Northampton, and Huntingdon, with part of Lincolnshire, and had their own princes, dependent on the kings of Mercia.

† The see of Canterbury was vacant four years between the death of Deusdedit and the consecration of Damian.

‡ The Southern Mercians, or Middle Angles, whom he governed as king during the life of his father.

the truth. Being an excellent youth, and most worthy of the title and person of a king, he was by his father elevated to the throne of that nation, and came to Oswy, king of the Northumbrians, requesting to have his daughter Elfleda given him to wife; but could not obtain his desires unless he would embrace the faith of Christ, and be baptized, with the nation which he governed. When he heard the preaching of truth, the promise of the heavenly kingdom, and the hope of resurrection and future immortality, he declared that he would willingly become a Christian, even though he should be refused the virgin; being chiefly prevailed on to receive the faith by King Oswy's son Alfrid, who was his relation and friend, and had married his sister Cyneberga, the daughter of King Penda.

Accordingly he was baptized by Bishop Finan, with all his earls and soldiers, and their servants, that came along with him, at a noted village belonging to the king, called At the Wall.* And having received four priests, who for their erudition and good life were deemed proper to instruct and baptize his nation, he returned home with much joy. These priests were Cedd and Adda, and Betti and Diuma; the last of whom was by nation a Scot, the others English. Adda was brother to Utta, whom we have mentioned before, a renowned priest, and abbat of the monastery of Gateshead.† The aforesaid priests, arriving in the province with the prince, preached the word, and were willingly listened to; and many, as well of the nobility as the common sort, renouncing the abominations of idolatry, were baptized daily.

Nor did King Penda obstruct the preaching of the word among his people, the Mercians, if any were willing to hear it; but, on the contrary, he hated and despised those whom he perceived not to perform the works of faith, when they had once received the faith, saying, "They were contemptible and wretched who did not obey their God, in

---

* Generally supposed to be Walton, but Smith thinks it is Waubottle, near Newcastle. The expression, "At the wall," is a corruption not unusual in the case of towns whose names are imperfectly understood by new comers. Thus Constantinople is called by the Turks, Stamboul, which is only a corruption of ES TAN POLIN.

† Gateshead is supposed to have been a Roman station called *Gabrosentum*, which signifies Goat's Head. It is situated on the southern bank of the Tyne, opposite to Newcastle.

whom they believed." This was begun two years before the death of King Penda.

But when he was slain, and Oswy, the most Christian king, succeeded him in the throne, Diuma, one of the aforesaid four priests, was made bishop of the Midland Angles, as also of the Mercians,* being ordained by Bishop Finan ; for the scarcity of priests was the occasion that one prelate was set over two nations. Having in a short time gained many people to our Lord, he died among the Midland Angles, in the country called Feppingum ; and Ceollach, of the Scottish nation, succeeded him in the bishopric. This prelate, not long after, left his bishopric, and returned to the island of Hii, which, among the Scots, was the chief and head of many monasteries. His successor in the bishopric was Trumhere, a religious man, and educated in the monastic life of the English nation, but ordained bishop by the Scots, which happened in the days of King Wulfhere, of whom we shall speak hereafter.

CHAP. XXII.

How the East Saxons again received the faith, which they had before cast off under King Sigebert, through the preaching of Cedd. [A.D. 653.]

At that time, also, the East Saxons, at the instance of King Oswy, again received the faith, which they had formerly cast off when they expelled Mellitus, their bishop. For Sigebert, who reigned next to Sigebert surnamed The Little, was then king of that nation, and a friend to King Oswy, who, when he often came to him into the province of the Northumbrians, used to endeavour to persuade him that those could not be gods that had been made by the hands of men ; that a stock or a stone could not be proper matter to form a god, the remains whereof were either burned in the fire, or framed into any vessels for the use of men, or else were cast out as refuse, trampled on and bruised to dust. That God is rather to be understood as of incomprehensible majesty and invisible to human eyes, almighty, eternal, the Creator of heaven and earth, and of mankind ; who governs and

* This see was fixed at Repton, formerly called Repington, in Derbyshire, the capital of the kingdom of Mercia, and was probably the see of the first four bishops of Mercia. It was afterwards, when St. Chad was bishop, removed to Lichfield where it has continued to this day. See p. 174.

will judge the world in righteousness ; whose everlasting
seat is in heaven, and not in vile and fading matter ; and
that it ought in reason to be concluded, that all those who
have learned and obeyed the will of Him by whom they
were created, will receive from Him eternal rewards. King
Oswy having often, in a friendly and brotherly manner, said
this and much more to the like effect, at. length, with the
consent of his friends, he believed, and after consulting with
those about him, and exhorting them, they all agreed and
gave their approbation, and were baptized with him by
Bishop Finan, in the king's village above spoken of, which
is called At the Wall, because it is close by the wall with
which the Romans formerly divided the island of Britain, at
the distance of twelve miles from the eastern sea.

King Sigebert, being now become a citizen of the eternal
kingdom, returned to the seat of his temporal kingdom, requesting of Oswy that he would give him some teachers,
who might convert his nation to the faith of Christ, and
baptize them.   Oswy, accordingly, sending into the province
of the Midland Angles, invited to him the man of God,
Cedd,* and, giving him another priest for his companion,
sent them to preach to the East Saxons.   When these two,
travelling to all parts of that country, had gathered a numerous church to our Lord, it happened that Cedd returned
home, and came to the church of Lindisfarne to confer with
Bishop Finan ; who, finding how successful he had been in
the work of the Gospel, made him bishop of the church or
the East Saxons, calling to him two other bishops to assist
at the ordination.   Cedd, having received the episcopal dignity, returned to his province, and pursuing the work he had
begun with more ample authority, built churches† in several
places, ordaining priests and deacons to assist him in the
work of faith, and the ministry of baptizing, especially in
the city which, in the language of the Saxons, is called

* Brother to St. Chad, bishop of Lichfield.

† These churches did not at all resemble the parish churches which, in
after times, the lords of the soil appear to have built for the use of themselves and their tenantry ; on the contrary, there is much show of probability that they were chapels or oratories dependent upon the two larger
churches which Cedd built at Ithancestir and at Tilbury, in both which
places he collected together a number of persons, and taught them to observe, if not a strictly monastic, yet a *regular* discipline.

Ithancestir,* as also in that which is named Tilaburg ;† the
first of which places is on the bank of the Pante, the other
on the bank of the Thames, where, gathering a flock of
servants of Christ, he taught them to observe the discipline
of regular life, as far as those rude people were then
capable.

Whilst the doctrine of everlasting life was thus, for a
considerable time, making progress, to the joy of the king
and of all the people, it happened that the king, at the
instigation of the enemy of all good men, was murdered by
his own kindred. They were two brothers who did this
wicked deed ; and being asked what had moved them to it,
had nothing else to answer, but that they had been incensed
against the king, and hated him, because he was too apt to
spare his enemies, and easily to forgive the wrongs they had
done him, upon their entreaty. Such was the crime for
which the king was killed, because he observed the precepts
of the Gospel with a devout heart ; in which innocent death,
however, his real offence was also punished, according to the
prediction of the man of God. For one of those earls that
murdered him was unlawfully married, which the bishop not
being able to prevent or correct, he excommunicated him, and
commanded all that would give ear to him not to enter within
his house, nor to eat of his meat. The king made slight of
this inhibition, and being invited by the earl, went to an
entertainment at his house, and when he was going thence,
the bishop met him. The king, beholding him, immediately
dismounted from his horse, trembling, and fell down at his
feet, begging pardon for his offence ; for the bishop, who was
likewise on horseback, had also alighted. Being much
incensed, he touched the king, lying in that humble posture,
with the rod he held in his hand, and using his pontifical
authority, spoke thus : " I say to you, forasmuch as you
would not refrain from the house of that wicked and
condemned person, you shall die in that very house." Yet it
is to be believed, that such a death of a religious man not
only blotted out his offence, but also added to his merit ;

* On the river Pante, now called Blackwater river, near Maldon,
Essex. There are now no remains of the city.
† Tilbury, near the Thames, opposite to Gravesend. St. Cedd resided
here when engaged in baptizing the East Saxons.

because it happened on account of his pious observance of the commands of Christ.

Sigebert was succeeded in the kingdom by Suidhelm, the son of Sexbald, who was baptized by the same Cedd, in the province of the East Angles, at the king's country-seat, called Rendlesham,* that is, Rendil's Mansion ; and Ethelwald, king of the East Angles, brother to Anna, king of the same people, was his godfather.

CHAP. XXIII.

Bishop Cedd, having a place given him by King Ethelwald, consecrates the same to our Lord with prayer and fasting. Of his death. [A.D. 659.]

THE same man of God, whilst he was bishop among the East Saxons, was also wont several times to visit his own country, Northumberland, to make exhortations. Ethelwald, the son of King Oswald, who reigned among the Deiri, finding him a holy, wise, and good man, desired him to accept some land to build a monastery, to which the king himself might frequently resort, to offer his prayers and hear the word, and be buried in it when he died ; for he believed that he should receive much benefit by the prayers of those who were to serve God in that place. The king had before with him a brother of the same bishop, called Celin, a man no less devoted to God, who, being a priest, was wont to administer to him the word and the sacraments of the faith ; by whose means he chiefly came to know and love the bishop. That prelate, therefore, complying with the king's desires, chose himself a place to build a monastery among craggy and distant mountains, which looked more like lurking-places for robbers and retreats for wild beasts, than habitations for men ; to the end that, according to the prophecy of Isaiah, "In the habitations where before dragons dwelt, might be grass with reeds and rushes ;" that is, that the fruits of good works should spring up, where before beasts were wont to dwell, or men to live after the manner of beasts.

The man of God, desiring first to cleanse the place for the monastery from former crimes, by prayer and fasting, that it might become acceptable to our Lord, and so to lay the foundations, requested of the king that he would give

* Rendlesham, in Suffolk.

him leave to reside there all the approaching time of Lent,
to pray. All which days, except Sundays, he fasted till the
evening, according to custom, and then took no other
sustenance than a little bread, one hen's egg, and a little milk
mixed with water. This, he said, was the custom of those
of whom he had learned the rule of regular discipline; first,
to consecrate to our Lord, by prayer and fasting, the places
which they had newly received for building a monastery or a
church. When there were ten days of Lent still remaining,
there came a messenger to call him to the king; and he, that
the religious work might not be intermitted, on account of
the king's affairs, entreated his priest, Cynebil, who was also
his own brother, to complete that which had been so piously
begun. Cynebil readily complied, and when the time of
fasting and prayer was over, he there built the monastery,
which is now called Lestingau,* and established therein the
religious customs of Lindisfarne, where they had been
educated.

Cedd for many years having charge of the bishopric in
the aforesaid province, and of this monastery, over which he
had placed superiors, it happened that he came thither at a
time when there was a mortality, and fell sick and died. He
was first buried in the open air; but in the process of time a
church was built of stone in the monastery, in honour of the
Mother of God, and his body interred in the same, on the
right hand of the altar.

The bishop left the monastery to be governed after him
by his brother Chad, who was afterwards made bishop,† as
shall be said in its place. For the four brothers we have
mentioned, Cedd and Cynebil, Celin and Ceadda, [Chad,]
which is a rare thing to be met with, were all celebrated
priests of our Lord, and two of them also came to be bishops.
When the brethren who were in his monastery, in the

---

* It has been supposed that this monastery was situated at Lastingham,
Cleaveland, Yorkshire. Dugdale (i. 342) says, it was situated in the
deanery of Rydale and archdeaconry of Cleaveland, at no great distance
from Whitby. John of Tinemouth places the foundation in the year 648;
Bede in 660. It was completely ruined in the Danish wars, about 870.—The
beautiful old Saxon church at Lastingham, remarks Mr. Stevenson, if not
the original building of Cedd or his brother Chad, is one of the oldest
churches in the kingdom.

† First bishop of York, and then of Lichfield.

province of the East Saxons, heard that the bishop was dead
in the province of the Northumbrians, about thirty men of
that monastery came thither, being desirous either to live
near the body of their father, if it should please God,
or to die there and be buried. Being lovingly received by
their brethren and fellow soldiers in Christ, all of them died
there by the aforesaid pestilence, except one little boy, who
was delivered from death by his father's prayers. For when
he had lived there a long time after, and applied himself to
the reading of sacred writ, he was informed that he had not
been regenerated by the water of baptism, and being then
washed in the laver of salvation, he was afterwards promoted
to the order of priesthood, and proved very useful to many
in the church. I do not doubt that he was delivered at the
point of death, as I have said, by the intercession of his
father, whilst he was embracing his beloved corpse, that so
he might himself avoid eternal death, and by teaching,
exhibit the ministry of life and salvation to others of the
brethren.

CHAP. XXIV.

*King Penda being slain, the Mercians received the faith of Christ, and
Oswy gave possessions and territories to God, for building monasteries,
in acknowledgment for the victory obtained.* [A.D. 655.]

AT this time, King Oswy was exposed to the fierce and intolerable irruptions of Penda, king of the Mercians, whom we have
so often mentioned, and who had slain his brother; at length,
necessity compelling him, he promised to give him greater
gifts that can be imagined, to purchase peace; provided that
the king would return home, and cease to destroy the provinces of his kingdom. That perfidious king refused to
grant his request, and resolved to extirpate all his nation,
from the highest to the lowest; whereupon he had recourse
to the protection of the Divine goodness for deliverance from
his barbarous and impious foe, and binding himself by a vow,
said, "If the pagan will not accept of our gifts, let us offer
them to him that will, the Lord our God." He then vowed,
that if he should come off victorious, he would dedicate his
daughter to our Lord in holy virginity, and give twelve farms
to build monasteries. After this he gave battle with a very

small army against superior forces: indeed, it is reported
that the pagans had three times the number of men; for they
had thirty legions, led on by most noted commanders.   King
Oswy and his son Alfrid met them with a very small army,
as has been said, but confiding in the conduct of Christ; his
other son, Egfrid, was then kept an hostage at the court of
Queen Cynwise, in the province of the Mercians.   King
Oswald's son Ethelwald, who ought to have assisted them,
was on the enemy's side, and led them on to fight against his
country and uncle; though, during the battle, he withdrew,
and waited the event in a place of safety.   The engagement
beginning, the pagans were defeated, the thirty commanders,
and those who had come to his assistance, were put to flight,
and almost all of them slain; among whom was Ethelhere,
brother and successor to Anna, king of the East Angles, who
had been the occasion of the war, and who was now killed,
with all his soldiers.   The battle was fought near the river
Vinwed,* which then, with the great rains, had not only filled
its channel, but overflowed its banks, so that many more
were drowned in the flight than destroyed by the sword.

Then King Oswy, pursuant to the vow he had made to
our Lord, returned thanks to God for the victory, and gave
his daughter Elfleda, who was scarce a year old, to be consecrated to him in perpetual virginity; delivering also twelve
small portions of land, wherein earthly warfare should cease,
and in which there should be a perpetual residence and subsistence for monks to follow the warfare which is spiritual,
and pray diligently for the peace of his nation.   Of those possessions six were in the province of the Deiri, and the other
six in that of the Bernicians.   Each of the said possessions
contained ten families, that is, a hundred and twenty in all.
The aforesaid daughter of King Oswy, thus dedicated to
God, was put into the monastery, called Heruteu,† or, "The
Island of the Hart," where, at that time, the Abbess Hilda‡
presided, and, two years after, having acquired a possession
of ten families, at the place called Streaneshalch,§ she built a
monastery there, in which the aforesaid king's daughter was

* Winwidfield, near Leeds.   † Now Hartlepool.
‡ Grandniece of Edwin, king of Northumbria.
§ Whitby, in the North Riding of Yorkshire.

first a learner, and afterwards a teacher of the monastic life; till, being sixty years of age, the blessed virgin departed to the nuptials and embraces of her heavenly bridegroom. In that same monastery, she and her father, Oswy, her mother, Eanfleda; her mother's father, Edwin, and many other noble persons, are buried in the church of the holy Apostle Peter. King Oswy concluded the aforesaid war in the country of Loidis,* in the thirteenth year of his reign, on the 15th of November, to the great benefit of, both nations; for he both delivered his own people from the hostile depredations of the pagans, and, having cut off the wicked king's head, converted the Mercians and the adjacent provinces to the grace of the Christian faith.

Diuma was made the first bishop of the Mercians, as also of Lindisfarne and the Midland Angles, as has been said above, and he died and was buried among the Midland Angles. The second was Ceollach, who, quitting the episcopal office whilst still alive, returned into Scotland, to which nation he belonged as well as Bishop Diuma. The third was Trumhere, an Englishman, but taught and ordained by the Scots, being abbat in the monastery that is called Ingethlingum,† and is the place where King Oswin was killed, as has been said above; for Queen Eanfleda, his kinswoman, in satisfaction for his unjust death, begged of King Oswy that he would give the aforesaid servant of God a place there to build a monastery, because he also was kinsman to the slaughtered king; in which monastery continual prayers should be offered up for the eternal health of the kings, both of him that had been slain, and of him that caused it to be done. The same King Oswy governed the Mercians, as also the people of the other southern provinces, three years after he had slain King Penda; and he likewise subdued the greater part of the Picts to the dominion of the English.

At which time he gave to the above-mentioned Peada, son to King Penda, who was his kinsman, the kingdom of the Southern Mercians, consisting, as is reported, of 5,000 families, divided by the river Trent from the Northern Mercians, whose land contained 7,000 families; but that Peada was the next spring very wickedly killed, by the treachery, as is

---

* Leeds.   † Gilling, Yorkshire.

said, of his wife, during the very time of celebrating Easter.
Three years after the death of King Penda, Immin, and
Eafa, and Eadbert, generals of the Mercians, rebelled against
King Oswy, setting up for their king, Wulfhere, son to the
said Penda, a youth, whom they had kept concealed; and
expelling the officers of the foreign king, they at once
recovered their liberty and their lands ; and being thus free,
together with their king, they rejoiced to serve Christ the
true King, that they might obtain the everlasting kingdom
which is in heaven.   This king governed the Mercians seventeen years, and had for his first bishop Trumhere, above
spoken of;   the second Jaruman;   the third Chad;* the
the fourth Winfrid.   All these, succeeding each other
regularly under King Wulfhere, discharged the episcopal
duties to the Mercian nation.

CHAP. XXV.

*How the controversy arose about the due time of keeping Easter, with those
that came out of Scotland.* [A.D. 652.]

In the meantime, Bishop Aidan being dead, Finan, who was
ordained and sent by the Scots, succeeded him in the bishopric, and built a church in the Isle of Lindisfarne, the episcopal see; nevertheless, after the manner of the Scots, he made
it, not of stone, but of hewn oak, and covered it with reeds;
and the same was afterwards dedicated in honour of St.
Peter the Apostle, by the reverend Archbishop Theodore.
Eadbert,† also bishop of that place, took off the thatch, and
covered it, both roof and walls, with plates of lead.

At this time, a great and frequent controversy happened
about the observance of Easter;‡ those that came from Kent
or France affirming, that the Scots kept Easter Sunday contrary to the custom of the universal church.   Among them
was a most zealous defender of the true Easter, whose name
was Ronan, a Scot by nation, but instructed in ecclesiastical
truth, either in France or Italy, who, disputing with Finan,
convinced many, or at least induced them to make a more

---

* St. Chad removed the see from Repton (see p. 145) to Lichfield, as
related in book iv. c. 3.

† Eadbert was consecrated bishop of Lindisfarne, A.D. 688. See book
iv. c. 29.   ‡ See ante, page 104.

strict inquiry after the truth; yet he could not prevail upon Finan, but, on the contrary, made him the more inveterate by reproof, and a professed opposer of the truth, being of a hot and violent temper. James, formerly the deacon of the venerable Archbishop Paulinus, as has been said above, kept the true and Catholic Easter, with all those that he could persuade to adopt the right way. Queen Eanfleda and her followers also observed the same as she had seen practised in Kent, having with her a Kentish priest that followed the Catholic mode, whose name was Romanus. Thus it is said to have happened in those times that Easter was twice kept in one year; and that when the king having ended the time of fasting, kept his Easter, the queen and her followers were still fasting, and celebrating Palm Sunday. This difference about the observance of Easter, whilst Aidan lived, was patiently tolerated by all men, as being sensible, that though he could not keep Easter contrary to the custom of those who had sent him, yet he industriously laboured to practise all works of faith, piety, and love, according to the custom of all holy men; for which reason he was deservedly beloved by all, even by those who differed in opinion concerning Easter, and was held in veneration, not only by indifferent persons, but even by the bishops, Honorius of Canterbury, and Felix of the East Angles.

But after the death of Finan, who succeeded him, when Colman, who was also sent out of Scotland, came to be bishop, a greater controversy arose about the observance of Easter, and the rules of ecclesiastical life. Whereupon this dispute began naturally to influence the thoughts and hearts of many, who feared, lest having received the name of Christians, they might happen to run, or to have run, in vain. This reached the ears of King Oswy and his son Alfrid; for Oswy, having been instructed and baptized by the Scots, and being very perfectly skilled in their language, thought nothing better than what they taught. But Alfrid, having been instructed in Christianity by Wilfrid, a most learned man, who had first gone to Rome to learn the ecclesiastical doctrine, and spent much time at Lyons with Dalfin, archbishop of France, from whom also he had received the ecclesiastical tonsure, rightly thought this man's doctrine ought to be preferred before all the traditions of the Scots. For this reason he had also given him a monastery of forty families, at a place called Rhypum;* which place, not long before, he had given to those that followed the system of the Scots for a monastery; but forasmuch as they afterwards, being left to their choice, prepared to quit the place rather than alter their opinion, he gave the place to him, whose life and doctrine were worthy of it.

Agilbert, bishop of the West Saxons,† above-mentioned, a friend to King Alfrid and to Abbat Wilfrid, had at that time come into the province of the Northumbrians, and was making some stay among them; at the request of Alfrid, made Wilfrid a priest in his monastery. He had in his company a priest, whose name was Agatho. The controversy being there started, concerning Easter, or the tonsure, or other ecclesiastical affairs, it was agreed, that a synod should be held in the monastery of Streaneshalch,‡ which signifies the Bay of the Lighthouse, where the Abbess Hilda, a woman devoted to God, then presided; and that there this controversy should be decided. The kings, both father and son, came thither, bishop Colman§ with his Scottish clerks, and Agilbert with the priests Agatho and Wilfrid, James and Romanus were on their side; but the Abbess Hilda and her followers were for the Scots, as was also the venerable Bishop Cedd,‖ long before ordained by the Scots, as has been said above, and he was in that council a most careful interpreter for both parties.

King Oswy first observed, that it behoved those who served one God to observe the same rule of life; and as they all expected the same kingdom in heaven, so they ought not to differ in the celebration of the Divine mysteries; but rather to inquire which was the truest tradition, that the same might be followed by all; he then commanded his bishop, Colman, first to declare what the custom was which he observed, and whence it derived its origin. Then Colman said, "The Easter which I keep, I received from my elders, who sent me bishop hither; all our forefathers, men beloved of God, are known to have kept it after the same manner; and that

---

* Ripon.   † His see was at Dorchester, near Oxford.
‡ Afterwards called Whitby.   § Third bishop of Lindisfarne.
‖ Bishop of London, or East Saxons.

the same may not seem to any contemptible or worthy to be
rejected, it is the same which St. John the Evangelist, the
disciple beloved of our Lord, with all the churches over
which he presided, is recorded to have observed." Having
said thus much, and more to the like effect, the king commanded Agilbert to show whence his custom of keeping
Easter was derived, or on what authority it was grounded.
Agilbert answered, "I desire that my disciple, the priest
Wilfrid, may speak in my stead; because we both concur
with the other followers of the ecclesiastical tradition that
are here present, and he can better explain our opinion in the
English language, than I can by an interpreter."

Then Wilfrid, being ordered by the king to speak,
delivered himself thus:—"The Easter which we observe,
we saw celebrated by all at Rome, where the blessed apostles,
Peter and Paul, lived, taught, suffered, and were buried; we
saw the same done in Italy and in France, when we travelled
through those countries for pilgrimage and prayer. We
found the same practised in Africa, Asia, Egypt, Greece, and
all the world, wherever the church of Christ is spread abroad,
through several nations and tongues, at one and the same
time; except only these and their accomplices in obstinacy,
I mean the Picts and the Britons, who foolishly, in these two
remote islands of the world, and only in part even of them,
oppose all the rest of the universe." When he had so said,
Colman answered, "It is strange that you will call our
labours foolish, wherein we follow the example of so great
an apostle, who was thought worthy to lay his head on our
Lord's bosom, when all the world knows him to have lived
most wisely." Wilfrid replied, "Far be it from us to charge
John with folly, for he literally observed the precepts of the
Jewish law, whilst the church still Judaized in many points,
and the apostles were not able at once to cast off all the
observances of the law which had been instituted by God.
In which way it is necessary that all who come to the faith
should forsake the idols which were invented by devils, that
they might not give scandal to the Jews that were among
the Gentiles. For this reason it was, that Paul circumcised
Timothy, that he offered sacrifice in the temple, that he
shaved his head with Aquila and Priscilla at Corinth; for
no other advantage than to avoid giving scandal to the Jews.

Hence it was, that James said, to the same Pául, ' You see, brother, how many thousands of the Jews have believed; and they are all zealous for the law. And yet, at this time, the Gospel spreading throughout the world, it is needless, nay, it is not lawful, for the faithful either to be circumcised, or to offer up to God sacrifices of flesh.' So John, pursuant to the custom of the law, began the celebration of the feast of Easter, on the fourteenth day of the first month, in the evening, not regarding whether the same happened on a Saturday, or any other day. But when Peter preached at Rome, being mindful that our Lord arose from the dead, and gave the world the hopes of resurrection, on the first day after the Sabbath, he understood that Easter ought to be observed, so as always to stay till the rising of the moon on the fourteenth day of the first moon, in the evening, according to the custom and precepts of the law, even as John did. And when that came, if the Lord's day, then called the first day after the Sabbath, was the next day, he began that very evening to keep Easter, as we all do at this day.* But if the Lord's day did not fall the next morning after the fourteenth moon, but on the sixteenth, or the seventeenth, or any other moon till the twenty-first, he waited for that, and on the Saturday before, in the evening, began to observe the holy solemnity of Easter. Thus it came to pass, that Easter Sunday was only kept from the fifteenth moon to the twenty-first. Nor does this evangelical and apostolic tradition abolish the law, but rather fulfil it ; the command being to keep the passover from the fourteenth moon of the first month in the evening to the twenty-first moon of the same month in the evening ; which observance all the successors of St. John in Asia, since his death, and all the church throughout the world, have since followed ; and that this is the true Easter, and the only one to be kept by the faithful, was not newly decreed by the council of Nice, but only confirmed afresh ; as the Church History informs us.

"Thus it appears, that you, Colman, neither follow the example of John, as you imagine, nor that of Peter, whose traditions you knowingly contradict ; and that you neither

* A complete and rather diffuse explanation of the controversy concerning Easter has been lately written by Professor De Morgan, of University College, London.

agree with the law nor the Gospel in the keeping of your Easter. For John, keeping the Paschal time according to the decree of the Mosaic law, had no regard to the first day after the Sabbath, which you do not practise, who celebrate Easter only on the first day after the Sabbath. Peter kept Easter Sunday between the fifteenth and the twenty-first moon, which you do not, but keep Easter Sunday from the fourteenth to the twentieth moon ; so that you often begin Easter on the thirteenth moon in the evening, whereof neither the law made any mention, nor did our Lord, the Author and Giver of the Gospel, on that day, but on the fourteenth, either eat the old passover in the evening, or deliver the sacraments of the New Testament, to be celebrated by the church, in memory of his passion. Besides, in your celebration of Easter, you utterly exclude the twenty-first moon, which the law ordered to be principally observed. Thus, as I said before, you agree neither with John nor Peter, nor with the law, nor the Gospel, in the celebration of the greatest festival."

To this Colman rejoined: "Did Anatolius, a holy man, and much commended in church history, act contrary to the law and the Gospel, when he wrote, that Easter was to be celebrated from the fourteenth to the twentieth ? Is it to be believed that our most reverend Father Columba and his successors, men beloved by God, who kept Easter after the same manner, thought or acted contrary to the Divine writings ? Whereas there were many among them, whose sanctity is testified by heavenly signs and the working of miracles, whose life, customs, and discipline I never cease to follow, not questioning their being saints in heaven."

"It is evident," said Wilfrid, "that Anatolius was a most holy, learned, and commendable man ; but what have you to do with him, since you do not observe his decrees ? For he, following the rule of truth in his Easter, appointed a revolution of nineteen years, which either you are ignorant of, or if you know it, though it is kept by the whole church of Christ, yet you despise it. He so computed the fourteenth moon in the Easter of our Lord, that according to the custom of the Egyptians, he acknowledged it to be the fifteenth moon in the evening ; so in like manner he assigned the twentieth to Easter-Sunday, as believing that to be the twenty-first moon, when the sun had set, which rule and distinction of his it appears you are ignorant of, in that you sometimes keep Easter before the full of the moon, that is, on the thirteenth day.   Concerning your Father Columba and his followers, whose sanctity you say you imitate, and whose rules and precepts you observe, which have been confirmed by signs from heaven, I may answer, that when many, on the day of judgment, shall say to our Lord, 'That in his name they prophesied, and cast out devils, and wrought many wonders,' our Lord will reply, 'That he never knew them.'   But far be it from me, that I say so of your fathers, because it is much more just to believe what is good, than what is evil, of persons whom one does not know.   Wherefore I do not deny those to have been God's servants, and beloved by him, who with rustic simplicity, but pious intentions, have themselves loved him.   Nor do I think that such keeping of Easter was very prejudicial to them, as long as none came to show them a more perfect rule ; and yet I do believe that they, if any catholic adviser had come among them, would have as readily followed his admonitions, as they are known to have kept those commandments of God, which they had learned and knew.

"But as for you and your companions, you certainly sin, if, having heard the decrees of the Apostolic See, and of the universal church, and that the same is confirmed by holy writ, you refuse to follow them ; for, though your fathers were holy, do you think that their small number, in a corner of the remotest island, is to be preferred before the universal church of Christ throughout the world ?   And if that Columba of yours, (and, I may say, ours also, if he was Christ's servant,) was a holy man and powerful in miracles, yet could he be preferred before the most blessed prince of the apostles, to whom our Lord said, 'Thou art Peter, and upon this rock I will build my church, and the gates of hell shall not prevail against it, and to thee I will give the keys of the kingdom of heaven ?'"

When Wilfrid had spoken thus, the king said, "Is it true, Colman, that these words were spoken to Peter by our Lord?"   He answered, "It is true, O king!"   Then says he, "Can you show any such power given to your Columba?"   Colman answered, "None."   Then added the king, "Do you both agree that these words were principally directed to Peter, and that the keys of heaven were given to him by our Lord?" They both answered, "We do." Then the king concluded, "And I also say unto you, that he is the door-keeper, whom I will not contradict, but will, as far as I know and am able, in all things obey his decrees, lest, when I come to the gates of the kingdom of heaven, there should be none to open them, he being my adversary who is proved to have the keys." The king having said this, all present, both great and small, gave their assent, and renouncing the more imperfect institution, resolved to conform to that which they found to be better.

CHAP. XXVI.

Colman, being worsted, returned home; Tuda succeeded him in the bishopric; the state of the church under those teachers. [A.D. 664.]

THE disputation being ended, and the company broken up, Agilbert returned home. Colman, perceiving that his doctrine was rejected, and his sect despised, took with him such as would not comply with the Catholic Easter and the tonsure,* (for there was much controversy about that also,) and went back into Scotland, to consult with his people what was to be done in this case. Cedd, forsaking the practices of the Scots, returned to his bishopric, having submitted to the Catholic observance of Easter. This disputation happened in the year of our Lord's incarnation 664, which was the twenty-second year of the reign of King Oswy, and the thirtieth of the episcopacy of the Scots among the English; for Aidan was bishop seventeen years, Finan ten, and Colman three.

* The tonsure, properly so called, does not appear to have been adopted for the first three centuries of the church; but originated with the earliest professors of the monastic institutions as a distinctive token of their renunciation of the pleasures of the world. Towards the close of the fifth century it began to be considered, both in the Greek and Latin churches, as a necessary rite for admission into the clerical office; but who were the originators of the circular and semicircular modes is not known. The Roman clergy shaved the crown of the head, which was surrounded by a circle of hair, supposed to represent the wreath of thorns forced by the cruelty of his persecutors on the temples of the Messiah, and which they pleaded had descended to them from St. Peter. The Scottish priests permitted the hair to grow on the back, and shaved the forepart of the head from ear to ear in the form of a crescent, which their opponents called in derision, the tonsure of Simon Magus.

When Colman was gone back into his own country, God's servant, Tuda, was made bishop of the Northumbrians* in his place, having been instructed and ordained bishop among the Southern Scots, having also the ecclesiastical tonsure of his crown, according to the custom of that province, and observing the Catholic time of Easter. He was a good and religious man, but governed his church a very short time; he came out of Scotland whilst Colman was yet bishop, and, both by word and example, diligently taught all. persons those things that appertain to the faith and truth. But Eata, who was abbat of the monastery of Melrose,† a most reverend and meek man, was appointed abbat over the brethren that stayed in the church of Lindisfarne, when the Scots went away; they say, Colman, upon his departure, requested and obtained this of King Oswy, because Eata was one of Aidan's twelve boys of the English nation, whom he received when first made bishop there, to be instructed in Christ; for the king much loved Bishop Colman on account of his singular discretion. This is the same Eata, who, not long after, was made bishop of the same church of Lindisfarne. Colman carried home with him part of the bones of the most reverend Father Aidan, and left part of them in the church where he had presided, ordering them to be interred in the sacristy.

The place which he governed shows how frugal he and his predecessors were, for there were very few houses besides the church found at their departure; indeed, no more than were barely sufficient for their daily residence; they had also no money, but cattle; for if they received any money from rich persons, they immediately gave it to the poor; there being no need to gather money, or provide houses for the entertainment of the great men of the world; for such never resorted to the church, except to pray and hear the word of God. The king himself, when opportunity offered, came only with five or six servants, and having performed his devotions in the church, departed. But if they happened to take a repast there, they were satisfied with only the plain and daily food of the brethren, and required

* Fourth bishop of Lindisfarne. He was the last of the Scottish bishops, as they are termed, who had the government of this see.

† Near Jedburgh, Roxburghshire.

M

no more; for the whole care of those teachers was to serve God, not the world—to feed the soul, and not the belly.

For this reason the religious habit was at that time in great veneration; so that wheresoever any clergyman or monk happened to come, he was joyfully received by all persons, as God's servant; and if they chanced to meet him upon the way, they ran to him, and bowing, were glad to be signed with his hand, or blessed with his mouth. Great attention was also paid to their exhortations; and on Sundays they flocked eagerly to the church, or the monasteries, not to feed their bodies, but to hear the word of God; and if any priest happened to come into a village, the inhabitants flocked together to hear from him the word of life; for the priests and clergymen went into the village on no other account than to preach, baptize, visit the sick, and, in few words, to take care of souls; and they were so free from worldly avarice, that none of them received lands and possessions for building monasteries, unless they were compelled to do so by the temporal authorities; which custom was for some time after observed in all the churches of the Northumbrians. But enough has now been said on this subject.

CHAP. XXVII.

Egbert, a holy man of the English nation, led a monastic life in Ireland.
[A.D. 664.]

IN the same year of our Lord's incarnation, 664, there happened an eclipse of the sun, on the third of May, about ten o'clock in the morning. In the same year, a sudden pestilence* also depopulated the southern coasts of Britain, and afterwards extending into the province of the Northumbrians, ravaged the country far and near, and destroyed a great multitude of men. To which plague the aforesaid priest Tuda fell a victim, and was honourably buried in the monastery of Pegnaleth.† This pestilence did no less harm in the island of Ireland. Many of the nobility, and of the lower ranks of

* Called the Yellow Plague.
† In the Saxon Chronicle, it is called Wagele. Probably Finchale, in the parish of St. Oswald's, on the Western bank of the Wear, near Durham.

the English nation, were there at that time, who, in the days of the Bishops Finan and Colman, forsaking their native island, retired thither, either for the sake of Divine studies, or of a more continent life ; and some of them presently devoted themselves to a monastical life, others chose rather to apply themselves to study, going about from one master's cell to another. The Scots willingly received them all, and took care to supply them with food, as also to furnish them with books to read, and their teaching, gratis.[*]

Among these were Ethelhun and Egbert, two youths of great capacity, of the English nobility. The former of whom was brother to Ethelwin, a man no less beloved by God, who also afterwards went over into Ireland to study, and having been well instructed, returned into his own country, and being made bishop in the province of Lindsey,[†] long governed that church worthily and creditably. These two being in the monastery which in the language of the Scots is called Rathmelsigi,[‡] and having lost all their companions, who were either cut off by the mortality, or dispersed into other places, fell both desperately sick of the same distemper, and were grievously afflicted. Of these, Egbert,[§] (as I was informed by a priest venerable for his age, and of great veracity, who declared he had heard those things from his own mouth,) concluding that he was at the point of death, went out of his chamber, where the sick lay, in the morning, and sitting alone in a convenient place, began seriously to reflect upon his past actions, and, being full of compunction at the remembrance of his sins, bedewed his face with tears, and prayed fervently to God that he might not die yet, before he could make amends for the offences which he had committed in his infancy and younger years, or might further exercise himself in good works. He also made a vow that he would, for the sake of God, live in a strange place, so as never to return into the island of Britain, where he was born ; that besides the canonical times of singing psalms, he would, unless prevented by corporeal infirmity,

[*] The reader, who has heard much of the early civilization of Ireland, will remember that the description given in the text applies to a period no earlier than the seventh century.

[†] Sidnacester, probably between Lincoln and Gainsborough. See pages 99 and 127.   [‡] Now Melfont, Ireland.

[§] Appointed abbat of Iona, A.D. 716. See book v. c. 22.

M 2

say the whole Psalter daily to the praise of God; and that he would every week fast one whole day and a night. Returning home, after his tears, prayers, and vows, he found his companion asleep, and going to bed himself, began to compose himself to rest. When he had lain quiet awhile, his comrade awaking, looked on him, and said, "Alas! Brother Egbert, what have you done? I was in hopes that we should have entered together into life everlasting; but know that what you prayed for is granted." For he had learned in a vision what the other had requested, and that his prayer was granted.

In short, Ethelhun died the next night; but Egbert, shaking off his distemper, recovered and lived a long time after to grace the priestly office, which he had received, by his worthy behaviour; and after much increase of virtue, according to his desire, he at length, in the year of our Lord's incarnation 729, being ninety years of age, departed to the heavenly kingdom. He led his life in great perfection of humility, meekness, continence, simplicity, and justice. Thus he was a great benefactor, both to his own nation, and to those of the Scots and Picts among whom he lived a stranger, by his example of life, his industry in teaching, his authority in reproving, and his piety in giving away much of what he received from the bounty of the rich. He also added this to his vow above-mentioned; during Lent, he would eat but one meal a day, allowing himself nothing but bread and thin milk, and even that by measure. That milk, new the day before, he kept in a vessel, and the next day skimming off the cream, drank the rest, as has been said, with a little bread. Which sort of abstinence he likewise always observed forty days before the nativity of our Lord, and as many after the solemnity of Pentecost, that is, of the Quinquagesima.

CHAP. XXVIII.

Tuda being dead, Wilfrid was ordained, in France, and Chad, in the province of the West Saxons, to be bishops of the Northumbrians. [A.D. 665.]

IN the meantime, King Alfrid* sent the priest, Wilfrid, to the king of France,† to be consecrated bishop over him and

---

* King of Deira.   † Cloitaire, king of Neustria.

his people. That prince sent him to be ordained by Agilbert, who, as was said above, having left Britain, was made bishop of the city of Paris, and by him Wilfrid was honourably consecrated, several bishops meeting together for that purpose in a village belonging to the king, called Compiegne.* He made some stay in the parts beyond the sea, after his consecration, and Oswy, following the example of the king his son, sent a holy man, of modest behaviour, well read in the Scripture, and diligently practising those things which he had learned therein, to be ordained bishop of the church of York. This was a priest called Ceadda [Chad], brother to the reverend prelate Cedd, of whom mention has been often made, and abbat of the monastery of Lestingau.† With him the king also sent his priest Eadhed, who was afterwards, in the reign of Egfrid, made bishop of the church of Ripon. On arriving in Kent, they found that Archbishop Deusdedit was departed this life, and no other prelate as yet appointed in his place; whereupon they proceeded to the province of the West Saxons, where Wini was bishop, and by him the person above-mentioned was consecrated bishop; two bishops of the British nation, who kept Easter Sunday according to the canonical manner, from the fourteenth to the twentieth day of the moon, as has been said, being taken to assist at the ordination; for at that time there was no other bishop in all Britain canonically ordained, besides that Wini.‡

Chad, being thus consecrated bishop, began immediately to devote himself to ecclesiastical truth and to chastity; to apply himself to humility, continence, and study; to travel about, not on horseback, but after the manner of the apostles, on foot, to preach the Gospel in towns, the open country, cottages, villages, and castles; for he was one of the disciples of Aidan, and endeavoured to instruct his people, by the same actions and behaviour, according to his and his

---

* A royal villa. According to the ceremonial of the Gallican church, Wilfrid was carried in a golden chair by his brother bishops, singing hymns of joy; none but bishops being allowed to touch the chair.

† Lastingham. See book iii. c. 23, page 149.

‡ Theodore, archbishop of Canterbury, expressing some doubts of the validity of St. Chad's consecration, subsequently completed it, when he was appointed to the see of Lichfield. See book iv. c. 2, page 173.

brother Cedd's example. Wilfrid also being made a bishop, came into Britain, and in like manner by his doctrine brought into the English Church many rules of Catholic observance. Whence it followed, that the Catholic institutions daily gained strength, and all the Scots that dwelt in England either conformed to these, or returned into their own country.

CHAP. XXIX.

How the priest Wighard was sent from Britain to Rome, to be consecrated archbishop, of his death there, and of the letters of the Apostolic Pope giving an account thereof. [A.D. 665.]

AT this time the most noble King Oswy, of the province of the Northumbrians, and Egbert of Kent, having consulted together about the state of the English Church, (for Oswy, though educated by the Scots, perfectly understood that the Roman was the Catholic and Apostolic Church,) with the consent of the holy church of the English nation, accepted of a good man, and fit priest, to be made a bishop, called Wighard, one of Bishop Deusdedit's clergy, and sent him to Rome to be ordained bishop, to the end that he, having received the degree of an archbishop, might ordain Catholic prelates for the churches of the English nation throughout all Britain. But Wighard, arriving at Rome, was cut off by death, before he could be consecrated bishop, and the following letter was sent back into Britain to King Oswy :—

"*To the most excellent Lord, our son, Oswy, king of the Saxons, Vitalian, bishop, servant of the servants of God.* We have received your excellency's pleasing letters ; by reading whereof we understand your most pious devotion and fervent love to obtain everlasting life ; and that by the protecting hand of God you have been converted to the true and apostolic faith, hoping that as you reign in your nation, so you will hereafter reign in Christ. Blessed be the nation, therefore, that has been found worthy to have such a wise king and worshipper of God ; forasmuch as he is not himself alone a worshipper of God, but also studies day and night the conversion of all his subjects to the Catholic and apostolic faith, to the redemption of his own soul. Who will not

rejoice at hearing such pleasant things? Who will not be
delighted at such good works? Because your nation has
believed in Christ the Almighty God, according to the words
of the Divine prophets, as it is written in Isaiah, 'In that
day there shall be a root of Jesse, which shall stand for an
ensign of the people; to him shall the Gentiles seek.' And
again, 'Listen, O isles, unto me, and hearken ye people from
afar.' And a little after, 'It is a light thing that thou
shouldst be my servant to raise up the tribes of Jacob, and
to restore the preserved of Israel. I will also give thee for
a light to the Gentiles, that thou mayest be my salvation to
the ends of the earth.' And again, 'Kings shall see, princes
also shall arise and worship.' And presently after, 'I have
given thee for a covenant of the people, to establish the
earth, and possess the desolate heritages; that thou mayest
say to the prisoners, Go forth; to them that are in darkness,
Show yourselves.' And again, 'I the Lord have called thee
in righteousness, and will hold thine hand, and will keep
thee, and give thee for a light of the Gentiles, and for a
covenant of the people; to open the blind eyes, to bring out
the prisoner from the prison, and them that sit in darkness
from the prison-house.'

"Behold, most excellent son, how plain it is, not only of
you, but also of all the nations of the prophets, that they
shall believe in Christ, the Creator of all things. Wherefore it behoves your highness, as being a member of Christ,
in all things, continually to follow the pious rule of the
prince of the apostles, in celebrating Easter, and in all
things delivered by the blessed apostles, Peter and Paul,
whose doctrine daily enlightens the hearts of believers, even
as the two heavenly lights, the sun and moon, daily illumine
all the earth."

And after some lines, wherein he speaks of celebrating
Easter uniformly throughout all the world, he adds,—

"We have not been able now to find, considering the length
of the journey, a man, docile, and qualified in all respects to
be a bishop, according to the tenor of your letters. But as
soon as such a proper person shall be found, we will send
him well instructed to your country, that he may, by word
of mouth, and through the Divine oracles, with the assistance of God, root out all the enemy's tares throughout your

island. We have received the presents sent by your highness to the blessed prince of the apostles, for an eternal memorial, and return you thanks, and always pray for your
safety with the clergy of Christ. But he that brought
these presents has been removed out of this world, and is
buried at the church of the apostles, for whom we have been
much concerned, because he died here. However, we have
ordered the blessed gifts of the holy martyrs, that is, the
relics of the blessed apostles, Peter and Paul, and of the holy
martyrs, Laurentius, John, and Paul, and Gregory, and Pan-
cratius,* to be delivered to the bearers of these our letters,
to be by them delivered to you. And to your consort also,
our spiritual daughter, we have by the aforesaid bearers sent
a cross, with a gold key to it, made out of the most holy
chains of the apostles, Peter and Paul; at whose pious
endeavours all the Apostolic See rejoices with us, as much as
her pious works shine and blossom before God.

"We therefore desire your highness will hasten, according
to our wish, to dedicate all your island to Christ our God;
for you certainly have for your protector, the Redeemer of
mankind, our Lord Jesus Christ, who will prosper you in all
things, that you may bring together a new people of Christ;
establishing there the Catholic and apostolic faith. For it is
written, 'Seek first the kingdom of God and his righteousness, and all these things shall be added to you.' Truly
your highness seeks, and shall no doubt obtain, that all your
islands shall be made subject to you, as is our wish and
desire. Saluting your excellency with fatherly affection, we
always pray to the Divine Goodness, that it will vouchsafe
to assist you and yours in all good works, that you may reign
with Christ in the world to come. May the Heavenly Grace
preserve your excellency in safety!"

In the next book we shall have a more suitable occasion
to show who was found out and consecrated in Wighard's
place.

---

* St. Pancras, who suffered martyrdom during the Diocletian persecution, A.D. 304.

CHAP. XXX.

*The East Saxons, during a pestilence, returning to idolatry, are imme-
diately brought back from their error by the Bishop Jaruman.*
[A.D. 665.]

AT the same time, the Kings Sighere and Sebbi, though
subject to Wulfhere, king of the Mercians, governed the
province of the East Saxons* after Suidhelm, of whom we
have spoken above. That province labouring under the
aforesaid mortality, Sighere, with that part of the people that
was under his dominion, forsook the mysteries of the Christian faith, and turned apostate. For the king himself, and
many of the commons and great men, being fond of this life,
and not seeking after another, or rather not believing that
there was any other, began to restore the temples that had
been abandoned, and to adore idols, as if they might by those
means be protected against the mortality. But Sebbi, his
companion and co-heir in the kingdom, with his people, very
devoutly preserved the faith which he had embraced, and, as
we shall show hereafter, ended his faithful life with much
felicity.

King Wulfhere, understanding that the faith of the province was partly profaned, sent Bishop Jaruman,† who was
successor to Trumhere, to correct that error, and restore the
province to the truth. He proceeded with much discretion,
(as I was informed by a priest who bore him company in
that journey, and had been his fellow labourer in the word)
for he was a religious and good man, and travelling through
all the country, far and near, reduced both the aforesaid king
and people to the way of righteousness, so that, either forsaking or destroying the temples and altars which they had
erected, they opened the churches, and rejoiced in confessing
the name of Christ, which they had opposed, being more
desirous to die in him with the faith of the resurrection, than
to live in the filth of apostacy among their idols. These
things being performed, the priests and teachers returned
home with joy.

* Each ruled over a separate part of the East Saxons, under the supremacy of Mercia.   † Bishop of Lichfield. See page 153.

BOOK IV.

CHAPTER I.

Deusdedit, archbishop of Canterbury, dying, Wighard was sent to Rome to succeed him in that dignity; but he dying there, Theodore was ordained archbishop, and sent into Britain with the Abbat Hadrian. [A.D. 664.]

In the above-mentioned year of the aforesaid eclipse, which was presently followed by the pestilence, in which also Bishop Colman, being overcome by the unanimous consent of the Catholics, returned home, Deusdedit, the sixth bishop of the church of Canterbury, died on the 14th of July. Erconbert, also, king of Kent, departed this life the same month and day; leaving his kingdom to his son Egbert, which he held nine years. The see then became vacant for some considerable time, until, the priest Wighard, a man skilled in ecclesiastical discipline, of the English race, was sent to Rome by the said King Egbert, and Oswy, king of the Northumbrians, as was briefly mentioned in the foregoing book, with a request that he might be ordained bishop of the church of England; sending at the same time presents to the apostolic pope, and many vessels of gold and silver. Arriving at Rome, where Vitalian presided at that time over the Apostolic See, and having made known to the aforesaid pope the occasion of his journey, he was not long after snatched away, with almost all his companions that went with him, by a pestilence which happened at that time.

But the apostolic pope having consulted about that affair, made diligent inquiry for some one to send to be archbishop of the English churches. There was then in the Niridian monastery, which is not far from the city of Naples in Campania, an abbat, called Hadrian, by nation an African, well versed in holy writ, experienced in monastical and ecclesiastical discipline, and excellently skilled both in the Greek and and Latin tongues. The pope, sending for him, commanded him to accept of the bishopric, and repair into Britain; he answered, that he was unworthy of so great a dignity, but said he could name another, whose learning and age were fitter for the episcopal office. And having proposed to the

pope a certain monk, belonging to a neighbouring monastery
of virgins, whose name was Andrew, he was by all that knew
him judged worthy of a bishopric; but bodily infirmity prevented his being advanced to the episcopal station. Then
again Hadrian was pressed to accept of the bishopric; but he
desired a respite for a time, to see whether he could find
another fit to be ordained bishop.

There was at that time in Rome, a monk, called Theodore,
well known to Hadrian, born at Tarsus in Cilicia, a man well
instructed in worldly and Divine literature, as also in Greek
and Latin;* of known probity of life, and venerable for age,
being sixty-six years old. Hadrian offered him to the pope
to be ordained bishop, and prevailed; but upon these conditions, that he should conduct him into Britain, because he
had already travelled through France twice upon several
occasions, and was, therefore, better acquainted with the way,
and was, moreover, sufficiently provided with men of his
own; as also that being his fellow labourer in doctrine, he
might take special care that Theodore should not, according
to the custom of the Greeks, introduce any thing contrary to
the true faith into the church where he presided. Hadrian,
being ordained subdeacon, waited four months for his hair to
grow, that it might be shorn into the shape of a crown; for
he had before the tonsure of St. Paul,† the apostle, after the
manner of the eastern people. He was ordained by Pope
Vitalian, in the year of our Lord 668, on Sunday, the 26th
of March, and on the 27th of May was sent with Hadrian
into Britain.

They proceeded by sea to Marseilles, and thence by land
to Arles, and having there delivered to John, archbishop of
that city, Pope Vitalian's letters of recommendation, were
by him detained till Ebrin, the king's mayor of the palace,
sent them a pass to go where they pleased. Having received
the same, Theodore repaired to Agilbert, bishop of Paris, of
whom we have spoken above, and was by him kindly received, and long entertained. But Hadrian went first to
Emme, and then to Faro, bishops of Sens and Meaux, and
lived with them a considerable time; for the hard winter

---

* Hadrian is termed by William of Malmsbury, "a fountain of letters
and a river of arts."   † This tonsure consisted in shaving the whole head.

had obliged them to rest wherever they could. King Egbert, being informed by messengers that the bishop they had asked of the Roman prelate was in the kingdom of France, sent thither his præfect, Redfrid, to conduct him; who, being arrived there, with Ebrin's leave, conveyed him to the port of Quentavic ;* where, being indisposed, he made some stay, and as soon as he began to recover, sailed over into Britain. But Ebrin detained Hadrian, suspecting that he went on some message from the emperor to the kings of Britain, to the prejudice of the kingdom, of which he at that time took especial care; however, when he found that he really had no such commission, he discharged him, and permitted him to follow Theodore. As soon as he came, he received from him the monastery of St. Peter the apostle,† where the archbishops of Canterbury are usually buried, as I have said before; for at his departure, the apostolic lord had ordered that he should provide for him in his diocese, and give him a suitable place to live in with his followers.

CHAP. II.

Theodore visits all places; the churches of the English begin to be instructed in holy literature, and in the Catholic truth; Putta is made bishop of the church of Rochester in the room of Damianus. [A.D. 669.]

THEODORE arrived at his church the second year after his consecration, on Sunday, the 27th of May, and held the same twenty-one years, three months, and twenty-six days. Soon after, he visited all the island, wherever the tribes of the Angles inhabited, for he was willingly entertained and heard by all persons; and everywhere attended and assisted by Hadrian, he taught the right rule of life, and the canonical custom of celebrating Easter. This was the first archbishop whom all the English church obeyed. And forasmuch as both of them were, as has been said before, well read both in sacred and in secular literature, they gathered a crowd of disciples, and there daily flowed from them rivers of knowledge to water the hearts of their hearers; and, together with the books of holy writ, they also taught them the arts of ecclesiastical poetry, astronomy, and arithmetic. A testi-

* St. Quentin, province of Picardy.
† Afterwards called St. Augustine's. This was, for some time after, the most distinguished seat of learning in the south of England. See p. 60.

mony of which is, that there are still living at this day some
of their scholars, who are as well versed in the Greek and
Latin tongues as in their own, in which they were born.
Nor were there ever happier times since the English came
into Britain; for their kings, being brave men and good
Christians, they were a terror to all barbarous nations, and
the minds of all men were bent upon the joys of the heavenly
kingdom of which they had just heard; and all who desired
to be instructed in sacred reading had masters at hand to
teach them.

From that time also they began in all the churches of the
English to learn sacred music, which till then had been
only known in Kent. And, excepting James above-mentioned, the first singing-master in the churches of the Northumbrians was Eddi, surnamed Stephen,* invited from
Kent by the most reverend Wilfrid, who was the first of the
bishops of the English nation that taught the churches of
the English the Catholic mode of life.

Theodore, visiting all parts, ordained bishops in proper
places, and with their assistance corrected such things as he
found faulty. Among the rest, when he upbraided Bishop
Chad that he had not been duly consecrated, he, with great
humility, answered, "If you know I have not duly received
episcopal ordination, I willingly resign the office, for I never
thought myself worthy of it; but, though unworthy, in
obedience submitted to undertake it." Theodore, hearing
his humble answer, said that he should not resign the bishopric, and he himself completed his ordination after the Catholic manner. But at the time when Deusdedit died, and a
bishop for the church of Canterbury was by request ordained
and sent, Wilfrid was also sent out of Britain into France to
be ordained; and because he returned before Theodore, he
ordained priests and deacons in Kent till the archbishop
should come to his see. Being arrived in the city of Rochester, where the see had been long vacant† by the death
of Damianus, he ordained a person better skilled in ecclesiastical discipline, and more addicted to simplicity of life than
active in worldly affairs. His name was Putta, and he was
extraordinarily skilful in the Roman style of church music,

* Author of the Life of Wilfrid, published in Gale's collection of Scrip-
tores, vol. i. p. 40.　　　† It had been vacant five years.

which he had learned from the disciples of the holy Pope
Gregory.

CHAP. III.

*How Chad, above-mentioned, was made Bishop of the Mercians. Of his
life, death, and burial.* [A.D. 669.]

AT that time, the Mercians were governed by King Wulfhere, who, on the death of Jaruman, desired of Theodore to
supply him and his people with a bishop; but Theodore
would not obtain a new one for them, but requested of King
Oswy that Chad might be their bishop. He then lived
retired at his monastery, which is at Lestingau, Wilfrid
filling the bishopric of York, and of all the Northumbrians,
and likewise of the Picts, as far as the dominions of King
Oswy extended. And, seeing that it was the custom of that
most reverend prelate to go about the work of the Gospel to
several places rather on foot than on horseback, Theodore
commanded him to ride whenever he had a long journey to
undertake; and finding him very unwilling to omit his former pious labour, he himself, with his hands, lifted him on
the horse; for he thought him a holy man, and therefore
obliged him to ride wherever he had need to go. Chad
having received the bishopric of the Mercians and Lindisfarne,* took care to administer the same with great rectitude
of life, according to the example of the ancients. King
Wulfhere also gave him land of fifty families, to build a
monastery, at the place called Ad Barve,† or "At the
Wood," in the province of Lindsey, wherein marks of the
regular life instituted by him continue to this day.

He had his episcopal see in the place called Lichfield,‡

* A diocese not much less in extent than the Northumbrian kingdom,
having all the counties which compose the midland circuit, and Staffordshire, with part of Shropshire and Cheshire besides.

† Barton-upon-Humber, Lincolnshire, where there is still standing a very
ancient Saxon Church, dedicated to St. Peter.

‡ This place is called by Ingulphus and Henry of Huntingdon, *Lichfeld*,
which means "the field of the dead," from the traditionary martyrdom of
1000 Christians here during the Diocletian persecution. In the reign of
Offa, this see not only obtained the precedence of all the Mercian bishoprics, but, through the interest of Offa with Pope Adrian, was made for a
short time the archi-episcopal see, [A.D. 789,] and invested with the greater
part of the jurisdiction of Canterbury.

in which he also died, and was buried, and where the see of
the succeeding bishops of that province still continues. He
had built himself a habitation not far from the church,
wherein he was wont to pray and read with seven or eight
of the brethren, as often as he had any spare time from the
labour and ministry of the word. When he had most gloriously governed the church in that province two years and
a half, the Divine Providence so ordaining, there came round
a season like that of which Ecclesiastes says, " That there is
a time to cast stones, and a time to gather them ; " for there
happened a mortality sent from heaven, which, by means of
the death of the flesh, translated the stones of the church
from their earthly places to the heavenly building. And
when, after many of the church of that most reverend prelate had been taken out of the flesh, his hour also drew near
wherein he was to pass out of this world to our Lord, it
happened one day that he was in the aforesaid dwelling with
only one brother, called Owini, his other companions being
upon some reasonable occasion returned to the church. Now
Owini was a monk of great merit, having forsaken the world
with the pure intention of obtaining the heavenly reward ;
worthy in all respects to have the secrets of our Lord revealed to him, and worthy to have credit given by his hearers
to what he said, for he came with Queen Etheldrid from the
province of the East Angles, and was her prime minister,
and governor of her family. As the fervour of his faith
increased, resolving to renounce the world, he did not go
about it slothfully, but so fully forsook the things of this
world, that, quitting all he had, clad in a plain garment, and
carrying an axe and hatchet in his hand, he came to the
monastery of that most reverend prelate, called Lestingau ;*
denoting, that he did not go to the monastery to live idle, as
some do, but to labour, which he also confirmed by practice ;
for as he was less capable of meditating on the Holy Scriptures, he the more earnestly applied himself to the labour of
his hands. In short, he was received by the bishop into the
house aforesaid, and there entertained with the brethren, and
whilst they were engaged within in reading, he was without,
doing such things as were necessary.

One day when he was thus employed abroad, and his com-

* Lastingham. See p. 149.

panions were gone to the church, as I began to state, the bishop was alone reading or praying in the oratory of that place, when on a sudden, as he afterwards said, he heard the voice of persons singing most sweetly and rejoicing, and appearing to descend from heaven. Which voice he said he first heard coming from the south-east, and that afterwards it drew near him, till it came to the roof of the oratory where the bishop was, and entering therein, filled the same and all about it. He listened attentively to what he heard, and after about half an hour, perceived the same song of joy to ascend from the roof of the said oratory, and to return to heaven the same way it came, with inexpressible sweetness. When he had stood some time astonished, and seriously revolving in his mind what it might be, the bishop opened the window of the oratory, and making a noise with his hand, as he was often wont to do, ordered him to come in to him. He accordingly went hastily in, and the bishop said to him, "Make haste to the church, and cause the seven brothers to come hither, and do you come with them." When they were come, he first admonished them to preserve the virtue of peace among themselves, and towards all others ; and indefatigably to practise the rules of regular discipline, which they had either been taught by him, or seen him observe, or had noticed in the words or actions of the former fathers. Then he added, that the day of his death was at hand ; for, said he, "that amiable guest, who was wont to visit our brethren, has vouchsafed also to come to me this day, and to call me out of this world. Return, therefore, to the church, and speak to the brethren, that they in their prayers recommend my passage to our Lord, and that they be careful to provide for their own, the hour whereof is uncertain, by watching, prayer, and good works."

When he had spoken thus much and more, and they, having received his blessing, had gone away in sorrow, he who had heard the heavenly song returned alone, and prostrating himself on the ground, said, "I beseech you, father, may I be permitted to ask a question ?"—"Ask what you will," answered the bishop. Then he added, "I entreat you to tell me what song of joy was that which I heard coming upon this oratory, and after some time returning to heaven ?" The bishop answered. "If you heard the singing, and know of the coming of the heavenly company, I command you, in the name of our Lord, that you do not tell the same to any before my death.   They were angelic spirits, who came to call me to my heavenly reward, which I have always longed after, and they promised they would return seven days hence, and take me away with them."   Which was accordingly fulfilled, as had been said to him ; for being presently seized with a languishing distemper, and the same daily increasing, on the seventh day, as had been promised to him, when he had prepared for death by receiving the body and blood of our Lord, his soul being delivered from the prison of the body, the angels, as may justly be believed, attending him, he departed to the joys of heaven.

It is no wonder that he joyfully beheld the day of his death, or rather the day of our Lord, which he had always carefully expected till it came ; for notwithstanding his many merits of continence, humility, teaching, prayer, voluntary poverty, and other virtues, he was so full of the fear of God, so mindful of his last end in all his actions, that, as I was informed by one of the brothers who instructed me in Divinity, and who had been bred in his monastery, and under his direction, whose name was Trumhere, if it happened that there blew a strong gust of wind when he was reading or doing any other thing, he immediately called upon God for mercy, and begged it might be extended to all mankind.   If the wind grew stronger, he closed his book, and prostrating himself on the ground, prayed still more earnestly.   But, if it proved a violent storm of wind or rain, or else that the earth and air were filled with thunder and lightning, he would repair to the church, and devote himself to prayers and repeating of psalms till the weather became calm.   Being asked by his followers why he did so, he answered, "Have not you read—'The Lord also thundered in the heavens, and the Highest gave forth his voice.   Yea, he sent out his arrows and scattered them ; and he shot out lightnings, and discomfited them.'   For the Lord moves the air, raises the winds, darts lightning, and thunders from heaven, to excite the inhabitants of the earth to fear him ; to put them in mind of the future judgment ; to dispel their pride, and vanquish their boldness, by bringing into their thoughts that dreadful time, when the heavens and the earth being in a

N

flame, he will come in the clouds, with great power and majesty, to judge the quick and the dead. Wherefore," said he, "it behoves us to answer his heavenly admonition with due fear and love ; that, as often as he lifts his hand through the trembling sky, as it were to strike, but does not yet let it fall, we may immediately implore his mercy ; and searching the recesses of our hearts, and cleansing the filth of our vices, we may carefully behave ourselves so as never to be struck." *

With this revelation and account of the aforesaid brother, concerning the death of this prelate, agrees the discourse of the most reverend Father Egbert, above spoken of, who long led a monastic life with the same Chad, when both were youths, in Ireland, praying, observing continency, and meditating on the Holy Scriptures. But when he afterwards returned into his own country, the other continued in a strange country for our Lord's sake till the end of his life. A long time after, Hygbald, a most holy and continent man, who was an abbat in the province of Lindsey, came out of Britain to visit him, and whilst these holy men were discoursing of the life of the former fathers, and rejoicing to imitate the same, mention was made of the most reverend prelate, Chad, whereupon Egbert, said, "I know a man in this island, still in the flesh, who, when that prelate passed out of this world, saw the soul of his brother Cedd, with a company of angels, descending from heaven, who, having taken his soul along with them, returned thither again." Whether he said this of himself, or some other, we do not certainly know ; but the same being said by so great a man, there can be no doubt of the truth thereof.

Chad died on the 2nd of March, and was first buried by St. Mary's Church, but afterwards, when the church of the most holy prince of the apostles, Peter, was built, his bones were translated into it.† In both which places, as a testimony of his virtue, frequent miraculous cures are wont to be wrought. And of late, a certain distracted person, who had been wandering about everywhere, arrived there in the evening, unknown or unregarded by the keepers of the

* Jeremy Taylor has some excellent remarks on this pious custom of St. Chad, in his Life of Christ, Discourse xviii.

† In 1148 they were removed to the present Cathedral of Lichfield.

place, and having rested there all the night, went out in his perfect senses the next morning, to the surprise and delight of all ; thus showing that a cure had been performed on him through the goodness of God. The place of the sepulchre is a wooden monument, made like a little house, covered, having a hole in the wall, through which those that go thither for devotion usually put in their hand and take out some of the dust, which they put into water and give to sick cattle or men to drink, upon which they are presently eased of their infirmity, and restored to health. In his place, Theodore ordained Winfrid, a good and modest man, to preside, as his predecessors had done, over the bishoprics of the Mercians, the Midland Angles, and the Lindisfarnes,* of all which, Wulfhere, who was still living, was king. Winfrid was one of the clergy of the prelate he had succeeded, and had for a considerable time filled the office of deacon under him.

CHAP. IV.

Bishop Colman, having left Britain, built two monasteries in Scotland ; the one for the Scots, the other for the English he had taken along with him. [A.D. 667.]

IN the meantime, Colman, the Scottish bishop, departing from Britain, took along with him all the Scots he had assembled in the isle of Lindisfarne, and also about thirty of the English nation, who had been all instructed in the monastic life ; and leaving some brothers in his church, he repaired first to the isle of Hii (Iona), whence he had been sent to preach the word of God to the English nation. Afterwards he retired to a small island, which is to the west of Ireland, and at some distance from its coast, called in the language of the Scots, Inisbofinde,† the Island of the White Heifer. Arriving there, he built a monastery, and placed in it the monks he had brought of both nations ; who not agreeing among themselves, by reason that the Scots, in the summer season, when the harvest was to be brought in,

---

* On the death of Peada, Wulfhere succeeded to the united kingdoms of the Mercians and Middle Angles (see p. 143), which were considered as two distinct kingdoms. The bishopric of the Mercians was fixed at Repton, afterwards removed to Lichfield. See note at page 145.

† A small island on the Irish coast still retaining its ancient name.

leaving the monastery, wandered about through places with
which they were acquainted; but returned again the next
winter, and would have what the English had provided to be
in common; Colman sought to put an end to this dissension,
and travelling about far and near, he found a place in the
island of Ireland fit to build a monastery, which, in the
language of the Scots, is called Mageo,* and bought a small
part of it of the earl to whom it belonged, to build his
monastery thereon; upon condition, that the monks residing
there should pray to our Lord for him who let them have the
place.   Then building a monastery, with the assistance of
the earl and all the neighbours, he placed the English there,
leaving the Scots in the aforesaid island.   This monastery is
to this day possessed by English inhabitants; being the same
that, grown up from a small beginning to be very large, is
generally called Mageo; and as all things have long since
been brought under a better method, it contains an exemplary
society of monks, who are gathered there from the province
of the English, and live by the labour of their hands, after
the example of the venerable fathers, under a rule and a
canonical abbat, in much continency and singleness of life.

CHAP. V.

*Of the death of the kings Oswy and Egbert, and of the synod held at
Hertford, in which Archbishop Theodore presided.* [A. D. 670.]

IN the year of the incarnation of our Lord 670, being the
second year after Theodore arrived in England, Oswy, king
of the Northumbrians, fell sick, and died, in the fifty-eighth
year of his age.†   He at that time bore so great affection to
the Roman apostolical institution, that had he recovered of
his sickness, he had designed to go to Rome, and there to
end his days at the Holy Places, having entreated Bishop Wilfrid, by the promise of a considerable donation in money, to
conduct him on his journey.   He died on the 15th of February, leaving his son Egfrid his successor in the kingdom.
In the third year of his reign, Theodore assembled a synod
of bishops, and many other teachers of the church, who
loved and were acquainted with the canonical statutes of the

---

* Now annexed to the archbishopric of Tuam.
† With Oswy expired the title and the authority of Bretwalda.

fathers. When they were met together, he began, as became
a prelate, to enjoin the observance of such things as were
agreeable to the unity and the peace of the church. The
purport of which synodical proceedings is as follows :—

"In the name of our Lord God and Saviour Jesus Christ,
who reigns for ever and for ever, and governs his church, it
was thought meet that we should assemble, according to the
custom of the venerable canons, to treat about the necessary
affairs of the church. We met on the 24th day of September, the first indiction,* at a place called Hertford, myself,
Theodore, the unworthy bishop of the see of Canterbury,
appointed by the Apostolic See, our fellow priest and most
reverend brother, Bisi, bishop of the East Angles ; also by
his proxies, our brother and fellow priest, Wilfrid, bishop of
the nation of the Northumbrians, as also our brothers and
fellow priests, Putta, bishop of the Kentish castle, called
Rochester ; Eleutherius, bishop of the West Saxons, and
Winfrid, bishop of the province of the Mercians. When
we were all met together, and were sat down in order, I
said, 'I beseech you, most dear brothers, for the love and
fear of our Redeemer, that we may all treat in common for
our faith ; to the end that whatsoever has been decreed and
defined by the holy and reverend fathers, may be inviolably
observed by all.' This and much more I spoke tending to
the preservation of the charity and unity of the church ; and
when I had ended my discourse, I asked every one of them
in order, whether they consented to observe the things that
had been formerly canonically decreed by the fathers ? To
which all our fellow priests answered, 'It so pleases us, and
we will all most willingly observe with a cheerful mind whatever is laid down in the canons of the holy fathers.' I then
produced the said book of canons, and publicly showed them
ten chapters in the same, which I had marked in several
places, because I knew them to be of the most importance
to us, and entreated that they might be most particularly
received by them all.

* We learn from Bede's work, De Temporum Ratione, c. 46, that the
English indiction began on the 24th of September. Now the year 673, or
rather from the 24th of Sept. A.D. 672 to the 24th of Sept. 673, was the
first indiction. It appears therefore that the Synod of Hertford fell on
the last day of the indiction. Perhaps, as Professor Hussey remarks, the
24th of September might be reckoned as belonging to either indiction.

"Chapter I. That we all in common keep the holy day of Easter on the Sunday after the fourteenth moon of the first month.

"II. That no bishop intrude into the diocese of another, but be satisfied with the government of the people committed to him.

"III. That it shall not be lawful for any bishop to trouble monasteries dedicated to God, nor to take anything forcibly from them.

"IV. That monks do not remove from one place to another, that is, from monastery to monastery, unless with the consent of their own abbat; but that they continue in the obedience which they promised at the time of their conversion.

"V. That no clergyman, forsaking his own bishop, shall wander about, or be anywhere entertained without letters of recommendation from his own prelate. But if he shall be once received, and will not return when invited, both the receiver, and the person received, be under excommunication.

"VI. That bishops and clergymen, when travelling, shall be content with the hospitality that is afforded them; and that it be not lawful for them to exercise any priestly function without leave of the bishop in whose diocese they are.

"VII. That a synod be assembled twice a year; but in regard that several causes obstruct the same, it was approved by all, that we should meet on the 1st of August once a year, at the place called Clofeshoch.*

"VIII. That no bishop, through ambition, shall set himself before another; but that they shall all observe the time and order of their consecration.

"IX. It was generally set forth, that more bishops should be made, as the number of believers increased; but this matter for the present was passed over.

"X. Of marriages; that nothing be allowed but lawful wedlock; that none commit incest; no man quit his true wife, unless, as the gospel teaches, on account of fornication. And if any man shall put away his own wife, lawfully joined to him in matrimony, that he take no other, if he wishes to be a good Christian, but continue as he is, or else be reconciled to his own wife.

* Cliff, in Kent, or Abingdon, Berks.

"These chapters being thus treated of and defined by all, to the end, that for the future, no scandal of contention might arise from any of us, or that things be falsely set forth, it was thought fit that every one of us should, by subscribing his hand, confirm all the particulars so laid down. Which definitive judgment of ours, I dictated to be written by Titillus our notary. Done in the month and indiction aforesaid. Whosoever, therefore, shall presume in any way to oppose or infringe this decision, confirmed by our consent, and by the subscription of our hands, according to the decree of the canons, must take notice, that he is excluded from all sacerdotal functions, and from our society. May the Divine Grace preserve us in safety, living in the unity of his holy church."

This synod was held in the year from the incarnation of our Lord 673. In which year, Egbert, king of Kent, died in the month of July; his brother Lothere succeeded him on the throne, which he had held eleven years and seven months. Bisi, the bishop of the East Angles,* who is said to have been in the aforesaid synod, was successor to Boniface, before spoken of, a man of much sanctity and religion; for when Boniface died, after having been bishop seventeen years, he was by Theodore substituted in his place. Whilst he was still alive, but hindered by much sickness from administering his episcopal functions, two bishops, Ecci and Badwin were elected and consecrated in his place; from which time to the present, that province has had two bishops.

CHAP. VI.

Winfrid being deposed, Sexwulf was put into his See, and Earconwald made bishop of the East Saxons. [A.D. 674.]

NOT long after, Theodore, the archbishop, taking offence at some disobedience of Winfrid, bishop of the Mercians,† deposed him from his bishopric when he had been possessed of it but a few years, and in his place made Sexwulf bishop,

* His see was at Dunwich, Suffolk, (see p. 99), and during his life this diocese was divided, Bishop Badwin being placed at North Elmham, and Bishop Ecci at Dunwich. In 955 the two sees were reunited; in 1075 it was removed to Thetford, and finally in 1094 to Norwich.

† Bishop of Lichfield.

who was founder and abbat of the monastery of Medesham-stead,* in the country of the Girvii.   Winfrid, thus deposed, returned to his monastery of Ad Barve,† and there ended his life in holy conversation.

He then also appointed Earconwald bishop of the East Saxons, in the city of London, over whom at that time presided Sebbi and Sighere, of whom mention has been made above.   This Earconwald's life and conversation, as well when he was bishop as before his advancement to that dignity, is reported to have been most holy, as is even at this time testified by heavenly miracles; for to this day, his horse-litter, in which he was wont to be carried when sick, is kept by his disciples, and continues to cure many of agues and other distempers; and not only sick persons who are laid in that litter, or close by it, are cured; but the very chips of it, when carried to the sick, are wont immediately to restore them to health.

This man, before he was made bishop, had built two famous monasteries, the one for himself, and the other for his sister Ethelberga, and established them both in regular discipline of the best kind.   That for himself was in the county of Surrey, by the river Thames, at a place called Ceortesei,‡ that is, the Island of Ceorot; that for his sister in the province of the East Saxons, at the place called Bercingum,§ wherein she might be a mother and nurse of devout women. Being put into the government of that monastery, she behaved herself in all respects as became the sister of such a brother, living herself regularly, and piously, and orderly, providing for those under her, as was also manifested by heavenly miracles.

* The monastery of Medeshamstead, " the home in the meadow," afterwards Burgh St. Peter, now Peterborough, was one of the numerous ecclesiastical foundations scattered over the wide extent of the Fen land, which served as a natural barrier between the kingdoms of East Anglia and Mercia.   Peada, king of Mercia, is agreed to have been the first founder about A.D. 650, and which was completed by Wulfhere.   See Saxon Chron. A.D. 657, and Chronicon Angliæ Petriburgense, 8vo. Londini, 1845, passim.

† See book iv. ch. 3, page 174.   ‡ Chertsey.   § Barking in Essex.

CHAP. VII.

How it was indicated by a heavenly light where the bodies of the Nuns should be buried in the monastery of Barking. [A.D. 676.]

IN this monastery many miracles were wrought, which have been committed to writing by many, from those who knew them, that their memory might be preserved, and following generations edified; some whereof we have also taken care to insert in our Ecclesiastical History. When the mortality, which we have already so often mentioned, ravaging all around, had also seized on that part of this monastery where the men resided, and they were daily hurried away to meet their God, the careful mother of the society began often to inquire in the convent, of the sisters, where they would have their bodies buried, and where a church-yard should be made when the same pestilence should fall upon that part of the monastery in which God's female servants were divided from the men, and they should be snatched away out of this world by the same destruction. Receiving no certain answer, though she often put the question to the sisters, she and all of them received a most certain answer from heaven. For one night, when the morning psalm was ended, and those servants of Christ were gone out of their oratory to the tombs of the brothers who had departed this life before them, and were singing the usual praises to our Lord, on a sudden a light from heaven, like a great sheet, came down upon them all, and struck them with so much terror, that they, in consternation, left off singing. But that resplendent light, which seemed to exceed the sun at noon-day, soon after rising from that place, removed to the south side of the monastery, that is, to the westward of the oratory, and having continued there some time, and covered those parts in the sight of them all, withdrew itself up again to heaven, leaving conviction in the minds of all, that the same light, which was to lead or to receive the souls of those servants of God into heaven, was intended to show the place in which their bodies were to rest, and await the day of the resurrection. This light was so great, that one of the eldest of the brothers, who at the same time was in their oratory with another younger than himself, related in the morning, that the rays

of light which came in at the crannies of the doors and
windows, seemed to exceed the utmost brightness of day-
light itself.

CHAP. VIII.

*A little boy, dying in the same monastery, called upon a virgin that was to
follow him; another at the point of leaving her body, saw some small
part of the future glory.* [A.D. 676.]

THERE was, in the same monastery, a boy, not above three
years old, called Esica; who, by reason of his infant age,
was bred up among the virgins dedicated to God, and there
to pursue his studies.   This child being seized by the aforesaid pestilence, when he was at the last gasp, called three
times upon one of the virgins consecrated to God, directing
his words to her by her own name, as if she had been
present, Eadgith; Eadgith! Eadgith! and thus ending his
temporal life, entered into that which is eternal.   The virgin,
whom he called, was immediately seized, where she was, with
the same distemper, and departing this life the same day on
which she had been called, followed him that called her into
the heavenly country.

Likewise, one of those same servants of God, being ill of
the same disease, and reduced to extremity, began on a sudden, about midnight, to cry out to them that attended her,
desiring they would put out the candle that was lighted
there; which, when she had often repeated, and yet no one
did it, at last she said, "I know you think I speak this in
a raving fit, but let me inform you it is not so; for I tell you,
that I see this house filled with so much light, that your
candle there seems to me to be dark."   And when still no
one regarded what she said, or returned any answer, she
added, "Let that candle burn as long as you will; but take
notice, that it is not my light, for my light will come to me
at the dawn of the day."   Then she began to tell, that a
certain man of God, who had died that same year, had
appeared to her, telling her that at the break of day she
should depart to the heavenly light.   The truth of which
vision was made out by the virgin's dying as soon as the day
appeared.

CHAP. IX.

Of the signs which were shown from heaven when the mother of that con-
gregation departed this life. [A. D. 676.]

WHEN Ethelberga, the pious mother of that holy congregation, was about to be taken out of this world, a wonderful
vision appeared to one of the sisters, called Tortgith; who,
having lived many years in that monastery, always endeavoured, in all humility and sincerity, to serve God, and
took care to assist the same mother in keeping up regular
discipline, by instructing and reproving the younger ones.
Now, in order that her virtue might be perfected in affliction,
according to the apostle, she was suddenly seized with a most
grievous distemper, under which, through the good providence of our Redeemer, she suffered very much for the space
of nine years; to the end, that whatever stain of vice remained amidst her virtues, either through ignorance or
neglect, might all be eradicated by the fire of long tribulation.   This person, going out of her chamber one night, just
at the first dawn of the day, plainly saw as it were a human
body, which was brighter than the sun, wrapped up in a
sheet, and lifted up on high, being taken out of the house in
which the sisters used to reside.   Then looking earnestly to
see what it was that drew up the glorious body which she
beheld, she perceived it was drawn up as it were by cords
brighter than gold, until, entering into the open heavens, it
could no longer be seen by her.   Reflecting on this vision,
she made no doubt that some one of the society would soon
die, and her soul be lifted up to heaven by her good works
as it were by golden cords, which accordingly happened; for
a few days after, the beloved of God, Ethelberga, mother of
that society, was delivered out of the prison of the flesh; and
her life is known to have been such that no person who knew
her ought to question but that the heavenly kingdom was
open to her, when she departed from this world.

There was also, in the same monastery, a certain nun, of
noble worldly origin, and much nobler in the love of the
world to come; who had, for many years, been so disabled
in all her body, that she could not move a single limb.   Being informed that the venerable abbess's body was carried

into the church, till it could be buried, she desired to be
carried thither, and to be bowed down towards it, after the
manner of one praying ; which being done, she spoke to her
as if she had been living, and entreated her that she would
obtain of the mercy of our compassionate Creator, that she
might be delivered from such great and lasting pains ; nor
was it long before her prayer was heard : for being taken
out of the flesh twelve days after, she exchanged her temporal afflictions for an eternal reward. Three years after the
death of this lady, the above-mentioned servant of Christ,
Tortgith, was so far spent with the distemper before mentioned, that her bones would scarcely hang together ; and,
at last, when the time of her dissolution was at hand, she
not only lost the use of her other limbs, but also of her
tongue ; which having continued three days and as many
nights, she was, on a sudden, relieved by a spiritual vision,
opened her mouth and eyes, and looking up to heaven, began
thus to direct her discourse to the vision which she saw :
" Your coming is very acceptable to me, and you are wel-
come !" Having so said, she was silent awhile, as it were,
waiting for the answer of the person she saw and spoke to ;
then, as if displeased, she said, " I am not pleased with this ;"
then pausing awhile, she said again, " If it cannot be to-
day, I beg the delay may not be long ;" and again holding
her peace a short while, she concluded thus ; " If it is positively so decreed, and the resolution cannot be altered, I beg
that it may be no longer deferred than this next night."
Having so said, and being asked by those about her to whom
she talked, she said, " With my most dear mother, Ethelberga ;" by which they understood, that she was come to
acquaint her that the time of her departure was at hand ;
for, as she had desired, after one day and night, she was delivered from the bonds and infirmity of the flesh, and entered
the joys of eternal salvation.

CHAP. X.

*A blind woman, praying in the burial-place of that monastery, was re-
stored to her sight.* [A.D. 676.]

HILDELITH, a devout servant of God, succeeded Ethelberga
in the office of abbess, and presided over that monastery

many years, till she was of an extreme old age, with exemplary conduct, in the observance of regular discipline, and in the care of providing all things for the public use.   The narrowness of the place where the monastery is built, led her to think that the bones of the male and female servants of Christ, which had been there buried, should be taken up, and translated into the church of the blessed mother of God, and interred in one place : whoever wishes to read it, may find in the book from which we have gathered these things, how often a brightness of heavenly light was seen there, and a fragrancy of wonderful odour smelled, and what other miracles were wrought.

However, I think it by no means fit to pass over the miraculous cure, which the same book informs us was wrought in the church-yard of the said religious house. There lived in that neighbourhood a certain earl, whose wife was seized with a dimness in her eyes, which at length became so bad, that she could not see the least glimpse of light : having continued some time in total darkness, on a sudden she bethought herself that she might recover her lost sight, if she were carried to the monastery of the nuns, and there pray for the same, at the relics of the saints. Nor did she lose any time in performing what she had thought of : for being conducted by her maids to the monastery, which was very near, and professing that she had perfect faith that she should be there healed, she was led into the burial-place, and having long prayed there on her knees, she did not fail to be heard, for as she rose from prayer, before she went out of the place, she received the gift of sight which she had desired ; and whereas she had been led thither by her servants, she now returned home joyfully without help : as if she had lost her sight to no other end than that she might make it appear how great light the saints enjoyed in heaven, and how great was the power of their virtue.

CHAP. XI

Sebbi, king of the same province, ends his life in a monastery. [A.D. 694.]

AT that time, as the same little book informs us, Sebbi, a devout man, of whom mention has been made above, governed the kingdom of the East Saxons. He was much addicted to religious actions, almsgivings, and frequent prayer; preferring a private and monastic life to all the wealth and honours of his kingdom, which sort of life he would also long before have undertaken, had not his wife positively refused to be divorced from him; for which reason many were of opinion, and often said so, that a person of such a disposition ought rather to have been a bishop than a king. When he had been thirty years a king, and a soldier of the heavenly kingdom, he fell into a violent sickness, of which he died, and admonished his wife, that they should then at least jointly devote themselves to the service of God, since they could no longer enjoy, or rather serve, the world. Having with much difficulty obtained this of her, he repaired to Waldhere, bishop of London, who had succeeded Earconwald, and with his blessing received the religious habit, which he had long desired. He also carried to him a considerable sum of money, to be given to the poor, reserving nothing to himself, but rather coveting to remain poor in spirit for the sake of the kingdom of heaven.

When the aforesaid distemper increased upon him, and he perceived the day of his death to be drawing near, being a man of a royal disposition, he began to apprehend lest, when under pain, and at the approach of death, he might be guilty of anything unworthy of his person, either in words, or any motion of his limbs. Wherefore, calling to him the aforesaid bishop of London, in which city he then was, he entreated him that none might be present at his death, besides the bishop himself, and two of his attendants. The bishop having promised that he would most willingly perform the same, not long after the man of God composed himself to sleep, and saw a comforting vision, which took from him all anxiety for the aforesaid uneasiness; and, moreover, showed him on what day he was to depart this life. For, as he afterwards related, he saw three men in bright garments come to him; one of whom sat down before his bed, whilst his companions stood and inquired about the state of the sick man they came to see: he who was sitting in front of the bed said, that his soul should depart his body without any pain, and with a great splendour of light; and declared that he should die the third day after; both which particulars happened, as he had been informed by the vision; for on the third day after, he suddenly fell, as it were, into a slumber, and breathed out his soul·without any sense or pain.

A stone coffin having been provided for burying his body, when they came to lay it in the same, they found his body a span longer than the coffin. Hereupon they hewed away the stone, and made the coffin about two fingers longer; but neither would it then contain the body. Under this difficulty of entombing him, they had thoughts either to get another coffin, or else to shorten the body, by bending it at the knees, if they could. But a wonderful event, caused by Providence, prevented the execution of either of those designs; for on a sudden, in the presence of the bishop, and Sighard, the son of the king who had turned monk, and who reigned after him jointly with his brother Suefred, and of a considerable number of men, that same coffin was found to answer the length of the body, insomuch that a pillow might also be put in at the head; and at the feet the coffin was four fingers longer than the body. He was buried in the church of the blessed Apostle of the Gentiles,* by whose instructions he had learned to hope for heavenly things.

CHAP. XII.

Hedda succeeds Eleutherius in the bishopric of the West Saxons; Cuichelm succeeds Putta in that of Rochester, and is himself succeeded by Gebmund; and who were then bishops of the Northumbrians.
[A.D. 673.]

ELEUTHERIUS was the fourth bishop of the West Saxons;† for Birinus was the first, Agilbert the second, and Wini the third. When Kenwalk, in whose reign the said Eleutherius was made bishop, died, his under-rulers took upon them the kingdom of the people, and dividing it among themselves, held it ten years; and during their rule he died, and Hedda succeeded him in the bishopric, having been consecrated by Theodore, in the city of London; during whose prelacy, Cadwalla,‡ having subdued and removed those rulers, took upon him the government. When he had reigned two years, and whilst the same bishop still governed the church, he quitted his sovereignty for the love of the heavenly kingdom,

* St. Paul's, London.   † Winchester bishopric.   ‡ King of Wessex.

and, going away to Rome, ended his days there, as shall be said more fully hereafter.

In the year of our Lord's incarnation 676, when Ethelred, king of the Mercians, ravaged Kent with a powerful army, and profaned churches and monasteries, without regard to religion, or the fear of God, he among the rest destroyed the city of Rochester; Putta, who was bishop, was absent at that time, but when he understood that his church was ravaged, and all things taken away, he went to Sexwulf, bishop of the Mercians,* and having received of him a certain church, and a small spot of land, ended his days there in peace; in no way endeavouring to restore his bishopric, because (as has been said above) he was more industrious in spiritual than in worldly affairs; serving God only in that church, and going wherever he was desired, to teach church music. Theodore consecrated Cuichelm bishop of Rochester in his stead; but he, not long after, departing from his bishopric for want of necessaries, and withdrawing to other parts, Gebmund was substituted in his place.

In the year of our Lord's incarnation, 678, which is the eighth of the reign of Egfrid, in the month of August, appeared a star, called a comet, which continued for three months, rising in the morning, and darting out, as it were, a pillar of radiant flame. The same year a dissension† broke out between King Egfrid and the most reverend prelate, Wilfrid, who was driven from his see, and two bishops substituted in his stead, to preside over the nation of the Northumbrians, namely, Bosa, to preside over the nation of the Deiri; and Eata over that of the Bernicians; the former having his see in the city of York, the latter in the church of Hagulstad, or else Lindisfarne; both of them promoted to the episcopal dignity from a society of monks. With them also was Edhed ordained bishop in the province of Lindsey,‡ which King Egfrid had but newly subdued, having overcome and vanquished Wulfhere; and this was the first bishop of its own which that province had; the second was Ethelwin; the

---

* Lichfield.

† It appears that this dissension was caused by Ermenburga, Egfrid's queen, who was jealous lest the splendour of Wilfrid's monasteries and his stately buildings should diminish the regal honours of her husband.

‡ Sidnacester. See page 127.

third Edgar; the fourth Cynebert, who is there at present.
Before Edhed, Sexwulf was bishop as well of that province
as of the Mercians and Midland Angles; so that, when expelled from Lindsey, he continued in the government of
those provinces. Edhed, Bosa, and Eata, were ordained at
York by archbishop Theodore; who also, three years after
the departure of Wilfrid, added two bishops to their number;
Tumbert, in the church of Hagulstad, Eata still continuing
in that of Lindisfarne; and Trumwine in the province of
the Picts, which at that time was subject to the English.*
Edhed returning from Lindsey, because Ethelred had recovered that province, was placed by him over the church of
Ripon.

CHAP. XIII.

Bishop Wilfrid converts the province of the South Saxons to Christ.
[A.D. 681.]

BEING expelled from his bishopric, and having travelled in
several parts, Wilfrid went to Rome. He afterwards returned to Britain; and though he could not, by reason of
the enmity of the aforesaid king, be received into his own
country or diocese, yet he could not be restrained from
preaching the Gospel; for, taking his way into the province
of the South Saxons, which extends from Kent on the west
and south, as far as the West Saxons, and contains land of
7000 families, who at that time, were still pagans, he administered to them the word of faith, and the baptism of salvation.   Ethelwalch, king of that nation, had been, not long

---

* There is some difficulty connected with the above statement of the
venerable historian, respecting the division of Wilfrid's diocese. Some
maintain (Wharton, Anglia Sacra, i. 693,) that the diocese of Lindisfarne,
with Hexham severed from it, was left to Wilfrid; while others make Hexham and Lindisfarne to have been one diocese conferred on Eata. It
seems more probable that Theodore divided the diocese into four bishoprics,
giving York to Bosa, Hexham and Lindisfarne to Eata, (which were
again divided in 684, when Tumbert was appointed to Hexham,) Lindsey
to Edhed (whose see was at Sidnacester), and Abercorn, or Whitherne, in
the Pictish territory, to Trumwine.
† The South Saxons were converted to Christianity much later than the
other Saxon kingdoms in Britain, probably because they were cut off by
downs and marshes from communication with the rest of the island.

before, baptized in the province of the Mercians, by the persuasion of King Wulfhere, who was present, and was also his godfather, and as such gave him two provinces, viz. the Isle of Wight, and the province of Meanwara,* in the nation of the West Saxons. The bishop, therefore, with the king's consent, or rather to his great satisfaction, baptized the principal generals and soldiers of that country; and the priests, Eappa, and Padda, and Burghelm, and Eadda, either then, or afterwards, baptized the rest of the people. The queen, whose name was Ebba, had been christened in her own island, the province of the Wiccii.† She was the daughter of Eanfrid, the brother of Eanher, who were both Christians, as were their people; but all the province of the South Saxons were strangers to the name and faith of God. There was among them a certain monk of the Scottish nation, whose name was Dicul,‡ who had a very small monastery, at the place called Bosanham,§ encompassed with the sea and woods, and in it five or six brothers, who served our Lord in poverty and humility; but none of the natives cared either to follow their course of life, or hear their preaching.

But Bishop Wilfrid, by preaching to them, not only delivered them from the misery of perpetual damnation, but also from an inexpressible calamity of temporal death, for no rain had fallen in that province in three years before his arrival, whereupon a dreadful famine ensued, which cruelly destroyed the people. In short, it is reported, that very often, forty or fifty men, being spent with want, would go together to some precipice, or to the sea-shore, and there, hand in hand, perish by the fall, or be swallowed up by the waves. But on the very day on which the nation received the baptism of faith, there fell a soft but plentiful rain; the earth revived again, and the verdure being restored to the

There are strong appearances of the sea having formerly run up into the land on both the east and west of this county; and in many districts of the county primæval manners still are found.

* A district comprehending almost the eastern moiety of Hampshire.

† Inhabitants of Gloucester, Worcester, and part of Warwickshire.

‡ One of the companions of Fursey, mentioned in book iii. c. 19. Was he also the Dicuil, author of a geographical work still extant!

§ Bosham, or Bosanham, four miles from Chichester, in Sussex, still retains its ancient name.

fields, the season was pleasant and fruitful. Thus the former superstition being rejected, and idolatry exploded, the hearts and flesh of all rejoiced in the living God, and became convinced that He who is the true God had, through his heavenly grace, enriched them with wealth, both temporal and spiritual. For the bishop, when he came into the province, and found so great misery from famine, taught them to get their food by fishing; for their sea and rivers abounded in fish, but the people had no skill to take them, except eels alone. The bishop's men having gathered eel-nets everywhere, cast them into the sea, and by the blessing of God took three hundred fishes of several sorts, which, being divided into three parts, they gave a hundred to the poor, a hundred to those of whom they had the nets, and kept a hundred for their own use. By this benefit the bishop gained the affections of them all, and they began more readily at his preaching to hope for heavenly goods, seeing that by his help they had received those which are temporal.

At this time, King Ethelwalch gave to the most reverend prelate, Wilfrid, land of eighty-seven families, to maintain his company who were in banishment, which place is called Selsey,* that is, the Island of the Sea-Calf. That place is encompassed by the sea on all sides, except the west, where is an entrance about the cast of a sling in width; which sort of place is by the Latins called a peninsula, by the Greeks, a chersonesus. Bishop Wilfrid, having this place given him, founded therein a monastery, which his successors possess to this day, and established a regular course of life, chiefly of the brethren he had brought with him; for he both in word and actions performed the duties of a bishop in those parts during the space of five years, until the death of King Egfrid. And forasmuch as the aforesaid king, together with the said place, gave him all the goods that were therein, with the lands and men, he instructed them in the faith of Christ, and baptized them all. Among whom were two hundred and fifty men and women slaves, all of whom he, by baptism, not only rescued from the servitude of the

* Selsey, eight miles south from Chichester, Sussex. Eadbert, abbat of this monastery, in 711, was consecrated first bishop of the South Saxons, and fixed his see at this place; but Bishop Stigand, in 1070, procured its translation to Chichester.

Devil, but gave them their bodily liberty also, and exempted them from the yoke of human servitude.

CHAP. XIV.

How a pestilential mortality ceased through the intercession of King Oswald. [A.D. 681.]

IN this monastery, at that time, certain manifestations of the heavenly grace are said to have been shown forth; for the tyranny of the devil having been recently exploded, the faith of Christ began to prevail therein. Of which number I have thought it proper to perpetuate the memory of one which the most reverend Bishop Acca was wont to relate to me, affirming it had been told him by most creditable brothers of the same monastery. About the same time that this province of the South Saxons embraced the faith of Christ, a grievous mortality ran through many provinces of Britain; which, also, by the Divine dispensation, reached to the aforesaid monastery, then governed by the most reverend and religious priest of Christ, Eappa; and many, as well of those that had came thither with the bishop, as of those that had been called to the faith of the same province of the South Saxons, were snatched away out of this world. The brethren, in consequence, though fit to keep a fast of three days, and to implore the Divine goodness, that it would vouchsafe to extend mercy to them, either by delivering those that were in danger by the distemper from death, or by delivering those who departed this life from eternal damnation.

There was at that time in the monastery, a little boy, of the Saxon nation, lately called to the faith, who had been seized with the same distemper, and had long kept his bed. On the second day of the fasting and praying, it happened that the said boy was, about the second hour of the day, left alone in the place where he lay sick, and through the Divine disposition, the most blessed princes of the apostles vouchsafed to appear to him; for he was a lad of an extraordinarily mild and innocent disposition, and with sincere devotion observed the mysteries of the faith which he had received. The apostles therefore, saluting him in a most affectionate manner, said, "My child, do not fear death, about which you are so uneasy; for we will this day conduct you to

the heavenly kingdom; but you are first to stay till the masses
are said, that having received the body and blood of our
Lord, to support you on your journey, and being so discharged through sickness and death, you may be carried up
to the everlasting joys in heaven.

"Call therefore to you the priest, Eappa, and tell him,
that the Lord has heard your prayers and devotion, and has
favourably accepted of your fast, and not one more shall die
of this plague, either in the monastery or its adjacent possessions; but all your people who any where labour under this
distemper, shall be eased of their pain, and restored to their
former health, except you alone, who are this day to be delivered by death, and to be carried into heaven, to behold our
Lord Christ, whom you have faithfully served: this favour
the Divine mercy has vouchsafed to grant you, through the
intercession of the godly and dear servant of God, King
Oswald, who formerly ruled over the nation of the Northumbrians, with the authority of a temporal king, and such devotion of Christian piety as leads to the heavenly kingdom; for
this very day that king was killed in war by the infidels, and
taken up to the everlasting joys of souls in heaven, and associated among the number of the elect. Let them look in
their books, wherein the departure of the dead is set down,
and they will find that he was, this day, as we have said,
taken out of this world. Let them, therefore, celebrate
masses in all the oratories of this monastery, either in thanksgiving for their prayers being heard, or else in memory of
the aforesaid King Oswald, who once governed their nation;
and therefore he humbly offered up his prayers to our Lord
for them, as for strangers of his nation; and let all the
brethren, assembling in the church, communicate in the
heavenly sacrifices, and so let them cease to fast, and refresh
themselves with food."

The boy called the priest, and repeated all these words to
him; the priest particularly inquired after the habit and form
of the men that had appeared to him. He answered, "Their
habit was noble, and their countenances most pleasant and
beautiful, such as I had never seen before, nor did I think
there could be any men so graceful and comely. One of
them indeed was shorn like a clerk, the other had a long
beard; and they said that one of them was called Peter, the

other Paul; and both of them the servants of our Lord and Saviour Jesus Christ, sent by him from heaven to protect our monastery." The priest believed what the boy said, and going thence immediately, looked in his chronicle, and found that King Oswald had been killed on that very day. He then called the brethren, ordered dinner to be provided, masses to be said, and all of them to communicate as usual; causing also part of the Lord's oblation of the same sacrifice to be carried to the sick boy.

Soon after this, the boy died, on that same day; and by his death proved that what he had heard from the apostles of God was true. A further testimony of the truth of his words was, that no person besides himself, belonging to the same monastery, died at that time. By which vision, many that heard of it were wonderfully excited to implore the Divine mercy in adversity, and to adopt the wholesome remedy of fasting. From that time, the day of the nativity of that king and soldier of Christ began to be yearly honoured with the celebration of masses, not only in that monastery, but in many other places.

CHAP. XV.

King Cædwalla, having slain Ethelwalch, king of the West Saxons,* wasted that Province with rapine and slaughter. [A.D. 685.]

IN the meantime, Cædwalla, a daring young man, of the royal race of the Gewissæ,† who had been banished his country, came with an army, slew Ethelwalch, and wasted that country with much slaughter and plundering; but he was soon expelled by Berthun and Andhun, the king's commanders, who afterwards held the government of that province. The first of them was afterwards killed by the same Cædwalla, when he was king of the Gewissæ, and the province was more entirely subdued: Ina, likewise, who reigned after Cædwalla, kept that country under the like servitude for several years; for which reason, during all that time, they had no bishop of their own; but their first bishop, Wilfrid, having been recalled home, they were subject to the bishop of the Gewissæ, i. e. the West Saxons, in the city of Winchester.‡

---

* This should be South-Saxons. See page 193. † West Saxons.

‡ The churches of Sussex were only subject to the Winchester see for about twenty-five years. See book v. ch. 18.

CHAP. XVI.

How the Isle of Wight received Christian inhabitants, and two royal youths of that island were killed immediately after baptism. [A.D. 686.]

AFTER Cædwalla had possessed himself of the kingdom of the Gewissæ, he also took the Isle of Wight, which till then was entirely given over to idolatry, and by cruel slaughter endeavoured to destroy all the inhabitants thereof, and to place in their stead people from his own province; having bound himself by a vow, though he was not yet, as is reported, regenerated in Christ, to give the fourth part of the land, and of the booty, to our Lord, if he took the island, which he performed by giving the same for our Lord to the use of Bishop Wilfrid, who happened at the time to have accidentally come thither out of his own nation. The measure of that island, according to the computation of the English, is of twelve hundred families, and accordingly the bishop had given him land of three hundred families. The part which he received, he committed to one of his clerks called Bernwin, who was his sister's son, assigning him a priest, whose name was Hiddila, who might administer the word and baptism of salvation to all that would be saved.

Here I think it ought not to be omitted that the first fruits of the natives of that island who, by believing, secured their salvation, were two royal youths, brothers to Atwald, king of the island, who were honoured by the particular grace of God. For when the enemy approached, they made their escape out of the island, and passed over into the neighbouring province of the Jutes;* where, being conducted to the place called At the Stone,† as they thought to be concealed from the victorious king, they were betrayed and ordered to be killed. This being made known to a certain abbat and priest, whose name was Cynebert, who had a monastery not far from thence, at a place called Reodford,‡ that is, the Ford of Reeds, he came to the king, who then lay privately in those parts, to be cured of the wounds which he had received whilst he was fighting in the Isle of Wight, and

---

* See p. 24.
+ Now Stoneham, between Winchester and Southampton.
‡ Now Redbridge, situated at the head of the Southampton water.

begged of him, that if the lads must inevitably be killed, he might be allowed first to instruct them in the mysteries of the faith. The king consented, and the bishop having taught them the word of truth, and cleansed their souls by baptism, made the entrance into the kingdom of heaven sure to them. Then the executioner being at hand, they joyfully underwent the temporal death, through which they did not doubt they were to pass to the life of the soul, which is everlasting. Thus, after all the provinces of the island of Britain had embraced the faith of Christ, the Isle of Wight also received the same; yet being under the affliction of foreign subjection, no man there received the ministry, or rank of a bishop, before Daniel, who is now bishop of the West Saxons.*

The island is situated opposite the division between the South Saxons and the Gewissæ, being separated from it by a sea, three miles over, which is called Solente. In this narrow sea, the two tides of the ocean, which flow round Britain from the immense northern ocean, daily meet and oppose one another beyond the mouth of the river Homelea,† which runs into that narrow sea, from the lands of the Jutes, which belong to the country of the Gewissæ; after this meeting and struggling together of the two seas, they return into the ocean from whence they come.

CHAP. XVII.

Of the Synod held in the plain of Heathfield, where Archbishop Theodore presided. [A.D. 680.]

ABOUT this time, Theodore being informed that the faith of the church at Constantinople was much perplexed by the heresy of Eutyches,‡ and desiring to preserve the churches of the English, over which he presided, from that infection, an assembly of many venerable priests and doctors was convened, at which he diligently inquired into their doctrines, and found they all unanimously agreed in the Catholic faith. This he took care to have committed to writing by the authority of the synod, as a memorial, and for the instruction of

---

* Winchester.   † The Hamble.
‡ Called Monothelitism, which maintained that the divine and human nature of Jesus Christ were so united, as to form only *one* nature, yet without any change, confusion, or mixture of the two natures.

succeeding generations; the beginning of which instrument
is as follows:—

"In the name of our Lord and Saviour Jesus Christ, in
the tenth year of the reign of our most pious lord, Egfrid,
king of the Northumbrians, the seventeenth of October, the
eighth indiction; and in the sixth year of the reign of
Ethelfrid, king of the Mercians, in the seventeenth year of
the reign of Aldhulf, of the East Angles, in the seventh year
of the reign of Lothair, king of Kent; Theodore, by the
grace of God, archbishop of the island of Britain, and of the
city of Canterbury, being president, and the other venerable
bishops of the island of Britain sitting with him, the holy
Gospels being laid before them, at the place which, in the
Saxon tongue, is called Heathfield,* we conferred together,
and expounded the true and orthodox faith, as our Lord
Jesus in the flesh delivered the same to his disciples, who
saw him present, and heard his words, and as it is delivered
in the creed of the holy fathers, and by all holy and universal synods in general, and by the consent of all approved
doctors of the Catholic church; we, therefore, following
them jointly and orthodoxly, and professing accordance to
their divinely inspired doctrine, do believe, and do, according
to the holy fathers, firmly confess, properly and truly, the
Father, and Son, and Holy Ghost, a trinity consubstantial in
unity, and unity in trinity, that is, one God subsisting in
three consubstantial persons, of equal honour and glory."

And after much more of this sort, appertaining to the confession of the true faith, this holy synod added to its instrument, "We have received the five holy and general councils
of the blessed fathers acceptable to God; that is, of 318
bishops, who were assembled at Nice, against the most impious Arius and his tenets; and at Constantinople, of 150,
against the madness of Macedonius and Eudoxius, and their
tenets; and at Ephesus, first of 200, against the most wicked
Nestorius, and his tenets; and at Chalcedon, of 360, against
Eutyches and Nestorius, and their tenets; and again, at
Constantinople, in a fifth council, in the reign of Justinian
the younger, against Theodorus and Theodoret, and the epistles of Iba, and their tenets, against Cyril;" and again a
little lower, "the synod held in the city of Rome, in the time

* Now Bishop's Hatfield, in Hertfordshire.

of the blessed Pope Martin, in the eighth indiction, and in
the ninth year of the most pious Emperor Constantine, we
receive : and we glorify our Lord Jesus Christ, as they glorified him, neither adding nor diminishing any thing ;
anathematizing those with our hearts and mouths whom
they anathematized, and receiving those whom they received,
glorifying God the Father, who is without beginning, and
his only begotten Son generated from eternity, and the Holy
Ghost proceeding from the Father and the Son in an ineffa-
ble manner, as those holy apostles, prophets, and doctors,
whom we have above-mentioned, did declare. And all we,
who, with Archbishop Theodore, have thus expounded the
Catholic faith, have also subscribed thereto."

CHAP. XVIII

Of John, the singer of the apostolic see, who came into Britain to teach.
[A.D. 680.]

AMONG those who were present at this synod, was the venerable John, archchanter of the church of the holy Apostle
Peter, and abbat of the monastery of St. Martin, who came
lately from Rome, by order of Pope Agatho, together with
the most reverend Abbat Biscop, surnamed Benedict, of
whom mention has been made above, and this John, with
the rest, signed the declaration of the Catholic faith. For
the said Benedict, having built a monastery in Britain, in
honour of the most blessed prince of the apostles, at the
mouth of the river Were,* went to Rome with Ceolfrid, his
companion and fellow-labourer in that work, who was after
him abbat of the same monastery ; he had been several times
before at Rome, and was now honourably received by Pope
Agatho of blessed memory ; from whom he also obtained the
confirmation of the immunities of this monastery, being a
bull of privilege signed by apostolical authority, pursuant to
what he knew to be the will and grant of King Egfrid, by
whose consent and gift of land he had built that monastery.

He then received the aforesaid Abbat John to be conducted into Britain, that he might teach in his monastery
the method of singing throughout the year, as it was prac-

* Now called Monk-Wearmouth. Venerable Bede passed the early
part of his monastic life in this establishment.

tised at St. Peter's at Rome. The Abbat John did as he had been commanded by the pope, teaching the singers of the said monastery the order and manner of singing and reading aloud, and committing to writing all that was requisite throughout the whole course of the year for the celebration of festivals; all which are still observed in that monastery, and have been copied by many others elsewhere. The said John not only taught the brothers of that monastery; but such as had skill in singing resorted from almost all the monasteries of the same province to hear him; and many invited him to teach in other places.

Besides singing and reading, he had also been directed by the pope, carefully to inform himself concerning the faith of the English church, and to give an account thereof at his return to Rome. For he also brought with him the decision of the synod of the blessed Pope Martin and 105 bishops, held not long before at Rome, principally against those who taught but one will and operation in Christ, and gave it to be transcribed in the aforesaid monastery of the most religious Abbat Benedict. The men who followed such opinion, much perplexed the faith of the church of Constantinople at that time; but by the help of God they were then discovered and subdued. Wherefore, Pope Agatho, being desirous to be informed concerning the state of the church in Britain, as well as in other provinces, and to what extent it was clear from the contagion of heretics, gave this affair in charge to the most reverend Abbat John, then appointed to go to Britain. The synod we have spoken of having been called for this purpose in Britain, the Catholic faith was found untainted in them all, and a copy of the same given him to carry to Rome.

But in his return to his own country, soon after crossing the sea, he fell sick and died; and his body, for the sake of St. Martin, in whose monastery he presided, was by his friends carried to Tours, and honourably buried; for he had been kindly entertained there when he went into Britain, and earnestly entreated by the brethren, that in his return to Rome he would take that road, and give them a visit. In short, he was there supplied with some to conduct him on his way, and assist him in the work enjoined him. Though he died by the way, yet the testimony of the faith of the

English nation was carried to Rome, and most agreeably received by the apostolic pope, and all those that heard or read it.

CHAP. XIX.

How Queen Etheldrida always preserved her virginity, and her body suffered no corruption in the grave. [A.D. 660.]

KING Egfrid took to wife, Etheldrida, the daughter of Anna, king of the East Angles, of whom mention has been often made; a man very religious, and in all respects renowned for his inward disposition and actions. She had before been given in marriage to another, viz. to Tonbert, chief of the Southern Girvii;* but he died soon after he had received her, and she was given to the aforesaid king. Though she lived with him twelve years, yet she preserved the glory of perfect virginity, as I was informed by Bishop Wilfrid, of blessed memory, of whom I inquired, because some questioned the truth thereof; and he told me that he was an undoubted witness of her virginity, forasmuch as Egfrid promised he would give many lands and much money, if he could persuade the queen to consent to pay the marriage duty, for he knew the queen loved no man so much as himself; and it is not to be doubted that the same might in one instance take place in our age, which true histories tell us happened several times in former ages, through the assistance of the same Lord who has promised to continue with us unto the end of the world; for the miraculous circumstance that her flesh, being buried, could not suffer corruption, is a token that she had not been defiled by familiarity with man.

She had long requested the king, that he would permit her to lay aside worldly cares, and to serve only the true King, Christ, in a monastery; and having at length with difficulty prevailed, she went as a nun into the monastery of the Abbess Ebba,† who was aunt to King Egfrid, at the place called the city Coludi,‡ having taken the veil from the hands of the aforesaid Bishop Wilfrid; but a year after she

---

* See note at page 143
† Ebba was the daughter of King Ethelfrid, and the sister of Oswald, and half-sister of King Oswy.   ‡ Coldingham, Berwickshire.

was herself made abbess in the country called Ely, where, having built a monastery,[*] she began, by works and examples of a heavenly life, to be the virgin mother of very many virgins dedicated to God. It is reported of her, that from the time of her entering into the monastery, she never wore any linen but only woollen garments, and would rarely wash in a hot bath, unless just before any of the great festivals, as Easter, Whitsuntide, and the Epiphany, and then she did it last of all, after having, with the assistance of those about her, first washed the other servants of God there present; besides, she seldom did eat above once a day, excepting on the great solemnities, or some other urgent occasion, unless some considerable distemper obliged her. From the time of matins she continued in the church at prayer till it was day; some also say, that by the spirit of prophecy, she, in the presence of all, not only foretold the pestilence of which she was to die, but also the number of those that should be then snatched away out of her monastery. She was taken to our Lord, in the midst of her flock, seven years after she had been made abbess; and, as she had ordered, was buried among them, in such a manner as she had died, in a wooden coffin.

She was succeeded in the office of abbess by her sister Sexberga,[†] who had been wife to Erconbert, king of Kent; who, when her sister had been buried sixteen years, thought fit to take up her bones, and, putting them into a new coffin, to translate them into the church. Accordingly she ordered some of the brothers to provide a stone to make a coffin of; they accordingly went on board ship, because the country of Ely is on every side encompassed with the sea or marshes, and has no large stones, and came to a small abandoned city, not far from thence, which, in the language of the English, is called Grantchester,[‡] and presently, near the city walls,

[*] Aldwulf, king of the East Angles, and brother to Etheldrida, supplied the funds for building this monastery. Bentham conjectures that the superintendence of the wall was committed to Bishop Wilfrid, from whom Etheldrida received the benediction as abbess. After the Norman Conquest, Ely was made a bishop's see, A.D. 1107.

[†] Before Sexberga retired to Ely, she founded a monastery in the Isle of Sheppey, for seventy-seven nuns, over whom she placed an abbess, her daughter Ermenilda, queen dowager of Mercia.

[‡] Near Cambridge. The coffin found here was a relic of ancient Roman art.

they found a white marble coffin, most beautifully wrought, and neatly covered with a lid of the same sort of stone. Concluding therefore that God had prospered their journey, they returned thanks to him, and carried it to the monastery.

The body of the holy virgin and spouse of Christ, when her grave was opened, being brought into sight, was found as free from corruption as if she had died and been buried on that very day; as the aforesaid Bishop Wilfrid, and many others that know it, can testify. But the physician, Cynefrid, who was present at her death, and when she was taken up out of the grave, was wont of more certain knowledge to relate, that in her sickness she had a very great swelling under her jaw. "And I was ordered," said he, "to lay open that swelling, to let out the noxious matter in it, which I did, and she seemed to be somewhat more easy for two days, so that many thought she might recover from her distemper; but the third day the former pains returning, she was soon snatched out of the world, and exchanged all pain and death for everlasting life and health. And when so many years after her bones were to be taken out of the grave, a pavilion being spread over it, all the congregation of brothers were on the one side, and of sisters on the other, standing about it singing, and the abbess, with a few, being gone to take up and wash the bones, on a sudden we heard the abbess within loudly cry out, 'Glory be to the name of the Lord.' Not long after they called me in, opening the door of the pavilion, where I found the body of the holy virgin taken out of the grave and laid on a bed, as if it had been asleep; then taking off the veil from the face, they also showed the incision which I had made, healed up; so that, to my great astonishment, instead of the open gaping wound with which she had been buried, there then appeared only an extraordinarily slender scar.

"Besides, all the linen cloths in which the body had been buried, appeared entire and as fresh as if they had been that very day wrapped about her chaste limbs." It is reported, that when she was much troubled with the aforesaid swelling and pain in her jaw, she was much pleased with that sort of distemper, and wont to say, "I know that I deservedly bear the weight of my sickness on my neck, for I remember, when I was very young, I bore there the needless weight of jewels; and therefore I believe the Divine goodness would have me endure the pain in my neck, that I may be absolved from the guilt of my needless levity, having now, instead of gold and precious stones, a red swelling and burning on my neck." It happened also that by the touch of that linen, devils were expelled from bodies possessed, and other distempers were sometimes cured; and the coffin she was first buried in is reported to have cured some of distempers in the eyes, who, praying with their heads touching that coffin, presently were delivered from the pain or dimness in their eyes. They washed the virgin's body, and having clothed it in new garments, brought it into the church, and laid it in the coffin that had been brought, where it is held in great veneration to this day. The coffin was found in a wonderful manner, as fit for the virgin's body as if it had been made purposely for her, and the place for the head particularly cut, exactly fit for her head, and shaped to a nicety.

Ely is in the province of the East Angles, a country of about six hundred families, in the nature of an island, enclosed, as has been said, either with marshes or waters, and therefore it has its name from the great plenty of eels taken in those marshes; there the aforesaid servant of Christ desired to have a monastery, because, as we have before observed, she was descended from that same province of the East Angles.

CHAP. XX.

A Hymn on the aforesaid Holy Virgin. [A.D. 660.]

I THINK it proper to insert in this history a hymn of virginity, which I composed in elegiac verse several years ago, in praise and honour of the same queen and spouse of Christ; and therefore truly a queen, because the spouse of Christ; and to imitate the method of the Holy Scripture, in whose history many poetical pieces are inserted which are known to be composed in metre.

> Hail, Triune Power, who rulest every age,
> Assist the numbers which my pen engage.
> Let Maro wars in loftier numbers sing,
> I sound the praises of our heavenly King.

Chaste is my verse, nor Helen's rape I write ;
Light tales like these, but prove the mind as light.
See ! from on high the God descends, confined
In Mary's womb, to rescue lost mankind.
Behold ! a spotless maid a God brings forth,
A God is born, who gave e'en nature birth !
The virgin-choir the mother-maid resound,
And chaste themselves, her praises shout around.
Her bright example numerous vot'ries raise,
Tread spotless paths, and imitate her ways.
The blessed Agatha and Eulalia trust
Sooner to flames, than far more dangerous lust.
Tecla and chaste Euphemia overcame
The fear of beasts to save a virgin name.
Agnes and sweet Cecilia, joyful maids,
Smile while the pointed swords their breasts invades.
Triumphing joy attends the peaceful soul,
Where heat, nor rain, nor wishes mean control.
Thus Etheldrida, pure from sensual crime,
Bright shining star ! arose to bless our time.
Born of a regal race, her sire a king,
More noble honour to her lord shall bring.
A queen her name, her hand a sceptre rears,
But greater glories wait above the spheres.
What man wouldst thou desire ! See Christ is made
Her spouse, her blessed Redeemer weds the maid.
While you attend the heavenly Mother's train,
Thou shalt be mother of a heavenly reign.
The holy maid who twelve years sat a queen,
A cloister'd nun devote to God was seen.
Noted for pious deeds, her spotless soul
Left the vile world, and soar'd above the pole.
Sixteen Novembers since was the blest maid
Entomb'd, whose flesh no putrid damps invade.
Thy grace, O Christ ! for in the coffin's found
No tainted vest wrapping the corpse around.
The swelling dropsy, and dire atrophy,
A pale disease from the blest vestments fly.
Rage fires the fiend, who whilom Eve betray'd,
While shouting angels hail the glorious maid.
See ! wedded to her God, what joy remains,
In earth, or heaven, see ! with her God she reigns !
Behold ! the spouse, the festal torches shine,
He comes ! behold ! what joyful gifts are thine !
Thou a new song on the sweet harp shalt sing,
A hymn of praise to thy celestial King.
None from the flock of the throned Lamb shall move,
Whom grateful passion bind, and heavenly love.

CHAP. XXI.

Bishop Theodore made peace between the kings Egfrid and Ethelred.
[A.D. 679.]

IN the ninth year of the reign of King Egfrid, a great
battle was fought between him and Ethelred, king of the
Mercians, near the river Trent, and Elfwin, brother to King
Egfrid, was slain, a youth about eighteen years of age, and
much beloved by both provinces, for King Ethelred had
married his sister Osthritha. There was now reason to expect
a more bloody war, and more lasting enmity between those
kings and their fierce nations ; but Theodore, the bishop,
beloved of God, relying on the Divine assistance, by his
wholesome admonitions extinguished the dangerous fire that
was breaking out ; so that the kings and their people on both
sides being appeased, no man was put to death, but only
the usual mulct paid to the king for his brother that had been
killed ; and this peace continued long after between those
kings and their kingdoms.

CHAP. XXII.

How a certain captive's chains fell off when masses were sung for him.
[A.D. 679.]

IN the aforesaid battle, wherein Elfwin, the king's brother,
was killed, a memorable fact is known to have happened,
which I think ought not to be passed by in silence ; for the
relation of the same will conduce to the salvation of many.
In that battle, one Imma, a youth belonging to the king, was
left as dead, and having lain so all that day and the next
night among the dead bodies, at length he came to himself,
and sitting, bound up his wounds in the best way he could.
Then having rested awhile, he stood up, and began to go off
to seek some friends that might take care of him ; but in so
doing he was discovered and taken by some of the enemy's
army, and carried before their lord, who was an earl
belonging to King Ethelred. Being asked by him who he
was, and fearing to own himself a soldier, he answered, "He
was a peasant, poor and married, and that he came to the
army with others to bring provisions to the soldiers." The
earl entertained him, and ordered his wounds to be dressed ;
and when he began to recover, to prevent his escaping, he

P

ordered him to be bound; but that could not be performed, for as soon as they that bound him were gone, his bonds were all loosened.

He had a brother called Tunna, who was a priest and abbat of a monastery in the city which from him is still called Tunnacester.* Hearing that his brother had been killed in the fight, he went to see whether he could find his body; and finding another very like him in all respects, concluding it to be his, he carried the same to his monastery, and buried it honourably, and took care often to say masses for the absolution of his soul; the celebration whereof occasioned what I have said, that none could bind him but he was presently loosed again. In the meantime, the earl that kept him was amazed, and began to inquire why he could not be bound; whether he had any spells about him, as are spoken of in fabulous stories. He answered, "He knew nothing of those contrivances; but I have," said he, "a brother who is a priest in my country, and I know that he, supposing me to be killed, causes masses to be said for me; and if I were now in the other life, my soul there, through his intercession, would be delivered from pain."

Having continued with the earl some time, those who attentively observed him, by his countenance, mien, and discourse, took notice, that he was not of the meaner sort, as he had said, but of some quality. The earl then privately sending for him, pressed to know who he was, promising to do him no harm, if he would ingenuously confess his quality. Which when he had done, declaring that he had been the king's servant, the earl answered, "I perceived by your answers that you were no peasant. And now you deserve to die, because all my brothers and relations were killed in that fight; yet I will not put you to death, because it will be a breach of my promise."

As soon, therefore, as he was recovered, he sold him at London, to a Freson, but he could not be bound by him the whole way as he was led along; but though his enemies put

---

* Perhaps Tovecester, of the Domesday-book, "a city and fortified place on the river Tove," which is considered to have been a Roman station, and on the north side of which are the ruins of a Saxon tower. It is now called Towcester, a market town in Northamptonshire. The letters *n* and *v* are repeatedly confounded together in deciphering old MSS.

several sorts of bonds on him, they were all loosed. The buyer, perceiving that he could in no way be bound, gave him leave to ransom himself if he could; now it was at the third hour (nine in the morning) when the masses were wont to be said, that his bonds were generally loosed. He, having taken an oath that he would either return, or send him the money for his ransom, went into Kent to King Lothaire, who was son to the sister of Queen Etheldrida, above spoken of, for he had once been her servant. From him he obtained the price of his ransom, and as he had promised, sent it to his master.

Returning afterwards into his own country, and coming to his brother, he gave him an exact account of all his fortunes, good and bad; and by his relation he understood, that his bonds had been generally loosed at those times when masses had been celebrated for him; and that other advantages which had accrued to him in his time of danger, had been conferred on him from Heaven, through the intercession of his brother, and the oblation of his saving sacrifice. Many persons, on hearing this account from the aforesaid man, were stirred up in the faith and devotion of piety either to prayer, or to alms-giving, or to offer up to our Lord the sacrifice of the holy oblation, for the deliverance of their friends who had departed this world; for they understood and knew that such saving sacrifice was available for the eternal redemption both of body and soul. This story was also told me by some of those who had heard it related by the person himself to whom it happened; therefore, I have thought fit to insert it in my Ecclesiastical History as I had it related to me.

CHAP. XXIII.

Of the life and death of the Abbess Hilda. [A.D. 680.]

In the year of the incarnation of our Lord 680, the most religious servant of Christ, Hilda, abbess of the monastery that is called Streaneshalch,* as above-mentioned, after having performed many heavenly works on earth, passed from thence to receive the rewards of the heavenly life, on the 17th of November, at the age of sixty-six years; the first

* Whitby, see pages 151, 155.

thirty-three of which she spent living most nobly in the
secular habit; and more nobly dedicated the remaining half
to our Lord in a monastic life.   For she was nobly born,
being the daughter of Hereric, nephew to King Edwin, with
which king she also embraced the faith and mysteries of
Christ, at the preaching of Paulinus, the first bishop of the
Northumbrians, of blessed memory, and preserved the same
undefiled till she attained to the sight of him in heaven.

Resolving to quit the secular habit, and to serve him
alone, she withdrew into the province of the East Angles,
for she was allied to the king; being desirous to pass over
from thence into France, to forsake her native country and
all she had, and so live a stranger for our Lord in the
monastery of Cale,* that she might with more ease attain
to the eternal kingdom in heaven; because her sister Here-
suid, mother to Aldwulf, king of the East Angles, at that
time living in the same monastery, under regular discipline,
was waiting for her eternal reward.   Being led by her example, she continued a whole year in the aforesaid province,
with the design of going abroad; afterwards, Bishop Aidan
being recalled home, he gave her the land of one family on
the north side of the river Wear; where for a year she also
led a monastic life, with very few companions.

After this she was made abbess in the monastery called
Heruteu,† which monastery had been founded, not long before, by the religious servant of Christ, Heiu,‡ who is said
to have been the first woman that in the province of the
Northumbrians took upon her the habit and life of a nun,
being consecrated by Bishop Aidan; but she, soon after she
had founded that monastery, went away to the city of Cal-
cacestir,§ and there fixed her dwelling.   Hilda, the servant
of Christ, being set over that monastery, began immediately
to reduce all things to a regular system, according as she
had been instructed by learned men; for Bishop Aidan, and
other religious men that knew her and loved her, frequently
visited and diligently instructed her, because of her innate
wisdom and inclination to the service of God.

When she had for some years governed this monastery,

---

* Chelles, ten miles from Paris.   See iii. 8, p. 121.   † Hartlepool.
See p. 151.   ‡ Leland and Cressy confound Heiu with St. Bega or Bees.
§ Tadcaster, Newton Kyme, or Ingleby Abberforth.

wholly intent upon establishing a regular life, it happened that she also undertook either to build or to arrange a monastery in the place called Streaneshalch, [Whitby,*] which work she industriously performed; for she put this monastery under the same regular discipline as she had done the former; and taught there the strict observance of justice, piety, chastity, and other virtues, and particularly of peace and charity; so that, after the example of the primitive church, no person was there rich, and none poor, all being in common to all, and none having any property. Her prudence was so great, that not only indifferent persons, but even kings and princes, as occasion offered, asked and received her advice; she obliged those who were under her direction to attend so much to reading of the Holy Scriptures, and to exercise themselves so much in works of justice, that many might be there found fit for ecclesiastical duties, and to serve at the altar.

In short, we afterwards saw five bishops taken out of that monastery, and all of them men of singular merit and sanctity, whose names were Bosa, Hedda, Oftfor, John, and Wilfrid.† We have above taken notice, that the first of them was consecrated bishop at York; of the second, it is to be observed that he was appointed bishop of Dorchester. Of the two last we shall speak hereafter, as they were consecrated: the first was bishop of Hagulstad, the second of the church of York; of the third, we will here take notice that, having applied himself to the reading and observation of the Scriptures in both the monasteries of Hilda, at length, being desirous to attain to greater perfection, he went into Kent, to Archbishop Theodore, of blessed memory; where having spent some more time in sacred studies, he also re-

---

* Camden, speaking of Whitby, says, "Here are found stones resembling snakes rolled up, the sports of nature, which she, as one observes, amuses herself with creating when weary of producing realities and serious productions. You would think they had once been snakes, covered over with a crust of stone. Report ascribes them to the prayers of Hilda, as if changed by her, who in the early Saxon church opposed with all her might the tonsure of priests and the celebration of Easter according to the Roman ritual." Brit. edit. Gough, 1789, vol. iii. p. 17.

† Bosa was bishop of York; Hedda of Dorchester, and translated to Winchester; Oftfor of Worcester; John (the famous St. John of Beverley, book v. c. 2,) of Hexham, translated to York; Wilfrid of York.

solved to go to Rome, which, in those days, was reckoned of
great moment : returning thence into Britain, he took his
way into the province of the Wiccii, where King Osric then
ruled,* and continued there a long time, preaching the word
of faith, and making himself an example of good life to all
that saw and heard him.   At that time, Bosel, the bishop
of that province,† laboured under such weakness of body,
that he could not perform the episcopal functions ; for which
reason, this Oftfor was, by universal consent, chosen bishop
in his stead, and by order of King Ethelred, consecrated by
Bishop Wilfrid,‡ of blessed memory, who was then bishop
of the Midland Angles, because Archbishop Theodore was
dead, and no other bishop ordained in his place.   Before the
aforesaid man of God, Bosel, Tatfrid, a most learned and
industrious man, and of excellent ability, had been chosen
bishop there, from the same abbess's monastery, but had
been snatched away by an untimely death, before he could
be ordained.

Thus this servant of Christ, Abbess Hilda, whom all that
knew her called Mother, for her singular piety and grace,
was not only an example of good life, to those that lived in
her monastery, but afforded occasion of amendment and salvation to many who lived at a distance, to whom the fame
was brought of her industry and virtue ; for it was necessary that the dream which her mother, Bregusuit, had,
during her infancy, should be fulfilled.   At the time that
her husband, Hereric, lived in banishment, under Cerdic,
king of the Britons, where he was also poisoned, she fancied,
in a dream, that she was seeking for him most carefully,
and could find no sign of him any where ; but, after having
used all her industry to seek him, she found a most precious
jewel under her garment, which, whilst, she was looking on
it very attentively, cast such a light as spread itself throughout all Britain ; which dream was brought to pass in her
daughter that we speak of, whose life was a bright example,
not only to herself, but to all who desired to live well.

* Osric probably had the supremacy of the whole of the province of
Wiccii, or Magesetania, (Gloucestershire and Worcestershire) ; although
Oswald may have held Worcestershire as an appanage.
† Bosel was appointed the first bishop of Worcester, A.D. 679.
‡ Wilfrid was now restored to the see of York.

When she had governed this monastery many years, it pleased Him who has made such merciful provision for our salvation, to give her holy soul the trial of a long sickness, to the end that, according to the apostle's example, her virtue might be perfected in infirmity. Falling into a fever, she fell into a violent heat, and was afflicted with the same for six years continually; during all which time she never failed either to return thanks to her Maker, or publicly and privately to instruct the flock committed to her charge; for by her own example she admonished all persons to serve God dutifully in perfect health, and always to return thanks to him in adversity, or bodily infirmity. In the seventh year of her sickness, the distemper turning inwards, she approached her last day, and about cockcrowing, having received the holy communion to further her on her way, and called together the servants of Christ that were within the same monastery, she admonished them to preserve evangelical peace among themselves, and with all others; and as she was making her speech, she joyfully saw death approaching, or if I may speak in the words of our Lord, passed from death to life.

That same night it pleased Almighty God, by a manifest vision, to make known her death in another monastery, at a distance from hers, which she had built that same year, and is called Hackness.* There was in that monastery, a certain nun called Begu,† who, having dedicated her virginity to God, had served him upwards of thirty years in monastical conversation. This nun, being then in the dormitory of the sisters, on a sudden heard the well-known sound of a bell in the air, which used to awake and call them to prayers, when any one of them was taken out of this world, and opening her eyes, as she thought, she saw the top of the house open, and a strong light pour in from above; looking earnestly

---

* Hackness, thirteen miles from Whitby, was a cell belonging to Whitby Abbey, which at the dissolution contained four monks of the Benedictine order. Hilda erected several cells or smaller convents as appanages to Whitby.

† St. Bega, better known as St. Bees, from the monastery built by her, at the place named after her, near Copeland Forest, Cumberland. There is a legendary account of her printed in the Carlisle Tracts, from the Cottonian MSS. Faust. B. 4, fol. 122—139, as well as in the Lives of English Saints, No. VI.

upon that light, she saw the soul of the aforesaid servant of God in that same light, attended and conducted to
heaven by angels.　Then awaking, and seeing the other
sisters lying round about her, she perceived that what she
had seen was either in a dream or a vision ; and rising immediately in a great fright, she ran to the virgin who then presided in the monastery instead of the abbess, and whose
name was Frigyth, and, with many tears and sighs, told her
that the Abbess Hilda, mother of them all, had departed this
life, and had in her sight ascended to eternal bliss, and to
the company of the inhabitants of heaven, with a great
light, and with angels conducting her.　Frigyth having
heard it, awoke all the sisters, and calling them to the
church, admonished them to pray and sing psalms for her
soul ; which they did during the remainder of the night ;
and at break of day, the brothers came with news of her
death, from the place where she had died.　They answered
that they knew it before, and then related how and when
they had heard it, by which it appeared that her death had
been revealed to them in a vision the very same hour that
the others said she had died.　Thus it was by Heaven happily ordained, that when some saw her departure out of this
world, the others should be acquainted with her admittance
into the spiritual life which is eternal.　These monasteries
are about thirteen miles distant from each other.

It is also reported, that her death was, in a vision, made
known the same night to one of the holy virgins who loved
her most passionately, in the same monastery where the said
servant of God died.　This nun saw her soul ascend to heaven in the company of angels ; and this she declared, the
very same hour that it happened, to those servants of Christ
that were with her ; and awakened them to pray for her
soul, even before the rest of the congregation had heard of
her death.　The truth of which was known to the whole
monastery in the morning.　This same nun was at that time
with some other servants of Christ, in the remotest part of
the monastery, where the women newly converted were wont
to be upon trial, till they were regularly instructed, and
taken into the society of the congregation.

CHAP. XXIV.

*There was in the same monastery a brother, on whom the gift of writing
verses was bestowed by heaven.* [A.D. 680.]

THERE was in this abbess's monastery a certain brother, particularly remarkable for the grace of God, who was wont to
make pious and religious verses, so that whatever was interpreted to him out of Scripture, he soon after put the same
into poetical expressions of much sweetness and humility, in
English, which was his native language.   By his verses the
minds of many were often excited to despise the world, and
to aspire to heaven.   Others after him attempted, in the
English nation, to compose religious poems,* but none could
ever compare with him, for he did not learn the art of poetry
from men, but from God; for which reason he never could
compose any trivial or vain poem, but only those which relate
to religion suited his religious tongue; for having lived in a
secular habit till he was well advanced in years, he had never
learned any thing of versifying; for which reason being sometimes at entertainments, when it was agreed for the sake of
mirth that all present should sing in their turns, when he saw
the instrument come towards him, he rose up from table and
returned home.

Having done so at a certain time, and gone out of the
house where the entertainment was, to the stable, where he
had to take care of the horses that night, he there composed
himself to rest at the proper time; a person appeared to him
in his sleep, and saluting him by his name, said, "Cædmon,
sing some song to me."   He answered, "I cannot sing; for
that was the reason why I left the entertainment, and retired
to this place, because I could not sing."   The other who
talked to him, replied, "However you shall sing."—"What
shall I sing?" rejoined he.   "Sing the beginning of created
beings," said the other.   Hereupon he presently began to

* From what Bede says of Cædmon and his imitators, and from some
other circumstances, it seems probable that the vernacular religious feeling
was composed chiefly during the years which intervened between the age of
the poet (A.D. 680,) and that of the historian (A.D. 731.)—*Wright's Essay
on the Literature of the Anglo-Saxons.*

sing verses to the praise of God, which he had never heard, the purport whereof was thus :—We are now to praise the Maker of the heavenly kingdom, the power of the Creator and his counsel, the deeds of the Father of glory. How he, being the eternal God, became the author of all miracles, who first, as almighty preserver of the human race, created heaven for the sons of men as the roof of the house, and next the earth. This is the sense, but not the words in order as he sang them in his sleep; for verses, though never so well composed, cannot be literally translated out of one language into another, without losing much of their beauty and loftiness. Awaking from his sleep, he remembered all that he had sung in his dream, and soon added much more to the same effect in verse worthy of the Deity.

In the morning he came to the steward, his superior, and having acquainted him with the gift he had received, was conducted to the abbess, by whom he was ordered, in the presence of many learned men, to tell his dream, and repeat the verses, that they might all give their judgment what it was, and whence his verse proceeded. They all concluded, that heavenly grace had been conferred on him by our Lord. They expounded to him a passage in holy writ, either historical, or doctrinal, ordering him, if he could, to put the same into verse.* Having undertaken it, he went away, and returning the next morning, gave it to them composed in most excellent verse; whereupon the abbess, embracing the grace of God in the man, instructed him to quit the secular habit, and take upon him the monastic life; which being accordingly done, she associated him to the rest of the brethren in her monastery, and ordered that he should be taught the whole series of sacred history. Thus Cædmon, keeping in mind all he heard, and as it were chewing the cud, converted the same into most harmonious verse; and sweetly repeating the same, made his masters in their turn his hearers. He sang the creation of the world, the origin of man, and all the history of Genesis: and made many verses on the departure of the children of Israel out of Egypt, and their entering

---

* A part of one of Cædmon's poems is preserved in King Alfred's Saxon version of Bede's History. The original may be seen in Turner's Anglo-Saxons, (book ix. c. 1, vol. iii. p. 302,) with a literal translation.

into the land of promise, with many other histories from holy
writ; the incarnation, passion, resurrection of our Lord, and
his ascension into heaven; the coming of the Holy Ghost,
and the preaching of the apostles; also the terror of future
judgment, the horror of the pains of hell, and the delights of
heaven; besides many more about the Divine benefits and
judgments, by which he endeavoured to turn away all men
from the love of vice, and to excite in them the love of, and
application to, good actions; for he was a very religious man,
humbly submissive to regular discipline, but full of zeal
against those who behaved themselves otherwise; for which
reason he ended his life happily.

For when the time of his departure drew near, he laboured
for the space of fourteen days under a bodily infirmity which
seemed to prepare the way, yet so moderate that he could
talk and walk the whole time. In his neighbourhood was
the house to which those that were sick, and like shortly to
die, were carried. He desired the person that attended him,
in the evening, as the night came on in which he was to depart this life, to make ready a place there for him to take his
rest. This person, wondering why he should desire it,
because there was as yet no sign of his dying soon, did what he
had ordered. He accordingly went there, and conversing
pleasantly in a joyful manner with the rest that were in the
house before, when it was past midnight, he asked them,
whether they had the Eucharist there? They answered,
"What need of the Eucharist? for you are not likely to die,
since you talk so merrily with us, as if you were in perfect
health."—"However," said he, "bring me the Eucharist."
Having received the same into his hand, he asked, whether
they were all in charity with him, and without any enmity
or rancour? They answered, that they were all in perfect
charity, and free from anger; and in their turn asked him,
whether he was in the same mind towards them? He
answered, "I am in charity, my children, with all the servants
of God." Then strengthening himself with the heavenly
viaticum, he prepared for the entrance into another life, and
asked, how near the time was when the brothers were to be
awakened to sing the nocturnal praises of our Lord? They
answered, "It is not far off." Then he said, "Well, let us
wait that hour;" and signing himself with the sign of the

cross, he laid his head on the pillow, and falling into a slumber, ended his life so in silence.

Thus it came to pass, that as he had served God with a simple and pure mind, and undisturbed devotion, so he now departed to his presence, leaving the world by a quiet death; and that tongue, which had composed so many holy words in praise of the Creator, uttered its last words whilst he was in the act of signing himself with the cross, and recommending himself into his hands, and by what has been here said, he seems to have had foreknowledge of his death.

CHAP. XXV.

Of the vision that appeared to a certain man of God before the monastery of the city Coludi was burned down. [A.D. 679.]

AT this time, the monastery of virgins, called the city of Coludi, above-mentioned, was burned down, through carelessness; and yet all that knew the same, might observe that it happened through the malice of those who dwelt in it, and chiefly of those who seemed to be the greatest. But there wanted not a warning of the approaching punishment from the Divine goodness, by which they might have stood corrected, and by fasting, prayers, and tears, like the Ninevites, have averted the anger of the just Judge.

There was in that monastery a man of the Scottish race, called Adamnan,* leading a life entirely devoted to God in continence and prayer, insomuch that he never took any food or drink, except only on Sundays and Thursdays; but often spent whole nights in prayer. This austerity of life he had first adopted from necessity to correct his evil propensities; but in process of time the necessity became a custom.

For in his youth he had been guilty of some wicked action, for which, when he came to himself, he conceived extraordinary horror, and dreaded lest he should be punished for the same by the upright Judge. Repairing, therefore, to a priest, who he hoped might show him the way of salvation, he confessed his guilt, and desired to be advised how he might avoid the future wrath of God. The priest having heard his offence, said, "A great sore requires much

---

* Not the abbat of Iona mentioned in book v. c. 15. It is said that the monk of Coldingham survived the burning of the monastery three years.

attention in the cure ; and, therefore, give yourself up as far as you are able to fasting, reading of psalms, and prayer, to the end, that thus preventing the wrath of our Lord, in confession, you may find him merciful." Being highly affected with the grief of a guilty conscience, and desiring, as soon as possible, to be loosed from the inward fetters of sin, which lay heavy upon him, he answered, "I am young in years, and strong of body, and shall, therefore, easily bear whatever you shall enjoin me to do, so that I may be saved in the day of our Lord ; though you should command me to spend the whole night in prayer standing, and to pass the whole week in abstinence." The priest replied, "It is too much for you to hold out the whole week without bodily sustenance ; but it is sufficient to fast two or three days ; do this till I come again to you in a short time, when I will more fully show you what you are to do, and how long to continue your penance." Having so said, and prescribed the measure of his penance, the priest went away, and upon some sudden occasion passed over into Ireland, whence he derived his origin, and returned no more to him, as he had appointed. Remembering this injunction and his own promise, he totally addicted himself to tears, penance, holy watching, and continence ; so that he only fed on Thursdays and Sundays, as has been said ; and ate nothing all the other days of the week. When he heard that his priest was gone to Ireland, and had died there, he ever after observed that same abstinence, according to his direction ; and as he had begun that course through the fear of God, in penitence for his guilt, so he still continued the same unremittingly for the Divine love, and in hope of his reward.

Having practised this carefully for a long time, it happened that he had gone on a certain day to a distance from the monastery, accompanied by one of the brothers ; and as they were returning from this journey, when they drew near to the monastery, and beheld its lofty buildings, the man of God burst out into tears, and his countenance discovered the trouble of his heart. His companion, perceiving it, asked what was the reason, to which he answered : "The time is at hand, when a devouring fire shall consume all the structures which you here behold, both public and private." The other, hearing these words, as soon as they came into the monastery, told them to Ebba, the mother of the congregation. She, with good cause, being much concerned at that prediction, called the man to her, and narrowly inquired of him how he came to know it. He answered, "Being busy one night lately in watching and singing psalms, I on a sudden saw a person unknown standing by me, and being startled at his presence, he bade me not to fear, and speaking to me in a familiar manner, 'You do well,' said he, 'in that you spend this night-time of rest, not in giving yourself up to sleep, but in watching and prayer.' I answered, 'I know I have great need of wholesome watching, and earnest praying to our Lord to pardon my transgressions.' He replied, 'You are in the right, for you and many more do need to redeem their sins by good works, and when they cease from labouring about temporal affairs, then to labour the more eagerly for the desire of heavenly goods; but this very few do; for I, having now visited all this monastery regularly, have looked into every one's chambers and beds, and found none of them except yourself busy about the care of his soul; but all of them, both men and women, either indulge themselves in slothful sleep, or are awake in order to commit sin; for even the cells that were built for praying or reading, are now converted into places of feasting, drinking, talking, and other delights; the very virgins dedicated to God, laying aside the respect due to their profession, whensoever they are at leisure, apply themselves to weaving fine garments, either to use in adorning themselves like brides, to the danger of their condition, or to gain the friendship of strange men; for which reason, a heavy judgment from heaven is deservedly ready to fall on this place and its inhabitants by devouring fire.'" The abbess said, "Why did you not sooner acquaint me with what you knew?" He answered, "I was afraid to do it, out of respect to you, lest you should be too much afflicted; yet you may have this comfort, that the calamity will not happen in your days." This vision being divulged abroad, the inhabitants of that place were for a few days in some little fear, and leaving off their sins, began to punish themselves; but after the abbess's death they returned to their former wickedness, nay, they became more wicked; and when they thought themselves in peace and security, they soon felt the effects of the aforesaid judgment.

That all this fell out thus, was told me by my most reverend fellow-priest, Edgils, who then lived in that monastery.* Afterwards, when many of the inhabitants had departed thence, on account of the destruction, he lived a long time in our monastery, and died there. We have thought fit to insert this in our History, to admonish the reader of the works of our Lord, how terrible he is in his counsels on the sons of men, lest we should at some time or other indulge in the pleasures of flesh, and dreading the judgment of God too little, fall under his sudden wrath, and either be severely afflicted with temporal losses, or else being more severely tried, be snatched away to eternal perdition.

CHAP. XXVI.

Of the death of the Kings Egfrid and Lothere. [A.D. 684.]

IN the year of our Lord's incarnation 684, Egfrid, king of the Northumbrians, sending Beort, his general, with an army, into Ireland, miserably wasted that harmless nation, which had always been most friendly to the English; insomuch that in their hostile rage they spared not even the churches or monasteries. Those islanders, to the utmost of their power, repelled force with force, and imploring the assistance of the Divine mercy, prayed long and fervently for vengeance; and though such as curse cannot possess the kingdom of God, it is believed, that those who were justly cursed on account of their impiety, did soon suffer the penalty of their guilt from the avenging hand of God; for the very next year, that same king, rashly leading his army to ravage the province of the Picts,† much against the advice of his friends, and particularly of Cuthbert, of blessed memory, who had been lately ordained bishop, the enemy made show as if they fled, and the king was drawn into the straits of inaccessible mountains,‡ and slain, with the greatest part of his forces, on the 20th of May, in the fortieth year of his age, and the fifteenth of his reign. His friends, as has been said, advised him not to engage in this war; but he having the year before refused to listen to the most reverend father, Egbert, advising

---

* After the destruction of Coldingham monastery Edgils went to Wearmouth.

† The Britons of Strath Clyde.   ‡ At Drumnechtan, county of Forfar.

him not to attack the Scots, who did him no harm, it was
laid upon him as a punishment for his sin, that he should not
now regard those who would have prevented his death.

From that time the hopes and strength of the English
crown "began to waver and retrograde;" for the Picts recovered their own lands, which had been held by the English
and the Scots that were in Britain, and some of the Britons
their liberty, which they have now enjoyed for about forty-
six years. Among the many English that then either fell
by the sword, or were made slaves, or escaped by flight out
of the country of the Picts, the most reverend man of God,
Trumwine, who had been made bishop over them, withdrew
with his people that were in the monastery of Abercurnig,*
seated in the country of the English, but close by the arm
of the sea which parts the lands of the English and the
Scots.† Having recommended his followers, wheresoever he
could, to his friends in the monasteries, he chose his own
place of residence in the monastery, which we have so often
mentioned, of men and women servants of God, at Streaneshalch ;‡ and there he, for several years, led a life in all
monastical austerity, not only to his own, but to the benefit
of many, with a few of his own people ; and dying there, he
was buried in the church of St. Peter the Apostle, with the
honour due to his life and rank. The royal virgin, Elfled,
with her mother, Eanfled, whom we have mentioned before,
then presided over that monastery ; but when the bishop
came thither, this devout woman found in him extraordinary
assistance in governing, and comfort to herself. Alfrid succeeded Egfrid in the throne, being a man most learned in
Scripture, said to be brother to the other, and son to
King Oswy : he nobly retrieved the ruined state of the kingdom, though within narrower bounds.

The same year, being the 685th from the incarnation of
our Lord, Lothere, king of Kent, died on the sixth of February, when he had reigned twelve years after his brother
Egbert, who had reigned nine years : he was wounded in

---

* Abercornig, i.e. Aber-Caran-ey, the "island on the Caron;" Abercorn.
See pp. 20, 193.
+ This passage leaves no doubt as to the boundary of the Pictish terri-
tory. For the appointment of Trumwine, see book iv. c. 12, p. 193.
‡ Whitby.

battle with the South Saxons, whom Edric, the son of Egbert, had raised against him, and died whilst his wound was being dressed. After him, the same Edric reigned a year and a half. On his death, kings of doubtful title, or foreigners, 'for some time wasted the kingdom, till the lawful king, Wictred, the son of Egbert, being settled in the throne, by his piety and zeal delivered his nation from foreign invasion.

CHAP. XXVII.

Cuthbert, a man of God, is made bishop; and how he lived and taught whilst still in a monastic life. [A. D. 685.]

THE same year that King Egfrid departed this life, he (as has been said) promoted to the bishopric of the church of Lindisfarne, the holy and venerable Cuthbert,[*] who had for many years led a solitary life, in great continence of body and mind, in a very small island, called Farne,[†] distant almost nine miles from that same church, in the ocean. From his very childhood he had always been inflamed with the desire of a religious life; but he took upon him the habit and name of a monk when he was a young man: he first entered into the monastery of Melrose, which is on the bank of the river Tweed, and was then governed by the Abbat Eata, a meek and simple man, who was afterwards made bishop of the church of Hagulstad or Lindisfarne,[‡] as has been said above, over which monastery at that time was placed Boisil, a priest of great virtue and of a prophetic spirit. Cuthbert, humbly submitting himself to this man's direction, from him received both the knowledge of the Holy Scriptures, and example of good works.

After he had departed to our Lord, Cuthbert was placed over that monastery, where he instructed many in regular life, both by the authority of a master, and the example of his own behaviour. Nor did he afford admonitions and an example of a regular life to his monastery alone, but endeavoured to convert the people round about far and near from

---

[*] The Life of St. Cuthbert, written by Venerable Bede, has been already published by the Editor in "Bede's Minor Historical Works," and will be again given in a volume of "Anglo-Saxon Biographies, Letters," &c., uniform with the present. † See note at p. 135. ‡ See pp. 192, 3.

the life of foolish custom, to the love of heavenly joys; for
many profaned the faith which they had received by their
wicked actions; and some also, in the time of a mortality,
neglecting the sacraments of faith which they had received,
had recourse to the false remedies of idolatry, as if they
could have put a stop to the plague sent from God, by en-
chantments, spells, or other secrets of the hellish art.   In
order to correct the error of both sorts, he often went out of
the monastery, sometimes on horseback, but oftener on foot,
and repaired to the neighbouring towns, where he preached
the way of truth to such as were gone astray; which had
been also done by Boisil in his time.   It was then the custom of the English people, that when a clerk or priest came
into the town, they all, at his command, flocked together to
hear the word; willingly heard what was said, and more
willingly practised those things that they could hear or
understand.   But Cuthbert was so skilful an orator, so fond
was he of enforcing his subject, and such a brightness
appeared in his angelic face, that no man present presumed
to conceal from him the most hidden secrets of his heart,
but all openly confessed what they had done; because they
thought the same guilt could not be concealed from him, and
wiped off the guilt of what they had so confessed with worthy
fruits of penance, as he commanded.   He was wont chiefly
to resort to those places, and preach in such villages, as being seated high up amid craggy uncouth mountains, were
frightful to others to behold, and whose poverty and bar-
barity rendered them inaccessible to other teachers; which
nevertheless he, having entirely devoted himself to that pious
labour, did so industriously apply himself to polish with his
doctrine, that when he departed out of his monastery, he
would often stay a week, sometimes two or three, and sometimes a whole month, before he returned home, continuing
among the mountains to allure that rustic people by his
preaching and example to heavenly employments.

This venerable servant of our Lord, having thus spent
many years in the monastery of Melrose, and there become
conspicuous by many miracles, his most reverend abbat,
Eata, removed him to the isle of Lindisfarne, that he might
there also, by the authority of a superior and his own
example, instruct the brethren in the observance of regular

discipline; for the same reverend father then governed that
place also as abbat; for, from ancient times, the bishop was
wont to reside there with his clergy, and the abbat with his
monks, who were likewise under the care of the bishop;
because Aidan, who was the first bishop of the place, being
himself a monk, brought monks thither, and settled the monastic institution there; as the blessed Father Augustine is
known to have done before in Kent, the most reverend Pope
Gregory writing to him, as has been said above, to this
effect :—"But since, my brother, having been instructed in
monastic rules, you must not live apart from your clergy
in the church of the English, which has been lately, through
the help of God, converted to the faith; you must, therefore, establish that course of life, which was among our
ancestors in the primitive church, among whom, none called
anything that he possessed his own; but all things were in
common to them."

CHAP. XXVIII.

*The same St. Cuthbert, being an Anchorite, by his prayers obtained a
spring in a dry soil, and had a crop from seed sown by himself out of
season.* [A.D. 664.]

AFTER this, Cuthbert, advancing in his meritorious and devout intentions, proceeded even to the adoption of a hermit's
life of solitude, as we have mentioned. But forasmuch as
we several years ago wrote enough of his life and virtues,
both in heroic verse and prose, it may suffice at present only
to mention this, that when he was about to repair to the
island, he made this protestation to the brothers, saying, "If
it shall please the Divine goodness to grant me, that I may
live in that place by the labour of my hands, I will willingly
reside there; but if not, I will, by God's permission, very
soon return to you." The place was quite destitute of water,
corn, and trees; and being infested by evil spirits, very ill
suited for human habitation; but it became in all respects
habitable, at the desire of the man of God; for upon his
arrival the wicked spirits withdrew. When he had there,
after expelling the enemies, with the assistance of the
brethren, built himself a small dwelling, with a trench about
it, and the necessary cells and an oratory, he ordered the

brothers to dig a pit in the floor of the dwelling, although the ground was hard and stony, and no hopes appeared of any spring. Having done this upon the faith and at the request of the servant of God, the next day it appeared full of water, and to this day affords plenty of its heavenly bounty to all that resort thither. He also desired that all instruments for husbandry might be brought him, and some wheat; and having sown the same at the proper season, neither stalk, nor so much as a leaf, sprouted from it by the next summer. Hereupon the brethren visiting him according to custom, he ordered barley to be brought him, in case it were either the nature of the soil, or the Divine will, that such grain should rather grow there. He sowed it in the same field just as it was brought him, after the proper time of sowing, and consequently without any likelihood of its coming to good; but a plentiful crop immediately came up, and afforded the man of God the means which he had so ardently desired of supporting himself by his own labour.

When he had here served God in solitude many years, the mound which encompassed his habitation being so high, that he could from thence see nothing but heaven, to which he so ardently aspired, it happened that a great synod was assembled in the presence of King Egfrid, near the river Alne, at a place called Twyford,* which signifies "the two fords," in which Archbishop Theodore, of blessed memory, presided, Cuthbert was, by the unanimous consent of all, chosen bishop of the church of Lindisfarne. They could not, however, persuade him to leave his monastery, though many messengers and letters were sent to him; at last the aforesaid king himself, with the most holy Bishop Trumwine, and other religious and great men, passed over into the island; many also of the brothers of the same isle of Lindisfarne assembled together for the same purpose: they all knelt, conjured him by our Lord, and with tears and entreaties, till they drew him, also in tears, from his retreat, and forced him to the synod. Being arrived there, after much opposition, he was overcome by the unanimous resolution of all present, and submitted to take upon himself the episcopal dignity; being chiefly prevailed upon by the mention that Boisil, the servant of God, when he had prophetically fore-

* In Northumberland.

told all things that were to befall him, had also predicted
that he should be a bishop. However, the consecration was
not appointed immediately ; but after the winter, which was
then at hand, it was performed at Easter, in the city of
York, and in the presence of the aforesaid King Egfrid ;
seven bishops meeting on the occasion, among whom, Theodore, of blessed memory, was primate. He was first elected
bishop of the church of Hagulstad, in the place of Tumbert,
who had been deposed from the episcopal dignity ; but in
regard that he chose rather to be placed over the church of
Lindisfarne, in which he had lived, it was thought fit that
Eata should return to the see of the church of Hagulstad,
to which he had been first ordained, and that Cuthbert
should take upon him the government of the church of
Lindisfarne.*

Following the example of the apostles, he became an ornament to the episcopal dignity, by his virtuous actions ; for
he both protected the people committed to his charge, by
constant prayer, and excited them, by most wholesome
admonitions, to heavenly practices ; and, which is the
greatest help in teachers, he first showed in his behaviour
what he taught was to be performed by others ; for he was
much inflamed with the fire of Divine charity, modest in the
virtue of patience, most diligently intent on devout prayers,
and affable to all that came to him for comfort. He thought
it equivalent to praying, to afford the infirm brethren the
help of his exhortations, well knowing that he who said
" Thou shalt love the Lord thy God," said likewise, " Thou
shalt love thy neighbour as thyself." He was also remarkable for penitential abstinence, and always intent upon heavenly things, through the grace of humility : lastly, when he
offered up to God the sacrifice of the saving victim, he com-

* Eata was appointed to the see of Lindisfarne, united with that of
Hexham. Other authors affirm (Wharton's Anglia Sacra, and Hutchin-
son's Durham, i. 13) that Lindisfarne for fourteen years wanted its proper
bishop ; as Chad on his consecration made York the bishop's residence,
and assumed the dignity of metropolitan. In the year 684, however, the
two sees were again divided, and Tumbert was appointed to Hexham, from
which he was afterwards dismissed, and Cuthbert appointed his successor.
(See p. 193.) Godwin states, that Eata, understanding that the see of
Lindisfarne would be more acceptable to Cuthbert than that of Hexham,
voluntarily resigned it in his favour.—*Dugdale's Monast. Anglic.* i. 220.

mended his prayer to God, not with a loud voice, but with
tears drawn from the bottom of his heart.

Having spent two years in his bishopric, he returned to
his island and monastery, being advertised by a Divine
oracle, that the day of his death, or rather of his life, was
drawing near; as he, at that time, with his usual simplicity,
signified to some persons, though in terms which were
somewhat obscure, but which were nevertheless afterwards
plainly understood; while to others he declared the same
openly.

CHAP. XXIX.

*St. Cuthbert foretold to the anchorite, Herebert, that his death was at
hand.* [A.D. 687.]

THERE was a certain priest, venerable for the probity of his
life and manners, called Herebert, who had long been united
with the man of God, Cuthbert, in the bonds of spiritual
friendship. This man leading a solitary life in the island of
that great lake from which the river Derwent flows, was
wont to visit him every year, and to receive from him spiritual
advice. Hearing that Bishop Cuthbert was come to the city
of Lugubalia,*.he repaired thither to him, according to custom, being desirous to be still more and more inflamed in
heavenly desires through his wholesome admonitions. Whilst
they alternately entertained one another with the delights of
the celestial life, the bishop, among other things, said,
"Brother Herebert, remember at this time to ask me all the
questions you wish to have resolved, and say all you design;
for we shall see one another no more in this world. For
I am sure that the time of my dissolution is at hand, and I
shall speedily put off this tabernacle of the flesh." Hearing
these words, he fell down at his feet, and shedding tears,
with a sigh, said, "I beseech you, by our Lord, not to forsake
me; but that you remember your most faithful companion,
and entreat the Supreme Goodness that, as we served him
together upon earth, we may depart together to see his bliss
in heaven. For you know that I have always endeavoured

* Otherwise called Luel. See Sim. Dun. i. 9, Carlisle, Old Penryth in
Cumberland.

to live according to your directions, and whatsoever faults I have committed, either through ignorance or frailty, I have instantly submitted to correction according to your will." The bishop applied himself to prayer, and having presently had intimation in the spirit that he had obtained what he asked of the Lord, he said, "Rise, brother, and do not weep, but rejoice, because the Heavenly Goodness has granted what we desired."

The event proved the truth of this promise and prophecy, for after their parting at that time, they no more saw one another in the flesh; but their souls quitting their bodies on the very same day, that is, on the 20th of March, they were immediately again united in spirit, and translated to the heavenly kingdom by the ministry of angels. But Herebert was first prepared by a tedious sickness, through the dispensation of the Divine Goodness, as may be believed, to the end that if he was any thing inferior in merit to the blessed Cuthbert, the same might be made up by the chastising pain of a long sickness, that being thus made equal in grace to his intercessor, as he departed out of the body at the very same time with him, so he might be received into the same seat of eternal bliss.

The most reverend father died in the isle of Farne, earnestly entreating the brothers that he might also be buried in that same place, where he had served God a considerable time. However, at length yielding to their entreaties, he consented to be carried back to the isle of Lindisfarne, and there buried in the church. This being done accordingly, the venerable Bishop Wilfrid held the episcopal see of that church one year, till such time as one was chosen to be ordained in the room of Cuthbert. Afterwards Edbert was consecrated, a man renowned for his knowledge in the Divine writings, as also for keeping the Divine precepts, and chiefly for almsgiving, so that, according to the law, he every year gave the tenth part, not only of four-footed beasts, but also of all corn and fruit, as also of garments, to the poor.

CHAP. XXX.

St. Cuthbert's body was found altogether uncorrupted after it had been buried eleven years; his successor in the bishopric departed this world not long after. [A.D. 698].

IN order to show with how much glory the man of God, Cuthbert, lived after death, his holy life having been before his death signalized by frequent miracles; when he had been buried eleven years, Divine Providence put it into the minds of the brethren to take up his bones, expecting, as is usual with dead bodies, to find all the flesh consumed and reduced to ashes, and the rest dried up, and intending to put the same into a new coffin, and to lay them in the same place, but above the pavement, for the honour due to him. They acquainted Bishop Edbert with their design, and he consented to it, and ordered that the same should be done on the anniversary of his burial. They did so, and opening the grave, found all the body whole, as if it had been alive, and the joints pliable, more like one asleep than a dead person; besides, all the vestments the body had on were not only found, but wonderful for their freshness and gloss. The brothers seeing this, with much amazement hastened to tell the bishop what they had found; he being then alone in a place remote from the church, and encompassed by the sea. There he always used to spend the time of Lent, and was wont to continue there with great devotion, forty days before the birth of our Lord, in abstinence, prayer, and tears. There also his venerable predecessor, Cuthbert, had some time sorved God in private, before he went to the isle of Farne a

They brought him also some part of the garments that had covered his holy body; which presents he thankfully accepted, and attentively listening to the miracles, he with wonderful affection kissed those garments, as if they had been still upon his father's body, and said, "Let the body be put into new garments in lieu of these you have brought, and so lay it into the coffin you have provided; for I am certain that the place will not long remain empty, having been sanctified with so many miracles of heavenly grace; and how happy is he to whom our Lord, the author and giver of all bliss, shall grant the privilege of lying in the same."

The bishop having said this and much more, with many tears
and great humility, the brothers did as he had commanded
them, and when they had dressed the body in new garments,
and laid it in a new coffin, they placed it on the pavement of
the sanctuary.   Soon after, God's beloved bishop, Edbert,
fell grievously sick, and his distemper daily increasing, in a
short time, that is, on the 6th of May, he also departed to
our Lord, and they laid his body in the grave of the holy
father Cuthbert, placing over it the coffin, with the uncorrupted remains of that father.   The miracles sometimes
wrought in that place testify the merits of them both; some
of which we before preserved the memory of in the book of
his life, and have thought fit to add some more in this History, which have lately come to our knowledge.

CHAP. XXXI.

Of one that was cured of a palsy at the tomb of St. Cuthbert.   [A.D. 698.]

THERE was in that same monastery a brother whose name
was Bethwegen,* who had for a considerable time waited
upon the guests of the house, and is still living, having the
testimony of all the brothers and strangers resorting thither,
of being a man of much piety and religion, and serving the
office put upon him only for the sake of the heavenly reward.   This man, having on a certain day washed the
mantles or garments which he used in the hospital, in the sea,
was returning home, when on a sudden, about half way, he
was seized with a sudden distemper in his body, insomuch
that he fell down, and having lain some time, he could
scarcely rise again.   When at last he got up, he felt one half
of his body, from the head to the foot, struck with palsy,
and with much difficulty got home by the help of a staff.
The distemper increased by degrees, and as night approached,
became still worse, so that when day returned, he could
scarcely rise or go alone.   In this weak condition, a good
thought came into his mind, which was to go to the church,
the best way he could, to the tomb of the reverend father
Cuthbert, and there, on his knees, to beg of the Divine Goodness either to be delivered from that disease, if it were for

---

* Badudegn, Baduthegn, and Beadotheng, are the other forms of this
name : all of them are equally harsh to the ears of modern Englishmen.

his good, or if the Divine Providence had ordained him longer to lie under the same for his punishment, that he might bear the pain with patience and a composed mind.

He did accordingly, and supporting his weak limbs with a staff, entered the church, and prostrating himself before the body of the man of God, he, with pious earnestness, prayed, that, through his intercession, our Lord might be propitious to him. In the midst of his prayers, he fell as it were into a stupor, and, as he was afterwards wont to relate, felt a large and broad hand touch his head, where the pain lay, and by that touch, all the part of his body which had been affected with the distemper, was delivered from the weakness, and restored to health down to his feet. He then awoke, and rose up in perfect health, and returning thanks to God for his recovery, told the brothers what had happened to him; and to the joy of them all, returned the more zealously, as if chastened by his affliction, to the service which he was wont before so carefully to perform. The very garments which had been on Cuthbert's body, dedicated to God, either whilst living, or after he was dead, were not exempt from the virtue of performing cures, as may be seen in the book of his life and miracles, by such as shall read it.

CHAP. XXXII.

Of one who was cured of a distemper in his eye at the relics of St. Cuthbert. [A.D. 698.]

Nor is that cure to be passed over in silence, which was performed by his relics three years ago, and was told me by the brother himself, on whom it was wrought. It happened in the monastery, which, being built near the river Dacore,* has taken its name from the same, over which, at that time, the religious Suidbert presided as abbat. In that monastery was a youth whose eyelid had a great swelling on it, which growing daily, threatened the loss of the eye. The surgeons applied their medicines to ripen it, but in vain. Some said it ought to be cut off; others opposed it, for fear of worse consequences. The brother having long laboured under this malady, and seeing no human means likely to save his eye, but that, on the contrary, it grew daily worse, was cured on

* Dacre, Cumberland, five miles from Penrith.

a sudden, through the Divine Goodness, by the relics of the holy father, Cuthbert; for the brethren, finding his body uncorrupted, after having been many years buried, took some part of the hair, which they might, at the request of friends, give or show, in testimony of the miracle.

One of the priests of the monastery, named Thridred, who is now abbat there, had a small part of these relics by him at that time. One day in the church he opened the box of relics, to give some part to a friend that begged it, and it happened that the youth who had the distempered eye was then in the church; the priest, having given his friend as much as he thought fit, delivered the rest to the youth to put it into its place. Having received the hairs of the holy head, by some fortunate impulse, he clapped them to the sore eyelid, and endeavoured for some time, by the application of them, to soften and abate the swelling. Having done this, he again laid the relics into the box, as he had been ordered, believing that his eye would soon be cured by the hairs of the man of God, which had touched it; nor did his faith disappoint him. It was then, as he is wont to relate it, about the second hour of the day; but he, being busy about other things that belonged to that day, about the sixth hour of the same, touching his eye on a sudden, found it as sound with the lid, as if there never had been any swelling or deformity on it.

BOOK V.

CHAPTER I.

How Ethelwald, successor to Cuthbert, leading an eremetical life, calmed a tempest when the brethren were in danger at sea.   [A.D. 687.]

THE venerable Ethelwald, who had received the priesthood in the monastery of Inhrypum,* and had, by actions worthy of the same, sanctified his holy office, succeeded the man of God, Cuthbert, in the exercise of a solitary life, having practised the same before he was bishop, in the isle of Farne. For the more certain demonstration of the life

* Ripon.

which he led, and his merit, I will relate one miracle of
his, which was told me by one of these brothers for and
on whom the same was wrought; viz. Guthfrid, the venerable servant and priest of Christ, who, afterwards, as abbat,
presided over the brethren of the same church of Lindisfarne, in which he had been educated.

"I came," says he, "to the island of Farne, with two
others of the brethren, to speak with the most reverend
father, Ethelwald. Having been refreshed with his discourse, and taken his blessing, as we were returning home,
on a sudden, when we were in the midst of the sea, the fair
weather which was wafting us over was checked, and there
ensued so great and dismal a tempest, that neither the sails
nor oars were of any use to us, nor had we anything to expect but death. After long struggling with the wind and
waves to no effect, we looked behind us to see whether it
was practicable at least to recover the island from whence
we came, but we found ourselves on all sides so enveloped
in the storm, that there was no hope of escaping. But looking out as far as we could see, we observed, on the island of
Farne, Father Ethelwald, beloved of God, come out of his
cavern to watch our course; for, hearing the noise of the
storm and raging sea, he was come out to see what would
become of us. When he beheld us in distress and despair,
he bowed his knees to the Father of our Lord Jesus Christ,
in prayer for our life and safety; upon which, the swelling
sea was calmed, so that the storm ceased on all sides, and a
fair wind attended us to the very shore. When we had
landed, and had dragged upon the shore the small vessel that
brought us, the storm, which had ceased a short time for our
sake, immediately returned, and raged continually during the
whole day; so that it plainly appeared that the brief cessation
of the storm had been granted from Heaven at the request of
the man of God, in order that we might escape."

The man of God remained in the isle of Farne twelve
years, and died there; but was buried in the church of St.
Peter and Paul, in the isle of Lindisfarne, beside the bodies
of the aforesaid bishops. These things happened in the days
of King Alfred, who ruled the nation of the Northumbrians
eighteen years after his brother Egfrid.

CHAP. II.

How Bishop John cured a dumb man by blessing him.   [A.D. 685.]

IN the beginning of the aforesaid reign, Bishop Eata died,
and was succeeded in the prelacy of the church of Hagulstad
by John,* a holy man, of whom those that familiarly knew
him are wont to tell many miracles ; and more particularly,
the reverend Berthun, a man of undoubted veracity, and
once his deacon, now abbat of the monastery called Inderawood,† that is, in the wood of the Deiri : some of which
miracles we have thought fit to transmit to posterity.   There
is a certain building in a retired situation, and enclosed by a
narrow wood and a trench, about a mile and a half from the
church of Hagulstad, and separated from it by the river
Tyne, having a burying-place dedicated to St. Michael the
Archangel, where the man of God used frequently, as occasion offered, and particularly in Lent, to reside with a few
companions.   Being come thither once at the beginning of
Lent, to stay, he commanded his followers to find out some
poor person labouring under any grievous infirmity, or want,
whom he might keep with him during those days, by way of
alms, for so he was always used to do.

There was in a village not far off, a certain dumb youth,
known to the bishop, for he often used to come into his
presence to receive alms, and had never been able to speak
one word.   Besides, he had so much scurf and scabs on his
head, that no hair ever grew on the top of it, but only some
scattered hairs in a circle round about.   The bishop caused
this young man to be brought, and a little cottage to be made
for him within the enclosure of the dwelling, in which he
might reside, and receive a daily allowance from him.

---

* Afterwards called St. John of Beverley.
† The modern Beverley.   This town is twenty-nine miles from York,
the site of the ancient *Petuaria*, and was inhabited by the Britons before
the invasion of Cæsar.   The place, from the woods with which it was formerly covered, was called *Deirwalde*, implying the forest of the Deiri.
This monastery was erected for the use of both sexes, and placed under the
government of Berthun.   In 867 it was destroyed by the Danes ; but in
the early part of the tenth century it was restored by Athelstan, who made
it collegiate, with privilege of sanctuary, and a charter of liberties to the
townsmen.

When one week of Lent was over, the next Sunday he
caused the poor man to come in to him, and ordered him to
put his tongue out of his mouth and show it him; then laying hold of his chin, he made the sign of the cross on his
tongue, directing him to draw it back into his mouth and to
speak. "Pronounce some word," said he; "say yea,"
which, in the language of the Angles, is the word of affirming and consenting, that is, yes. The youth's tongue was
immediately loosed, and he said what he was ordered. The
bishop, then pronouncing the names of the letters, directed
him to say A; he did so, and afterwards B, which he also
did. When he had named all the letters after the bishop,
the latter proceeded to put syllables and words to him, which
being also repeated by him, he commanded him to utter
whole sentences, and he did it. Nor did he cease all that
day and the next night, as long as he could keep awake, as
those who were present relate, to talk something, and to
express his private thoughts and will to others, which he
could never do before; after the manner of the cripple, who,
being healed by the Apostles Peter and John, stood up leap-
ing, and walked, and went with them into the temple, walking, and skipping, and praising the Lord, rejoicing to have
the use of his feet, which he had so long wanted. The
bishop, rejoicing at his recovery of speech, ordered the physician to take in hand the cure of his scurfed head. He did
so, and with the help of the bishop's blessing and prayers, a
good head of hair grew as the flesh was healed. Thus the
youth obtained a good aspect, a ready utterance, and a beautiful head of hair, whereas before he had been deformed,
poor, and dumb. Thus rejoicing at his recovery, the bishop
offered to keep him in his family, but he rather chose to
return home.

CHAP. III.

The same bishop, John, by his prayers, healed a sick maiden. [A.D. 686.]

THE same Berthun told another miracle of the bishop's.
When the reverend Wilfrid, after a long banishment, was
admitted to the bishopric of the church of Hagulstad, and
the aforesaid John, upon the death of Bosa, a man of great
sanctity and humility, was, in his place, appointed bishop of

York, he came, once upon a time, to the monastery of Virgins, at the place called Wetadun,* where the Abbess Hereberga then presided. "When we were come thither," said he, "and had been received with great and universal joy, the abbess told us, that one of the virgins, who was her daughter in the flesh, laboured under a grievous distemper, having been lately bled in the arm, and whilst she was engaged in study, was seized with a sudden violent pain, which increased so that the wounded arm became worse, and so much swelled, that it could not be grasped with both hands; and thus being confined to her bed, through excess of pain, she was expected to die very soon. The abbess entreated the bishop that he would vouchsafe to go in and give her his blessing; for that she believed she would be the better for his blessing or touching her. He asked when the maiden had been bled? and being told that it was on the fourth day of the moon, said, 'You did very indiscreetly and unskilfully to bleed her on the fourth day of the moon; for I remember that Archbishop Theodore, of blessed memory, said, that bleeding at that time was very dangerous, when the light of the moon and the tide of the ocean is increasing; and what can I do to the girl if she is like to die?'

"The abbess still earnestly entreated for her daughter, whom she dearly loved, and designed to make abbess in her stead, and at last prevailed with him to go in to her. He accordingly went in, taking me with him to the virgin, who lay, as I said, in great anguish, and her arm swelled so fast that there was no bending of the elbow; the bishop stood and said a prayer over her, and having given his blessing, went out. Afterwards, as we were sitting at table, some one came in and called me out, saying, 'Coenberg' (that was the virgin's name) 'desires you will immediately go back to her.' I did so, and entering the house, perceived her countenance more cheerful, and like one in perfect health. Having seated myself down by her, she said, Would you like me to call for something to drink?'—'Yes, said I, 'and am very glad if you can.' When the cup was brought, and we had both drunk, she said, 'As soon as the bishop had said the prayer, given me his blessing, and gone out, I immediately began to mend; and though I have not

* That is, "Wettown," now Watton, in Yorkshire.

yet recovered my former strength, yet all the pain is quite gone from my arm, where it was most intense, and from all my body, as if the bishop had carried it away with him; though the swelling of the arm still seems to remain.' When we departed from thence, the cure of the pain in her limbs was followed by the assuaging of the swelling; and the virgin being thus delivered from torture and death, returned praise to our Lord and Saviour, with his other servants who were there."

CHAP. IV.

The same bishop healed an earl's wife that was sick, with holy water.
[A.D. 686.]

THE same abbat related another miracle, similar to the former, of the aforesaid bishop. "Not very far from our monastery, that is, about two miles off, was the country-house of one Puch, an earl, whose wife had languished near forty days under a very acute disease, insomuch that for three weeks she could not be carried out of the room where she lay. It happened that the man of God was, at that time, invited thither by the earl to consecrate a church;* and when that was done, the earl desired him to dine at his house. The bishop declined, saying, "He must return to the monastery, which was very near." The earl, pressing him more earnestly, vowed he would also give alms to the poor, if the bishop would break his fast that day in his house. I joined my entreaties to his, promising in like manner to give alms for the relief of the poor, if he would go and dine at the earl's house, and give his blessing. Having at length, with much difficulty, prevailed, we went in to dine. The bishop had sent to the woman that lay sick some of the holy water, which he had blessed for the consecration of the church, by one of the brothers that went along with me, ordering him to give her some to drink, and wash the place where her greatest pain was, with some of the same. This being done, the woman immediately got up in health, and perceiving that she had not only been delivered from her tedious distemper, but at the same time recovered the strength which she had lost, she presented the cup to the

* At South Burton, Yorkshire.

bishop and to us, and continued serving us with drink as she had begun till dinner was over ; following the example of Peter's mother-in-law, who, having been sick of a fever, arose at the touch of our Lord, and having at once received health and strength, ministered to them."

CHAP. V.

The same bishop recovered one of the earl's servants from death. [A.D. 686.]

AT another time also, being called to consecrate Earl Addi's church,* when he had performed that duty, he was entreated by the earl to go in to one of his servants, who lay dangerously ill, and having lost the use of all his limbs, seemed to be just at death's door ; and indeed the coffin had been provided to bury him in. The earl urged his entreaties with tears, earnestly praying that he would go in and pray for him, because his life was of great consequence to him ; and he believed that if the bishop would lay his hand upon him and give him his blessing, he would soon mend. The bishop went in, and saw him in a dying condition, and the coffin by his side, whilst all that were present were in tears. He said a prayer, blessed him, and on going out, as is the usual expression of comforters, said, " May you soon recover." Afterwards, when they were sitting at table, the lad sent to his lord, to desire he would let him have a cup of wine, because he was thirsty. The earl, rejoicing that he could drink, sent him a cup of wine, blessed by the bishop ; which, as soon as he had drunk, he immediately got up, and, shaking off his late infirmity, dressed himself, and going in to the bishop, saluted him and the other guests, saying, " He would also eat and be merry with them." They ordered him to sit down with them at the entertainment, rejoicing at his recovery. He sat down, ate and drank merrily, and behaved himself like the rest of the company ; and living many years after, continued in the same state of health. The aforesaid abbat says this miracle was not wrought in his presence, but that he had it from those who were there.

* At North Burton, Yorkshire

R

CHAP. VI.

The same bishop, by his prayers and blessing, delivered from death one of his clerks, who had bruised himself by a fall. [A.D. 686.]

Nor do I think that this further miracle, which Herebald, the servant of Christ, says was wrought upon himself, is to be passed over in silence. He was then one of that bishop's clergy, but now presides as abbat in the monastery at the mouth of the river Tyne. "Being present," said he, "and very well acquainted with his course of life, I found it to be most worthy of a bishop, as far as it is lawful for men to judge ; but I have known by the experience of others, and more particularly by my own, how great his merit was before Him who is the judge of the heart ; having been by his prayer and blessing brought back from the gates of death to the way of life. For, when in the prime of my youth, I lived among his clergy, applying myself to reading and singing, but not having yet altogether withdrawn my heart from youthful pleasures, it happened one day that as we were travelling with him, we came into a plain and open road, well adapted for galloping our horses. The young men that were with him, and particularly those of the laity, began to entreat the bishop to give them leave to gallop, and make trial of the goodness of their horses. He at first refused, saying, 'it was an idle request ;' but at last, being prevailed on by the unanimous desire of so many, 'Do so,' said he, 'if you will, but let Herebald have no part in the trial.' I earnestly prayed that I might have leave to ride with the rest, for I relied on an excellent horse, which he had given me, but I could not obtain my request.

"When they had several times galloped backwards and forwards, the bishop and I looking on, my wanton humour prevailed, and I could no longer refrain, but though he forbade me, I struck in among them, and began to ride at full speed ; at which I heard him call after me, 'Alas ! how much you grieve me by riding after that manner.' Though I heard him, I went on against his command ; but immediately the fiery horse taking a great leap over a hollow place, I fell, and lost both sense and motion, as if I had been dead ; for there was in that place a stone, level with the ground, covered with only a small turf, and no other stone to

be found in all that plain ; and it happened, as a punishment
for my disobedience, either by chance, or by Divine Providence so ordering it, that my head and hand, which in falling
I had clapped to my head, hit upon that stone, so that my
thumb was broken and my skull cracked, and I lay, as I said,
like one dead.

"And because I could not move, they stretched a canopy
for me to lie in.. It was about the seventh hour of the day,
and having lain still, and as it were dead from that time till
the evening, I then revived a little, and was carried home by
my companions, but lay speechless all the night, vomiting
blood, because something was broken within me by the fall.
The bishop was very much grieved at my misfortune, and
expected my death, for he bore me extraordinary affection.
Nor would he stay that night, as he was wont, among his
clergy ; but spent it all in watching and prayer alone, imploring the Divine goodness, as I imagine, for my health.
Coming to me in the morning early, and having said a
prayer over me, he called me by my name, and as it were
waking me out of a heavy sleep, asked, 'Whether I knew
who it was that spoke to me ?' I opened my eyes and said,
'I do ; you are my beloved bishop.'—'Can you live ?' said
he. I answered, 'I may, through your prayers, if it shall
please our Lord.'

"He then laid his hand on my head, with the words of
blessing, and returned to prayer ; when he came again to see
me, in a short time, he found me sitting and able to talk ;
and, being induced by Divine instinct, as it soon appeared,
began to ask me, 'Whether I knew for certain that I had
been baptized ?' I answered, 'I knew beyond all doubt that
I had been washed in the laver of salvation, to the remission
of my sins, and I named the priest by whom I knew myself
to have been baptized.' He replied, 'If you were baptized
by that priest, your baptism is not perfect ; for I know him,
and that having been ordained priest, he could not, by reason of the dulness of his understanding, learn the ministry
of catechising and baptizing ; for which reason I commanded
him altogether to desist from his presumptuous exercising of
the ministry, which he could not duly perform.' This said,
he took care to catechise me at that very time ; and it happened that he blew upon my face, on which I presently

R 2

found myself better. He called the surgeon, and ordered him to close and bind up my skull where it was cracked; and having then received his blessing, I was so much better that I mounted on horseback the next day, and travelled with him to another place; and being soon after perfectly recovered, I received the baptism of life."

He continued in his see thirty-three years, and then ascending to the heavenly kingdom, was buried in St. Peter's Porch, in his own monastery, called Inderawood, in the year of our Lord's incarnation 721. For having, by his great age, become unable to govern his bishopric, he ordained Wilfrid, his priest, bishop of the church of York, and retired to the aforesaid monastery, and there ended his days in holy conversation.

CHAP. VII.

Cædwalla, king of the West Saxons, went to Rome to be baptized; his successor Ina also devoutly repaired to the same church of the holy apostles. [A.D. 688.]

In the third year of the reign of Alfrid, Cædwalla, king of the West Saxons, having most honourably governed his nation two years, quitted his crown for the sake of our Lord and his everlasting kingdom, and went to Rome, being desirous to obtain the peculiar honour of being baptized in the church of the blessed apostles, for he had learned that in baptism alone, the entrance into heaven is opened to mankind; and he hoped at the same time, that laying down the flesh, as soon as baptized, he should immediately pass to the eternal joys of heaven; both which things, by the blessing of our Lord, came to pass according as he had conceived in his mind. For coming to Rome, at the time that Sergius was pope, he was baptized on the holy Saturday before Easter Day, in the year of our Lord 689, and being still in his white garments, he fell sick, and departed this life on the 20th of April, and was associated with the blessed in heaven. At his baptism, the aforesaid pope had given him the name of Peter, to the end, that he might be also united in name to the most blessed prince of the apostles, to whose most holy body his pious love had brought him from the utmost bounds of the earth. He was likewise buried in his church, and by

the pope's command an epitaph written on his tomb, wherein
the memory of his devotion might be preserved for ever, and
the readers or hearers might be inflamed with religious desire by the example of what he had done.

The epitaph was this:—

High state and place, kindred, a wealthy crown,
Triumphs, and spoils in glorious battles won,
Nobles, and cities walled, to guard his state,
High palaces, and his familiar seat,
Whatever honours his own virtue won,
Or those his great forefathers handed down,
Cædwal armipotent, from heaven inspir'd,
For love of heaven hath left, and here retir'd;
 Peter to see, and Peter's sacred chair,
The royal pilgrim travelled from afar,
Here to imbibe pure draughts from his clear stream,
And share the influence of his heavenly beam;
Here for the glories of a future claim,
Converted, chang'd his first and barbarous name.
And following Peter's rule, he from his Lord
Assumed the name at father Sergius' word,
At the pure font, and by Christ's grace made clean,
In heaven is free from former taints of sin.
Great was his faith, but greater God's decree,
Whose secret counsels mortal cannot see:
Safe came he, e'en from Britain's isle, o'er seas,
And lands, and countries, and through dangerous ways,
Rome to behold, her glorious temple see,
And mystic presents offer'd on his knee.
Now in the grave his fleshly members lie,
His soul, amid Christ's flock, ascends the sky.
Sure wise was he to lay his sceptre down,
And gain in heaven above a lasting crown.

Here was deposited Cædwalla, called also Peter, king of the Saxons, on
the twelfth day of the kalends of May, the second indiction. He lived
about thirty years, in the reign of the most pious emperor, Justinian, in the
fourth year of his consulship, in the second year of our apostolic lord,
Pope Sergius.

When Cædwalla went to Rome, Ina succeeded him on
the throne, being of the blood royal; and having reigned
thirty-seven years over that nation, he gave up the kingdom
in like manner to younger persons, and went away to Rome,
to visit the blessed apostles, at the time when Gregory was
pope, being desirous to spend some time of his pilgrimage
upon earth in the neighbourhood of the holy place, that he

might be more easily received by the saints into heaven. The same thing, about the same time, was done through the zeal of many of the English nation, noble and ignoble, laity and clergy, men and women.

CHAP. VIII.

Archbishop Theodore dies, Berthwald succeeds him as archbishop, and, among many others whom he ordained, he made Tobias, a most learned man, bishop of the church of Rochester. [A.D. 690.]

THE year after that in which Cædwalla died at Rome, that is, 690 after the incarnation of our Lord, Archbishop Theodore, of blessed memory, departed this life, old and full of days for he was eighty-eight years of age; which number of years he had been wont long before to foretell to his friends that he should live, the same having been revealed to him in a dream. He held the bishopric twenty-two years, and was buried in St. Peter's church, where all the bodies of the bishops of Canterbury are buried. Of whom, as well as of his companions, of the same degree, it may rightly and truly be said, that their bodies are interred in peace, and their names shall live from generation to generation. For to say all in few words, the English churches received more advantage during the time of his pontificate, than ever they had done before. His person, life, age, and death, are plainly described to all that resort thither, by the epitaph on his tomb, consisting of thirty-four heroic verses. The first whereof are these:

> Here rests fam'd Theodore, a Grecian name,
> Who had o'er England an archbishop's claim;
> Happy and blessed, industriously he wrought,
> And wholesome precepts to his scholars taught.

The four last are as follow:—

> And now it was September's nineteenth day,
> When, bursting from its ligaments of clay,
> His spirit rose to its eternal rest,
> And joined in heaven the chorus of the blest.

Berthwald succeeded Theodore in the archbishopric, being abbat of the monastery of Raculph,* which lies on the north side of the mouth of the river Genlade.† He was a man learned in the Scriptures, and well instructed in ecclesiasti-

* Reculver.   † The Inlade.

cal and monastic discipline, yet not to be compared to his predecessor. He was chosen bishop in the year of our Lord's incarnation 692, on the first day of July, Withred and Suebhard being kings in Kent; but he was consecrated the next year, on Sunday the 29th of June, by Godwin, metropolitan bishop of France, and was enthroned on Sunday the 31st of August. Among the many bishops whom he ordained was Tobias,* a man learned in the Latin, Greek, and Saxon tongues, otherwise also possessing much erudition, whom he consecrated in the stead of Gebmund, bishop of that see, deceased.

CHAP. IX.

Egbert, a holy man, would have gone into Germany to preach, but could not; Wictbert went, but meeting with no success, returned into Ireland, from whence he came. [A.D. 689.]

AT that time the venerable servant of Christ, and priest, Egbert, whom I cannot name but with the greatest respect, and who, as was said before, lived a stranger in Ireland to obtain hereafter a residence in heaven, proposed to himself to do good to many, by taking upon him the apostolical work, and preaching the word of God to some of those nations that had not yet heard it; many of which nations he knew there were in Germany, from whom the Angles or Saxons, who now inhabit Britain, are known to have derived their origin; for which reason they are still corruptly called Garmans by the neighbouring nation of the Britons. Such are the Frisons,† the Rugins, the Danes, the Huns, the Ancient Saxons, and the Boructuars‡ (or Bructers). There are also in the same parts many other nations still following pagan rites, to whom the aforesaid soldier of Christ designed to repair, sailing round Britain, and to try whether he could deliver any of them from Satan, and bring them over to Christ; or if this

---

* Ninth bishop of Rochester.

† Among all the German nations none maintained their liberty against the Romans, with greater success and courage, than the Frisons, who having formerly occupied a large tract of country on the coasts of the German ocean, crossed the Rhine into Belgic Gaul, and possessed themselves of those provinces about the mouth of the Rhine, which the Catti, who were also originally Germans, then held.

‡ The Boructuars seem to have inhabited the territory of Berg, and the neighbouring country toward Cologne.

could not be done, to go to Rome, to see and adore the hallowed thresholds of the holy apostles and martyrs of Christ.

But the Divine oracles and certain events proceeding from heaven obstructed his performing either of those designs; for when he had made choice of some most courageous companions, fit to preach the word of God, as being renowned for their learning and virtue; when all things were provided for the voyage, there came to him on a certain day in the morning one of the brethren, formerly disciple and minister in Britain to the beloved priest of God, Boisil, when the said Boisil was superior of the monastery of Melrose, under the Abbat Eata, as has been said above. This brother told him the vision which he had seen that night. " When after the morning hymns," said he, " I had laid me down in my bed, and was fallen into a slumber, my former master and loving tutor, Boisil, appeared to me, and asked, ' Whether I knew him?' I said, ' I do; you are Boisil.' He answered, ' I am come to bring Egbert a message from our Lord and Saviour, which nevertheless must be delivered to him by you. Tell him, therefore, that he cannot perform the journey he has undertaken; for it is the will of God that he should rather go to instruct the monasteries of Columba.' " Now Columba was the first teacher of Christianity to the Picts beyond the mountains northward, and the founder of the monastery in the island Hii, which was for a long time much honoured by many tribes of the Scots and Picts; wherefore he is now by some called Columbkill, the name being compounded from Columb and Cell.* Egbert, having heard the vision, ordered the brother that had told it him, not to mention it to any other, lest it should happen to be an illusion. However, when he considered of it with himself, he apprehended that it was real; yet would not desist from preparing for his voyage to instruct those nations.

A few days after the aforesaid brother came again to him, saying, " That Boisil had that night again appeared to him after matins, and said, ' Why did you tell Egbert that which

* I am happy to acknowledge an error which I had inadvertently committed in the former editions of this work by translating this passage as if the name Columbkill belonged to the island, instead of the abbat. My acknowledgments are due to the reviewer, in the British Critic, who detected the mistake. See p. 113.

I enjoined you in so light and cold a manner ? However, go now and tell him, that whether he will or no, he shall go to Columb's monastery, because their ploughs do not go straight ; and he is to bring them into the right way.' " Hearing this, Egbert again commanded the brother not to reveal the same to any person. Though now assured of the vision, he nevertheless attempted to undertake his intended voyage with the brethren. When they had put aboard all that was requisite for so long a voyage, and had waited some days for a fair wind, there arose one night on a sudden so violent a storm, that the ship was run aground, and part of what had been put aboard spoiled. However, all that belonged to Egbert and his companions was saved. Then he, saying, like the prophet, "This tempest has happened upon my account," laid aside the undertaking and stayed at home.

However, Wictbert, one of his companions, being famous for his contempt of the world and for his knowledge, for he had lived many years a stranger in Ireland, leading an eremitical life in great purity, went abroad, and arriving in Frisland, preached the word of salvation for the space of two years successively to that nation and to its king, Rathbed ; but reaped no fruit of all his great labour among his barbarous auditors. Returning them to the beloved place of his peregrination, he gave himself up to our Lord in his wonted repose, and since he could not be profitable to strangers by teaching them the faith, he took care to be the more useful to his own people by the example of his virtue.

CHAP. X.

Wilbrord, preaching in Frisland, converted many to Christ ; his two companions, the Hewalds, suffered martyrdom. [A.D. 690.]

WHEN the man of God, Egbert, perceived that neither he himself was permitted to preach to the Gentiles, being withheld, on account of some other advantage to the church, which had been foretold him by the Divine oracle ; nor that Wictbert, when he went into those parts, had met with any success ; he nevertheless still attempted to send some holy and industrious men to the work of the word, among whom was Wilbrord, a man eminent for his merit and rank in the priesthood. They arrived there, twelve in number, and turning aside to Pepin, duke of the Franks, were graciously received by him; and as he had lately subdued the Hither Frisland, and expelled King Rathbed, he sent them thither to preach, supporting them at the same time with his authority, that none might molest them in their preaching, and bestowing many favours on those who consented to embrace the faith. Thus it came to pass, that with the assistance of the Divine grace, they in a short time converted many from idolatry to the faith of Christ.

Two other priests of the English nation, who had long lived strangers in Ireland, for the sake of the eternal kingdom, following the example of the former, went into the province of the Ancient Saxons, to try whether they could there gain any to Christ by preaching. They both bore the same name, as they were the same in devotion, Hewald being the name of both, with this distinction, that, on account of the difference of their hair, the one was called Black Hewald and the other White Hewald. They were both piously religious, but Black Hewald was the more learned of the two in Scripture. On entering that province, these men took up their lodging in a certain steward's house, and requested that he would conduct them to his lord,* for that they had a message, and something to his advantage, to communicate to him; for those Ancient Saxons have no king, but several lords that rule their nation; and when any war happens, they cast lots indifferently, and on whomsoever the lot falls, him they follow and obey during the war; but as soon as the war is ended, all those lords are again equal in power. The steward received and entertained them in his house some days, promising to send them to his lord, as they desired.

But the barbarians finding them to be of another religion, by their continual prayer and singing of psalms and hymns, and by their daily offering the sacrifice of the saving oblation,—for they had with them sacred vessels and a consecrated table for an altar,—they began to grow jealous of them, lest if they should come into the presence of their chief, and converse with him, they should turn his heart from their gods, and convert him to the new religion of the Christian faith; and thus by degrees all their province

* Originally called " Ealdorman," or Senior. Satrap is the Latin term, used by Bede.

should change its old worship for a new. Hereupon they, on a sudden, laid hold of them and put them to death; the White Hewald they slew immediately with the sword; but the Black they put to tedious torture and tore limb from limb, throwing them into the Rhine. The chief, whom they had desired to see, hearing of it, was highly incensed, that the strangers who desired to come to him had not been allowed; and therefore he sent and put to death all those peasants and burnt their village. The aforesaid priests and servants of Christ suffered on the 3rd of October.

Nor did their martyrdom want the honour of miracles; for their dead bodies having been cast into the river by the pagans, as has been said, were carried against the stream for the space of almost forty miles, to the place where their companions were. Moreover, a long ray of light, reaching up to heaven, shined every night over the place where they arrived, in the sight of the very pagans that had slain them. Moreover, one of them appeared in a vision by night to one of his companions, whose name was Tilmon, a man of illustrious and of noble birth, who from a soldier was become a monk, acquainting him that he might find their bodies in that place, where he should see rays of light reaching from heaven to the earth; which turned out accordingly; and their bodies being found, were interred with the honour due to martyrs; and the day of their passion or of their bodies being found, is celebrated in those parts with proper veneration. At length, Pepin, the most glorious general of the Franks, understanding these things, caused the bodies to be brought to him, and buried them with much honour in the church of the city of Cologne, on the Rhine. It is reported, that a spring gushed out in the place where they were killed, which to this day affords a plentiful stream.

CHAP. XI

How the venerable Swidbert in Britain, and Wilbrord at Rome, were ordained bishops for Frisland.   [A.D. 692.]

AT their first coming into Frisland, as soon as Wilbrord found he had leave given him by the prince to preach, he made haste to Rome, where Pope Sergius then presided over the apostolical see, that he might undertake the desired work

of preaching the Gospel to the Gentiles, with his licence and
blessing ; and hoping to receive of him some relics of the
blessed apostles and martyrs of Christ ; to the end, that when
he destroyed the idols, and erected churches in the nation to
which he preached, he might have the relics of saints at
hand to put into them, and having deposited them there,
might accordingly dedicate those places to the honour of
each of the saints whose relics they were.   He was also desirous there to learn or to receive from thence many other
things which so great a work required.   Having obtained
all that he wanted, he returned to preach.

At which time, the brothers who were in Frisland, attending the ministry of the word, chose out of their own number
a man, modest of behaviour, and meek of heart, called Swidbert, to be ordained bishop for them.   He, being sent into
Britain, was consecrated by the most reverend Bishop Wilfrid, who, happening to be then driven out of his country,
lived in banishment among the Mercians ; for Kent had no
bishop at that time, Theodore being dead, and Berthwald,
his successor, who was gone beyond the sea, to be ordained,
not having returned.

The said Swidbert, being made bishop, returned from Britain not long after, and went among the Boructuarians ; and
by his preaching brought many of them into the way of
truth ; but the Boructuarians being not long after subdued
by the Ancient Saxons, those who had received the word
were dispersed abroad ; and the bishop himself repaired to
Pepin, who, at the request of his wife, Blithryda, gave him
a place of residence in a certain island on the Rhine, which,
in their tongue, is called Inlitore ;* where he built a monastery, which his heirs still possess, and for a time led a most
continent life, and there ended his days.

When they who went over had spent some years teaching
in Frisland, Pepin, with the consent of them all, sent the
venerable Wilbrord to Rome, where Sergius was still pope,
desiring that he might be consecrated archbishop over the
nation of the Frisons ; which was accordingly done, in the
year of our Lord's incarnation 696.   He was consecrated in
the church of the Holy Martyr Cecilia, on her feast-day ;

* Or Keiserswerdt, six miles from Dusseldorf.

the pope gave him the name of Clement, and sent him back to his bishopric, fourteen days after his arrival at Rome.

Pepin gave him a place for his episcopal see, in his famous castle, which in the ancient language of those people is called Wiltaburg, that is, the town of the Wilts ; but, in the French tongue, Utrecht.* The most reverend prelate having built a church there,† and preaching the word of faith far and near, drew many from their errors, and erected several churches and monasteries. For not long after he constituted other bishops in those parts, from among the brethren that either came with him or after him to preach there ; some of which are now departed in our Lord ; but Wilbrord himself, surnamed Clement, is still living, venerable for old age, having been thirty-six years a bishop, and sighing after the rewards of the heavenly life, after the many spiritual conflicts which he has waged.‡

CHAP. XII.

Of one among the Northumbrians, who rose from the dead, and related the things which he had seen, some exciting terror and others delight. [A. D. 696.]

AT this time a memorable miracle, and like to those of former days, was wrought in Britain ; for, to the end that the living might be saved from the death of the soul, a certain person, who had been some time dead, rose again to life, and related many remarkable things he had seen ; some of which I have thought fit here briefly to take notice of. There was a master of a family in that district of the Northumbrians which is called Cuningham, who led a religious life, as did also all that belonged to him. This man fell sick, and his distemper daily increasing, being brought to extremity, he died in the beginning of the night ; but in the morning early, he suddenly came to life again, and sat up, upon which all those that sat about the body weeping, fled away in a

---

* Bede seems to confound Utrecht with Wiltenburgh, which is three miles from it.

† The church of our Saviour. Wilbrord also restored the church of St. Martin, which subsequently became the cathedral.

‡ Wilbrord laboured in his diocese for about half a century, and died, according to Mabillon, in 740 or 741 ; but according to Dr. Smith, in 745.

great fright, only his wife, who loved him best, though in a great consternation and trembling, remained with him. He, comforting her, said, "Fear not, for I am now truly risen from death, and permitted again to live among men ; however, I am not to live hereafter as I was wont, but from henceforward after a very different manner." Then rising immediately, he repaired to the oratory of the little town, and continuing in prayer till day, immediately divided all his substance into three parts ; one whereof he gave to his wife, another to his children, and the third, belonging to himself, he instantly distributed among the poor. Not long after, he repaired to the monastery of Melrose, which is almost enclosed by the winding of the river Tweed, and having been shaven, went into a private dwelling, which the abbat had provided, where he continued till the day of his death, in such extraordinary contrition of mind and body, that though his tongue had been silent, his life declared that he had seen many things either to be dreaded or coveted, which others knew nothing of.

Thus he related what he had seen. "He that led me had a shining countenance and a bright garment, and we went on silently, as I thought, towards the north-east. Walking on, we came to a vale of great breadth and depth, but of infinite length ; on the left it appeared full of dreadful flames, the other side was no less horrid for violent hail and cold snow flying in all directions ; both places were full of men's souls, which seemed by turns to be tossed from one side to the other, as it were by a violent storm ; for when the wretches could no longer endure the excess of heat, they leaped into the middle of the cutting cold ; and finding no rest there, they leaped back again into the middle of the unquenchable flames. Now whereas an innumerable multitude of deformed spirits were thus alternately tormented far and near, as far as could be seen, without any intermission, I began to think that this perhaps might be hell, of whose intolerable flames I had often heard talk. My guide, who went before me, answered to my thought, saying, 'Do not believe so, for this is not the hell you imagine.'

"When he had conducted me, much frightened with that horrid spectacle, by degrees, to the farther end, on a sudden

I saw the place begin to grow dusk and filled with darkness.
When I came into it, the darkness, by degrees, grew so
thick, that I could see nothing besides it and the shape and
garment of him that led me. As we went on through the
shades of night, on a sudden there appeared before us frequent globes of black flames, rising as it were out of a great
pit, and falling back again into the same. When I had been
conducted thither, my leader suddenly vanished, and left me
alone in the midst of darkness and this horrid vision, whilst
those same globes of fire, without intermission, at one time
flew up and at another fell back into the bottom of the
abyss ; and I observed that all the flames, as they ascended,
were full of human souls, which, like sparks flying up with
smoke, were sometimes thrown on high, and again, when the
vapour of the fire ceased, dropped down into the depth
below. Moreover, an insufferable stench came forth with
the vapours, and filled all those dark places.

"Having stood there a long time in much dread, not
knowing what to do, which way to turn, or what end I
might expect, on a sudden I heard behind me the noise of a
most hideous and wretched lamentation, and at the same
time a loud laughing, as of a rude multitude insulting captured enemies. When that noise, growing plainer, came up
to me, I observed a gang of evil spirits dragging the howl-
ing and lamenting souls of men into the midst of the darkness, whilst they themselves laughed and rejoiced. Among
those men, as I could discern, there was one shorn like a
clergyman, a layman, and a woman. The evil spirits that
dragged them went down into the midst of the burning pit ;
and as they went down deeper, I could no longer distinguish
between the lamentation of the men and the laughing of the
devils, yet I still had a confused sound in my ears. In the
meantime, some of the dark spirits ascended from that flaming abyss, and running forward, beset me on all sides, and
much perplexed me with their glaring eyes and the stinking
fire which proceeded from their mouths and nostrils ; and
threatened to lay hold on me with burning tongs, which they
had in their hands, yet they durst not touch me, though they
frightened me. Being thus on all sides enclosed with enemies and darkness, and looking about on every side for
assistance, there appeared behind me, on the way that I

came, as it were, the brightness of a star shining amidst the
darkness ; which increased by degrees, and came rapidly
towards me : when it drew near, all those evil spirits, that
sought to carry me away with their tongs, dispersed and
fled.

"He, whose approach put them to flight, was the same
that led me before ; who, then turning towards the right,
began to lead me, as it were, towards the south-east, and
having soon brought me out of the darkness, conducted me
into an atmosphere of clear light. While he thus led me in
open light, I saw a vast wall before us, the length and
height of which, in every direction, seemed to be altogether
boundless. I began to wonder why we went up to the wall,
seeing no door, window, or path through it. When we
came to the wall, we were presently, I know not by what
means, on the top of it, and within it was a vast and delightful field, so full of fragrant flowers that the odour of its delightful sweetness immediately dispelled the stink of the dark
furnace, which had pierced me through and through. So
great was the light in this place, that it seemed to exceed
the brightness of the day, or the sun in its meridian height.
In this field were innumerable assemblies of men in white,
and many companies seated together rejoicing. As he led
me through the midst of those happy inhabitants, I began to
think that this might, perhaps, be the kingdom of heaven,
of which I had often heard so much. He answered to my
thought, saying, 'This is not the kingdom of heaven, as you
imagine.'

"When we had passed those mansions of blessed souls and
gone farther on, I discovered before me a much more beautiful light, and therein heard sweet voices of persons singing,
and so wonderful a fragrancy proceeded from the place, that
the other which I had before thought most delicious, then
seemed to me but very indifferent; even as that extraordinary brightness of the flowery field, compared with this,
appeared mean and inconsiderable. When I began to hope
we should enter that delightful place, my guide, on a sudden
stood still; and then turning back, led me back by the way
we came.

"When we returned to those joyful mansions of the souls
in white, he said to me, 'Do you know what all these things

are which you have seen ?' I answered, I did not; and then
he replied, 'That vale you saw so dreadful for consuming
flames and cutting cold, is the place in which the souls of
those are tried and punished, who, delaying to confess and
amend their crimes, at length have recourse to repentance at
the point of death, and so depart this life; but nevertheless
because they, even at their death, confessed and repented,
they shall all be received into the kingdom of heaven at the
day of judgment; but many are relieved before the day of
judgment, by the prayers, alms, and fasting, of the living,
and more especially by masses. That fiery and stinking pit,
which you saw, is the mouth of hell, into which whosoever
falls shall never be delivered to all eternity. This flowery
place, in which you see these most beautiful young people, so
bright and merry, is that into which the souls of those are
received who depart the body in good works, but who are
not so perfect as to deserve to be immediately admitted into
the kingdom of heaven; yet they shall all, at the day of
judgment, see Christ, and partake of the joys of his kingdom ;
for whoever are perfect in thought, word and deed, as soon as
they depart the body, immediately enter into the kingdom of
heaven; in the neighbourhood whereof that place is, where
you heard the sound of sweet singing, with the fragrant
odour and bright light. As for you, who are now to return
to your body, and live among men again, if you will endeavour nicely to examine your actions, and direct your
speech and behaviour in righteousness and simplicity, you
shall, after death, have a place or residence among these joyful troops of blessed souls; for when I left you for a while, it
was to know how you were to be disposed of.' When he
had said this to me, I much abhorred returning to my body,
being delighted with the sweetness and beauty of the place I
beheld, and with the company of those I saw in it. However, I durst not ask him any questions; but in the meantime, on a sudden, I found myself alive among men."

Now these and other things which this man of God saw,
he would not relate to slothful persons and such as lived
negligently; but only to those who, being terrified with the
dread of torments, or delighted with the hopes of heavenly
joys, would make use of his words to advance in piety. In
the neighbourhood of his cell lived one Hemgils, a monk,

s

eminent in the priesthood, which he honoured by his good
works: he is still living, and leading a solitary life in Ireland, supporting his declining age with coarse bread and cold
water. He often went to that man, and asking several questions, heard of him all the particulars of what he had seen
when separated from his body; by whose relation we also
came to the knowledge of those few particulars which we
have briefly set down. He also related his visions to King
Alfrid, a man most learned in all respects, and was by him
so willingly and attentively heard, that at his request he was
admitted into the monastery above-mentioned, and received
the monastic tonsure; and the said king, when he happened
to be in those parts, very often went to hear him. At that
time the religious and humble abbat and priest, Ethelwald,
presided over the monastery, and now with worthy conduct
possesses the episcopal see of the church of Lindisfarne.

He had a more private place of residence assigned him in
that monastery, where he might apply himself to the service
of his Creator in continual prayer. And as that place lay
on the bank of the river, he was wont often to go into the
same to do penance in his body, and many times to dip quite
under the water, and to continue saying psalms or prayers in
the same as long as he could endure it, standing still sometimes up to the middle, and sometimes to the neck in water;
and when he went out from thence ashore, he never took off
his cold and frozen garments till they grew warm and dry
on his body. And when in the winter the half-broken pieces
of ice were swimming about him, which he had himself
broken, to make room to stand or dip himself in the river,
those who beheld it would say, "It is wonderful, brother
Drithelm, (for so he was called,) that you are able to endure
such violent cold;" he simply answered, for he was a man
of much simplicity and indifferent wit, "I have seen greater
cold." And when they said, "It is strange that you will
endure such austerity;" he replied, "I have seen more
austerity." Thus he continued, through an indefatigable
desire of heavenly bliss, to subdue his aged body with daily
fasting, till the day of his being called away; and thus he
forwarded the salvation of many by his words and example.

CHAP. XIII.

Of another, who before his death saw a book containing all his sins, which was showed him by devils. [A.D. 704—709.]

IT happened quite the contrary with one in the province of the Mercians, whose visions and words, and also his behaviour, were neither advantageous to others nor to himself. In the reign of Coenred, who succeeded Ethelred, there was a layman in a military employment, no less acceptable to the king for his worldly industry, than displeasing to him for his private neglect of himself. The king often admonished him to confess and amend, and to forsake his wicked courses, before he should lose all time for repentance and amendment by a sudden death. Though frequently warned, he despised the words of salvation, and promised he would do penance at some future time. In the meantime, falling sick he was confined to his bed, and began to feel very severe pains. The king coming to him (for he loved the man), earnestly exhorted him, even then, before death, to repent of his offences. He answered, "He would not then confess his sins, but would do it when he was recovered of his sickness, lest his companions should upbraid him of having done that for fear of death, which he had refused to do in health." He thought he then spoke very bravely, but it afterwards appeared that he had been miserably deluded by the wiles of the Devil.

The distemper still increasing, when the king came again to visit and instruct him, he cried out with a lamentable voice, "What will you have now? What are ye come for? for you can no longer do me any good." The king answered, "Do not talk so; behave yourself like a man in his right mind."—"I am not mad," replied he, "but I have now all the guilt of my wicked conscience before my eyes."—"What is the meaning of that?" rejoined the king. "Not long since," said he, "there came into this room two most beautiful youths, and sat down by me, the one at my head, and the other at my feet. One of them produced a very small and most curious book, and gave it me to read; looking into it, I there found all the good actions I had ever done in my life written down, and they were very few and inconsiderable. They took back the book and said nothing to me. Then, on a sudden, appeared an army of wicked and deformed spirits, encompassing this house without, and filling it within. Then he, who, by the blackness of his dismal face, and his sitting above the rest, seemed to be the chief of them, taking out a book horrid to behold, of a prodigious size, and of almost insupportable weight, commanded one of his followers to bring it to me to read. Having read it, I found therein most plainly written in black characters, all the crimes I ever committed, not only in word and deed, but even in the least thought; and he said to those men in white, who sat by me, 'Why do you sit here, since you most certainly know that this man is ours?' They answered, 'You are in the right; take and add him to the number of the damned.' This said, they immediately vanished, and two most wicked spirits rising, with forks in their hands, one of them struck me on the head, and the other on the foot. These strokes are now with great torture penetrating through my bowels to the inward parts of my body, and as soon as they meet I shall die, and the devils being ready to snatch me away, I shall be dragged into hell."

Thus talked that wretch in despair, and dying soon after, he is now in vain suffering in eternal torments that penance which he refused to suffer during a short time, that he might obtain forgiveness. Of whom it is manifest, that (as the holy Pope Gregory writes of certain persons) he did not see these things for his own sake, since they availed him only for the instruction of others, who, knowing of his death, should be afraid to put off the time of repentance, whilst they have leisure, lest, being prevented by sudden death, they should depart impenitent. His having books laid before him by the good or evil spirits, was done by Divine dispensation, that we may keep in mind that our actions and thoughts are not lost in the wind, but are all kept to be examined by the Supreme Judge, and will in the end be shown us either by friendly or hostile angels. As to the angels first producing a white book, and then the devils a black one; the former a very small one, the latter one very large; it is to be observed, that in his first years he did some good actions, all which he nevertheless obscured by the evil actions of his youth. If, on the contrary, he had taken care in his youth to correct the errors of his more tender years, and to cancel them in God's sight by doing well, he might have been associated to the number of those of whom the Psalm says, "Blessed are those whose iniquities are forgiven, and whose sins are hid." This story, as I learned it of the venerable Bishop Pechthelm,* I have thought proper to relate in a plain manner, for the salvation of my hearers.

CHAP. XIV.

Of another, who being at the point of death, saw the place of punishment appointed for him in hell. [A.D. 704.]

I KNEW a brother myself, would to God I had not known him, whose name I could mention if it were necessary, and who resided in a noble monastery, but lived himself ignobly. He was frequently reproved by the brethren and elders of the place, and admonished to adopt a more regular life; and though he would not give ear to them, he was long patiently borne with by them, on account of his usefulness in temporal works, for he was an excellent carpenter; he was much addicted to drunkenness, and other pleasures of a lawless life, and more used to stop in his workhouse day and night, than to go to church to sing and pray, and hear the word of life with the brethren. For which reason it happened to him according to the saying, that he who will not willingly and humbly enter the gate of the church, will certainly be damned, and enter the gate of hell whether he will or no. For he falling sick, and being reduced to extremity, called the brethren, and with much lamentation, and like one damned, began to tell them, that he saw hell open, and Satan at the bottom thereof; as also Caiaphas, with the others that slew our Lord, by him delivered up to avenging flames. "In whose neighbourhood," said he, "I see a place of eternal perdition provided for me, miserable wretch." The brothers, hearing these words, began seriously to exhort him, that he should repent even then whilst he was in the flesh. He answered in despair, "I have no time now to change my course of life, when I have myself seen my judgment passed."

Whilst uttering these words, he died without having re-

* Bishop of Whithern, in Galloway. See book v. c. 23.

ceived the saving viaticum, and his body was buried in the remotest parts of the monastery, nor did any one dare either to say masses or sing psalms, or even to pray for him. How far has our Lord divided the light from darkness! The blessed martyr, Stephen, being about to suffer death for the truth, saw the heavens open, the glory of God revealed, and Jesus standing on the right hand of God. And where he was to be after death, there he fixed the eyes of his mind, that he might die with the more satisfaction. On the contrary, this carpenter, of a dark mind and actions, when death was at hand, saw hell open and witnessed the damnation of the Devil and his followers; the unhappy wretch also saw his own prison among them, to the end that, despairing of his salvation, he might die the more miserably; but might by his perdition afford cause of salvation to the living who should hear of it. This happened lately in the province of the Bernicians, and being reported abroad far and near, inclined many to do penance for their sins without delay, which we hope may also be the result of this our narrative.

CHAP. XV.

Several churches of the Scots, at the instance of Adamnan, conformed to the Catholic Easter; the same person wrote a book about the holy places. [A.D. 703.]

At this time a great part of the Scots in Ireland, and some also of the Britons in Britain, through the goodness of God, conformed to the proper and ecclesiastical time of keeping Easter. Adamnan, priest and abbat of the monks that were in the isle of Hii, was sent ambassador by his nation to Alfrid, king of the English,* where he made some stay, observing the canonical rites of the church, and was earnestly admonished by many, who were more learned than himself, not to presume to live contrary to the universal custom of the Church, either in relation to the observance of Easter, or any other decrees whatsoever, considering the small number of his followers, seated in so distant a corner of the world; in consequence of this he changed his mind, and readily preferred those things which he had seen and heard in the English churches, to the customs which he and

* Of Northumbria.

his people had hitherto followed. For he was a good and
wise man, and remarkably learned in Holy Scripture. Returning home, he endeavoured to bring his own people that
were in the isle of Hii, or that were subject to that monastery, into the way of truth, which he had learned and embraced with all his heart; but in this he could not prevail.
He then sailed over into Ireland, to preach to those people,
and by modestly declaring the legal time of Easter, he reduced many of them, and almost all that were not under the
dominion of those of Hii, to the Catholic unity, and taught
them to keep the legal time of Easter.

Returning to his island, after having celebrated the canonical Easter in Ireland, he most earnestly inculcated the observance of the Catholic time of Easter in his monastery, yet
without being able to prevail; and it so happened that he
departed this life before the next year came round, the
Divine goodness so ordaining it, that as he was a great lover
of peace and unity, he should be taken away to everlasting
life before he should be obliged, on the return of the time of
Easter, to quarrel still more seriously with those that would
not follow him in the truth.

This same person wrote a book about the holy places,
most useful to many readers; his authority, from whom he
procured his information, was Arculf, a French bishop, who
had gone to Jerusalem for the sake of the holy places; and
having seen all the Land of Promise, travelled to Damascus,
Constantinople, Alexandria, and many islands, and returning
home by sea, was by a violent storm forced upon the western
coast of Britain. After many other accidents, he came to
the aforesaid servant of Christ, Adamnan, who, finding him
to be learned in the Scriptures, and acquainted with the holy
places, entertained him zealously, and attentively gave ear to
him, insomuch that he presently committed to writing all
that Arculf said he had seen remarkable in the holy places.
Thus he composed a work beneficial to many, and particularly to those who, being far removed from those places
where the patriarchs and apostles lived, know no more of
them than what they learn by reading. Adamnan presented
this book to King Alfrid, and through his bounty it came to
be read by lesser persons. The writer thereof was also well
rewarded by him, and sent back into his country. I believe

it will be acceptable to our readers if we collect some particulars from the same, and insert them in our History.*

CHAP. XVI.

The account given by the aforesaid book of the place of our Lord's nativity, passion, and resurrection. [A. D. 704.]

He wrote concerning the place of the nativity of our Lord, to this effect. "Bethlehem, the city of David, is seated on a narrow ridge, encompassed on all sides with valleys, being a thousand paces in length from east to west, the wall low without towers, built along the edge of the plain on the summit. In the east angle thereof is a sort of natural half cave, the outward part whereof is said to have been the place where our Lord was born ; the inner is called our Lord's Manger. This cave within is all covered with rich marble, over the place where our Lord is said particularly to have been born, and over it is the great church of St. Mary." He likewise wrote about the place of his Passion and Resurrection in this manner. "Entering the city of Jerusalem on the north side, the first place to be visited, according to the disposition of the streets, is the church of Constantine, called the Martyrdom. It was built by the Emperor Constantine, in a royal and magnificent manner, on account of the cross of our Lord having been found there by his mother Helen. From thence, to the westward, appears the church of Golgotha, in which is also to be seen the rock which once bore the cross with our Saviour's body fixed on it, and now it bears a large silver cross, with a great brazen wheel hanging over it surrounded with lamps. Under the place of our Lord's cross, a vault is hewn out of the rock, in which sacrifice is offered on an altar for honourable persons deceased, their bodies remaining meanwhile in the street. To the westward of this is the Anastasis, that is, the round church of our Saviour's resurrection, encompassed with three walls, and supported by twelve columns. Between each of the walls is a broad space, containing three altars at three differ-

---

* Besides the work "On the Holy Places," [De Locis Sanctis,] Adamnan is the reputed author of a "Life of Saint Columba ; " but I have strong doubts of Adamnan's having written it. I propose shortly to publish the original text of both these works.

ent points of the middle wall; to the north, the south, and
the west, it has eight doors or entrances through the three
opposite walls; four whereof front to the north-east, and
four to the south-east. In the midst of it is the round tomb
of our Lord cut out of the rock, the top of which a man
standing within can touch; the entrance is on the east;
against it is still laid that great stone. To this day it bears
the marks of the iron tools within, but on the outside it is all
covered with marble to the very top of the roof, which is
adorned with gold, and bears a large golden cross. In the
north part of the monument, the tomb of our Lord is hewed
out of the same rock, seven feet in length, and three palms
above the floor; the entrance being on the south side, where
twelve lamps burn day and night, four within the sepulchre,
and eight above on the right hand side. The stone that was
laid at the entrance to the monument, is now cleft in two;
nevertheless, the lesser part of it stands as a square altar
before the door of the monument; the greater part makes
another square altar at the east end of the same church, and
is covered with linen cloths. The colour of the said monument and sepulchre appears to be white and red."

CHAP. XVII.

Of the place of our Lord's ascension, and the tombs of the patriarchs.
[A.D. 704.]

CONCERNING the place of our Lord's ascension, the aforesaid
author writes thus. "Mount Olivet is equal in height to
Mount Sion, but exceeds it in breadth and length; bearing
few trees besides vines and olive trees, and is fruitful in
wheat and barley, for the nature of that soil is not calculated
for bearing things of large or heavy growth, but grass and
flowers. On the very top of it, where our Lord ascended
into heaven, is a large round church, having about it three
vaulted porches. For the inner house could not be vaulted
and covered, because of the passage of our Lord's body; but
it has an altar on the east side, covered with a narrow roof.
In the midst of it are to be seen the last prints of our Lord's
feet, the sky appearing open above where he ascended; and
though the earth is daily carried away by believers, yet still
it remains as before, and retains the same impression of the

feet. Near this lies an iron wheel, as high as a man's neck, having an entrance towards the west, with a great lamp hanging above it on a pulley, and burning night and day. In the western part of the same church are eight windows ; and eight lamps, hanging opposite to them by cords, cast their light through the glass as far as Jerusalem ; this light is said to strike the hearts of the beholders with a sort of joy and humility. Every year, on the day of the Ascension, when mass is ended, a strong blast of wind is said to come down, and to cast to the ground all that are in the church."

Of the situation of Hebron, and the tombs of the fathers, he writes thus. "Hebron, once the city and metropolis of David's kingdom, now only showing what it was by its ruins, has, one furlong to the east of it, a double cave in the valley, where the tombs of the patriarchs are enclosed with a square wall, their heads lying to the north. Each of the tombs is covered with a single stone, worked like the stones of a church, and of a white colour, for three patriarchs. Adam's is of more mean and common workmanship, and lies not far from them at the farthest northern extremity. There are also some poorer and smaller monuments of three women. The hill Mamre is a thousand paces from the monuments, and is full of grass and flowers, having a flat plain on the top. In the northern part of it, Abraham's oak, being a stump about twice as high as a man, is enclosed in a church."

Thus much have we collected from the works of the aforesaid writer, keeping to the sense of his words, but more briefly delivered, and have thought fit to insert in our History. Whosoever desires to see more of the contents of that book, may see it either in the same, or in that which we have lately epitomized from it.

CHAP. XVIII.

The South Saxons received Eadbert and Eolla, and the West Saxons, Daniel and Aldhelm, for their bishops. Of the writings of the same Aldhelm. [A.D. 705.]

In the year of the incarnation of our Lord 705, Alfrid, king of the Northumbrians, died just before the end of the twentieth year of his reign. His son Osred, a boy about eight years of age, succeeding him in the throne, reigned eleven years. In the beginning of his reign, ·Hedda, bishop of the West Saxons,* departed to the heavenly kingdom; for he was a good and just man, and exercised his episcopal duties rather by his innate love of virtue, than by what he had gained from learning. The most reverend prelate, Pech-thelm, of whom we shall speak in the proper place,† and who was a long time either deacon or monk with his successor Aldhelm, is wont to relate that many miraculous cures have been wrought in the place where he died, through the merit of his sanctity; and that the men of that province used to carry the dust from thence for the sick, which, when they had put into water, the sprinkling or drinking thereof restored health to many sick men and beasts; so that the holy earth being frequently carried away, there was a considerable hole left.

Upon his death the bishopric of that province was divided into two dioceses. One of them was given to Daniel,‡ which he governs to this day; the other to Aldhelm,§ wherein he most worthily presided four years; both of them were well instructed, as well in ecclesiastical affairs as in the knowledge of the Scriptures. Aldhelm, when he was only a priest and abbat of the monastery of Malmesbury, by order of a synod of his own nation, wrote a notable book‖ against the error of the Britons, in not celebrating Easter at the proper time, and in doing several other things not consonant to the purity and the peace of the church; and by the reading of this book he persuaded many of them, who were subject to the West Saxons, to adopt the Catholic celebration of our Lord's resurrection. He likewise wrote a notable book on Virginity, which, in imitation of Sedulius, he composed double, that is, in hexameter verse and prose. He wrote some other books, as being a man most learned in all re-

* Winchester. See p. 191.   † In book v. c. 23.
‡ Daniel was bishop of Winchester, which included the counties of Hampshire, Surrey, Sussex, and the Isle of Wight.
§ Aldhelm was appointed to the new see of Sherborne, consisting of the counties of Dorset, Somerset, Wilts, Devon, and Cornwall. This see continued for more than three centuries, when it was removed first to Wilton, afterwards to Old Sarum, and finally to New Sarum, or Salisbury.
‖ This notable book of Bishop Aldhelm, is but a short tract of a few pages, published together with all his other works in " S. Aldhelmi Opera, 8vo. London, 1842;" forming vol. I. of " Patres Ecclesiæ Anglicanæ."

spects, for he had a clean style, and was, as I have said, wonderful for ecclesiastical and liberal erudition. On his death, Forthere was made bishop in his stead, and is living at this time, being likewise a man very learned in Holy Writ.

Whilst they were bishops, it was decreed in a synod, that the province of the South Saxons, which till then belonged to the diocese of the city of Winchester, where Daniel then presided, should also have an episcopal see, and a bishop of its own.* Eadbert, at that time abbat of the monastery of Bishop Wilfrid, of blessed memory, called Selsey, was consecrated their first bishop. On his death, Eolla succeeded in the bishopric. He also died some years since, and the bishopric has been discontinued to this day.

CHAP. XIX.

Coinred, king of the Mercians, and Offa, of the East Saxons, ended their days at Rome, in the monastic habit. Of the life and death of Bishop Wilfrid. [A.D. 709.]

In the fourth year of the reign of Osred, Coinred, who had for some time nobly governed the kingdom of the Mercians, did a much more noble act, by quitting the throne of his kingdom, and going to Rome, where being shorn, when Constantine was pope, and made a monk at the relics of the apostles, he continued to his last hour in prayers, fasting and alms-deeds. He was succeeded in the throne by Ceolred, the son of Ethelred, who had been king before Coinred. With him went the son of Sighere, king of the East Saxons above-mentioned, whose name was Offa, a youth of most lovely age and beauty, and most earnestly desired by all his nation to be their king. He, with like devotion, quitted his wife, lands, kindred and country, for Christ and for the Gospel, that he might "receive an hundred-fold in this life, and in the world to come life everlasting." He also, when they came to the holy places at Rome, receiving the tonsure, and adopting a monastic life, attained the long wished-for sight of the blessed apostles in heaven.

The same year that they departed from Britain, the cele-

* See pages 195, 198.

brated prelate, Wilfrid, died in the province of Undalum,*
after he had been bishop forty-five years. His body, being
laid in a coffin, was carried to his monastery, called Ripon,
and there buried in the church of the blessed Apostle Peter,
with the honour due to so great a prelate. We will now
turn back, and briefly mention some particulars of his life.
Being a boy of a good disposition, and behaving himself
worthily at that age, he conducted himself so modestly and
discreetly in all respects, that he was deservedly beloved,
respected, and cherished by his elders as one of themselves.
At fourteen years of age he preferred the monastic to the
secular life; which, when he had signified to his father, for
his mother was dead, he readily consented to his heavenly
wishes, and advised him to persist in his holy resolution.
Accordingly he came to the isle of Lindisfarne, and there
giving himself up to the service of the monks, he took care
diligently to learn and to perform those things which belong
to monastic purity and piety; and being of an acute understanding, he in a very short time learned the psalms and
some books, before he was shorn, but when he was already
become very remarkable for the greater virtues of humility
and obedience: for which he was deservedly beloved and
respected by his equals and elders. Having served God
some years in that monastery, and being a clear-sighted
youth, he observed that the way to virtue taught by the
Scots was not perfect, and he resolved to go to Rome, to
see what ecclesiastical or monastic rites were in use there.
The brethren being made acquainted therewith, commended
his design, and advised him to put it into execution. He
then repaired to Queen Eanfled, to whom he was well
known, and who had got him into that monastery by her
advice and assistance, and acquainted her that he was desirous to visit the churches of the apostles. She, being
pleased with the youth's resolution, sent him into Kent, to
King Earconbert, who was her uncle's son, requesting that
he would send him to Rome in an honourable manner. At
that time, Honorius, one of the disciples of the holy Pope
Gregory, and well instructed in ecclesiastical institutes, was

* Oundle, Northamptonshire. The monastery at this place, where Wilfrid died, is considered by some to have been a cell to the abbey of Peterborough, and part of its possessions.

archbishop there. Whilst he made some stay there, and, being a youth of an active spirit, diligently applied himself to learn those things which he undertook, another youth, called Biscop, or otherwise Benedict, of the English nobility, arrived there, being likewise desirous to go to Rome, of which we have before made mention.

The king gave him Wilfrid for a companion, with orders to conduct him to Rome. When they came to Lyons, Wilfrid was detained there by Dalfin, the bishop of that city; but Benedict hastened on to Rome. That prelate was delighted with the youth's prudent discourse, the gracefulness of his aspect, the alacrity of his behaviour, and the sedateness and gravity of his thoughts; for which reason he plentifully supplied him and his companions with all necessaries, as long as they stayed with him; and further offered to commit to him the government of a considerable part of France, to give him a maiden daughter of his own brother to wife, and to receive him as his adopted son. He returned thanks for the favour, which he was pleased to show to a stranger, and answered, that he had resolved upon another course of life, and for that reason had left his country and set out for Rome.

Hereupon the bishop sent him to Rome, furnishing him with a guide and plenty of all things requisite for his journey, earnestly requesting that he would come that way when he returned into his own country. Wilfrid arriving at Rome, by constantly applying himself to prayer and the study of ecclesiastical affairs, as he had before proposed to himself, gained the friendship of the most holy and learned Boniface, the archdeacon, who was also counsellor to the pope, by whose instruction he regularly learned the four Gospels, the true calculation of Easter, and many other things appertaining to ecclesiastical discipline, which he could not attain in his own country. When he had spent some months there, in successful study, he returned into France, to Dalfin; and having stayed with him three years, received from him the tonsure, and was so much beloved that he had thoughts of making him his heir; but this was prevented by the bishop's untimely death, and Wilfrid was reserved to be bishop of his own, that is, the English, nation; for Queen Baldhilda sent soldiers with orders to put the bishop to death; whom

Wilfrid, his clerk, attended to the place where he was to be beheaded, being very desirous, though the bishop opposed it, to die with him; but the executioners, understanding that he was a stranger, and of the English nation, spared him, and would not put him to death with his bishop.

Returning to England, he was admitted to the friendship of King Alfrid, who had always followed the catholic rules of the Church; and therefore finding him to be a Catholic, he gave him land of ten families at the place called Stanford;* and not long after, the monastery, of thirty families, at the place called Ripon; which place he had lately given to those that followed the doctrine of the Scots, to build a monastery upon. But, forasmuch as they afterwards, being left to their choice, would rather quit the place than adopt the catholic Easter, and other canonical rites, according to the custom of the Roman Apostolic Church, he gave the same to him, whom he found to follow better discipline and better customs.

At the same time, by the said king's command, he was ordained priest in the same monastery, by Agilbert, bishop of the West Saxons† above-mentioned, the king being desirous that a man of so much piety and learning should continue with him as priest and teacher; and not long after, having discovered and banished the Scottish sect, as was said above, he, with the advice and consent of his father Oswy, sent him into France, to be consecrated bishop, at about thirty years of age, the same Agilbert being then bishop of Paris, and eleven other bishops meeting at the consecration of the new bishop, that function was most honourably performed. Whilst he was yet beyond the sea, Chad, a holy man, was consecrated bishop of York, by command of King Oswy, as has been said above; and having ably ruled that church three years, he retired to govern his monastery of Lestingau, and Wilfrid was made bishop of all the province of the Northumbrians.‡

Afterwards, in the reign of Egfrid, he was expelled his bishopric, and others were consecrated bishops in his stead, of whom mention has been made above. Designing to go to Rome, to answer for himself before the pope, when he

---

* Now Stamford, Lincolnshire.   † Dorchester.   ‡ At York.

was aboard the ship, the wind blew hard west, and he was driven into Frisland, and honourably received by that barbarous people and their King Aldgist, to whom he preached Christ, and instructed many thousands of them in the word of truth, washing them from their abominations in the laver of salvation. Thus he there began the work of the Gospel which was afterwards finished by Wilbrord, a most reverend bishop of Jesus Christ. Having spent the winter there with his new converts, he set out again on his way to Rome, where his cause being tried before Pope Agatho and several bishops, he was by their universal consent, acquitted of what had been laid to his charge, and declared worthy of his bishopric.

At the same time, the said Pope Agatho assembling a synod at Rome, of one hundred and twenty-five bishops, against those that taught there was only one will and operation in our Lord and Saviour, ordered Wilfrid also to be summoned, and, when seated among the bishops, to declare his own faith and the faith of the province or island from whence he came; and they being found orthodox in their faith, it was thought fit to record the same among the acts of that synod, which was done in this manner : "Wilfrid, the beloved of God, bishop of the city of York, having referred to the Apostolic See, and being by that authority acquitted of every thing, whether specified against him or not, and having taken his seat in judgment, with one hundred and twenty-five other bishops in the synod, made confession of the true and catholic faith, and subscribed the same in the name of the northern part of Britain and Ireland, inhabited by the English and Britons, as also by the Scots and Picts."

After this, returning into Britain, he converted the province of the South Saxons from their idolatrous worship. He also sent ministers to the Isle of Wight; and in the second year of Alfrid, who reigned after Egfrid, was restored to his see and bishopric by that king's invitation. However, five years after, being again accused by that same king and several bishops, he was again expelled his diocese. Coming to Rome, together with his accusers, and being allowed to make his defence before a number of bishops and the apostolic Pope John, it was declared by the unanimous judgment of them all, that his accusers had in part laid false accusations to his charge; and the aforesaid pope undertook to write to the kings of the English, Ethelred and Alfrid, to cause him to be restored to his bishopric, because he had been falsely accused.

His acquittal was much forwarded by the reading of the synod of Pope Agatho, of blessed memory, which had been formerly held when Wilfrid was in Rome, and sat in council among the bishops, as has been said before. For that synod being, on account of the trial, by order of the apostolic pope, read before the nobility and a great number of the people for some days, they came to the place where it was written, "Wilfrid, the beloved of God, bishop of the city of York, having referred his cause to the Apostolic See, and being by that power cleared," &c., as above stated. This being read, the hearers were amazed, and the reader stopping, they began to ask of one another, who that Bishop Wilfrid was? Then Boniface, the pope's counsellor, and many others, who had seen him there in the days of Pope Agatho, said, he was the same bishop that lately came to Rome, to be tried by the Apostolic See, being accused by his people, and who, said they, having long since been here upon such like accusation, the cause and controversy between both parties being heard and discussed, was proved by Pope Agatho, of blessed memory, to have been wrongfully expelled from his bishopric, and so much honoured by him, that he commanded him to sit in the council of bishops which he had assembled, as a man of untainted faith and an upright mind. This being heard, the pope and all the rest said, that a man of such great authority, who had exercised the episcopal function near forty years, ought not to be condemned, but being cleared of all the crimes laid to his charge, to return home with honour.

Passing through France, on his way back to Britain, on a sudden he fell sick, and the distemper increasing, was so ill, that he could not ride, but was carried in his bed. Being thus come to the city of Meaux, in France, he lay four days and nights, as if he had been dead, and only by his faint breathing showed that he had any life in him; having continued so four days, without meat or drink, speaking or hearing, he, at length, on the fifth day, in the morning, as it were awakening out of a dead sleep, sat up in bed, and opening his eyes, saw numbers of brethren singing and weeping about him, and fetching a sigh, asked where Acca, the priest, was? This man, being called, immediately came in, and seeing him thus recovered and able to speak, knelt down, and returned thanks to God, with all the brethren there present. When they had sat awhile, and begun to discourse, with much reverence, on the heavenly judgments, the bishop ordered the rest to go out for an hour, and spoke to the priest, Acca, in this manner :—

"A dreadful vision has now appeared to me, which I wish you to hear and keep secret, till I know how God will please to dispose of me. There stood by me a certain person, remarkable for his white garments, telling me he was Michael, the Archangel, and said, 'I am sent to save you from death: for the Lord has granted you life, through the prayers and tears of your disciples, and the intercession of his blessed mother Mary, of perpetual virginity; wherefore I tell you, that you shall now recover from this sickness; but be ready, for I will return to visit you at the end of four years. But when you come into your country, you shall recover most of the possessions that have been taken from you, and shall end your days in perfect peace.'" The bishop accordingly recovered, at which all persons rejoiced, and gave thanks to God, and setting forward on his journey, arrived in Britain.

Having read the letters which he brought from the apostolic pope, Bertwald, the archbishop, and Ethelred, who had been formerly king, but was then an abbat, readily took his part; for the said Ethelred, calling to him Coinred, whom he had made king in his own stead, he requested of him to be friends with Wilfrid, in which request he prevailed; but Alfrid, king of the Northumbrians, refused to admit him. However he died soon after, and his son Osred obtained the crown, when a synod was assembled, near the river Nidd, and after some contesting on both sides, at length, by the consent of all, he was admitted to preside over his church; and thus he lived in peace four years, till the day of his death. He died on the 12th of October, in his monastery, which he had in the province of Undalum,* under the government of the Abbat Cuthbald; and by the ministry of the brethren, he was car-

* Oundle in Northamptonshire.

ried to his first monastery of Ripon, and buried in the church of Saint Peter the apostle, close by the south end of the altar, as has been mentioned above, with this epitaph over him :—

> Here the great prelate Wilfrid lies entomb'd,
> Who, led by piety, this temple rear'd
> To God, and hallow'd with blest Peter's name,
> To whom our Lord the keys of heaven consign'd.
> Moreover gold and purple vestments gave,
> And plac'd a cross,—a trophy shining brigh
> With richest ore—four books o'erwrought with gold,
> Sacred evangelists in order plac'd,
> And (suited well to these) a desk he rear'd,
> (Highly conspicuous) cas'd with ruddy gold.
> He likewise brought the time of Easter right,
> To the just standard of the canon law ;
> Which our forefathers fixed and well observ'd,
> But long by error chang'd, he justly plac'd.
> Into these parts a numerous swarm of monks
> He brought, and strictly taught their founder's rules.
> In lapse of years, by many dangers tossed ;
> At home by discords, and in foreign realms,
> Having sat bishop five and forty years,
> He died, and joyful sought the realms above ;
> That, blessed by Christ, and favour'd with his aid,
> The flock may follow in their pastor's path.*

CHAP. XX.

Albinus succeeded to the religious Abbat Hadrian, and Acca to Bishop Wilfrid. [A. D. 709.]

THE next year after the death of the aforesaid father (Wilfrid), that is, in the first year of King Osred, the most reverend father, Abbat Hadrian, fellow labourer in the word of God with Theodore the archbishop of blessed memory, died, and was buried in the church of the blessed Mother of God, in his own monastery,† this being the forty-first year from his being sent by Pope Vitalian with Theodore, and the thirty-ninth after his arrival in England. Of whose learning, as well as that of Theodore, one testimony among

---

* Eddi Stephanus, precentor of Canterbury, wrote the Life of Wilfrid, as did also Eadmer, secretary to St. Anselm. There is an extended account of him in Peck's History of Stamford, and in the Lives of the English Saints, No. VIII. † St. Augustine's, Canterbury.

others is, that Albinus,[*] his disciple, who succeeded him in
the government of his monastery, was so well instructed in
the study of the Scriptures, that he knew the Greek tongue
to no small perfection, and the Latin as thoroughly as the
English, which was his native language.

Acca, his priest, succeeded Wilfrid in the bishopric of the
church of Hagulstad; being himself a most active man, and
great in the sight of God and man, he much adorned and
added to the structure of his church, which is dedicated to
the Apostle St. Andrew. For he made it his business, and
does so still, to procure relics of the blessed apostles and
martyrs of Christ from all parts, to place them on altars,
dividing the same by arches in the walls of the church.
Besides which, he diligently gathered the histories of their
sufferings, together with other ecclesiastical writings, and
erected there a most numerous and noble library. He likewise industriously provided holy vessels, lights, and such
like things as appertain to the adorning of the house of God.
He in like manner invited to him a celebrated singer, called
Maban, who had been taught to sing by the successors of the
disciples of the blessed Gregory in Kent, for him to instruct
himself and his clergy, and kept him twelve years, to teach
such ecclesiastical songs as were not known, and to restore
those to their former state which were corrupted either by
want of use, or through neglect. For Bishop Acca himself
was a most expert singer, as well as most learned in Holy
Writ, most pure in the confession of the catholic faith, and
most observant in the rules of ecclesiastical institution; nor
did he ever cease to be so till he received the rewards of his
pious devotion, having been bred up and instructed among
the clergy of the most holy and beloved of God, Bosa, bishop
of York. Afterwards, coming to Bishop Wilfrid in hopes of
improving himself, he spent the rest of his life under him
till that bishop's death, and going with him to Rome, learned
there many profitable things concerning the government of
the holy church, which he could not have learned in his own
country.

* See page 2, where Bede acknowledges the assistance he received from
Albinus in the compilation of this work.

CHAP. XXI.

Abbat Ceolfrid sent the King of the Picts architects to build a church, and with them an epistle concerning the Catholic Easter and Tonsure. [A D. 710.]

AT that time, Naitan, king of the Picts, inhabiting the northern parts of Britain, taught by frequent meditation on the ecclesiastical writings, renounced the error which he and his nation had till then been under, in relation to the observance of Easter, and submitted, together with his people, to celebrate the catholic time of our Lord's resurrection. For performing this with the more ease and greater authority, he sought assistance from the English, whom he knew to have long since formed their religion after the example of the holy Roman Apostolic Church. Accordingly he sent messengers to the venerable Ceolfrid, abbat of the monastery of the blessed apostles, Peter and Paul, which stands at the mouth of the river Wear, and near the river Tyne, at the place called Jarrow, which he gloriously governed after Benedict, of whom we have before spoken ; desiring, that he would write him a letter containing arguments, by the help of which he might the better confute those that presumed to keep Easter out of the due time ; as also concerning the form and manner of tonsure for distinguishing the clergy ; not to mention that he himself possessed much information in these particulars. He also prayed to have architects sent him to build a church in his nation after the Roman manner, promising to dedicate the same in honour of St. Peter, the prince of the apostles, and that he and all his people would always follow the custom of the holy Roman Apostolic Church, as far as their remoteness from the Roman language and nation would allow. The reverend Abbat Ceolfrid, complying with his desires and request, sent the architects he desired, and the following letter :—

" *To the most excellent lord, and most glorious King Naitan, Abbat Ceolfrid, greeting in the Lord.* We most readily and willingly endeavour, according to your desire, to explain to you the catholic observance of holy Easter, according to what we have learned of the Apostolic See, as you, devout king, with a religious intention, have requested ; for

we know, that whenever the Church applies itself to learn,
to teach, and to assert the truth, which are the affairs of our
Lord, the same is given to it from heaven. For a certain
worldly writer* most truly said, that the world would be
most happy if either kings were philosophers, or philosophers
were kings. For if a worldly man could judge truly of the
philosophy of this world, and form a correct choice concerning the state of this world, how much more is it to be wished,
and most earnestly to be prayed for by the citizens of the
heavenly country, who are travelling through this world,
that the more powerful any persons are in this world, the
more they may labour to be acquainted with the commands
of Him who is the Supreme Judge, and by their example
and authority may induce those that are committed to their
charge, as well as themselves, to keep the same.

" There are three rules in the Sacred Writings, on account
of which it is not lawful for any human authority to change
the time of keeping Easter, which has been prescribed to us ;
two whereof are divinely established in the law of Moses ;
the third is added in the Gospel by means of the passion and
resurrection of our Lord. For the law enjoined, that the
Passover should be kept in the first month of the year, and
the third week of that month, that is, from the fifteenth day
to the one-and-twentieth. It is added, by apostolic institution, in the Gospel, that we are to wait for our Lord's day in
that third week, and to keep the beginning of the Paschal
time on the same. Which threefold rule whosoever shall
rightly observe, will never err in fixing the Paschal feast.
But if you desire to be more plainly and fully informed in all
these particulars, it is written in Exodus, where the people
of Israel, being about to be delivered out of Egypt, are commanded to keep the first Passover, that the Lord said to
Moses and Aaron, ' This month shall be unto you the beginning of months ; it shall be the first month of the year to
you. Speak ye unto all the congregation of Israel, saying,
In the tenth day of this month, they shall take to them every
man a lamb, according to the house of their fathers, a lamb
for an house.' And a little lower, ' And he shall keep it
until the fourteenth day of the same month ; and the whole
assembly of the congregation of Israel shall kill it in the

* Plato, in his Republic.

evening.' By which words it most plainly appears, that thus
in the Paschal observance mention is made of the fourteenth
day, not that the Passover is commanded to be kept on that
day : but the lamb is commanded to be killed on the evening
of the fourteenth day ; that is, on the fifteenth day of the
moon, which is the beginning of the third week, when the
moon appears in the sky. And because it was on the night
of the fifteenth moon, when, by the slaughter of the Egyptians, Israel was redeemed from a long captivity, therefore it
is said, 'Seven days shall ye eat unleavened bread.' By
which words all the third week of the same month is decreed
to be kept solemn. But lest we should think that those
same seven days were to be reckoned from the fourteenth to
the twentieth, God immediately adds, 'Even the first day ye
shall put away leaven out of your houses ; for whosoever
eateth leavened bread, from the first day until the seventh
day, that soul shall be cut off from Israel ;' and so on, till he
says, 'For in this self-same day I will bring your army out
of the land of Egypt.'

"Thus he calls that the first day of unleavened bread, in
which he was to bring their army out of Egypt. But it is
evident, that they were not brought out of Egypt on the
fourteenth day, in the evening whereof the lamb was killed,
and which is properly called the Passover or Phase, but on
the fifteenth day, as is most plainly written in the book of
Numbers. 'Departing therefore from Ramesse on the fifteenth day of the first month, the next day the Israelites
kept the Passover with a high hand.' Thus the seven
days of unleavened bread on the first whereof the people
of God were brought out of Egypt, are to be reckoned from
the beginning of the third week, as has been said, that is,
from the fourteenth day of the first month, till the one-and-
twentieth of the same month, that day included. But the
fourteenth day is noted down separately from this number,
by the name of the Passover, as is plainly made out by what
follows in Exodus: where when it is said, 'For in this same
day I will bring your army out of the land of Egypt ;' it is
presently added, 'You shall keep it a feast by an ordinance
for ever. In the first month, on the fourteenth day of the
month at even, ye shall eat unleavened bread, until the one-
and-twentieth day of the month at even. Seven days shall

there be no leaven found in your houses.' Now, who is
there that does not perceive, that there are not only seven
days, but rather eight, from the fourteenth to the one-and-
twentieth, if the fourteenth be also reckoned in the number?
But if, as by diligent study of Scriptures appears to be the
truth, we reckon from the evening of the fourteenth day to
the evening of the one-and-twentieth, we shall certainly
find, that the same fourteenth day gives its evening for the
beginning of the Paschal feast; so that the sacred solemnity
contains no more than only seven nights and as many days.
By which our definition is proved to be true, wherein we
said, that the Paschal time is to be celebrated in the first
month of the year, and the third week of the same. For it
is really the third week, because it begins on the evening of
the fourteenth day, and ends on the evening of the one-and-
twentieth.

"But since Christ our Paschal Lamb is slain, and has
made the Lord's day, which among the ancients was called
the first after the Sabbath, a solemn day to us for the joy of
his resurrection, the apostolic tradition has so inserted it into
the Paschal festivals as to decree, that nothing in the least
be anticipated, or detracted from the time of the legal Passover; but rather ordains, that the same first month should
be waited for, pursuant to the precept of the law, and accordingly the fourteenth day of the same, and the evening
thereof. And when this day should happen to fall on the
Sabbath, every one in his family should take a lamb, and
kill it in the evening, that is, that all the churches throughout the world, composing one catholic church, should provide
bread and wine for the mystery of the flesh and blood of the
unspotted Lamb 'that took away the sins of the world;' and
after the solemnity of reading the lessons and prayers of the
Paschal ceremonies, they should offer up these things to the
Lord, in hopes of future redemption. For that same night
in. which the people of Israel were delivered out of Egypt
by the blood of the Lamb, is the very same in which all the
people of God were, by Christ's resurrection, delivered from
eternal death. Then, on the morning of the Lord's day,
they should celebrate the first day of the Paschal festival;
for that is the day on which our Lord, with much joy of
pious revelation, made known the glory of his resurrection.

The same is the first day of unleavened bread, concerning
which it is distinctly written in Leviticus, 'In the fourteenth
day of the first month, at even, is the Lord's Passover. And
on the fifteenth day of the same month, is the feast of unleavened bread unto the Lord; seven days ye must eat unleavened bread; the first day shall be most solemn and holy.'

"If therefore it could be that the Lord's day should always happen on the fifteenth day of the first month, that is,
on the fifteenth moon, we might always celebrate Easter at
the very same time with the ancient people of God, though
the nature of the mystery be different, as we do it with one
and the same faith. But in regard that the day of the week
does not keep pace exactly with the moon, the apostolical
tradition, which was preached at Rome by St. Peter, and
confirmed at Alexandria by Mark the Evangelist, his interpreter, appointed that when the first month was come, and
in it the evening of the fourteenth day, we should also wait
for the Lord's day, which falls between the fifteenth and the
one-and-twentieth day of the same month. For on whichever of those days it shall fall, Easter will be properly kept
on the same; as it is one of those seven days on which the
unleavened bread is ordered to be kept. Thus it comes to
pass that our Easter never deviates from the third week of
the first month, but either observes the whole, or at least
some of the seven legal days of unleavened bread. For
though it takes in but one of them, that is, the seventh,
which the Scripture so highly commends, saying, 'But the
seventh day shall be more solemn and holy, ye shall do no
servile work therein,' none can lay it to our charge, that we
do not rightly keep our Lord's Paschal day, which we received from the Gospel, in the third week of the first month,
as the Law prescribes.

"The catholic reason of this observance being thus explained; the unreasonable error, on the other hand, of those
who, without any necessity, presume either to anticipate, or
to go beyond the term prescribed in the Law, is manifest.
For they that think the Lord's day of Easter is to be observed from the fourteenth day of the first month till the
twentieth moon, anticipate the time prescribed in the law,
without any necessary reason; for when they begin to celebrate the vigil of the holy night from the evening of the

thirteenth day, it is plain that they make that day the beginning of their Easter, whereof they find no mention in the
Law; and when they refuse to celebrate our Lord's Easter
on the one-and-twentieth day of the month, they wholly
exclude that day from their solemnity, which the Law often
recommends as memorable for the greater festival; and thus,
perverting the proper order, they place Easter day in the
second week, and sometimes keep it entirely in the same,
and never bring it to the seventh day of the third week.
And again, because they rather think that Easter is to be
kept on the sixteenth day of the said month, and so to the
two-and-twentieth, they no less erroneously, though the contrary way, deviate from the right way of truth, and as it
were avoiding to be shipwrecked on Scylla, they run on and
are drowned in the whirlpool of Charybdis. For when they
teach that Easter is to be begun at the rising of the sixteenth moon of the first month, that is, from the evening of
the fifteenth day, it is manifest that they altogether exclude
from their solemnity the fourteenth day of the same month,
which the Law firstly and chiefly recommends; so that they
scarcely touch upon the evening of the fifteenth day, on
which the people of God were delivered from the Egyptian
servitude, and on which our Lord, by his blood, rescued the
world from the darkness of sin, and on which being also
buried, he gave us hopes of a blessed repose after death.

"And the same persons, taking upon themselves the
penalty of their error, when they place the Lord's day of
Easter on the twenty-second day of the month, openly transgress and exceed the legal term of Easter, as beginning the
Easter on the evening of that day in which the Law appointed it to be finished and completed; and appoint that to
be the first day of Easter, whereof no mention is any where
found in the Law, viz. the first of the fourth week. And
they are sometimes mistaken, not only in defining and computing the moon's age, but also in finding the first month;
but this controversy is longer than can or ought to be contained in this letter. I will only say thus much, that by the
vernal equinox, it may always be found, without the chance
of an error, which is the first month of the year, according
to the lunar calculation, and which the last. But the equinox, according to the opinion of all the Eastern nations, and

particularly of the Egyptians, who exceed all other learned
men in that calculation, usually happens on the twelfth day
before the kalends of April, as we also prove by horological
inspection. Whatever moon therefore is at the full before
the equinox, being on the fourteenth or fifteenth day, the
same belongs to the last month of the foregoing year, and
consequently is not proper for the celebration of Easter; but
that moon which is full after the equinox, or on the very
equinox, belongs to the first month, and in it, without a
doubt, the ancients were wont to celebrate the Passover;
and we also ought to keep Easter when the Sunday comes.
And that this must be so, there is this cogent reason, because
it is written in Genesis, that 'God made two lights; a
greater light to rule the day, and a lesser light to rule the
night.' Or, as another edition has it, 'A greater light to
begin the day, and a lesser to begin the night.' The sun,
therefore, proceeding from the midst of the east, fixed the
vernal equinox by his rising, and afterwards the moon, when
the sun set in the evening, followed full from the midst of
the east; thus every year the same first month of the moon
must be observed in the like order, so that the full moon
must be either on the very day of the equinox, as was done
from the beginning, or after it is gone by. But if the full
of the moon shall happen to be but one day before the time
of the equinox, the aforesaid reason proves that such moon
is not to be assigned to the first month of the new year, but
rather to the last of the preceding, and that it is therefore
not proper for the celebration of the Paschal festival.

"Now if it will please you likewise to hear the mystical
reason in this matter, we are commanded to keep Easter in
the first month of the year, which is also called the month of
the new fruit, because we are to celebrate the mysteries of
our Lord's resurrection and our deliverance, with our minds
renewed to the love of heavenly things. We are commanded
to keep it in the third week of the same month, because
Christ, who had been promised before the Law, and under
the Law, came with grace, in the third age of the world, to
be slain as our Passover; and rising from the dead the third
day after the offering of his passion, he wished this to be
called the Lord's day, and the festival of his resurrection to
be yearly celebrated on the same. For we also, in this man-

ner only, can truly celebrate his solemnity, if we take care
with him to keep the Passover, that is, the passage out of
this world to the Father, by faith, hope, and charity.   We
are commanded to observe the full moon of the Paschal
month after the vernal equinox, to the end, that the sun may
first make the day longer than the night, and then the moon
may afford the world her full orb of light ; inasmuch as first
'the sun of righteousness, in whose wings is salvation,' that
is, our Lord Jesus, ·by the triumph of his resurrection, dispelled all the darkness of death, and so ascending into heaven, filled his Church, which is often signified by the name
of the moon, with the light of inward grace, by sending down
upon her his Spirit.   Which plan of salvation the prophet
had in his mind, when he said 'The sun was exalted and the
moon stood in her order.'

   "He, therefore, who shall contend that the full Paschal
moon can happen before the equinox, deviates from the doctrine of the Holy Scriptures, in the celebration of the great-
ost mysteries, and agrees with those who confide that they
may be saved without the grace of Christ forerunning them ;
and who presume to teach that they might have attained to
perfect righteousness, though the true light had never vanquished the darkness of the world, by dying and rising
again.   Thus, after the equinoctial rising of the sun, and
after the subsequent full moon of the first month, that is,
after the end of the fourteenth day of the same month, all
which, according to the law, ought to be observed, we still,
by the instruction of the Gospel, wait in the third week for
the Lord's day ; and thus, at length, we celebrate our due
Easter solemnity, to show that we do not, with the ancients,
honour the shaking off of the Egyptian yoke ; but that, with
devout faith and affection, we worship the redemption of the
whole world ; which having been prefigured in the deliverance of God's ancient people, was completed in Christ's
resurrection, to make it appear that we rejoice in the sure
and certain hope of the day of our own resurrection, which
we believe will happen on the same Lord's day.

   "Now this calculation of Easter, which we show you is to
be followed, is contained in a circle or revolution of nineteen
years, which began long since, that is, in the very times of
the apostles, especially at Rome and in Egypt, as has been

said above. But by the industry of Eusebius, who took his surname from the blessed martyr Pamphilus, it was reduced to a plainer system; insomuch that what till then used to be sent about to all the several churches by the patriarch of Alexandria, might, from that time forward, be most easily known by all men, the course of the fourteenth day of the moon being regularly ordered. This Paschal calculation, Theophilus, patriarch of Alexandria, composed for the Emperor Theodosius, for a hundred years to come. Cyril also, his successor, comprised a series of ninety-five years in five revolutions of nineteen years. After whom, Dionysius Exiguus added as many more, in the same manner, reaching down to our own time. The expiration of these is now drawing near, but there is so great a number of calculators, that even in our churches throughout Britain, there are many who, having learned the ancient rules of the Egyptians, can with great ease carry on those revolutions of the Paschal times for any distant number of years, even to five hundred and thirty-two years, if they will; after the expiration of which, all that belongs to the question of the sun and moon, of month and week, returns in the same order as before. We therefore forbear to send you those revolutions of the times to come, because you only desired to be instructed respecting the Paschal time, and declared you had enough of those catholic tables concerning Easter.

"But having said thus much briefly and succinctly, as you required concerning Easter, I also exhort you to take care to promote the tonsure, as ecclesiastical and agreeable to the Christian faith, for concerning that also you desired me to write to you; and we know indeed that the apostles were not all shorn after the same manner, nor does the Catholic Church, though it agrees in the same Divine faith, hope, and charity, agree in the same form of tonsure throughout the world: in fine, to look back to remote times, that is, the times of the patriarchs, Job, the example of patience, when, on the approach of tribulation, he shaved his head, made it appear that he had used, in time of prosperity, to let his hair grow; and Joseph, the great practiser and teacher of chastity, humility, piety, and other virtues, is found to have been shorn when he was to be delivered from servitude; by which it appears, that during the time of servitude, he

was in the prison without cutting his hair. Now you may
observe how each of these men of God differed in the manner of their appearance abroad, though their inward con-
sciences were alike influenced by the grace of virtue. But
though we may be free to confess, that the difference of tonsure is not hurtful to those whose faith is pure towards God,
and their charity sincere towards their neighbour, especially
since we do not read that there ever was any controversy
among the Catholic fathers about the difference of tonsure,
as there has been about the difference in keeping Easter, or
in matters of faith ; however, among all the tonsures that
are to be found in the Church, or among mankind at large,
I think none more worthy of being followed than that which
that disciple had on his head, to whom, on his confession,
our Lord said, ' Thou art Peter, and upon this rock I will
build my Church, and the gates of hell shall not prevail
against it, and to thee I will give the keys of the kingdom of
heaven.' Nor do I think any more worthy to be abhorred
and detested, by all the faithful, than that which that man
used, to whom Peter, when he would have bought the grace
of the Holy Ghost, said, ' Thy money be with thee to perdition, because thou thoughtest the gift of God to be purchased
for money ; there is no part or lot for thee in this speech.'
Nor do we shave ourselves in the form of a crown only because Peter was so shorn ; but because Peter was so shorn
in memory of the passion of our Lord ; therefore we also,
who desire to be saved by the same passion, do with him
bear the sign of the same passion on the top of our head,
which is the highest part of our body. For as all the
Church, because it was made a church by the death of him
that gave it life, is wont to bear the sign of his holy cross on
the forehead, to the end, that it may, by the constant protection of his sign, be defended from the assaults of evil spirits,
and by the frequent admonition of the same be instructed, in
like manner, to crucify its flesh with its vices and concupi-
scences ; so also it behoves those, who have either taken the
vows of monks, or have any degree among the clergy, to
curb themselves the more strictly by continence.

"Every one of them is likewise to bear on his head, by
means of the tonsure, the form of the crown which Christ in
his passion bore of thorns, in order that Christ may bear the

thorns and briars of our sins; that is, that he may remove
and take them from us; and also that they may at once show
that they, willingly, and with a ready mind, endure scoffs
and reproaches for his sake; to make it appear, that they
always expect 'the crown of eternal life, which God has promised to those that love him,' and that for the gaining thereof
they despise both the adversities and the prosperities of this
world.   But as for the tonsure which Simon Magus is said
to have used, what Christian will not immediately detest and
cast it off together with his magic?   Upon the top of the
forehead, it does seem indeed to resemble a crown; but when
you come to the neck, you will find the crown you thought
you had seen so perfect cut short; so that you may be satisfied such a distinction properly belongs not to Christians but
to Simoniacs, such as were indeed in this life thought worthy
of a perpetual crown of glory by erring men; but in that
life which is to follow this, are not only deprived of all hopes
of a crown, but are moreover condemned to eternal punishment.

"But do not think that I have said thus much, as judging
those who use this tonsure, are to be damned, in case they
favour the catholic unity in faith and actions; on the contrary, I confidently declare, that many of them have been
holy and worthy of God.   Of which number is Adamnan,
the abbat and renowned priest of Columba, who, when sent
ambassador by his nation to King Alfrid, came to see our
monastery, and discovering wonderful wisdom, humility, and
religion in his words and behaviour, among other things, I
said to him in discourse, 'I beseech you, holy brother, who
think you are advancing to the crown of life, which knows
no period, why do you, contrary to the habit of your faith,
wear on your head a crown that is terminated, or bounded?
And if you aim at the society of St. Peter, why do you
imitate the tonsure of him whom St. Peter anathematized?
and why do you not rather even now show that you imitate
to your utmost the habit of him with whom you desire to
live happy for ever.'   He answered, 'Be assured, my dear
brother, that though I have Simon's tonsure, according to the
custom of my country, yet I utterly detest and abhor the
Simoniacal wickedness; and I desire, as far as my little-
ness is capable of doing it, to follow the footsteps of the most

blessed prince of the apostles.' I replied, 'I verily believe it as you say; but let it appear by showing outwardly such things as you know to be his, that you in your hearts embrace whatever is from Peter the Apostle. For I believe your wisdom does easily judge, that it is much more proper to estrange your countenance, already dedicated to God, from resemblance to him whom in your heart you abhor, and of whose hideous face you would shun the sight; and, on the other hand, that it becomes you to imitate the outward resemblance of him, whom you seek to have for your advocate with God, as you desire to follow his actions and instructions.'

" This I then said to Adamnan, who indeed showed how much he had improved upon seeing the statutes of our churches, when, returning into Scotland, he afterwards by his preaching brought great numbers of that nation over to the catholic observance of the Paschal time ; though he was not yet able to gain the consent of the monks that lived in the island of Hii, over whom he presided. He would also have been mindful to amend the tonsure, if his authority had extended so far.

"But I also admonish your wisdom, O king, that you endeavour to make the nation, over which the King of kings, and Lord of lords, has placed you, observe in all points those things which appertain to the unity of the Catholic and Apostolic Church; for thus it will come to pass, that after your temporal kingdom has passed away, the blessed prince of the apostles will lay open to you and yours the entrance into the heavenly kingdom, where you will rest for ever with the elect. The grace of the eternal King preserve thee in safety, long reigning, for the peace of us all, my most beloved son in Christ."

This letter having been read in the presence of King Naitan, and many more of the most learned men, and carefully interpreted into his own language by those who could understand it, he is said to have much rejoiced at the exhortation; insomuch that, rising from among his great men that sat about him, he knelt on the ground, giving thanks to God that he had been found worthy to receive such a present from the land of the English ; and, said he, " I knew indeed before, that this was the true celebration of Easter, but now

I so fully know the reason for observing of this time, that I seem convinced that I knew little of it before. Therefore I publicly declare and protest to you that are here present, that I will for ever continually observe this time of Easter, with all my nation; and I do decree that this tonsure, which we have heard is most reasonable, shall be received by all the clergy in my kingdom." Accordingly he immediately performed by his regal authority what he had said. For the circles or revolutions of nineteen years were presently, by public command, sent throughout all the provinces of the Picts to be transcribed, learned and observed, the erroneous revolutions of eight-four years being every where suppressed. All the ministers of the altar and monks had the crown shorn, and the nation thus reformed, rejoiced, as being newly put under the direction of Peter, the most blessed prince of the apostles, and secure under his protection.

CHAP. XXII.

The Monks of Hii, and the monasteries subject to them, begin to celebrate the canonical Easter at the preaching of Egbert.   [A.D. 716.]

NOT long after, those monks also of the Scottish nation, who lived in isle of Hii, with the other monasteries that were subject to them, were by the assistance of our Lord brought to the canonical observation of Easter, and the right mode of tonsure. For in the year after the incarnation of our Lord 716, when Osred was slain, and Coenred took upon him the government of the kingdom of the Northumbrians, the holy father and priest, Egbert, beloved of God, and worthy to be named with all honour, whom we have often mentioned before, coming among them, was joyfully and honourably received. Being a most agreeable teacher, and devout in practising those things which he taught, and being willingly heard by all, he, by his pious and frequent exhortations, converted them from that inveterate tradition of their ancestors, of whom may be said those words of the apostle, "That they had the zeal of God, but not according to knowledge." He taught them to perform the principal solemnity after the catholic and apostolic manner, as has been said, under the figure of a perpetual circle; which appears to have been accomplished by a wonderful dispensation of the Divine

U

goodness; to the end, that the same nation which had willingly, and without envy, communicated to the English people the knowledge of the true Deity, should afterwards, by means of the English nation, be brought where they were defective to the true rule of life. Even as, on the contrary, the Britons, who would not acquaint the English with the knowledge of the Christian faith, now, when the English people enjoy the true faith, and are thoroughly instructed in its rules, continue inveterate in their errors, expose their heads without a crown, and keep the solemnity of Christ without the society of the Church.

The monks of Hii, by the instruction of Egbert, adopted the catholic rites, under Abbat Dunchad, about eighty years after they had sent Aidan to preach to the English nation.* This man of God, Egbert, remained thirteen years in the aforesaid island, which he had thus consecrated again to Christ, by kindling in it a new ray of Divine grace, and restoring it to the unity of ecclesiastical discipline. In the year of our Lord's incarnation 729, in which the Easter of our Lord was celebrated on the 24th of April, he performed the solemnity of the mass, in memory of the same resurrection of our Lord, and dying that same day, thus finished, or rather never ceases to celebrate, with our Lord, the apostles, and the other citizens of heaven, that greatest festival, which he had begun with the brethren, whom he had converted to the unity of grace. But it was a wonderful dispensation of the Divine Providence, that the venerable man not only passed out of this world to the Father, in Easter, but also when Easter was celebrated on that day, on which it had never been wont to be kept in those parts. The brethren rejoiced in the certain and catholic knowledge of the time of Easter, and rejoiced in the protection of their father, departed to our Lord, by whom they had been converted. He also congratulated his being so long continued in the flesh till he saw his followers admit, and celebrate with him, that as Easter day which they had ever before avoided. Thus the most reverend father being assured of their standing corrected, rejoiced to see the day of our Lord, and he saw it and was glad.

* Aidan was sent into England about a.d. 634. Vide pages 112, 116, 134, 135. Therefore the monks of Iona adopted the Catholic mode of keeping Easter about 714.

CHAP. XXIII.

Of the present state of the English nation, or of all Britain,
[A.D. 725—731.]

In the year of our Lord's incarnation 725, being the seventh
year of Osric, king of the Northumbrians, who succeeded
Coenred, Wictred, the son of Egbert, king of Kent, died on
the 23rd of April, and left his three sons, Ethelbert, Eadbert, and Alric, heirs of that kingdom, which he had governed thirty-four years and a half.   The next year died
Tobias, bishop of the church of Rochester, a most learned
man, as has been said before; for he was disciple to those
teachers of blessed memory, Theodore, the archbishop, and
Abbat Hadrian, by which means, as we have before observed, besides his erudition in ecclesiastical and general
literature, he learned both the Greek and Latin tongues to
such perfection, that they were as well known and familiar
to him as his native language.   He was buried in the porch
of St. Paul the Apostle, which he had built within the
church of St. Andrew for his own place of burial.   After
him Aldwulf took upon him the office of bishop, having
been consecrated by Archbishop Bertwald.

In the year of our Lord's incarnation 729, two comets
appeared about the sun, to the great terror of the beholders.
One of them went before the rising sun in the morning, the
other followed him when he set at night, as it were presaging much destruction to the east and west; one was the
forerunner of the day, and the other of the night, to signify
that mortals were threatened with calamities at both times.
They carried their flaming tails towards the north, as it
were ready to set the world on fire.   They appeared in
January, and continued nearly a fortnight.   At which time
a dreadful plague of Saracens ravaged France with miserable slaughter; but they not long after in that country
received the punishment due to their wickedness.*   In
which year the holy man of God, Egbert, departed to our
Lord, as has been said above, on Easter day; and imme-

---

* The great battle of Tours, in which Charles Martel defeated the Arabs,
was fought in A.D. 732.   This passage was therefore inserted by Bede after
he had finished his history, when he revised it in 734 or 735.

diately after Easter, that is, on the 9th of May, Osric, king
of the Northumbrians, departed this life, after he had reigned eleven years, and appointed Ceolwulf, brother to Coenred,
who had reigned before him, his successor; the beginning
and progress of whose reign were so filled with commotions,
that it cannot yet be known what is to be said concerning
them, or what end they will have.

In the year of our Lord's incarnation 731, Archbishop
Bertwald died of old age, on the 9th of January, having
held his see thirty-seven years, six months and fourteen
days. In his stead, the same year, Tatwine, of the province
of the Mercians, was made archbishop, having been a priest
in the monastery called Briudun.* He was consecrated in
the city of Canterbury by the venerable men, Daniel, bishop
of Winchester, Ingwald of London, Aldwin of Lichfield,
and Aldwulf of Rochester, on Sunday, the 10th of June,
being a man renowned for religion and wisdom, and notably
learned in Sacred Writ.

Thus at present,† the bishops Tatwine and Aldwulf preside in the churches of Kent; Ingwald in the province of
the East Saxons. In the province of the East Angles, Ald-
bert and Hadulac are bishops; in the province of the West

* Near the Bredon Hills in Worcestershire.
† The following list of the Saxon bishoprics at the time when Bede
closed his history, [A.D. 731,] will enable the reader to recognize those
which belonged to each separate kingdom :—

Kingdoms.	Sees.	Prelates.
Kent	Canterbury	Tatwine.
	Rochester	Aldwulf.
East Saxons	London	Ingwald.
East Angles	Dunwich	Aldbert.
	Elmham	Hadulac.
West Saxons	Winchester	Daniel.
	Sherborne	Forthere.
Mercia	Lichfield	Aldwin.
	Hereford	Walstod.
	Worcester	Wilfrid.
	Lindsey (Sidnacester)	Cunebert.
	Dorchester, removed to Leicester, A.D. 737	Vacant.
South Saxons	Selsey	Vacant.
Northumbria	York	Wilfrid II.
	Lindisfarne	Ethelwald.
	Hexham	Acca.
	Whitherne	Pechthelm.

Saxons, Daniel and Forthere are bishops; in the province of
the Mercians, Aldwin. Among those people who live beyond the river Severn to the westward, Walstod is bishop;
in the province of the Wiccians, Wilfrid; in the province of
the Lindisfarnes, Cynebert presides; the bishopric of the
Isle of Wight belongs to Daniel, bishop of Winchester.
The province of the South Saxons, having now continued
some years without a bishop, receives the episcopal ministry
from the prelate of the West Saxons. All these provinces,
and the others southward to the bank of the river Humber,
with their kings, are subject to King Ethelbald.

But in the province of the Northumbrians, where King
Ceolwulf reigns, four bishops now preside; Wilfrid in the
church of York, Ethelwald in that of Lindisfarne, Acca in
that of Hagulstad, Pechthelm in that which is called the
White House, which, from the increased number of believers, has lately become an episcopal see, and has him for
its first prelate.* The Picts also at this time are at peace
with the English nation, and rejoice in being united in peace
and truth with the whole Catholic Church. The Scots that
inhabit Britain, satisfied with their own territories, meditate
no hostilities against the nation of the English. The Britons, though they, for the most part, through innate hatred,
are adverse to the English nation, and wrongfully, and from
wicked custom, oppose the appointed Easter of the whole
Catholic Church; yet, from both the Divine and human
power withstanding them, can in no way prevail as they
desire; for though in part they are their own masters, yet
elsewhere they are also brought under subjection to the
English. Such being the peaceable and calm disposition
of the times, many of the Northumbrians, as well of the
nobility as private persons, laying aside their weapons, rather incline to dedicate both themselves and their children
to the tonsure and monastic vows, than to study martial
discipline. What will be the end hereof, the next age will

* Bede here speaks of Pechthelm as the *first* bishop of Whitherne,
which must be understood as the first under the Saxon dynasty; for in
book iii. ch. 4, page 114, he mentions St. Ninias as the founder of the
see, A.D. 412. There was probably an interruption in the succession of
the prelates during the three hundred years which intervened between the
death of St. Ninias and the appointment of Pechthelm, owing to the civil
wars and the invasion of the Saxons.

show. This is for the present the state of all Britain; in the year since the coming of the English into Britain about 285, but in the 731st year of the incarnation of our Lord, in whose reign may the earth ever rejoice; may Britain exult in the profession of his faith; and may many islands be glad, and sing praises in honour of his holiness!

CHAP. XXIV.

Chronological recapitulation of the whole work: also concerning the author himself.

I HAVE thought fit briefly to sum up those things which have been related more at large, according to the distinction of times, for the better preserving them in memory.

In the sixtieth year before the incarnation of our Lord, Caius Julius Cæsar, first of the Romans, invaded Britain, and was victorious, yet could not gain the kingdom.

In the year from the incarnation of our Lord, 46, Claudius, second of the Romans, invading Britain, had a great part of the island surrendered to him, and added the Orkney islands to the Roman empire.

In the year from the incarnation of our Lord 167, Eleutherius, being made bishop at Rome, governed the Church most gloriously fifteen years. Lucius, king of Britain, writing to him, requested to be made a Christian, and succeeded in obtaining his request.

In the year from the incarnation of our Lord 189, Severus, being made emperor, reigned seventeen years; he enclosed Britain with a trench from sea to sea.

In the year 381, Maximus, being made emperor in Britain, sailed over into Gaul, and slew Gratian.

In the year 409, Rome was crushed by the Goths, from which time Roman emperors began to reign in Britain.

In the year 430, Palladius was sent to be first the bishop of the Scots that believed in Christ, by Pope Celestine.

In the year 449, Martian being made emperor with Valentinian, reigned seven years; in whose time the English, being called by the Britons, came into Britain.

In the year 538, there happened an eclipse of the sun, on the 16th of February, from the first to the third hour.

In the year 540, an eclipse of the sun happened on the

20th of June, and the stars appeared during almost half an hour after the third hour of the day.

In the year 547, Ida began to reign; from him the royal family of the Northumbrians derives its original; he reigned twelve years.

In the year 565, the priest, Columba, came out of Scotland, into Britain, to instruct the Picts, and he built a monastery in the isle of Hii.

In the year 596, Pope Gregory sent Augustine with monks into Britain, to preach the word of God to the English nation.

In the year 597, the aforesaid teachers arrived in Britain; being about the 150th year from the coming of the English into Britain.

In the year 601, Pope Gregory sent the pall into Britain, to Augustine, who was already made bishop; he sent also several ministers of the word, among whom was Paulinus.

In the year 603, a battle was fought at Degsastane.

In the year 604, the East Saxons received the faith of Christ, under King Sabert, and Bishop Mellitus.

In the year 605, Gregory died.

In the year 616, Ethelbert, king of Kent, died.

In the year 625, the venerable Paulinus was, by Archbishop Justus, ordained bishop of the Northumbrians.

In the year 626, Eanfleda, daughter to King Edwin, was baptized with twelve others, on Whit-Saturday.

In the year 627, King Edwin was baptized, with his nation, at Easter.

In the year 633, King Edwin being killed, Paulinus returned to Kent.

In the year 640, Eadbald, king of Kent, died.

In the year 642, King Oswald was slain.

In the year 644, Paulinus, first bishop of York, but now of the city of Rochester, departed to our Lord.

In the year 651, King Oswin was killed, and Bishop Aidan died.

In the year 653, the Midland Angles, under their prince, Penda, received the mysteries of the faith.

In the year 655, Penda was slain, and the Mercians became Christians.

In the year 664, there happened an eclipse of the sun;

Earconbert, king of Kent, died; and Colman returned to the Scots; a pestilence arose; Ceadda and Wilfrid were ordained bishops of the Northumbrians.

In the year 668, Theodore was ordained bishop.

In the year 670, Oswy, king of the Northumbrians, died.

In the year 673, Egbert, king of Kent, died, and a synod was held at Hertford, in the presence of King Egfrid, Archbishop Theodore presiding : the synod did much good, and its decrees are contained in ten chapters.

In the year 675, Wulfhere, king of the Mercians, dying, when he had reigned seventeen years, left the crown to his brother Ethelred.

In the year 676, Ethelred ravaged Kent.

In the year 678, a comet appeared; Bishop Wilfrid was driven from his see by King Egfrid; and Bosa, Eata, and Eadhed were consecrated bishops in his stead.

In the year 679, Elfwine was killed.

In the year 680, a synod was held in the field called Hethfeld, concerning the Christian faith, Archbishop Theodore presiding ; John, the Roman abbat, was also present. The same year also the Abbess Hilda died at Streaneshalch.

In the year 685, Egfrid, king of the Northumbrians, was slain.

The same year, Lothere, king of Kent died.

In the year 688, Cædwalla, king of the West Saxons, went to Rome from Britain.

In the year 690, Archbishop Theodore died.

In the year 697, Queen Ostritha was murdered by her own people, that is, the nobility of the Mercians.

In the year 698, Berthred, the royal commander of the Northumbrians, was slain by the Picts.

In the year 704, Ethelred became a monk, after he had reigned thirty years over the nation of the Mercians, and gave up the kingdom to Coenred.

In the year 705, Alfrid, king of the Northumbrians, died.

In the year 709, Coenred, king of the Mercians, having reigned six years, went to Rome.

In the year 711, Earl Bertfrid fought with the Picts.

In the year 716, Osred, king of the Northumbrians, was killed; and Ceolred, king of the Mercians, died; and Egbert, the man of God, brought the monks of Hii to observe the Catholic Easter and ecclesiastical tonsure.

In the year 725, Withred, king of Kent, died.

In the year 729, comets appeared; the holy Egbert departed; and Osric died.

In the year 731, Archbishop Bertwald died.

The same year Tatwine was consecrated ninth archbishop of Canterbury, in the fifteenth year of Ethelbald, king of Kent.

THUS much of the Ecclesiastical History of Britain, and more especially of the English nation, as far as I could learn either from the writings of the ancients, or the tradition of our ancestors, or of my own knowledge, has, with the help of God, been digested by me, Bede, the servant of God, and priest of the monastery of the blessed apostles, Peter and Paul, which is at Wearmouth and Jarrow; who being born in the territory of that same monastery, was given, at seven years of age, to be educated by the most reverend Abbat Benedict, and afterwards by Ceolfrid; and spending all the remaining time of my life in that monastery, I wholly applied myself to the study of Scripture, and amidst the observance of regular discipline, and the daily care of singing in the church, I always took delight in learning, teaching, and writing. In the nineteenth year of my age, I received deacon's orders; in the thirtieth, those of the priesthood, both of them by the ministry of the most reverend Bishop John, and by order of the Abbat Ceolfrid. From which time, till the fifty-ninth year of my age, I have made it my business, for the use of me and mine, to compile out of the works of the venerable Fathers, and to interpret and explain according to their meaning these following pieces :—

On the Beginning of Genesis, to the Nativity of Isaac and the Reprobation of Ismael, three books.

Of the Tabernacle and its Vessels, and of the Priestly Vestments, three books.

On the first Part of Samuel, to the Death of Saul, four books.

Of the Building of the Temple, of Allegorical Exposition, like the rest, two books.

Item, on the Book of Kings, thirty Questions.

On Solomon's Proverbs, three books.

On the Canticles, seven books.

On Isaiah, Daniel, the twelve Prophets, and Part of Jeremiah, Distinctions of Chapters, collected out of St. Jerome's Treatise.

On Esdras and Nehemiah, three books.

On the Song of Habacuc, one book.

On the Book of the blessed Father Tobias, one Book of Allegorical Exposition concerning Christ and the Church.

Also, Chapters of Readings on Moses's Pentateuch, Joshua, and Judges.

On the Books of Kings and Chronicles.

On the Book of the blessed Father Job.

On the Parables, Ecclesiastes, and Canticles.

On the Prophets Isaiah, Esdras, and Nehemiah.

On the Gospel of Mark, four books.

On the Gospel of Luke, six books.

Of Homilies on the Gospel, two books.

On the Apostle, I have carefully transcribed in order all that I have found in St. Augustine's Works.

On the Acts of the Apostles, two books.

On the seven Catholic Epistles, a book on each.

On the Revelation of St. John, three books.

Also, Chapters of Readings on all the New Testament, except the Gospel.

Also a book of Epistles to different Persons, of which one is of the Six ages of the world ; one of the Mansions of the Children of Israel ; one on the Words of Isaiah, "And they shall be shut up in the prison, and after many days shall they be visited;" one of the Reason of the Bissextile, or Leap-Year, and of the Equinox, according to Anatolius.

Also, of the Histories of Saints. I translated the Book of the Life and Passion of St. Felix, Confessor, from Paulinus's Work in metre, into prose.

The Book of the Life and Passion of St. Anastasius, which was ill translated from the Greek, and worse amended by some unskilful person, I have corrected as to the sense.

I have written the Life of the Holy Father Cuthbert, who

was both monk and prelate, first in heroic verse, and then in prose.

The History of the Abbats of this Monastery, in which I rejoice to serve the Divine Goodness, viz. Benedict, Ceolfrid, and Huetbert, in two books.

The Ecclesiastical History of our Island and Nation in five books.

The Martyrology of the Birth-days of the Holy Martyrs, in which I have carefully endeavoured to set down all that I could find, and not only on what day, but also by what sort of combat, or under what judge they overcame the world.

A Book of Hymns in several sorts of metre, or rhyme.

A Book of Epigrams in heroic or elegiac verse.

Of the Nature of Things, and of the Times, one book of each.

Also, of the Times, one larger book.

A book of Orthography digested in Alphabetical Order.

Also a Book of the Art of Poetry, and to it I have added another little Book of Tropes and Figures ; that is, of the Figures and Manners of Speaking in which the Holy Scriptures are written.

And now, I beseech thee, good Jesus, that to whom thou hast graciously granted sweetly to partake of the words of thy wisdom and knowledge, thou wilt also vouchsafe that he may some time or other come to thee, the fountain of all wisdom, and always appear before thy face, who livest and reignest world without end.　　Amen !

HERE ENDS, BY GOD'S HELP,

THE FIFTH BOOK

OF THE ECCLESIASTICAL HISTORY

OF THE ENGLISH NATION.

(What follows appears to be by another hand.)

[In the year from the incarnation of our Lord 732, Egbert was made bishop of York, in the room of Wilfrid [II.]; Cunebert, bishop of Lindisfarians [Sidnacester ?] died.

A. D. 733, there happened an eclipse of the sun, on the 18th day before the kalends of September, about the third hour of the day; so that almost all the orb of the sun seemed to be covered with a black and horrid shield.

In the year from the incarnation of our Lord 733, archbishop Tatwine having received the pall by apostolical authority, ordained Alwich* and Sig-frid† bishops.

A. D. 734, the moon, on the 2nd before the kalends of February, about the time of cock-crowing, was, for about a whole hour, covered with a bloody red, after which a blackness followed, and she regained her light.

In the year from the incarnation of our Lord 734, bishop Tatwine died.

In the year from the incarnation of our Lord 735, Nothelm was ordained archbishop; and bishop Egbert, having received the pall from the apostolic see, was the first confirmed archbishop after Paulinus, and ordained Frithbert‡ and Frithwald‖ bishops; and the priest Bede died.

A. D. 737, too much drought rendered the land unfruitful, and Ceolwulf, voluntarily receiving the tonsure, left the kingdom to Eadbert.

A. D. 739, Ethelard, king of the West-Saxons, died, as did archbishop Nothelm.

A. D. 740, Cuthbert was consecrated in Nothelm's stead. Ethelbald, king of the Mercians, through impious fraud, wasted part of the Northumbrians, their king Eadbert, with his army, being employed against the Picts. Bishop Ethelwald died also, and Conwulf was consecrated in his stead. Amwin and Eadbert were slain.

A. D. 741, first a great drought happened in the country. Charles, king of the Franks, died; and his sons, Caroloman and Pepin, reigned in his stead.

A. D. 745, Bishop Wilfrid and Ingwald, bishop of London, departed to our Lord.

A. D. 747, the man of God, Herefrid, died.

A.D. 750, Cuthred, king of the West Saxons, rose up against king Ethelbald and Oenguse; Theneorus and Eanred died; Eadbert added the plain of Kyle and other places to his dominions.

A. D. 756, in the fifth year of king Eadbert, on the ides of January, there happened an eclipse of the sun; afterwards, the same year and month, on the 9th before the kalends of February the moon suffered an eclipse, being most horridly black.

A. D. 756, Boniface, called also Winfrid, bishop of the Franks, received the crown of martyrdom, with fifty-three others; and Redger was consecrated archbishop in his stead, by pope Stephen.

A. D. 757, Ethelbald, king of the Mercians, was miserably murdered, in the night, by his own tutors; Beonred began his reign; Cynewulf, king of the West-Saxons, died; and the same year, Offa, having vanquished Beonred, in a bloody manner, sought to gain the kingdom of the Mercians.

A. D. 758, Eadbert, king of the Northumbrians, receiving St. Peter's ton-sure for the love of God, and to gain the heavenly country by violence, left the kingdom to his son Oswulph.

A. D. 759, Oswulph was wickedly murdered by his own servants; and Ethel-wald, being chosen the same year by his people, entered upon the kingdom; in whose second year there happened a great tribulation of mortality, and con-tinued almost two years, several grievous distempers raging, but more espe-cially the dysentery.

A. D. 761, Oeng, king of the Picts, died; who, from the beginning to the end of his reign, continued a bloody tyrannical butcher: Oswin was also slain.

A. D. 765, King Alcred was advanced to the throne.

A. D. 766, Archbishop Egbert, of the royal race, and endued with Divine knowledge, as also Frithbert, both of them truly faithful prelates, departed to our Lord.]

* Sidnacester.   † Selsey.   ‡ Hexham.   ‖ Whitherne.

THE

ANGLO-SAXON CHRONICLE.

ANGLO-SAXON CHRONICLE.[*]

[THE island [†] of Britain is eight hundred miles long and two hundred miles broad : and here in this island are five tongues ; English, British, Scottish, Pictish, and Latin. The first inhabitants of this land were Britons ; they came from Armenia,[‡] and first settled in the south of Britain. Then befell it that Picts came from the south from Scythia, with long ships, not many, and first landed in North Hibernia, and there entreated the Scots that they might there abide. But they would not permit them, for they said that they could not all abide there together. And then the Scots said, 'We may nevertheless give you counsel. We know another island eastward of this, where ye may dwell if ye will, and if any one withstand you, we will assist you, so that you may subdue it.' Then went the Picts and subdued this land northwards ; the southern part the Britons had, as we before have said. And the Picts obtained wives for themselves of the Scots, on this condition, that they should always choose their royal lineage on the woman's side ; which they have held ever since. And then befell it in the course of years

* The Anglo-Saxon Chronicle is apparently the work of many successive hands, and extends in different copies from the time of Cæsar's invasion to the middle of the twelfth century. As it has been repeatedly printed, it may suffice here to repeat, that, with the exception of the insertions placed within brackets, the text to the year 975 is mostly taken from the MS. designated by the letter *A*.; from that period to 1079 from MSS. *A. C. D. E. F.* and *G.*, and from thence to the conclusion from MS. *E.*: and that such portions of the different MSS. as are concurrent with the text, but will not conveniently admit of collation, are given separately in a smaller type. These variations will sometimes convey the same information two or three times over : but it has been deemed advisable to retain all of them that the reader may have a more ample means of judging of the authority of this invaluable national record.

† This description of Britain is taken from Bede's Ecclesiastical History.　　　　　　　　　　‡ Armorica.

that some part of the Scots departed from Hibernia into Britain, and conquered some portion of the land. And their leader was called Reoda; from whom they are named Dalreodi.*]

Sixty years before Christ was born, Gaius Julius, emperor of the Romans, with eighty ships, sought Britain. There he was at first distressed by a fierce battle, and a large portion of his army was dispersed. And then he left his army to abide among the Scots,† and went south into Gaul, and there collected six hundred ships, with which he came again into Britain. And as they first rushed together, the emperor's 'gerrefa'‡ was slain: he was called Labienus. Then the Welsh took large and sharp stakes and drove them into the fording place of a certain river under water; this river was called Thames. When the Romans discovered this, then would they not go over the ford. Then fled the Britons to the wood-wastes, and the emperor conquered very many of their chief cities after a great struggle, and departed again into Gaul.

Before the incarnation of Christ sixty years, Gaius Julius the emperor, first of the Romans, sought the land of Britain; and he crushed the Britons in battle, and overcame them: and nevertheless he was unable to gain any empire there.

A.D. 1. Octavianus reigned fifty-six years; and in the forty-second year of his reign Christ was born.

A. 2. The three astrologers came from the eastern parts in order that they might worship Christ. And the children were slain at Bethlehem, in persecution of Christ by Herod.

A. 3. This year died Herod, having stabbed himself, and Archelaus his son succeeded to the government. And the child Christ was brought back again from Egypt.

A. 4. 5. §

---

* See the etymology of this name in a note at page 7.

† "This is an error, arising from the inaccurately written MSS. of Orosius and Bede; where *in Hybernia* and *in Hiberniam* occur for *in hiberna*. The error is retained in Wheloc's Bede."—INGRAM.

‡ "Tribune."—INGRAM.

§ These blank dates are found in the MSS. of the Saxon Chronicle, and are retained in this volume, for the sake of references which occur between the MSS. where the date happens to be blank, and others in which facts are assigned to them.

A. 6. From the beginning of the world to this year, five thousand and two hundred years were gone by.

A. 7.—10.

A. 11. This year Herod the son of Antipater obtained the government of Judea.

A. 12. Philip and Herod divided Lysia (between them), and Judea they divided into tetrarchies.

A. 12. This year Judea was divided into four tetrarchies.

A. 13.—15.

A. 16. This year Tiberius succeeded to the empire.

A. 17.—25.

A. 26. This year Pilate began to rule over the Jews.

A. 27.—29.

A. 30. This year Christ was baptized; and he converted Peter and Andrew, and James and John and Philip, and the twelve apostles.

A. 31. 32.

A. 33. This year Christ was crucified; being from the beginning of the world about five thousand two hundred and twenty-six years.

A. 34. This year St. Paul was converted, and St. Stephen stoned.

A. 35. This year the blessed apostle Peter established a bishop's see in the city of Antioch.

A. 36. 37.

A. 38. This year Pilate slew himself with his own hand.

A. 39. This year Caius obtained the empire.

A. 40. Matthew, in Judea, began to write his gospel.

A. 41.—44.

A. 45. This year the blessed apostle Peter established a bishop's see in Rome. This year James, the brother of John, was slain by Herod.

A. 46. This year Herod died; he who slew James, one year before his own death.

A. 46. This year the emperor Claudius came to Britain, and subdued a large part of the island; and he also added the island of Orkney to the dominion of the Romans.

A. 47. This year Claudius, second of the Roman kings, sought the land of Britain, and brought under his power the greater part of the island, and also subjected the Orkney Islands to the dominion of the Romans. This war he

effected in the fourth year of his reign : and in the same
year was the great famine in Syria, which was foretold in
the Acts of the Apostles through Agabus the prophet. Then
Nero succeeded to the empire after Claudius : he nearly lost
the island of Britain through his cowardice. Mark the
Evangelist begins to write the gospel in Egypt.

A. 47. This was in the fourth year of his reign, and in this same year
was the great famine in Syria which Luke speaks of in the book called
' Actus Apostolorum.'

A. 47. This year Claudius, king of the Romans, went with an army into
Britain, and subdued the island, and subjected all the Picts and Welsh to
the rule of the Romans.

A. 48. In this year there was a very severe famine.

A. 49. This year Nero began to reign.

A. 50. This year Paul was sent in bonds to Rome.

A. 51.—61

A. 62. This year James, the brother of our Lord, suffered
martyrdom.

A. 63. This year Mark the Evangelist died.

A. 64.—68.

A. 69. This year Peter and Paul suffered martyrdom.

A. 69. This year Peter suffered on the cross, and Paul was slain.

A. 70. This year Vespasian obtained the empire.

A. 71. This year Titus, the son of Vespasian, slew one
hundred and eleven thousand Jews in Jerusalem.

A. 72.—80.

A. 81. This year Titus succeeded to the empire, after
Vespasian ; he who said that he had lost the day on which
he had done no good.

A. 82. 83.

A. 84. This year Domitian, the brother of Titus, succeeded to the empire.

A. 84. This year John the Apostle wrote the book which is called
Apocalypse.

A. 85. 86.

A. 87. This year John the Evangelist wrote the book of
the Apocalypse in the island of Patmos.

A. 88.—99.

A. 100. This year Simon the apostle, the kinsman of
Christ, was crucified, and John the Evangelist rested in
death on that day at Ephesus.

A. 101. This year pope Clement died.

A. 102.—109.

A. 110. This year Ignatius the bishop suffered martyrdom.

A. 111.—115.

A. 116. This year Adrian the emperor began to reign.

A. 117.—136.

A. 137. This year Antoninus began to reign.

A. 138.—144.

A. 145. This year Marcus Antoninus and Aurelius his brother succeeded to the empire.

A. 146.—166.

A. 167. This year Eleutherius obtained the bishopric of Rome, and held it in great glory for twelve years.* To him Lucius, king of Britain. sent letters praying that he might be made a Christian : and he fulfilled that he requested. And they afterwards continued in the right faith till the reign of Diocletian.

A. 167. This year Eleutherius succeeded to the popedom, and held it fifteen years ; and in the same year Lucius, king of the Britons, sent and begged baptism of him. And he soon sent it him ; and they continued in the true faith until the time of Diocletian.

A. 168.—187.

A. 188. This year Severus succeeded to the empire, and went with an army into Britain, and subdued a great part of the island by battle ; and then, for the protection of the Britons, he built a rampart of turf, and a broad wall thereon, from sea to sea. He reigned seventeen years, and then ended his days at York. His son Bassianus succeeded to the empire : another son of his was called Geta ; he died.

A. 190.—198.

A. 199. In this year the Holy-rood† was found.

A. 200. Two hundred years.

A. 201.—285.

A. 286. This year St. Alban the martyr suffered.

---

* According to Muratori, Eleutherius presided from A. 170 to A. 185.

† "Those writers who mention this grand discovery of the holy cross, by Helena the mother of Constantine, disagree so much in their chronology, that it is a vain attempt to reconcile them to truth or to each other. This and the other notices of ecclesiastical matters, whether Latin or Saxon, from the year 190 to the year 380 of the Laud MS. and 381 of the printed Chronicle, may be safely considered as interpolations, probably posterior to the Norman Conquest."—INGRAM.

A. 287.—299.

A. 300. Three hundred years.

A. 301.—342.

A. 343. This year S. Nicolas died.

A. 344.—378.

A. 379. This year Gratian succeeded to the empire.

A. 380.

A. 381. This year Maximus the emperor obtained the empire; he was born in the land of Britain, and went thence into Gaul. And he there slew the emperor Gratian, and drove his brother, who was called Valentinian, out of the country. And Valentinian afterwards gathered an army and slew Maximus, and obtained the empire. In these days the heresy of Pelagius arose throughout the world.

A. 382.—408.

A. 409. This year the Goths took the city of Rome by storm, and after this the Romans never ruled in Britain; and this was about eleven hundred and ten years after it had been built. Altogether they ruled in Britain four hundred and seventy years since Caius Julius first sought the land.

A. 410.—417.

A. 418. This year the Romans collected all the treasures that were in Britain, and some they hid in the earth, so that no one has since been able to find them; and some they carried with them into Gaul.

A. 419.—422.

A. 423. This year Theodosius the younger succeeded to the empire.

A. 424.—429.

A. 430. This year Palladius * the bishop was sent to the Scots by pope Celestinus, that he might confirm their faith.

A. 430. This year Patrick was sent by pope Celestine to preach baptism to the Scots.

A. 431.—442.

A. 443. This year the Britons sent over sea to Rome, and begged for help against the Picts; but they had none, because they were themselves warring against Attila, king of the

* "Palladius and Patricius have been sometimes confounded together; so that it is difficult to assign to each his respective share of merit in the conversion of the Scots of Ireland."—INGRAM.

Huns. And then they sent to the Angles, and entreated the like of the ethelings of the Angles.

A. 444. This year St. Martin died.

A. 445.—447.

A. 448. This year John the Baptist revealed his head to two monks, who came from the east to offer up their prayers at Jerusalem, on the spot which was formerly Herod's residence.

A. 449. This year Martianus and Valentinus succeeded to the empire, and reigned seven years. And in their days Hengist and Horsa, invited by Vortigern, king of the Britons, landed in Britain on the shore which is called Wippidsfleet ; at first in aid of the Britons, but afterwards they fought against them. King Vortigern gave them land in the south-east of this country, on condition that they should fight against the Picts. Then they fought against the Picts, and had the victory wheresoever they came. They then sent to the Angles ; desired a larger force to be sent, and caused them to be told the worthlessness of the Britons, and the excellencies of the land. Then they soon sent thither a larger force in aid of the others. At that time there came men from three tribes in Germany ; from the Old-Saxons, from the Angles, from the Jutes. From the Jutes came the Kentish-men and the Wightwarians, that is, the tribe which now dwells in Wight, and that race among the West-Saxons which is still called the race of Jutes. From the Old-Saxons came the men of Essex and Sussex and Wessex. From Anglia, which has ever since remained waste betwixt the Jutes and Saxons, came the men of East Anglia, Middle Anglia, Mercia, and all North-humbria. Their leaders were two brothers, Hengist and Horsa : they were the sons of Wihtgils ; Wihtgils son of Witta, Witta of Wecta, Wecta of Woden : from this Woden sprang all our royal families, and those of the South-humbrians also.

A. 449. And in their days Vortigern invited the Angles thither, and they came to Britain in three ceols, at the place called Wippidsfleet:

A. 450.—454.

A. 455. This year Hengist and Horsa fought against king Vortigern   at   the   place   which   is   called   Ægels-threp, [Aylesford,] and his brother Horsa was there slain, and after that Hengist obtained the kingdom, and Æsc his son.

A. 456. This year Hengist and Æsc slew four troops of Britons with the edge of the sword, in the place which is named Creccanford, [Crayford].*

A. 457. This year Hengist and Æsc his son fought against the Britons at the place which is called Crecganford, [Crayford,] and there slew four thousand men; and the Britons then forsook Kent, and in great terror fled to London.

A. 458.—464.

A. 465. This year Hengist and Æsc fought against the Welsh near Wippidsfleet, [Ebbsfleet?] and there slew twelve Welsh ealdormen, and one of their own thanes was slain there, whose name was Wipped.

A. 466.—472.

A. 473. This year Hengist and Æsc fought against the Welsh, and took spoils innumerable; and the Welsh fled from the Angles like fire.

A. 474.—476.

A. 477. This year Ælla, and his three sons, Cymen, and Wlencing, and Cissa, came to the land of Britain with three ships, at a place which is named Cymenes-ora, and there slew many Welsh, and some they drove in flight into the wood that is named Andreds-lea.

A. 478.—481.

A. 482. This year the blessed abbat Benedict, by the glory of his miracles, shone in this world, as the blessed Gregory relates in his book of Dialogues.

A. 483. 484.

A. 485. This year Ælla fought against the Welsh near the bank of Mearcrædsburn.

A. 486. 487.

A. 488. This year Æsc succeeded to the kingdom, and was king of the Kentish-men twenty-four years.

A. 489. 490.

A. 491. This year Ælla and Cissa besieged Andreds-cester, and slew all that dwelt therein, so that not a single Briton was there left.

* The positions usually assigned to various places mentioned in the earlier portion of the Chronicle, are often very uncertain, depending chiefly on a supposed or real similarity of names. Where these, however, appear sufficiently probable, they are placed between brackets if otherwise, a quære is added.

A. 492.—494.

A. 495. This year two ealdormen came to Britain, Cerdic and Cynric his son, with five ships, at the place which is called Cerdics-ore, and the same day they fought against the Welsh.*

A. 496.—500.

A. 501. This year Port, and his two sons Bieda and Mægla, came to Britain with two ships, at a place which is called Portsmouth, and they soon effected a landing, and they there slew a young British man of high nobility.

A. 502.—507.

A. 508. This year Cerdic and Cynric slew a British king, whose name was Natan-leod, and five thousand men with him. After that the country was named Natan-lea, as far Cerdicsford, [Charford.]

A. 509. This year† St. Benedict the abbat, father of all monks, went to heaven.

A. 510.—513.

A. 514. This year the West-Saxons came to Britain with three ships, at the place which is called Cerdic's-ore, and Stuf and Whitgar fought against the Britons, and put them to flight.

A. 515.—518.

A. 519. This year Cerdic and Cynric obtained the kingdom of the West-Saxons ; and the same year they fought against the Britons where it is now named Cerdicsford. And from that time forth the royal offspring of the West-Saxons reigned.

A. 520.—526.

A. 527. This year Cerdic and Cynric fought against the Britons at the place which is called Cerdic's-lea.

A. 528. 529.

A. 530. This year Cerdic and Cynric conquered the island of Wight, and slew many men at Whit-garas-byrg, [Carisbrooke, in Wight.]

A. 531.—533.

A. 534. This year Cerdic, the first king of the West Saxons, died, and Cynric his son succeeded to the kingdom,

---

* Gibson here introduced into the text a long genealogy, which, as Dr. Ingram observes : "is not justified by a single MS."

† Benedict died, according to Mabillon, in 543.

and reigned from that time twenty-six years; and they gave the whole island of Wight to their two nephews, Stuf and Wihtgar.

A. 535.—537.

A. 538. This year, fourteen days before the Kalends of March, the sun was eclipsed from early morning till nine in the forenoon.

A. 539.

A. 540. This year the sun was eclipsed on the twelfth before the Kalends of July, and the stars showed themselves full-nigh half an hour after nine in the forenoon.

A. 541.—543.

A. 544. This year Wihtgar died, and they buried him in Wiht-gara-byrg.   [Carisbrooke.]

A. 545. 546.

A. 547. This year Ida began to reign, from whom arose the royal race of North-humbria; and he reigned twelve years, and built Bambrough, which was at first enclosed by a hedge, and afterwards by a wall. Ida was the son of Eoppa, Eoppa of Esa, Esa of Ingwi, Ingwi of Angenwit, Angenwit of Aloc, Aloc of Benoc, Benoc of Brond, Brond of Beldeg, Beldeg of Woden, Woden of Frithowald, Frithowald of Frithuwulf, Frithuwulf of Finn, Finn of Godwulf, Godwulf of Geat.

A. 548.—551.

A. 552. This year Cynric fought against the Britons at the place which is called Searo-byrig [Old Sarum], and he put the Britons to flight. Cerdic was Cynric's father, Cerdic was the son of Elesa, Elesa of Esla, Esla of Gewis, Gewis of Wig, Wig of Freawin, Freawin of Frithogar, Frithogar of Brond, Brond of Beldeg, Beldeg of Woden. And Ethelbert, the son of Ermenric was born; and in the thirtieth year of his reign he received baptism, the first of the kings in Britain.

A. 553.—555.

A. 556. This year Cynric and Ceawlin fought against the Britons at Berin-Byrig, [Banbury?]

A. 557.—559.

A. 560. This year Ceawlin succeeded to the kingdom of the West-Saxons, and Ida being dead, Alla succeeded to the kingdom of North-humbria, each of whom reigned thirty

years. Alla was the son of Iff, Iff of Usfrey, Usfrey of
Wilgis, Wilgis of Westerfalcon, Westerfalcon of Seafowl,
Seafowl of Sebbald, Sebbald of Sigeat, Sigeat of Swadd,
Swadd of Sygar, Sygar of Waddy, Waddy of Woden,
Woden of Frithuwulf.

A. 561—564.

A. 565. This year Ethelbert* succeeded to the kingdom
of the Kentish-men, and held it fifty-three years. In his
days the holy pope Gregory sent us baptism, that was in the
two and thirtieth year of his reign: and Columba, a mass-
priest, came to the Picts, and converted them to the faith of
Christ: they are dwellers by the northern mountains. And
their king gave him the island which is called Ii [Iona]:
therein are five hides of land, as men say. There Columba
built a monastery, and he was abbat there thirty-seven years,
and there he died when he was seventy-two years old. His
successors still have the place. The Southern Picts had
been baptized long before: bishop Ninia, who had been instructed at Rome, had preached baptism to them, whose
church and his monastery is at Whitherne, consecrated in the
name of St. Martin: there he resteth, with many holy men.
Now in Ii there must ever be an abbat, and not a bishop;
and all the Scottish bishops ought to be subject to him, because Columba was an abbat and not a bishop.

A. 565. This year Columba the presbyter came from the Scots among
the Britons, to instruct the Picts, and he built a monastery in the island of
Hii.

A. 566. 567.

A. 568. This year Ceawlin, and Cutha, Ceawlin's brother,
fought against Ethelbert, and drove him into Kent, and they
killed two ealdormen at Wibban-dune [Wimbledon],† Oslaf
and Cnebba.

A. 569. 570.

A. 571. This year Cuthulf fought against the Britons
at Bedcanford [Bedford], and took four towns, Lygean-birg
[Lenbury], and Ægeles-birg [Aylesbury], and Bænesington
[Benson], and Egonesham [Eynsham]; and the same year
he died. Cutha was Ceawlin's brother.

* Bede [ii. 5,] says Ethelbert died on February 23, A.D. 616, after a
reign of fifty-six years. This would make it out that he succeeded to the
throne in A.D. 560.   † Or Worplesdon, Surrey.

A. 572.—576.

A. 577. This year Cuthwine and Ceawlin fought against the Britons, and they slew three kings, Comail, and Condidan, and Farinmeail, at the place which is called Deorham [Derham ?], and took three cities from them, Gloucester, and Cirencester, and Bath.

A. 578.—582.

A. 583. This year Mauricius succeeded to the empire of the Romans.

A. 584. This year Ceawlin and Cutha fought against the Britons at the place which is called Fethan-lea, [Frethern ?] and there was Cutha slain ; and Ceawlin took many towns, and spoils innumerable ; and wrathful he thence returned to his own.

A. 585.—587.

A. 588. This year King Ælle died, and Ethelric reigned after him five years.

A. 589.

590. At this period Ceol reigned five years.

591. This year in Britain was a great slaughter in battle at Woddesbeorg [Wemborow ?], and Ceawlin was expelled.

A. 592. This year Gregory succeeded to the popedom in Rome.

A. 593. This year Ceawlin, and Cwichelm, and Crida, perished ; and Ethelfrith succeeded to the kingdom of the North-humbrians ; he was the son of Æthelric, Æthelric of Ida.

A. 594. 595.

A. 596. This year Pope Gregory sent Augustine to Britain, with a great many monks, who preached the word of God to the nation of the Angles.

A. 597. This year Ceolwulf began to reign over the West-Saxons ; and he fought and contended incessantly against either the Angles, or the Welsh, or the Picts, or the Scots. He was the son of Cutha, Cutha of Cynric, Cynric of Cerdic, Cerdic of Elesa, Elesa of Esla, Esla of Gewis, Gewis of Wig, Wig of Freawine, Freawine of Frithogar, Frithogar of Brond, Brond of Beldeg, Beldeg of Woden. This year Augustine and his companions came to the land of the Angles.

A. 598.—600.

A. 601. This year Pope Gregory sent a pall to Archbishop Augustine in Britain, and also a great many religious teachers to assist him, and amongst them was Paulinus the bishop, who afterwards converted Edwin. king of the Northumbrians, to baptism.

A. 602.

A. 603. This year there was a battle at Egesanstane.*

A. 603. This year Æthan, king of the Scots, fought against the Dalreods and against Ethelfrith king of the North-humbrians, at Dægsanstane [Dawston1], and they slew almost all his army. There Theodbald, Ethelfrith's brother, was slain with all his band. Since then no king of the Scots has dared to lead an army against this nation. Hering, the son of Hussa, led the enemy thither.

A. 604. This year the East-Saxons received the faith and baptism under King Sebert and Bishop Mellitus.

A. 604. This year Augustine consecrated two bishops, Mellitus and Justus. He sent Mellitus to preach baptism to the East-Saxons, whose king was called Sebert son of Ricole, the sister of Ethelbert, and whom Ethelbert had there appointed king. And Ethelbert gave Mellitus a bishop's see in London, and to Justus he gave Rochester, which is twenty-four miles from Canterbury.

A. 605.

A. 606. This year Pope Gregory died, about ten years after he had sent us baptism ; his father was called Gordian, and his mother Silvia.

A. 607. This year Ceolwulf fought against the South-Saxons. And this year Ethelfrith led his army to Chester, and there slew numberless Welshmen : and so was fulfilled the prophecy of Augustine, wherein he saith, 'If the Welsh will not be at peace with us, they shall perish at the hands of the Saxons.' There also were slain two hundred priests, who came to pray for the army of the Welsh : their ealdor was called Scromail [Brocmail], who with some fifty escaped thence.

A. 608.—610.

A. 611. This year Cynegils succeeded to the kingdom of the West-Saxons, and held it thirty-one years. Cynegils was the son of Ceol, Ceol of Cutha, Cutha of Cynric.

A. 612. 613.

A. 614. This year Cynegils and Cuichelm fought at

* See Bede's Eccl. Hist. lib. i. c. 34, p. 61.

Beandune* [Bampton ?], and slew two thousand and sixty-five Welshmen.

A. 615

A. 616. This year Ethelbert, king of the Kentish-men, died; he was the first English king who received baptism, and he was the son of Eormenric; he reigned fifty-six years, and from the beginning of the world to this same year five thousand eight hundred years were gone by; and after him Eadbald his son succeeded to the kingdom; he forsook his baptismal vow, and lived after the manner of the heathens, so that he had his father's widow to wife. Then Laurentius, who was archbishop of Kent, was minded that he would go southwards over the sea, and leave it entirely. But the apostle Peter came to him by night and scourged him sorely, because he wished thus to forsake the flock of God, and commanded him to go to the king and preach the true faith to him; and he did so, and the king was converted and was baptized. In this king's days Laurentius, who was archbishop of Kent after Augustine, died, and was buried beside Augustine on the 4th Non. Feb. After him Mellitus, who formerly had been bishop of London, succeeded to the archbishopric: then the men of London, where Mellitus had been formerly, became heathens (again). And in about five years, during the reign of Eadbald, Mellitus departed to Christ. Then after him Justus succeeded to the archbishopric; and he consecrated Romanus to Rochester, where formerly himself had been bishop.

A. 616. In that time Laurentius was archbishop, and for the sorrowfulness which he had on account of the king's unbelief he was minded to forsake this country entirely, and go over sea; but St. Peter the apostle scourged him sorely one night, because he wished thus to forsake the flock of God, and commanded him to teach boldly the true faith to the king; and he did so, and the king turned to the right (faith). In the days of this same king, Eadbald, this Laurentius died. The holy Augustine, while yet in sound health, ordained him bishop, in order that the community of Christ, which was yet new in England, should not after his decease be at any time without an archbishop. After him Mellitus, who had been previously bishop of London, succeeded to the archbishopric. And within five years of the decease of Laurentius, while Eadbald still reigned, Mellitus departed to Christ.

* This is more likely to be Bampton in Oxfordshire, than Bampton in Devonshire, which is by far too remote to admit the supposition that the battle in question was fought there.

A. 617. This year Ethelfrid king of the North-humbrians was slain by Redwald king of the East-Angles, and Edwin the son of Alla succeeded to the kingdom, and subdued all Britain, the Kentish-men alone excepted. And he drove out the ethelings, sons of Ethelfrid; that is to say, first Eanfrid, Oswald, and Oswy, Oslac, Oswudu, Oslaf, and Offa.

A. 618.

A. 619. This year archbishop Laurentius died.

A. 620.—623.

A. 624. This year archbishop Mellitus died.

A. 625. This year Paulinus was ordained bishop of the North-humbrians by archbishop Justus on the xii. Kalends of August.

A. 625. This year archbishop Justus consecrated Paulinus bishop of the North-humbrians.

A. 626. This year Eumer came from Cuichelm king of the West-Saxons, thinking to stab king Edwin. But he stabbed Lilla his thane, and Forthhere, and wounded the king. And on the same night a daughter was born to Edwin: she was called Eanfled. Then the king made a vow to Paulinus that he would give his daughter to God, if he would obtain of God that he might kill his foe who had sent the assassin. And he then went with an army against the West-Saxons, and there killed five kings, and slew a great number of the people. And at Pentecost Paulinus baptized his daughter with twelve others. And within a twelvemonth the king and all his court were baptized at Easter; that year Easter fell on the second before the Ides of April. This was done at York, where he first ordered a church to be built of wood, which was consecrated in the name of St. Peter. There the king gave Paulinus a bishop's see, and there he afterwards commanded a larger church to be built of stone. And this year Penda succeeded to the kingdom [Mercia], and reigned thirty years; and he was fifty years (old) when he succeeded to the kingdom. Penda was the son of Pybba, Pybba of Creoda, Creoda of Cynewald, Cynewald of Cnebba, Cnebba of Icel, Icel of Eomær, Eomær of Angeltheow, Angeltheow of Offa, Offa of Wærmund, Wærmund of Wihtlæg, Wihtlæg of Woden.

A 627. This year king Edwin was baptized with his

people by Paulinus at Easter. And this Paulinus also preached baptism in Lindsey, where the first who believed was a certain great man called Blecca, with all his followers. And in this time Honorius, who sent Paulinus his pall, succeeded to the popedom after Boniface. And archbishop Justus died on the fourth before the Ides of November, and Honorius was consecrated archbishop of Canterbury by Paulinus at Lincoln. And to this Honorius the pope also sent a pall: and he sent a letter to the Scots, desiring that they should turn to the right Easter.

A. 627. This year, at Easter, Paulinus baptized Edwin king of the North-humbrians, with his people: and earlier within the same year, at Pentecost, he had baptized Eanfled daughter of the same king.

A. 628. This year Cynegils and Cuichelm fought against Penda at Cirencester; and then made a treaty.

A. 629.—631.

A. 632. This year Eorpwald was baptized.

A. 633. This year king Edwin was slain by Cadwalla and Penda at Heathfield [Hatfield Chase?] on the second before the Ides of October, and he reigned seventeen years; and his son Osfrid was also slain with him. And after that went Cadwalla and Penda and laid waste the whole country of the North-humbrians. When Paulinus saw that, he took Ethelberga, Edwin's widow, and departed in a ship to Kent. And Eadbald and Honorius received him very honourably, and gave him a bishop's see in Rochester; and he dwelt there till his end.

A. 634. This year Osric, whom Paulinus had formerly baptized, succeeded to the kingdom of Deira; he was the son of Elfric, Edwin's uncle. And Eanfrid the son of Ethelfrid succeeded to Bernicia. And this year also bishop Birinus first preached baptism to the West-Saxons under king Cynegils. Birinus came thither by command of Honorius the pope, and he there was bishop until his life's end. And this year also Oswald succeeded to the kingdom of the North-humbrians, and he reigned nine years; the ninth being numbered to him because of the heathenism which they practised who reigned over them the one year between him and Edwin.

A. 635. This year king Cynegils was baptized by Birinus

the bishop, at Dorchester, and Oswald king of the North humbrians was his godfather.

A. 636. This year king Cuichelm was baptized at Dorchester, and the same year he died. And bishop Felix preached the faith of Christ to the East-Angles.

A. 637. 638

A. 639. This year Birinus baptized king Cuthred at Dorchester, and received him as his (god) son.

A. 640. This year Eadbald, king of the Kentish-men, died, and he reigned twenty-five years. He had two sons, Ermenred and Earconbert, and Earconbert reigned there after his father. He overthrew all idolatry in his kingdom, and was the first of the English kings who established the Easter-fast. His daughter was called Earcongota, a holy woman and a wondrous person, whose mother was Sexberga, daughter of Anna, king of the East-Angles. And Ermenred begot two sons, who afterwards were martyred by Thunner.

A. 641.

A. 642. This year Oswald, king of the North-humbrians, was slain by Penda and the South-humbrians at Maserfeld on the Nones of August,* and his body was buried at Bardney. His sanctity and his miracles were afterwards manifested in various ways beyond this island, and his hands are at Bambrough, uncorrupted. And the same year that Oswald was slain, Oswy his brother succeeded to the kingdom of the North-humbrians, and he reigned two less (than) thirty years.

A. 643. This year Kenwalk succeeded to the kingdom of the West-Saxons, and held it thirty-one years; and Kenwalk commanded the old church at Winchester to be built in the name of St. Peter: and he was the son of Cynegils.

A. 644. This year Paulinus died, on the sixth before the Ides of October;† he was first archbishop of York, and afterwards at Rochester. He was bishop one less (than) twenty years, and two months and twenty-one days. And this year Oswin's uncle's son,‡ the son of Osric, succeeded to the kingdom of Deira, and reigned seven years.

---

* The 5th of August.   † The 10th of October.
‡ This is apparently corrupt, and should be read 'Oswin, the son of Osric, Edwin's uncle's son.' See Bede, iii. 1, and above An. 634.

A. 645. This year king Kenwalk was driven out of his kingdom by king Penda.

A. 646. This year king Kenwalk was baptized.

A. 647.

A. 648. This year Kenwalk gave Cuthred, his kinsman, three thousand hides of land by Ashdown, [Aston ?] Cuthred was the son of Cuichelm, Cuichelm of Cynegils. This year the minster was built at Winchester, which king Kenwalk caused to be made, and hallowed in the name of St. Peter.

A. 649.

A. 650. This year Agilbert, a native of Gaul, obtained the bishopric of the West-Saxons after Birinus the Romish bishop.

A. 650. This year Birinus the bishop died, and Agilbert the French-man was ordained.

A. 650. This year king Oswy ordered king Oswin to be slain, on the thirteenth before the Kal. of September; and about twelve days after this bishop Aidan died, on the second before the Kal. of September.

A. 651.

A. 652. This year Kenwalk fought at Bradford on the Avon.

A. 653. This year the Middle-Saxons, under Peada the ealdorman, received the true faith.

A. 654. This year king Anna was slain, and Botolph began to build a minster at Ycean-ho [Boston ?]. And this year archbishop Honorius died, on the second before the Kalends of October.

A. 655. This year king Oswy slew king Penda at Winwidfield, and thirty men of royal race with him, and some of them were kings, among whom was Ethelhere, brother of Anna, king of the East Angles. And the Mercians became Christians. From the beginning of the world to this time five thousand eight hundred and fifty years were agone; and Peada the son of Penda succeeded to the kingdom of the Mercians.

*In his time he and Oswy the brother of king Oswald came together, and agreed that they would rear a monastery to the glory of Christ and the honour of St. Peter. And they did so, and named it 'Medeshamstede' [Peterborough], because

* This is the first of many late additions to the Chronicle concerning the monastery of Peterborough. They occur in only one of the MSS.

there is a whirpool at this place, which is called Meadswell. And they began the foundations and wrought thereon, and then committed it to a monk who was called Sexwulf. He was greatly God's friend, and all the country loved him, and he was very nobly born, and rich in a worldly sense; but he is now much richer, being with Christ. And king Peada reigned no long time, for he was betrayed by his own wife at Easter.

This year Ithamar bishop of Rochester consecrated Deus-dedit to the see of Canterbury on the seventh before the Kalends of April.

A. 656.

A. 657. This year Peada died, and Wulfhere the son of Penda succeeded to the kingdom of the Mercians.

In his time the abbacy of Medeshamstede, which his brother had begun, waxed very rich. The king favoured it much for the love of his brother Peada, and for the love of Oswy his brother by baptism, and for the love of abbat Sexwulf. And he said that he would dignify and honour it, and this by the counsel of Ethelred and Merwal his brothers, and Kyneburg and Kyneswith his sisters, and by the counsel of the archbishop, who was called Deus-dedit, and by the counsel of all his witan, both clergy and laity, who were in his kingdom; and he did so.

Then the king sent after the abbat that he should come to him with all speed; and he did so. Then the king said to the abbat, 'Lo! I have sent for thee, beloved Sexwulf, for the behoof of my soul, and I will plainly tell thee for why. My brother Peada and my dear friend Oswy began a monastery to the glory of Christ and St. Peter. But my brother, as it has pleased Christ, is departed this life, and lo! my prayer to thee is, beloved friend, that they work diligently on the work, and I will find thee gold and silver, land and possessions, and all that behoveth thereto.' Then the abbat went home and began to build; and he so sped, by the grace of Christ, that in a few years the monastery was ready. When the king heard that said, he was very glad: he bade send throughout the nation after all his thanes, after the archbishop, and after the bishops, and after his earls, and after all who loved God, that they should come to him; and he set a day on which the monastery should be hallowed.

Y

At the hallowing of the monastery king Wulfhere was present, and his brother Ethelred, and his sisters Kyneburg and Kyneswith. And Deus-dedit archbishop of Canterbury hallowed the monastery, and Ithamar bishop of Rochester, and the bishop of London, who was called Wini, and the bishop of the Mercians, who was called Jaruman, and bishop Tuda. And there was Wilfrid the priest, who was afterwards a bishop : and all his thanes who were within his kingdom were there.

When the monastery had been hallowed in the name of St. Peter, St. Paul, and St. Andrew, then the king stood up before all his thanes, and said with a clear voice, 'Thanked be the high Almighty God for the worthy deed which here is done, and I will this day do honour to Christ and St. Peter ; and I desire that ye all assent to my words : I, Wulfhere, do this day give to St. Peter and abbat Sexwulf, and the monks of the monastery, these lands, and these waters, and meres, and fens, and wears, and all the lands which lie thereabout, which are of my kingdom, freely, so that none but the abbat and the monks shall have any claim upon them. This is the grant. From Medeshamstede to North-borough, and thence to the place which is called Foleys, and thence all the fen straight to Esendic, and from Esendic to the place which is called Fethermouth, and thence along the straight way ten miles to Ugdike, and thence to Ragwell, and from Ragwell five miles to the straight stream which goeth to Elm and to Wisbeach, and thence about three miles to Trokenholt, and from Trokenholt straight through all the fen to Derworth which is twenty miles long, and thence to Great Cross, and from Great Cross through a clear water called Bradney, and thence six miles to Paxlade, and thence onward through all the meres and fens which lie toward Huntingdon-port, and these meres and lakes, Shelfermere and Wittleseymere, and all the others which lie thereabout, with the land and the houses which are on the east-half of Shelfermere, and from thence all the fens to Medeshamstede, and from Medeshamstede to Welmsford, and from Welmsford to Clive, and thence to Easton, and from Easton to Stamford, and from Stamford even as the water runneth to the aforesaid North-borough.' These are the lands and the fens which the king gave to St. Peter's monastery.

Then said the king, 'This gift is little ; but it is my will that they shall hold it so royally and so freely that neither geld nor tribute be taken from it, except for the monks alone. And thus free I will make this minster, that it be subject to Rome alone ; and here it is my will that all of us who are unable to go to Rome shall visit St. Peter.'

While he was saying these words, the abbat desired of him that he would grant him what he should desire of him : and the king granted it. 'I have here 'godefrihte'* monks who wish to spend their lives as anchorites, if they knew where. And there is an island here, which is called Anchorets-isle, and my desire is, that we might build a minster there to the glory of St. Mary, so that those may dwell therein who wish to lead a life of peace and rest.'

Then the king answered, and said thus : 'Behold, Sexwulf, lo ! not only that one which thou hast desired, but all things which I know thee to desire on our Lord's behalf, I thus approve and grant. And I beg of thee, my brother Ethelred, and my sisters Kyneburg and Kyneswith, that ye be witnesses for your souls' redemption, and that ye write it with your fingers. And I beg all those who come after me, be they my sons, be they my brothers, or kings that come after me, that our gift may stand, even as they would be partakers of the life eternal, and would escape everlasting torment. Whosoever shall take from this our gift, or the gifts of other good men, may the heavenly gateward take from him in the kingdom of heaven ; and whosoever will increase it, may the heavenly gateward increase (his state) in the kingdom of heaven.'

These are the witnesses who were there, who subscribed it with their fingers on the cross of Christ, and assented to it with their tongues. King Wulfhere was the first who confirmed it by word, and afterwards subscribed it with his fingers on the cross of Christ ; and said thus : 'I, king Wulfhere, with the kings, and earls, and dukes, and thanes, the witnesses of my gift, do confirm it before the archbishop Deus-dedit with the cross of Christ. ✠' 'And I, Oswy king of the North-humbrians, the friend of this monastery and of abbat Sexwulf, approve of it with the cross of Christ. ✠'

* This word is rendered by Lye, "God-fearing," and by Ingram, simply "good."

'And I, king Sighere, grant it with the cross of Christ. ✠'
'And I, king Sibbi, subscribe it with the cross of Christ. ✠'
'And I, Ethelred, the king's brother, grant it with the cross
of Christ. ✠' 'And we, the king's sisters, Kyneburg and
Kyneswith, we approve it. ✠' 'And I, Deus-dedit
archbishop of Canterbury, grant it. ✠' After that, all the
others who were there assented to it with the cross of
Christ.✠ They were by name Ithamar bishop of Rochester,
and Wini bishop of London, and Jaruman who was bishop
of the Mercians, and bishop Tuda, and Wilfrid the priest,
who was afterwards bishop, and Eappa the priest, whom king
Wulfhere sent to preach Christianity in the Isle of Wight, and
abbat Sexwulf, and Immine the ealdorman, and Edbert the
ealdorman, and Herefrid the ealdorman, and Wilbert the
ealdorman, and Abon the ealdorman, Ethelbald, Brordan,
Wilbert, Elmund, Frethegis. These, and many others
who were there, servants of the king, all assented to it.
This writing was written six hundred and sixty-four years
after the birth of our Lord, (in) the seventh year of king
Wulfhere; the ninth year of archbishop Deus-dedit. They
then laid the curse of God, and the curse of all saints, and
of all Christian people (upon him) who should undo any
thing which there was done. 'So be it,' say all, 'Amen.'

When these things were done, the king sent to Rome to
Vitalian who then was pope, and desired that he should
grant by his rescript, and with his blessing, all the before-
mentioned things. And the pope sent this rescript, thus
saying, 'I, pope Vitalian, concede to thee king Wulfhere,
and archbishop Deus-dedit, and abbat Sexwulf, all the things
which ye desire, and I forbid that any king or any man have
any claim thereon, except the abbat alone ; nor let him obey
any man except the pope of Rome, and the archbishop of
Canterbury. If any one break this in any thing, may St.
Peter exterminate him with his sword : if any one observe
it, may St. Peter, with the keys of heaven, undo for him the
kingdom of heaven.' Thus the monastery at Medeshamstede
was begun, which since has been called Burh [Peterborough].

After that, another archbishop came to Canterbury, who
was called Theodore, a very good and a wise man, and he
held his synod with his bishops and with the clergy. There
was Winfred bishop of the Mercians deposed from his

bishopric, and abbat Saxulf was there chosen to be bishop, and Cuthbald, a monk of the same monastery, was chosen abbat. This synod was held six hundred and seventy-three years after the birth of our Lord.

A. 658. This year Kenwalk fought against the Welsh at Beonna [Pen]; and he drove them as far as Pedrida, [Petherton?] this was fought after he came from East-Anglia; he was there three years in exile. Thither had Penda driven him, and deprived him of his kingdom, because he had forsaken his sister.

A. 659.

A. 660. This year Bishop Agilbert departed from Kenwalk, and Wini held the bishopric* three years, and Agilbert obtained the bishopric of Paris in France by the Seine.

A. 661. This year, during Easter, Kenwalk fought at Pontesbury, and Wulfhere, the son of Penda, laid the country waste as far as Ashdown. And Cuthred the son of Cuichelm and king Cenbert† died in one year. And Wulfhere the son of Penda laid waste Wight, and gave the people of Wight to Ethelwald king of the South-Saxons, because Wulfhere had been his sponsor at baptism. And Eappa the mass-priest, by the command of Wilfrid and King Wulfhere, was the first of men who brought baptism to the people of the Isle of Wight.

A. 662. 663.

A. 664. This year the sun was eclipsed on the 5th before the Nones of May;‡ and Earconbert king of the Kentish-men died, and Egbert his son succeeded to the kingdom; and Colman,§ with his companions, went to his country. The same year there was a great pestilence in the island of Britain, and bishop‖ Tuda died of the pestilence, and was buried at Wagele.¶ And Chad and Wilfrid were ordained; and the same year archbishop Deus-dedit died.

A. 665. 666.

A. 667. This year Oswy and Egbert sent Wighard

---

* Of Wessex, at Winchester. See p. 191.

† "Father of Cædwalla, king of Wessex. See A. 685."—*Petrie.*

‡ May 3. "This happened on the 1st of May; but the error is Bede's."—*Petrie.*

§ Bishop of Lindisfarne.   ‖ Of Lindisfarne.   ¶ See note at p. 162.

the priest to Rome, that he might there be consecrated archbishop of Canterbury; but he died soon after he came
thither.

A. 667. This year Wighard went to Rome, even as King Oswy and
Egbert had sent him.

A. 668. This year Theodore was ordained an archbishop,
and sent to Britain.

A. 669. This year king Egbert gave Reculver to Bass
the mass-priest, that he might build a minster thereon.

A. 670. This year Oswy king of the North-humbrians
died, on the 15th before the Kalends of March;* and Egfrid
his son reigned after him; and Hlothere,† the nephew of
bishop Agilbert, obtained the bishopric over the West-
Saxons, and held it seven years. Bishop Theodore consecrated him. And Oswy was the son of Ethelfrid, Ethelfrid
of Ethelric, Ethelric of Ida, Ida of Eoppa.

A. 671. This year was the great destruction among the
birds.

A. 672. This year king Kenwalk died, and Sexburga his
queen reigned one year after him.

A. 673. This year Egbert, king of the Kentish-men
died; and the same year there was a Synod at Hertford, and
Saint Etheldrida began the minster at Ely.

A. 674. This year Escwin succeeded to the kingdom of
the West-Saxons; he was the son of Cenfus, Cenfus of
Cenferth, Cenferth of Cuthgils, Cuthgils of Ceolwulf, Ceolwulf of Cynric, Cynric of Cerdic.

A. 675. This year Wulfhere, the son of Penda, and
Escwin, the son of Cenfus, fought at Beadan-head; and
the same year Wulfhere died, and Ethelred succeeded to
the kingdom.

Now in his time he sent bishop Wilfrid to Rome to the
pope that then was, he was called Agatho, and showed him
by letter and by message how his brothers Peada and Wulfhere, and Sexwulf the abbat, had built a minster, which was
called Medeshamstede, and that they had freed it against
king and against bishop of all services; and he besought
him that he would assent to it with his rescript and with his
blessing. And then the pope sent his rescript to England,
thus saying:

* February 15th.　　† Eleutherius, bishop of Winchester. See p. 191.

"I, Agatho, pope of Rome, greet well the worshipful Ethelred, king of the Mercians, and the archbishop Theodore of Canterbury, and the bishop of the Mercians Sexwulf, who was formerly abbat, and all the abbats who are in England, with the greeting of God and my blessing. I have heard the desire of king Ethelred, and of archbishop Theodore, and of bishop Sexwulf, and of abbat Cuthbald; and it is my will that it be in all wise even as you have spoken. And I ordain, on behalf of God and St. Peter, and of all saints, and of every person in orders, that neither king, nor bishop, nor earl, nor any man have any claim, nor any tribute, geld, or military service; neither let any man exact any kind of service from the abbacy of Medeshamstede. I also ordain that the shire-bishop be not so bold that he perform any ordination or consecration within the abbacy unless the abbat beseech it of him, nor have any claim there for proxies, or synodals, or for any kind of thing. And it is my will that the abbat be holden as legate of Rome over all the island, and that whatsoever abbat shall be there chosen by the monks, he be consecrated by the archbishop of Canterbury. I will and concede that whatever man shall have made a vow to go to Rome, which he may be unable to fulfil, either from sickness or his Lord's need (of him), or from poverty, or be unable to come there from any other kind of need, be he of England, or of whatever other island he be, let him come to the minster at Medeshamstede, and have the same forgiveness of Christ and St. Peter, and of the abbat and of the monks, that he should have if he went to Rome. Now I beseech thee, brother Theodore, that thou cause to be commanded throughout all England, that a synod be gathered, and this decree, be read and observed. In like manner I command thee bishop Sexwulf, that even as thou didst desire that the minster be free, so I forbid thee and all the bishops that shall come after thee, from Christ and all his saints, that ye have any claim upon the minster, except so far as the abbat shall be willing. Now will I say in a word, that whoso observeth this rescript and this decree, let him be ever dwelling with God Almighty in the kingdom of heaven; and whoso breaketh through it, let him be excommunicated, and thrust down with Judas and with all the devils in hell, unless he turn to repentance. Amen!"

This rescript Pope Agatho and one hundred and twenty-five bishops sent to England by Wilfrid archbishop of York. This was done six hundred and eighty years after the birth of our Lord, and in the sixth year of king Ethelred.

The king then commanded the archbishop Theodore that he should appoint a meeting of all the witan at the place which is called Heathfield.* When they were there assembled, he caused the rescript to be read, which the pope had sent thither, and they all assented to and fully confirmed it.

Then said the king : "All those things which my brother Peada, and my brother Wulfhere, and my sisters Kyneburg and Kyneswith, gave and granted to St. Peter and the abbat, it is my will shall stand ; and I will in my day increase it for the good of their souls and of my own. Now to-day I give St. Peter at his minster, Medeshamstede, these lands and all that lieth there adjoining ; that is to say, Bredon, Repings, Cadney, Swineshead, Hanbury, Lodeshall, Scuffanhall, Cosford, Stratford, Wattleburn, Lushgard, Ethelhunisland, Bardney. These lands I give St. Peter all as freely as I myself possessed them, and so that none of my successors take anything therefrom. If any one shall do so, let him have the curse of the pope of Rome, and the curse of all bishops, and of all those who are here witnesses, and this I confirm with Christ's token.✠" "I, Theodore, archbishop of Canterbury, am witness to this charter of Medeshamstede, and I confirm it with my signature, and I excommunicate all those who shall break any part thereof, and I bless all those who shall observe it.✠" "I, Wilfrid, archbishop of York, I am witness to this charter, and I assent to the same curse.✠" "I, Sexwulf, who was first abbat and am now bishop, I give those my curse, and that of all my successors, who shall break through this." "I, Ostritha, wife of Ethelred, grant it." "I, Adrian, legate, assent to it." "I, Putta, bishop of Rochester, I subscribe it." "I, Waldhere, bishop of London, confirm it." "I, Cuthbald, abbat, assent to it, so that whoso shall break it, let him have the cursing of all bishops and of all Christian folk. Amen !"

A. 676. This year, in which Hedda succeeded to his bishopric ;† Escwin died, and Kentwin succeeded to the kingdom

* Bishop's Hatfield. See p. 201.   † Of Wessex, or Winchester.

of the West-Saxons : and Kentwin was the son of Cynegils,
Cynegils of Ceolwulf.   And Ethelred, king of the Mercians, laid waste Kent.

A. 677.

A. 678. This year the star (called) a comet appeared in
August, and shone like a sunbeam every morning for three
months ; and bishop Wilfrid was driven from his bishopric
by King Egfrid ; and two bishops were consecrated in his
stead ; Bosa to Deira, and Eata to Bernicia.   And Eadhed
was consecrated bishop over the men of Lindsey ; he was
the first of the bishops of Lindsey.*

A. 679. This year Elfwin was slain near the Trent,
where Egfrid and Ethelred fought ; and Saint Etheldrida died.   And Coldingham was burned by fire from
heaven.†

A. 680. This year archbishop Theodore appointed a
synod at Heathfield, because he wished to set forth aright
the Christian faith.   And the same year Hilda, abbess of
Whitby, died.

A. 681. This year Tumbert was consecrated bishop of
Hexham, and Trumwine of the Picts,‡ for at that time they
were subject to this country.

A. 682. In this year Kentwin drove the Britons to the
sea.

A. 683.

A. 684. Here in this year Egfrid sent an army against
the Scots, and Beort his ealdorman with it, and miserably
they plundered and burned the churches of God.

A. 685. This year king Egfrid commanded that Cuthbert should be consecrated a bishop ; and on the first day of
Easter, at York, archbishop Theodore consecrated him
bishop of Hexham ; because Tumbert had been deposed
from his bishopric.   This year Cædwalla began to contend for
the kingdom.   Cædwalla was the son of Cenbert, Cenbert
of Cadda, Cadda of Cutha, Cutha of Ceawlin, Ceawlin of Cynric, Cynric of Cerdic.   And Mul was the brother of Cædwalla,
and he was afterwards burned in Kent.   And the same year,
on the 13th before the Kalends of June, king Egfrid was
slain near the North-sea, and a great army with him.§   He
was king fifteen years, and Alfrid his brother succeeded to

*.-See p. 193.   † See p. 220.   ‡ Whithern.   § See p. 223.

the kingdom after him. Egfrid was the son of Oswy, Oswy of Ethelfrid, Ethelfrid of Ethelric, Ethelric of Ida, Ida of Eoppa. And Lothere, king of the Kentish-men, died the same year. And John was consecrated bishop of Hexham, and he was there until Wilfrid returned. Afterwards John succeeded to the bishopric of York, for bishop Bosa was dead. Then, after that, Wilfrid* his priest was consecrated bishop of York, and John retired to his minster at Derewood.† This year it rained blood in Britain, and milk and butter were turned into blood.

A. 685. And in this same year Cuthbert was consecrated bishop of Hexham by archbishop Theodore at York, because bishop Tumbert had been driven from the bishopric.

A. 686. This year Cædwalla and Mul his brother laid waste Kent and Wight. This Cædwalla gave to St. Peter's minster at Medeshamstede, Hook, which is in an island called Egborough; the then abbat of the monastery was called Egbald. He was the third abbat after Sexwulf. At that time Theodore was archbishop in Kent.

A. 687. This year Mul was burned in Kent, and twelve other men with him; and the same year Cædwalla again laid waste Kent.

A. 688. This year Ina succeeded to the kingdom of the West-Saxons, and held it thirty-seven years; and he built the minster at Glastonbury; and he afterwards went to Rome, and there dwelt to the end of his days: and the same year Cædwalla went to Rome, and received baptism from the pope,‡ and the pope named him Peter; and in about seven days he died. Now Ina was the son of Cenred, Cenred of Ceolwald, Ceolwald was Cynegil's brother, and they were sons of Cuthwine the son of Ceawlin, Ceawlin of Cynric, Cynric of Cerdic.

A. 688. This year king Cædwalla went to Rome, and received baptism of Pope Sergius, and he gave him the name of Peter, and in about seven days afterwards, on the twelfth before the Kalends of May, while he was yet in his baptismal garments, he died; and he was buried in St. Peter's church. And Ina succeeded to the kingdom of the West-Saxons after him, and he reigned twenty-seven years.

A. 689.

A. 690. This year archbishop Theodore died; he was

* Wilfrid II. See p. 293.   † Beverley. See p. 237.   ‡ Sergius.

bishop twenty-two years, and he was buried at Canterbury ; and Berthwald succeeded to the bishopric.   Before this the bishops had been Romans, but from this time they were English.

A. 691.

A. 692. This year Berthwald was chosen archbishop on the Kalends of July ; he was before that abbat of Reculver. There were then two kings in Kent, Withred and Webherd [Suebhard].

A. 693. This year Berthwald was consecrated archbishop by Guodun, bishop of the Gauls, on the 5th before the Nones of July. *   At this time Gebmund, bishop of Rochester, died, and archbishop Berthwald consecrated Tobias in his place ; and Drithelm departed this life.

A. 694. This year the Kentish-men compounded with Ina, and gave him thirty thousand pounds† for his friendship, because they had formerly burned Mul.   And Withred succeeded to the kingdom of the Kentish-men, and held it thirty-three years.   Withred was the son of Egbert, Egbert of Earconbert, Earconbert of Eadbald, Eadbald of Ethelbert.

As soon as he was king, he commanded a great council to be assembled at the place which is called Baccancelde,‡ in which sat Withred, king of the Kentish-men, and Berthwald, the archbishop of Canterbury, and Tobias, bishop of Rochester, and with them were assembled abbats and abbesses, and many wise men, all to consult about the bettering of God's churches in Kent.   Now began the king to speak, and said, "It is my will that all the minsters and the churches that were given and bequeathed to the glory of God in the days of faithful kings my predecessors, and in the days of my kinsmen, of King Ethelbert and those who followed after him,

---

* The 29th of June.

† " The reading of MSS. *B* and *F*, however excessive the sum may appear, has been placed in the text, because, unlike the 'thirty men' of *A.G*, or the 'thirty thousand' of *D.E*, it is intelligible without having recourse to conjecture.   The payment, whatever its amount may have been, was probably the legal compensation for the death of Mul . . . Of the early Latin writers, Ethelwald says, it was 30,000 solidi, ' per singulos constanti numero sexdecim nummis;' Florence, of Worcester, 3750 pounds ; and Malmesbury, 30,000 mancuses, which, at eight to the pound, would agree with Florence."—*Petrie*.   ‡ Beckenham, Kent.

do so remain to the glory of God, and firmly continue so to
all eternity for evermore.   For I, Withred, an earthly king,
instigated by the King of heaven, and burning with the zeal
of righteousness, have learned from the institutes of our
forefathers, that no layman has a right to possess himself of
a church, nor of any of the things which belong to a church.
And hence strictly and faithfully do we appoint and decree,
and in the name of the Almighty God and of all his saints
we forbid to all kings our successors, and to ealdormen, and
all laymen any lordship whatever over the churches, and
over all their possessions, which I, or my elders of olden
days, have given as an everlasting inheritance to the glory of
Christ and of our lady St. Mary, and of the holy apostles.
And observe, when it shall happen that a bishop, or an abbat,
or an abbess, shall depart this life, let it be made known to
the archbishop, and by his counsel and advice, let such an
one be chosen as shall be worthy.   And let the archbishop
inquire into the life and purity of him who is chosen to such
a duty, and in nowise let any one be chosen to such a duty
without the counsel of the archbishop.   It is the duty of
kings to appoint earls and ealdormen, shire-reeves and
doomsmen, and of the archbishop to instruct and advise the
community of God, and bishops, and abbats, and abbesses,
priests and deacons, to choose and appoint, and consecrate and
stablish them by good precepts and example, lest any of
God's flock stray and be lost.

A. 695. 696.

A. 697. This year the South-humbrians slew Ostritha,
Ethelred's queen, Egfrid's sister.

A. 698.

A. 699. This year the Picts slew Beort the ealdorman.

A. 700. 701.

A. 702. This year Kenred succeeded to the kingdom of
the South-humbrians.

A. 703. This year bishop Hedda died, and he held the
bishopric at Winchester twenty-seven years.

A. 704. This year Ethelred the son of Penda, king of
the Mercians, became a monk, and he had held the kingdom
twenty-nine years ; then Kenred succeeded to it.

A. 705. This year Alfrid king of the North-humbrians
died at Driffield on the nineteenth before the Kalends of

January: and bishop Sexwulf.* Then Osred his son succeeded to the kingdom.

A. 706.—708.

A. 709. This year bishop Aldhelm died, he was bishop† on the west of Selwood; and in the early days of Daniel the land of the West-Saxons was divided into two bishop-shires, and before that it had been one; the one ‡ Daniel held, the other § Aldhelm. After Aldhelm, Forthhere succeeded to it. And king Ceolred succeeded to the kingdom of the Mercians; and Kenred went to Rome, and Offa with him. And Kenred was there till the end of his life. And the same year bishop Wilfrid ‖ died at Oundle, and his body was carried to Ripon; he was bishop forty-five years; him king Egfrid had formerly driven away to Rome.

A. 710. This year Acca, Wilfrid's priest, succeeded to the bishopric ¶ which before he had held; and the same year Bertfrid the ealdorman fought against the Picts between Heugh and Carau. And Ina and Nun his kinsman fought against Gerent king of the Welsh; and the same year Higbald was slain.

A. 711.—713.

A. 714. This year Saint Guthlac died, and king Pepin.

A. 715. This year Ina and Ceolred fought at Wanborough. This year died king Dagobert.

A. 716. This year Osred king of the North-humbrians was slain on the southern border; he had the kingdom seven years after Alfrid; then Kenred succeeded to the kingdom, and held it two years, then Osric, who held it eleven years; and the same year Ceolred king of the Mercians died, and his body lies at Lichfield, and Ethelred's the son of Penda at Bardney. Then Ethelbald succeeded to the kingdom of the Mercians, and held it forty-one years. Ethelbald was the son of Alwy, Alwy of Eawa, Eawa of Pybba, whose genealogy is written before.** And that pious man Egbert converted the monks in the island of Hii to the right faith, so that they observed Easter duly, and the ecclesiastical tonsure.

A. 717.

A. 718. This year Ingild the brother of Ina died, and their sisters were Cwenburga and Cuthburga. And Cuthburga

* Of Lichfield.　　　† Of Sherborne.　‡ Winchester.
§ Sherborne. See p. 267.　‖ Of Hexham.　¶ Hexham.　**A. 626.

built the monastery at Wimburn; and she was given in marriage to Alfrid king of the North-humbrians; but they separated during his life-time.

A. 719. 720.

A. 721. This year bishop Daniel * went to Rome; and the same year Ina slew Cynewulf the etheling. And this year the holy bishop John † died; he was bishop thirty-three years, eight months, and thirteen days; and his body rests at Beverley.

A. 722. This year queen Ethelburga razed Taunton, which Ina had previously built; and Ealdbert the exile departed into Surry and Sussex, and Ina fought against the South-Saxons.

A. 723. 724.

A. 725. This year Withred king of the Kentish-men died on the ninth before the Kalends of May; he reigned thirty-four years; his genealogy is above: and Egbert succeeded to the kingdom of Kent; and Ina fought against the South-Saxons, and there slew Ealdbert the etheling, whom he before had driven into exile.

A. 726.

A. 727. This year Tobias bishop of Rochester died, and in his place archbishop Berthwald consecrated Aldwulf bishop.

A. 728. This year Ina went to Rome, and there gave (up) his life, and Ethelard his kinsman succeeded to the kingdom of the West-Saxons, and held it fourteen years. And the same year Ethelard and Oswald the etheling fought; and Oswald was the son of Ethelbald, Ethelbald of Cynebald, Cynebald of Cuthwin, Cuthwin of Ceawlin.

A. 729. This year the star (called) a comet appeared, and Saint Egbert died in Ii.

A. 729. And the same year Osric died; he was king eleven years: then Ceolwulf succeeded to the kingdom, and held it eight years.

A. 730. This year Oswald the etheling died.

A. 731. This year Osric king of the North-humbrians was slain, and Ceolwulf succeeded to the kingdom, and held it eight years,‡ and Ceolwulf was the son of Cutha, Cutha of Cuthwin, Cuthwin of Leodwald, Leodwald of Egwald,

* Of Winton.   † Of York.
‡ Osric's death is rightly placed by another MS. in 729.

Egwald of Aldhelm, Aldhelm of Ocga, Ocga of Ida, Ida of Eoppa.   And archbishop Berthwald died on the Ides of January ;* he was bishop thirty-seven years six months and fourteen days.   And the same year Tatwine was consecrated archbishop ;† he had been before a priest at Bredon among the Mercians.   Daniel bishop of Winchester, and Ingwald bishop of London, and Aldwin bishop of Lichfield, and Aldwulf bishop of Rochester consecrated him on the tenth of June : he had the archbishopric three years.

A. 732.

A. 733. This year Ethelbald conquered Somerton ; and the sun was eclipsed, and the whole disc of the sun was like a black shield.   And Acca was driven from his bishopric. ‡

A. 734. This year the moon was as if it had been sprinkled with blood ; and archbishop Tatwine and Bede died, and Egbert was consecrated bishop. §

A. 735. This year bishop Egbert received his pall at Rome.

A. 736. This year archbishop Nothelm received his pall from the bishop of the Romans. ‖

A. 737. This year bishop Forthere,¶ and queen Frithogitha ** went to Rome. And king Ceolwulf †† received Peter's tonsure, and gave his kingdom to Eadbert, his uncle's son ; he reigned twenty-one years ; and bishop Ethelwald ‡‡ and Acca died, and Conwulf was consecrated bishop.§§   And the same year king Ethelbald laid waste the land of the Northhumbrians.

A. 738. This year Eadbert the son of Eata, Eata being the son of Leodwald, succeeded to the kingdom of the Northhumbrians, and held it twenty-one years.   His brother was archbishop § Egbert the son of Eata ; and they both rest in one porch in the city of York.

A. 739. 740.

A. 741. This year king Ethelard died, and Cuthred his kinsman succeeded to the kingdom of the West-Saxons, and held it sixteen years ; and he contended strenuously against Ethelbald king of the Mercians.   And archbishop

---

* The 13th of January.   † Of Canterbury.   ‡ Hexham.
§ Of York.   ‖ Greg. III.   ¶ Of Winton.
** Of Wessex.   †† Of Northumbria.
‡‡ Of Lindisfarne.   §§ Of York.

Nothelm* died, and Cuthbert was consecrated archbishop; and Dun bishop to Rochester. This year York was burnt.

A. 742. This year a great synod was held at Cloveshou; and there was Ethelbald king of the Mercians, and archbishop Cuthbert, and many other wise men.

A. 743. This year Ethelbald king of the Mercians, and Cuthred king of the West-Saxons, fought against the Welsh.

A. 744. This year Daniel gave up the see of Winchester, and Hunferth succeeded to the bishopric : and stars were seen to shoot rapidly : and Wilfrid the younger,† who was bishop of York, died on the third before the Kalends of May ;‡ he was bishop thirty years.

A. 745. This year Daniel died : then forty-three years had elapsed since he obtained the bishopric.

A. 746. This year king Selred was slain.

A. 747.

A. 748. This year Cynric the etheling of the West-Saxons was slain : and Eadbert king of the Kentish-men died ; and Ethelbert, the son of king Withred, succeeded to the kingdom.

A. 749.

A. 750. This year Cuthred, king of the West-Saxons, fought against Ethelhun, the proud ealdorman.

A. 751.

A. 752. This year Cuthred, king of the West-Saxons, in the twelfth year of his reign, fought at Burford against Ethelbald king of the Mercians, and put him to flight.

A. 753. This year Cuthred, king of the West-Saxons, fought against the Welsh.

A. 754. This year Cuthred, king of the West-Saxons, died ; and Kineward obtained the bishopric of Winchester, after Hunferth: and the same year Canterbury was burned : and Sigebert his kinsman succeeded to the kingdom of the West-Saxons, and held it one year.

A. 755. This year Cynewulf, and the West-Saxon 'witan'

---

* Of Canterbury.

† Wilfrid the second, archbishop of York, is apparently confounded with the bishop of Worcester of the same name. The former was succeeded by Egbert in 734. See A. 734 and 776, and Bede, p. 299.

‡ The 29th of April.

deprived his kinsman Sigebert of his kingdom, except
Hampshire, for his unjust doings; and that he held until he
slew the ealdorman who longest abode by him.   And then
Cynewulf drove him into Andred, and he abode there until
a swine-herd stabbed him at Privets-flood [Privett, Hamp-
shire], and avenged the ealdorman Cumbra.

And Cynewulf fought very many battles against the
Welsh; and after he had held the kingdom about one and
thirty years, he purposed to expel an etheling, who was
named Cyneard: and Cyneard was Sigebert's brother.
And he then learned that the king with a small band was
gone to Merton to visit a woman; and he there beset him
and surrounded the chamber on every side, before the men
who were with the king discovered him.   And when the
king perceived this, he went to the door, and there manfully
defended himself, until he beheld the etheling, and then he
rushed out upon him and sorely wounded him; and they all
continued fighting against the king until they had slain
him.

And upon this, the king's thanes having discovered the
affray by the woman's cries, each, as he was ready, and with
his utmost speed ran to the spot.   And the etheling offered
money and life to each of them, and not one of them would
accept it; but they continued fighting till they all fell, except
one, a British hostage, and he was sorely wounded.

Then upon the morrow, the king's thanes, whom he had
left behind him, heard that the king was slain, then rode they
thither, and Osric his ealdorman, and Wiferth his thane, and
the men whom he had previously left behind.   And at the
town wherein the king lay slain they found the etheling, and
those within had closed the gates against them; but they
then went onward.   And he then offered them their own
choice of land and money if they would grant him the
kingdom, and showed them that their kinsman were with
him, men who would not desert him.   And they then said,
that no kinsman was dearer to them than their lord, and that
they never would follow his murderer.   And they then bade
their kinsmen that they should go away from him in safety;
but they said that the same had been bidden their companions
who before that had been with the king; then they said, that
they no more minded it 'than your companions who were

z

slain with the king.' And then they continued fighting around the gates until they made their way in, and slew the etheling, and all the men who were with him, except one who was the ealdorman's godson ; and he escaped with life, though he was wounded in several places.

And Cynewulf reigned thirty-one years, and his body lies at Winchester, and the etheling's at Axminster ; and their right paternal kin reaches to Cerdic.

And the same year Ethelbald king of the Mercians was slain at Seckington, and his body lies at Repton, and he reigned forty-one years ; and Bernred obtained the kingdom, and held it a little while and unhappily. And the same year Offa drove out Bernred and obtained the kingdom, and held it thirty-nine years ; and his son Egfert held it one hundred and forty-one days. Offa was the son of Thingferth, Thingferth of Enwulf, Enwulf of Osmod, Osmod of Eawa, Eawa of Pybba, Pybba of Creoda, Creoda of Cynewald, Cynewald of Cnebba, Cnebba of Icel, Icel of Eomær, Eomær of Angeltheow, Angeltheow of Offa, Offa of Wærmund, Wærmund of Wihtlæg, Wihtlæg of Woden.

A. 755. This year Cynewulf deprived king Sigebert of his kingdom; and Sigebert's brother, Cynehard by name, slew Cynewulf at Merton ; and he reigned thirty-one years. And in the same year Ethelbald king of the Mercians was slain at Repton. And Offa succeeded to the kingdom of the Mercians, Bernred being driven out.

A. 756.

A. 757. This year Eadbert king of the North-humbrians was shorn, and his son Oswulph succeeded to the kingdom, and reigned one year ; and he was slain by his household on the eighth before the Kal. of August.*

A. 758. This year archbishop Cuthbert died ; and he held the archbishopric eighteen years.†

A. 759. This year Bregowin was ordained archbishop at St. Michael's-tide, and held the see four years. And Moll Ethelwald succeeded to the kingdom of the Northhumbrians, and reigned six years, and then resigned it.

A. 760. This year Ethelbert king of the Kentish-men died ; he was the son of king Withred : and Ceolwulf also died.

A. 761. This year was the severe winter ; and Moll king

* The 25th of July.   † Of Canterbury.

of the North-humbrians slew Oswin at Edwin's Cliff on the eighth before the Ides of August.

A. 762. This year archbishop * Bregowin died.

A. 763. This year Lambert was ordained archbishop on the fortieth day after mid-winter,† and held the see twenty-six years. And Frithwald bishop of Whitherne died on the Nones of May.‡ He was consecrated at York on the eighteenth before the Kal. of September,§ in the sixth year of Ceolwulf's reign, and he was bishop twenty-nine years. Then Petwin was consecrated bishop of Whitherne at Adlingfleet, on the sixteenth before the Kalends of August.‖

A. 764. This year archbishop Lambert received his pall.

A. 765. This year Alcred succeeded to the kingdom of the North-humbrians, and reigned nine years.

A. 766. This year died archbishop Egbert at York on the 13th before the Kalends of December; he was bishop thirty-seven years; and Frithbert at Hexham; he was bishop thirty-three years; and Ethelbert was consecrated to York, and Alhmund to Hexham.

A. 767.

A. 768. This year king Eadbert the son of Eata, died on the thirteenth before the Kalends of September.

A. 769.—771.

A. 772. This year bishop Milred ¶ died.

A. 773. This year a fiery crucifix appeared in the heavens after sunset: and the same year the Mercians and the Kentish-men fought at Otford; and wondrous adders were seen in the land of the South-Saxons.

A. 774. This year at Easter-tide, the North-humbrians drove their king Alcred from York, and took Ethelred, the son of Moll, to be their lord; he reigned four years.

A. 775.

A. 776. This year bishop Petwin ** died on the thirteenth before the Kalends of October; he was bishop fourteen years.

A. 777. This year Cynewolf and Offa fought about Bensington, and Offa took the town; and the same year, on

* Canterbury.
‡ The 7th of May.
‖ The 17th of July.
** Of Whitherne.

† The 2nd of February.
§ The 15th of August.
¶ Of Worcester.

z 2

the seventeenth before the Kalends of July, Ethelbert was consecrated at York bishop of Whitherne.

In the days of king Offa there was an abbat of Medeshamstede called Beonna. The same Beonna, by the consent of all the monks of the minster, let to Cuthbert the ealdorman ten copy-lands at Swineshead, with lease, and with meadow, and with all that lay thereto, and on this condition: that Cuthbert should give the abbat therefore fifty pounds, and each year one day's entertainment, or thirty shillings in money; and furthermore, that after his decease the land should return to the minster. The witnesses of this were king Offa, and king Egfert, and archbishop Higbert,* and bishop Ceolwulf, and bishop Inwona, and abbat Beonna, and many other bishops and abbats, and many other great men. In the days of this same Offa there was an ealdorman who was called Brorda. He desired of the king that for love of him he would free a minster of his called Woking, because he wished to give it to Medeshamstede, and St. Peter, and the abbat that then was, who was called Pusa. Pusa succeeded Beonna, and the king loved him greatly. And the king then freed the minster Woking, against king, and against bishop, and against earl, and against all men, so that no one should have any claim there except St. Peter and the abbat. This was done in the king's town called Free-Richburn.

A. 778. This year Ethelbald and Herbert slew three high-reeves; Edulf, the son of Bosa, at Kings-cliff, and Cynewolf and Egga at Helathyrn, on the eleventh before the Kalends of April: and then Alfwold obtained the kingdom,† and drove Ethelred out of the country; and he reigned ten years.

A. 779.

A. 780. This year the Old-Saxons and the Franks fought; and the high-reeves of the North-humbrians burned Bern the ealdorman at Silton, on the eighth before the Kalends of January: and archbishop Ethelbert died at York, in whose place Eanbald was consecrated; and bishop Cynewolf gave up the bishopric of Lindisfarne. This year Alhmund, bishop of Hexham, died on the seventh before the Ides of September, and Tilbert was consecrated in his place on the

* Of Lichfield!   † Northumbria.

sixth before the Nones of October; and Higbald was consecrated at Sockbury bishop of Lindisfarne; and king Alfwold
sent to Rome for a pall, and invested Eanbald as archbishop.

A. 781.

A. 782. This year died Werburh, Ceolred's queen, and
Cynewolf, bishop of Lindisfarne; and there was a synod at
Acley.

A. 783.

A. 784. This year Cyneard slew king Cynewolf, and was
himself there slain, and eighty-four men with him; and
then Bertric obtained the kingdom of the West-Saxons,
and he reigned sixteen years, and his body lies at Wareham;
and his right paternal kin reaches to Cerdic. At this time
king Elmund reigned in Kent. This king Elmund was
the father of Egbert, and Egbert was father of Athulf.

A. 785. This year abbat Bothwin died at Ripon; and
this year there was a contentious synod at Chalk-hythe, and
archbishop Lambert gave up some portion of his bishopric,
and Higbert was elected by king Offa; and Egfert was
consecrated king. And at this time messengers were sent
from Rome by pope Adrian to England, to renew the faith
and the peace which St. Gregory had sent us by Augustine
the bishop; and they were worshipfully received, and sent
away in peace.

A. 786.

A. 787. This year king Bertric took to wife Eadburga,
king Offa's daughter; and in his days first came three ships
of Northmen, out of Hæretha-land [Denmark]. And then
the reve* rode to the place, and would have driven them to
the king's town, because he knew not who they were: and
they there slew him. These were the first ships of Danish-
men which sought the land of the English nation.

A. 788. This year a synod was assembled in the land of
the North-humbrians at Fingall, on the 4th before the
Nones of September; and abbat Albert died at Ripon.

A. 789. This year Alfwold, king of the Northumbrians,
was slain by Siga on the 8th before the Kalends of October;
and a heavenly light was frequently seen at the place where
he was slain; and he was buried at Hexham within the
church; and Osred, the son of Alcred succeeded to the

* Since called sheriff; i. e. the *reve*, or steward, of the shire.—INGRAM.

kingdom after him : he was his nephew. And a synod was assembled at Acley.

A. 790. This year archbishop Lambert died, and the same year abbat Athelard was chosen archbishop.* And Osred, king of the North-humbrians, was betrayed, and driven from the kingdom; and Ethelred, the son of Ethelwald, again obtained the government.

A. 791. This year Baldulf was consecrated bishop of Whitherne, on the 16th before the Kalends of August, by archbishop Eanbald,† and by bishop Ethelbert.‡

A. 792. This year Offa, king of the Mercians, commanded the head of king Ethelbert§ to be struck off. And Osred, who had been king of the Northumbrians, having come home after his exile, was seized and slain on the 18th before the Kalends of October ; and his body lies at Tinemouth. And king Ethelred took a new wife, who was called Elfleda, on the 3rd before the Kalends of October.

A. 793. This year dire forwarnings came over the land of the North-humbrians, and miserably terrified the people ; these were excessive whirlwinds, and lightnings ; and fiery dragons were seen flying in the air. A great famine soon followed these tokens ; and a little after that, in the same year, on the 6th before the Ides of January, the ravaging of heathen men lamentably destroyed God's church at Lindisfarne through rapine and slaughter. And Siga died on the 8th before the Kalends of March.

A. 794. This year Pope Adrian‖ and king Offa died ; and Ethelred, king of the North-humbrians, was slain by his own people on the 13th before the Kalends of May ; and bishop Ceolwulf¶ and bishop Eadbald went away from the land. And Egfert succeeded to the kingdom of the Mercians and died the same year. And Eadbert, who by a second name was named Pren, obtained the kingdom of Kent. And Ethelherd the ealdorman died on the Kalends of August ; and the heathens ravaged among the North-humbrians, and plundered Egfert's monastery at the mouth of the Wear ; and there one of their leaders was slain, and also some of their ships were wrecked by a tempest ; and many of them

* Of Canterbury,   † Of York.
‡ Of Hexham.   § Of East Anglia.
‖ Pope Adrian died December 25th, 795.   ¶ Of Lindsey.

were there drowned, and some came on shore alive, and they were soon slain at the river's mouth.

A. 795. This year the moon was eclipsed between cock-crowing and dawn, on the 5th before the Kalends of April; and Eardulf succeeded to the kingdom of the North-humbrians on the 2nd before the Ides of May; and he was afterwards con-secrated king, and raised to his throne on the 8th before the Kalends of June, at York, by archbishop Eanbald, and bishop Ethelbert,* and Higbald,† and Badulf,‡ bishops.

A. 796. This year Kenulf, king of the Mercians, laid waste Kent as far as the marshes, and took Pren their king, and led him bound into Mercia, and let his eyes be picked out and his hands be cut off. And Athelard, archbishop of Canterbury, appointed a synod, and confirmed and ratified, by the command of Pope Leo, all the things respecting God's ministers which were appointed in Withgar's days, and in other kings' days, and thus sayeth :

"I, Athelard, the humble archbishop of Canterbury, by the unanimous counsel of the whole synod, and with . . . of all . . . to the congregation of all the ministers to which in old days immunity was given by faithful men, in the name of God, and by his awful doom, I command, as I have com-mand of Pope Leo, that henceforth none dare to choose for themselves lords over God's heritage from amongst laymen. But even as it stands in the rescript which the pope has given, or those holy men have appointed who are our fathers and instructors concerning holy minsters, thus let them con-tinue inviolate, without any kind of gainsaying. If there be any man who will not observe this ordinance of God, and of our pope, and ours, and who despiseth and holdeth it for nought, let him know that he shall give account before the judgment-seat of God. And I, Athelard, archbishop, with twelve bishops, and three and twenty abbats, do confirm and ratify this same with Christ's rood-token."

And archbishop Eanbald died on the 4th before the Ides of August of the same year, and his body lies at York; and the same year died bishop Ceolwulf;§ and a second Ean-

* Of Hexham.   † Lindisfarne.
‡ Whitherne.   § Of Lindsey.

bald was consecrated in the place of the other on the 19th before the Kalends of September.

A. 796. This year Offa, king of the Mercians, died on the 4th before the Kalends of August; he reigned forty years.

A. 797. This year the Romans cut out the tongue of Pope Leo, and put out his eyes, and drove him from his see ; and soon afterwards, God helping, he was able to see and speak, and again was pope as he before was. And Eanbald received his pall on the 6th before the Ides of September ; and bishop Ethelbert* died on the 17th before the Kalends of November ; and Heandred was consecrated bishop in his place on the 3rd before the Kalends of November ; and bishop Alfun died at Sudbury, and he was buried in Dunwich, and Tidfrith was chosen after him ; and Siric, king of the East Saxons, went to Rome.   In this same year the body of Witburga was found at Dereham, all whole and uncorrupted, five and fifty years after she had departed from this life.

A. 798. This year there was a great fight at Whalley in the land of the North-humbrians, during Lent, on the 4th before the Nones of April, and there Alric, the son of Herbert, was slain, and many others with him.

A. 799. This year archbishop Athelard† and Kenebert bishop of the West-Saxons,‡ went to Rome.

A. 800. This year, on the 17th before the Kalends of February, the moon was eclipsed at the second hour of the night.   And king Bertric and Worr the ealdorman died, and Egbert succeeded to the kingdom of the West-Saxons. And the same day Ethelmund, ealdorman, rode over from the Wiccians, at Cynemæresford [Kempsford].   Then Woxtan the ealdorman with the men of Wiltshire met him. There was a great fight, and both the ealdormen were slain, and the men of Wiltshire got the victory.

A. 801.

A. 801. This year Beornmod was ordained bishop of Rochester.

A. 802. This year on the 13th before the Kalends of January the moon was eclipsed at dawn ; and Beornmod was ordained bishop of Rochester.§

* Of Hexham.   † Of Canterbury.   ‡ Winchester.
§ Placed in 801 by another MS.

A. 803. This year died Higbald bishop of Lindisfarne on the 8th before the Kalends of July, and Egbert II. was consecrated in his stead on the 3d before the Ides of June; and this year archbishop Athelard died in Kent, and Wulfred was ordained archbishop; and abbat Forthred died.

A. 804. This year archbishop Wulfred received his pall.

A. 805. This year king Cuthred died among the Kentishmen, and Colburga abbess,* and Herbert the ealdorman.

A. 806. This year the moon was eclipsed on the Kalends of September: and Eardulf king of the North-humbrians was driven from his kingdom; and Eanbert bishop of Hexham died. Also in the same year, on the 2d before the Nones of June, a cross appeared in the moon on a Wednesday at dawn; and afterwards in this year, on the third before the Kalends of September, a wonderful circle was seen about the sun.

A. 807. 808.

A. 809. This year the sun was eclipsed at the beginning of the fifth hour of the day on the 17th before the Kalends of August, the 2d day of the week, the 29th of the moon.

A. 810. 811.

A. 812. This year king Charlemagne died, and he reigned five and forty years; and archbishop Wulfred and Wigbert bishop of the West-Saxons† both went to Rome.

A. 813. This year archbishop Wulfred, with the blessing of pope Leo, returned to his own bishopric; and the same year king Egbert laid waste West-Wales from eastward to westward.

A. 814. This year the noble and holy pope ‡Leo died, and after him Stephen succeeded to the popedom.

A. 815.

A. 816. This year pope Stephen died, and after him Paschal was ordained pope; and the same year the English school at Rome§ was burned.

A. 817. 818.

A. 819. This year Kenulf king of the Mercians died,

---

* Of Berkeley.   † Sherborne.

‡ Leo III. died 11th June 816. *Eginhard, Ann.* Stephen IV. was consecrated on the 22d of the same month.

§ The Angle-School was a quarter near St. Peter's, where the English pilgrims at Rome resided. According to Anastasius, they called it their 'Borough,' (burgus). *V. Anastas. Bibliothecar. de Vita Stephani IV.*

and Ceolwulf succeeded to the kingdom ; and Eadbert the ealdorman died.

A. 820.

A. 821. This year Ceolwulf was deprived of his king-dom.*

A. 822. This year two ealdormen, Burhelm and Mucca, were slain ; and there was a synod at Cloveshoo.

A. 823. This year there was a battle between the Welsh and the men of Devon at Camelford :† and the same year Eg-bert king of the West-Saxons and Bernulf king of the Mercians fought at Wilton, and Egbert got the victory, and there was great slaughter made. He then sent from the army his son Ethelwulf, and Ealstan his bishop,‡ and Wulfherd his ealdorman, into Kent with a large force, and they drove Baldred the king northwards over the Thames. And the men of Kent, and the men of Surrey, and the South-Saxons, and the East-Saxons, submitted to him ; for ·for-merly they had been unjustly forced from his kin.   And the same year the king of the East-Angles and the people sought the alliance and protection of king Egbert for dread of the Mercians ; and the same year the East-Angles slew Bernulf king of Mercia.

A. 824.

A. 825. This year Ludecan king of the Mercians was slain, ‚and his five ealdormen with him ; and Withlaf succeeded to the kingdom.

A. 826.

A. 827. This year the moon was eclipsed § on the mass-night of midwinter.   And the same year king Egbert conquered the kingdom of the Mercians, and all that was south of the Humber ; and he was the eighth king who was Bretwalda.   Ælla king of the South-Saxons was the first who had thus much dominion ; the second was Ceawlin king of the West-Saxons ; the third was Ethelbert king of the Kentish-men ; the fourth was Redwald king of the East-Angles ; the fifth was Edwin king of the North-humbrians ; the sixth was Oswald who reigned after him ; the seventh was Oswy, Oswald's brother ; the eighth was Egbert king of the West-Saxons.   And Egbert led an army to Dore

* Mercia.   † In Cornwall.   ‡ Sherborne.
§ The eclipse happened on the 25th of December, 828.

against the North-humbrians, and they there offered him obedience and allegiance, and with that they separated.

A. 828. This year Withlaf again obtained the kingdom of the Mercians, and bishop Ethelwald* died; and the same year king Egbert led an army against the North-Welsh, and he forced them to obedient subjection.

A. 829. This year archbishop Wulfred died, and after him abbat Theologild was chosen to the archbishopric,† on the 7th before the Kalends of May; and he was consecrated upon a Sunday, the 5th before the Ides of June: and he died on the 3rd before the Kalends of September.

A. 830. This year Ceolnoth was chosen bishop,‡ and ordained; and abbat Theologild died.

A. 831. This year archbishop Ceolnoth received his pall.

A. 832. This year the heathen men ravaged Sheppey.

A. 833. This year king Egbert fought against the men of thirty-five ships at Charmouth, and there was great slaughter made, and the Danish-men maintained possession of the field. And Herefrith§ and Wigthun,‖ two bishops, died; and Dudda and Osmod, two ealdormen, died.

A. 834.

A. 835. This year a great hostile fleet came to the West-Welsh,¶ and they united together, and made war upon Egbert king of the West-Saxons. As soon as he heard of it he went thither with an army, and fought against them at Hengeston, and there he put to flight both the Welsh and the Danish-men.

A. 836. This year king Egbert died; before he was king, Offa king of the Mercians, and Bertric, king of the West-Saxons, drove him out of England into France for three years; and Bertric assisted Offa, because he had his daughter for his queen. And Egbert reigned thirty-seven years and seven months: and Ethelwulf the son of Egbert succeeded to the kingdom of the West-Saxons; and he gave his son Athelstan the kingdoms of the Kentish-men, and of the East-Saxons, and of the men of Surrey, and of the South-Saxons.

A. 836. And Ethelstan his other son succeeded to the kingdom of the Kentish-men, and to Surrey, and to the kingdom of the South-Saxons.

· * Of Lichfield.   † Of Canterbury.   ‡ Of Canterbury.
§ Of Selsey.   ‖ Of Winchester.   ¶ Cornwall.

A. 837. This year Wulfherd the ealdorman fought at
Hamtun [Southampton], against the forces of thirty-five
ships, and there made great slaughter, and got the victory ;
and the same year Wulfherd died. And the same year
Ethelhelm the ealdorman fought against the Danish army
at Portland-isle with the men of Dorset, and for a good
while he put the enemy to flight ; but the Danish-men had
possession of the field, and slew the ealdorman.

A. 838. This year Herebert the ealdorman was slain by
the heathen men, and many with him among the Marsh-
men ; and afterwards, the same year, in Lindsey, and in
East-Anglia, and in Kent, many men were slain by the
enemy.

A. 839. This year there was great slaughter at London,
and at Canterbury, and at Rochester.

A. 840. This year king Ethelwulf fought at Charmouth
against the crews of thirty-five ships, and the Danish-men
maintained possession of the field. And Louis the emperor
died.

A. 841.—844.

A. 845. This year Eanwulf the ealdorman, with the men
of Somerset, and bishop Ealstan,* and Osric the ealdorman, with the men of Dorset, fought at the mouth of the
Parret against the Danish army, and there made great
slaughter, and got the victory.

A. 846.—850.

A. 851. This year Ceorl the ealdorman, with the men of
Devonshire, fought against the heathen men at Wembury,†
and there made great slaughter and got the victory. And
the same year king Athelstan and Elchere the ealdormen
fought on shipboard, and slew a great number of the enemy
at Sandwich in Kent, and took nine ships, and put the others
to flight ; and the heathen men, for the first time, remained
over winter in Thanet. And the same year came three
hundred and fifty ships to the mouth of the Thames, and the
crews landed and took Canterbury and London by storm,
and put to flight Berthwulf, king of the Mercians, with
his army, and then went south over the Thames into Surrey ;
and there king Ethelwulf and his son Ethelbald, with the
army of the West-Saxons, fought against them at Ockley,

* Of Sherborne.   † Near Plymouth.

and there made the greatest slaughter among the heathen army that we have heard reported to the present day, and there got the victory.

A. 852. At this time Ceolred, abbat of Medeshamstede and the monks let to Wulfred the land of Sempringham, on this condition, that after his decease the land should return to the minster, and that Wulfred should give the land of Sleaford to Medeshamstede, and each year should deliver into the minster sixty loads of wood, and twelve of coal and six of faggots, and two tuns full of pure ale, and two beasts fit for slaughter, and six hundred loaves, and ten measures of Welsh ale, and each year a horse, and thirty shillings, and one day's entertainment. At this agreement were present king Burhred, and archbishop Ceolred, and bishop Tunbert, and bishop Cenred, and bishop Aldhun, and abbat Witred, and abbat Wertherd, and Ethelherd, the ealdorman, and Hunbert, the ealdorman, and many others.

A. 853. This year Burhred, king of the Mercians, and his council, begged of king Ethelwulf that he would assist him so that he might make the North-Welsh obedient to him. He then did so; and went with an army across Mercia among the North-Welsh, and made them all obedient to him. And the same year king Ethelwulf sent his son Alfred to Rome. Leo [IV.] was then pope of Rome; and he consecrated him king, and took him for his son at confirmation. Then, in the same year, Ealhere, with the men of Kent, and Huda, with the men of Surry, fought in Thanet, against the heathen army; and at first they were victorious; and many there were slain, and drowned on either hand, and both the ealdormen were killed. And upon this after Easter Ethelwulf, king of the West-Saxons, gave his daughter to Burhred king of the Mercians.

A. 854.

A. 855. This year the heathen men, for the first time, remained over winter in Sheppey: and the same year king Ethelwulf gave by charter the tenth part of his land throughout his realm for the glory of God and his own eternal salvation. And the same year he went to Rome in great state, and dwelt there twelve months, and then returned homewards. And then Charles, king of the Franks, gave him his daughter to wife; and after that he came to his people, and they were glad of it. And about two years after he came from France he died, and his body lies at Winchester. And he reigned eighteen years and a half. And Ethelwulf was the son of Egbert, Egbert of Elmund, Elmund of Eafa, Eafa of Eoppa, Eoppa of Ingild; Ingild was Ina's brother, king of the West-Saxons, he who held the kingdom thirty-seven years, and afterwards went to St. Peter, and there resigned his life; and they were the sons of Kenred, Kenred of Ceolwald, Ceolwald of Cutha, Cutha of Cuthwin, Cuthwin of Ceawlin, Ceawlin of Cynric, Cynric of Cerdic, Cerdic of Elesa, Elesa of Esla, Esla of Gewis, Gewis of Wig, Wig of Freawin, Freawin of Frithogar, Frithogar of Brond, Brond of Beldeg, Beldeg of Woden, Woden of Frithowald, Frithowald of Frealaf, Frealaf of Frithuwulf, Frithuwulf of Finn, Finn of Godwulf, Godwulf of Geat, Geat of Tætwa, Tætwa of Beaw, Beaw of Sceldi, Sceldi of Heremod, Heremod of Itermon, Itermon of Hathra, Hathra of Guala, Guala of Bedwig, Bedwig of Sceaf, that is, the son of Noah, he was born in Noah's ark; Lamech, Methusalem, Enoh, Jared, Malalahel, Cainion, Enos, Seth, Adam the first man, and our Father, that is, Christ. Amen. Then Ethelwulf's two sons succeeded to the kingdom; Ethelbald succeeded to the kingdom of the West-Saxons; and Ethelbert to the kingdom of the Kentish-men, and to the kingdom of the East-Saxons, and to Surry, and to the kingdom of the South-Saxons; and then Ethelbald reigned five years. Alfred his third son he had sent to Rome: and when Pope Leo [IV.] heard say that Ethelwulf was dead, he consecrated Alfred king, and held him as his spiritual son at confirmation, even as his father Ethelwulf had requested on sending him thither.

A. 855. And on his return homewards he took to (wife) the daughter of Charles, king of the French, whose name was Judith, and he came home safe. And then in about two years he died, and his body lies at Winchester; and he reigned eighteen years and a half, and he was the son of Egbert. And then his two sons succeeded to the kingdom; Ethelbald to the kingdom of the West-Saxons, and Ethelbert to the kingdom of the Kentish-men, and of the East-Saxons, and of Surry, and of the South-Saxons. And he reigned five years.

A. 856.—859.

A. 860. This year died king Ethelbald, and his body lies

at Sherborne; and Ethelbert succeeded to all the realm of his brother, and he held it in goodly concord and in great tranquillity. And in his days a large fleet came to land, and the crews stormed Winchester. And Osric the ealdorman, with the men of Hampshire, Ethelwulf the ealdorman, with the men of Berkshire, fought against the army, and put them to flight, and had possession of the place of carnage. And Ethelbert reigned five years, and his body lies at Sherborne.

A. 861. This year died St. Swithun the bishop.*

A. 862.—864.

A. 865. This year the heathen army sat down in Thanet, and made peace with the men of Kent, and the men of Kent promised them money for the peace; and during the peace and the promise of money the army stole away by night, and ravaged all Kent to the eastward.

A. 866. This year Ethelred, Ethelbert's brother, succeeded to the kingdom of the West-Saxons: and the same year a great heathen army came to the land of the English nation, and took up their winter quarters among the East-Angles, and there they were horsed; and the East-Angles made peace with them.

A. 867. This year the army went from East-Anglia over the mouth of the Humber to York in North-humbria. And there was much dissension among that people, and they had cast out their king Osbert, and had taken to themselves a king, Ælla, not of royal blood; but late in the year they resolved that they would fight against the army; and therefore they gathered a large force, and sought the army at the town of York, and stormed the town, and some of them got within, and there was an excessive slaughter made of the North-humbrians, some within, some without, and the kings were both slain: and the remainder made peace with the army. And the same year bishop Ealstan died; and he had the bishopric of Sherborne fifty years, and his body lies in the town.

A. 868. This year the same army went into Mercia to Nottingham, and there took up their winter quarters. And Burhred king of the Mercians, and his 'witan,' begged of Ethelred king of the West-Saxons, and of Alfred his brother,

* Winchester.

that they would help them, that they might fight against the army. And then they went with the West-Saxon power into Mercia as far as Nottingham, and there met with the army within the fortress; and besieged them therein: but there was no great battle; and the Mercians made peace with the army.

A. 869. This year the army again went to York, and sat there one year.

A. 870. This year the army rode across Mercia into East-Anglia, and took up their winter quarters at Thetford: and the same winter king Edmund fought against them, and the Danes got the victory, and slew the king, and subdued all the land, and destroyed all the minsters which they came to. The names of their chiefs who slew the king were Hingwar and Hubba. At that same time they came to Medesham-stede, and burned and beat it down, slew abbat and monks, and all that they found there. And that place, which before was full rich, they reduced to nothing. And the same year died archbishop Ceolnoth. Then went Ethelred and Alfred his brother, and took Athelred bishop of Wiltshire, and appointed him archbishop of Canterbury, because formerly he had been a monk of the same minster of Canterbury. As soon as he came to Canterbury, and he was stablished in his arch-bishopric, he then thought how he might expel the clerks who (were) there within, whom archbishop the Ceolnoth had (be-fore) placed there for such need . . . as we shall relate. The first year that he was made archbishop there was so great a mortality, that of all the monks whom he found there within, no more than five monks survived. Then for the . . . . he (commanded) his chaplains, and also some priests of his vills, that they should help the few monks who there survived to do Christ's service, because he could not so readily find monks who might of themselves do the service; and for this reason he commanded that the priests, the while, until God should give peace in this land, should help the monks. In that same time was this land much distressed by frequent battles, and hence the archbishop could not there effect it, for there was warfare and sorrow all his time over England; and hence the clerks remained with the monks. Nor was there ever a time that monks were not there within, and they ever had lordship over the priests. Again the archbishop

Ceolnoth thought, and also said to those who were with him, 'As soon as God shall give peace in this land, either these priests shall be monks, or from elsewhere I will place within the minister as many monks as may do the service of themselves : for God knows that I . . . .)*

'A. 871. This year the army came to Reading in Wessex ; and three days after this, two of their earls rode forth. Then Ethelwulf the ealdorman met them at Englefield, and there fought against them, and got the victory : and there one of them, whose name was Sidrac, was slain. About three days after this, king Ethelred and Alfred his brother led a large force to Reading, and fought against the army, and there was great slaughter made on either hand. And Ethelwulf the ealdorman was slain, and the Danish-men had possession of the place of carnage. And about four days after this, king Ethelred and Alfred his brother fought against the whole army at Ashdown ; and they were in two bodies : in the one were Bagsac and Halfdene the heathen kings, and in the other were the earls. And then king Ethelred fought against the division under the kings, and there king Bagsac was slain ; and Alfred his brother against the division under the earls, and there earl Sidrac the elder was slain, earl Sidrac the younger, and earl Osbern, and earl Frene, and earl Harold ; and both divisions of the army were put to flight, and many thousands slain : and they continued fighting until night. And about fourteen days after this, king Ethelred and Alfred his brother fought

---

* As this portion of the text is slightly defective, the Latin narrative is subjoined : Cum autem venisset Cantuariam, statim cogitare cœpit quomodo possit ejicere clericos de ecclesia Christi, quos Ceolnothus pro tali necessitate compulsus ibi posuit. Primo igitur anno ordinationis suæ tanta mortalitas facta est in ecclesia Christi, ut de tota congregatione monachorum non remanerent nisi quinque. Qua de causa quia ita subito non potuit invenire tot monachos qui ibi servitium Dei facere possent, ex simplicitate cordis præcepit capellanis clericis suis, ut essent cum eis usque quod Deus pacificaret terram, quæ tunc nimis erat turbata propter nimias tempestates bellorum. Accepit etiam de villis suis presbyteros, ut essent cum monachis, ita tamen ut monachi semper haberent dominatum super clericos. Cogitavit idem archiepiscopus et sæpe suis dixit, quia statim cum Deus pacem nobis dederit, aut isti clerici monachi fient, aut ego ubicumque monachos inveniam quos reponam. Scit enim Deus, inquit quod aliter facere non possum. Sed nunquam temporibus suis pax fuit in Anglia, et ideo remanserunt clerici cum monachis, nec ullo tempore fuit ecclesia sine monachis. Sed nec iste Æthelredus archiepiscopus potuit facere.

A A

against the army at Basing, and there the Danes obtained
the victory. And about two months after this, king Ethelred
and Alfred his brother fought against the army at Marden;
and they were in two bodies, and they put both to flight,
and during a great part of the day were victorious; and there
was great slaughter on either hand; but the Danes had possession of the place of carnage: and there bishop Heah-
mund* was slain, and many good men : and after this battle
there came a great army in the summer to Reading. And
after this, over Easter, king Ethelred died; and he reigned
five years and his body lies at Winburn-minster.

Then Alfred the son of Ethelwulf, his brother, succeeded
to the kingdom of the West-Saxons. And about one month
after this, king Alfred with a small band fought against the
whole army at Wilton, and put them to flight for a good part
of the day; but the Danes had possession of the place of
carnage. And this year nine general battles were fought
against the army in the kingdom south of the Thames,
besides which, Alfred the king's brother, and single
ealdormen, and king's thanes, oftentimes made incursions on
them, which were not counted: and within the year nine
earls and one king were slain. And that year the West-
Saxons made peace with the army.

A. 871. And the Danish-men were overcome : and they had two
heathen kings, Bagsac and Halfdene, and many earls ; and there was
king Bagsac slain, and these earls ; Sidrac the elder, and also Sidrac the
younger, Osbern, Frene, and Harold ; and the army was put to flight.

A. 872. This year the army went from Reading to
London, and there took up their winter-quarters : and then
the Mercians made peace with the army.

A. 873. This year the army went into North-humbria,
and took up their winter-quarters at Torksey in Lindsey :
and then the Mercians made peace with the army.

A. 874. This year the army went from Lindsey to Repton,
and there took up their winter-quarters, and drove king
Burhred over sea about twenty-two years after he had
obtained the kingdom ; and subdued the whole country : and
Burhred went to Rome, and there remained ; and his body
lies in St. Mary's church at the English school. And that
same year they committed the kingdom of the Mercians to

* Of Sherborne.

the keeping of Ceolwulf, an unwise king's-thane ; and he swore oaths, to them, and delivered hostages that it should be ready for them on whatever day they would have it, and that he would be ready both in his own person and with all who would follow him, for the behoof of the army.

A. 875. This year the army went from Repton : and Halfdene went with some of the army into North-humbria, and took up winter-quarters by the river Tyne.   And the army subdued the land, and oft-times spoiled the Picts, and the Strathclyde Britons.   And the three kings, Gothrun, and Oskytel, and Anwind, went with a large army from Repton to Cambridge, and sat down there one year.   And that summer king Alfred went out to sea with a fleet, and fought against the forces of seven ships, and one of them he took, and put the rest to flight.

A. 876. This year the army stole away to Wareham, a fortress of the West-Saxons.   And afterwards the king made peace with the army; and they delivered to the king hostages from among the most distinguished men of the army ; and then they swore oaths to him on the holy ring, which they never before would do to any nation, that they would speedily depart his kingdom.   And notwithstanding this, that part of the army which was horsed stole away by night from the fortress to Exeter.   And that year Halfdene apportioned the lands of North-humbria : and they thenceforth continued ploughing and tilling them.   This year Rolla overran Normandy with his army, and he reigned fifty years.

A. 876. And in this same year the army of the Danes in England swore oaths to king Alfred upon the holy ring, which before they would not do to any nation ; and they delivered to the king hostages from among the most distinguished men of the army, that they would speedily depart from his kingdom ; and that by night they broke.

A. 877. This year the army came to Exeter from Wareham ; and the fleet sailed round westwards : and then a great storm overtook them at sea, and there one hundred and twenty ships were wrecked at Swanwich.   And king Alfred with his forces rode after the army which was mounted, as far as Exeter ; and they were unable to overtake them before they were within the fortress, where they could not be come at.   And they there delivered to him hostages as many as he would have, and swore many oaths : and then they observed the peace well. And afterwards, during harvest, the army went into Mercia, and some part of it they apportioned, and some they delivered to Ceolwulf.

A. 878. This year, during midwinter, after twelfth night, the army stole away to Chippenham, and overran the land of the West-Saxons, and sat down there ; and many of the people they drove beyond sea, and of the remainder the greater part they subdued and forced to obey them, except king Alfred : and he, with a small band, with difficulty retreated to the woods and to the fastnesses of the moors. And the same winter the brother of Hingwar and of Halfdene came with twenty-three ships to Devonshire in Wessex; and he was there slain, and with him eight hundred and forty men of his army : and there was taken the war-flag which they called the RAVEN. After this, at Easter king Alfred with a small band constructed a fortress at Athelney ; and from this fortress, with that part of the men of Somerset which was nearest to it, from time to time they fought against the army. Then in the seventh week after Easter he rode to Brixton, on the east side of Selwood ; and there came to meet him all the men of Somerset, and the men of Wiltshire, and that portion of the men of Hampshire which was on this side of the sea ; and they were joyful at his presence. On the following day he went from that station to Iglea [Iley], and on the day after this to Heddington, and there fought against the whole army, put them to flight, and pursued them as far as their fortress : and there he sat down fourteen days. And then the army delivered to him hostages, with many oaths, that they would leave his kingdom, and also promised him that their king should receive baptism : and this they accordingly fulfilled. And about three weeks after this king Gothrun came to him, with some thirty men who were of the most distinguished in the army, at Aller, which is near Athelney : and the king was his godfather at baptism ; and his chrism-loosing* was at Wedmore : and he was twelve days with the king ; and he greatly honoured him and his companions with gifts.

A. 879. This year the army went to Cirencester from

* Apparently the removal of the fillet which, covering the chrism on the forehead, was bound round the head at confirmation.

Chippenham, and sat there one year. And that year a body of pirates drew together, and sat down at Fulham on the Thames. And that same year the sun was eclipsed during one hour of the day.*

A. 880. This year the army went from Cirencester to East Anglia, and settled in the land, and apportioned it. And that same year the army, which previously had sat down at Fulham, went over sea to Ghent in France, and sat there one year.

A. 881. This year the army went further into France, and the French fought against them: and then was the army there horsed after the battle.

A. 882. This year the army went up along the banks of the Maese far into France, and there sat one year. And that same year king Alfred went out to sea with his ships, and fought against the forces of four ships of Danish men, and took two of the ships, and the men were slain that were in them; and the forces of two ships surrendered to him, and they were sorely distressed and wounded before they surrendered to him.

A. 883. This year the army went up the Scheldt to Condé, and sat there one year. And Marinus the pope then sent 'lignum Domini' to king Alfred; and that same year Sighelm and Athelstan carried to Rome the alms which the king had vowed to send thither, and also to India, to St. Thomas and to St. Bartholomew, when they sat down against the army at London; and there, thanks be to God, they largely obtained the object of their prayer after the vow.

A. 884. This year the army went up the Somme to Amiens, and there sat one year. This year † the benevolent bishop Ethelwold died.

A. 885. ‡This year the fore-mentioned army divided itself into two; the one part went eastward, the other part

* The eclipse happened on the 14th of March, 880.

† The account of the death of Ethelwold bishop of Winchester, here inserted in MS. F., is anticipated a century by the carelessness of the scribe: the name of his successor in the Latin puts this beyond all doubt. See A. 984.

‡ Asser omits the events of A. 884 of the Chronicle, and places those of 885 under that year. At any rate the foreign transactions are rightly so placed.

to Rochester, and besieged the city, and wrought another fortress about themselves. And, notwithstanding this, the townsmen defended the city till king Alfred came out with his forces. Then went the army to their ships, and abandoned their fortress; and they were there deprived of their horses, and soon after, in that same manner, departed over sea. And that same year king Alfred sent a fleet from Kent to East-Anglia. So soon as they came to the mouth of the Stour, there met them sixteen ships of pirates; and they fought against them, and captured all the ships and killed the men. As they afterwards returned homeward with the booty, a large fleet of pirates met them, and then fought against them that same day, and the Danish-men had the victory. That same year, before mid-winter, *Charles king of the French died; he was killed by a wild boar; and one year before this, his brother† died: he too had the western kingdom: and they were both sons of Louis, who likewise had the western kingdom, and died that year when the sun was eclipsed: he was son of Charles‡ whose daughter Ethelwulf, king of the West-Saxons, had for his queen. And that same year a large fleet drew together against the Old Saxons; and there was a great battle twice in that year, and the Saxons had the victory, and the Frisians were there with them. That same year Charles§ succeeded to the western kingdom, and to all the kingdom on this side the Wendel-sea [Tuscan Sea], and beyond this sea, in like manner as his great-grandfather had it, with the exception of the Lid-wiccas [Bretons]. Charles was Louis's son; Louis was Charles's brother, who was father of Judith, whom king Ethelwulf had; and they were sons of Louis, Louis was son of the elder Charles, Charles was Pepin's son. And that same year died the good Pope Marinus, who, at the prayer of Alfred king of the West-Saxons, freed the English school; and he sent him great gifts, and part of the rood on which Christ suffered. And that same year the army in East-Anglia broke the peace with king Alfred.

A. 886. This year the army which before had drawn eastward, went westward again, and thence up the Seine, and there took up their winter quarters near the town of Paris. That same year king Alfred repaired London; and

---

* Carloman.   † Louis III.   ‡ The Bald.   § The Fat.

all the English submitted to him, except those who were
under the bondage of the Danish-men; and then he committed the town to the keeping of Ethered the ealdorman.

A. 887. This year the army went up through the bridge
at Paris, and thence up along the Seine as far as the Marne,
and thence up the Marne to Chezy, and then sat down, there,
and on the Yonne, two winters in the two places. And that
same year Charles * king of the French died; and six weeks
before he died, Arnulf his brother's son bereaved him of the
kingdom. And then was that kingdom divided into five,
and five kings were consecrated thereto. This, however,
was done by permission of Arnulf: and they said that they
would hold it from his hand, because none of them on the
father's side was born thereto except him alone. Arnulf
then dwelt in the land east of the Rhine: and Rodulf then
succeeded to the middle kingdom,† and Oda to the western
part, and Beorngar and Witha‡ to the land of the Lombards
and to the lands on that side of the mountain: and that they
held in great discord, and fought two general battles, and oft
and many times laid waste the land, and each repeatedly
drove out the other. And that same year that the army
went up beyond the bridge at Paris, Ethelhelm the ealdorman § carried the alms of the West-Saxons and of king
Alfred to Rome.

A. 888. This year Beeke the ealdorman carried the alms
of the West-Saxons and of king Alfred to Rome; and queen
Ethelswith, who was king Alfred's sister, died on the way
to Rome, and her body lies at Pavia. And that same year
Athelred archbishop of Canterbury, and Ethelwold the ealdorman died in the same month.

A. 889. In this year there was no journey to Rome, except that king Alfred sent two couriers with letters.

A. 890. This year abbat Bernhelm carried the alms of
the West-Saxons and of king Alfred to Rome. And Gothrun the Northern king died, whose baptismal name was
Athelstan; he was king Alfred's godson, and he abode in
East-Anglia, and first settled that country. And that same
year the army went from the Seine to St. Lo, which is between Brittany and France; and the Bretons fought against
them, and had the victory, and drove them out into a river,

* The Fat.   † Burgundy.   ‡ Guido.   § Of Wilts.

and drowned many of them. This year Plegmund was chosen of God and of all the people to be archbishop of Canterbury.

A. 891. This year the army went eastward; and king Arnulf, with the East-Franks and Saxons and Bavarians, fought against that part which was mounted before the ships came up, and put them to flight. And three Scots came to king Alfred in a boat without any oars from Ireland, whence they had stolen away, because they desired for the love of God to be in a state of pilgrimage, they recked not where. The boat in which they came was made of two hides and a half; and they took with them provisions sufficient for seven days; and then about the seventh day they came on shore in Cornwall, and soon after went to king Alfred. Thus they were named: Dubslane, and Macbeth, and Maelinmun. And Swinney, the best teacher among the Scots, died.

A. 892. And that same year after Easter, about Rogation week or before, the star appeared which in Latin is called *cometa*; some men say in English that it is a hairy star, because a long radiance streams from it, sometimes on the one side, and sometimes on each side.

A. 893. In this year the great army, about which we formerly spoke,* came again from the eastern kingdom westward to Boulogne, and there was shipped; so that they came over in one passage, horses and all; and they came to land at Limne-mouth with two hundred and fifty ships. This port is in the eastern part of Kent, at the east end of the great wood which we call Andred; the wood is in length from east to west one hundred and twenty miles, or longer, and' thirty miles broad: the river of which we before spoke flows out of the weald. On this river they towed up their ships as far as the weald, four miles from the outward harbour, and there stormed a fortress: within the fortress a few churls were stationed, and it was in part only constructed. Then soon after that Hasten with eighty ships landed at the mouth of the Thames, and wrought himself a fortress at Milton; and the other army did the like at Appledore.

A. 894. In this year, that was about a twelve-month after these had wrought the fortress in the eastern district, the North-humbrians and the East-Angles had given oaths to ·

* See back at A.D. 891.

king Alfred, and the East-Angles six hostages ; and nevertheless, contrary to their plighted troth, as oft as the other
armies went out with all their force, they also went out,
either with them or on their own part.   On this king Alfred
gathered together his forces, and proceeded until he encamped between the two armies, as near as he could for the
wood fastnesses, and for the water fastnesses, so that he
might be able to reach either of them in case they should
seek any open country.   From this time the enemy always
went out along the weald in bands and troops, by whichever
border was at the time without forces : and they also were
sought out by other bands, almost every day, either by day
or night, as well from the king's force as also from the towns.
The king had divided his forces into two, so that one half
was constantly at home, the other half in the field ; besides
those men whose duty it was to defend the towns.   The army
did not come out of their stations with their whole force
oftener than twice : once when they first came to land, before the forces were assembled ; a second time when they
would go away from their stations.   Then had they taken
much booty, and would at that time go northward over the
Thames into Essex towards their ships.   Then the king's
forces outrode and got before them, and fought against them
at Farnham, and put the army to flight, and retook the
booty ; and they fled over the Thames, where there was no
ford ; then up along the Colne into an island.   Then the
forces there beset them about so long as they there had any
provisions : but at length they had stayed their term of service, and had consumed their provisions ; and the king was
then on his way thitherwards with the division which
warred under him.   While he was on his way thither, and
the other force was gone homewards, and the Danish-men
remained there behind, because their king had been wounded
in the battle, so that they could not carry him away, then
those who dwell among the North-humbrians and among the
East-Anglians gathered some hundred ships and went about
south ; and some forty ships about to the north, and besieged a fortress in Devonshire by the north sea ; and those
who went about to the south besieged Exeter.   When the
king heard that, then turned he westward towards Exeter
with all his force, except a very strong body of the people.

eastward. These went onwards until they came to London; and then with the townsmen, and the aid which came to them from the west, they went east to Bamfleet. Hasten was then come there with his band which before sat at Milton; and the great army was also come thereto, which before sat at Appledore near Limne-mouth. The fortress at Bamfleet had been ere this constructed by Hasten, and he was at that time gone out to plunder; and the great army was therein. Then came they thereto, and put the army to flight, and stormed the fortress, and took all that was within it, as well the property, as the women, and the children also, and brought the whole to London; and all the ships they either broke in pieces or burned, or brought to London or to Rochester; and they brought the wife of Hasten and his two sons to the king: and he afterwards gave them up to him again, because one of them was his godson, and the other Ethered, the ealdorman's. They had become their godfathers before Hasten came to Bamfleet, and at that time Hasten had delivered to him hostages and taken oaths: and the king had also given him many gifts; and so likewise when he gave up the youth and the woman. But as soon as they came to Bamfleet, and the fortress was constructed, then plundered he that very part of the king's realm which was in the keeping of Ethered his compeer; and again, this second time, he had gone out to plunder that very same district when his fortress was stormed. Now the king with his forces had turned westward towards Exeter, as I said before, and the army had beset the city; but when he arrived there, then went they to their ships. While the king was thus busied with the army there, in the west, and both the other armies had drawn together at Shoebury in Essex, and there had constructed a fortress, then both together went up along the Thames, and a great addition came to them, as well from the East-Anglians as from the North-humbrians. They then went up along the Thames till they reached the Severn; then up along the Severn. Then Ethered the ealdorman, and Ethelm the ealdorman, and Ethelnoth the ealdorman, and the king's thanes who were then at home in the fortified places, gathered forces from every town east of the Parret, and as well west as east of Selwood, and also north of the Thames, and west of the

Severn, and also some part of the North-Welsh people.
When they had all drawn together, then they came up with
the army at Buttington on the banks of the Severn, and there
beset them about, on either side, in a fastness.   When they
had now sat there many weeks on both sides of the river,
and the king was in the west in Devon, against the fleet,
then were the enemy distressed for want of food ; and having eaten a great part of their horses, the others being
starved with hunger, then went they out against the men
who were encamped on the east bank of the river, and fought
against them : and the Christians had the victory.   And
Ordhelm a king's thane was there slain, and also many other
king's thanes were slain ; and of the Danish-men there was
very great slaughter made ; and that part which got away
thence was saved by flight.   When they had come into
Essex to their fortress and to their ships, then the survivors
again gathered a great army from among the East-Angles
and the North-humbrians before winter, and committed their
wives and their ships and their wealth to the East-Angles,
and went at one stretch, day and night, until they arrived at
a western city in Wirall, which is called Lega-ceaster
[Chester].   Then were the forces unable to come up with
them before they were within the fortress : nevertheless
they beset the fortress about for some two days, and took all
the cattle that was there without, and slew the men whom
they were able to overtake without the fortress, and burned
all the corn, and with their horses ate it every evening.
And this was about a twelve-month after they first came
hither over sea.

A. 895. And then soon after that, in this year, the army
from Wirall went among the North-Welsh, for they were
unable to stay there : this was because they had been deprived both of the cattle and of the corn which they had
plundered.   When they had turned again out of North-
Wales, with the booty which they had there taken, then
went they over Northumberland and East-Anglia, in
such wise that the forces could not overtake them before
they came to the eastern parts of the land of Essex, to an
island that is out on the sea, which is called Mersey.   And
as the army which had beset Exeter again turned homewards,
then spoiled they the South-Saxons near Chichester ; and

the townsmen put them to flight, and slew many hundreds
of them, and took some of their ships. Then that same
year, before winter, the Danish-men who had sat down in
Mersey, towed their ships up the Thames, and thence up the
Lea. This was about two years after they had come hither
over sea.

A. 896. In that same year the fore-mentioned army constructed a fortress on the Lea, twenty miles above London.
After this, in summer, a great body of the townsmen, and
also of other people, went onwards until they arrived at the
Danish fortress; and there they were put to flight, and
some four king's thanes were slain. Then after this, during
harvest, the king encamped near to the town, while the
people reaped the corn, so that the Danish-men might not
deprive them of the crop. Then on a certain day the king
rode up along the river, and observed where the river might
be obstructed, so that they would be unable to bring out
their ships. And they then did thus: they constructed two
fortresses on the two sides of the river. When they had
already begun the work, and had encamped before it,
then perceived the army that they should not be able to
bring out their ships. They then abandoned them, and
went across the country till they arrived at Bridgenorth by
the Severn; and there they constructed a fortress. Then
the forces rode westwards after the army: and the men of
London took possession of the ships; but all which they
could not bring away, they broke up, and those which were
worthy of capture they brought to London: moreover the
Danish-men had committed their wives to the keeping of the
East-Angles before they went out from their fortress. Then
sat they down for the winter at Bridgenorth. This was
about three years after they had come hither over sea to
Limne-mouth.

A. 897. After this, in the summer of this year, the army
broke up, some for East-Anglia, some for North-humbria;
and they who were moneyless procured themselves ships
there, and went southwards over sea to the Seine. Thanks
be to God, the army had not utterly broken down the English nation; but during the three years it was much more
broken down by the mortality among cattle and among men,
and most of all by this, that many of the most eminent

king's thanes in the land died during the three years ; some
of whom were, Swithulf, bishop of Rochester, and Ceol-
mund, ealdorman of Kent, and Bertulf, ealdorman of
Essex, and Wulfred, ealdorman of Hampshire, and Eal-
hard, bishop of Dorchester, and Eadulf, the king's thane in
Sussex, and Bernwulf, the governor of Winchester, and
Eadulf, the king's horse-thane, and many also besides these,
though I have named the most distinguished.   That same
year the armies from among the East-Anglians and from
among the North-humbrians harassed the land of the West-
Saxons, chiefly on the south coast, by prædatory bands ;
most of all by their esks, which they had built many
years before.   Then king Alfred commanded long ships to
be built to oppose the esks ; they were full-nigh twice as
long as the others ; some had sixty oars, and some had more ;
they were both swifter and steadier, and also higher than the
others.   They were shapen neither like the Frisian nor the
Danish, but so as it seemed to him they would be most efficient.
Then some time in the same year, there came six ships to the
Isle of Wight, and there did much harm, as well as in Devon,
and elsewhere on the sea-coast.   Then the king commanded
nine of the new ships to go thither, and they obstructed their
passage from the port towards the outer sea.   Then went
they with three of their ships out against them ; and three
lay in the upper part of the port in the dry ; for the men
were gone ashore.   Then took they two of the three
ships at the outer part of the port, and killed the men, and
the other ship escaped ; in that also the men were killed except five : they got away because the other ships were
aground.   They also were aground very disadvantageously :
three lay aground on that side of the deep on which the
Danish ships were aground, and all the rest upon the other
side, so that no one of them could get to the others.   But
when the water had ebbed many furlongs from the ships,
then the Danish-men went from their three ships to the
other three which were left by the tide on their side, and
then they there fought against them.   There was slain Lu-
cumon, the king's reeve, and Wulfheard, the Frisian, and
Ebb, the Frisian, and Ethelere, the Frisian, and Ethelferth,
the king's neat-herd, and of all the men, Frisians and English, seventy-two ; and of the Danish-men, one hundred and

twenty. Then, however, the flood-tide came to the Danish
ships before the Christians could shove theirs off, and they
therefore rowed them out : nevertheless, they were damaged
to such a degree that they could not row round the Sussex
land ; and there the sea cast two of them on shore, and the
men were led to the king at Winchester ; and he commanded
them to be there hanged : and the men who were in the
single ship came to East-Anglia, sorely wounded. That
same summer no less than twenty ships, with their crews,
wholly perished upon the south coast. That same year died
Wulfric, the king's horse-thane ; he was also "Wealh-
reeve."

A. 898. In this year died Ethelm, ealdorman of Wiltshire,
nine days before midsummer ; and this year died Elstan,
who was bishop of London.

A. 899. 900.

A. 901. This year died ALFRED, the son of Ethelwulf, six
days before the mass of All Saints. He was king over the whole
English nation, except that part which was under the dominion of the Danes ; and he held the kingdom one year
and a half less than thirty years. And then Edward his
son succeeded to the kingdom. Then Ethelwald, the æthe-
ling, his uncle's son, seized the castle at Wimborne* and that at
Twineham,† without leave of the king and of his "witan."
Then rode the king with his forces until he encamped at
Badbury, near Wimborne ; and Ethelwald sat within the
vill, with the men who had submitted to him ; and he had
obstructed all the approaches towards him, and said that he
would do one of two things—or there live, or there lie.
But notwithstanding that, he stole away by night, and
sought the army in North-humbria ; and they received him
for their king, and became obedient to him. And the king
commanded that he should be ridden after ; but they were
unable to overtake him. They then beset the woman whom
he had before taken, without the king's leave, and against
the bishop's command ; for she had previously been consecrated a nun. And in this same year Ethelred, who was
ealdorman of Devonshire, died, four weeks before king
Alfred.

* Dorsetshire.
† Christchurch, New Forest division of Southampton.

A. 902. And that same year was the battle at the Holme, between the Kentish-men and the Danish-men.

A. 902. This year Elswitha died.

A. 903. This year died Athulf, the ealdorman, brother of Elswitha, king Edward's mother ; and Virgilius, abbat of the Scots ; and Grimbald, the mass-priest, on the 8th before the Ides of July. And this same year was the consecration of the New-minster at Winchester, and St. Judoc's advent.

A. 904. This year Ethelwald came hither over sea with the ships that he was able to get, and he was submitted to in Essex. This year the moon was eclipsed.

A. 905. This year Ethelwald enticed the army in East-Anglia to break the peace, so that they ravaged over all the land of Mercia until they came to Cricklade, and there they went over the Thames, and took, as well in Bradon as thereabout, all that they could lay hands on, and then turned homewards again. Then king Edward went after them, as speedily as he could gather his forces, and overran all their land between the dikes and the Ouse, all as far north as the fens. When, after this, he would return thence, then commanded he it to be proclaimed through his whole force, that they should all return together. Then the Kentish-men remained there behind, notwithstanding his orders, and seven messengers whom he had sent to them. Then the army there came up to them, and there fought them : and there Siwulf the ealdorman, and Sigelm the ealdorman, and Eadwold the king's thane, and Kenwulf the abbat, and Sigebright son of Siwulf, and Eadwold son of Acca, were slain, and likewise many with them, though I have named the most distinguished. And on the Danish side were slain Eohric their king, and Ethelwald the etheling, who had enticed him to break the peace, and Byrtsige son of Brithnoth the etheling, and Ysopk the 'hold' [governor ?], and Oskytel the hold, and very many with them, whom we are now unable to name. And there was great slaughter made on either hand ; and of the Danish-men there were more slain, though they had possession of the place of carnage. And Elhswitha died that same year. This year a comet appeared on the thirteenth before the Kalends of November.

A. 906. In this year died Alfred, who was governor of

Bath. And in the same year peace was concluded at Hitch-ingford, even as king Edward ordained, as well with the East-Angles as with the North-humbrians.

A. 906. This year king Edward, from necessity, concluded a peace both with the army of East-Anglia and of North-humbria.

A. 907. This year Chester was repaired.

A. 908. This year died Denewulf, who was bishop at Winchester.

A. 909. This year St. Oswald's body was removed from Bardney into Mercia.

A. 910. This year Frithstan succeeded to the bishopric at Winchester : and, after that, bishop Asser died ; he was bishop at Sherborne. And that same year king Edward sent out a force both of West-Saxons and of Mercians, and they greatly spoiled the army of the north, as well of men as of every kind of cattle, and slew many of the Danish-men : and they were therein five weeks. In this year the Angles and the Danes fought at Tootenhall on the eighth before the Ides of August, and the Angles obtained the victory. And that same year Ethelfled built the fortress at Bramsbury.

A. 910. This year the army of the Angles and of the Danes fought at Tootenhall. And Ethelred ealdor of the Mercians died ; and king Edward took possession of London, and of Oxford, and of all the lands which owed obedience thereto. And a great fleet came hither from the south, from the Lidwiccas, [Brittany,] and greatly ravaged by the Severn ; but they there, afterwards, almost all perished.

A. 911. This year the army among the North-humbrians broke the peace, and despised whatever peace king Edward and his 'witan' offered them, and overran the land of Mercia. And the king had gathered together some hundred ships, and was then in Kent, and the ships went south-east along the sea-coast towards him. Then thought the army that the greatest part of his force was in the ships, and that they should be able to go, unfought, wheresoever they chose. When the king learned that, that they were gone out to plunder, then sent he his forces after them, both of the West-Saxons and of the Mercians ; and they overtook the army as they were on their way homewards, and then fought against them, and put them to flight, and slew many thousands of them ; and there were slain king Ecwils, and king Halfdene and Ohter the earl, and Scurf the earl, and Othulf the hold, and Benesing the hold, and Anlaf the black, and Thurferth the hold, and Osferth the collector and Guthferth the hold, and Agmund the hold, and Guthferth.

A. 911. Then the next year after this died Ethelred lord of the Mercians.

A. 912. This year died Ethered ealdorman of the Mercians; and king Edward took possession of London and of Oxford, and of all the lands which owed obedience thereto. This year Ethelfled lady of the Mercians came to Scærgate on the holy eve, 'Invention of the Holy Cross,' and there built the fortress; and the same year, that at Bridgenorth.

A. 913. In this year, about Martinmas,* king Edward commanded the northern fortress to be built at Hertford, between the Memer, the Benewic, and the Lea. And then after that, during the summer, between Rogation-days and midsummer, king Edward went with some of his forces to Maldon in Essex, and there encamped, whilst the fortress at Witham was wrought and built; and a good part of the people who were before under the dominion of the Danish-men submitted to him: and in the meanwhile some part of his force constructed the fortress at Hertford, on the south side of the Lea. This year, by the help of God, Ethelfled lady of the Mercians went with all the Mercians to Tamworth, and there built the fortress early in the summer; and after this before Lammas, that at Stafford.

A. 914. Then after this, in the next year, that at Eddesbury, early in the summer; and afterwards, in the same year, late in harvest, that at Warwick.

A. 915. Then after this, in the next year, after mid-winter, that at Cherburg, and that at Warburton; and that same year, before mid-winter, that at Runcorn.

A. 915. This year was Warwick built.

A. 916. This year abbat Egbert was guiltlessly slain, be-fore midsummer, on the sixteenth before the Kalends of July: the same day was the feast of the martyr St. Ciricius and his fellows. And about three days after this, Ethelfled sent her forces among the Welsh, and stormed Brecknock,

---

* Florence of Worcester seems to understand this as relating to the festival of St. Martin of Tours, 11 Nov. and places Maldon, &c. as well as the events of 917 of the text, under the year 914.

and there took the king's wife, and some four and thirty persons.

A. 917. In this year, after Easter, the army rode forth from Northampton and Leicester, and broke the peace, and slew many men at Hockerton, and there about. And then very speedily after that, when the one came home, then they got ready another troop which rode out against Leighton : and then the inhabitants were aware of them, and fought against them, and put them to full flight, and retook all which they had seized, and also a great portion of their horses and of their weapons. This year, before Lammas, Ethelfled, lady of the Mercians, God helping her, got possession of the fortress which is called Derby, with all that owed obedience thereto ; and there also were slain, within the gates, four of her thanes, which to her was a cause of sorrow.

A. 918. This year, in the early part of the year, by God's help, she got into her power, by treaty, the fortress at Leicester, and the greater part of the army which owed obedience thereto became subject to her ; and the people of York had also covenanted with her, some having given a pledge, and some having bound themselves by oath, that they would be at her command. In this year a great fleet came over hither from the south, from the Lidwiccas, [Brittany,] and with it two earls, Ohtor and Rhoald : and they went west about till they arrived within the mouth of the Severn, and they spoiled the North-Welsh everywhere by the sea-coast where they then pleased. And in Archenfield they took bishop* Cameleac, and led him with them to their ships ; and then king Edward ransomed him afterwards with forty pounds. Then after that, the whole army landed, and would have gone once more to plunder about Archenfield. Then met them the men of Hereford and of Gloucester, and of the nearest towns, and fought against them and put them to flight, and slew the earl Rhoald, and a brother of Ohter the other earl, and many of the army, and drove them into an inclosure, and there beset them about, until they delivered hostages to them that they would depart from king Edward's dominion. And the king had so ordered it that his forces sat down against them on the south side of Severn-mouth, from the Welsh coast westward, to the mouth of the Avon eastward ; so that on

* Of Llandaff.

that side they durst not anywhere attempt the land. Then,
nevertheless, they stole away by night on some two occasions ;
once, to the east of Watchet, and another time to Porlock.
But they were beaten on either occasion, so that few of them
got away, except those alone who there swam out to the
ships. And then they sat down, out on the island of Bradan-
relice, [Flat-holms,] until such time as they were quite destitute of food; and many men died of hunger, because they
could not obtain any food. Then they went thence to Deo-
mod, [S. Wales,] and then out to Ireland : and this was
during harvest. And then after that, in the same year,
before Martinmas, king Edward went with his forces to
Buckingham, and there sat down four weeks ; and, ere he
went thence, he erected both the forts on either side of the
river. And Thurkytel the earl sought to him to be his lord,
and all the captains, and almost all the chief men who owed
obedience to Bedford, and also many of those who owed
obedience to Northampton.

A. 918. But very shortly after they had become so, she died at Tamworth, twelve days before midsummer, the eighth year of her having rule
and right lordship over the Mercians ; and her body lies at Gloucester,
within the east porch of St. Peter's church. [See end of A.D. 922.]

A. 918. This year died Ethelfled the lady of the Mercians.

A. 919. In this year, before Martinmas, king Edward
went with his forces to Bedford, and gained the town ; and
almost all the townsmen who formerly dwelt there submitted
to him : and he sat down there four weeks, and commanded
the town to be built on the south side of the river before he
went thence.

A. 919. This year also the daughter of Ethelred, lord of the Mercians,
was deprived of all dominion over the Mercians, and carried into Wessex,
three weeks before mid-winter : she was called Elfwina.

A. 920. In this year, before midsummer, king Edward
went to Maldon, and built the town, and fortified it before he
departed thence. And that same year Thurkytel the earl
went over sea into France, together with such men as would
follow him, with the peace and aid of king Edward.

A. 921. In this year, before Easter, king Edward gave
orders to take possession of the town at Towcester, and to
fortify it. And again, after that, in the same year, during
Rogation days, he commanded the town at Wigmore to

be built. That same summer, between Lammas and midsummer, the army from Northampton and from Leicester,
and thence north, broke the peace, and went to Towcester,
and fought against the town the whole day; and they thought
that they should be able to take it by storm. But, nevertheless, the people who were within defended it until a larger
force came to them : and then they departed from the town
and went away. Then, again very soon after that, they went
out once more by night with a predatory band, and came
upon men who were unprepared, and took no small number
as well of men as of cattle between Burnham wood and Ayles-
bury. At that same time went out the army from Huntingdon and from the East-Angles, and constructed the fortress
at Tempsford, and abode, and built there; and forsook the
other at Huntingdon, and thought that from thence they
could, by warfare and hostility, get more of the land again.
And they went forth until they arrived at Bedford : and
then the men who were there within went out against them,
and fought with them and put them to flight, and slew a
good part of them. Then again, after that, a large army
once more drew together from East-Anglia and from Mercia,
and went to the town at Wigmore, and beset it round
about, and fought against it the greater part of the day,
and took the cattle thereabout. And nevertheless, the
men who were within the town defended it ; and then the
army left the town and went away. Then, after that, in
the same summer, much people, within king Edward's
dominion, drew together out of the nearest towns, who could
go thither, and went to Tempsford, and beset the town, and
fought against it till they took it by storm, and slew the king,
and Toglos the earl, and Mann the earl, his son, and his
brother, and all those who were there within and would defend themselves; and took the others, and all that was
therein. Then, very soon after this, much people drew
together during harvest, as well from Kent as from Surrey
and from Essex, and from each of the nearest towns, and
went to Colchester, and beset the town, and fought against
it until they mastered it, and slew all the people there within,
and took all that was there, except the men who fled away
over the wall. Then after that, once again during the
same harvest, a large army drew together out of East-Anglia,

as well of the land-force as of the pirates whom they had enticed to their aid; and they thought that they should be able
to avenge their wrongs. And they went to Maldon, and
beset the town, and fought against it until more aid came to
the help of the townsmen from without; and then the army
left the town and went away. And then the men from the
town went out after them, and those also who came from
without to their aid; and they put the army to flight, and
slew many hundreds of them, as well of the pirates as of
the others. Then, very shortly after, during the same
harvest, king Edward went with the forces of the West-
Saxons to Passoham, and sat down there while they encompassed the town at Towcester with a stone wall. And Thurferth the earl, and the captains, and all the army which owed
obedience to Northampton, as far north as the Welland, submitted to him, and sought to him to be their lord and protector. And when one division of the forces went home,
then another went out, and took possession of the town of
Huntingdon, and repaired and rebuilt it, by command of
king Edward, where it had been previously demolished; and
all who were left of the inhabitants of that country submitted
to king Edward, and sought his peace and his protection.
And after this, still in the same year, before Martinmas, king
Edward went with the forces of the West-Saxons to Colchester, and repaired the town, and rebuilt it where it had
been before broken down; and much people submitted to
him, as well among the East-Anglians as among the East
Saxons, who before were under the dominion of the Danes.
And all the army among the East-Anglians swore union
with him, that they would all that he would, and would
observe peace towards all to which the king should grant his
peace, both by sea and by land. And the army which owed
obedience to Cambridge chose him specially to be their
lord and protector; and confirmed it with oaths, even as he
then decreed it. This year king Edward built the town at
Gladmouth. This year king Sihtric slew Neil his brother.

A. 922. In this year, between Rogation days and midsummer, king Edward went with his forces to Stamford,
and commanded the town to be built upon the south side of
the river: and all the people which owed obedience to the
northern town submitted to him, and sought to him to be

their lord. And then, during the sojourn which he there
made, Ethelfled his sister died there, at Tamworth, twelve
days before midsummer. And then he took possession of
the town at Tamworth; and all the people of the land of
Mercia, who before were subject to Ethelfled, submitted to
him; and the kings of the North-Welsh, Howel, and Cle-
dauc, and Jothwel, and all the North-Welsh race, sought to
him to be their lord. Then went he thence to Nottingham
and took possession of the town, and commanded it to be
repaired and occupied as well by English as by Danes.
And all the people who were settled in Mercia, as well Danish as English, submitted to him.

A. 923. In this year, after harvest, king Edward went
with his forces to Thelwall, and commanded the town to be
built, and occupied, and manned; and commanded another
force also of Mercians, the while that he sat there, to take
possession of Manchester in North-humbria, and repair and
man it. This year died archbishop Plegmund. This year
king Reginald won York.

A. 924. In this year, before midsummer, king Edward
went with his forces to Nottingham, and commanded the
town to be built on the south side of the river, over against
the other, and the bridge over the Trent, between the two
towns: and then he went thence into Peakland, to Bake-
well, and commanded a town to be built nigh thereunto,
and manned. And then chose him for father and for lord,
the king of the Scots and the whole nation of the Scots, and
Reginald and the son of Eadulf and all those who dwell in
North-humbria, as well English as Danes, and North-men
and others, and also the king of the Strath-clyde Britons,
and all the Strath-clyde Britons.

A. 924. This year Edward was chosen for father and for lord by the
king of the Scots, and by the Scots, and king Reginald, and by all the
North-humbrians, and also the king of the Strath-clyde Britons, and by
all the Strath-clyde Britons.

A. 924. This year king Edward died among the Mercians at Farndon;
and very shortly, about sixteen days after this, Elward his son died at
Oxford; and their bodies lie at Winchester. And Athelstan was chosen
king by the Mercians, and consecrated at Kingston. And he gave his sister
to Ofse [Otho], son of the king of the Old-Saxons.

A. 925. This year king Edward died, and Athelstan his
son succeeded to the kingdom. And St. Dunstan was born:

and Wulfhelm succeeded to the archbishopric of Canterbury.
This year king Athelstan and Sihtric king of the North-
humbrians came together at Tamworth, on the 3d before the
Kalends of February; and Athelstan gave him his sister.

A. 925. This year Bishop Wulfhelm was consecrated. And that same
year king Edward died.

A. 926. This year fiery lights appeared in the north part
of the heavens. And Sihtric perished: and king Athelstan obtained the kingdom of the North-humbrians. And
he ruled all the kings who were in this island: first, Howel
king of the West-Welsh; and Constantine king of the Scots;
and Owen king of the Monmouth people; and Aldred, son of
Ealdulf, of Bambrough: and they confirmed the peace by
pledge, and by oaths, at the place which is called Eamot,
on the 4th before the Ides of July; and they renounced all
idolatry, and after that submitted to him in peace.

A. 927. This year king Athelstan expelled king Guth-
frith. And this year Archbishop Wulfhelm went to Rome.

A. 928. William succeeded to Normandy, and held it
fifteen years.

A. 929. 930.

A. 931. This year Brinstan was ordained bishop of Winchester on the 4th before the Kalends of June; and he held
the bishopric two years and a half.

A. 931. This year died Frithstan bishop of Winchester, and Brinstan
was blessed in his place.

A. 932. This year died bishop Frithstan.

A. 933. This year Edwin the etheling was drowned at
sea. This year king Athelstan went into Scotland, as well
with a land army as with a fleet, and ravaged a great part
of it. And bishop Brinstan died at Winchester on the
feast of All-Hallows.

A. 934. This year bishop Elphege succeeded to the
bishopric of Winchester.

A. 935. 936.

A. 937.

Here Athelstan, king,
of earls the lord,
of heroes the bracelet-giver,

and his brother eke,
Edmund etheling,
life-long-glory

in battle won
with edges of swords
near Brumby.
The board-walls they clove,
they hewed the war-lindens,
  Hamora lafan'
offspring of Edward,
such was their noble nature
from their ancestors,
that they in battle oft
'gainst every foe
the land defended,
hoards and homes.
The foe they crushed,
the Scottish people
and the shipmen
fated fell.
The field 'dæniede'
with warriors' blood,
since the sun up
at morning-tide,
mighty planet,
glided o'er grounds,
God's candle bright,
the eternal Lord's,
till the noble creature
sank to her settle.
There lay many a warrior
by javelins strewed;
northern man
over shield shot;
so the Scots eke,
weary, war-sad.
West-Saxons onwards
throughout the day,
in bands,
pursued the footsteps
of the loathed nations.
They hewed the fugitives
behind, amain,
with swords mill-sharp.

Mercians refused not
the hard hand-play
to any heroes
who with Anlaf,
over the ocean,
in the ship's bosom,
this land sought
fated to the fight.
Five lay
on the battle-stead,
youthful kings,
by swords in slumber laid:
so seven eke
of Anlaf's earls;
of the army countless,
shipmen and Scots.
There was made flee
the North-men's chieftain,
by need constrained,
to the ship's prow
with a little band.
The bark drove afloat:
the king departed
on the fallow flood,
his life preserved.
So there eke the sage
came by flight
to his country north,
Constantine,
hoary warrior.
He had no cause to exult
in the communion of swords.
Here was his kindred band
of friends o'erthrown
on the folk-stead,
in battle slain;
and his son he left
on the slaughter-place,
mangled with wounds,
young in the fight:
he had no cause to boast,

hero grizzly-haired,
of the bill-clashing,
the old deceiver;
nor Anlaf the moor,   [mies;
with the remnant of their ar-
they had no cause to laugh
that they in war's works
the better men were
in the battle-stead,
at the conflict of banners,
meeting of spears,
concourse of men,
traffic of weapons;   [field
that they on the slaughter-
with Edward's
offspring played.

The North-men departed
in their nailed barks;
bloody relic of darts,
on roaring ocean
o'er the deep water
Dublin to seek,
again Ireland,
shamed in mind.

So too the brothers,
both together,
king and etheling,
their country sought,
West-Saxons' land,

in the war exulting.
They left behind them,
the corse to devour,
the sallowy kite
and the swarthy raven
with horned nib,
and the dusky 'pada,'
erne white-tailed,
the corse to enjoy,
greedy war-hawk,
and the grey beast,
wolf of the wood.

Carnage greater has not been
in this island
ever yet
of people slain,
before this,
by edges of swords,
as books us say,
old writers,
since from the east hither,
Angles and Saxons
came to land,
o'er the broad seas
Britain sought,
mighty war-smiths,
the Welsh o'ercame,
earls most bold,
this earth obtained.

A. 937. This year king Athelstan and Edmund his brother led a force to Brumby, and there fought against Anlaf; and, Christ helping, had the victory: and they there slew five kings and seven earls.

A. 938. 939.

A. 940. This year king Athelstan died at Gloucester on the 6th before the Kalends of November, about forty-one years, except one day, after king Alfred died. And Edmund the etheling, his brother, succeeded to the kingdom, and he was then eighteen years of age: and king Athelstan reigned fourteen years and ten weeks. Then was Wulfhelm archbishop in Kent.

A. 941. This year the North-humbrians were false to

their plighted troth, and chose Anlaf of Ireland to be their king.

Here Edmund king,
ruler of Angles,
protector of men,
Mercia obtained,
dear deed-doer,
as the Dor flows,
course of the white-well,
and Humber's river,
broad sea-stream.
Five towns,
Leicester,
and Lincoln,
and Nottingham,
so Stamford eke,
and Derby,
to Danes were erewhile,
under North-men,
by need constrained,
of heathen men
in captive chains,
a long time ;
until again redeemed them,
for his worthiness,
the bulwark of warriors,
offspring of Edward,
Edmund king.

A. 941. This year king Edmund received king Anlaf at baptism ; and that same year, a good long space after, he received king Reginald at the bishop's hands.

A. 942. This year king *Anlaf died.

A. 943. This year Anlaf stormed Tamworth, and great carnage was on either hand ; and the Danes had the victory, and much booty they led away with them : there during the pillage was Wulfrun taken. This year king Edmund besieged king Anlaf and archbishop Wulfstan in Leicester ; and he would have taken them, were it not that they broke out by night from the town. And, after that, Anlaf acquired king Edmund's friendship ; and king Edmund then received king Anlaf at baptism, and he royally gifted him. And that same year, after a good long time, he received king Reginald at the bishop's hands. This year king Edmund delivered Glastonbury to St. Dunstan, where he afterwards became the first abbat.

A. 944. This year king Edmund subdued all Northumberland under his power, and expelled two kings, Anlaf, son of Sihtric, and Reginald, son of Guthferth.

A. 945. This year king Edmund ravaged all Cumberland, and granted it all to Malcolm king of the Scots, on the

* See Hen. Huntingdon and Simeon of Durham. A. 941. There were several chiefs of that name at this period : Anlaf the son of Guthferth, Anlaf the son of Sihtric, and Anlaf Cuaran, mentioned A. 949.

condition, that he should be his fellow-worker as well by sea
as by land.

A. 946. This year king Edmund died on St. Augustine's
mass-day. That was widely known how he his days ended:
that Leofa stabbed him at Puckle-church. And Aelfleda
at Damerham, Elgar's daughter, the ealdorman, was then
his queen: and he had the kingdom six years and a half.
And then after him his brother Edred the etheling succeeded to the kingdom, and subdued all Northumberland
under his power: and the Scots gave him oaths, that they
would all that he would.

A. 947. This year king Edred came to Tadden's-cliff,
and there Wulfstan the archbishop and all the North-humbrian "witan" plighted their troth to the king: and within
a little while they belied it all, both pledge and also oaths.

A. 948. This year king Edred ravaged all Northumberland, because they had taken Eric to be their king: and
then, during the pillage, was the great minster burned at
Ripon that St. Wilfrid built. And as the king went
homewards, then the army of York overtook him: the rear
of the king's forces was at Chesterford; and there they
made great slaughter. Then was the king so wroth that he
would have marched his forces in again and wholly destroyed
the land. When the North-humbrian "witan" understood
that, then forsook they Eric, and made compensation for
the deed with king Edred.

A. 949. This year Anlaf Curran came to Northumberland.

A. 950.

A. 951. This year died Elphege bishop of Winchester, on
St. Gregory's mass-day. This same blessed St. Dunstan. . . .

A. 952. In this year king Edred commanded archbishop
Wulfstan to be brought into the fastness at Jedburgh,
because he had been oft accused to the king: and in this
year also the king commanded great slaughter to be made in
the town of Thetford, in revenge of the abbat Edelm, whom
they had before slain. This year the North-humbrians expelled king Anlaf, and received Eric, Harold's son.

A. 953.

A. 954. This year the North-humbrians expelled Eric,
and Edred obtained the kingdom of the North-humbrians.

This year archbishop Wulfstan again obtained a bishopric at Dorchester.

A. 955. This year died king Edred on St. Clement's mass-day, at Frome, and he rests in the Old-minster [Winchester]; and he reigned nine years and a half. And then Edwy succeeded to the kingdom, king Edmund's and St. Elfgiva's son. And he banished St. Dunstan out of the land.

A. 955. And Edwy succeeded to the kingdom of the West-Saxons, and Edgar his brother succeeded to the kingdom of the Mercians: and they were the sons of King Edmund and of S. Elfgiva.

A. 956.

A. 957. This year died Wulfstan archbishop of York, on the 17th before the Kalends of January, and he was buried at Oundle. And in the same year abbat Dunstan was driven away over sea. This year Edgar the etheling succeeded to the kingdom of the Mercians.

A. 958. In this year archbishop Odo* separated king Edwy and Elfgiva, because they were too nearly related. This year died king Edwy on the Kalends of October; and Edgar his brother succeeded to the kingdom, as well of the West-Saxons as of the Mercians, and of the North-humbrians; and he was then sixteen years of age.

In his days
it prospered well,
and God him granted
that he dwelt in peace
the while that he lived;
and he did as behoved him,
diligently he earned it.
He upreared God's glory wide,
and loved God's law,
and bettered the public peace,
most of the kings
who were before him
in man's memory.
And God him eke so helped,
that kings and earls
gladly to him bowed,
and were submissive
to that that he willed;
and without war
he ruled all
that himself would.
He was wide
throughout nations
greatly honoured,
because he honoured
God's name earnestly,
and God's law pondered
much and oft,
and God's glory reared
wide and far,
and wisely counselled,
most oft, and ever,
for God and for the world,
of all his people.

* Of Canterbury.

One misdeed he did
all too much
that he foreign
vices loved,
and heathen customs
within this land
brought too oft,
and outlandish men
hither enticed,

and harmful people
allured to this land.
But God grant him
that his good deeds
be more availing
than his misdeeds,
for his soul's protection
on the longsome course.

A. 959. This year Edgar sent after St. Dunstan, and gave him the bishopric at Worcester; and afterwards the bishopric at London.

A. 960.

A. 961. This year departed Odo the Good, archbishop; and St. Dunstan succeeded to the archbishopric.

A. 962. This year died Elfgar, the king's kinsman, in Devonshire, and his body rests at Wilton. And king Sifferth killed himself, and his body lies at Wimborne. And then, within the year, there was a great mortality, and the great fever was in London; and Paul's minster was burnt, and that same year was again built up. In this same year Athelmod the mass-priest went to Rome, and there died, on the 18th before the Kalends of September.

A. 963. This year died Wulfstan the deacon, on Childermass-day, and after that died Gyric the mass-priest. In this same year abbat Ethelwold* succeeded to the bishopric at Winchester, and he was consecrated on the vigil of St. Andrew: it was Sunday that day. In the year after he was consecrated, then made he many minsters, and drove the clerks out of the bishopric, because they would not observe any rule, and he set monks there. He made there two abbacies; one of monks, one of nuns; all which was within Winchester. Afterwards, then came he to the king, Edgar, and begged of him that he would give him all the minsters which heathen men had formerly broken down, because he would restore them: and the king cheerfully granted it. And then the bishop came first to Ely, where St. Etheldrida lies, and caused the minster to be made: then he gave it to one of his monks, who was named Britnoth. He then consecrated him abbat, and there set monks to serve God where

* Of Abingdon.

previously had been nuns : he bought then many villages
of the king, and made it very rich.   After that came bishop
Ethelwold to the minster which was called Medeshamstede,
which formerly had been destroyed by heathen men : he
found nothing there but old walls and wild woods.   There
found he, hidden in the old walls, writings that abbat
Hedda had erewhile written, how king Wulfhere and
Ethelred his brother had built it, and how they had freed it
against king and against bishop, and against all secular services, and how the pope Agatho had confirmed the same by
his rescript, and the archbishop Deus-dedit.   Then caused
he the minster to be built ; and set there an abbat, who was
called Adulf, and caused monks to be there where before
was nothing.   Then came he to the king, and caused him
to look at the writings which before were found ; and the
king answered then and said :

"I, Edgar, grant and give to-day, before God and before
the archbishop Dunstan, freedom to St. Peter's minster,
Medeshamstede, from king and from bishop : and all the
villages which lie thereto ; that is to say, Eastfield, and
Dodthorp, and Eye, and Paston.   And thus I free it, that
no bishop have there any command, without the abbat of the
minster.   And I give the town which is called Oundle, with
all which thereto lieth, that is to say, that which is called
'the Eight-hundreds,' and market and toll, so freely, that
neither king, nor bishop, nor earl, nor sheriff, have there
any command, nor any man except the abbat alone, and him
whom he thereto appointeth.   And I give to Christ and St.
Peter, and through the prayer of bishop Ethelwold, these
lands ; that is to say, Barro, Warmington, Ashton, Ketter-
ing, Castor, Eylesworth, Walton, Witherington, Eye, Thorp;
and one moneyer in Stamford.   These lands, and all the
others that belong to the minster, them declare I free : that
is, with sack and sock, toll and team, and infangthief ; these
rights, and all others, them declare I the shire of Christ and St.
Peter.   And I give the two parts of Whittlesey-mere, with the
waters and with the wears and fens, and so through Meerlade straight to the water which is called Nen, and so eastward to King's-delf.   And I will that a market be in the
same town, and that no other be between Stamford and Huntingdon.   And I will that the toll be thus given : first, from

Whittlesey-mere all as far as the king's toll of Norman-cross-hundred, and then back again from Whittlesey-mere, through Meerlade, straight to the Nen, and so as the water runneth to Crowland, and from Crowland to Must, and from Must to King's-delf, and to Whittlesey-mere.   And I will that all liberties, and all the remissions that my predecessors have given, that they stand ; and I sign and confirm it with Christ's rood-token." ⚜

Then Dunstan the archbishop of Canterbury answered, and said : "I grant that all the things which here are given and spoken of, and all the things which thy predecessors and mine have conceded, those will I that they stand ; and whosoever this breaketh, then give I him the curse of God, and of all saints, and of all ordained heads, and of myself, unless he come to repentance.   And I give, in acknowledgment, to St. Peter, my mass-hackel, and my stole, and my 'reef,' for the service of Christ."   "I, Oswald, archbishop of York, assent to all these words by the holy rood which Christ suffered on." ⚜   "I, Ethelwold, bishop, bless all who shall observe this ; and I excommunicate all who shall break this, unless he come to repentance."   Here was Elfstan bishop, Athulf bishop, and Eskwi abbat, and Osgar abbat, and Ethelgar abbat, and Elfere the ealdorman, Ethelwin the ealdorman, Britnoth ; Oslac the ealdorman, and many other great men : and all assented to it, and all signed it with Christ's cross. ⚜   This was done after the birth of our Lord nine hundred and seventy-two years, of the king's reign the sixteenth year.

Then the abbat Aldulf bought lands, numerous and many, then greatly enriched the minster withal ; and then was he there so long as until the archbishop Oswald of York was dead, and then he was chosen archbishop.   And then, soon, another abbat was chosen of the self-same minster, who was called Kenulf : he was afterwards bishop at Winchester. And he first made the wall about the minster : then gave he that to name Peterborough, which before was called Medeshamstede : he was there until he was appointed bishop at Winchester.   Then another abbat was chosen of the self-same minster, who was called Elfsy : Elfsy was then abbat, from that time, fifty years.   He took up St. Kyneburg and St. Kyneswith, who lay at Castor, and St. Tibba, who lay at

Ryhall, and brought them to Peterborough, and made an offering of them all to St. Peter in one day; and preserved them all the while he was there.

A. 963. This year, by king Edgar, St. Ethelwold was chosen to the bishoprick at Winchester. And the archbishop of Canterbury, St. Dunstan, consecrated him bishop on the first Sunday of Advent; that was on the 3rd before the Kalends of December.

A. 964. This year king Edgar expelled the priests at Winchester from the Old-minster and from the New-minster, and from Chertsey, and from Milton, and filled them with monks; and he appointed abbat Ethelgar abbat to the New-minster, and Ordbert to Chertsey, and Cyneward to Milton.

A. 964. This year were the canons driven out of the Old-minster by king Edgar, and also from the New-minster, and from Chertsey and from Milton; and he appointed thereto monks and abbats: to the New-minster Ethelgar, to Chertsey Ordbert, to Milton Cyneward.

A. 965. In this year king Edgar took Elfrida for his queen; she was daughter of Ordgar the ealdorman.

A. 966. This year Thored, Gunner's son, ravaged Westmoreland. And that same year Oslac obtained an ealdordom.

A. 967.

A. 968. In this year king Edgar ordered all Thanetland to be ravaged.

A. 969. 970.

A. 971. This year died archbishop Oskytel: he was first consecrated bishop of Dorchester, and afterwards of York; by favour of king Edred, and of all his 'witan,' he was consecrated archbishop; and he was a bishop twenty-two years; and he died on the mass-night of All-Hallows, ten days before Martin-mass, at Thame. And abbat Thurkytel his kinsman, carried the bishop's body to Bedford, because he was then, at that time, abbat there.

A. 972. This year died Edmund the etheling, and his body lies at Rumsey.

A. 972. This year Edgar the etheling was consecrated king at Bath, on Pentecost's mass-day, on the 5th before the Ides of May, the thirteenth year since he had obtained the kingdom; and he was then one less than thirty years of age. And soon after that, the king led all his ship-forces to Chester; and there came to meet him six kings, and they all plighted their troth to him, that they would be his fellow-workers by sea and by land.

A. 973.
Here was Edgar,
ruler of Angles,
in full assembly,
hallowed king,
at the old city
Akemanscester ;
but it the islanders,
beorns, by another word,
name Bath.
There was much bliss
on that blessed day
to all occasioned,
which children of men
name and call
Pentecost's day.
There was a heap of priests ;
of monks a large band,
as I have heard,
of sage ones, gathered :
and then agone was
ten hundred years,
told in numbers,
from the birth-tide
of the glorious King,
Pastor of light.
but that there remaining
then still was,
of yearly-tale,
as writings say,
seven and twenty :
so nigh had to the Victor-lord
a thousand run out
when this befel.
And himself, Edmund's
offspring, had
nine and twenty,
guardian 'gainst evil works,
years in the world
when this was done,

and then in the thirtieth, was
hallowed ruler.
A. 974.
A. 975.
Here, ended
the joys of earth,
Edgar, of Angles king
chose him another light,
beauteous and winsome
and left this frail,
this barren life.
Children of men name,
men on the earth,
every where, that month,
in this land,
those who erewhile were
in the art of numbers
rightly taught,
July month,
when the youth departed,
on the eighth day,
Edgar, from life,
bracelet giver to heroes.
And then his son succeeded
to the kingdom,
a child un-waxen,
of earls the prince.
to whom was Edward name.
And him, a glorious chief.
ten days before,
departed from Britain,
the good bishop,*
through nature's course,
to whom was Cyneward name.
Then was in Mercia,
as I have heard,
widely and every where,
the glory of the Lord
laid low on earth :
many were expelled,

* Of Wells.

C C

sage servants of God;
that was much grief
to him who in his breast bore
a burning love
of the Creator, in his mind.
Then was the Source of wonders
too oft contemned;
the Victor-lord,
heaven's Ruler.   [through
Then men his law broke
and then was eke driven out,
beloved hero,
Oslac from this land,
o'er rolling waters,
o'er the ganet's-bath;
hoary-haired hero,
wise and word-skilled,
o'er the water's throng,
o'er the whale's domain,

of home bereaved.
And then was seen,
high in the heavens,
a star in the firmament,
which lofty-souled
men, sage minded,
call widely,
cometa by name;
men skilled in arts,
wise truth-bearers.
Throughout mankind was
the Lord's vengeance
widely known,
famine o'er earth.
That again heaven's Guardian,
bettered, Lord of angels,
gave again bliss
to each isle-dweller,
through earth's fruits.

A. 975. The 8th before the Ides of
     July.
   Here Edgar died,
ruler of Angles,
West-Saxons' joy,
and Mercians' protector.
   Known was it widely
throughout many nations.
'Thæt' offspring of Edmund,
o'er the ganet's-bath.

honoured far,
   Kings him widely
bowed to the king,
as was his due by kind.
   No fleet was so daring,
nor army so strong,
that 'mid the English nation
took from him aught,
the while that the noble king
ruled on his throne.

And this year Edward, Edgar's son, succeeded to the kingdom; and then soon, in the same year, during harvest, appeared 'cometa' the star; and then came in the following year a very great famine, and very manifold commotions among the English people.

In his days,
for his youth,
God's gainsayers
God's law broke;
Eldfere, ealdorman,
and others many;
and rule monastic quashed,
and minsters dissolved,
and monks drove out,
and God's servants put down,

whom Edgar, king, ordered erewhile
the holy bishop
Ethelwold to stablish;
and widows they plundered,
many times and oft:
and many unrighteousnesses,
and evil unjust-deeds
arose up afterwards:
and ever after that
it greatly grew in evil.

And at that time, also, was Oslac the great earl banished from England.

A. 976. This year was the great famine among the English nation.

A. 977. This year, after Easter, was the great council at Kirtlington; and there died bishop Sideman, by a sudden death, on the 2d before the Kalends of May. He was bishop in Devonshire, and he desired that the resting-place of his body should be at Crediton, at his episcopal seat. Then commanded king Edward and archbishop Dunstan that he should be borne to St. Mary's minster, which is at Abingdon: and so too was it done: and he is moreover honourably buried on the north side, in St. Paul's chapel.

A. 978. In this year all the chief 'witan' of the English nation fell at Calne from an upper chamber, except the holy archbishop Dunstan, who alone supported himself upon a beam; and there some were grievously maimed, and some did not escape with life. In this year was King Edward martyred; and Ethelred the etheling, his brother, succeeded to the kingdom, and he was in the same year consecrated king. In that year died Alfwold; he was bishop of Dorset, and his body lies in the minster at Sherborne.

A. 979. In this year was Ethelred consecrated king at Kingston, on the Sunday, fourteen days after Easter; and there were at his consecration two archbishops, and ten suffragan-bishops. That same year was seen a bloody cloud, oftentimes, in the likeness of fire; and it was mostly apparent at midnight, and so in various beams was coloured: when it began to dawn, then it glided away.

A. 979. This year was king Edward slain at even-tide, at Corfe-gate, on the 15th before the Kalends of April, and then was he buried at Wareham, without any kind of kingly honours.

There has not been 'mid Angles
a worse deed done
than this was,
since they first
Britain-land sought.
Men him murdered,
but God him glorified.
He was in life
an earthly king;
he is now after death
a heavenly saint.
Him would not his earthly
kinsmen avenge,
but him hath his heavenly Father
greatly avenged.
The earthly murderers
would his memory
on earth blot out,
but the lofty Avenger
hath his memory
in the heavens
and on earth wide-spread.
They who would not erewhile
to his living
body bow down,
they now humbly
on knees bend
to his dead bones.

Now we may understand
that men's wisdom
and their devices,

and their councils,
are like nought
'gainst God's resolves.

This year Ethelred succeeded to the kingdom ; and he was very quickly after that, with much joy of the English witan, consecrated king at Kingston.

A. 980. In this year abbat Ethelgar* was consecrated bishop on the 6th before the Nones of May, to the episcopal seat at Selsey.   And in the same year was Southampton ravaged by a ship-force, and the most part of the townsmen slain, and led captive.   And that same year was Thanet-land ravaged by a ship force, and the most part of the townsmen slain, and led captive.   And that same year was Legecester-shire [Chester] ravaged by a northern ship-force.   In this year St. Dunstan and Alfere the ealdorman fetched the holy king's body, St. Edward's, from Wareham, and bore it with much solemnity to Shaftsbury.

A. 981. In this year St. Petroc's-stowe [Padstow] was ravaged ; and that same year was much harm done everywhere by the sea-coast, as well among the men of Devon as among the Welsh.   And in the same year died Elfstan bishop of Wiltshire, and his body lies in the minster at Abingdon ; and Wulfgar then succeeded to the bishopric. And in the same year died abbat Womare† at Ghent.

A. 981. This year came first the seven ships, and ravaged Southampton.

A. 982. In this year landed among the men of Dorset three ships of pirates ; and they ravaged in Portland.   That same year London was burnt ; and in the same year died two ealdormen, Ethelmer in Hampshire, and Edwin in Sussex ; and Ethelmer's body lies at Winchester, in the New-minster, and Edwin's in the minster at Abingdon.   This same year died two abbesses in Dorset, Herelufu at Shaftesbury, and Wulfwina at Wareham.   And that same year went Otho the Roman emperor to Greek-land [Calabria], and there met he a large force of Saracens, coming up from the sea, and they would then go plundering the Christian people.   And then the Emperor fought against them, and there was great slaughter made on either hand ; and the emperor had possession of the place of carnage : and nevertheless he was there much harassed before he turned thence : and as he homeward went, then died

* Of New-minster.   † Of St. Peter's.

his brother's son, who was named Otho, and he was Leo-dulf the etheling's son, and Leodulf was the elder Otho's son and king Edward's daughter's son.

A. 983. This year died Alfere the ealdorman, and Alfric succeeded to the same ealdorman-ship.* And Pope Benedict [VII.] died.

A. 984. This year died the benevolent bishop of Winchester, Ethelwold, father of monks, on the Kalends of August; and the consecration of the succeeding bishop, Elphege [II.], who by another name was called Godwin, was on the 14th before the Kalends of November; and he took the episcopal seat at Winchester, on the day of the two apostles Simon and Jude.

A. 985. This year was Alfric the ealdorman banished the land. And in the same year was Edwin consecrated abbat of the minster at Abingdon.

A. 986. This year the king laid waste the bishopric of Rochester. This year first came the great murrain among cattle in the English nation.

A. 987.

A. 988. This year was Watchet ravaged, and Goda, the Devonshire thane, slain, and with him much slaughter made. And this year departed the holy archbishop Dunstan, and passed to the heavenly life: and bishop Ethelgar† succeeded, after him, to the archbishopric ;‡ and little while after that he lived, but one year and three months.

A. 989.

A. 990. This year Siric was consecrated archbishop,§ and afterwards went to Rome for his pall. And abbat Eadwin‖ died; and abbat Wulfgar succeeded to the abbacy.

A. 991. This year was Ipswich ravaged; and after that, very shortly, was Britnoth the ealdorman slain at Maldon. And in that year it was decreed that tribute, for the first time, should be given to the Danish-men, on account of the great terror which they caused by the sea-coast; that was at first ten thousand pounds: this counsel was first given by archbishop Siric.

A. 992. This year Oswald the holy archbishop¶ left this, and passed to the heavenly life: and Ethelwin the ealdor-

---

* Mercia.   † Of Selsey.   ‡ Of Canterbury.
§ Of Canterbury.   ‖ Of Abingdon.   ¶ Of York.

man* died in the same year. Then decreed the king and all his witan that all the ships which were worth anything should be gathered together at London. And the king then committed the forces to the leading of Elfric the ealdorman, and of Thorod the earl, and of bishop Elfstan,† and of bishop Escwy;‡ and they were to try if they could any where betrap the army about. Then sent the ealdorman Elfric and directed the army to be warned; and then during the night of which they should have joined battle by day, then fled he by night from the forces, to his great disgrace: and the army then escaped, except one ship, whose crew was there slain. And then the ships from East-Anglia, and from London met the army, and there they made great slaughter of them; and took the ship, all armed and equipped, in which the ealdorman was. And then after the decease of archbishop Oswald, abbat Aldulf, of Peterborough, succeeded to the bishopric of York, and of Worcester; and Kenulf to the abbacy of Peterborough.

A. 992. This year Oswald the blessed archbishop died, and Abbat Eadulf succeeded to York and to Worcester. And this year the king and all his witan decreed that all the ships which were worth anything should be gathered together at London, in order that they might try if they could any where betrap the army from without. But Ælfric the ealdorman, one of those in whom the king had most confidence, directed the army to be warned; and in the night, as they should on the morrow have joined battle, the self-same Ælfric fled from the forces; and then the army escaped.

A. 993. In this year was Bambrough entered by storm, and much booty there taken. And after that the army came to the mouth of the Humber, and there wrought much evil, as well in Lindsey as in Northumbria. Then a very large force was gathered together; and as they should have joined battle, then the leaders, first of all, began the flight; that was Frene, and Godwin, and Frithgist. In this year the king ordered Elfgar, son of Elfric the ealdorman, to be blinded.

A. 993. In this year came Olave with ninety-three ships to Staines, and ravaged there about, and then went thence to Sandwich, and so thence to Ipswich, and that all over-ran; and so to Maldon. And there Britnoth the ealdorman came against them with his forces, and fought against them: and they there slew the ealdorman, and had possession of the place of

* Of E. Anglia.   † Of London.   ‡ Of Dorc ester.

carnage. And after that peace was made with them; and him [Anlaf] the king afterwards received at the bishop's hands, through the instruction of Siric bishop of the Kentish-men, and of Ælphege [II.] of Winchester.

A. 994. In this year came Olave and Sweyn to London, on the nativity of St. Mary, with ninety-four ships; and they then continued fighting stoutly against the city, and would also have set fire to it. But they there sustained: more harm and evil than they ever supposed that any citizens would be able to do unto them. But the holy mother of God, on that day, shewed her mercy to the citizens and delivered them from their foes. And they then went thence, and wrought the utmost evil that ever any army could do, by burning, and plundering, and by man-slaying, both by the sea-coast and among the East-Saxons, and in the land of Kent, and in Sussex, and in Hampshire. And at last they took to themselves horses, and rode as far as they would, and continued doing unspeakable evil. Then the king and his witan decreed that they should be sent to, and promised tribute and food, on condition that they should cease from their plundering: which terms they accepted. And then all the army came to Southampton, and there took up their winter-quarters: and there they were victualled from all the realm of the West-Saxons, and they were paid sixteen thousand pounds of money. Then the king sent bishop Elphege [II.]* and Ethelwerd the ealdorman after king Olave, and the while, hostages were delivered to the ships; and they then led Olave with much worship to the king at Andover. And king Ethelred received him at the bishop's hands, and royally gifted him. And then Olave made a covenant with him, even as he also fulfilled, that he never again would come hostilely to the English nation.

A. 995. In this year appeared 'cometa,' the star, and archbishop Sigic died: and Alfric bishop of Wiltshire† was chosen‡ on Easter-day, at Amesbury, by king Ethelred and by all his witan. This Alfric was a very wise man, so that there was no sager man in England. Then went Alfric to his archiepiscopal seat; and when he came thither he was received by those men in orders who were most unacceptable to him, that was, by clerks. And soon (he sent for) all the wisest men he anywhere knew of, and also the old men who

* Of Winchester.   † Afterwards Salisbury.   ‡ To Canterbury.

were able to say the soothest how each thing had been in
this land in the days of their elders; in addition to what
himself had learned from books and from wise men. Him
told the very old men, as well clergy as laity, that their
elders had told them how it had been established by law
soon after St. Augustine came to this land. When Augustine had obtained the bishopric in the city,* then was he
archbishop over all king Ethelbert's kingdom, as it is related in Historia Anglorum†...... make (a bishop's) see by
the king's aid in .... was begun by the old Romans ... and
to sprout forth. In that company the foremost were Mellitus, Justus, Paulinus, Rufinianus. By these sent the blessed
pope the pall, and therewith a letter, and instruction how he
should consecrate bishops, and in which place in Britain he
should seat them. And to the king (also) he sent letters
and many worldly gifts of divers things. And the churches
which they had got ready he commanded to be consecrated in
the name of our Lord and Saviour Christ and St. Mary;
and for himself there fix a dwelling-place, and for all his
after-followers; and that he (should) place therein men of
the same order that he had sent thither, and of which he
himself was, and also that each........ monks who should
fill the archiepiscopal seat at Canterbury, and that be ever
observed by God's leave and blessing and by St. Peter's, and
by all who came after him. When this embassy came again
to king Egelbert and to Augustine, they were very pleased
with such instruction. And the archbishop then consecrated the minster in Christ's name and St. Mary's, (on)
the day which is called the mass-day of the two martyrs,
Primus et Felicianus, and there within placed monks all as
St. Gregory commanded: and they God's service continently
performed; and from the same monks bishops were taken for
each..... as thou mayst read in Historia Anglorum.‡ Then
was archbishop Alfric very blithe, that he had so many witnesses (who) stood best at that time with the king. Still
more, the same witan who were with the archbishop said:
Thus also we .... monks have continued at Christ-Church
during Augustine's days, and during Laurentius', Mellitus',
Justus', Honorius', Deusdedit, Theodore's, Berthwold's, Tatwine's, Nothelm's, Cuthbert's, Bregwine's, Lambert's, ...

   * Canterbury.   † Bede, b. i. c. 25.   ‡ Bede, b. i. c. 33.

Athelard's, Wulfred's, Theologild's. But the (first) year when
Ceolnoth came to the archbishopric, there was such a mortality that there remained no more than five monks within
Christ-Church. During all his time there was war and sorrow in this land, so that no man could think of anything else
but . . . . . Now, God be thanked, it is in the king's power
and thine, whether they may be longer there within, because
they (might) never better be brought thereout than now may
be done, if it is the king's will and thine. The archbishop
then, without any staying, with all (these) men, went anon
to the king and showed him all, so as we here before have
related. Then was the king very glad (at these) tidings,
and said to the archbishop and to the others, 'It seemeth
advisable to me that thou shouldst go first of all to Rome
after thy (pall, and that) thou show to the pope all this, and,
after that, act by his counsel:' And they all answered, that
that was the best counsel. When (the priests) heard this,
then resolved they that they should take two from among
themselves and send to the pope; and they should offer him
great gifts and silver, on condition that he should give them
the arch(-pall). But when they came to Rome, then would
not the pope do that, because they brought him no letter
either from the king or from the people, and commanded
them to go, lo! where they would. (So soon as) the priests
had gone thence, came archbishop Alfric to Rome, and the
pope received him with much worship, and commanded him
on the morrow to perform mass at St. Peter's altar, and the
pope himself put on him his own pall, and greatly honoured
him. When this was done, the archbishop began telling the
pope all about the clerks, how it had happened, and how
they were within the minster at his archbishopric. And
the pope related to him again how the priests had come to
him, and offered great gifts, in order that he should give
them the pall. And the pope said, 'Go now to England
again with God's blessing, and St. Peter's and mine; and as
thou comest home, place in thy minster men of that order
which St. Gregorius commanded Augustine therein to place,
by God's command, and St. Peter's and mine.' Then the
archbishop with this returned to England. As soon as he
came home, he entered his archiepiscopal seat, and after that
went to the (king) and the king and all his people thanked

God for his return, and that he so had succeeded as was pleasing to them all. He then went again to Canterbury, and drove the clerks out of the minster, and there within placed monks, all as the pope commanded him.

A. 996. In this year was Alfric consecrated archbishop to Christ-Church.* This year was Wulstan ordained bishop of London.

A. 997. In this year the army went about Devonshire into Severn-mouth, and there ravaged, as well among the Cornish-men as among the North-Welsh, and among the men of Devon; and then landed at Watchet, and there wrought much evil by burning and by man-slaying. And after that they again went about Penwithstert, on the south side, and went then into the mouth of the Tamar, and then went up until they came to Liddyford, and burned and destroyed every thing which they met with; and they burned Ordulf's minster at Tavistock, and brought unspeakable booty with them to their ships. This year archbishop Alfric went to Rome after his arch-pall.

A. 998. This year the army went again eastward into Frome-mouth, and everywhere there they went up as far as they would into Dorset. And forces were often gathered against them; but, as soon as they should have joined battle, then was there ever, through some cause, flight begun; and in the end they ever had the victory. And then at another time they sat down in the Isle of Wight, and got their food the while from Hampshire and from Sussex.

A. 999. This year the army again came about into Thames, and went then up along the Medway, and to Rochester. And then the Kentish forces came there to meet them, and they there stoutly joined battle: but alas! that they too quickly yielded and fled; for they had not the support which they should have had. And the Danish-men had possession of the place of carnage; and then they took horse and rode wheresoever they themselves would, and full nigh all the West-Kentish men they ruined and plundered. Then the king, with his witan, decreed that, with a ship force and also with a land force, they should be attacked. But when the ships were ready, then the miserable crew delayed from day to day, and distressed the poor people who lay in

* Canterbury.

the ships : and ever as it should have been forwarder, so was
it later from one time to another ; and ever they let their
enemies' forces increase, and ever the people retired from the
sea, and they ever went forth after them.   And then in the
end, these expeditions both by sea and land effected nothing,
except the people's distress and waste of money, and the
emboldening of their foes.

A. 1000. In this year the king went into Cumberland,
and ravaged it well nigh all.   And his ships went out about
Chester, and should have come to meet him, but they were
not able : then ravaged they Anglesey.   And the hostile
fleet went this summer to Richard's dominions.*

A. 1001. In this year was much hostility in the land of
the English through the ship-force, and well nigh every
where they ravaged and burned, so that they advanced
in one course until they came to the town of Alton ; and
then there came against them the men of Hampshire, and
fought against them.   And there was Ethelwerd the king's
high-steward slain, and Leofric at Whitchurch, and Leofwin
the king's high-steward, and Wulfhere the bishop's thane, and
Godwin at Worthy, bishop Elfsy's son,† and of all men,
one and eighty ; and there were of the Danish-men many
more slain, though they had possession of the place of carnage.   And they went thence west until they came to
Devon ; and there Paley came to meet them, with the ships
which he could gather, because he had fled from king Ethelred, contrary to all the plighted troth that he had given him ;
and the king had also well gifted him with houses, and with
gold and with silver.   And they burned Teignton, and also
many other good towns which we are unable to name ; and
there, afterwards, peace was made with them.   And they
then went thence to Exmouth, so that they proceeded upwards in one course until they came to Pen : and there
Cole the king's high-reve, and Edsy the king's-reve, went
against them with the forces which they were able to gather
together ; and they there were put to flight, and there were
many slain : and the Danish-men had possession of the place
of carnage.   And the morning after, they burned the village
of Pen and at Clifton, and also many goodly towns which we
are unable to name, and then went again east until they

* Normandy.   † See note at p. 413.

came to the Isle of Wight; and on the morning after, they
burned the town at Waltham, and many other small towns;
and soon after a treaty was entered into with them, and they
made peace.

A. 1001. This year the army came to Exmouth, and then went up to
the town, and there continued fighting stoutly; but they were very strenuously resisted.   Then went they through the land, and did all as was their
wont; destroyed and burnt.   Then was collected a vast force of the people of Devon and of the people of Somerset, and they then came together
at Pen.   And so soon as they joined battle, then the people gave
way: and there they made great slaughter, and then they rode over the
land, and their last incursion was ever worse than the one before: and then
they brought much booty with them to their ships. And thence they went
into the Isle of Wight, and there they roved about, even as they themselves
would, and nothing withstood them: nor any fleet by sea durst meet them;
nor land force either, went they ever so far up.   Then was it in every
wise a heavy time, because they never ceased from their evil doings.

A. 1002. In this year the king decreed, and his witan,
that tribute should be paid to the fleet, and peace made with
them, on condition that they should cease from their evil-
doings.   Then sent the king to the fleet Leofsy the
ealdorman; and he then settled a truce with them by the
king's word, and his witan's, and that they should receive
food and tribute.   And that they then accepted: and then
were they paid twenty-four thousand pounds.   Then during
this, Leofsy the ealdorman slew Eafy the king's high-steward;
and the king then banished him the land.   And then in the
same Lent came the lady, Richard's * daughter, Emma
Elfgive, hither to land: and in the same summer archbishop
Aldulf † died.   And in that year the king ordered all the
Danish-men who were in England to be slain.   This was
done on St. Brice's mass-day; because it was made known
to the king that they would treacherously bereave him of his
life, and afterwards all his witan; and after that have his
kingdom without any gainsaying.

A. 1003. This year was Exeter entered by storm, through
the French churl Hugh, whom the ‡ lady had appointed her
steward: and then the army entirely ruined the town, and
there took much booty.   And in the same year the army
went up into Wiltshire.   Then was gathered a very large
force from Wiltshire and from Hampshire, and very

* Duke of Normandy.   † Of York.   ‡ Emma.

resolutely they came in presence of the army. Then should
the ealdorman Elfric have led the forces, but he then had
recourse to his old devices : as soon as they were so near that
either army could look on the other, then feigned he himself
sick, and began by retching to spew, and said that he was
grievously ill : and thus deceived the people whom he should
have led ; as it is said : When the leader groweth feeble,
then is all the army greatly hindered. When Sweyn saw
that they were not unanimous, and that they all separated,
then led he his army into Wilton ; and they spoiled the town,
and burned it ; and he went then to Salisbury, and thence
went to the sea again, where he knew that his sea-horses
were.

A. 1004. This year came Sweyn with his fleet to
Norwich, and entirely spoiled and burned the town. Then
decreed Ulfkytel, with the witan of East-Anglia, that it were
better that they should purchase peace of the army before
they did very much harm in the land ; because they had
come unawares, and he had not time that he might gather
his forces. Then during the truce which ought to have been
between them, then stole the army up from their ships, and
went their way to Thetford. When Ulfkytel understood
that, then sent he word that the ships should be hewed in
pieces, but they in whom he trusted failed to do it, and he
then gathered his forces secretly, as he best might. And
the army then came to Thetford, within three weeks of their
having before plundered Norwich, and were one day there
within, and plundered and burned the town. And then on the
morrow, as they would have gone to their ships, then came
Ulfkytel with his band, in order that they might there join
battle with them. And they there stoutly joined battle,
and much slaughter was there made on either hand. There
were the chief among the East-Anglian people slain ; but if
the full force there had been, they never again had gone to
their ships ; inasmuch as they themselves said, that they
never had met a worse hand-play among the English nation
than Ulfkytel had brought to them.

A. 1005. In this year was the great famine throughout
the English nation ; such, that no man ever before recollected
one so grim. And the fleet in this year went from this land
to Denmark ; and staid but a little space ere it came again.

A. 1006. This year died archbishop Alfric, and after him bishop Elphege [II.] succeeded to the archbishopric:* and bishop Brithwin succeeded to the bishopric of Wiltshire.†   And in the same year was Wulfgeat deprived of all his possessions, and Wulfeah and Ufgeat were blinded, and Elfelm the ealdorman was slain ; and bishop Kenulf‡ died.   And then, after mid-summer, then came the great fleet to Sandwich, and did all as they had been before wont ; they ravaged, and burned, and destroyed, wherever they went.   Then the king commanded all the people of Wessex and of Mercia to be called out ; and then they lay out all the harvest in the field against the army.   But it availed nothing the more than it oft before had done : but for all this the army .went wheresoever itself would, and the forces did every kind of harm to the inhabitants ; so that neither profited them, nor the home army nor the foreign army.   When it became winter, then went the forces home ; and the army then came, over St. Martin's-mass, to their quarters in the Isle of Wight, and procured themselves there from all parts that which they needed.   And then, at mid-winter, they went to their ready store, throughout Hampshire into Berkshire, to Reading : and they did their old wont ; they lighted their war-beacons as they went.   Then went they to Wallingford, and that all burned, and were then one day in Cholsey : and they went then along Ashdown to Cuckamsley-hill, and there abode, as a daring boast ; for it had been often said, if they should reach Cuckamsley-hill, that they would never again get to the sea : then they went homewards another way.   Then were forces assembled at Kennet, and they there joined battle : and they soon brought that band to flight, and afterwards carried their booty to the sea.   But there might the Winchester-men see an army daring and fearless, as they went by their gates towards the sea, and fetched themselves food and treasures over fifty miles from the sea.   Then had the king gone over Thames into Shropshire, and there took his abode during the mid-winter's tide.   Then became the dread of the army so great, that no man could think or discover how they could be driven out of the land, or this land maintained against them ; for they had every shire in

* Of Canterbury.   † Afterwards the diocese of Salisbury.
‡ Of Winchester.

Wessex sadly marked, by burning and by plundering. Then
the king began earnestly with his witan to consider what
might seem most advisable to them all, so that this land
might be saved, before it was utterly destroyed. Then the
king and his witan decreed, for the behoof of the whole
nation, though it was hateful to them all, that they needs
must pay tribute to the army. Then the king sent to the
army, and directed it to be made known to them, that he
would that there should be a truce between them, and that
tribute should be paid, and food given them. And then all
that they accepted: and then were they victualled from
throughout the English nation.

A. 1006. This year Elphege [II.] was consecrated archbishop.*

A. 1007. In this year was the tribute delivered to the
army, that was thirty-six thousand pounds. In this year
also was Edric appointed ealdorman over the kingdom of
Mercia. This year bishop Elphege went to Rome after his
pall.

A. 1008. This year the king commanded that ships should
be speedily built throughout the English nation : that is then,
from three hundred hides and from ten hides, one vessel ; and
from eight hides, a helmet and a coat of mail.

A. 1009. In this year were the ships ready about which
we before spake ; and there were so many of them as never
before, according as books say unto us, had been among the
English nation in any king's days. And they were all
brought together to Sandwich, and there they were to lie
and defend this land against every foreign army. But still
we had not the good fortune nor the worthiness, that the
ship-force could be of any use to this land, any more than it
oft before had been. Then befell it at this same time, or a
little before, that Brihtric, Edric the ealdorman's brother,
accused [of treason] to the king Wulfnoth the "child" of the
South-Saxons, father of Godwin the earl. He then went out,
and enticed ships unto him, until he had twenty ; and he then
ravaged every where by the south coast, and wrought every
kind of evil. Then it was told unto the ship-forces that
they might be easily taken, if they would go about it. Then
Brihtric took with him eighty ships, and thought that he
should acquire great fame if he could seize Wulfnoth alive

* Of Canterbury.

or dead. But as they were on their way thither, then came
such a wind against them as no man before remembered, and
the ships it then utterly beat, and smashed to pieces, and
cast upon the land; and soon came Wulfnoth, and burned
the ships. When this was thus known in the other ships
where the king was, how the others had fared, then was it as
if it had been all hopeless ; and the king went his way home;
and the ealdormen and the nobility, and thus lightly left
the ships ; and then afterwards, the people who were in the
ships brought them to London : and they let the whole
nation's toil thus lightly pass away ; and no better was that
victory on which the whole English nation had fixed their
hopes. When this ship-expedition had thus ended, then
came, soon after Lammas, the vast hostile army, which we
have called Thurkill's army, to Sandwich ; and they soon
went their way to Canterbury, and the city would soon
have subdued, if the citizens had not first desired peace of
them : and all the people of East-Kent made peace with the
army, and gave them three thousand pounds. And then,
soon after that, the army went forth till they came to the Isle of
Wight ; and thence every where in Sussex, and in Hampshire,
and also in Berkshire, they ravaged and plundered *as their
wont is.** Then the king commanded the whole nation to be
called out ; so that they should be opposed on every side :
but lo ! nevertheless, they marched as they pleased. Then,
upon a certain occasion, the king had got before them with
all his forces, as they would go to their ships ; and all the
people were ready to attack them. But it was then prevented
through Edric the ealdorman, *as it ever is still.** Then,
after St. Martin's-mass, they went once more into Kent,
and took up their winter-quarters on the Thames, and obtained their food from Essex, and from the shires which
were there nearest, on both sides of the Thames. And oft
they fought against the city of London : but praise be to
God that it yet stands sound, and they there ever met
with ill fare. And then, after mid-winter, took they their
way upwards through Chiltern, and so to Oxford, and burned
the city ; and betook themselves then, on both sides of the

---

* These expressions in the present tense afford a strong proof that the
original records of these transactions are nearly coeval with the transactions
themselves. Later MSS. use the past tense.—INGRAM.

Thames, towards their ships. Then were they warned that there were forces gathered at London against them : then went they over at Staines. And thus they went the whole winter ; and during Lent they were in Kent, and repaired their ships.

A. 1010. This year, after Easter, came the fore-mentioned army into East-Anglia, and landed at Ipswich, and went forthwith where they understood Ulfkytel was with his forces. This was on the day, called the first of the ascension of our Lord. The East Angles soon fled. Then stood Cambridge-shire firmly against them. There was slain Athelstan the king's son-in-law, and Oswy and his son, and Wulfric, Leofwin's son, and Eadwy, Efy's brother, and many other good thanes, and numberless of the people : the flight first began at Thurkytel Myrehead. And the Danes had possession of the place of carnage : and there were they horsed ; and afterwards had dominion over East-Anglia, and the land three months ravaged and burned ; and they even went into the wild fens, and they destroyed men and cattle, and burned throughout the fens : and Thetford they burned, and Cambridge. And after that they went southward again to the Thames, and the men who were horsed rode towards the ships ; and after that, very speedily, they went westward into Oxfordshire, and thence into Buckinghamshire, and so along the Ouse until they came to Bedford, and so onwards to Temsford ; and ever burning as they went. Then went they again to their ships with their booty. And when they went to their ships, then ought the forces again to have gone out against them, until they should land ; but then the forces went home : and when they were eastwards, then were the forces kept westwards ; and when they were southwards, then were our forces northwards. Then were all the witan summoned to the king, and they were then to counsel how this land might be defended. But although something might be then counselled, it did not stand even one month : at last there was no chief who would assemble forces, but each fled as he best might ; nor, at the last, would even one shire assist another. Then before St. Andrew's mass-day, came the enemy to Northampton, and they soon burned the town and took there-about as much as they themselves would ; and thence they went over Thames into Wessex, and so by

Cannings-marsh, burning all the way. When they had gone so far as they then would, then came they at mid-winter to their ships.

A. 1011. In this year sent the king and his witan to the army, and desired peace, and promised them tribute and food, on condition that they would cease from their plundering. They had then over-run, 1st, East-Anglia, and 2d, Essex, and 3d, Middlesex, and 4th, Oxfordshire, and 5th, Cambridge-shire; and 6th, Hertfordshire, and 7th, Buckinghamshire, and 8th, Bedfordshire, and 9th, half of Huntingdonshire, and 10th, much of Northamptonshire; and south of Thames, all Kent, and Sussex, and Hastings, and Surry, and Berkshire, and Hampshire, and much of Wiltshire. All these misfortunes befel us through unwise counsel, that they were not in time offered tribute, or fought against; but when they had done the most evil, then peace and truce were made with them. And nevertheless, for all the truce and tribute, they went everywhere in bands, and plundered our miserable people, and robbed and slew them. And then in this year, between the Nativity of St. Mary and St. Michael's-mass, they besieged Canterbury, and got into it through treachery, because Elfmar betrayed it, whose life the archbishop Elphege had before saved. And there they took the archbishop Elphege, and Elfward the king's steward, and the abbess Leo-fruna,[*] and bishop Godwin.[†] And abbat Elfmar[‡] they let go away. And they took there within all the men in orders, and men and women: it is not to be told to any man how many there were. And they remained within the city afterwards as long as they would. And when they had thoroughly searched the city, then went they to their ships, and led the archbishop with them.

Was then captive	erewhile saw bliss,
he who erewhile was	in that hapless city,
head of the English race	whence to us came first
and Christendom.	Christendom and bliss,
There might then be seen	'fore God, and 'fore the world.
misery, where men oft	

And they kept the archbishop with them so long as until the time that they martyred him.

A. 1012. In this year came Edric the ealdorman, and all

* Of S. Mildred's.   † Godwin III. of Rochester.   ‡ Of St. Augustine's.

the chief witan, clergy and laity, of the English people to
London, before Easter; Easter-day was then on the Ides
of April; and they were there then so long as until all
the tribute was paid, after Easter; that was eight and forty
thousand pounds. Then on the Saturday was the army
greatly excited against the bishop, because he would not promise them any money: but he forbade that any thing should
be given for him. They had also drunk deeply, for wine
had been brought there from the south. Then took they the
bishop, led him to their hustings on the eve of Sunday, the
octaves of Easter, which was on the 13th before the Kalends of
May; and there they then shamefully slaughtered him:
they cast upon him bones and the horns of oxen, and then
one of them struck him with an axe-iron on the head, so that
with the blow he sank down; and his holy blood fell on the
earth, and his holy soul he sent forth to God's kingdom.
And on the morrow the body was carried to London, and
the bishops Ednoth* and Elfhun,† and the townsmen, received it with all reverence, and buried it in St. Paul's
minster; and there God now manifesteth the miraculous
powers of the holy martyr. When the tribute was paid, and
oaths of peace were sworn, then the army separated widely,
in like manner as before it had been gathered together. Then
became subject to the king five and forty ships of the army,
and covenanted with him that they would defend this country,
and that he should feed and clothe them.

A. 1013. In the year after that in which the archbishop
Elphege was martyred, the king appointed bishop Living to
be archbishop of Canterbury. And in this same year,
before the month of August, came king Sweyn with his
fleet to Sandwich, and went then, very soon, about East-
Anglia into the mouth of the Humber, and so upward along
Trent, until he came to Gainsborough. And then, soon,
Utred the earl and all the North-humbrians submitted to
him, and all the people in Lindsey, and afterwards the people
in the Five Boroughs,‡ and soon after, all the army north of
Watling-street; and hostages were delivered to him from
every shire. After he had learned that all the people were

* Of Dorchester.   † Of London.
‡ Namely, Leicester, Lincoln, Nottingham, Stamford, and Derby. See
A. 942, 1015.

obedient to him, then bade he that his army should be
victualled and horsed ; and he then afterwards went southward with all the forces. and committed the ships and the
hostages to his son Canute. And after he came over Watling-
street, they wrought the most evil that any army could do.
Then went he to Oxford, and the townsmen soon submitted,
and delivered hostages ; and thence to Winchester, and they
did the like. Then went he thence eastward to London, and
much of his people was drowned in the Thames, because
they kept not to any bridge. When he came to the city,
then would not the townsmen submit, but held out against
him with all their might, because king Ethelred was therein,
and Thurkill with him. Then went king Sweyn thence to
Wallingford, and so over the Thames westward to Bath, and
sat down there with his forces. And Ethelmar the ealdorman came thither, and the western thanes with him, and they
all submitted to Sweyn, and delivered hostages for themselves. And when he had thus succeeded, then went he
northward to his ships ; and then all the people held him for
full king. And after that the townsmen of London submitted, and delivered hostages, because they dreaded lest he
should utterly undo them. Then Sweyn ordered a full-tri-
bute and provisions for his army during the winter ; and
Thurkill ordered the like for the army which lay at Greenwich : and for all that, they plundered as oft as they would.
Then was this people nothing benefited either from the south
or from the north. Then was king Ethelred some while
with the fleet which lay in the Thames ; and the lady* then
departed over sea to her brother Richard,† and Elfsy, abbat of
Peterborough, with her. And the king sent bishop Elfhun
with the ethelings, Edward and Alfred, over sea, that he
might have charge of them. Then departed the king from
the fleet at mid-winter into the Isle of Wight, and was there
during that tide ; and after that tide he went over the sea to
Richard, and was there with him until such time as Sweyn
was dead. And the while that the lady was with her brother
beyond sea, Elfsy, abbat of Peterborough, who was there with
her, went to the minster which is called Boneval, where St.
Florentine's body lay. There found he a poor place, a poor
abbat, and poor monks ; for they had been plundered. Then

* Emma.   † Duke of Normandy.

bought he there of the abbat and of the monks St. Florentine's body, all except the head, for five hundred pounds ;
and then when he came home again, then made he an offering of it to Christ and St. Peter.

A. 1014. In this year king Sweyn ended his days, at
Candlemas, on the third before the Nones of February.   And
that same year Alwy was consecrated bishop of London, at
York, on St. Juliana's mass-day.   And all the fleet then
chose Canute for king.   Then counselled all the witan who
were in England, clergy and laity, that they should send
after king Ethelred ; and they declared that no lord were
dearer to them than their natural lord, if he would rule them
better than he had before done.   Then sent the king his
son Edward hither with his messengers, and ordered them to
greet all his people ; and said that he would be to them a
loving lord, and amend all those things which they all abhorred, and each of those things should be forgiven which
had been done or said to him, on condition that they all, with
one consent, would be obedient to him, without deceit.   And
they then established full friendship, by word and by pledge,
on either half, and declared every Danish king an outlaw
from England for ever.   Then, during Lent, king Ethelred
came home to his own people ; and he was gladly received
by them all.   Then, after Sweyn was dead, Canute sat with
his army at Gainsborough until Easter ; and it was agreed
between him and the people of Lindsey that they should find
him horses, and that afterwards they should all go out together, and plunder.   Then came king Ethelred thither, to
Lindsey, with his full force, before they were ready : and
then they plundered, and burned, and slew all the people
whom they could reach.   And Canute went away out with his
fleet, and thus the poor people were deceived through him,
and then he went southward until he came to Sandwich ;
and there he caused the hostages to be put on shore who had
been delivered to his father, and cut off their hands, and
ears, and noses.   And besides all these evils, the king
ordered the army which lay at Greenwich to be paid twenty-
one thousand pounds.   And in this year, on the eve of St.
Michael's mass, came the great sea-flood wide throughout
this land, and ran so far up as it never before had done, and
washed away many towns, and a countless number of people.

A. 1015. In this year was the great council at Oxford;
and there Edric the ealdorman betrayed Sigeferth and
Morcar, the chief thanes in the Seven Boroughs. He allured
them into his chamber, and there within they were cruelly
slain. And the king then took all their possessions, and
ordered Sigeferth's relict to be taken, and to be brought to
Malmesbury. Then, after a little space, Edmund the
etheling went there and took the woman, contrary to the
king's will, and had her for his wife. Then, before the
Nativity of St. Mary, the etheling went thence, from the
west, north to the Five Boroughs, and soon took possession of
all Sigeferth's property, and Morcar's; and the people all
submitted to him. And then, during the same time, came
king Canute to Sandwich; and soon after went about Kent
into Wessex, until he came to the mouth of the Frome: and
then he ravaged in Dorset, and in Wiltshire, and in Somerset. Then lay the king sick at Corsham. Then gathered
Edric the ealdorman forces, and the etheling Edmund in
the north. When they came together, then would the
ealdorman betray the etheling, but he was not able: and
they then parted without a battle on that account, and gave
way to their foes. And Edric the ealdorman then enticed
forty ships from the king, and then went over to Canute. And
the men of Wessex submitted, and delivered hostages, and
horsed the army; and then was it there until mid-winter.

A. 1016. In this year came Canute with his army, and
Edric the ealdorman with him, over Thames into Mercia at
Cricklade. And then they went to Warwickshire, during
the midwinter's tide, and ravaged, and burned, and slew all
that they could come at. Then began the etheling Edmund
to gather his forces. When the forces were assembled, then
would it not content them except it so were that the king
were there with them, and they might have the help of the
citizens of London: then gave they up the expedition,
and each man went him away home. Then after that tide,
the forces were again called out, so that each man, who
was able to go, should come forth, under full penalties;
and they sent to the king at London, and prayed him
that he would come to meet the forces with such help as
he could gather. When they all had come together, then
it availed them nothing more than it oft before had done.

Then was it made known to the king that they would betray him; they who ought to have been of aid to him. Then left he the forces and returned to London. Then rode the etheling Edmund into North-humbria to Utred the earl, and every man thought that they would assemble forces against king Canute. Then marched they into Staffordshire, and into Shropshire, and to Chester; and they plundered on their part, and Canute on his part. He went out through Buckinghamshire into Bedfordshire, and thence to Hunting-donshire, and so into Northamptonshire along the fens to Stamford, and then into Lincolnshire; then thence to Nottinghamshire, and so to North-humbria towards York. When Utred heard this, then left he off his plundering, and hastened northwards, and then submitted, from need, and all the North-humbrians with him; and he delivered hostages: and, notwithstanding, they slew him, through the counsel of Edric the ealdorman, and Thurkytel, son of Nafan, with him. And then, after that, king Canute appointed Eric to be his earl in North-humbria, in like manner as Utred had been; and afterwards went southward, by another way, all to the west: and then before Easter, came all the army to their ships. And the etheling Edmund went to London to his father. And then, after Easter, went king Canute with all his ships towards London. Then befell it that king Ethelred died, before the ships arrived. He ended his days on St. George's mass day, and he held his kingdom with great toil and under great difficulties the while that his life lasted. And then, after his end, all the peers who were in London, and the citizens, chose Edmund to be king: and he strenuously defended his kingdom the while that his time lasted. Then came the ships to Greenwich at Rogation days. And within a little space they went to London, and they dug a great ditch on the south side, and dragged their ships to the west side of the bridge; and then afterwards they ditched the city around, so that no one could go either in or out: and they repeatedly fought against the city; but the citizens strenuously withstood them. Then had the king Edmund, before that, gone out; and then he over-ran Wessex, and all the people submitted to him. And soon after that he fought against the army at Pen, near Gillingham. And a second battle he fought, after mid-summer, at Sherston; and there much slaughter was made on either side, and the armies of themselves separated. In that battle was Edric the ealdorman, and Ælmer darling, helping the army against king Edmund. And then gathered he his forces for the third time, and went to London, all north of Thames, and so out through Clayhanger; and relieved the citizens, and drove the army in flight to their ships. And then, two days after, the king went over at Brentford, and there fought against the army, and put them to flight: and there many of the English people were drowned, from their own carelessness; they who went before the forces, and would take booty. And after that the king went into Wessex, and collected his forces. Then went the army, soon, to London, and beset the city around, and strongly fought against it, as well by water as by land. But the Almighty God delivered it.

The enemy went then, after that, from London, with their ships, into the Orwell, and there went up, and proceeded into Mercia, and destroyed and burned whatsoever they over-ran, as is their wont, and provided themselves with food: and they conducted, as well their ships as their droves, into the Medway. Then king Edmund assembled, for the fourth time, all his forces, and went over the Thames at Brentford, and went into Kent; and the army fled before him, with their horses, into Sheppey: and the king slew as many of them as he could overtake. And Edric the ealdorman went then to meet the king at Aylesford: than which no measure could be more ill-advised.

The army then went again up into Essex, and passed into Mercia, and destroyed whatever it over-ran.

When the king learned that the army was upward, then assembled he, for the fifth time, all the English nation, and followed after them, and overtook them in Essex, at the down which is called Assingdon: and there they strenuously joined battle. Then did Edric the ealdorman, as he had oft before done, begin the flight first with the Maisevethians, and so betrayed his royal lord and the whole people of the English race. There Canute had the victory; and all the English nation fought against him. There was slain bishop Ednoth,[*] and abbat Wulsy, and Elfric the ealdorman,

* Of Dorchester.

and Godwin the ealdorman of Lindsey, and Ulfkytel of East-Anglia, and Ethelward, son of Ethelwine* the ealdorman; and all the nobility of the English race was there destroyed.

Then, after this battle, went king Canute up with his army into Gloucestershire, where he learned that king Edmund was.

Then advised Edric the ealdorman, and the counsellors who were there, that the kings should be mutually reconciled. And they delivered hostages mutually; and the kings came together at Olney near Deerhurst, and then confirmed their friendship as well by pledge as by oath, and settled the tribute for the army. And they then separated with this reconcilement: and Edmund obtained Wessex, and Canute Mercia and the northern district. The army then went to their ships with the things they had taken. And the men of London made a truce with the army, and bought themselves peace: and the army brought their ships to London, and took up their winter-quarters therein. Then, at St. Andrew's mass, died king Edmund; and his body lies at Glastonbury, with his grandfather Edgar. And in the same year died Wulfgar, abbat of Abingdon; and Ethelsy succeeded to the abbacy.

A. 1017. In this year king Canute obtained the whole realm of the English race, and divided it into four parts: Wessex to himself, and East-Anglia to Thurkill, and Mercia to Edric, and North-humbria to Eric. And in this year was Edric the ealdorman slain in London, very justly, and Norman, son of Leofwin the ealdorman, and Ethelward, son of Ethelmar the great, and Britric, son of Elphege, in Devonshire. And king Canute banished Edwy the etheling, and afterwards commanded him to be slain, and Edwy king of the churls. And then, before the Kalends of August, the king commanded the relict of king Ethelred, Richard's daughter, to be fetched for his wife; that was Elfgive in English, Emma in French.

A. 1017. This year Canute was chosen king.

: A. 1018. In this year the tribute was delivered throughout the whole English nation; that was altogether, two and

---

* Called Ethelsy in some MSS.

seventy thousand pounds, besides that which the townsmen of London paid, which was ten and a half thousand pounds. And then some of the army went to Denmark, and forty ships remained with king Canute. And the Danes and the Angles agreed, at Oxford, to live under Edgar's law. And this year abbat Ethelsy died at Abingdon, and Ethelwine succeeded him.

A. 1019. This year king Canute went with forty ships to Denmark, and there abode all the winter.

A. 1019. And this winter died archbishop Elfstan:[*] he was named Living; and he was a very provident man, both as to God and as to the world.

A. 1020. In this year died archbishop Living: and king Canute came again to England. And then, at Easter, there was a great council at Cirencester: then was outlawed Ethelward the ealdorman, and Edwy, king of the churls. And in this year went the king to Assingdon, and archbishop Wulstan [II.],[†] and Thurkyl the earl, and many bishops and also abbats, and many monks with them, and consecrated the minster at Assingdon. And Ethelnoth the monk, who was dean at Christ-Church, was in the same year, on the Ides of November, consecrated bishop at Christ-Church,[‡] by archbishop Wulfstan.

A. 1020. And caused to be built there a minster of stone and lime, for the souls of the men who there were slain, and gave it to one of his priests, whose name was Stigand.

A. 1021. In this year, at Martin-mass, king Canute outlawed Thurkyl the earl. And bishop Elfgar,[§] the almsgiver, died on Christmas-morn.

A. 1022. This year king Canute went out with his ships to the Isle of Wight. Archbishop Ethelnoth went to Rome, and was there received by Benedict, the honourable pope, with much worship; and he, with his own hands, put his pall upon him, and very honourably consecrated him archbishop, and blessed him, on the Nones of October. And the archbishop soon after, on the self-same day, sang mass therewith: and then thereafter was honourably entertained by the same pope, and also himself took the pall from St. Peter's altar;

[*] Of Canterbury.   [†] Of York.
[‡] Canterbury.   [§] Of Elmham.

and then afterwards he blithely went home to his country. And abbat Leofwine, who had been unjustly driven out from Ely, was his companion; and he cleared himself of everything that was said against him, as the pope instructed him, in the presence of the archbishop, and of all the fellowship which was with him.

A. 1022. And afterwards with the pall he there performed mass as the pope instructed him: and he feasted after that with the pope; and afterwards went home with a full blessing.

A. 1023. This year king Canute came again to England, and Thurkyl and he were reconciled; and he committed Denmark and his son to the keeping of Thurkyl; and the king took Thurkyl's son with him to England. This year died archbishop Wulfstan:* and Elfric succeeded him; and archbishop Ethelnoth blessed him at Canterbury. This year king Canute, within London, in St. Paul's minster, gave full leave to archbishop Ethelnoth and Bishop Brithwine,† and to all the servants of God who were with them, that they might take up from the tomb the archbishop St. Elphege. And they then did so, on the sixth before the Ides of June. And the illustrious king, and the archbishop and suffragan bishops, and earls, and very many clergy, and also laity, carried, in a ship, his holy body over the Thames to Southwark, and there delivered the holy martyr to the archbishop and his companions; and they then, with a worshipful band and sprightly joy, bore him to Rochester. Then, on the third day, came Emma the lady, with her royal child Harda-Canute: and then they all, with much state and bliss, and songs of praise, bore the holy archbishop into Canterbury; and then worshipfully brought him into Christ's Church, on the third before the Ides of June. Again, after that, on the eighth day, the seventeenth before the Kalends of July, archbishop Ethelnoth, and bishop Elfsy,‡ and bishop Brithwine, and all those who were with them, deposited St. Elphege's holy body on the north side of Christ's altar, to the glory of God, and the honour of the holy archbishop, and the eternal health of all who there daily seek to his holy body with a devout heart and with all humility. God Almighty have mercy on all Christian men, through St. Elphege's holy merits.

* Of York.　　† Of Sherborne.　　‡ Of Winchester.

A. 1023. And he caused St. Elphege's remains to be borne from London to Canterbury.

A. 1023. And the same year archbishop Ethelnoth bore St. Elphege's, the archbishop's, remains to Canterbury, from London.

A. 1024.

A. 1025. This year king Canute went to Denmark, with his ships, to the holm by the holy river. And there came against him Ulf and Eglaf, and a very great army, as well a land-army as a fleet from Sweden. And there very many men were destroyed on king Canute's side, as well of Danish-men as of English: and the Swedes had possession of the place of carnage.

A. 1026. This year bishop Elfric* went to Rome, and received his pall of Pope John, on the 2d before the Ides of November.

A. 1027

A. 1028. This year king Canute went from England, with fifty ships of English thanes, to Norway, and drove king Olave out of the land, and possessed himself of all that land.

A. 1029. This year king Canute came home again to England. And so soon as he came to England, he gave to Christ-Church at Canterbury the haven at Sandwich, and all the dues that arise thereof, on either side of the haven : so that, lo! when the flood is all at the highest, and all at the fullest, if a ship be floating so nigh the land as it nighest may, and there be a man standing in the ship, and he have a taper ax in his . . . .

A. 1030.' This year was king Olave slain in Norway by his own people ; and afterwards was sainted. And in this year, before that, died Hacon, the doughty earl, at sea.

A. 1030. This year came king Olave again into Norway, and the people gathered against him, and fought against him ; and he was there slain.

A. 1031. This year king Canute went to Rome. And so soon as he came home then went he into Scotland : and the king of the Scots, Malcolm [II.], submitted to him, and became his man, but that he held only a little while, and two other kings, Macbeth and Jehmar. And Robert, earl of Normandy, went to Jerusalem, and there died ; and William, who was afterwards king in England, succeeded to Normandy, though he was a child.

* Of York.

A. 1032. In this year appeared the wild fire, such as no man before remembered; and moreover on all sides it did harm, in many places. And in the same year died Elfsy,* bishop at Winchester; and Alwyn, the king's priest, succeeded thereto.

A. 1033. This year died bishop Leofsy, and his body rests at Worcester: and Brihtege was raised to his see.† In this year died Merewith bishop of Somerset ;‡ and he is buried at Glastonbury.

A. 1034. This year died bishop Etheric,§ and he lies at Ramsey. This same year died Malcolm [II.], king in Scotland.

A. 1035. This year died king Canute; and Harold, his son, succeeded to the kingdom. He departed at Shaftesbury, on the 2d before the Ides of November; and they bore him thence to Winchester, and there they buried him. And Elfgive, Emma, the lady, then sat there within: and Harold, who said that he was son of Canute and of the other Elfgive, though it was not true; he sent thither, and caused to be taken from her all the best treasures, which she could not withhold, that king Canute had possessed; and nevertheless she still sat there within, as long as she could.

A. 1036. This year Alfred the innocent etheling, son of king Ethelred, came in hither, and would go to his mother, who sat at Winchester; but that neither Godwin the earl, nor the other men who had much power, would allow him because the cry was then greatly in favour of Harold, though that was unjust.

But Godwin him then let,
and him in bonds set;   [ed;
and his companions he dispers-
and some divers ways slew; .
some they for money sold,
some cruelly slaughtered,
some did they bind,
some did they blind,
some did they mutilate,
some did they scalp:
nor was a bloodier deed
done in this land
since the Danes came,
and here accepted peace.
Now is our trust in
the beloved God,
that they are in bliss,
blithely with Christ,
The etheling still lived,
who were without guilt
so miserably slain.
every ill they him vowed,
until it was decreed
that he should be led

* Godwin and Dugdale make Elfsy or Elsinus. to be translated to Canterbury, 1038.   † Worcester.   ‡ Wells.   § Of Dorchester.

to Ely-bury,	After that him they buried,
thus bound.	as well was his due
Soon as he came to land,	full worthily,
in the ship he was blinded;	as he worthy was,
and him thus blind	at the west end,
they brought to the monks:	the steeple well-nigh,
and he there abode	in the south aisle.
the while that he lived.	His soul is with Christ.

A. 1036. This year died king Canute at Shaftesbury, and he is buried at Winchester in the Old-minster: and he was king over all England very nigh twenty years. And soon after his decease there was a meeting of all the witan at Oxford; and Leofric the earl, and almost all the thanes north of the Thames, and the 'lithsmen' at London, chose Harold for chief of all England, him and his brother Hardecanute who was in Denmark. And Godwin the earl and all the chief men of Wessex withstood it as long as they could; but they were unable to effect any thing in opposition to it. And then it was decreed that Elfgive, Hardecanute's mother, should dwell at Winchester with the king's, her son's, household, and hold all Wessex in his power; and Godwin the earl was their man. Some men said of Harold that he was son of king Canute and of Elfgive daughter of Elfelm the ealdorman, but it seemed quite incredible to many men; and he was nevertheless full king over all England.

A. 1037. This year was Harold chosen king over all, and Hardecanute forsaken, because he stayed too long in Denmark; and then they drove out his mother Elfgive, the queen, without any kind of mercy, against the stormy winter: and she came then to Bruges beyond sea; and Baldwin the earl* there well received her, and there kept her the while she had need. And before, in this year, died Eafy the noble dean at Evesham.

A. 1037. This year was driven out Elfgive, king Canute's relict; she was king Hardecanute's mother; and she then sought the protection of Baldwin south of the sea, and he gave her a dwelling in Bruges, and protected and kept her, the while that she there was.

A. 1038. This year died Ethelnoth the good archbishop,† and bishop Ethelric in Sussex,‡ who desired of God that he would not let him live, any while, after his beloved father Ethelnoth; and accordingly, within seven days after, he departed, and bishop Elfric in East-Anglia,§ and bishop Briteagus in Worcestershire on the 13th before the Kalends of January. And then bishop Eadsine succeeded to the arch-

* Of Flanders.   † Of Canterbury   ‡ Selsey.   § Elmham.

bishopric, and Grinketel to the bishopric in Sussex, and
bishop Living to Worcestershire and to Gloucestershire.

A. 1038. This year died Ethelnoth, the good archbishop, on the Kalends of November, and a little after, Ethelric bishop in Sussex, and then
before Christmas, Briteagus bishop in Worcestershire, and soon after, Elfric
bishop in East-Anglia.

A. 1039. This year was the great wind: and bishop
Brithmar died at Lichfield. And the Welsh slew Edwin
brother of Leofric the earl, and Thurkil, and Elfget, and
very many good men with them. And this year also came
Hardecanute to Bruges, where his mother was.

A. 1039. This year king Harold died at Oxford, on the 16th before the
Kalends of April, and he was buried at Westminster. And he ruled England four years and sixteen weeks; and in his days sixteen ships were retained in pay, at the rate of eight marks for each rower, in like manner as had
been before done in the days of king Canute. And in this same year came
king Hardecanute to Sandwich, seven days before midsummer. And he was
soon acknowledged as well by English as by Danes; though his advisers
afterwards grievously requited it, when they decreed that seventy-two ships
should be retained in pay, at the rate of eight marks for each rower. And
in this same year the sester of wheat went up to fifty-five pence, and even
further.

A. 1040. This year died king Harold. Then sent they
after Hardecanute to Bruges; thinking that they did well.
And he then came hither with sixty ships before midsummer,
and then imposed a very heavy tribute, so that it could hardly
be levied; that was eight marks for each rower, and all were
then averse to him who before had desired him; and moreover he did nothing royal during his whole reign. He
caused the dead Harold to be taken up, and had him cast into
a fen. This year archbishop Eadsine went to Rome.

A. 1040. This year was the tribute paid; that was twenty-one
thousand pounds and ninety-nine pounds. And after that they paid to
thirty-two ships, eleven thousand and forty-eight pounds. And, in
this same year, came Edward, son of king Ethelred, hither to land, from
Weal-land; he was brother of king Hardecanute: they were both sons of
Elfgive; Emma, who was daughter of earl Richard.

A. 1041. This year Hardecanute caused all Worcestershire
to be ravaged, on account of his two household servants, who
demanded the heavy impost; when the people slew them in the
town within the minster. This year, soon after, came from
beyond sea Edward, his brother on the mother's side, king

Ethelred's son, who before for many years had been driven
from his country; and yet was he sworn king: and he
then abode thus in his brother's family while he lived.
And in this year also Hardecanute betrayed Eadulf the earl,[*]
while under his protection : and he became then a belier of
his "wed." And this year bishop Egelric[†] was ordained at
York, on the 3rd before the Ides of January.

A. 1041. This year died king Hardecanute at Lambeth, on the 6th before
the Ides of June: and he was king over all England two years wanting ten
days; and he is buried in the Old-minster at Winchester with king Canute
his father. And his mother, for his soul, gave to the New-minster the
head of St. Valentine the martyr. And before he was buried, all people
chose Edward for king .at London : may he hold it the while that God
shall grant it to him ! And all that year was a very heavy time, in many
things and divers, as well in respect to ill seasons as to the fruits of the
earth. And so much cattle perished in the year as no man before remembered, as well through various diseases as through tempests. And in this
same time died Elsinus abbat of Peterborough ; and then Arnwius the monk
was chosen abbat, because he was a very good man, and of great simplicity.

A. 1042. This year died king Hardecanute as he stood at
his drink, and he suddenly fell to the earth with a terrible
convulsion : and then they who were there nigh took hold of
him ; and he after that spake not one word : and he died on
the 6th before the Ides of June. And all people then acknowledged Edward for king, as was his true natural right.

A. 1043. This year was Edward consecrated king at Winchester, on the first day of Easter, with much pomp ; and
then was Easter on the third before the Nones of April.
Archbishop Eadsine consecrated him, and before all the people
well instructed him ; and for his own need, and all the people's, well admonished him. And Stigand the priest was
blessed bishop of the East-Angles.[‡] And soon after, the
king caused all the lands which his mother possessed to be
seized into his hands, and took from her all that she possessed in gold, and in silver, and in things unspeakable, because she had before held it too closely with him. And soon
after, Stigand was deposed from his bishopric, and all that
he possessed was seized into the king's hands, because he
was nearest to his mother's counsel, and she went just as he
advised her, as people thought.

---

[*] Of Northumbria.   [†] Of Durham.   [‡] Elmham.

A. 1043. This year was Edward consecrated king at Winchester on the first day of Easter. And this year, fourteen days before Andrew's-mass, the king was advised to ride from Gloucester, and Leofric the earl, and Godwin the earl, and Sigwarth [Siward] the earl, with their followers, to Winchester, unawares upon the lady [Emma]; and they bereaved her of all the treasures which she possessed, they were not to be told, because before that she had been very hard with the king her son; inasmuch as she had done less for him than he would, before he was king, and also since: and they suffered her after that to remain therein.

This year king Edward took the daughter [Edgitha] of Godwin the earl for his wife. And in this same year died bishop Brithwin, and he held the bishopric thirty-eight years, that was the bishopric of Sherborne, and Herman the king's priest succeeded to the bishopric. And in this year Wulfric was hallowed abbat of St. Augustine's at Christmas, on Stephen's mass-day, by leave of the king, and, on account of his great infirmity, of abbat Elfstan.

A. 1044. This year archbishop Eadsine* gave up the bishopric by reason of his infirmity, and he blessed thereto Siward abbat of Abingdon, as bishop, by the king's leave and counsel, and Godwin's the earl's: it was known to few men else before it was done, because the archbishop thought that some other man would obtain or buy it whom he could less trust in, and be pleased with, if more men should know of it. And in this year was a very great famine over all England, and corn was so dear as no man before remembered; so that the sester of wheat went up to sixty pence, and even further. And in the same year the king went out to Sandwich with thirty-five ships: and Athelstan the churchwarden obtained the abbacy at Abingdon. And Stigand re-obtained his bishopric. And in the same year king Edward took Edgitha, daughter of Godwin the earl, to wife, ten days before Candlemas.

A. 1044. This year died Living bishop in Devonshire, and Leofric succeeded thereto: he was the king's priest. And in this same year died Elfstan abbat of St. Augustine's, on the third before the Nones of July. And in this same year was outlawed Osgod Clapa.

A. 1045. In this year died bishop Brithwin† on the 10th before the Kalends of May; and king Edward gave the bishopric to Herman his priest. And in the same summer king Edward went out with his ships to Sandwich; and there so great a force was gathered, that no man had.

* Of Canterbury.
† Of Ramsbury, afterwards removed to Salisbury.

E E

seen a greater fleet in this land. And in this same year died bishop Living* on the 13th before the Kalends of April; and the king gave the bishopric to Leofric his priest. This year died Elfward bishop of London, on the 8th before the Kalends of August. He was first abbat of Evesham, and greatly advanced the minster whilst he was there. He went then to Ramsey, and there gave up his life. And Manni was chosen abbat,† and ordained on the 4th before the Ides of August. And in this year was driven out Gunnilde, the noble woman, king Canute's niece; and she, after that, stayed at Bruges a long while, and afterwards went to Denmark.

A. 1045. This year died Grimkytel bishop in Sussex, and Heca the king's priest succeeded thereto. And in this year died Alwyn, bishop of Winchester, on the 4th before the Kalends of September; and Stigand, bishop to the north,‡ succeeded thereto. And in the same year Sweyn the earl went out to Baldwin's land§ to Bruges and abode there all the winter; and then in summer he went out.

A. 1046. In this year Sweyn the earl went into Wales, and Griffin the Northern king‖ went with him; and they delivered hostages to him. As he was on his way homewards, then commanded he to be brought unto him the abbess of Leominster: and he had her as long as he listed; and after that he let her go home. And in this same year Osgod Clapa was outlawed before mid-winter. And in this same year, after Candlemas, came the severe winter, with frost and with snow, and with all kinds of tempestuous weather, so that there was no man then alive who could remember so severe a winter as this was, as well through mortality of men as murrain of cattle; even birds and fishes perished through the great cold and famine.

A. 1046. This year died Brithwin, bishop in Wiltshire, and Herman was appointed to his see. In that year king Edward gathered a large ship-force at Sandwich, on account of the threatening of Magnus in Norway: but his and Sweyn's contention in Denmark hindered his coming here.

A. 1046. This year died Athelstan, abbat of Abingdon, and Sparhawk, monk of St. Edmund's-bury, succeeded him. And in this same year died bishop Siward, and archbishop Eadsine again obtained the whole bishopric.¶ And in this same year Lothen and Irling came with twenty-five ships to Sandwich, and there took unspeakable booty, in men, and in

* Of Crediton.   † Of Evesham.   ‡ Of Elmham.
§ Flanders.   ‖ Of North Wales.   ¶ Of Canterbury.

gold, and in silver, so that no man knew how much it all was. And they then went about Thanet, and would there do the like; but the land's-folk strenuously withstood them, and denied them as well landing as water; and thence utterly put them to flight. And they betook themselves then into Essex, and there they ravaged, and took men, and property, and whatsoever they might find. And they betook themselves then east to Baldwine's land, and there they sold what they had plundered; and after that went their way east, whence they before had come.

A. 1046. In this year was the great synod at St. Remi's [Rheims]. Thereat was Leo the pope, and the archbishop of Burgundy [Lyons], and the archbishop of Besançon, and the archbishop of Treves, and the archbishop of Rheims; and many men besides, both clergy and laity. And king Edward sent thither bishop Dudoc,* and Wulfric abbat of St. Augustine's,+ and abbat Elfwin,+ that they might make known to the king what should be there resolved on for Christendom. And in this same year king Edward went out to Sandwich with a great fleet. And Sweyn the earl, son of Godwin the earl, came in to Bosham with seven ships; and he obtained the king's protection, and he was promised that he should be held worthy of every thing which he before possessed. Then Harold the earl, his brother, and Beorn the earl contended that he should not be held worthy of any of the things which the king had granted to them: but a protection of four days was appointed him to go to his ships. Then befell it during this, that word came to the king that hostile ships lay westward, and were ravaging. Then went Godwin the earl west about with two of the king's ships; the one commanded Harold the earl, and the other Tosty his brother; and forty-two of the people's ships. Then Harold the earl was removed from the king's ship which Harold the earl before had commanded. Then went they west to Pevensey, and lay there weather-bound. Upon this, after two days, then came Sweyn the earl thither, and spoke with his father, and with Beorn the earl, and begged of Beorn that he would go with him to the king at Sandwich, and help him to the king's friendship: and he granted it. Then went they as if they would go to the king. Then whilst they were riding, then begged Sweyn of him that he would go with him to his ships: saying that his seamen would depart from him unless he should at the soonest come thither. Then went they both where his ships lay. When they came thither, then begged Sweyn the earl of him that he would go with him on ship-board. He strenuously refused, so long as until his seamen seized him, and threw him into the boat, and bound him, and rowed to the ship, and put him there aboard. Then they hoisted up their sails and ran west to Exmouth, and had him with them until they slew him: and they took the body and buried it in a church. And then his friends and litsmen came from London, and took him up, and bore him to Winchester to the Old-minster: and he is there buried with king Canute his uncle. And Sweyn went then east to Baldwin's land, and sat down there all the winter at Bruges, with his full protection. And in the same year died Eadnoth [II.] bishop‡ of the north; and Ulf was made bishop.

A. 1047. In this year died bishop Grinketel; he was

---

* Of Wells.   + Of Ramsey.   ‡ Of Dorchester.

bishop* in Sussex, and he lies in Christ-Church, at Canterbury; and king Edward gave the bishopric to Heca his priest. And in this same year died bishop Alwyn† on the 4th before the Kalends of September; and king Edward gave the bishopric to bishop Stigand. And Athelstan abbat of Abingdon died in the same year, on the 4th before the Kalends of April: then was Easter-day on the 3rd before the Nones of April. And there was over all England a very great mortality in the same year.

A. 1047. This year died Living the eloquent bishop, on the 10th before the Kalends of April, and he had three bishoprics; one in Devonshire, and in Cornwall, and in Worcester. Then Leofric‡ succeeded to Devonshire and to Cornwall, and bishop Aldred to Worcester. And in this year Osgod, the master of the horse, was outlawed: and Magnus§ won Denmark.

A. 1047. In this year there was a great council in London at Mid-lent, and nine ships of lightermen were discharged, and five remained behind. In this same year came Sweyn the earl into England. And in this same year was the great synod at Rome, and king Edward sent thither bishop Heroman and bishop Aldred; and they came thither on Easter eve. And afterwards the pope held a synod at Vercelli, and bishop Ulf came thereto; and well nigh would they have broken his staff, if he had not given very great gifts; because he knew not how to do his duty so well as he should. And in this year died archbishop Eadsine, on the 4th before the Kalends of November.

A. 1048. In this year was a great earthquake wide throughout England. In the same year Sandwich and the Isle of Wight were ravaged, and the chief men that were there slain. And after that king Edward and the earls went out with their ships. And in the same year bishop Siward resigned the bishopric on account of his infirmity, and went to Abingdon, and archbishop Eadsine again received the bishopric:| and he [Siward] died within eight weeks after, on the 10th before the Kalends of November.

A. 1048. This year was the severe winter: and this year died Alwyn, bishop of Winchester, and bishop Stigand was raised to his see. And before that, in the same year, died Grinketel, bishop in Sussex, and Heca the priest succeeded to the bishopric. And Sweyn also sent hither, begging assistance against Magnus, king of Norway; that fifty ships should be sent to his aid. But it seemed unadvisable to all people: and it was then hindered by reason that Magnus had a great ship force. And he then drove out Sweyn, and with much man-slaying won the land: and the

---

* Of Selsey.   † Of Winchester.
‡ Leofric removed the see to Exeter.
§ King of Norway. || Of Canterbury.

Danes paid him much money and acknowledged him as king. And that same year Magnus died.

A. 1048. In this year king Edward appointed Robert, of London, archbishop of Canterbury, during Lent. And in the same Lent he went to Rome after his pall : and the king gave the bishopric of London to Sparhafoc abbat of Abingdon ; and the king gave the abbacy of Abingdon to bishop Rodulf, his kinsman. Then came the archbishop from Rome one day before St. Peter's-mass-eve, and entered on his archiepiscopal see at Christ's Church on St. Peter's mass-day ; and soon after went to the king. Then came abbat Sparhafoc to him with the king's writ and seal, in order that he should consecrate him bishop of London. Then the archbishop refused, and said that the pope had forbidden it him. Then went the abbat to the archbishop again for that purpose, and there desired episcopal ordination ; and the archbishop constantly refused him, and said that the pope had forbidden it him. Then went the abbat to London, and occupied the bishopric which the king before had granted him, with his full leave, all the summer and the harvest. And then came Eustace* from beyond sea soon after the bishop, and went to the king, and spoke with him that which he then would, and went then homeward. When he came to Canterbury, east, then took he refreshment there, and his men, and went to Dover. When he was some mile or more on this side of Dover, then he put on his breast-plate, and so did all his companions, and went to Dover. When they came thither, then would they lodge themselves where they chose. Then came one of his men, and would abide in the house of a householder against his will, and wounded the householder ; and the householder slew the other. Then Eustace got upon his horse, and his companions upon theirs ; and they went to the householder, and slew him within his own dwelling ; and they went up towards the town, and slew, as well within as without, more than twenty men. And the townsmen slew nineteen men on the other side, and wounded they knew not how many. And Eustace escaped with a few men, and went again to the king, and made known to him, in part, how they had fared. And the king became very wroth with the townsmen. And the king sent off Godwin the earl, and bade him go into Kent in a hostile manner to Dover : for Eustace had made it appear to the king, that it had been more the fault of the townsmen than his : but it was not so. And the earl would not consent to the inroad, because he was loath to injure his own people. Then the king sent after all his council, and bade them come to Gloucester, nigh the aftermass of St. Mary. Then had the Welshmen erected a castle in Herefordshire among the people of Sweyn the earl, and wrought every kind of harm and disgrace to the king's men there about which they could. Then came Godwin the earl, and Sweyn the earl, and Harold the earl, together at Beverstone, and many men with them, in order that they might go to their royal lord, and to all the peers who were assembled with him, in order that they might have the advice of the king and his aid, and of all this council, how they might avenge the king's disgrace, and the whole nation's. Then were the Welshmen with the king beforehand, and accused the earls, so that they might not come within his eyes' sight ; because they said that they were coming thither in order to betray the king. Thither had come

* Earl of Boulogne.

Siward the earl * and Leofric the earl,† and much people with them, from the north, to the king ; and it was made known to the earl Godwin and his sons, that the king and the men who were with him, were taking counsel concerning them : and they arrayed themselves on the other hand resolutely, though it were loathful to them that they should stand against their royal lord.   Then the peers on either side decreed that every kind of evil should cease : and the king gave the peace of God and his full friendship to either side.   Then the king and his peers decreed that a council of all the nobles should be held for the second time in London at the harvest equinox ; and the king directed the army to be called out, as well south of the Thames as north, all that was in any way most eminent.   Then declared they Sweyn the earl an outlaw, and summoned Godwin the earl and Harold the earl, to the council, as quickly as they could effect it.   When they had come thither, then were they summoned into the council.   Then required he safe conduct and hostages, so that he might come, unbetrayed, into the council and out of the council.   Then the king demanded all the thanes whom the earls before had ; and they granted them all into his hands.   Then the king sent again to them, and commanded them that they should come with twelve men to the king's council.   Then the earl again required safe conduct and hostages, that he might defend himself against each of those things which were laid to him.   Then were the hostages refused him ; and he was allowed a safe conduct for five nights to go out of the land.   And then Godwin the earl and Sweyn the earl went to Bosham, and shoved out their ships, and betook themselves beyond sea, and sought Baldwin's protection, and abode there all the winter.   And Harold the earl went west to Ireland, and was there all the winter within the king's protection.   And soon after this happened, then put away the king the lady who had been consecrated his queen,‡ and caused to be taken from her all which she possessed, in land, and in gold, and in silver, and in all things, and delivered her to his sister at Wherwell.   And abbat Sparhafoc was then driven out of the bishopric of London, and William the king's priest was ordained thereto.   And then Odda was appointed earl over Devonshire, and over Somerset, and over Dorset, and over the Welsh. And Algar, the son of Leofric the earl, was appointed to the earldom which Harold before held.

A. 1049.   In this year the emperor gathered a countless force against Baldwin§ of Bruges : by reason that he had destroyed the palace at Nimeguen, and also, that he had done many other injuries to him : the force was not to be told which he had gathered.   There was Leo [IX.] the pope of Rome, and many great men of many nations.   He sent also to king Edward, and begged the aid of his ships, in order that he should not suffer him to escape from him by water.   And he went then to Sandwich, and there continued lying with a great fleet, until the emperor obtained of Bald-

---

* Of Northumbria.   † Of Mercia.
‡ Editha.   § Earl of Flanders.

win all that he would. Thither came back again Sweyn
the earl to king Edward, and requested land of him, from
which he might maintain himself. But Harold his brother
contended, and Beorn the earl, that they should not give
up to him any thing which the king had given to them.
He came hither with false pretences ; saying that he would
be his man, and begged of Beorn the earl that he would aid
him : but the king refused him every thing. Then went
Sweyn to his ships at Bosham ; and Godwin the earl went
from Sandwich with forty-two ships to Pevensey, and Beorn
the earl went forth with him ; and then the king gave leave
to all the Mercians to go home : and they did so. Then was
it made known to the king, that Osgod lay at Ulps with
thirty-nine ships. Then the king sent after the ships which
lay at the Nore, that he might send after him. But
Osgod fetched his wife from Bruges, and went back again
with six ships ; and the others landed in Essex, at Eadulf-
ness, and there did harm, and went again to their ships.
Then lay Godwin the earl and Beorn the earl at Pevensey,
with their ships. Then came Sweyn the earl with fraud,
and begged of Beorn the earl that he would be his companion
to the king at Sandwich ; saying that he would swear oaths
to him, and be faithful to him. Then Beorn concluded that,
on account of their kindred, he would not deceive him. Then
took he three companions with him, and they then rode to
Bosham, as if they would go to Sandwich, where Sweyn's
ships lay. And they soon bound him, and led him on ship-
board ; and then went to Dartmouth, and there caused him to
be slain and deeply buried. But him his kinsman Harold
thence fetched and bore to Winchester, and there buried with
king Canute his uncle. And then the king and all the army
declared Sweyn an outlaw. Eight ships he had before he
murdered Beorn ; after that, all forsook him except two :
and then he went to Bruges, and there abode with Baldwin.
And in this year died Eadnoth, the good bishop, in Oxfordshire,* and Oswy abbat of Thorney, and Wulfnoth abbat of
Westminster : and king Edward gave the bishopric to Ulf
his priest, and unworthily bestowed it. And in this same
year king Edward discharged nine ships from pay ; and
they went away, ships and all ; and five ships remained be-

* Dorchester.

hind, and the king promised them twelve months' pay. And in the same year went bishop Heroman[*] and bishop Aldred[†] to Rome, to the pope, on the king's errand.

A. 1049. This year Sweyn came again to Denmark, and Harold, uncle of Magnus, went to Norway after Magnus was dead ; and the Normans acknowledged him : and he sent hither to land concerning peace. And Sweyn also sent from Denmark, and begged of king Edward the aid of his ships. They were to be at least fifty ships : but all people opposed it. And this year also there was an earthquake, on the Kalends of May, in many places in Worcester, and in Wick, and in Derby, and elsewhere ; and also there was a great mortality among men, and murrain among cattle : and moreover, the wild-fire did much evil in Derbyshire and elsewhere.

A. 1050. In this year came the bishops home from Rome: and Sweyn the earl was inlawed. And in this same year died archbishop Eadsine, on the fourth before the Kalends of November ; and also, in this same year, Alfric archbishop of York, on the eleventh before the Kalends of February ; and his body lies at Peterborough. Then king Edward held a council in London at Mid-lent, and appointed Robert archbishop of Canterbury, and abbat Sparhafoc to London; and gave to bishop Rodulf, his kinsman, the abbacy at Abingdon. And the same year he discharged all the lightermen from pay.

A. 1050. Thither also came Sweyn the earl, who before had gone from this land to Denmark, and who there had ruined himself with the Danes. He came thither with false pretences ; saying that he would again be obedient to the king. And Beorn the earl promised him that he would be of assistance to him. Then, after the reconciliation of the emperor and of Baldwin, many of the ships went home, and the king remained behind at Sandwich with a few ships ; and Godwin the earl also went with forty-two ships from Sandwich to Pevensey, and Beorn the earl went with him. Then was it made known to the king that Osgod lay at Ulps with thirty-nine ships ; and the king then sent after the ships which before had gone home, that he might send after him. And Osgod fetched his wife from Bruges, and they went back again with six ships. And the others landed in Sussex[‡] at Eadulf-ness, and there did harm, and went again to their ships : and then a strong wind came against them, so that they were all destroyed, except four, whose crews were slain beyond sea. While Godwin the earl and Beorn the earl lay at Pevensey, then came Sweyn the earl, and begged Beorn the earl, with fraud, who was his uncle's son, that he would be his companion to the king at Sandwich, and better his affairs with him. He went then, on account of the relationship, with three companions, with him ; and he led him then towards Bosham, where his ships lay : and then they bound him, and led him on ship-board. Then went he thence with

---

[*] Of Ramsbury.   Heroman removed the see to Salisbury.
[†] Of Worcester.   [‡] Essex.

him to Dartmouth, and there ordered him to be slain, and deeply buried. Afterwards he was found, and borne to Winchester, and buried with king Canute his uncle. A little before that, the men of Hastings and thereabout, fought two of his ships with their ships; and slew all the men, and brought the ships to Sandwich to the king. Eight ships he had before he betrayed Beorn; after that all forsook him except two. In the same year arrived in the Welsh Axa, from Ireland, thirty-six ships, and thereabout did harm, with the help of Griffin the Welsh king. The people were gathered together against them; bishop Aldred * was also there with them; but they had too little power. And they came unawares upon them at very early morn; and there they slew many good men, and the others escaped with the bishop: this was done on the fourth before the Kalends of August. This year died, in Oxfordshire, Oswy abbat of Thorney, and Wulfnoth abbat of Westminster; and Ulf the priest was appointed as pastor to the bishopric which Eadnoth had held; but he was after that driven away; because he did nothing bishop-like therein: so that it shameth us now to tell more about it. And bishop Siward died: he lieth at Abingdon. And this year was consecrated the great minster at Rheims: there was pope Leo [IX.] and the emperor; † and there they held a great synod concerning God's service. St. Leo the pope presided at the synod: it is difficult to have a knowledge of the bishops who came there, and how many abbats: and hence, from this land were sent two—from St. Augustine's and from Ramsey.

A. 1051. In this year came archbishop Robert hither over sea with his pall. And in this same year were banished Godwin, the earl, and all his sons from England; and he went to Bruges and his wife, and his three sons, Sweyn, and Tosty, and Grith: and Harold and Leofwine went to Ireland, and there dwelt during the winter. And in this same year died the old lady, king Edward's mother, and Hardecanute's, who was called Emma, on the second before the Ides of March; and her body lies in the Old-minster,‡ with king Canute.

A. 1051. In this year died Eadsine archbishop of Canterbury; and the king gave to Robert the Frenchman, who before had been bishop of London, the archbishopric. And Sparhafoc abbat of Abingdon succeeded to the bishopric of London; and it was afterwards taken from him before he was consecrated. And bishop Heroman and bishop Aldred went to Rome.

A. 1052. This year came Harold, the earl, from Ireland, with his ships to the mouth of the Severn, nigh the boundaries of Somerset and Devonshire, and there greatly ravaged; and the people of the land drew together against him, as well from Somerset as from Devonshire; and he put them to flight, and there slew more than thirty good thanes, besides

* Of Worcester.   † Hen. III.   ‡ Winchester.

other people : and soon after that he went about Penwithstert. And then king Edward caused forty vessels to be
fitted out. They lay at Sandwich many weeks ; they were
to lie in wait for Godwin, the earl, who had been at Bruges
during the winter ; and, notwithstanding, he came hither to
land first, so that they knew it not. And during the time
that he was here in the land, he enticed to him all the men
of Kent, and all the boatmen from Hastings and everywhere there by the sea-coast, and all the East-end, and Sussex, and Surrey, and much else in addition thereto. Then all
declared that they with him would die and live. When the
fleet which lay at Sandwich, learned this concerning Godwin's voyage, then set they out after him. And he escaped
them, and concealed himself wherever he then could ; and
the fleet went again to Sandwich, and so homeward to London. Then when Godwin learned that the fleet which lay
at Sandwich was gone home, then went he once more to the
Isle of Wight, and lay thereabout by the sea-coast so long as
until they came together, he and his son earl Harold. And
they did not much harm after they came together, except
that they seized provisions : but they enticed to them all the
land-folk by the sea-coast and also up the country ; and they
went towards Sandwich, and collected ever forth with them
all the boatmen which they met with, and then came to
Sandwich, with an overflowing army. When king Edward
learned that, then sent he up after more help ; but they came
very late. And Godwin advanced ever towards London
with his fleet until he came to Southwark, and there abode
some time until the flood-tide came up. During that time
he also treated with the townsmen, that they should do
almost all that he would. When he had mustered all
his host, then came the flood-tide ; and they then soon drew
their anchors, and held their way through the bridge by the
south shore, and the land-force came from above, and arrayed
themselves along the strand : and they then inclined with
the ships towards the north shore, as if they would hem the
king's ships about. The king also had a great land-force on
his side, in addition to his shipmen ; but it was loathful to
almost all of them that they should fight against men of
their own race ; for there was little else there which was of
much account except Englishmen, on either side ; and more-

over they were unwilling that this land should be still more
exposed to outlandish men, by reason that they themselves
destroyed each other. Then decreed they that wise men
should be sent between them ; and they settled a truce on
either side. And Godwin landed, and Harold his son, and
from their fleet as many as to them seemed fitting. Then
there was a general council : and they gave his earldom
clean to Godwin, as full and as free as he before possessed it,
and to his sons also all that they before possessed, and to his
wife and his daughter as full and as free as they before possessed it. And they then established between them full
friendship, and to all the people they promised good law.
And then they outlawed all the Frenchmen who before had
instituted unjust law, and judged unjust judgments, and
counselled ill counsel in this land ; except so many as they
agreed upon, whom the king liked to have with him, who
were true to him and to all his people. And bishop Robert,*
and bishop William,† and bishop Ulf,‡ with difficulty
escaped, with the Frenchmen who were with them, and thus
got over sea. And Godwin, the earl, and Harold, and the
queen,§ sat down in their possessions. Sweyn had gone
before this to Jerusalem from Bruges ; and he died on his
way home at Constantinople on Michael's-mass. It was on
the Monday after St. Mary's-mass that Godwin with his
ships came to Southwark ; and the morning after, on the
Tuesday, they were reconciled, as it here before stands.
Godwin then grew sick soon after he landed ; and he afterwards departed : but he did all too little penance for the
property of God which he held belonging to many holy
places. And the same year came the strong wind, on Thomas's-mass-night, and did much harm in many parts. Moreover Rees, the Welsh king's‖ brother, was slain.

A. 1052. This year died Alfric, archbishop of York, a very pious man,
and wise. And in the same year king Edward abolished the tribute,
which king Ethelred had before imposed : that was in the nine-and-
thirtieth year after he had begun it. That tax distressed all the English
nation during so long a time, as it here above is written ; that was ever before other taxes which were variously paid, and wherewith the people were
manifestly distressed. In the same year Eustace ¶ landed at Dover : he

* Of Canterbury.   † Of London.   ‡ Of Dorchester.
§ Editha.   ‖ Of South Wales.   ¶ Earl of Boulogne.

had king Edward's sister to wife. Then went his men inconsiderately
after quarters, and a certain man of the town they slew ; and another man
of the town their companion ; so that there lay seven of his companions.
And much harm was there done on either side, by horse and also by
weapons, until the people gathered together : and then they fled away
until they came to the king at Gloucester ; and he gave them protection.
When Godwin, the earl, understood that such things should have happened in his earldom, then began he to gather together people over all his
earldom,* and Sweyn, the earl, his son, over his, and Harold, his other son,
over his earldom ; and they all drew together in Gloucestershire, at Lang-
tree, a great force and countless, all ready for battle against the king, unless Eustace were given up, and his men placed in their hands, and also
the Frenchmen who were in the castle. This was done seven days before
the latter mass of St. Mary. Then was king Edward sitting at Gloucester.
Then sent he after Leofric, the earl,† and north after Siward the earl,‡ and
begged their forces. And then they came to him ; first with a moderate aid,
but after they knew how it was there, in the south, then sent they north over
all their earldoms, and caused to be ordered out a large force for the help
of their lord ; and Ralph, also, over his earldom : and then came they all
to Gloucester to help the king, though it might be late. Then were they
all so united in opinion with the king that they would have sought out
Godwin's forces if the king had so willed. Then thought some of them
that it would be a great folly that they should join battle ; because there
was nearly all that was most noble in England in the two armies, and they
thought that they should expose the land to our foes, and cause great destruction among ourselves. Then counselled they that hostages should be
given mutually ; and they appointed a term at London, and thither the
people were ordered out over all this north end, in Siward's earldom, and
in Leofric's, and also elsewhere ; and Godwin, the earl, and his sons were
to come there with their defence. Then came they to Southwark, and a
great multitude with them, from Wessex ; but his band continually dimin-
ished the longer he stayed. And they exacted pledges for the king from
all the thanes who were under Harold, the earl, his son ; and then they
outlawed Sweyn, the earl, his other son. Then did it not suit him to come
with a defence to meet the king, and to meet the army which was with him.
Then went he by night away ; and the king on the morrow held a council,
and, together with all the army, declared him an outlaw, him and all
his sons. And he went south to Thorney, and his wife, and Sweyn his son,
and Tosty and his wife, Baldwin's relation of Bruges, and Grith his son.
And Harold, the earl, and Leofwine, went to Bristol in the ship which
Sweyn, the earl, had before got ready for himself, and provisioned. And
the king sent bishop Aldred§ to London with a force ; and they were to
overtake him ere he came on ship-board : but they could not or they would
not. And he went out from Avonmouth, and met with such heavy weather
that he with difficulty got away ; and there he sustained much damage.
Then went he forth to Ireland when fit weather came. And Godwin,

---

* Godwin's earldom consisted of Wessex, Sussex, and Kent : Sweyn's
of Oxford, Gloucester, Hereford, Somerset, and Berkshire : and Harold's
of Essex, East-Anglia, Huntingdon. and Cambridgeshire.
   † Of Mercia.   ‡ Of Northumbria.   § Of Worcester.

and those who were with him, went from Thorney to Bruges, to Baldwin's
land, in one ship, with as much treasure as they might therein best stow for
each man.   It would have seemed wondrous to every man who was in
England if any one before that had said that it should end thus; for he had
been erewhile to that degree exalted, as if he ruled the king and all England ; and his sons were earls and the king's darlings, and his daughter
wedded and united to the king : she was brought to Wherwell, and they
delivered her to the abbess.   Then, soon, came William, the earl,* from
beyond sea, with a great band of Frenchmen; and the king received
him, and as many of his companions as it pleased him ; and let him away
again.   This same year was given to William, the priest, the bishopric of
London, which before had been given to Sparhafoc.

A. 1052. This year died Elfgive, the lady, relict of king Ethelred and
of king Canute, on the second before the Nones of March.   In the same
year Griffin, the Welsh king, plundered in Herefordshire, until he came
very nigh to Leominster ; and they gathered against him, as well the
landsmen as the Frenchmen of the castle, and there were slain of the
English very many good men, and also of the Frenchmen ; that was on
the same day, on which, thirteen years before, Eadwine had been slain by
his companions.

A. 1052. In this year died Elfgive Emma, king Edward's mother and
king Hardecanute's.   And in this same year, the king decreed, and his
council, that ships should proceed to Sandwich; and they set Ralph, the
earl, and Odda, the earl,† as head-men thereto.   Then Godwin, the earl,
went out from Bruges with his ships to Ysendyck, and left it one day before
Midsummer's-mass eve, so that he came to Ness, which is south of Romney.   Then came it to the knowledge of the earls out at Sandwich ; and
they then went out after the other ships, and a land-force was ordered out
against the ships.   Then during this, Godwin, the earl, was warned, and
then he went to Pevensey ; and the weather was very severe, so that
the earls could not learn what was become of Godwin, the earl.   And then
Godwin, the earl, went out again, until he came once more to Bruges ; and
the other ships returned again to Sandwich.   And then it was decreed that
the ships should return once more to London, and that other earls and
commanders should be appointed to the ships.   Then was it delayed so
long that the ship-force all departed, and all of them went home.   When
Godwin, the earl, learned that, then drew he up his sail, and his fleet, and
then went west direct to the Isle of Wight, and there landed and ravaged so
long there, until the people yielded them so much as they laid on them.
And then they went westward until they came to Portland, and there they
landed, and did whatsoever harm they were able to do.   Then was Harold
come out from Ireland with nine ships ; and then landed at Porlock, and
there much people was gathered against him ; but he failed not to procure
himself provisions.   He proceeded further, and slew there a great number
of the people, and took of cattle, and of men, and of property as it suited
him.   He then went eastward to his father : and then they both went eastward until they came to the Isle of Wight, and there took that which was
yet remaining for them.   And then they went thence to Pevensey, and
got away thence as many ships as were there fit for service, and so onwards

* Of Normandy.   † Of Devon.

until he came to Ness, and got all the ships which were in Romney, and in
Hythe, and in Folkstone.   And then they went east to Dover, and there
landed, and there took ships and hostages, as many as they would, and so
went to Sandwich and did "hand" the same ; and everywhere hostages
were given them, and provisions wherever they desired.   And then they
went to North-mouth, and so toward London ; and some of the ships went
within Sheppey, and there did much harm, and went their way to King's
Milton, and that they all burned, and betook themselves then toward
London after the earls.   When they came to London, there lay the king
and all the earls there against them, with fifty ships.   Then the earls sent
to the king, and required of him, that they might be held worthy of each
of those things which had been unjustly taken from them.   Then the king,
however, resisted some while ; so long as until the people who were with
the earl were much stirred against the king and against his people, so that
the earl himself with difficulty stilled the people.   Then bishop Stigand
interposed with God's help, and the wise men as well within the town as
without ; and they decreed that hostages should be set forth on either side:
and thus was it done.   When archbishop Robert and the Frenchmen
learned that, they took their horses and went, some west to Pentecost's
castle, some north to Robert's castle.   And archbishop Robert and bishop
Ulf went out at East-gate, and their companions, and slew and otherwise
injured many young men, and went their way direct to Eadulf's-ness ; and
he there put himself in a crazy ship, and went direct over sea, and left his
pall and all Christendom here on land, so as God would have it, inasmuch as
he had before obtained the dignity so as God would not have it.   Then there
was a great council proclaimed without London : and all the earls and the
chief men who were in this land were at the council.   There Godwin bore
forth his defence, and justified himself, before king Edward his lord, and
before all people of the land, that he was guiltless of that which was
laid against him, and against Harold his son, and all his children.   And
the king gave to the earl and his children his full friendship, and full earldom, and all that he before possessed, and to all the men who were with
him.   And the king gave to the lady* all that she before possessed.   And
they declared archbishop Robert utterly an outlaw, and all the Frenchmen, because they had made most of the difference between Godwin, the
earl, and the king.   And bishop Stigand obtained the archbishopric of
Canterbury.   In this same time Arnwy, abbot of Peterborough, left the
abbacy, in sound health, and gave it to Leofric the monk, by leave of the
king and of the monks ; and abbat Arnwy lived afterwards eight years.
And abbat Leofric then (enriched) the minster, so that it was called the
Golden-borough.   Then it waxed greatly, in land, and in gold, and in silver.

A. 1052.   And went so to the Isle of Wight, and there took all the ships
which could be of any service, and hostages, and betook himself so eastward.
And Harold had landed with nine ships at Porlock, and slew there much
people, and took cattle, and men, and property, and went his way eastward
to his father, and they both went to Romney, to Hythe, to Folkstone, to
Dover, to Sandwich, and ever they took all the ships which they found,
which could be of any service, and hostages, all as they proceeded ; and
went then to London.

* Editha.

A. 1053. In this year was the king at Winchester at Easter, and Godwin, the earl, with him, and Harold, the earl, his son, and Tosty. Then, on the second day of Easter, sat he with the king at the feast : then suddenly sank he down by the footstool, deprived of speech, and of all his power, and he was then carried into the king's chamber, and they thought it would pass over : but it did not so ; but he continued on, thus speechless and powerless, until the Thursday, and then resigned his life : and he lies there within the Old-minster. And his son Harold succeeded to his earldom, and resigned that which he before held ; and Elgar succeeded thereto. This same year died Wulfsy, bishop of Lichfield, and Leofwine, abbat of Coventry succeeded to the bishopric ; and Egelward, abbat of Glastonbury, died, and Godwin, abbat of Winchcomb. Moreover, the Welshmen slew a great number of the English people, of the wardmen, near Westbury. In this year there was no archbishop in this land ; but bishop Stigand held the bishopric of Canterbury at Christchurch, and Kynsey of York ; and Leofwine and Wulfwy went over sea, and caused themselves to be there ordained bishops ; Wulfwy obtained the bishopric which Ulf had,* he being yet living and driven from it.

A. 1053. This year was the great wind on Thomas's-mass-night, and also the whole midwinter there was much wind ; and it was decreed that Rees, the Welsh king's brother, should be slain, because he had done harm; and his head was brought to Gloucester on Twelfth-day eve. And the same year, before All Hallows-mass, died Wulfsy, bishop of Lichfield, and Godwin, abbat of Winchcomb, and Egelward, abbat of Glastonbury, all within one month, and Leofwine succeeded to the bishopric of Lichfield, and bishop Aldred† took the abbacy at Winchcomb, and Egelnoth succeeded to the abbacy at Glastonbury. And the same year died Elfric, Odda's brother at Deorhurst ; and his body resteth at Pershore. And the same year died Godwin the earl ; and he fell ill as he sat with the king at Winchester. And Harold his son succeeded to the earldom which his father before held ; and Elgar, the earl, succeeded to the earldom which Harold before held.

A. 1053. In this year died Godwin, the earl, on the 17th before the Kalends of May, and he is buried at Winchester, in the Old-minster ; and Harold, the earl, his son, succeeded to the earldom, and to all that which his father had held : and Elgar, the earl, succeeded to the earldom which Harold before held.

A. 1054. This year went Siward the earl‡ with a great army into Scotland, and made much slaughter of the Scots,

* Dorchester.　　† Of Worcester.　　‡ Of Northumbria.

and put them to flight : and the king escaped. Moreover, many fell on his side, as well Danish-men as English, and also his own son.* The same year was consecrated the minster at Evesham, on the 6th before the Ides of October. In the same year bishop Aldred† went south over sea into Saxony, and was there received with much reverence. That same year died Osgod Clapa suddenly, even as he lay on his bed. In this year died Leo [IX.] the holy pope of Rome. And in this year there was so great a murrain among cattle, as no man remembered for many years before. And Victor [II.] was chosen pope.

1054. This year went Siward the earl with a great army into Scotland, both with a ship-force and with a land-force, and fought against the Scots, and put to flight king Macbeth, and slew all who were the chief men in the land, and led thence much booty, such as no man before had obtained. But his son Osborn, and his sister's son Siward, and some of his house-carls, and also of the king's, were there slain, on the day of the Seven Sleepers. The same year went bishop Aldred to Cologne, over sea, on the king's errand ; and he was there received with much worship by the emperor,‡ and there he dwelt well nigh a year ; and either gave him entertainment, both the bishop of Cologne and the emperor. And he gave leave to bishop Leofwine§ to consecrate the minster at Evesham on the 6th before the Ides of October. In this year died Osgod suddenly in his bed. And this year died St. Leo the pope ; and Victor was chosen pope in his stead.

A. 1055. In this year died Siward the earl at York, and his body lies within the minster at Galmanho,‖ which himself had before built, to the glory of God and of all his saints.   Then, within a little time after, was a general council in London, and Elgar the earl, Leofric the earl's son, was outlawed without any kind of guilt ; and he went then to Ireland, and there procured himself a fleet, which was of eighteen ships, besides his own : and they went then to Wales, to king Griffin,¶ with that force ; and he received him into his pro- tection.   And then, with the Irishmen and with Welshmen, they gathered a great force : and Ralph the earl gathered a great force on the other hand at Hereford-port.   And they sought them out there : but before there was any spear thrown, the English people fled because they were on horses ;

* Osborn.   † Of Worcester.
‡ Henry III.   § Of Lichfield.
‖ A Saxon abbey, merged afterwards in St. Mary's at York.
¶ Of North Wales.

and there great slaughter was made, about four hundred men or five; and they made none on the other side. And they then betook themselves to the town, and that they burned; and the great minster which Athelstan the venerable bishop before caused to be built, that they plundered and bereaved of relics and of vestments, and of all things; and slew the people, and some they led away. Then a force was gathered from well nigh throughout all England, and they came to Gloucester, and so went out, not far, among the Welsh; and there they lay some while: and Harold the earl caused the ditch to be dug about the port* the while. Then, during this, then spoke they concerning peace; and Harold the earl, and those who were with him, came to Bilsley: and there peace and friendship was established between them. And then they inlawed Elgar the earl, and gave him all that before had been taken from him; and the fleet went to Chester, and there awaited their pay, which Elgar had promised them. The man-slaying was on the ninth before the Kalends of November. In the same year died Tremerin the Welsh bishop,† soon after that ravaging; he was bishop Athelstan's coadjutor from the time that he had become infirm.

A. 1055. In this year died Siward the earl at York, and he lies at Galmanho, in the minster which himself caused to be built, and consecrated in God's and Olave's name. And Tosty succeeded to the earldom which he had held. And archbishop Kynsey‡ fetched his pall from pope Victor. And soon thereafter was outlawed Elgar the earl, son of Leofric the earl, well-nigh without guilt. But he went to Ireland and to Wales, and procured himself there a great force, and so went to Hereford: but there came against him Ralph the earl, with a large army. And with a slight conflict he put them to flight, and much people slew in the flight: and they went then into Hereford-port, and that they ravaged, and burned the great minster which bishop Athelstan had built, and slew the priests within the minster, and many in addition thereto, and took all the treasures therein, and carried them away with them. And when they had done the utmost evil, this counsel was counselled: that Elgar the earl should be inlawed, and be given his earldom, and all that had been taken from him. This ravaging happened on the 9th before the Kalends of November. In the same year died Tremerin the Welsh bishop,§ soon after that ravaging: and he was bishop Athelstan's coadjutor from the time that he had become infirm.

A. 1055. In this year died Siward the earl: and then was summoned a general council, seven days before Mid-lent; and they outlawed Elgar the earl, because it was cast upon him that he was a traitor to the king and to

---

* Hereford.   † Of St. David's.   ‡ Of York.   § Of St. David's.

all the people of the land.   And he made a confession of it before all the men who were there gathered ; though the word escaped him unintentionally.   And the king gave the earldom to Tosty, son of earl Godwin, which Siward the earl before held.   And Elgar the earl sought Griffin's protection in North-Wales.   And in this year Griffin and Elgar burned St. Elthelbert's minster, and all the town of Hereford.

A. 1056.   This year bishop Egelric gave up his bishopric at Durham, and went to St. Peter's minster, Peterborough ; and his brother Egelwine succeeded thereto.   This year died Athelstan the venerable bishop, on the 4th before the Ides of February, and his body lies at Hereford-port ; and Leofgar was appointed bishop ; he was the mass-priest of Harold the earl.   He wore his knapsack during his priesthood until he was a bishop.   He forsook his chrism and his rood, his ghostly weapons, and took to his spear and his sword, after his bishophood ; and so went to the field against Griffin the Welsh king : and there was he slain, and his priests with him, and Elnoth the sheriff and many good men with them ; and the others fled away.   This was eight days before midsummer.   It is difficult to tell the distress, and all the marching, and the camping, and the travail and destruction of men, and also of horses, which all the English army endured, until Leofric the earl* came thither, and Harold the earl, and bishop Aldred,† and made a reconciliation there between them ; so that Griffin swore oaths that he would be to king Edward a faithful and unbetraying underking.   And bishop Aldred succeeded to the bishopric which Leofgar had before held eleven weeks and four days. In the same year died Cona‡ the emperor.   This year died Odda the earl,§ and his body lies at Pershore, and he was ordained a monk before his end ; a good man he was and pure, and right noble.   And he died on the 2nd before the Kalends of September.

A. 1057.
Here came Edward etheling
to Angle-land ;
he was king Edward's
brother's son,
Edmund king,
who Ironside was called

for his valour.
This etheling Canute king
had sent away
to Unger-land∥
to be betrayed :
but he there grew up
to a good man,

---

* Of Mercia.   † Of Worcester.   ‡ Hen. III.
§ Of Devon.   ∥ Hungary.

as God him granted.
and him well became ;
so that he obtained   [wife,
the emperor's kinswoman to
and by her, fair
offspring he begot :
she was Agatha hight.
Nor wist we
for which cause
that done was,
that he might not

his kinsman Edward
king behold.
Alas ! that was a rueful case
and harmful
for all this nation
that he so soon
his life did end   [came
after that he to Angle-land·
for the mishap
of this wretched nation.

In the same year died Leofric the earl,[*] on the second before
the kalends of October ; he was very wise for God and also
for the world, which was a blessing to all this nation.   He
lies at Coventry ; and his son Elgar succeeded to his government.   And within the year died Ralph, the earl[†] on the
12th before the kalends of January ; and he lies at Peterborough.   Moreover, bishop Heca died in Sussex, and Agel-
ric was raised to his see.[‡]   And this year pope Victor died,
and Stephen [IX.] was chosen pope.

A. 1057. In this year Edward etheling, king Edmund's son, came hither
to land, and soon after died : and his body is buried within St. Paul's minster at London.   And pope Victor died, and Stephen [IX.] was chosen
pope : he was abbat of Mont-Cassino.   And Leofric the earl died, and
Elgar his son succeeded to the earldom which the father before held.

A. 1058. This year Elgar, the earl,[§] was banished ; but
he soon came in again, with violence, through Griffin's[||] aid.
And this year came a fleet from Norway : it is tedious to
tell how all these matters went.   In the same year bishop
Aldred[¶] consecrated the minster at Gloucester, which himself
had raised to the glory of God and of St. Peter ; and so he
went to Jerusalem with such splendour as none other had
displayed before him, and there devoted himself to God : and
a worthy gift he also offered at our Lord's tomb ; that was a
golden chalice of five marks of very wonderful work.   In
the same year died Pope Stephen [IX.], and Benedict
[X.] was appointed pope : he sent a pall to bishop Stigand.

* Of Mercia.   † Of Hereford.
‡ Selsey.   § Of Mercia.
|| King of North Wales.   ¶ Of Worcester.

Algeric was ordained bishop of Sussex,* and abbat Siward of Rochester.

A. 1058. This year died Pope Stephen, and Benedict was consecrated pope: the same sent hither to land a pall to archbishop Stigand. And in this year died Heca, bishop of Sussex; and archbishop Stigand ordained Algeric, a monk at Christchurch, bishop of Sussex, and abbat Siward bishop of Rochester.

A. 1059. In this year was Nicholas [II.] chosen pope, he had before been bishop of the town of Florence; and Benedict was driven away, who had there before been pope. And in this year was the steeple consecrated at Peterborough, on the 16th before the Kalends of November.

A. 1060. In this year there was a great earthquake on the Translation of St. Martin: and king Henry died in France. And Kynsey, archbishop of York, departed on the 11th before the Kalends of January, and he lies at Peterborough; and bishop Aldred succeeded to the bishopric, and Walter succeeded to the bishopric of Herefordshire: and bishop Dudoc also died; he was bishop in Somerset;† and Giso the priest was appointed in his stead.

A. 1061. This year bishop Aldred went to Rome after his pall, and he received it from Pope Nicholas. And Tosty and his wife also went to Rome: and the bishop and the earl suffered much distress as they came homeward. And this year died Godwin, bishop of St. Martin's;‡ and Wulfric abbat of St. Augustine's, on the 14th before the Kalends of April [May?]. And Pope Nicholas died, and Alexander [II.] was chosen pope: he had been bishop of Lucca.

A. 1061. In this year died Dudoc, bishop of Somerset, and Giso succeeded. And in the same year died Godwin, bishop of St. Martin's, on the 7th before the Ides of March. And in the self-same year died Wulfric, abbat of St. Augustine's, within the Easter week, on the 14th before the Kalends of May. When word came to the king that abbat Wulfric was departed, then chose he Ethelsy the monk thereto, from the Old-Minster, who then followed archbishop Stigand, and was consecrated abbat at Windsor, on St. Augustine's mass-day.

A. 1062.

A. 1063. In this year, after midwinter, Harold, the earl, went from Gloucester to Rhyddlan, which was Griffin's, and burned the vill, and his ships, and all the stores which thereto belonged, and put him to flight. And then, at Roga-

* Selsey.   † Wells.   ‡ At Canterbury.

tion-tide, Harold went with his ships from Bristol about
Wales ; and the people made a truce and delivered hostages ;
and Tosty went with a land-force against them : and they
subdued the land.   But in this same year, during harvest,
was king Griffin slain, on the Nones of August, by his own
men, by reason of the war that he warred with Harold the
earl.   He was king over all the Welsh race : and his head
was brought to Harold the earl, and Harold brought it to the
king, and his ship's head, and the rigging therewith.   And
king Edward committed the land to his two brothers, Bleth-
gent and Rigwatle ; and they swore oaths, and delivered
hostages to the king and to the earl, that they would be
faithful to him in all things, and be everywhere ready for
him, by water and by land, and make such renders from the
land as had been done before to any other king.

A. 1063. This year went Harold the earl, and his brother Tosty the
earl, as well with a land-force as a ship-force, into Wales, and they subdued the land ; and the people delivered hostages to them, and submitted ;
and went afterwards and slew their king Griffin, and brought to Harold his
head: and he appointed another king thereto.

A. 1064.

A. 1065. In this year, before Lammas, Harold the earl
ordered a building to be erected in Wales at Portskeweth,
after he had subdued it ; and there he gathered much good ;
and thought to have king Edward there for the purpose of
hunting.   But when it was all ready, then went Caradoc,
Griffin's son, with the whole force which he could procure,
and slew almost all the people who there had been building ;
and they took the good which there was prepared.   We wist
not who first devised this ill counsel.   This was done on St.
Bartholomew's mass-day.   And soon after this, all the thanes
in Yorkshire and in Northumberland gathered themselves
together, and outlawed their earl, Tosty, and slew his household men, all that they might come at, as well English as
Danish : and they took all his weapons at York, and gold,
and silver, and all his treasures which they might any where
there hear of, and sent after Morkar, the son of Elgar the
earl, and chose him to be their earl : and he went south with
all the shire, and with Nottinghamshire, and Derbyshire,
and Lincolnshire, until he came to Northampton : and his
brother Edwin came to meet him with the men who were

in his earldom, and also many Britons came with him.
There came Harold, the earl, to meet them ; and they laid
an errand upon him to king Edward, and also sent messengers with'him, and begged that they might have Morkar for
their earl.   And the king granted it, and sent Harold again
to them at Northampton, on the eve of St. Simon's and
St. Jude's mass ; and he made known the same to them, and
delivered a pledge thereof unto them : and he there renewed
Canute's law.   But the northern men did much harm
about Northampton whilst he went on their errand, inasmuch as they slew men and burned houses and corn ; and
took all the cattle which they might come at, that was many
thousand : and many hundred men they took and led north
with them ; so that that shire, and the other shires which
there are nigh, were for many years the worse.   And Tosty
the earl, and his wife, and all those who would what he
would, went south over sea with him to Baldwin, the earl,
and he received them all ; and they were all the winter
there.   And king Edward came to Westminster at midwinter, and there caused to be consecrated the minster which himself had built to the glory of God and of St. Peter, and of
all God's saints ; and the church-hallowing was on Childer-
mass-day.   And he died on Twelfth-day eve, and him they
buried on Twelfth-day eve, in the same minster, as it hereafter sayeth.

Here Edward king,
of Angles lord,
sent his stedfast
soul to Christ,
in God's protection,
spirit holy.
He in the world here
dwelt awhile
in royal majesty
mighty in council.
Four-and-twenty,
lordly ruler !
of winters numbered,
he wealth dispensed ;
and he a prosperous tide,
ruler of heroes,
distinguished governed,
Welsh and Scots,
and Britons also,
son of Ethelred,
Angles and Saxons,
chieftains bold.
Where'er embrace
cold ocean-waves,
there all to Edward,
noble king !
obeyed faithfully,
the warrior-men.
Aye was blithe-mind
the harmless king,
though he long erst
of land bereaved,

in exile dwelt
wide o'er the earth,
since Canute o'ercame
the race of Ethelred,
and Danes wielded
the dear realm
of Angle-land,
eight-and-twenty
of winters numbered,
wealth dispensed.
After forth-came,
in vestments lordly,
king with the chosen good,
chaste and mild,
Edward the noble :
the realm he guarded,
land and people,
until suddenly came

death the bitter,
and so dear a one seized.
This noble, from earth
angels carried,
stedfast soul,
into heaven's light.
And the sage ne'ertheless,
the realm committed
to a highly-born man,
Harold's self,
the noble earl !
He in all time
obeyed faithfully
his rightful lord
by words and deeds,
nor aught neglected
which needful was
to his sovereign-king.

And this year also was Harold consecrated king ; and he with little quiet abode therein, the while that he wielded the realm.

A. 1065. And the man-slaying was on St. Bartholomew's mass-day. And then, after Michael's-mass, all the thanes in Yorkshire went to York, and there slew all earl Tosty's household servants whom they might hear of, and took his treasures : and Tosty was then at Britford with the king. And then, very soon thereafter, was a great council at Northampton ; and then at Oxford on the day of Simon and Jude. And there was Harold the earl, and would work their reconciliation if he might, but he could not : but all his earldom him unanimously forsook and outlawed, and all who with him lawlessness upheld, because he robbed God first, and all those bereaved over whom he had power of life and of land. And they then took to themselves Morkar for earl ; and Tosty went then over sea, and his wife with him, to Baldwin's land, and they took up their winter residence at St. Omer's.

A. 1066. In this year king Harold came from York to Westminster, at that Easter which was after the mid-winter in which the king died ; and Easter was then on the day, 16th before the Kalends of May. Then was, over all England, such a token seen in the heavens, as no man ever before saw. Some men said that it was cometa the star, which some men call the haired star ; and it appeared first on the eve Litania Major, the 8th before the Kalends of May, and so shone all the seven nights. And soon after came in Tosty the earl from beyond sea into the Isle of Wight, with so great a fleet as he might procure ; and there they yielded him as well money as food. And king Harold, his brother, gathered so great a ship-force, and also a land-force, as no king here in the land had before done ; because it was made known to him that William the bastard would come hither and win this land ; all as it afterwards happened. And the while, came Tosty the earl into Humber with sixty ships ; and Edwin the earl came with a land-force and drove him out. And the boatmen forsook him ; and he went to Scotland with twelve vessels. And there met him Harold king of Norway with three hundred ships ; and Tosty submitted to him and became his man. And they then went both into Humber, until they came to York ; and there fought against them Edwin the earl, and Morkar the earl, his brother: but the Northmen had the victory. Then was it made known to Harold king of the Angles that this had thus happened: and this battle was on the vigil of St. Matthew. Then came Harold our king unawares on the Northmen, and met with them beyond York, at Stanford-bridge, with a great army of English people ; and there during the day was a very severe fight on both sides. There was slain Harold the Fair-haired, and Tosty the earl ; and the Northmen who were there remaining were put to flight ; and the English from behind hotly smote them, until they came, some, to their ships, some were drowned, and some also burned ; and thus in divers ways they perished, so that there were few left : and the English had possession of the place of carnage. The king then gave his protection to Olave, son of the king of the Norwegians, and to their bishop, and to the earl of Orkney, and to all those who were left in the ships : and they then went up to our king, and swore oaths that they ever would observe peace and friendship towards this land ; and the king let them go home with twenty-four ships. These two general battles were fought within five days. Then came William earl of Normandy into Pevensey, on the eve of St. Michael's-mass : and soon after they were on their way, they constructed a castle at Hasting's-port. This was then made known to king Harold, and he then gathered a great force, and came to meet him at the estuary of Appledore ; and William came

against him unawares, before his people were set in order.
But the king nevertheless strenuously fought against him
with those men who would follow him ; and there was great
slaughter made on either hand. There was slain king
Harold, and Leofwin the earl, his brother, and Girth the
earl, his brother, and many good men ; and the Frenchmen
had possession of the place of carnage, all as God granted
them for the people's sins. Archbishop Aldred and the
townsmen of London would then have child Edgar for king,
all as was his true natural right : and Edwin and Morcar
vowed to him that they would fight together with him. But
in that degree that it ought ever to have been forwarder, so
was it from day to day later and worse ; so that at the end
all passed away. This fight was done on the day of Calixtus the pope. And William the earl went afterwards again
to Hastings, and there awaited to see whether the people
would submit to him. But when he understood that they
would not come to him, he went upwards with all his army
which was left to him, and that which afterwards had come
from over sea to him ; and he plundered all that part which
he over-ran, until he came to Berkhampstead. And there
came to meet him archbishop Aldred,* and child Edgar,
and Edwin the earl, and Morcar the earl, and all the
chief men of London ; and then submitted, for need, when
the most harm had been done : and it was very unwise that
they had not done so before ; since God would not better it,
for our sins : and they delivered hostages, and swore oaths
to him ; and he vowed to them that he would be a loving
lord to them : and nevertheless, during this, they plundered
all that they over-ran. Then, on mid-winter's day, archbishop Aldred consecrated him king at Westminster ; and he
gave him a pledge upon Christ's book, and also swore, before
he would set the crown upon his head, that he would govern
this nation as well as any king before him had at the best
done, if they would be faithful to him. Nevertheless, he
laid a tribute on the people, very heavy ; and then went, during Lent, over sea to Normandy, and took with him archbishop Stigand, and Aylnoth, abbat of Glastonbury, and
child Edgar, and Edwin the earl, and Morkar the earl,
and Waltheof the earl, and many other good men of Eng-

* Of York.

land. And bishop Odo* and William the earl remained here
behind, and they built castles wide throughout the nation,
and poor people distressed; and ever after it greatly grew
in evil. May the end be good when God will!

A. 1066. This year died king Edward, and Harold the earl succeeded
to the kingdom, and held it forty weeks and one day. And this year came
William, and won England. And in this year Christ-Church† was burned.
And this year appeared a comet on the 14th before the Kalends of May.

A. 1066....‡And then he [Tosty] went thence, and did harm everywhere
by the sea-coast where he could land, as far as Sandwich. Then was it
made known to king Harold, who was in London, that Tosty his brother
was come to Sandwich. Then gathered he so great a ship-force, and also
a land force, as no king here in the land had before gathered, because it
had been soothly said unto him, that William the earl from Normandy,
king Edward's kinsman, would come hither and subdue this land: all as
it afterwards happened. When Tosty learned that king Harold was
on his way to Sandwich, then went he from Sandwich, and took some of
the boatmen with him, some willingly and some unwillingly; and went
then north into Humber, and there ravaged in Lindsey, and there slew
many good men. When Edwin the earl and Morcar the earl understood
that, then came they thither, and drove him out of the land. And he went
then to Scotland: and the king of Scots protected him, and assisted him
with provisions; and he there abode all the summer. Then came king
Harold to Sandwich, and there awaited his fleet, because it was long before
it could be gathered together. And when his fleet was gathered together,
then went he into the Isle of Wight, and there lay all the summer and the
harvest; and a land-force was kept every where by the sea, though in the
end it was of no benefit. When it was the Nativity of St. Mary, then were
the men's provisions gone, and no man could any longer keep them there.
Then were the men allowed to go home, and the king rode up, and the
ships were despatched to London; and many perished before they came
thither. When the ships had reached home, then came king Harold from
Norway, north into Tyne, and unawares, with a very large ship-force, and
no small one; that might be, or more. And Tosty the earl came to him
with all that he had gotten, all as they had before agreed; and then they
went both, with all the fleet, along the Ouse, up towards York. Then was
it made known to king Harold in the south, as he was come from on ship-
board, that Harold king of Norway and Tosty the earl were landed near
York. Then went he northward, day and night, as quickly as he could
gather his forces. Then, before that king Harold could come thither, then
gathered Edwin the earl and Morcar the earl from their earldom as great a
force as they could get together; and they fought against the army, and
made great slaughter: and there was much of the English people slain,
and drowned, and driven away in flight; and the Northmen had possession
of the place of carnage. And this fight was on the vigil of St. Matthew
the apostle, and it was Wednesday. And then, after the fight, went Harold king of Norway, and Tosty the earl, into York, with as much people

---

. * Odo, bishop of Bayeux, half brother of king William, and William
Fitz Osbert, created earl of Hereford.   † Canterbury.

‡ Continued after "money as food," in page 440.

as seemed meet to them. And they delivered hostages to them from the city, and also assisted them with provisions; and so they went thence to their ships, and they agreed upon a full peace, so that they should all go with him south, and this land subdue. Then, during this, came Harold king of the Angles, with all his forces, on the Sunday, to Tadcaster, and there drew up his force, and went then on Monday throughout York; and Harold king of Norway, and Tosty the earl, and their forces, were gone from their ships beyond York to Stanfordbridge, because it had been promised them for a certainty, that there, from all the shire, hostages should be brought to meet them. Then came Harold king of the English against them, unawares, beyond the bridge, and they there joined battle, and very strenuously, for a long time of the day, continued fighting: and there was Harold king of Norway and Tosty the earl slain, and numberless of the people with them, as well of the Northmen as of the English: and the Northmen fled from the English. Then was there one of the Norwegians who withstood the English people, so that they might not pass over the bridge, nor obtain the victory. Then an Englishman aimed at him with a javelin, but it availed nothing ; and then came another under the bridge, and pierced him terribly inwards under the coat of mail. Then came Harold, king of the English, over the bridge, and his forces onward with him, and there made great slaughter, as well of Norwegians as of Flemings. And the king's son, Edmund, Harold let go home to Norway, with all the ships.

A. 1066. In this year was consecrated the minster at Westminster, on Childer-mass-day. And king Edward died, on the eve of Twelfth-day ; and he was buried on Twelfth-day, within the newly consecrated church at Westminster. And Harold the earl succeeded to the kingdom of England, even as the king had granted it to him, and men also had chosen him thereto ; and he was crowned as king on Twelfth-day. And that same year that he became king, he went out with a fleet against William ;* and the while, came Tosty the earl into Humber with sixty ships. Edwin the earl came with a land-force and drove him out; and the boatmen forsook him. And he went to Scotland with twelve vessels ; and Harold the king of Norway met him with three hundred ships, and Tosty submitted to him; and they both went into Humber, until they came to York. And Morcar the earl, and Edwin the earl, fought against them; and the king of the Norwegians had the victory. And it was made known to king Harold how it there was done, and had happened ; and he came there with a great army of English men, and met him at Stanfordbridge, and slew him and the earl Tosty, and boldly overcame all the army. And the while, William the earl landed at Hastings, on St. Michael's-day : and Harold came from the north, and fought against him before all his army had come up : and there he fell, and his two brothers, Girth and Leofwin; and William subdued this land. And he came to Westminster, and archbishop Aldred consecrated him king, and men paid him tribute, and delivered him hostages, and afterwards bought their land. And then was Leofric abbat of Peterborough in that same expedition ; and there he sickened, and came home, and was dead soon thereafter, on All-hallows-mass-night; God be merciful to his soul ! In his day was all bliss and all good in Peterborough; and he was dear to all people, so that the king gave to St. Peter and to him the abbacy at Burton, and that of Coventry, which Leofric the earl, who

* Earl of Normandy.

was his uncle, before had made, and that of Crowland, and that of Thorney. And he conferred so much of good upon the minster of Peterborough, in gold, and in silver, and in vestments, and in land, as never any other did before him, nor any after him. After, Golden-borough became a wretched borough. Then chose the monks for abbat Brand the provost, by reason that he was a very good man, and very wise, and sent him then to Edgar the etheling, by reason that the people of the land supposed that he should become king: and the etheling granted it him then gladly. When king William heard say that, then was he very wroth, and said that the abbat had despised him. Then went good men between them, and reconciled them, by reason that the abbat was a good man. Then gave he the king forty marks of gold for a reconciliation; and then thereafter, lived he a little while, but three years. After that came every tribulation and every evil to the minster. God have mercy on it !

A. 1067. This year the king came back to England on St. Nicolas's day, and on the same day Christ's Church, Canterbury, was consumed by fire. Bishop Wulfwy also died, and lies buried at his see of Dorchester. Child Edric and the Britons were unsettled this year, and fought with the men of the castle at Hereford, to whom they did much harm. The king this year imposed a heavy tax on the unfortunate people ; but, notwithstanding, he let his men plunder all the country which they passed through : after which he marched to Devonshire and besieged Exeter eighteen days. Many of his army were slain there : but he had promised them well and performed ill : the citizens surrendered the city, because the thanes had betrayed them. This summer the child Edgar, with his mother Agatha, his sisters Margaret and Christina, Merlesweyne and several good men, went to Scotland under the protection of king Malcolm, who received them all. Then it was that king Malcolm desired to have Margaret to wife : but, the child Edgar and all his men refused for a long time ; and she herself also was unwilling, saying that she would have neither him nor any other person, if God would allow her to serve him with her carnal heart, in strict continence, during this short life. But the king urged her brother until he said yes ; and indeed he did not dare to refuse, for they were now in Malcolm's kingdom. So that the marriage was now fulfilled, as God had foreordained, and it could not be otherwise, as he says in the Gospel, that not a sparrow falls to the ground, without his foreshowing. The prescient Creator knew long before what he would do with her, namely that she should increase the glory of God in this land, lead the king out of the wrong into the right path, bring him and his people to a better way, and suppress all the bad customs which the nation formerly followed. These things she afterwards accomplished. The king therefore married her, though against her will, and was pleased with her manners, and thanked God who had given him such a wife. And being a prudent man he turned himself to God and forsook all impurity of conduct, as St. Paul, the apostle of the Gentiles, says : " *Salvabitur vir*," &c. which means in our language " Full oft the unbelieving husband is sanctified and healed through the believing wife, and so belike the wife through the believing husband." The queen above-named afterwards did many things in this land to promote the glory of God, and conducted herself well in her noble rank, as always was her custom. She was sprung from a noble line of ancestors, and her father was Edward Etheling, son of king Edmund. This Edmund was the son of Ethelred, who was the son of Edgar, the son of Edred ; and so on in that royal line. Her maternal kindred traces up to the emperor Henry, who reigned at Rome.

This year Harold's mother, Githa, and the wives of many good men with her, went to the Steep Holmes, and there abode some time ; and afterwards went from thence over sea to St. Omer's.

This Easter the king came to Winchester; and Easter was then on the tenth day before the Kalends of April. Soon after this the lady Matilda came to this country, and archbishop Eldred consecrated her queen at Westminster on Whitsunday. It was then told the king, that the people in the North had gathered together and would oppose him there. Upon this he went to Nottingham, and built a castle there, and then advanced to York, where he built two castles : he then did the same at Lincoln, and everywhere in those parts. Then earl Cospatric and all the best men went into Scotland. During these things one of Harold's sons came with a fleet from Ireland unexpectedly into the mouth of the river Avon, and soon plundered all that neighbourhood. They went to Bristol, and would have stormed the town, but the inhabitants opposed them bravely. Seeing they could get nothing from the town, they went to their ships with the

booty they had got by plundering, and went to Somersetshire,
where they went up the country. Ednoth, master of the
horse, fought with them, but he was slain there, and many
good men on both sides ; and those who were left departed
thence.

A. 1068. This year king William gave the earldom of
Northumberland to earl Robert, and the men of that country
came against him, and slew him and 900 others with him.
And then Edgar etheling marched with all the Northumbrians to York, and the townsmen treated with him; on
which king William came from the south with all his troops,
and sacked the town, and slew many hundred persons. He
also profaned St. Peter's minster, and all other places, and
the etheling went back to Scotland.

After this came Harold's sons from Ireland, about Midsummer, with sixty-four ships and entered the mouth of the
Taff, where they incautiously landed. Earl Beorn came
upon them unawares with a large army, and slew all their
bravest men : the others escaped to their ships, and Harold's
sons went back again to Ireland.

A. 1069. This year died Aldred archbishop of York, and
he lies buried in his cathedral church. He died on the
festival of Protus and Hyacinthus, having held the see with
much honour ten years, all but fifteen weeks.

Soon after this, three of the sons of Sweyne came from
Denmark with 240 ships, together with earl Osbern and
earl Thorkill, into the Humber ; where they were met by
child Edgar and earl Waltheof, and Merle-Sweyne, and
earl Cospatric with the men of Northumberland and all the
landsmen, riding and marching joyfully with an immense
army ; and so they went to York, demolished the castle, and
found there large treasures. They also slew many hundred
Frenchmen, and carried off many prisoners to their ships ;
but, before the shipmen came thither, the Frenchmen had
burned the city, and plundered and burnt St. Peter's minster.
When the king heard of this, he went northward with all
the troops he could collect, and laid waste all the shire ;
whilst the fleet lay all the winter in the Humber, where the
king could not get at them. The king was at York on
midwinter's day, remaining on land all the winter, and at
Easter he came to Winchester.

This year bishop Egelric being at Peterborough, was accused and sent to Westminster; and his brother bishop Egelwin was outlawed. And the same year Brand abbat of Peterborough died on the fifth before the Kalends of December.

A. 1070. This year Lanfranc abbat of Caen came to England, and in a few days he was made archbishop of Canterbury. He was consecrated * at his metropolis on the

* In the second year after Lanfranc's consecration he went to Rome. pope Alexander so greatly honoured him, that contrary to his custom he rose to meet him, and gave him two palls in token of especial favour: Lanfranc received one of them from the altar after the Roman manner, and the pope, with his own hands, gave him the other, in which he himself had been accustomed to perform mass. In the presence of the pope, Thomas brought forwards a calumny touching the primacy of the see of Canterbury, and the subjection of certain bishops. Lanfranc briefly and clearly states the conclusion to which this affair was afterwards brought in England, in an epistle to the aforesaid pope Alexander. This year a general council was held at Winchester, in which he deposed Wulfric, abbat of the new monastery, and made many regulations touching Christian discipline. A few days afterwards, he consecrated Osbern at London as bishop of Exeter, and Scotland at Canterbury as abbat of St. Augustine's.

In his third year he consecrated Peter at Gloucester as bishop of Lichfield or Chester. This year also a great council was held at a place called Pennenden Heath [near Maidstone], in which Lanfranc proved that he and his church held their lands and their rights by sea and by land, as freely as the king held his: excepting in three cases: to wit, if the highway be dug up; if a tree be cut so as to fall upon it; and if murder be committed and blood spilt: when a man is taken in these misdeeds, the fine paid shall belong to the king; otherwise their vassals shall be free from regal exactions.

In his fourth year he consecrated Patrick at London as bishop of Dublin, in Ireland, from whom he received a profession of obedience, and he moreover gave him very memorable letters to the kings of Ireland.

In his fifth year a general council was held at London, the proceedings of which Lanfranc committed to writing, at the request of many.

In his sixth year he gave the bishopric of Rochester to Ernost, a monk of Christ church, whom he also consecrated at London. A council was held at Winchester: and the same year Ernost departed this life.

In his seventh year, he gave the bishopric of Rochester to Gundulph, whom he consecrated at Canterbury. This year Thomas archbishop of York sent letters to Lanfranc, requesting that he would send two bishops to consecrate a certain priest, who had come to him with letters from the Orkneys, to the intent that he might be made bishop of those islands. Lanfranc consenting to this, commanded Wolstan bishop of Worcester, and Peter bishop of Chester, to go to York, and to assist Thomas in completing the ceremony.

In his eighth year, a council was held at London, in which Lanfranc deposed Ailnoth abbat of Glastonbury.

fourth before the Kalends of September, by eight bishops his suffragans; the rest who were absent signifying through messengers, and by writing, why they could not be

In his eleventh year, a council was held at Gloucester, wherein, by the king's order, and with the consent of Lanfranc, Thomas archbishop of York consecrated William to the bishopric of Durham; and because he could not be attended by the Scotch bishops his suffragans, the bishops Wolstan, Osbern, Giso, and Robert assisted at this ceremony by the command of Lanfranc. At this time Lanfranc sent letters rich in sacred lore to bishop Donald in Ireland.

In his sixteenth year Lanfranc consecrated Donatus, his monk at Canterbury, to the bishopric of Dublin, by the desire of the king, clergy, and people of Ireland. This year a council was held at Gloucester, wherein Lanfranc deposed Wulstcetel abbat of Croyland. He consecrated Robert to the bishopric of Chester, and William to that of Elmham, in one day, at Canterbury. At Winchester also he consecrated Maurice as bishop of London, who brought noble gifts to his mother church at Canterbury a few days afterwards.

In the eighteenth year of Lanfranc's prelacy, on the death of king William beyond sea, he acknowledged his son William, as he had done his father, and consecrated and crowned him in St. Peter's church, which is in the western part of London. The same year, and at his metropolitan city of Canterbury, he examined and consecrated Godfrey as bishop of Chichester, Wydo also as abbat of St. Augustine's and John as bishop of Wells. The next day Lanfranc on his own authority, and taking with him Odo bishop of Bayeux the king's brother, who was then at Canterbury, conducted the abbat Wydo to St. Augustine's and commanded the brothers of the order to receive him as their own abbat and pastor; but they, with one accord, answered that they would neither submit to him nor receive him. Thus Lanfranc came leading the abbat, and when he found that the monks were obstinate in resistance, and that they would not obey him, he commanded that all the refractory should come out one by one. When therefore nearly all had left the monastery, Lanfranc and his suite led in the abbat with much pomp, placed him in the chair, and delivered the church up to him. He also seized the prior, Elfrin by name, and as many others as he thought fit, and he put them forthwith into claustral imprisonment at Canterbury; but he sent those who had the greatest influence, and were the authors of this scandal, to the castle to be confined there. After he had returned home having finished all, he was informed that the monks who had left the monastery were assembled, near St. Mildred's church. Hereupon he sent to them, saying, that if they would, they might return to the church before the ninth hour, but that if they delayed longer, they would not be allowed free entrance, but he treated as renegadoes. Having heard this message they doubted whether to return or to remain, but at the hour of refection, when they became hungry, many repenting of their obstinacy sent to Lanfranc and promised submission. These he treated with lenity, and desired that they should return directly and confirm by oath their profession of obedience to the aforesaid abbat. Thus they returned and swore faithfulness and obedience to the abbat Wydo, upon

there. This year Thomas, who had been chosen as bishop of York, came to Canterbury, that he might be consecrated there after the old form, but when Lanfranc craved the

the relics of St. Augustine. Lanfranc seized those who remained behind and placed them in various monasteries of England, confining them till he brought them to profess their submission. About the same time, he seized one of them named Alfred, who had attempted to flee, and confined him loaded with irons at Canterbury, together with some of his fellows : and he exercised upon them the utmost severity of their order. But when these monks were thought to be sufficiently humbled and had promised amendment, Lanfranc taking pity on them, had them brought from the several places whither he had banished them, and reconciled them to their abbat.

The same year the dissensions were renewed, and the monks plotted the death of their abbat, but one of them, named Columban, being taken, Lanfranc caused him to be brought to him. As he stood there before him, Lanfranc asked if he desired to murder his abbat. And the monk forthwith replied, " Yes ! if I could I would certainly kill him." Then Lanfranc commanded that he should be tied up naked by the gates of St. Augustine's and suffer flagellation before all the people, that his cowl should then be torn off, and that he should be driven out of the city. This order was executed, and thenceforth, during Lanfranc's life, sedition was repressed by the dread of his severity.

In the nineteenth year of his prelacy, died the venerable archbishop Lanfranc, and he was buried at his metropolitan see of Canterbury, of which he had been possessed eighteen years, nine months, and two days. His deeds, his buildings, alms, and labours, are only in part recounted in the writing which is read on his anniversary, for they were very numerous. After his death the monks of St. Augustine's, openly rebelling against their aforesaid abbat Wydo, stirred up the citizens of Canterbury, who, with an armed force, attempted to slay him in his house. But his family made resistance, and when many had been wounded, and some killed on both sides, the abbat with much difficulty escaped unhurt from amongst them, and fled for refuge to the mother church of Canterbury (Christ's church.) On the report of this disturbance Walkelin bishop of Winchester, and Gundolf bishop of Rochester, suffragans to the see of Canterbury, with some noblemen sent by the king, hastened to Canterbury, that they might take vengeance on the delinquents ; and when they had inquired into the causes of the sedition, and had found the monks unable to clear themselves, they condemned them to suffer public punishment because they had transgressed openly. But the prior and monks of Christ's church, moved with piety, pleaded against the sentence, lest, if they were to receive their discipline before all the people, they should henceforth be accounted infamous, and so their profession and office come to be despised. Wherefore it was granted on their intercession, that the punishment should take place in the church, into which the populace should not be admitted, but those only who were appointed to see it executed. And two monks of Christ's church, Wydo and Norman, were called in, and they inflicted the punishment at the command of the bishops. Then the rebellious monks were dispersed into various monasteries of England; and twenty-four monks

confirmation of his subjection by oath, he refused, and said
that he was not obliged to give it. Then was the archbishop
Lanfranc wroth, and he commanded the bishops, who were
there at his behest to assist at the ceremony, and all the
monks, to unrobe themselves ; and they did as he desired:
so this time Thomas returned home without consecration. It
happened soon after this, that the archbishop Lanfranc went
to Rome, and Thomas with him : and when they were come
thither, and had said all that they desired on other subjects,
Thomas began his speech, saying how he had come to
Canterbury, and how the archbishop had desired of him an
oath of obedience, and that he had refused it. Then the
archbishop Lanfranc began to make manifest with clear
reasoning, that he had a right to demand that which he
required : and he proved the same with strong arguments
before the Pope Alexander, and before all the council then
assembled : and thus they departed home. After this,
Thomas came to Canterbury, and humbly performed all that
the archbishop required, and thereupon he received the
blessing. This year earl Waltheof made peace with the
king. And during Lent in the same year the king caused all
the monasteries in England to be despoiled of their treasures.
The same year king Sweyn came from Denmark into the
Humber, and the people of those parts came to meet him and
made an alliance with him, for they believed that he would
conquer the land. Then the Danish bishop Christien, and
earl Osbern, and their Danish retainers, came into Ely, and
all the people of the fens joined them, for they believed that
they should conquer the whole country. Now the monks of
Peterborough were told that some of their own men, namely,

of Christ's church were substituted in their place, together with the prior,
named Anthony, who had been sub-prior at Christ's church. The townsmen
who entered the abbat's hall in arms were seized, and those who were con-
victed of having struck him lost their eyes.

After the death of Lanfranc the see remained vacant four years, nine
months, and nine days, during which time it suffered much adversity. At
length, in the year of our Lord's incarnation 1093, and on the second before
the Nones of March, the archbishopric of Canterbury was given to Anselm
abbat of Bec, a good and an upright man, of great learning, and amongst
the most noted of his time. He came to Canterbury on the seventh before
the Kalends of October, his earlier arrival having been prevented by many
sufficient causes, and he was consecrated on the second before the Nones of
December.

Hereward and his train, would pillage the monastery, because they had heard that the king had given the abbacy to a French abbat named Turold, and that he was a very stern man, and that he was come into Stamford with all his French followers.   There was, at that time, a church-warden named Ywar; who took all that he could by night, gospels, mass-robes, cassocks, and other garments, and such other small things as he could carry away, and he came before day to the abbat Turold, and told him that he sought his protection, and told how the outlaws were coming to Peterborough, and he said that he had done this at the desire of the monks.   Then early in the morning all the outlaws came with many ships, and they endeavoured to enter the monastery, but the monks withstood them, so that they were not able to get in.   Then they set fire to it, and burned all the monks' houses, and all those in the town, save one : and they broke in through the fire at Bolhithe-gate,* and the monks came before them and desired peace.   However they gave no heed to them, but went into the monastery, and climbed up to the holy crucifix, took the crown from our Lord's head, which was all of the purest gold, and the footstool of red gold from under his feet.   And they climbed up to the steeple, and brought down the table † which was hidden there ; it was all of gold and silver.   They also seized two gilt shrines, and nine of silver, and they carried off fifteen great crosses of gold and silver. And they took so much gold and silver, and so much treasure in money, robes, and books, that no man can compute the amount ; saying they did this because of their allegiance to the monastery : and afterwards they betook themselves to their ships and went to Ely, where they secured their treasures.   The Danes believed that they should overcome the Frenchmen, and they drove away all the monks, leaving only one named Leofwin the Long, and he lay sick in the hospital. Then came the abbat Turold, and eight score Frenchmen with him, all well armed ; and when he arrived he found all burnt both within and without, excepting the church itself ; and all the outlaws were then embarked, knowing that he would come thither. This happened on the fourth day before

* Bulldyke Gate.
† Ingram so translates the word, referring to a Gallo-Norman poem published by Sharpe.   Gibson, Lye, and Miss Gurney read " cope."

the Nones of June. Then the two kings, William and Sweyn, made peace with each other, on which the Danes departed from Ely, carrying with them all the aforesaid treasure. When they were come into the midst of the sea, there arose a great storm, which dispersed all the ships in which the treasures were: some were driven to Norway, some to Ireland, and others to Denmark, and all the spoils that reached the latter country, being the table * and some of the shrines and crosses, and many of the other treasures, they brought to one of the king's towns called——, and laid it all up in the church. But one night, through their carelessness and drunkenness the church was burned, with all that was in it. Thus was the monastery of Peterborough burned and pillaged. May Almighty God have pity on it in his great mercy: and thus the abbat Turold came to Peterborough, and the monks returned thither and performed Christian worship in the church, which had stood a full week without service of any kind. When bishop Egelric† heard this, he excommunicated all the men who had done this evil. There was a great famine this year; and this summer the fleet from the Humber sailed into the Thames, and lay there two nights, and it afterwards held on its course to Denmark. And earl Baldwin died, and his son Arnulf succeeded him; and earl William‡ and the French king should have been his support: but earl Robert came and slew his kinsman Arnulf, and the earl; put the king to flight, and slew many thousands of his men.

A. 1071. This year earl Edwin and earl Morcar fled, and wandered through the woods and fields. Then earl Morcar took ship and went to Ely; and earl Edwin was slain treacherously by his own men: and bishop Egelwine,§ and Siward Barn, and many hundreds with them, came into Ely. And when king William heard this, he called out a fleet and army; and he surrounded that land, and he made a bridge and entered in, his fleet lying off the coast. Then all the outlaws surrendered; these were, bishop Egelwine and earl Morcar, and all who were with them, excepting only Hereward, and his followers whom he led off with great valour. And the king seized their ships, and arms, and much

---

* Or cope: see the last note.   † Of Selsey.
‡ Fitz-Osberne.   § Of Durham.

treasure; and he disposed of the men as he would; and he sent bishop Egelwine to Abingdon, where he died early in the winter.

A. 1072. This year king William led an army and a fleet against Scotland, and he stationed the ships along the coast and crossed the Tweed with his army; but he found nothing to reward his pains. And king Malcolm came and treated with king William, and delivered hostages, and became his liege-man; and king William returned home with his forces. Bishop Egelric died this year; he had been consecrated to the archbishopric of York, of which he was unjustly deprived, and the see of Durham was given to him; this he held as long as he chose, and then resigned it and went to the monastery of Peterborough, and there he spent twelve years. Then after king William had conquered England, he removed Egelric from Peterborough, and sent him to Westminster, and he died on the Ides of October, and he is buried in the abbey, in the aisle of St. Nicholas.

A. 1073. This year king William carried an army of English and French over sea, and conquered the province of Maine: and the English did great damage, for they destroyed the vineyards and burned the towns, and they laid waste that province, the whole of which submitted to William; and they afterwards returned home to England.

A. 1074. This year king William went over sea to Normandy; and child Edgar came into Scotland from Flanders on St. Grimbald's mass-day. King Malcolm and Margaret his sister received him there with much pomp. Also Philip, king of France, sent him a letter inviting him to come, and offering to give him the castle of Montreuil, as a place to annoy his enemies from. After this, king Malcolm and his sister Margaret gave great presents and much treasure to him and his men, skins adorned with purple, sable-skin, grey-skin and ermine-skin-pelisses, mantles, gold and silver vessels, and escorted them out of his dominions with much ceremony. But evil befell them at sea; for they had hardly left the shore, when such rough weather came on, and the sea and wind drove them with such force upon the land, that their ships went to pieces and they saved their lives with much difficulty. They lost nearly all their riches and some of their men were taken by the French : but the boldest of them escaped back to Scotland, some on foot and some mounted on wretched horses. King Malcolm advised Edgar to send to king William beyond the sea, and request his friendship.   Edgar did so, and the king acceded to his request and sent to fetch him. Again, king Malcolm and his sister made them handsome presents, and escorted them with honour out of their dominions.   The sheriff of York met him at Durham, and went all the way with him, ordering him to be provided with meat and fodder at all the castles which they came to, until they reached the king beyond the sea.   There king William received him with much pomp, and he remained at the court, enjoying such privileges as the king granted him.

A. 1075. This year king William gave the daughter of William Fitz-Osberne in marriage to earl Ralph : the said Ralph was a Welchman on his mother's side, and his father was an Englishman named Ralph, and born in Norfolk. Then the king gave the earldom of Norfolk and Suffolk to his son, who brought his wife to Norwich, but

> There was that bride-ale
> The source of man's bale.

For earl Roger and earl Waltheof were there, and bishops and abbats, and they took counsel to depose the king of England.   And this was soon reported to the king then in Normandy, and it was told him withal that earl Roger and earl Ralph were the heads of the conspiracy, and that they had brought over the Britons to their side, and had sent eastward to Denmark for a fleet to assist them.   And earl Roger departed to his earldom in the west, and gathered his people together in rebellion against the king, but he was checked in his attempt.   And earl Ralph also being in his earldom would have marched forth with his people ; but the garrisons of the castles of England, and the inhabitants of the country came against him, and prevented his effecting any thing, on which he took ship at Norwich : and his wife remained in the castle, and held it till she had obtained terms, and then she departed from England with all her adherents. And after this the king came to England, and he took his kinsman earl Roger and put him in prison ; and earl Waltheof went over the sea and betrayed himself, but he asked forgiveness and offered a ransom. The king let him off lightly until he came to England, when he had him seized. And soon afterwards two hundred ships arrived from Denmark, commanded by two chieftains, Canute the son of Sweyn, and earl Hacco, but they durst not risk a battle with king William, but chose rather to go to York, where they broke into St. Peter's minster, and having taken thence much treasure, went away again. They then crossed over the sea to Flanders, but all who had been concerned in the act perished, namely earl Hacco and many others with him. And the lady Edgitha died at Winchester seven nights before Christmas, and the king caused her to be brought to Westminster with great pomp, and to be laid by her lord king Edward. And the king was at Westminster during Christmas, and there all the Britons who had been at the bridal feast at Norwich were brought to justice; some were blinded, and others banished. Thus were the traitors to William subdued.

1076. This year Sweyn king of Denmark died, and Harold his son succeeded to the kingdom. And the king gave Westminster to Vitalis, who had before been abbat of Bernay.* Earl Waltheof was beheaded at Winchester on the mass-day of St. Petronilla,† and his body was carried to Croyland, where it now lies. And the king went over sea and led his army into Brittany, and besieged the castle of Dol, and the Britons defended it till the king of France came up, and then William departed, having lost both men and horses and much treasure.

---

* Or Berneges. A cell to the abbey of Fescamp, in Normandy.

† "II. Kal. Jun. or the 31st of May. This notice of St. Petronilla, whose name and existence seem scarcely to have been known to the Latin historians, we owe exclusively to the valuable MS. c. t. b. iv. Yet if ever female saint deserved to be commemorated as a conspicuous example of early piety and Christian zeal, it must be Petronilla. She was no less a person than the daughter of St. Peter himself; who, being solicited to marry a nobleman at Rome of the name of Flaccus, and on her refusal allowed three days to deliberate, after passing the whole time in fasting and prayer, and receiving the sacrament at the hands of Nicomedes the priest, expired on the third day! This is no Romish legend of modern growth, for her name appears in the martyrology of Bede, and in the most venerable records of primitive Christianity."—INGRAM. And yet, the reader, who shall receive even the existence of Petronilla in any other light than as a fable, must possess a credulity which will enable him to realize all the impostures with which ecclesiastical history abounds.

1077. This year a peace was made between the king of France and William king of England, but it lasted only a little while. And this year, one night before the assumption of St. Mary, there was a more dreadful fire in London than had ever happened since the town was built. And the moon was eclipsed, three nights before candlemas: the same year died Egelwig abbat of Evesham, on the fourteenth day before the Kalends of March, which was the mass-day of St. Juliana; and Walter became bishop in his stead. Bishop Herman also died on the tenth day before the Kalends of March. He was bishop in Berkshire, Wiltshire, and Dorsetshire. Also in this year king Malcolm won the mother of Malslaythe and all his best men and all his treasure and his oxen and himself hardly escaped.... There was also this year a dry summer, and wild-fire burned many towns, and many cities were ruined by it.

A. 1078.

A. 1079. This year king William's son Robert, fled from his father to his uncle Robert in Flanders, because his father would not let him govern his earldom in Normandy; which he himself, and with his consent Philip king of France, had given to him. The best men of that land had sworn allegiance to him and taken him for their lord. And the same year king William fought against his son Robert without the borders of Normandy near a castle called Gerberoy, and there king William was wounded, and the horse on which he sat was killed, and he that brought him another horse, namely, Tookie Wiggodson, was killed with a dart, and his son William was also wounded, and many men were slain, but Robert returned to Flanders. We will not say more at present of the harm that he did to his father.

This year, between the two festivals of St. Mary, king Malcolm invaded England with a large army, and laid waste Northumberland as far as the Tyne; and he slew many hundred men, and carried home much money and treasure and many prisoners.

A. 1080. This year Walcher bishop of Durham was slain at a gemot, and a hundred French and Flemings with him: Walcher himself was born in Lorraine. The Northumbrians perpetrated this in the month of May.

A. 1081. This year the king led an army into Wales, and there he set free many hundred persons.

A. 1082. This year the king arrested bishop Odo. And there was a great famine this year.

A. 1083. This year a quarrel arose in Glastonbury between the abbat Thurstan and his monks. It was first caused by the abbat's unwise conduct, in that he treated his monks ill in many respects, but the monks were lovingly-minded towards him, and begged him to govern them in right and in kindness, and they would be faithful and obedient to him. But the abbat would none of this, and wrought them evil, and threatened worse. One day the abbat went into the chapter-house, and spoke against the monks, and would have taught them amiss;* and he sent for laymen, and they came in all armed upon the monks in the chapter-house. Then the monks were greatly terrified and knew not what to do, and some ran for refuge into the church and locked the doors from within; but the others followed them, and would have dragged them forth when they durst not come out. Rueful things happened there on that day, for the French broke into the choir and threw darts towards the altar where the monks were collected, and some of their servants went upon the upper floor† and shot down arrows towards the chancel, so that many arrows stuck in the crucifix which stood above the altar, and the wretched monks lay around the altar, and some crept under it, and they called earnestly upon God and besought his mercy, since they could obtain no mercy at the hands of men. What can we say, but that they shot without ceasing, and others broke down the doors, and rushed in, and they slew some of the monks and wounded many, so that the blood ran down from the altar on the steps, and from the steps to the floor? Three were smitten to death and eighteen wounded. And the same year Matilda the wife of king William died on the day after the feast of All Saints. And the same year after Christmas the king caused a great and heavy tax to be raised throughout England, even seventy-two pence upon every hide of land.

* He wished to substitute the chant of William of Feschamp for that called the Gregorian.
† Probably along the open galleries in the upper story of the choir, commonly called the triforium.

A. 1084. This year Wulfwold abbat of Chertsey died on the 13th day before the Kalends of May.

A. 1085. This year men said and reported as certain, that Canute king of Denmark, the son of king Sweyn, was coming hither, and that he designed to conquer this land, with the assistance of Robert earl of Flanders, whose daughter he had married. When king William, who was then in Normandy, heard this, for England and Normandy were both his, he hastened hither with a larger army of horse and foot, from France and Brittany, than had ever arrived in this land, so that men wondered how the country could feed them all. But the king billeted the soldiers upon his subjects throughout the nation, and they provided for them, every man according to the land that he possessed. And the people suffered much distress this year: and the king caused the country near the sea to be laid waste, that if his enemies landed they might the less readily find any plunder. Afterwards when he had received certain information that they had been stopped,* and that they would not be able to proceed in this enterprise, he let part of his forces return to their own homes, and he kept part in this land through the winter. At midwinter the king was at Gloucester with his witan; and he held his court there five days; and afterwards the archbishop and clergy held a synod during three days; and Maurice was there chosen to the bishopric of London, William to that of Norfolk, and Robert to that of Cheshire; they were all clerks of the king. After this the king had a great consultation, and spoke very deeply with his witan concerning this land, how it was held and what were its tenantry. He then sent his men over all England, into every shire, and caused them to ascertain how many hundred hides of land it contained, and what lands the king possessed therein, what cattle there were in the several counties, and how much revenue he ought to receive yearly from each. He also caused them to write down how much land belonged to his archbishops, to his bishops, his abbats, and his earls, and, that I may be brief, what property every

* Because there was a mutiny in the Danish fleet; which was carried to such a height, that the king, after his return to Denmark, was slain by his own soldiers. Vide *Antiq. Celto-Scand.* p. 228. See also our Chronicle, A.D. 1087.—INGRAM.

inhabitant of all England possessed in land or in cattle, and how much money this was worth. So very narrowly did he cause the survey to be made, that there was not a single hide nor a rood of land, nor—it is shameful to relate that which he thought no shame to do—was there an ox, or a cow, or a pig passed by, and that was not set down in the accounts,* and then all these writings were brought to him.

· A. 1086. This year the king wore his crown and held his court at Winchester at Easter, and he so journeyed forward that he was at Westminster during Pentecost, and there he dubbed his son Henry a knight. And afterwards he travelled about, so that he came to Salisbury at Lammas; and his witan, and all the land-holders of substance in England, whose vassals soever they were, repaired to him there, and they all submitted to him, and became his men, and swore oaths of allegiance, that they would be faithful to him against all others. Thence he proceeded to the Isle of Wight because he was to cross over to Normandy; and this he afterwards did; but first, according to his custom, he extorted immense sums from his subjects, upon every pretext he could find, whether just or otherwise. Then he went over to Normandy, and king Edward's kinsman Edgar etheling left him, because he received no great honour from him: may Almighty God give him glory hereafter. And the etheling's sister Christina went into the monastery of Romsey, and took the holy veil. And the same was a very heavy year, and very disastrous and sorrowful; for there was a pestilence among the cattle, and the corn and fruits were checked; and the weather was worse than may easily be conceived: so violent was the thunder and lightning, that many persons were killed: and things ever grew worse and worse with the people. May Almighty God mend them, when such is his will!

A. 1087. The year 1087 after the birth of Christ our Saviour, and the one and twentieth of king William's reign, during which he governed and disposed of the realm of England even as God permitted him, was a very grievous time of scarcity in this land. There was also so much illness,

---

* This is the famous Doomsday Book, or Rotulus Wintoniæ, called also Liber Wintoniæ. At the end of it is the date, *Anno millesimo octogesimo sexto ab incarnatione Dei, vigesimo vero regni Willelmi, &c.*

that almost every other man was afflicted with the worst of evils, that is, a fever; and this so severe, that many died of it. And afterwards, from the badness of the weather which we have mentioned before, there was so great a famine throughout England, that many hundreds died of hunger. Oh, how disastrous, how rueful were those times! when the wretched people were brought to the point of death by the fever, then the cruel famine came on and finished them. Who would not deplore such times, or who is so hard-hearted that he will not weep for so much misery? But such things are, on account of the sins of the people, and because they will not love God and righteousness. Even so was it in those days; there was little righteousness in this land amongst any, excepting the monks alone, who fared well. The king and the chief men loved much, and over much, to amass gold and silver, and cared not how sinfully it was gotten, so that it came into their hands. The king sold out his lands as dear as dearest he might, and then some other man came and bid more than the first had given, and the king granted them to him who offered the larger sum; then came a third and bid yet more, and the king made over the lands to him who offered most of all; and he cared not how iniquitously his sheriffs extorted money from the miserable people, nor how many unlawful things they did. And the more men spake of rightful laws, the more lawlessly did they act. They raised oppressive taxes, and so many were their unjust deeds, it were hard to number them. And the same year, before harvest, St. Paul's holy minster, the residence of the bishops of London, was burnt, together with many other monasteries, and the greater and handsomer part of the whole city. At the same time likewise almost all the principal towns of England were burnt down. Oh, how sad and deplorable was this year, which brought forth so many calamities!

The same year also, before the assumption of St. Mary, king William marched with an army out of Normandy into France, and made war upon his own lord king Philip, and slew a great number of his people, and burned the town of Mante, and all the holy monasteries in it, and two holy men who served God as anchorites were burned there. This done king William returned into Normandy. Rueful deeds he did, and ruefully he suffered. Wherefore ruefully? He fell sick and became grievously ill. What can I say? The sharpness of death, that spareth neither rich nor poor, seized upon him. He died in Normandy the day after the nativity of St. Mary, and he was buried in Caen, at St. Stephen's monastery, which he had built and had richly endowed. Oh, how false, how unstable, is the good of this world! He, who had been a powerful king and the lord of many territories, possessed not then, of all his lands, more than seven feet of ground; and he, who was erewhile adorned with gold and with gems, lay then covered with mould. He left three sons: Robert the eldest was earl of Normandy after him; the second, named William, wore the crown of England after his father's death; and his third son was Henry, to whom he bequeathed immense treasures.

If any would know what manner of man king William was, the glory that he obtained, and of how many lands he was lord; then will we describe him as we have known him, we, who have looked upon him, and who once lived in his court.* This king William, of whom we are speaking, was a very wise and a great man, and more honoured and more powerful than any of his predecessors. He was mild to those good men who loved God, but severe beyond measure towards those who withstood his will. He founded a noble monastery on the spot where God permitted him to conquer England, and he established monks in it, and he made it very rich. In his days the great monastery at Canterbury was built, and many others also throughout England; moreover this land was filled with monks who lived after the rule of St. Benedict; and such was the state of religion in his days that all that would, might observe that which was prescribed by their respective orders. King William was also held in much reverence: he wore his crown three times every year when he was in England: at Easter he wore it at Winchester, at Pentecost at Westminster, and at Christmas at Gloucester. And at these times, all the men of England were with him, archbishops, bishops, abbats, and earls, thanes, and knights. So also, was he a very stern and a wrathful man, so that none durst do anything

---

* From this we learn that this part of the Chronicle was written by a contemporary and eye-witness of the facts which he relates.

against his will, and he kept in prison those earls who acted
against his pleasure.   He removed bishops from their sees,
and abbats from their offices, and he imprisoned thanes, and
at length he spared not his own brother Odo.   This Odo
was a very powerful bishop in Normandy, his see was that
of Bayeux, and he was foremost to serve the king.   He
had an earldom in England, and when William was in
Normandy he was the first man in this country, and him
did he cast into prison.   Amongst other things the good
order that William established is not to be forgotten; it
was such that any man, who was himself aught, might travel over the kingdom with a bosom-full of gold unmolested;
and no man durst kill another, however great the injury he
might have received from him.   He reigned over England,
and being sharp-sighted to his own interest, he surveyed the
kingdom so thoroughly that there was not a single hide of
land throughout the whole, of which he knew not the pos-
sessor, and how much it was worth, and this he afterwards
entered in his register.*   The land of the Britons † was
under his sway, and he built castles therein; moreover he
had full dominion over the Isle of Man (Anglesey): Scotland also was subject to him from his great strength; the
land of Normandy was his by inheritance, and he possessed
the earldom of Maine; and had he lived two years longer
he would have subdued Ireland by his prowess, and that
without a battle.   Truly there was much trouble in these
times, and very great distress; he caused castles to be built,
and oppressed the poor.   The king was also of great stern-
ness, and he took from his subjects many marks of gold, and
many hundred pounds of silver, and this, either with or
without right, and with little need.   He was given to
avarice, and greedily loved gain.   He made large forests
for the deer, and enacted laws therewith, so that whoever
killed a hart or a hind should be blinded.   As he forbade
killing the deer, so also the boars; and he loved the tall
stags as if he were their father.   He also appointed con-

* This is certainly an evident allusion to the compilation of Doomsday
Book already described, A.D. 1085, as Gibson observes; and it is equally
clear to me, that the composition of this part of the Chronicle is by a
different hand.—INGRAM.

† Wales.

cerning the hares, that they should go free. The rich complained and the poor murmured, but he was so sturdy that he recked nought of them; they must will all that the king willed, if they would live; or would keep their lands; or would hold their possessions; or would be maintained in their rights. Alas! that any man should so exalt himself, and carry himself in his pride over all! May Almighty God show mercy to his soul, and grant him the forgiveness of his sins! We have written concerning him these things, both good and bad, that virtuous men might follow after the good, and wholly avoid the evil, and might go in the way that leadeth to the kingdom of heaven.

We may write of many events which happened during this year. In Denmark, the Danes who were formerly accounted the most loyal of people, turned to the greatest possible perfidy and treachery, for they chose king Canute, and submitted to him, and swore oaths of allegiance, and afterwards they shamefully murdered him in a church.* It also came to pass in Spain, that the heathen men went forth, and made war upon the Christians, and brought great part of the country into subjection to themselves. But the Christian king, whose name was Alphonso, sent to all countries and begged assistance. And allies flocked to him from every Christian land, and they went forth, and slew or drove away all the heathens, and they won their land again by the help of God. The same year also many great men died in this land: Stigand bishop of Chichester, and the abbat of St. Augustine's, and the abbats of Bath and of Pershore, and the lord of them all William king of England, concerning whom we have spoken above.

After his death, his son William, of the same name with his father, took to himself the government, and was consecrated king in Westminster by archbishop Lanfranc three days before Michælmas: and all the men of England acknowledged him, and swore oaths of allegiance to him. This done, the king went to Winchester and examined the treasury, and the hoards which his father had amassed; gold and silver, vessels of plate, palls, gems, and many other valu-

* A church at Odensee, dedicated to St. Alban, whose relics had been brought from England by this Canute.

ables that are hard to be numbered. The king did as his father before he died commanded him ; he distributed treasures amongst all the monasteries of England, for the sake of his father's soul : to some he gave ten marks of gold, and to others six, and sixty pennies to every country church, and a hundred pounds of money was sent into every county to be divided among the poor for his soul's sake. And before he died he had also desired that all who had been imprisoned during his reign should be released. And the king was at London during midwinter.

A. 1088. This year the land was much disturbed, and filled with treason, so that the principal Frenchmen here would have betrayed their lord the king, and have had his brother Robert instead, who was earl of Normandy. Bishop Odo was the chief man in the conspiracy, together with bishop Gosfrith, and William bishop of Durham. The king esteemed the bishop so highly, that the affairs of all England were directed after his counsel, and according to his pleasure, but the bishop purposed to do by him as Judas Iscariot did by our Lord. And earl Roger was concerned in this conspiracy, and many others with him, all Frenchmen. This plot was concerted during Lent ; and as soon as Easter came they marched forth, and plundered, and burned, and laid waste the lands of the crown ; and they ruined the estates of those who remained firm in their allegiance. And each of the head conspirators went to his own castle, and manned and victualled it, as best he might. Bishop Gosfrith and Robert the peace-breaker went to Bristol, and having plundered the town, they brought the spoils into the castle ; and afterwards they sallied forth and plundered Bath, and all the surrounding country, and they laid waste all the lordship of Berkeley. And the chief men of Hereford and all that county, and the men of Shropshire, with many from Wales, entered Worcestershire, and went on plundering and burning, till they approached the county town, and they were resolved to burn this also, and to plunder the cathedral, and to seize the king's castle for themselves. The worthy bishop Wulstan seeing this, was much distressed in mind, because the castle was committed to his keeping. Nevertheless his retainers, few as they were, marched out, and through the mercy of God, and the good desert of the bishop, they slew

or took captive five hundred men, and put all the rest to
flight. The bishop of Durham did as much harm as he
could in all the northern parts: one of the conspirators
named Roger, threw himself into Norwich castle, and spread
devastation throughout that country: Hugo also was in no
respect less formidable to Leicestershire and Northampton.
Bishop Odo, with whom these commotions originated, departed to his earldom of Kent, which he ravaged, and he
wholly laid waste the lands of the king and the archbishop,
and brought all the plunder into his castle at Rochester.
When the king had heard all this, and with what treason
they were acting towards him, he was greatly disturbed in
mind; and he sent for the English, and laid his necessities
before them, and entreated their assistance. He promised
them better laws than had ever been in this land, and forbade
all unjust taxes, and guaranteed to his subjects their woods
and hunting. But these concessions were soon done away.
Howbeit the English came to the aid of their lord the king,
and they then marched towards Rochester, desiring to seize
bishop Odo, for they thought that if they had him who was
the head of the conspiracy in their power, they might with
greater ease subdue the others. Then they came to Tun-
bridge castle, in which were the knights of bishop Odo and
many others, who resolved to hold out against William. But
the English came on, and stormed the castle, and the garrison
capitulated. They then proceeded towards Rochester believing that the bishop was there: but the king was told
that he was departed to his castle at Pevensey, and the king
and his troops went after him, and he besieged that castle
full six weeks with a very large army.

In the meantime Robert earl of Normandy, the king's
brother, gathered together a great multitude, and thought
that he should win England with the aid of the disaffected of
this country. And he sent some of his troops to this land,
intending to follow them himself. But the English who
guarded the sea attacked these men, and slew and drowned
more than any one can number. At length provisions became scarce in the castle, on which the insurgents prayed for
a truce and surrendered the place to the king, and the bishop
took an oath that he would depart from England, and never
return unless the king sent for him, and that he would also

give up Rochester castle. After this the bishop proceeded
thither that he might deliver up that fortress, and the king
sent his men with him, but then the soldiers who were in the
castle arose, and seized the bishop, and the king's men, whom
they put into confinement. There were very good knights
in this castle : Eustace the younger, the three sons of earl
Roger, and all the best born of this land, and of Normandy.
When the king knew this, he set forth with all the troops
then with him, and he sent over all England and commanded
that every man of mark, French or English, from town and
from country, should come and join him. Many were those
who flocked to him, and he marched to Rochester and besieged the castle till the garrison capitulated. Bishop Odo
and those who were with him departed over sea, and thus the
bishop lost the station he held in this land. The king afterwards sent an army to Durham, and besieged the castle, and
the bishop capitulated, and surrendered it, and he gave up
his bishopric and went to Normandy. Many Frenchmen
also left their lands, and went over sea, and the king gave
their estates to those who had held fast to him.

A. 1089. This year the venerable father and patron of
monks, archbishop Lanfranc, departed this life, but we trust
that he has entered into the kingdom of heaven. There
was also a great earthquake throughout England on the 3rd
day before the Ides of August.* And it was a very late
year both as to the corn, and fruits of all kind, so that many
men reaped their corn about Martinmas, and even later.

A. 1090. Things being in the state we have described,
as regarding the king, his brother, and his people, William
considered how he might take the surest vengeance on his
brother Robert, harass him most, and win Normandy from
him. To this end, he gained the castle and port of St. Valery
by stratagem or bribery, and also Albemarle castle, and he
placed his knights in them, and they did much harm, ravaging and burning the country. After this he got possession
of more castles in that land, and in these also he stationed his
knights. When Robert earl of Normandy found that his
sworn liege-men revolted and gave up their castles to his
great injury, he sent to his lord Philip king of France, who

* The 11th of August.

came into Normandy with a large army; and the king and
the earl with an innumerable force besieged a castle defended
by the king of England's soldiers : but king William of England sent to Philip king of France, and he, for love of William or for his great bribes, deserted his vassal earl Robert
and his land, and returned to France, leaving things as they
were.   During all these transactions, England was greatly
oppressed by unlawful taxes, and many other grievances.

   A. 1091. This year king William held his court at Westminster at Christmas, and the following Candlemas he departed
from England to Normandy, bent on his brother's ruin : but
whilst he was in that country, peace was made between them,
on condition that the earl should give up Feschamp, the earldom
of Eu, and Cherbourg, to William, and withal that the king's
men should be unmolested in those castles of which they had
possessed themselves in the earl's despite.   And the king, on
his side, promised to reduce to their obedience the many
castles conquered by their father, which had since revolted
from the earl, and also to establish him in the possession of
all their father's territories abroad, excepting those places
which the earl had then given up to the king.   Moreover all
who had lost their lands in England on account of the earl
were to regain them by this treaty, and the earl also was to
receive certain estates in England then specified.   It was
also agreed that if the earl died leaving no legitimate son the
king should be heir of all Normandy, and in like manner if
the king died, that the earl should be heir of all England.
Twelve of the chief men on the part of the king, and twelve
on that of the earl, guaranteed this treaty by oath ; yet it was
observed but a short time. During this peace Edgar etheling
was dispossessed of those lands which the earl had granted him,
and he departed and went from Normandy into Scotland, to
the king his brother-in-law, and his sister.   Whilst king William was out of England, Malcolm king of Scotland invaded
this country, and ravaged great part of it, till the good men to
whom the keeping of the land was entrusted, sent their troops
against him and drove him back.   When king William heard
this in Normandy, he hastened to return, and he came to England and his brother earl Robert with him. And they called
out a fleet and army, but almost all the ships were lost, a few
days before Michaelmas, ere they reached Scotland. And

the king and his brother proceeded with the army : and when king Malcolm heard that they sought to attack him, he marched with his array out of Scotland into Lothian in England, and remained there. And when king William approached, earl Robert and Edgar etheling mediated a peace between the kings, on condition that king Malcolm should repair to our king, and become his vassal, and in all the like subjection as to his father before him ; and this he confirmed by oath. And king William promised him all the lands and possessions that he held under his father. By this peace Edgar etheling was reconciled to the king. And the kings separated in great friendship, but this lasted during a short time only. Earl Robert abode here with the king till Christmas drew near, and in this time he found little good faith as to the fulfilment of the treaty, and two days before the feast he took ship from the Isle of Wight and sailed to Normandy, and Edgar etheling with him.

A. 1092. This year king William went northward to Carlisle with a large army, and he repaired the city, and built the castle. And he drove out Dolfin, who had before governed that country ; and having placed a garrison in the castle, he returned into the south, and sent a great number of rustic Englishmen thither, with their wives and cattle, that they might settle there and cultivate the land.

A. 1093. This year, in Lent, king William was very sick at Gloucester, insomuch that he was universally reported to be dead : and he made many good promises in his illness ; that he would lead his future life in righteousness—that the churches of God he would guard and free—and never more sell them for money—and that he would have all just laws in his kingdom. And he gave the archbishopric of Canterbury, which he had hitherto kept in his own hands, to Anselm, who was before this abbat of Bec, and the bishopric of Lincoln to his chancellor Robert ; and he granted lands to many monasteries, but afterwards, when recovered, he took them back, and he neglected all the good laws that he had promised us. After this the king of Scotland sent desiring that the stipulated conditions might be performed ; and king William summoned him to Gloucester, and sent hostages to him in Scotland, and afterwards Edgar etheling and others met him, and brought him with much honour to the court.

But when he came there, he could neither obtain a conference with our king nor the performance of the conditions formerly promised him, and therefore they departed in great enmity: and king Malcolm returned home to Scotland, and as soon as he came thither, he assembled his troops and invaded England, ravaging the country with more fury than behoved him: and Robert, earl of Northumberland, with his men, lay in wait for him, and slew him unawares. He was killed by Moræl of Bambrough, the earl's steward, and king Malcolm's own godfather:* his son Edward, who, had he lived, would have been king after his father, was killed with him. When the good queen Margaret heard that her most beloved lord, and her son, were thus cut off, she was grieved in spirit unto death, and she went with her priest into the church, and having gone through all befitting rites, she prayed of God that she might give up the ghost. And then the Scots chose† Dufenal, the brother of Malcolm, for their king, and drove out all the English who had been with king Malcolm. When Duncan, the son of king Malcolm, heard all this, for he was in king William's court, and had remained here from the time that his father gave him as an hostage to our king's father, he came to the king, and did such homage as the king required; and thus, with his consent, he departed for Scotland, with the aid that he could muster, both English and French, and he deprived his kinsman Dufenal of the throne, and was received as king. But then some of the Scotch again gathered themselves together, and slew nearly all his men, and he himself escaped with few others. They were afterwards reconciled on this condition, that Duncan should never more bring English or Frenchmen into that country.

A. 1094. This year, at Christmas, king William held his

---

* Ingram translates the original " godsib" baptismal friend, and adds the following note, " literally a gossip; but such are the changes which words undergo in their meaning as well as in their form, that a title of honour, formerly implying a spiritual relationship in God, is now applied only to those whose conversation resembles the contemptible tittle-tattle of a christening:—Gibson translates it a ' susceptor,' i. e. an undertaker."

† " From this expression it is evident, that though preference was naturally and properly given to hereditary claims, the monarchy of Scotland, as well as of England, was in principle elective. The doctrine of hereditary, of divine, of indefeasible right, is of modern growth."—INGRAM.

court at Gloucester; and there came messengers to him out
of Normandy, from his brother Robert, and they said that
his brother renounced all peace and compact if the king
would not perform all that they had stipulated in the treaty;
moreover they called him perjured and faithless unless he
would perform the conditions, or would go to the place
where the treaty had been concluded and sworn to, and
there clear himself. Then at Candlemas the king went to
Hastings, and whilst he waited there for a fair wind, he
caused the monastery on the field of battle* to be consecrated; and he took the staff from Herbert Losange,† bishop
of Thetford.—After this, in the middle of Lent, he went
over sea to Normandy. When he came thither he and his
brother, earl Robert, agreed that they would meet in peace,
and they did so, to the end that they might be reconciled.
But afterwards, when they met, attended by the same men
who had brought about the treaty, and had sworn to see it
executed, these charged all the breach of faith upon the
king; he would not allow this, neither would he observe the
treaty, on which they separated in great enmity. And the
king then seized the castle of Bures, and took the earl's men
who were in it, and he sent some of them over to this country. And on the other hand the earl, with the assistance of
the king of France, took the castle of Argences, in which he
seized Roger the Poitou and seven hundred of the king's
soldiers; and he afterwards took the castle of Hulme; and
frequently did each burn the towns and take captive the
people of his rival. Then the king sent hither and ordered
out 20,000 Englishmen to aid him in Normandy, but when
they reached the sea they were desired to return, and to give
to the king's treasury the money that they had received;
this was half a pound for each man, and they did so. And
in Normandy, after this, the earl, with the king of France,
and all the troops that they could collect, marched towards
Eu, where king William then was, purposing to besiege him
therein, and thus they proceeded until they came to Lune-

* Battle Abbey.
† Commonly called Herbert de Losinga. His letters are of much historical interest: they were supposed to be lost, until they were recently
discovered by Robert Anstruther in the Brussels library, and published
8vo, Bruxellis, apud Vandale, et Londini apud D. Nutt.

ville, and there the king of France turned off through treachery, and on this the whole army dispersed. In the meantime king William sent for his brother Henry, who was in the castle of Damfront, and because he could not pass through Normandy in security, he sent ships for him, with Hugo, earl of Chester. And when they should have made for Eu, where the king was, they directed their course instead to England, and landed at Hampton* on the eve of All Saints' day; and they then remained in this country, and were in London at Christmas.

The same year also the Welsh gathered themselves together, and made war upon the French in Wales, or in the neighbouring parts, where they had been before deprived of their lands, and they stormed many fortresses and castles, and slew the men, and afterwards their numbers increased so much, that they divided themselves into many bodies; Hugo, earl of Shropshire, fought with one division and put it to flight, but nevertheless the others abstained not, during the whole year, from committing every outrage in their power. This year also the Scots conspired against their king Duncan, and slew him, and they afterwards took his uncle Dufenal a second time for their king; through whose instructions and instigation Duncan had been betrayed to his death.

A. 1095. This year king William was at Whitsand during the first four days of Christmas, and after the fourth day he set sail and landed at Dover. And the king's brother Henry remained in this country till Lent, and then he went over sea to Normandy, with much treasure to be employed in the king's service against their brother, earl Robert : and he gained ground upon the earl continually, and did much damage to his lands and subjects. Then at Easter the king held his court at Winchester, and Robert earl of Northumberland would not repair thither; therefore the king's anger was greatly stirred up against him, and he sent to him, and sternly commanded that if he would remain in peace he should come to his court at Pentecost. This year Easter fell on the 8th before the Kalends of April, and after Easter,

* Now called Southampton, to distinguish it from Northampton; but the common people, in both neighbourhoods, generally say " Hampton" to this day.—INGRAM.

on the night of the feast of St. Ambrose, the 2nd before the
Nones of April, there was seen all over the country a great
multitude of stars falling from heaven during nearly the whole
of the night, not one or two at a time, but so thickly that no
man might number them. After this, at Pentecost, the king
was at Windsor, and all his witan with him, excepting the
earl of Northumberland, for the king would neither give
hostages nor pledge his troth that he should come and go in
security. On this the king called out an army, and marched
against the earl into Northumberland, and as soon as he
came thither he seized almost all the chief men of the earl's
court in a certain fortress, and he put them in confinement.
And he besieged Tinmouth castle until he took it, and there
he seized the earl's brother, and all who were with him:
thence he proceeded to Bambrough, and there he besieged
the earl; and when the king found that he could not reduce
him, he caused a castle to be built over against Bambrough,
and called it in his speech, *Malveisin*, which is in English,
"the evil neighbour," and he garrisoned it strongly, and
afterwards he departed southward. Then one night, soon
after the king's return into the south, the earl went out of
Bambrough towards Tinmouth: but those in the new castle,
being aware of his design, pursued and attacked him, and
they wounded him, and afterwards took him prisoner, and some
of his followers were slain, and some taken alive. In the
meantime the king was told that the Welsh had stormed a
certain castle in Wales, called Montgomery, and had slain
earl Hugo's men who defended it; on this he commanded
another army to be called out in haste, and after Michaelmas
he proceeded into Wales. He divided his forces, and his
troops made their way through all parts of the country, and
met at Snowdon, on All Saints' day. But the Welsh ever
fled before him to the mountains and moors, so that no man
could get near them, and the king at length returned homewards, because he could do no more there that winter. When
the king came back, he commanded his people to take Robert
earl of Northumberland, and lead him to Bambrough, and to
put out both his eyes, unless the besieged would surrender
the castle, which was defended by his wife, and his steward
Morel, who was also his kinsman. On this, the castle was
given up, and Morel was received at William's court; and

through him many were discovered, both clergy and laity,
who had aided this rebellion with their counsel. Then the
king ordered some of them to be imprisoned before Christmas, and he straightly commanded throughout the kingdom,
that all who held lands of him should be at his court, on
that festival, as they would retain his protection. And the
king had earl Robert brought to Windsor, and confined there
in the castle. This year also, a little before Easter, the
pope's legate came to England; this was Walter, bishop of
Albano, a man of a very virtuous life, and at Pentecost he
presented archbishop Anselm with his pall from pope Urban,
and he received it at his metropolitan city of Canterbury.
And bishop Walter remained here great part of this year,
and on his return the Romescot,* which had not been paid for
many years before, was sent with him. This year also the
weather was very unseasonable, so that the fruits of the
earth were much injured over all the country.

A. 1096. This year king William held his Christmas
court at Windsor; and William bishop of Durham died
there on New Year's day. And the king and all his witan
were at Salisbury on the octaves of the Epiphany. There
Geoffry Bainard accused William of Eu, the king's relation,
saying that he had been concerned in the conspiracy against
the king, and for this cause he fought with him and overcame him in single combat, and after he was vanquished the
king commanded that his eyes should be put out; and the
king also caused his steward named William, who was his
aunt's son, to be hanged on the gallows. Then also Eoda
earl of Champagne, the king's uncle, and many others, were
deprived of their lands, and some were brought to London,
and there executed. At Easter, this year, there was a very
great stir in this country and in many others also, through
Urban, who was called pope, though he was not in possession of the see of Rome; and an innumerable multitude of
men, with their wives and children, departed to go and conquer the heathen nations. The king and his brother, earl
Robert, were reconciled in consequence of this expedition, so
that the king went over sea, and received from the earl all
Normandy for a sum of money, according to contract. And
thereupon the earl departed, and with him went the earls of

* Commonly called Peter's pence.

Flanders and of Boulogne, and many other headmen.* And earl Robert and those who accompanied him abode in Apulia that winter. But of those who went by Hungary, many thousands perished miserably there, or on the road, and many, rueful and hunger-bitten, toiled homewards against winter. These were very hard times to all the English, as well because of the manifold taxes, as of the very grievous famine which sorely afflicted the land. This year also the nobles who had charge of this country frequently sent forth armies into Wales, and thus they greatly oppressed many, and for no purpose, but with much loss of men and of money.

A. 1097. This year king William was in Normandy at Christmas, and before Easter he sailed for this land, intending to hold his court at Winchester, but he was kept at sea by bad weather till Easter eve; and Arundel was the first place to which he came, therefore he held his court at Windsor. After this, he marched into Wales with a large army, and his troops penetrated far into the country by means of some Welshmen who had come over to him, and were his guides. And William remained there from Midsummer till near August, to his great loss of men and horses and many other things.

When the Welsh had revolted from the king, they chose several leaders from among themselves, one of these was named Cadwgan, he was the most powerful of them all, and was the son of king Griffin's brother. The king, seeing that he could not effect his purpose, returned into England, and he forthwith caused castles to be built on the marches. Then at Michaelmas, on the 4th before the Nones of October, an uncommon star appeared shining in the evening, and soon going down: it was seen in the south-west, and the light which streamed from it seemed very long, shining towards the south-east; and it appeared after this manner nearly all the week. Many allowed that it was a comet. Soon after this, Anselm archbishop of Canterbury obtained permission from the king, though against his inclination, to leave this country and go over sea, because it seemed to him that in this nation little was done according to right, or after his desires. And at Martinmas the king went over sea to

---

* "Headmen or chiefs." The term is still retained with a slight variation in the north of Europe, as ' the *hetman* Platoff, of celebrated memory.' —INGRAM.

Normandy; but whilst he waited for a fair wind, his train did as much injury in the county in which they were detained, as any prince's retinue, or even an army could have committed in a peaceable land.

This year was in all respects a very heavy time, and the weather was singularly bad at the seasons when men should till their lands and gather in the harvest; and the people had nevertheless no respite from unjust taxes. Many shires, moreover, which are bound to duty in works at London, were greatly oppressed in making the wall around the tower, in repairing the bridge which had been almost washed away, and in building the king's hall at Westminster. These hardships fell upon many. This year also, at Michaelmas, Edgar etheling, with the king's aid, led an army into Scotland, and won that country by hard fighting, and drove out the king Dufnal, and established his kinsman Edgar the son of king Malcolm and queen Margaret, as king in fealty to William, and then he returned into England.

A. 1098. This year king William was in Normandy at Christmas; and Walkelin bishop of Winchester, and Baldwin abbat of St. Edmund's, both died during this festival. This year also died Turold abbat of Peterborough. Moreover in the summer of this year a spring of blood burst out at Finchamstead, in Berkshire, according to the declaration of many men of credit, who said that they had seen it. And earl Hugo was slain in Anglesey by foreign pirates; his brother Robert succeeded him, having obtained this of the king. Before Michaelmas-day the heaven appeared as it were on fire, almost all the night. This was a year of much distress, caused by the manifold oppressive taxes; nearly all the crops in the marsh lands failed also from the great rains, which ceased not the whole year.

A. 1099. This year king William was in Normandy at Christmas; and at Easter he came hither; and at Pentecost he held his court for the first time in the new building at Westminster, and there he gave the bishopric of Durham to his chaplain Ranulf, who had long been the chief manager and director of all the king's councils held in England. And soon afterwards William went over sea, and drove earl Elias from Maine, and brought that province into subjection; and at Michaelmas he returned to this land. This year also, on

St. Martin's day, there was so very high a tide, and the damage was so great in consequence, that men remembered not the like to have ever happened before, and the same day was the first of the new moon. And Osmond bishop of Salisbury died during Advent.

A. 1100. This year, at Christmas, king William held his court in Gloucester; and at Easter in Winchester; and at Pentecost in Westminster. And at Pentecost blood was observed gushing from the earth, at a certain town of Berkshire, even as many asserted who declared that they had seen it. And after this, on the morning after Lammas-day, king William was shot with an arrow by his own men, as he was hunting, and he was carried to Winchester and buried there.* This was in the thirteenth year from his accession. He was very powerful, and stern over his lands and subjects, and towards all his neighbours, and much to be dreaded, and through the counsels of evil men which were always pleasing to him, and through his own avarice, he was ever vexing the people with armies and with cruel taxes; for in his days all justice sank, and all unrighteousness arose, in the sight of God and the world. He trampled on the church of God, and as to the bishoprics and abbacies, the incumbents of which died in his reign, he either sold them outright, or kept them in his own hands, and set them out to renters; for he desired to be the heir of every one, churchman or layman, so that the day on which he was killed he had in his own hands the archbishopric of Canterbury, the bishoprics of Winchester and Salisbury, and eleven abbacies, all let out to farm, and in fine, however long I may delay mention of it,† all that was abominable to God and oppressive to men was common in this island in William's time: and therefore he was hated by almost all his people, and abhorred by God as his end showeth, in that he died in the midst of his unrighteousness, without repentance or any reparation made for his evil deeds. He was slain on a Thursday, and buried the next morning: and after he was buried, the witan who were then near at hand, chose his brother Henry as king,

* His monument is still to be seen there, a plain gravestone of black marble, of the common shape called "dos d'âne," such as are now frequently seen, though of inferior materials, in the church-yards of villages, and are only one remove from the grassy sod.—INGRAM.

† Ingram renders this, "though I may be tedious."

and he forthwith gave the bishopric of Winchester to William Giffard, and then went to London; and on the Sunday following he made a promise to God and all the people, before the altar at Westminster, that he would abolish the injustice which prevailed in his brother's time, and that he would observe the most equitable of the laws established in the days of any of the kings before him : and after this Maurice bishop of London consecrated him as king, and all the men of this land submitted to him, and swore oaths and became his liege-men.   And soon afterwards, the king, by the advice of those about him, caused Ranulf bishop of Durham to be taken and brought into the Tower of London, and confined there.   Then before Michaelmas Anselm archbishop of Canterbury came to this land; king Henry having sent for him by the advice of his witan, because he had left the country on account of the injustice done him by king William.   And soon afterwards the king took for his wife Maud the daughter of Malcolm king of Scotland and of the good queen Margaret king Edward's kinswoman, of the true royal line of England ; and on Martinmas day she was given to him with great pomp at Westminster, and archbishop Anselm wedded her to Henry, and afterwards consecrated her as queen.   And soon after this Thomas archbishop of York died.   This year also, in the autumn, earl Robert came home into Normandy, and Robert earl of Flanders and Eustace earl of Boulogne also returned from Jerusalem, and on earl Robert's arrival in Normandy he was joyfully received by all the people, excepting those in the castles which were garrisoned with king Henry's men, and against these he had many contests and struggles.

A. 1101. This year, at Christmas, king Henry held his court at Westminster, and at Easter at Winchester.   And soon afterwards the chief men of this land entered into a league against the king, both from their own great treachery, and through Robert earl of Normandy who had hostile designs upon this land.   And then the king sent out ships to annoy and hinder his brother; but some of them failed at time of need, and deserted from the king, and submitted to earl Robert.   At Midsummer the king posted himself with all his troops at Pevensey to oppose his brother, and he waited for him there.   And in the meantime earl Robert

landed at Portsmouth twelve nights before Lammas, and the
king marched against him with all his forces ; but the chief
men interfered and made peace between them, on condition
that the king should give up all those places in Normandy
which he then detained from his brother by force of arms ;
and that all who had lost their lands in England on the earl's
account should have them again, and that earl Eustace
should also have his father's estates in this country, and that
earl Robert should receive yearly 3000 marks of silver from
England; and it was stipulated by this treaty that whichever
of the brothers outlived the other, he should inherit all
England together with Normandy, unless the deceased left
legitimate issue.   And twelve men of the highest rank on
either side confirmed this treaty by oath : and the earl
afterwards remained here till after Michaelmas ; and his men
did much harm wherever they went, whilst the earl stayed in
this land. This year also, at Candlemas, bishop Ranulf
escaped by night from the Tower of London, in which he
was confined, and went to Normandy.   It was at his suggestion chiefly, that earl Robert was incited to invade this
land.

A. 1102. This year king Henry was at Westminster
during the feast of the Nativity, and at Easter he was at
Winchester. And soon afterwards a difference arose between
the king and Robert of Belesme, who held the earldom of
Shrewsbury in this country, which his father earl Roger had
enjoyed before him, and who had other great possessions
both here and abroad ; and the king went and besieged
Arundel Castle, and when he found that he should not be
able to take it speedily, he caused castles to be built before
it, and garrisoned with his men ; and then he led all
his troops to Bridgenorth, and remained there till he had
reduced the castle, and deprived earl Robert of his lands,
and he took from him all that he possessed in England; so
the earl departed over sea, and the king's soldiers were
disbanded and returned home. On the Michaelmas following
the king was at Westminster, with all the head men of this
land, both clergy and laity ; and archbishop Anselm held a
synod, at which many decrees were made touching the
Christian religion; and many abbats, both French and
English, lost their staffs and their abbacies, because they

had obtained them unlawfully, or had lived unrighteously therein.   And the same year, in Pentecost week, there came robbers, some from Auvergne, some from France, and some from Flanders, and they brake into the monastery of Peterborough, and carried off much treasure of gold and silver; crosses, chalices, and candlesticks.

A. 1103. This year king Henry was at Westminster at Christmas.   And soon afterwards the bishop William Giffard departed from this land, because he would not against right receive consecration from Gerard archbishop of York.   And at Easter the king held his court at Winchester; and afterwards, Anselm archbishop of Canterbury journeyed to Rome, as he and the king had agreed.   This year also earl Robert of Normandy came to this land, to speak with the king, and before he departed hence he gave up the 3000 marks which king Henry should have paid him yearly according to the treaty.   This year blood was seen gushing out of the earth at Hampstead,* in Berkshire.   This was a year of much distress from the manifold taxes, and also from a mortality among the cattle, and from the failure of the crops, both of the corn and all fruits of trees.   In the morning also of St. Lawrence's day, the wind did so much damage to all the fruit of this land, that no man remembered the like to have ever happened before.   The same year died Matthias abbat of Peterborough, who had not lived more than one year after he was made abbat.   After Michaelmas, on the 12th before the Kalends of November, he was received in procession as abbat, and the same day the year following he died at Gloucester, and there he was buried.

A. 1104. This year, at Christmas, king Henry held his court at Westminster, at Easter at Winchester, at Pentecost again at Westminster.   This year the first day of Pentecost was on the Nones of June, and on the Tuesday after, at midday, there appeared four circles of a white colour round the sun, one under the other as if they had been painted.   All who saw it wondered, because they never remembered such before.   An alliance was afterwards formed between Robert earl of Normandy and Robert of Belesme,† whom king Henry had deprived of his estates, and driven out of Eng-

* Finchamstead.   † Hence the English name Bellamy.

land, and from this, the king of England and the earl of
Normandy became at variance.   And the king sent his
people over sea into Normandy, and the head men of that
country received them, and admitted them into their castles
in treachery to their lord the earl, and they greatly annoyed
the earl by plundering and burning his territories.   This
year also, William earl of Moreton (Mortaigne) departed to
Normandy, and being there, he took arms against the king,
on which the king confiscated all his possessions and estates
in this country.   It is not easy to describe the misery of this
land, which it suffered at this time through the various and
manifold oppressions and taxes that never ceased or slack-
ened : moreover wherever the king went his train fell to
plundering his wretched people, and withal there was much
burning and manslaughter.   By all this was the anger of
God provoked, and this unhappy nation harassed.

A. 1105. This year, at Christmas, king Henry held his
court at Windsor, and the following Lent he went over sea
to Normandy against his brother earl Robert.   And whilst
he remained there he won Caen and Bayeux from his brother,
and almost all the castles and chief men of that land became
subject to him ; and in the autumn he came again to this
country.   And all that he had conquered in Normandy remained to him afterwards in peace and subjection, excepting
those places which lay in the neighbourhood of William earl
of Moreton,* and which he harassed continually as much as
harass he might, in revenge for the loss of his estates in
England.   Then before Christmas Robert de Belesme came
hither to the king.   This was a year of great distress from
the failure of the fruits, and from the manifold taxes which
never ceased, either before the king went abroad, while he
was there, or again after his return.

A. 1106. This year at Christmas, king Henry was at
Westminster, and there he held his court, and during this
festival Robert de Belesme departed from the king in enmity,
and left this country for Normandy.   After this, and before
Lent, the king was at Northampton, and his brother earl
Robert of Normandy came to him there ; and because the

---

* " De Moritonio" is the Latin title; the town of Mortaigne in Normandy is the place from which it is taken.

king would not give up that which he had won from the earl
in Normandy, they separated in enmity, and the earl soon
went again over sea.   In the first week of Lent, on the
evening of Friday, the 14th before the Kalends of March, a
strange star appeared, and it was seen a while every evening
for a long time afterwards.   This star appeared in the south-
west, it seemed small and dim, but the light that stood from
it was very bright, and like an exceedingly long beam shining
to the north-east ; and one evening it seemed as if a beam
from over against the star darted directly into it.   Some
persons said that they observed more unknown stars at this
time, but we do not write this as a certainty because we saw
them not ourselves.   One night, the morrow being the day
of our Lord's supper, that is, the Thursday before Easter,
two moons appeared before day in the heavens, the one in
the east and the other in the west, both full ; and the same
day was the 14th of the moon.   At Easter the king was at
Bath, and at Pentecost at Salisbury, because he would not
hold his court over sea during his absence from this country.
After this before August, the king went into Normandy, and
almost all the inhabitants bowed to his will, excepting Robert
de Belesme, and the earl of Mortaigne, and a few other
chiefs who yet held with the earl of Normandy : the king
therefore came with an army, and besieged a castle of the
earl of Mortaigne called Tinchebrai.   Whilst the king was
besieging this castle, Robert earl of Normandy and his army
came upon him on Michaelmas eve, and with him were
Robert de Belesme and William earl of Mortaigne, and all
who wished well to their cause, but strength and victory
were with the king.   The earl of Normandy was taken,
together with the earl of Mortaigne and Robert de Stutte-
ville ; and they were afterwards sent to England, and kept
in confinement ; Robert de Belesme was put to flight, and
William Crispin was taken, with many others ; Edgar etheling who had gone over from the king to the earl a short
time before, was also taken ; but the king afterwards let him
depart unhurt.   After this, the king subdued the whole of
Normandy, and brought it under his own will and power.
This year also there was a very terrible and sinful war
between the emperor of Saxony and his son, during which
the father died, and the son succeeded to the empire.

I I

A. 1107. This year king Henry was in Normandy at Christmas and reduced that land, and having settled the government, he came to England the following Lent ; and he held his court at Windsor at Easter, and at Pentecost he held it at Westminster. And in the beginning of August he was again at Westminster, and there he gave away bishoprics and abbacies, disposing of such as were without elders and pastors, both in England and Normandy ; the number of these was so great that no man remembered that so many were ever before given away at one time. And amongst others who then received abbacies, Ernulf prior of Canterbury obtained that of Peterborough. This was about the seventh year of king Henry's reign, and the one and fortieth year that the French ruled in this land. Many said that they saw various tokens in the moon this year, and his* light waxing and waning contrary to nature. This year died Maurice bishop of London, and Robert abbat of St. Edmund's Bury, and Richard abbat of Ely. This year also Edgar king of Scotland died on the Ides of January, and his brother Alexander succeeded to the kingdom with king Henry's consent.

A. 1108. This year, at Christmas, king Henry was at Westminster ; and at Easter at Winchester ; and at Pentecost again at Westminster. After this, before August, he went into Normandy. And Philip king of France dying on the Nones of August, his son Louis succeeded him, and there were afterwards many battles between the kings of France and of England, whilst Henry remained in Normandy. This year also Gerard archbishop of York died before Pentecost, and Thomas was afterwards appointed as his successor.

A. 1109. This year king Henry was in Normandy both at Christmas and at Easter ; and before Pentecost he came hither and held his court at Westminster, at which place the stipulations were ratified, and the oaths sworn, relative to the marriage of his daughter with the emperor. There was much thunder this year, and that very terrible. And Anselm archbishop of Canterbury died on the 11th before the Kalends of April, and the first day of Easter was on the greater Litany.

* The moon is of the masculine gender, and the sun feminine, in Anglo-Saxon, as in Arabic. See A.D. 1110.

A. 1110. This year, at Christmas, king Henry held his court at Westminster; and at Easter he was at Marlborough; and at Pentecost he held his court for the first time in the New Windsor. This year, before Lent, the king sent his daughter with manifold treasures over sea, and gave her to the emperor. On the fifth night of the month of May the moon appeared shining brightly in the evening, and afterwards his light waned by little and little, and early in the night he was so wholly gone that neither light, nor circle, nor any thing at all of him was to be seen, and thus it continued till near day, and then he appeared shining full and bright; he was a fortnight old the same day: the sky was very clear all the night, and the stars shone very brightly all over the heavens, and the fruit trees were greatly injured by that night's frost. After this, in the month of June, there appeared a star in the north-east, and its light stood before it to the south-west, and it was seen thus for many nights, and ever as the night advanced it mounted upwards and was seen going off to the north-west. This year Philip de Brause,* and William Mallet, and William Baynard, were deprived of their lands. This year also died earl Elias, who held Maine in fee-tail† of king Henry; but on his death the earl of Anjou took possession of that province, and kept it against the king's will. This was a year of much distress from the taxes which the king raised for his daughter's dowry, and from the bad weather by which the crops were greatly injured, and nearly all the fruit on the trees destroyed throughout the country.—This year men first began to work at the new monastery of Chertsey.

A. 1111. This year king Henry wore not his crown at Christmas, nor at Easter, nor at Pentecost. And in August he was called over sea to Normandy, by the hostility of certain of his enemies on the marches of France, and principally by that of the earl of Anjou, who held Maine against him: and after his arrival many were the intrigues and great the

* This is the term used by Miss Gurney. Dr. Ingram renders it Braiose; the Anglo-Saxon is Brause; the Latin, Braiosa. Is not the modern name Bracy derived from this root?

† That is, the territory was not a fee-simple, but subject to *taillage*, or taxation; and that particular species is probably here intended, which is called in old French "en queuage," an expression not very different from that in the text above.—INGRAM.

burning and plundering carried on by either party against
the other.—This year Robert earl of Flanders died and his
son Baldwin succeeded him. The winter was very long this
year, a heavy and a severe time, by which the fruits of the
earth were much injured ; and there was the greatest pestilence among the cattle ever remembered.

A. 1112. All this year king Henry remained in Normandy, on account of the war in which he was engaged with
France, and with the earl of Anjou, who held Maine against
him. And whilst he was there he deprived the earl of Evreux and William Crispin of their lands, and drove them out
of Normandy : and he restored to Philip de Brause the estates which had been taken from him, and he caused Robert
de Belesme to be seized and put into prison. This was a
very good year as to the crops, the trees and fields being very
fruitful ; but it was a very heavy and a sorrowful time, by
reason of a dreadful pestilence among men.

A. 1113. This year king Henry was in Normandy at
Christmas, at Easter, and at Pentecost. And in the summer
he sent hither Robert de Belesme, to be confined in Wareham
castle, and he himself came to this land soon afterwards.

A. 1114. This year, at Christmas, king Henry held his
court at Windsor, and he held no court again this year.
And at Midsummer he entered Wales with an army, and the
Welsh came and treated with the king, and he caused castles
to be built in that country. And in September he went over
sea to Normandy. In the end of May, this year, a strange
star with a long light was seen shining for many nights.
This year also there was so great an ebb of the tide every
where in one day, as no man remembered before, so that
men went through the Thames both riding and walking, east
of London bridge. This year there were very high winds in
the month of October, and more especially on the night of
the octaves of St. Martin, as was apparent in all woods and
towns. This year also the king gave the archbishopric of
Canterbury to Ralph bishop of Rochester ; and Thomas [II.]
archbishop of York died, and the king's chaplain Thurstan
succeeded him. At this time the king went towards the sea,
and he would have gone over but he was detained by the
weather. In the meanwhile he sent his writ to Ernulf abbat of Peterborough, desiring him to come to him with speed,

for that he would speak with him on something of importance. On Ernulf's arrival, the king and the archbishops and bishops, and the English nobility who attended the king, forced him to accept the bishopric of Rochester; he withstood them long, but his resistance availed nothing. And the king commanded the archbishop to take him to Canterbury, and to consecrate him as bishop whether he would or not. This was done in the town called Burne* on the 17th before the Kalends of October. When the monks of Peterborough heard this, they were so sorry as never before, because Ernulf was a very good and a mild man, and did much good within the monastery and out of it whilst he remained there. May Almighty God be ever with him! Soon afterwards, at the request of the archbishop of Canterbury, the king gave that abbacy to a monk of Sieyes named John. And soon after this the king and the archbishop sent him to Rome for the archbishop's pall, and with him a monk named Warner, and the archdeacon John the archbishop's nephew, and they sped well on their journey. This was done on the 11th before the Kalends of October, at the town called Rugenor (Rowner, near Gosport), and the same day the king took ship at Portsmouth.

A. 1115. This year, during Christmas, king Henry was in Normandy, and whilst he was there he caused all the chief men of Normandy to do homage and swear oaths of allegiance to his son William, whom he had by his queen; and afterwards in the month of July he returned hither. This year the winter was so severe with snow and with frost, that no man then living remembered a harder: and it occasioned much disease among the cattle. This year pope Paschal sent hither a pall to archbishop Ralph, and he received it with much pomp at his see of Canterbury. Anselm an abbat of Rome, the nephew of archbishop Anselm, and John abbat of Peterborough, brought the pall from Rome.

A. 1116. This year, at Christmas, king Henry was at St. Alban's, and there he caused the monastery to be consecrated; and at Easter he was at Wudiham.† This year

* "East Bourne, in Sussex, where the king was waiting for a fair wind to carry him over sea."—INGRAM. "Sittingburn."—MISS GURNEY.
† Odiham.

also, the winter being severe and long, it was a very heavy time for the cattle and all things. And soon after Easter the king went over sea, and much treachery was practised, and there was plundering and taking of castles between France and Normandy. The chief cause of enmity was that king Henry aided his nephew earl Theobald de Blois, who was then at war with his lord Louis king of France. This was a very calamitous year, the crops being spoiled by the heavy rains, which came on just before August and lasted till Candlemas. Mast also was so scarce this year that none was to be heard of in all this land, or in Wales: moreover this land and nation were many times sorely oppressed by the taxes which the king raised both within the towns and out of them. This year also the whole of the monastery of Peterborough was burnt, with all the houses, excepting the chapter-house and the dormitory: and the greater part of the town was burnt also. All this happened on a Friday, being the 2nd day before the Nones of August.

A. 1117. All this year king Henry abode in Normandy, because of the war with the king of France and his other neighbours: then in the summer the king of France, and the earl of Flanders with him, entered Normandy with an army and remained in the country one night, and went away again in the morning without fighting. And Normandy was greatly oppressed by taxes and by the levies of troops that king Henry raised to oppose them. This nation also was sorely aggrieved in like manner, to wit, by the manifold taxes. This year also there was a violent storm of thunder and lightning, rain and hail, on the night before the Kalends of December; and on the 3rd night before the Ides of December the moon appeared for a long time as it were bloody, and then it was darkened. Also, on the night of the 17th before the Kalends of January the heaven appeared very red, as if it were burning. And on the octave of St. John the Evangelist's day there was a great earthquake in Lombardy, by which many monasteries, towers, and houses were thrown down, and the inhabitants suffered greatly. This was a very bad year for the corn, through the rains which ceased scarcely at all. And Gilbert abbat of Westminster died on the 8th before the Ides of December, and Farit* abbat of Abingdon

* Faricius is the Latin name. Is he the same who wrote the life of

died on the 7th before the Kalends of March.   And in the
same year. . . . . .

A. 1118. All this year king Henry was in Normandy,
being at war with the king of France, and with the earl of
Anjou, and with the earl of Flanders.   And the earl of
Flanders was wounded in Normandy, on which he returned
to Flanders.   The king was greatly impoverished by this
war, and lost much money and land, and he was most
harassed by his own men, who continually revolted and betrayed him, and went over to his enemies, and treacherously
gave up their castles in the king's despite.   England paid
dearly for all this by the manifold taxes which ceased not all
this year.   This year, one evening in Epiphany week, there
was dreadful lightning which caused many deaths.   And
queen Matilda died at Westminster on the Kalends of May,
and was buried there.   And Robert earl of Mellent died
also this year.   This year also, on St. Thomas's day, there
was so exceedingly high a wind that none who then lived
remembered a greater, and this might be seen everywhere
from the state of the houses and of the trees.   Pope Paschal
also died this year, and John of Gaëta, whose other name
was Gelasius, succeeded to the popedom.

A. 1119. All this year king Henry remained in Normandy,
and was greatly perplexed by the war with the king of France,
and by the treachery of his own men, who were continually
revolting from him, till at length the two kings with their
forces met in Normandy.   The king of France was there put
to flight and all his best men taken, and many of king
Henry's vassals who with the garrisons of their castles had
been against him, now submitted, and were reconciled to
him, and some of the castles he took by force.   This year,
William the son of king Henry and of queen Matilda went
to Normandy to his father, and the daughter of the earl of
Anjou was there given and wedded to him.   On Michaelmas
eve there was a great earthquake in some parts of this land;
and it was felt most in Gloucestershire and Worcestershire.
The same year pope Gelasius died on this side of the mountains, and he was buried at Cluny ; and the archbishop of
Vienne was chosen pope, his name was Calixtus.   He

bishop Aldhelm, published in the end of my edition of Aldhelm's works!
[Aldhelmi Opera, Oxon. Lond. et Cant. 1845.]

afterwards came to Rheims, in France, on the feast of St.
Luke the evangelist, and held a council there. And
Thurstan archbishop of York journeyed thither, and because
he received consecration from the pope, against right, and to
the prejudice of the see of Canterbury, and against the
king's will, Henry wholly forbade his return to England;
and being thus deprived of his archbishopric, he proceeded
with the pope towards Rome. This year also Baldwin earl
of Flanders died of the wound which he had received in
Normandy, and was succeeded by Charles the son of his
aunt and of St. Canute, king of Denmark.

A. 1120. This year peace was made between the kings of
England and of France, and after this all king Henry's own
men in Normandy made their peace with him; also the earls
of Flanders and of Ponthieu. Then the king ordered and
disposed of his castles and land in Normandy after his own
will; and so, before Advent, he returned to England. And
the king's two sons William and Richard were drowned in
the passage, together with Richard earl of Chester, and
Ottuel his brother; and very many of the king's court,
stewards, and chamberlains, and butlers, and other men in
office, and an innumerable multitude of all ranks, were also
lost. The manner of their death was a twofold grief to their
friends, first because they lost their lives so suddenly, and
next that few of their bodies were ever found. And this
year that remarkable light twice came upon our Lord's
sepulchre at Jerusalem, once at Easter, and again on the
Assumption of St. Mary, according to the report of men of
credit, who came from thence. And Thurstan archbishop of
York was reconciled to the king through the pope, and he
came to this land, and was put in possession of his archbishopric, though much against the will of the archbishop of
Canterbury.

A. 1121. This year, at Christmas, king Henry was at
Bramton, and before Candlemas Athelis was given him to
wife at Windsor, and afterwards consecrated queen; she was
the daughter of the duke of Louvain. And the moon was
eclipsed on the night before the Nones of April, being the
fourteenth day of the moon. And the king was at Berkley
at Easter, and the Pentecost following he held a great court
at Westminster, and in the summer he entered Wales with

an army, and the Welsh came to meet him, and made a treaty with him on his own terms. This year the earl of Anjou returned from Jerusalem to his own land, and after this he sent hither to fetch away his daughter who had been married to the king's son William. And on the night of Christmas eve there was a very high wind throughout this land, as might be seen plainly in its effects.

A. 1122. This year king Henry was at Norwich at Christmas, and at Easter he was at Northampton. And the town of Gloucester was burned the Lent before, for while the monks were singing mass, the deacon having begun the gospel " *Prœteriens Jesus*," the fire fell on the top of the steeple,* and burned the whole monastery, and all the treasures in it, excepting a few books and three vestments : this happened on the eighth before the Ides of March. And there was a very high wind on the Tuesday after Palm Sunday, the eleventh before the Kalends of April : after this many strange tokens were noticed throughout England, and many ghosts were seen and heard. And on the night of the eighth before the Kalends of August, there was a great earthquake throughout Somersetshire and Gloucestershire. Again on the sixth before the Ides of September, St. Mary's day, there was a very high wind, which continued from nine in the morning till dark night. The same year Ralph archbishop of Canterbury died on the thirteenth before the Kalends of November. After this many shipmen were at sea, and on the water, and said that they saw a fire in the north-east, large and broad, near the earth, and that it grew in height unto the welkin, and the welkin divided into four parts and fought against it, as it would have quenched it ; nevertheless the fire flamed up to heaven. They observed this fire at day-break, and it lasted until it was light every where : this was on the seventh before the Ides of December.

A. 1123. This year king Henry was at Dunstable at Christmas, and the messengers from the earl of Anjou came to him there, and he proceeded thence to Woodstock, and his

---

* By steeple we are here to understand not a spire, but a tower ; spires not being then invented. I believe 'spear' is the word in Saxon to express what we mean by a spire ; 'stepel,' or 'steopel,' signifying only a steep, lofty, or perpendicular structure ; and our old antiquarians very properly make a distinction between a spire-steeple and a tower-steeple."—INGRAM.

bishops and all his court with him. Now it fell out on a
Wednesday, being the fourth before the Ides of January,
that the king rode in his deer-park, and Roger bishop of
Salisbury was on one side of him, and Robert Bloet bishop
of Lincoln on the other; and they rode there talking. Then
the bishop of Lincoln sank down, and said to the king,
"My lord king! I am dying," and the king alighted from his
horse, and took him between his arms, and bade them bear
him to his inn, and he soon lay there dead; and they took
his body with much pomp to Lincoln, and Robert bishop of
Chester,* who was called Pecceth, buried him before St.
Mary's altar. Soon after this the king sent his writs over
all England, and desired his bishops, his abbats, and his
thanes, that they should all come to the meeting of his witan
at Gloucester, on Candlemas-day, and they obeyed; and
when they were there assembled the king bade them choose
to themselves whomsoever they would as archbishop of
Canterbury, and that he would confirm their choice. Then
the bishops spake among themselves, and said that they
would never more have a man of any monastic order as
archbishop over them. And they all with one accord went
to the king, and entreated that they might choose one of the
clergy for their archbishop, and to this the king consented.
All this had been set on foot by the bishop of Salisbury, and
by the bishop of Lincoln before he died, for they never loved
the rule of monks, but were ever against monks and their
rule. And the prior and monks of Canterbury and all
others of the monastic order who were there, resisted this
proceeding two full days, but in vain, for the bishop of
Salisbury † was very powerful, and swayed all England, and
he was against them with all his might. Then they chose a
clerk named William of Curboil, he was a canon of a
monastery called Chiche; ‡ and they brought him before the
king, who gave him the archbishopric, and he was received

---

* Or Lichfield. Peter, the bishop of that see in 1075 removed it to
Chester, where it remained for a short period. Hence the bishops are
frequently styled bishops of Chester. The present bishopric of Chester
was not founded till 1541.

† Roger, bishop of Salisbury, was Lord Chief Justice, Lord Chancellor,
and Lord Treasurer.

‡ "St. Osythe, in Essex; a priory rebuilt A. 1118, for canons of the
Augustine order, of which there are considerable remains."—INGRAM.

by all the bishops; but the monks and earls, and almost all
the thanes who were there, would not acknowledge him.
At this same time the messengers of the earl departed from
the king dissatisfied, nothing regarding his gifts.   At this
time also a legate arrived from Rome; his name was Henry,
and he was abbat of the monastery of St. John of Angelo.
He came for the Romescot; and told the king that a clerk
had no right to be set over monks, and that therefore they
had formerly chosen the archbishop in the chapter, as was
befitting; but, for love of the bishop of Salisbury, the king
would not undo his act.   Soon afterwards, the archbishop
went to Canterbury, and was received, though unwillingly,
and he was forthwith consecrated there by the bishop of
London, and Ernulf bishop of Rochester, and William
Giffard bishop of Winchester, and Bernard bishop of Wales
(St. David's), and Roger bishop of Salisbury.   Then early
in Lent the archbishop journeyed to Rome for his pall, and
Bernard bishop of Wales, and Sefred abbat of Glastonbury,
and Anselm abbat of St. Edmund's, and John archdeacon of
Canterbury, and Giffard who was the king's court-chaplain,
went with him.   Thurstan archbishop of York went to Rome
at the same time by order of the pope, and he arrived three
days before the archbishop of Canterbury, and was received
with much honour.   Then came the archbishop of Canterbury, and it was a full week before he could obtain an
audience of the pope, because the pope had been given to
understand that he had received the archbishopric in opposition to the monks of the monastery, and against right; but
that which overcometh all the world, namely gold and
silver,* overcame Rome also, and the pope relented and gave

* "How fortunate for the writer that the pope and his cardinals did not
understand Saxon!   The boldness of this remark might otherwise have
procured him the distinguished honour of an excommunication.   Matthew
Paris has a similar remark, but less openly expressed, respecting the
venality of the Roman see: ' _quæ nulli deese consuevit, dummodo albi
aliquid vel rubei intercedat. An._ 1103.'   Dr. Ingram might have quoted
an equally elegant compliment paid to the cardinals, " _quorum nares
odor luori quæstus causa infœcavit,_" by Alan of Tewkesbury, if the orthodox editor of the Brussels edition of Vita Sancti Thomæ had not carefully
expunged the passage: I have only done justice to historical accuracy by
restoring the offensive words in " _Vita Sancti Thomæ_, vol. i. p. 359, _edii.
Oxon. et Lond._' "

him his pall, and the archbishop swore obedience in all things
that he should impose, on the heads of St. Peter and St.
Paul, and the pope then sent him home with his blessing.
Whilst the archbishop was abroad, the king gave the
bishopric of Bath to the queen's chancellor, named Godfrey;
he was of Louvain: this was done at Woodstock on the
Annunciation of St. Mary.   Soon afterwards the king went
to Winchester, where he remained during the festival of
Easter ; and while there he gave the bishopric of Lincoln to
a clerk named Alexander, who was a nephew of the bishop
of Salisbury, and he did this all for love of that bishop.
Then the king proceeded to Portsmouth, and stayed there over
Pentecost week ; and as soon as he had a fair wind he sailed
for Normandy, having committed all England to the care
and administration of Roger bishop of Salisbury.   The king
was in Normandy all this year, and a great war broke out
between him and his thanes, for earl Waleram of Mellent,
and Amalric, and Hugh of Montfort, and William of Romare,
and many others revolted from him and held their castles
against him ; and the king on his part opposed them with
vigour, and the same year he won from Waleram his castle
of Pont-Audemer, and from Hugh that of Montfort, and
after this his affairs continued to prosper more and more.   The
same year, before the bishop of Lincoln came to his see,
nearly the whole town of Lincoln was burnt, with a great
number of persons, both men and women, and so much harm
was done that no man could tell another how great the
damage was.   This happened on the fourteenth before the
Kalends of June.

A. 1124. All this year king Henry was in Normandy,
being detained there by his great wars with Louis king of
France, and the earl of Anjou, and with his own subjects
most of all.   Then it befell on the day of the annunciation of
St. Mary, that Waleram earl of Mellent was going from one
of his castles called Beaumont, to another, Watteville, and
Amalric the steward of the king of France, and Hugh the
son of Gervais, and Hugh of Montfort, and many other good
knights went with him.   Then the king's knights from all
the neighbouring castles came against them, and fought with
them, and put them to flight, and they took the earl Waleram,
and Hugh the son of Gervais, and Hugh of Montfort, and

five and twenty other knights, and brought them to the king;
and the king caused earl Waleram and Hugh the son of
Gervais to be confined in the castle of Rouen, and he sent
Hugh of Montfort to England, and caused him to be put in
strong bonds in that of Gloucester, and as many of the others
as he thought fit he sent north and south to his castles for
confinement. Then the king went on, and won all earl
Waleram's castles in Normandy, and all the others which his
enemies held against him. All this was on account of the
son of Robert earl of Normandy named William. The same
William had married the younger daughter of Fulk earl of
Anjou, and for this cause the king of France, and all the
earls and great men held with him, and said that the king
did wrongfully keep his brother Robert in confinement, and
that he had unjustly driven his son William out of Normandy. This year there was much unseasonable weather
which injured the corn and all fruits in England, so that,
between Christmas and Candlemas, one acre's seed of wheat,
that is, two seedlips, sold for six shillings, and one of barley,
that is, three seedlips, for six shillings, and one acre's seed of
oats, being four seedlips, for four shillings. It was thus,
because corn was scarce, and the penny* was so bad, that
the man who had a pound at the market, could hardly, for
any thing, pass twelve of these pennies. The same year, the
holy bishop of Rochester Ernulf, who had been abbat of
Peterborough, died on the Ides of March. After this died
Alexander king of Scotland, on the 9th before the Kalends of
May, and his brother David, then earl of Northamptonshire,
succeeded him, and held at the same time both the kingdom
of Scotland and the English earldom. And the pope of
Rome called Calixtus died on the 19th before the Kalends of
January, and Honorius succeeded to the popedom. The
same year, after St. Andrew's day, and before Christmas,
Ralph Basset, and the king's thanes held a witenagemot at
Huncothoe, in Leicestershire, and there they hanged more
thieves than had ever before been executed within so short
a time, being in all four and forty men: and they deprived
six men of their eyes and certain other members.† Many

---

* The pennies were of silver at this time.

† " Of here ægon and of here stanes."—*Original text.*

men of truth said that several of them suffered with great
injustice, but our Lord God Almighty, who seeth and
knoweth all hidden things, seeth that the miserable people is
oppressed with all unrighteousness ; first men are bereaved
of their property, and then they are slain.   Full heavy a
year was this ; he who had any property was bereaved of it
by heavy taxes and assessments, and he who had none,
starved with hunger.

A. 1125. Before Christmas, this year, king Henry sent
from Normandy to England, and commanded that all the
mint-men of England should be deprived of their limbs,
namely of their right hands and of certain other members.
And this because a man might have a pound, and yet not be
able to spend one penny at a market.   And Roger bishop of
Salisbury sent over all England, and desired all of them to
come to Winchester at Christmas ; and when they came
thither his men took them one by one, and cut off their right
hands.   All this was done within the twelve days, and with
much justice, because they had ruined this land with the great
quantity of bad metal which they all bought.   This year the
pope of Rome sent John of Crema, a cardinal, to this land.   He
first came to the king in Normandy, and the king received him
with much honour, and commended him to William archbishop
of Canterbury, who conducted him to Canterbury ; and he was
there received with much pomp, and a great procession, and
he sang the high mass at Christ's altar on Easter day ; and then
he journeyed over all England, to all the bishoprics and
abbacies, and he was honourably received every where, and
all gave him great and handsome gifts ; and in September
he held his council in London full three days, (beginning) on
the Nativity of St. Mary, with the archbishops, bishops, and
abbats, and the clergy and laity, and he sanctioned the laws
which archbishop Anselm had made, and he enacted many
others, though they remained in force but a little while.
Thence he went over sea soon after Michaelmas, and so to
Rome.   William archbishop of Canterbury, and Thurstan
archbishop of York, and Alexander bishop of Lincoln, and
John bishop of Lothian (Glasgow), and Geoffrey abbat of
St. Alban's accompanied him, and were received with great
honour by the pope Honorius, and they remained there the
whole winter.   The same year there was so great a flood on

St. Lawrence's day, that many towns were deluged, and men drowned, the bridges were broken up, and the corn fields and meadows spoiled; and there was famine and disease upon men and cattle; and it was so bad a season for all fruits as had not been for many years before. The same year John abbat of Peterborough died on the 2nd before the Ides of October.

A. 1126. This year king Henry was in Normandy till after harvest; and he came to this land between the nativity of St. Mary, and Michaelmas, accompanied by the queen, and by his daughter whom he had before given in marriage to the emperor Henry of Lorrain. He brought with him the earl Waleram, and Hugh the son of Gervais, and he imprisoned the earl at Bridge-north, and he afterwards sent him to Wallingford, and he sent Hugh to Windsor, and caused him to be kept in strong bonds. And after Michaelmas David king of Scotland came hither, and king Henry received him with much honour, and he abode through the year in this land. The same year the king caused his brother Robert to be taken from Roger bishop of Salisbury, and delivered to his son Robert earl of Gloucester, and he caused him to be removed to Bristol, and put into the castle. All this was done through the advice of his daughter, and of her uncle David king of Scotland.

A. 1127. This year, at Christmas, king Henry held his court at Windsor, and David, king of Scotland, was there, and all the head men of England, both clergy and laity. And the king caused the archbishops, bishops, abbats, earls, and all the thanes who were present, to swear to place England and Normandy, after his death, in the hands of his daughter the princess, who had been the wife of the emperor of Saxony. And then he sent her to Normandy, accompanied by her brother Robert, earl of Gloucester, and by Brian, the son of the earl Alan Fergan; and he caused her to be wedded to the son of the earl of Anjou, named Geoffrey Martell. Howbeit this displeased all the French and the English, but the king did it to have the alliance* of

---

* Miss Gurney renders this " to obtain peace from," following Gibson, who turns ' sibbe' into Latin by pacem, which Ingram justly disapproves of, on the ground that the powerful Henry would hardly fear so small a potentate as the earl of Anjou.

the earl of Anjou and aid against his nephew William. The same year Charles, earl of Flanders, was slain in Lent by his own men, as he lay before the altar in a church, and prayed to God during mass. And the king of France brought William, the son of the earl of Normandy, and gave him the earldom, and the men of Flanders received him. The same William had before taken to wife the daughter of the earl of Anjou, but they were afterwards divorced because of their nearness of kin, and this through the interference of Henry, king of England; he afterwards married the sister of the king of France, and on this account the king gave him the earldom of Flanders. The same year Henry gave the abbacy of Peterborough to an abbat named Henry of Poitou, who was in possession of the abbacy of St. Jean d'Angeli; and all the archbishops and bishops said that this grant was against right, and that he could not have in hand two abbacies. But the same Henry made the king believe that he had given up his abbey on account of the great disquietude of the land, and that he had done so by the order and with the leave of the pope of Rome, and of the abbat of Cluny, and because he was legate for collecting the Rome-scot. Nevertheless it was not so, but he wished to keep both abbeys in his own hands, and he did hold them as long as it was the will of God. In his clerical state he was bishop of Soissons, afterwards he was a monk at Cluny, then prior of the same monastery, and next he was prior of Sevigny; after this, being related to the king of England and to the earl of Poitou, the earl gave him the abbey of St. Jean d'Angeli. Afterwards, by his great craft, he obtained the archbishopric of Besançon, and kept possession of it three day; and then lost he it right worthily, in that he had gotten it with all injustice. He then obtained the bishopric of Saintes, which was five miles from his own abbey, and he kept this for nearly a week, but here again the abbat of Clugny displaced him, as he had before removed him from Besançon. Now he bethought himself, that if he could be sheltered in England, he might have all his will, on which he besought the king, and said to him that he was an old man, and completely broken, and that he could not endure the wrongs and oppressions of that land, and he asked the king himself, and through all his friends, by name for the

abbacy of Peterborough.   And the king granted it to him,
forasmuch as he was his kinsman, and in that he had been
one of the first to swear oaths, and to bear witness, when the
son of the earl of Normandy and the daughter of the earl of
Anjou were divorced on the plea of kindred.   Thus vex-
atiously was the abbacy of Peterborough given away at London, between Christmas and Candlemas; and so Henry
went with the king to Winchester, and thence he came to
Peterborough, and there he lived even as a drone in a hive;
as the drone eateth and draggeth forward to himself all that
is brought near, even so did he; and thus he sent over sea
all that he could take from religious or from secular, both
within and without; he did there no good, nor did he leave
any there.   Let no man think lightly of the marvel that we
are about to relate as a truth, for it was full well known
over all the country.   It is this; that as soon as he came
there,* it was on the Sunday, when men sing " *Exurge
quare O Domine;*" several persons saw and heard many
hunters hunting.—These hunters were black, and large, and
loathly, and their hounds were all black, with wide eyes, and
ugly, and they rode on black horses and on black bucks.
This was seen in the very deer-park of the town of Peterborough, and in all the woods from the same town to Stamford; and the monks heard the blasts of the horns which
they blew in the night.   Men of truth kept in the night
their watch on them, and said that there might well be about
twenty or thirty horn-blowers.   This was seen and heard
from the time that the abbat came thither, all that Lent,
until Easter.   Such was his entrance, of his exit we can say
nothing yet: God knoweth it.

A. 1128. All this year king Henry was in Normandy, on
account of the war between him and his nephew the earl of
Flanders; but the earl was wounded in battle by a servant,
and being so wounded he went to the monastery of St. Ber-
tin, and forthwith he was made a monk, and lived five days
after, and then died, and was buried there: God rest his
soul !   He was buried on the 6th before the Kalends of

---

* ' Thaer' in the original, not ' thider.'   Dr. Ingram remarks, that this
is the first instance of the negligent use of the word ' there' for " thither.'
But use is second nature, and in conversation at least, the former of these
words has entirely superseded the latter.

August. The same year died Randulph Passeflambàrd bishop of Durham, and he was buried there on the Nones of September. And this year the aforesaid abbat Henry went home to his own monastery in Poitou, with the king's leave. He had given the king to understand that he would wholly quit that monastery, and that country, and abide with him in England, and at his monastery at Peterborough. But so it was not, for he spake thus guilefully, wishing to remain there a twelvemonth or more, and then to return again. May Almighty God have mercy upon this wretched place! The same year Hugh of the Temple came from Jerusalem to the king in Normandy, and the king received him with much honour, and gave him much treasure in gold and silver, and afterwards he sent him to England, and there he was well received by all good men, and all gave him treasures; and in Scotland also: and they sent in all a great sum of gold and silver by him to Jerusalem. And he invited the people out to Jerusalem, and there went with him and after him so great a number, as never before since the first expedition in the days of pope Urban. Yet this availed little: he said that there was a furious war between the Christians and the heathens, and when they came there it was nothing but leasing. Thus were all these people miserably betrayed.

A. 1129. This year the king sent to England after earl Waleram, and after Hugh the son of Gervase; and there they gave him hostages, and Hugh went home to France his own country, and Waleram remained with the king, and the king gave him all his lands, excepting his castle alone. Then the king came to England in harvest, and the earl came with him, and they were as great friends as they had been enemies before. Then soon, by the king's counsel and consent, William archbishop of Canterbury sent over all England, and commanded the bishops, and abbats, and archdeacons, and all the priors, monks, and canons of all the cells of England, and all who had the charge and oversight of the Christian religion, that they should come to London at Michaelmas, to hold conference upon all God's rights. When they came thither, the meeting began on the Monday and lasted till the Friday, and it came out that it was all concerning the wives of archdeacons and priests, that they should part with them by St. Andrew's day; and that he who would not do this, should forego his church, his house, and his home, and never be permitted again to claim them. This was ordered by William archbishop of Canterbury, and all the bishops of England: and the king gave them leave to depart, and so they went home, and these decrees were in no respect observed, for all kept their wives, by the king's permission, even as before. The same year William Giffard bishop of Winchester died, and was buried there on the 8th before the Kalends of February; and after Michaelmas the king gave the bishopric to his nephew Henry abbat of Glastonbury, and he was consecrated by William archbishop of Canterbury on the fifteenth before the Kalends of December. The same year died pope Honorius, and before he was well dead, two popes were chosen. The one was named Peter, he was a monk of Clugny, and descended from the greatest men of Rome, and the Romans and the duke of Sicily held with him; the other was named Gregory, he was a clerk, and he was driven from Rome by the other pope and his kinsmen, and he was acknowledged by the emperor of Saxony, by the king of France, by Henry king of England, and by all on this side of the mountains. There was now so great a division in Christendom, that the like had never been before. May Christ appoint good counsel for his miserable people! The same year there was a great earthquake on St. Nicholas's night, a little before day.

A. 1130. This year the monastery of Canterbury was consecrated by archbishop William, on the 4th before the Nones of May. The following bishops were there: John of Rochester, Gilbert Universal of London, Henry of Winchester, Alexander of Lincoln, Roger of Salisbury, Simon of Worcester, Roger of Coventry, Godfrey of Bath, Everard of Norwich, Sigefrid of Chichester, Bernard of St. David's, Owen of Evreux, in Normandy, and John of Siezes. On the fourth day after this, king Henry was at Rochester, and nearly the whole town was burnt down; and archbishop William and the aforesaid bishops consecrated St. Andrew's monastery. And king Henry went over sea to Normandy during harvest. The same year Henry abbat of Angeli came to Peterborough after Easter, and said that he had wholly given up that monastery. After him, the

abbat of Clugny named Peter came to England with the
king's leave, and he was received with much honour wherever he went; he came to Peterborough, and there the abbat
Henry promised that he would obtain for him the monastery
of Peterborough, and that it should be annexed to Clugny;
but as it is said in the proverb:

> "The hedge still stands
> That parts the lands."

May Almighty God frustrate evil counsels! And soon
afterwards the abbat of Clugny went home to his own
country. This year was Angus slain by the Scottish army,
and a great number of persons with him. There was God's
right wrought upon him, for that he was all forsworn.

A. 1131. This year, on a moonlight night* after Christmas, during the first sleep, the northern half of the heaven
was, as it were, a burning fire; so that all who saw it were
more afeared† than ever they were before; this happened on
the 3rd before the Ides of January. The same year there
was so great a pestilence amongst animals over all England,
as had not been in the memory of man; it chiefly fell on
cattle and on swine, so that in the town where ten or twelve
ploughs had been going, not one remained, and the man, who
had possessed two or three hundred swine, had not one left
him. After this the hens died; and flesh-meat became
scarce, and cheese and butter. God mend the state of
things when such is his will! And king Henry came home
to England before harvest, after the feast of St. Peter *ad vin-
cula*. The same year before Easter the abbat Henry went
from Peterborough over sea to Normandy, and there he
spoke with the king, and told him that the abbat of Clugny
had commanded him to come over, and resign to him the
abbey of Angely; and that then, with his leave, he would
return home: and so he went to his own monastery and
abode there till Midsummer-day. And on the day after the
feast of St. John, the monks chose an abbat from among
themselves, and brought him into the church in procession;
they sang *Te Deum laudamus*, rang the bells, and set him
on the abbat's seat, and did all obedience to him, even as

* "Luna splendente."—GIBS. "Monday night."—INGRAM.
† The original Anglo-Saxon has it so, 'offaerd.'

they would to their abbat; and the earl and all the chief
men and the monks drove the other abbat Henry out of the
monastery, and well they might, for in five and twenty years
they had never known a good day.   All his great craftiness
failed him here, and now it behoved him to creep into any
corner, and to consider if perchance there yet remained some
slippery device, by which he might once more betray Christ
and all Christian people.   Then went he to Clugny, and
there they kept him, so that he could go neither east nor
west; the abbat of Clugny saying that they had lost St.
John's minster through him, and his great sottishness;
wherefore seeing he could give no better compensation, he
promised and swore on the holy relics, that if he might proceed to England he would obtain for them the monastery of
Peterborough, and would establish there a prior of Clugny,
a churchwarden, a treasurer, and a keeper of the robes, and
that he would make over to them all things both within and
without the monastery.   Thus he went into France and
abode there all the year.   May Christ provide for the
wretched monks of Peterborough, and for that miserable
place, for now do they stand in need of the help of Christ
and of all Christian people.

A. 1132. This year king Henry returned to this land:
then the abbat Henry came, and accused the monks of Peterborough to the king, because he desired to subject that monastery to Clugny; so that the king was well nigh beguiled,
and sent for the monks; but by God's mercy, and through
the bishops of Salisbury and Lincoln, and the other great
men who were there, he found out that the abbat dealt
treacherously.   When he could do no more, he wished
that his nephew might be abbat of Peterborough, but this
was not the will of Christ.   It was not very long after
this that the king sent for him, and made him give up the
abbey of Peterborough, and depart out of the country, and
the king granted the abbacy to a prior of St. Neot's named
Martin, and he came to the monastery, right worshipfully
attended, on St. Peter's day.

A. 1135. This year, at Lammas, king Henry went over
sea: and on the second day, as he lay asleep in the ship, the
day was darkened universally, and the sun became as if it
were a moon three nights old, with the stars shining round it

at mid-day. Men greatly marvelled, and great fear fell on them, and they said that some great event should follow thereafter—and so it was, for the same year the king died in Normandy, on the day after the feast of St. Andrew. Soon did this land fall into trouble, for every man greatly began to rob his neighbour as he might. Then king Henry's sons and his friends took his body, and brought it to England, and buried it at Reading. He was a good man, and great was the awe of him; no man durst ill treat another in his time : he made peace for men and deer. Whoso bare his burden of gold and silver, no man durst say to him ought but good. In the meantime his nephew Stephen de Blois had arrived in England, and he came to London, and the inhabitants received him, and sent for the archbishop, William Corboil, who consecrated him king on midwinter-day. In this king's time was all discord, and evil-doing, and robbery ; for the powerful men who had kept aloof, soon rose up against him; the first was Baldwin de Redvers, and he held Exeter against the king, and Stephen besieged him, and afterwards Baldwin made terms with him. Then the others took their castles, and held them against the king, and David, king of Scotland, betook him to Wessington [Derbyshire], but notwithstanding his array, messengers passed between them, and they came together, and made an agreement, though it availed little.

A. 1137. This year king Stephen went over sea to Normandy, and he was received there because it was expected that he would be altogether like his uncle, and because he had gotten possession of his treasure, but this he distributed and scattered foolishly. King Henry had gathered together much gold and silver, yet did he no good for his soul's sake with the same. When king Stephen came to England, he held an assembly at Oxford; and there he seized Roger bishop of Salisbury, and Alexander bishop of Lincoln, and Roger the chancellor, his nephew, and he kept them all in prison till they gave up their castles. When the traitors perceived that he was a mild man, and a soft, and a good, and that he did not enforce justice, they did all wonder. They had done homage to him, and sworn oaths, but they no faith kept; all became forsworn, and broke their allegiance, for every rich man built his castles, and defended them against him, and they filled the land full of castles. They greatly oppressed the wretched people by making them work at these castles, and when the castles were finished they filled them with devils and evil men. Then they took those whom they suspected to have any goods, by night and by day, seizing both men and women, and they put them in prison for their gold and silver, and tortured them with pains unspeakable, for never were any martyrs tormented as these were. They hung some up by their feet, and smoked them with foul smoke; some by their thumbs, or by the head, and they hung burning things on their feet. They put a knotted string about their heads, and twisted it till it went into the brain. They put them into dungeons wherein were adders and snakes and toads, and thus wore them out. Some they put into a crucet-house, that is, into a chest that was short and narrow, and not deep, and they put sharp stones in it, and crushed the man therein so that they broke all his limbs. There were hateful and grim things called Sachenteges in many of the castles, and which two or three men had enough to do to carry. The Sachentege was made thus: it was fastened to a beam, having a sharp iron to go round a man's throat and neck, so that he might no ways sit, nor lie, nor sleep, but that he must bear all the iron. Many thousands they exhausted with hunger. I cannot and I may not tell of all the wounds, and all the tortures that they inflicted upon the wretched men of this land; and this state of things lasted the nineteen years that Stephen was king, and ever grew worse and worse. They were continually levying an exaction from the towns, which they called Tenserie,* and when the miserable inhabitants had no more to give, then plundered they, and burnt all the towns, so that well mightest thou walk a whole day's journey nor ever shouldest thou find a man seated in a town, or its lands tilled.

Then was corn dear, and flesh, and cheese, and butter, for there was none in the land—wretched men starved with hunger—some lived on alms who had been erewhile rich: some fled the country—never was there more misery, and never acted heathens worse than these. At length they spared neither church nor churchyard, but they took all that was valuable therein, and then burned the church and all together. Neither did they spare the lands of bishops, nor of

* A payment to the superior lord for protection.

abbats, nor of priests; but they robbed the monks and the
clergy, and every man plundered his neighbour as much as
he could. If two or three men came riding to a town, all
the township fled before them, and thought that they were
robbers. The bishops and clergy were ever cursing them,
but this to them was nothing, for they were all accursed, and
forsworn, and reprobate. The earth bare no corn, you
might as well have tilled the sea, for the land was all ruined
by such deeds, and it was said openly that Christ and his
saints slept. These things, and more than we can say,
did we suffer during nineteen years because of our sins.
Through all this evil time the abbat Martin held his abbacy
for twenty years and a half and eight days, with many difficulties: and he provided the monks and guests with all
necessaries, and kept up much alms in the house; and withal
he wrought upon the church, and annexed thereto lands and
rents, and enriched it greatly, and furnished it with robes:
and he brought the monks into the new monastery on St.
Peter's day with much pomp. This was in the year 1140
of our Lord's incarnation, the twenty-third year after the
fire. And he went to Rome and was well received there by
pope Eugenius, from whom he obtained sundry privileges, to
wit, one for all the abbey lands, and another for the lands
that adjoin the monastery, and had he lived longer he meant
to have done as much for the treasurer's house. And he regained certain lands that powerful men possessed by force;
he won Cotingham and Easton from William Malduit, who
held Rockingham castle, and from Hugh of Walteville he
won Hirtlingbery, and Stanwick, and sixty shillings yearly
out of Oldwinkle. And he increased the number of monks,
and planted a vineyard, and made many works, and improved the town; and he was a good monk and a good man,
and therefore God and good men loved him. Now will we
relate some part of what befell in king Stephen's time. In
his reign the Jews of Norwich bought a Christian child
before Easter, and tortured him with all the torments wherewith our Lord was tortured, and they crucified him on Good
Friday for the love of our Lord, and afterwards buried him.
They believed that this would be kept secret, but our Lord
made manifest that he was a holy martyr, and the monks took
him and buried him honourably in the monastery, and he

performed manifold and wonderful miracles through the
power of our Lord, and he is called St. William.

A. 1138. This year David king of Scotland entered this
land with an immense army resolving to conquer it, and
William earl of Albemarle, to whose charge the king had
committed York, and other trusty men, came against him
with few troops, and fought with him, and they put the king
to flight at the Standard, and slew a great part of his
followers.

A. 1140. This year Stephen attempted to take Robert
earl of Gloucester the son of king Henry, but failed, for
Robert was aware of his purpose. After this, in Lent, the
sun and the day were darkened about noon, when men eat,
so that they lighted candles to eat by. This was on the 13th
before the Kalends of April, and the people were greatly astonished. After this William archbishop of Canterbury
died, and the king made Theobald, abbat of Bec, archbishop.
Then there arose a very great war between the king and
Randolph earl of Chester, not because the king did not give
him all that he could ask, even as he did to all others, but
that the more he gave them, the worse they always carried
themselves to him. The earl held Lincoln against the king,
and seized all that belonged to the king there, and the king
went thither, and besieged him and his brother William de
Romare in the castle: and the earl stole out and went for
Robert earl of Gloucester, and brought him thither with a
large army; and they fought furiously against their lord on
Candlemas-day, and they took him captive, for his men betrayed him and fled, and they led him to Bristol, and there
they put him into prison and close confinement. Now was
all England more disturbed than before, and all evil was in
the land. After this, king Henry's daughter, who had been
empress of Germany, and was now countess of Anjou, arrived, and she came to London, and the citizens would have
seized her, but she fled with much loss. Then Henry bishop
of Winchester, king Stephen's brother, spake with earl
Robert and with the empress, and swore them oaths that he
never more would hold with the king his brother, and he
cursed all those that did hold with him, and he said that he
would give up Winchester to them, and he made them come
thither. But when they were in that place Stephen's queen

brought up her strength and besieged them, till there was so great a famine in the town, they could endure it no longer. Then stole they out and fled, and the besiegers were aware of them, and followed them, and they took Robert earl of Gloucester and led him to Rochester, and imprisoned him there : and the empress fled into a monastery. Then wise men, friends of the king and of the earl, interfered between them, and they settled that the king should be let out of prison for the earl, and the earl for the king ; and this was done. After this the king and earl Randolph were reconciled at Stamford, and they took oaths and pledged their troth, that neither would betray the other : but this promise was set at nought, for the king afterwards seized the earl in Northampton through wicked counsel, and put him in prison, but he set him free soon after, through worse, on condition that he should swear on the cross, and find hostages that he would give up all his castles. Some he did deliver up, and others not ; and he did worse than he should have done in this country. Now was England much divided, some held with the king and some with the empress, for when the king was in prison the earls and the great men thought that he would never more come out, and they treated with the empress, and brought her to Oxford, and gave her the town. When the king was out of prison he heard this, and he took his army and besieged her in the tower, and they let her down from the tower by night with ropes, and she stole away, and she fled : and she went on foot to Wallingford. After this she went over sea, and all the Normans turned from the king to the earl of Anjou, some willingly, and some against their will ; for he besieged them till they gave up their castles, and they had no help from the king. Then the king's son Eustace went to France, and took to wife the sister of the king of France : he thought to obtain Normandy through this marriage, but little he sped, and that of right, for he was an evil man, and did more harm than good wherever he went : he spoiled the lands, and laid thereon heavy taxes : he brought his wife to England, and put her into the castle of ———— ;* she was a good woman but she had little bliss with him, and it was not the will of Christ that he

* " The MS. is here deficient ; but .... b for ' byrig' is discernible."
—INGRAM.

should bear rule long, and he died, and his mother also.
And the earl of Anjou died, and his son Henry succeeded
him ; and the queen of France was divorced from the king,
and she went to the young earl Henry and he took her to
wife, and received all Poitou with her.   Then he came into
England with a great army and won castles ; and the king
marched against him with a much larger army, howbeit they
did not fight, but the archbishop and wise men went between
them and made a treaty on these terms : that the king should
be lord and king while he lived, and that Henry should be
king after his death, and that he should consider him as his
father, and the king him as his son, and that peace and concord should be between them, and in all England.   The king,
and the earl, and the bishop, and the earls, and all the great
men swore to observe these and the other conditions that
were then made.   The earl was received with much honour
at Winchester and at London, and all did homage to him, and
swore to keep the peace, and it soon became a very good
peace, such as never was in this land.   Then the king was
more powerful here than ever he was ; and the earl went
over sea, and all the people loved him, because he did good
justice, and made peace.

A. 1154.   This year king Stephen died, and he was buried
with his wife and his son at Faversham ; they had built that
monastery.   When the king died the earl was beyond sea,
and no man durst do other than good for very dread of him.
When he came to England he was received with much honour, and was consecrated king at London on the Sunday before Christmas, and he held a great court there : and on the
same day that Martin abbat of Peterborough should have
gone thither he sickened, and he died on the 4th before the
Nones of January.   And that day the monks chose another
abbat from among themselves.   He is named William de
Walteville, a good clerk, and a good man, and well beloved
of the king and of all good people : and they buried the
abbat honourably in the church, and soon afterwards the
abbat elect and the monks went to the king at Oxford, and
the king gave him the abbacy, and he departed soon afterwards to Peterborough, where he remained with the abbat
before he came home.   And the king was received at Peter-

borough with great respect, and in full procession ; so he was also at Ramsey, at Thorney, and at . . . . and Spalding, and . . . .*

* The MS. is defective. Ramsey and Thorney are elicited from some faint traces in the Laud MS. which seem to have escaped the penetration of Gibson.   The last paragraph, if Gibson's reading be correct, appears to relate to some building which the abbat and monks of Peterborough had begun about this time. See Gunton's *History of Peterborough Minster*, and Cont. Hug. Candid. *ap.* Sparke, pp. 92, 93.

END OF ANGLO-SAXON CHRONICLE.

INDEX.

J. HADDON, PRINTER, CASTLE STREET, FINSBURY.

BOUNDARIES OF THE ANGLO-SAXON KINGDOMS.

Founded.	Kingdoms.	Modern Counties.
457	KENT	Kent.
491	SUSSEX	Sussex.
519	WESSEX	Surrey, Hants, with the Isle of Wight, Berks, Wilts, Dorset, Somerset, Devon, and part of Cornwall.
527	ESSEX	Essex, Middlesex, and southern part of Hertfordshire.
	NORTHUMBRIA	
547	BERNICIA	Northumberland, and the south-eastern counties of Scotland.
560	DEIRA	Cumberland, Durham, Westmoreland, York, and Lancaster.
571	EAST-ANGLIA	Norfolk, Suffolk, Cambridge, and part of Bedfordshire.
585	MERCIA	Chester, Derby, Nottingham, Lincoln, Shropshire, Stafford, Leicester, Rutland, Northampton, Huntingdon, Hereford, Worcester, Warwick, Gloucester, Oxford, Buckingham, and parts of Hertford and Bedford.

N.B. The boundaries varied frequently according to the fortunes of the reigning kings in the petty contests which they waged one against the other.

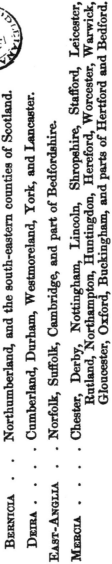

Ingram Content Group UK Ltd.
Milton Keynes UK
UKHW021103210423
420563UK00005B/244